CORPORATE AND PARTNERSHIP TAXATION

CORPORATE AND PARTNERSHIP TAXATION

Fourth Edition

By

STEPHEN SCHWARZ

Professor of Law
Hastings College of the Law

DANIEL J. LATHROPE

Professor of Law
Hastings College of the Law

BLACK LETTER SERIES®

THOMSON

WEST

Mat #18548348

Black Letter Series and Black Letter Series design appearing on the front cover are registered trademarks used herein under license.

COPYRIGHT © 1991, 1994 WEST PUBLISHING CO.
COPYRIGHT © 1997 WEST GROUP
COPYRIGHT © 2003 By WEST GROUP
        610 Opperman Drive
        P.O. Box 64526
        St. Paul, MN 55164–0526
        1–800–328–9352

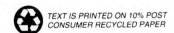

PUBLISHER'S PREFACE

This "Black Letter" is designed to help a law student recognize and understand the basic principles and issues of law covered in a law school course. It can be used both as a study aid when preparing for classes and as a review of the subject matter when studying for an examination.

Each "Black Letter" is written by experienced law school teachers who are recognized national authorities in the subject covered.

The law is succinctly stated by the authors of this "Black Letter." In addition, the exceptions to the rules are stated in the text. The rules and exceptions have purposely been condensed to facilitate quick and easy recollection. For an in-depth study of a point of law, citations to major student texts are given. In addition, a Text Correlation Chart provides a convenient means of relating material contained in the Black Letter to appropriate sections of the casebook the student is using in his or her law school course.

If the subject covered by this text is a code or code-related course, the code section or rule is set forth and discussed wherever applicable.

FORMAT

The format of this "Black Letter" is specially designed for review. (1) **Text.** First, it is recommended that the entire text be studied and, if deemed necessary, supplemented by the student texts cited. (2) **Capsule Summary.** The Capsule Summary is an abbreviated review of the subject matter which can be used both before and after studying the main body of the text. The headings in the Capsule Summary follow the main text of the "Black Letter." (3) **Table of Contents.** The Table of Contents is in outline form to help you organize the details of the subject and the Summary of Contents gives you a final overview of the materials. (4) **Practice Examination.** The Practice Examination in Appendix B gives you the opportunity of testing yourself with the type of questions asked on an exam and comparing your answer with a model answer.

In addition, a number of other features are included to help you understand the subject matter and prepare for examinations:

Short Questions and Answers: This feature is designed to help you spot and recognize issues in the examination. We feel that issue recognition is a major ingredient in successfully writing an examination.

Perspective: In this feature, the authors discuss their approach to the topic, the approach used in preparing the materials, and any tips on studying for and writing examinations.

Analysis: This feature, at the beginning of each section, is designed to give a quick summary of a particular section to help you recall the subject matter and to help you determine which areas need the most extensive review.

Examples: This feature is designed to illustrate, through fact situations, the law just stated. This, we believe, should help you analytically approach a question on the examination.

Glossary: This feature is designed to refamiliarize you with the meaning of a particular legal term. We believe that the recognition of words of art used in an examination helps you to better analyze the question. In addition, when writing an examination you should know the precise definition of a word of art you intend to use.

We believe that the materials in this "Black Letter" will facilitate your study of a law school course and assure success in writing examinations not only for the course but for the bar examination. We wish you success.

THE PUBLISHER

SUMMARY OF CONTENTS

TABLE OF CONTENTS

APPENDICES

CAPSULE SUMMARY

PART ONE: GENERAL CONSIDERATIONS

I. INTRODUCTION

A. Forms of Business Organization

The most common forms for a business organization in the United States are:

1. Sole proprietorships, which are businesses owned and operated by a single individual.

2. Corporations, which are fictitious legal entities that offer limited liability to their owners.

3. Partnerships, including general and limited partnerships, limited liability partnerships, and joint ventures.

4. Limited liability companies, a popular business entity form that provides limited liability for all of its members.

B. Conceptual Taxation Models

1. Aggregate Concept

The aggregate concept treats the assets of a business as owned directly by its individual owners, who are each responsible for a proportionate share of the liabilities of the business. The business organization itself is not a taxable entity.

2. Entity Concept

The entity concept treats a business organization as a taxable entity that is separate and apart from its owners. Transactions between the owners and the entity are generally taxable events.

3. Hybrid Concepts

Some taxing models adopt a hybrid approach, treating an organization as an entity for some purposes and an aggregate for others.

C. Overview of Taxing Regimes Under the Code

1. Subchapter C

Subchapter C embodies an entity approach by treating most corporations as separate taxable entities and by providing rules that govern transactions between corporations and their shareholders.

2. Subchapter K

Subchapter K applies a hybrid approach to partnerships and their partners. Partnerships do not pay taxes but pass through their income and deductions to their partners. A partnership is treated as an accounting entity, however, for purposes of determining its income and filing of returns. A modified entity approach is applied in various substantive contexts.

3. Subchapter S

Subchapter S is a hybrid model governing the treatment of eligible corporations that make an "S" election. S corporations are pass-through entities that generally are not subject to tax.

4. Specialized Tax Regimes

The Code includes other specialized tax regimes tailored for particular industries.

D. Influential Policies

The taxation of business organizations has been shaped by four broad tax policy decisions that influence taxpayer behavior. The relationship of these policies has changed as a result of recent tax legislation.

1. The Double Tax

The double tax regime of Subchapter C increases the cost of operating a business as a C corporation and often provides an incentive for taxpayers to choose partnerships or S corporations for business and investment activities.

2. Rate Structure

For most of our tax history, the maximum individual tax rate has exceeded the highest corporate rate. This rate structure historically made the corporation a refuge from steeper individual rates and provided an incentive to operate as a C corporation. With the maximum individual rate now only slightly higher than the top corporate rate, the choice of entity is not as clear, and many closely held businesses may prefer to operate as partnerships, limited liability companies, or S corporations to avoid the double tax.

3. Preferential Capital Gains Rates

Whenever there is a significant capital gains rate preference, taxpayers are motivated to devise strategies to convert ordinary income into capital gains, such as "bailing out" C corporation profits at capital gains rates.

4. Nonrecognition

Many corporate and partnership transactions qualify for nonrecognition treatment because they are regarded as mere changes in form which result in a continuity of investment.

E. Pervasive Judicial Doctrines

In addition to the language of the Code, the courts frequently apply various "common law" doctrines in determining the tax consequences of a transaction.

1. Substance Over Form

The Supreme Court has admonished that the tax consequences of a transaction should be determined by economic substance rather than form. Despite this well accepted doctrine, the Code often permits a taxpayer to assure a desired tax result by utilizing a particular form.

2. Step Transactions

Under the step transaction doctrine, separate formal steps are combined into a single integrated transaction for tax purposes. The courts disagree as to how and when the doctrine should be applied.

3. Business Purpose

Under the business purpose doctrine, a transaction may be denied certain tax benefits, such as nonrecognition of gain, if it is not motivated by a corporate business purpose apart from tax avoidance. The doctrine has been extended through regulations to patrol against abusive partnership transactions and corporate tax shelters.

4. Sham Transaction

A sham is a transaction that never actually occurred or is devoid of substance. Sham transactions are not respected for tax purposes.

II. CLASSIFICATION

A. Introduction

1. Impact of Classification

The operation of many Code sections varies depending upon whether the taxpayer is an individual, a partnership, a corporation or some other type of entity. Thus, the classification of an organization for tax purposes may be extremely important.

2. The Role of State Law

The classification of entities for federal tax purposes is a matter of federal law and depends on standards in the Internal Revenue Code.

3. Principal Classification Issues

Classification issues generally arise in two settings:

a. determining whether a separate entity exists for federal tax purposes, and

b. determining whether an entity with more than one owner should be classified as a corporation or partnership, or whether a single-owner entity should be disregarded for federal tax purposes or classified as a corporation.

B. Existence of a Separate Entity

1. In General

The regulations provide that a joint venture or other contractual arrangement may create a separate entity for federal tax purposes if the participants carry on a trade, business, financial operation, or venture and divide the profits therefrom. This definition is derived from case law distinguishing partnerships from less formal relationships. A critical factor in determining whether a partnership exists is whether "the parties in good faith and acting with a business purpose intended to join together in the present conduct of the enterprise." Courts look at a list of factors to determine the intent of the parties. The critical factor frequently is whether the parties have a joint profit motive.

2. Joint Profit Motive

The existence of a joint profit motive may be difficult to determine and depends on the particular fact situation.

3. Separate Entity vs. Co–Ownership of Property

The "mere co-ownership" of property which is maintained, kept in repair, and rented or leased does not create a separate entity. A separate entity exists if co-owners lease space and in addition provide services to the tenants either directly or through an agent. The IRS has specified conditions that must be met to receive a ruling that undivided fractional interests in rental property are a co-ownership rather than a partnership. In limited circumstances, an unincorporated organization may make a statutory election to be excluded from partnership classification for tax purposes.

4. Separate Entities vs. Expense Sharing, Employment, Loan and Other Relationships

An expense sharing relationship does not constitute a separate entity for tax purposes. In situations where one person supplies services or capital to a business venture, the determination of whether there is a separate entity generally depends on whether the parties are sharing a joint profit as co-owners or co-proprietors.

C. Classification of Business Entities

1. Introduction

The Code defines a corporation as including "associations, joint-stock companies, and insurance companies." The interpretation of this definition has a rich and textured history.

2. The Classification Regulations

Historically, the classification regulations employed four corporate characteristics to classify a business organization as either an association taxable as a corporation or as a partnership. Since 1997, the regulations generally classify most unincorporated business entities as partnerships. Under the regulations, a business entity organized under a state corporation statute is taxed as a corporation. An unincorporated business entity, such as a limited liability company or limited partnership, with two or more members is classified as a partnership. An unincorporated business entity with one owner is disregarded and thus treated as a sole proprietorship, branch, or division of the owner for federal tax purposes. Every unincorporated entity has the option of electing to be taxed as a corporation.

3. Publicly Traded Partnerships

A "publicly traded partnership," as defined in § 7704(b), is generally classified as a corporation for federal tax purposes.

4. Trusts

The fact that a business is operated in a trust will not prevent it from being classified as a business entity. The critical question in determining whether a trust will be classified as a business entity is whether a business objective is present or whether the trust was established merely to protect and conserve trust property.

D. Choice of Entity Considerations

Taxation as a partnership and limited liability under state law frequently make a limited liability company a desirable vehicle for conducting a new closely held business enterprise. Other factors, such as state taxes, may make a limited partnership or S corporation the best entity if the goal is to avoid the double tax regime applicable to C corporations. For corporations intending to reinvest their earnings for the reasonable growth needs of the business, a C corporation may be more attractive because the top corporate rate is slightly lower than the highest marginal individual rates. Publicly traded companies almost always operate as C corporations.

PART TWO: CORPORATE TAXATION

III. THE C CORPORATION AS A TAXABLE ENTITY

A. The Corporate Income Tax

1. Introduction
A C corporation is a separate taxable entity, which computes its taxable income under general tax principles.

2. Rates
A C corporation is subject to tax under § 11 at rates of 15% on the first $50,000 of taxable income, 25% on the next $25,000, 34% on taxable income from $75,000 to $10,000,000, and 35% on taxable income over $10,000,000. Surtaxes phase out the tax savings from the lower brackets for corporations with substantial taxable income. Qualified personal service corporations are not eligible for the lower graduated rates.

3. Determination of Taxable Income
A C corporation's "taxable income" is its gross income less allowable deductions. Most business expenses are deductible under § 162. The § 465 at-risk limitations and the § 469 passive loss limitations apply only to closely-held C corporations. Corporate shareholders may deduct 70% (and sometimes 80% or 100%) of the dividends they receive. Corporate capital gains are taxed at the same rate as ordinary income, and capital losses are only deductible to the extent of capital gains, with a three-year carryback and five-year carryforward of the excess.

4. Taxable Year
C corporations may adopt either a fiscal or calendar year. Personal service corporations must use a calendar year unless they: (a) show a business purpose for a fiscal year, or (b) make a fiscal year election under § 444 and make certain required distributions to prevent any deferral benefits to their owner-employees.

5. Accounting Method
C corporations generally must use the accrual method, with certain exceptions for farming and personal service corporations and corporations with average annual gross receipts of less than $5 million.

6. Loss Disallowance Rules
Losses from sales or exchanges of property between a shareholder and a more-than–50%–owned corporation may not be deducted.

7. Forced Matching Rules

Accrual method corporations may not deduct payments made to cash method owner-employees until the recipient includes the item in income.

8. Credits

C corporations qualify for a variety of tax credits.

B. The Corporate Alternative Minimum Tax

1. Introduction

C corporations must pay an alternative minimum tax ("AMT") to the extent that it exceeds their regular tax liability. The AMT is 20% of alternative minimum taxable income ("AMTI") less an exemption amount. Certain "small corporations" are completely exempt from the corporate AMT.

2. Alternative Minimum Taxable Income

AMTI is a corporation's taxable income, recomputed after certain timing adjustments and increased by specified tax preference items. The principal adjustments are for depreciation and adjusted current earnings ("ACE"). AMTI and ACE are designed to reflect a more accurate measure of a corporation's economic performance.

3. The Exemption Amount

A corporation's AMT exemption amount is $40,000, reduced by 25% of AMTI in excess of $150,000.

4. Credits

The AMT may be reduced by a special AMT foreign tax credit. A corporation's regular tax may be reduced by a minimum tax credit. The minimum tax credit is allowed for all of a corporation's AMT, not merely AMT attributable to deferral preferences.

C. Disregard of the Corporate Entity

1. Introduction

Most cases reject efforts by taxpayers to disregard the corporate entity for tax purposes unless the corporation is clearly shown to be a mere dummy or agent.

2. The Business Activity Test

A corporation generally is regarded as a separate taxable entity if it engages in any business activity.

3. The *National Carbide* Factors

The Supreme Court set forth six factors in the *National Carbide* case to determine if a corporate entity should be ignored as an agent. Under the most important of these factors, a corporation was not a true agent if its relations with its principal were dependent on the fact that it was owned by the principal.

4. The *Bollinger* Factors

In the more recent *Bollinger* case, the Supreme Court concluded that a corporate entity would be respected as a true agent with respect to an asset (e.g., real estate) if it had a written agency agreement, functioned as an agent with respect to the asset for all purposes and disclosed its agency status in dealings with third parties.

IV. FORMATION OF A CORPORATION

A. Introduction

Section 351 provides that certain transfers of property to a newly formed or preexisting controlled (i.e. 80% owned) corporation are not taxable events. Unrecognized gain or loss is preserved through transferred and exchanged basis rules.

B. Requirements for Nonrecognition Under § 351

No gain or loss is recognized when one or more persons transfer "property" to a corporation solely in exchange for "stock" of that corporation, and the transferors, as a group, "control" the corporation "immediately after the exchange."

1. "Property"

"Property" includes cash, inventory, intangibles and accounts receivable. Stock issued for past, present or future services rendered to the corporation is not treated as having been issued in return for property.

2. "Transfer"

The transferor must transfer all substantial rights in the property to the corporation.

3. Solely in Exchange for "Stock"

"Stock" means an ownership interest in a corporation and does not include rights, warrants or convertible debt. Certain preferred stock with debt-like characteristics is treated as "other property" rather than stock for some purposes under § 351.

4. "Control"

"Control" is ownership of at least 80% of the total combined voting power of all classes of stock entitled to vote and at least 80% of each class of nonvoting stock. "Control" is determined by looking to all the transferors of property as a group.

5. "Immediately After the Exchange"

The control test is applied "immediately after the exchange." If a transferor of property disposes of stock pursuant to a prearranged binding agreement, the control test is applied after that disposition. A gift of stock after an incorporation exchange will not cause a transaction to fail the control requirement.

6. Special Problems

a. A service provider who receives stock for services recognizes ordinary income. The corporation may deduct the value of stock issued for services as a business expense unless the nature of the services requires the corporation to amortize or capitalize the expenditure. Timing of the income and deduction is determined under § 83.

b. If stock is received in exchange for a combination of services and property, all the stock may be counted in applying the 80% "control" test unless the property transferred is of relatively small value compared to the stock received for services. The Service does not consider property "of relatively small value" if it equals at least 10% of the value of the stock received for services.

c. Section 351 does not require shareholders to receive stock in proportion to the value of the property they transfer but, in disproportionate transfer situations, the true nature of the transaction (e.g., compensation, gift) must be determined.

d. Section 351 generally overrides all recapture of depreciation provisions. The recapture gain is preserved in the depreciable property received by the corporation.

e. No gain is recognized on the transfer of an installment obligation in a § 351 transaction.

f. Transfers to an "investment company," as defined in § 351(e), do not qualify for nonrecognition.

7. Basis and Holding Period

a. If property is transferred in a § 351 transaction solely in exchange for stock, the basis of the stock received is the same as the adjusted basis of the property transferred. If a transferor receives more than one class of stock, the aggregate exchanged basis is allocated to each class in proportion to its fair market value.

b. The transferor's holding period in stock received in exchange for capital or § 1231 assets includes the holding period of the transferred property. The holding period of stock received for other assets begins on the date of the exchange.

c. The basis of property received by a corporation in a § 351(a) exchange is the transferor's adjusted basis, and the corporation's holding period for all transferred assets includes the holding period of the transferor.

C. Treatment of Boot
1. In General
A transferor who receives property other than stock from the corporation in a transaction that otherwise qualifies under § 351 recognizes gain (but not loss)

to the extent of the cash and the fair market value of any other property received. The other property is known in tax jargon as "boot."

2. Allocation of Boot

If several assets are transferred in exchange for both stock and boot, the boot is allocated among the transferred assets to determine the gain recognized on each asset. Realized gain is recognized to the extent of the boot allocable to the asset, but realized loss is never recognized.

3. Installment Boot

A transferor who receives installment boot (e.g., a debt security of the corporation) may be able to report any recognized gain (except for depreciation recapture and certain other ordinary income) on the installment method.

4. Basis and Holding Period

If a transferor receives boot in a § 351 transaction, her basis in the stock received is the same as the basis of the property transferred, minus the cash and the fair market value of other boot received, plus any gain recognized on the exchange. Boot generally takes a fair market value basis. The basis of property received by the corporation is the transferor's adjusted basis plus any gain recognized by the transferor.

5. Transfer of Appreciated Boot

A corporation that transfers appreciated boot (other than its own debt obligations) in a § 351 transaction generally must recognize gain as if it had sold the property for its fair market value.

D. Assumption of Liabilities
1. In General

In a § 351 transaction, a corporation's assumption of liabilities is not treated as boot, but the liabilities are treated as money received for purposes of determining the transferor's stock basis.

2. Determination of Amount of Liabilities Assumed

A recourse liability is treated as assumed to the extent that, based on all the facts and circumstances, the transferee has agreed to and is expected to satisfy the liability, whether or not the transferor-shareholder has been relieved of it. A nonrecourse liability is treated as having been assumed by a corporate transferee when an asset is transferred subject to the liability. In some cases where more than one asset is subject to the same nonrecourse liability, the amount of a nonrecourse liability treated as assumed must be reduced.

3. Tax Avoidance Transactions

If the principal purpose of a liability assumption was tax avoidance or was not a bona fide business purpose, all liabilities assumed by the corporation are treated as boot.

4. Liabilities in Excess of Basis

If liabilities assumed by the corporation exceed the aggregate adjusted basis of all properties transferred by a particular transferor, the excess is treated as gain from the sale or exchange of property. For this purpose, debts that would be currently deductible if paid by the transferor (e.g., accounts payable) and certain contingent debts are not treated as "liabilities." Some courts have held that a taxpayer who transfers assets with liabilities in excess of basis may avoid gain recognition by transferring a promissory note with a face value equal to the excess.

5. Limit on Basis Increase Attributable to Liability Assumption

If a transferor of property in a § 351 transaction recognizes gain under § 357(b) or § 357(c), the basis of the property transferred to the corporation may not exceed the fair market value of the property. A special rule may further limit the basis increase when the transferor is not subject to U.S. tax and the liability secures more than one asset.

E. Incorporation of a Going Business

1. Assignment of Income Doctrine

The assignment of income doctrine does not override § 351 on the transfer of accounts receivable by a cash basis taxpayer in the absence of a tax avoidance purpose. The corporation includes the receivables in income when they are collected.

2. Accounts Payable and Contingent Liabilities

Accounts payable transferred by a cash basis taxpayer in a § 351 transaction are deductible by the corporation when they are paid. Contingent liabilities transferred in a § 351 transaction for which the transferor has not received any tax benefit are either deductible by the corporation or treated as capital expenditures, as appropriate.

3. Tax Benefit Rule

It is unlikely that the tax benefit rule overrides § 351, but the issue is not entirely settled.

4. Depreciation Methods

A corporation that acquires depreciable property in a § 351 transaction generally inherits the transferor's depreciation method and remaining recovery period.

F. Contributions to Capital

1. Capital Contribution Defined

A contribution to capital is a transfer of cash or other property to a corporation without the receipt of stock in exchange.

2. Treatment of the Contributor

A shareholder does not recognize gain or loss on a contribution to capital but the shareholder's stock basis is increased by the amount of cash and the adjusted basis of any contributed property.

3. **Treatment of the Corporation**

Contributions to capital are not taxable to the corporation, which takes a transferred basis in the contributed property. Special rules apply to capital contributions by nonshareholders.

G. **Collateral Issues**

1. **Avoidance of § 351**

Taxpayers occasionally may wish to avoid § 351 to recognize a loss, step-up the basis of property or "freeze" appreciation as capital gain. Avoidance techniques include breaking control or structuring the transaction as a taxable sale.

2. **Relationship to Other Code Sections**

A § 351 transaction also may qualify as a tax-free reorganization or have the effect of a dividend. When §§ 351 and 482 overlap, courts have held that § 482 takes precedence if necessary to clearly reflect income.

H. **Organizational Expenses**

1. **Amortization**

Expenses of organizing a corporation are nondeductible capital expenditures which, at the corporation's election, may be amortized over 60 months.

2. **Organizational Expenses Defined**

Examples of organizational expenses include fees for drafting the articles of incorporation and by-laws, state filing fees and other expenses of creating the entity. Costs of issuing or selling stock are not organizational expenses and thus may not be amortized.

V. **CAPITAL STRUCTURE**

A. **Introduction**

1. **Sources of Corporate Capital**

The two sources of corporate capital are "debt" and "equity." The combination of debt and equity used to finance a corporation's operations is its "capital structure." Equity is a corporate ownership interest evidenced by shares of stock. Debt instruments represent funds borrowed by the corporation from the holder of the debt obligation. Many classification controversies involve hybrid instruments having both debt and equity characteristics.

2. **Tax Differences Between Debt and Equity**

The principal tax differences between debt and equity are:

a. Interest paid on corporate debt is deductible while dividends are not deductible.

b. Repayment of debt principal is tax-free to the debt holder while redemptions of stock may be a dividend to the shareholder.

c.   Accumulation of earnings to repay debt principal may provide a defense against imposition of the accumulated earnings tax.

d.   Equity qualifies for nonrecognition of gain on formation under § 351 while corporate debt securities constitute boot.

e.   Losses on worthlessness of some types of stock (e.g., § 1244 stock) may qualify for ordinary loss treatment while losses on worthlessness of debt are usually capital losses.

f.   Dividends received by corporate shareholders qualify for the § 243 dividends received deduction while interest is fully taxable.

B.   Distinguishing Between Debt and Equity

1.   § 385

Section 385 authorizes the Treasury to promulgate regulations to distinguish between debt and equity for tax purposes. In so doing, it may treat an interest as part debt and part equity. The factors to be taken into account are:

a.   The form of the obligation;

b.   Subordination to outside debt;

c.   The debt/equity ratio of the corporation;

d.   Convertibility into stock;

e.   Proportionality—i.e., the relationship between debt and stock holdings.

The issuing corporation's classification of an interest as stock or debt is generally binding on all holders of the interest. No regulations are currently effective and thus debt vs. equity classification issues must be resolved under the case law or, in specialized situations, by narrowly tailored statutory rules.

2.   Case Law

Debt vs. equity classification issues are factual questions that are resolved by applying a list of factors, including:

a.   Form of the obligation.

b.   Proportionality.

c.   Debt–equity ratio.

d.   Intent of the parties to create a debtor-creditor relationship.

e.   Subordination.

The courts usually treat reclassified debt as equity in its entirety.

3.   Consequences of Reclassification
If debt is reclassified as equity, payments labeled as "interest" and repayments of "principal" are treated as constructive dividends.

4.   Shareholder Guaranteed Debt
The Service may treat shareholder guaranteed debt as equivalent to a loan from the outside lender to the shareholder followed by a contribution to capital, causing "interest" payments to the lender to be treated as a constructive dividend to the shareholder.

C.   Character of Loss on Corporate Investment
1.   In General
Because stock and debt instruments generally are capital assets, any loss on their sale or disposition is treated as a capital loss.

2.   Loss on Worthlessness of Debt
A loss on a debt that is a "security" under § 165(g) is a capital loss. Losses incurred by noncorporate taxpayers on other debts are usually treated as short-term capital losses from a nonbusiness bad debt.

3.   Loss on Worthlessness of Equity
Losses on § 1244 stock are ordinary losses, subject to various limitations. Other losses on equity investments are capital losses.

D.   Special Problems of Excessive Corporate Debt
1.   Junk Bonds
Junk bonds are unsecured high-yield corporate debt obligations. Certain junk bonds known as "applicable high yield discount obligations" are subject to special tax treatment, such as deferral of any interest deduction until actual payments are made in cash or other property.

2.   Earnings Stripping
Section 163(j) disallows a deduction for interest paid or accrued by a domestic corporation to certain related entities that are exempt from U.S. tax.

3.   Limitation on Net Operating Losses
Corporations may be limited in their ability to carry back net operating losses attributable to various debt-financed transactions.

VI.   NONLIQUIDATING DISTRIBUTIONS

A.   Introduction
1.   Distribution vs. Dividend
A "distribution" is any payment by a corporation to its shareholders with respect to their stock. "Dividends" are distributions out of the current or accumulated earnings and profits of a corporation.

2. **Dividends Under Corporate Law**
    Dividends as defined under corporate law have no bearing on whether a distribution is a dividend for federal tax purposes.

3. **Distributions and Dividends Under the Code**
    The three steps in determining whether a distribution is a dividend are:

    a. Determine the amount of the distribution, which is the cash received plus the fair market value of any other property received reduced by any liabilities assumed by the shareholder or liabilities to which the property is subject.

    b. Determine the amount of the dividend, which is that part of the distribution that is made out of "current earnings and profits" or post–1913 "accumulated earnings and profits."

    c. Include the dividend in the shareholder's gross income and treat any remaining portion of the distribution first as a tax-free return of capital and then as gain from a sale or exchange of the stock.

B. **Earnings and Profits ("E & P")**
    1. **The Concept**
        The principal function of E & P is to measure the extent to which a distribution is made from a corporation's economic income.

    2. **Determination of E & P**
        E & P are derived by starting with the corporation's taxable income for the year and making certain additions (e.g., tax-exempt interest), subtractions (e.g., federal income taxes) and adjustments (e.g., depreciation).

C. **Cash Distributions**
    1. **In General**
        Cash distributions are dividends to the extent they are made out of current or accumulated E & P. Current E & P are measured as of the end of the taxable year without reductions for distributions made during the year.

    2. **Current E & P Exceed Distributions**
        If current E & P exceed cash distributions made during the year, each cash distribution is a dividend.

    3. **Distributions Exceed Current E & P**
        If cash distributions exceed current E & P, a portion of each distribution is treated as coming from current E & P. The remainder of each distribution is a dividend to the extent of accumulated E & P available on the distribution date.

    4. **Accumulated E & P But Current Deficit**
        To determine available accumulated E & P, a current deficit must be ratably allocated against accumulated E & P as of the date of each distribution or, alternatively, the corporation can allocate the deficit to the time period in which it was actually incurred.

D. Property Distributions
1. Consequences to the Distributing Corporation
A corporation recognizes gain on the distribution of appreciated property as if it had sold the property for its fair market value, but it may not recognize loss on a distribution of loss property. No gain or loss is recognized on a distribution of a corporation's own obligations. Current E & P are increased by any gain recognized on the distribution. Accumulated E & P are decreased by the fair market value of appreciated property (less any liabilities assumed), by the adjusted basis of any distributed loss property, and by the principal amount of debt obligations.

2. Consequences to Shareholders
The amount of the distribution is the fair market value of the distributed property reduced by any liabilities to which the property is subject. The distributee shareholder's basis is the fair market value of the distributed property without reduction for liabilities.

E. Constructive Distributions
1. In General
Some transactions that are not formally labeled as "dividends" may be treated as constructive dividends if they provide economic benefits to shareholders.

2. Examples of Constructive Dividends
Examples of constructive dividends include unreasonable compensation, low-interest loans, bargain sales or leases, excessive payments to shareholders for purchases of corporate property, payment of a shareholder's personal expenses, and transfers between commonly controlled corporations.

F. Special Problems of Corporate Shareholders
1. The Dividends Received Deduction
Corporate shareholders generally may deduct 70% (or sometimes 80% or 100%) of dividends received from other domestic corporations.

2. Holding Period Requirements
The dividends received deduction is not available when the stock on which the dividend is paid has been held for less than 46 days.

3. Extraordinary Dividends
Corporate shareholders sometimes must reduce their stock basis by the untaxed portion of an "extraordinary dividend" or recognize gain if the untaxed portion exceeds the shareholder's stock basis. A dividend is "extraordinary" if it exceeds 5% of the shareholder's adjusted basis in preferred stock, 10% of the adjusted basis in any other stock, and in other more specialized situations.

4. Debt–Financed Portfolio Stock
The dividends received deduction is reduced to the extent that the dividend is attributable to debt-financed portfolio stock.

5. Earnings and Profits Adjustments

Although a corporation generally must make certain timing adjustments (e.g., for depreciation) in determining its E & P, those adjustments are not made in determining the tax consequences of distributions to 20% or more corporate shareholders.

6. Preacquisition Dividend Strips

A parent corporation that sells the stock of a subsidiary in a taxable transaction may be able to convert capital gain on the sale to partially deductible dividend income by causing the subsidiary to make a large distribution shortly prior to the sale. The success of the technique depends on the timing and source of the distribution.

VII. STOCK REDEMPTIONS AND PARTIAL LIQUIDATIONS

A. Introduction

1. Redemption Defined

A redemption is a repurchase of stock by its issuer.

2. Overview of Tax Consequences

The shareholder-level consequences of a redemption depend on whether the distribution resembles a dividend or a sale by the redeemed shareholders. Redemptions that do not qualify for sale or exchange treatment are treated as § 301 distributions and are dividends to the extent of E & P.

3. Tax Stakes to Shareholders

Individual shareholders usually prefer sale or exchange treatment because they can recover their basis in the redeemed stock and treat any gain as capital gain. A corporation generally recognizes gain on a distribution of appreciated property in a redemption, but it may not recognize loss on a distribution of property that has declined in value.

B. Constructive Ownership of Stock

For purposes of determining stock ownership under § 302, an individual or entity is considered as owning stock owned by certain related family members and entities under the attribution rules in § 318.

C. Redemptions Treated as Exchanges

A redemption is treated as a § 301 distribution unless it meets one of four tests for exchange treatment in § 302(b).

1. Substantially Disproportionate Redemptions

To qualify as a substantially disproportionate redemption, the redeemed shareholder must own less than 50% of the voting power of the corporation after the redemption and the shareholder's percentage of voting stock and common stock (whether or not voting) after the redemption must be less than 80% of his percentage ownership before the redemption.

2. **Complete Terminations of a Shareholder's Interest**

A redemption that completely terminates a shareholder's actual and constructive stock interest in the corporation is treated as an exchange. Individual shareholders or entities who completely terminate their actual stock interest may waive family attribution under § 318 if the following requirements are met:

a. Immediately after the distribution, the shareholder has no interest in the corporation other than as a creditor;

b. The shareholder does not acquire any such interest other than by bequest or inheritance within the 10–year period from the date of the distribution;

c. The shareholder agrees to notify the Service of any prohibited acquisition during the 10–year post-distribution period; and

d. No portion of the redeemed stock was acquired within the 10–year predistribution period from a § 318 related person, and no such related person who continues to own stock in the distributing corporation acquired any stock within that period from the redeemed shareholder, except that these conditions do not apply if the acquisition or disposition of stock was not motivated by tax avoidance.

3. **Redemptions Not Essentially Equivalent to a Dividend**

A redemption is not essentially equivalent to a dividend if it results in a meaningful reduction of the shareholder's proportionate interest in the corporation. A significant loss of control (e.g., from more than 50% to less than 50%) is an example of a meaningful reduction, as is virtually any reduction in control or voting rights of an isolated minority shareholder.

4. **Partial Liquidations**

Distributions in partial liquidation are treated as exchanges to individual but not corporate shareholders. A partial liquidation results from a genuine contraction of the corporation's business, including the termination of a trade or business that the corporation has actively conducted for the five-year period preceding the distribution. A distribution of the stock of a subsidiary or the proceeds of sale of such stock does not qualify as a partial liquidation.

D. **Specific Tax Consequences of Redemptions**
   1. **Consequences to Shareholders**

   Redemptions that qualify for exchange treatment are treated as if the shareholder sold the redeemed stock to an outsider. Redemptions not qualifying for exchange treatment are treated as § 301 distributions and thus are dividends to the extent of the distributing corporation's E & P and a reduction of basis or capital gain to the extent of the balance of the distribution. Shareholders take a fair market value basis in any property distributed in a redemption.

2. Consequences to Distributing Corporation

The distributing corporation recognizes gain (but not loss) on a distribution of property in redemption of its stock. It increases its E & P by any gain recognized. If a redemption is treated as a § 301 distribution, E & P are reduced by the amount of money and the fair market value of the distributed property. If a redemption is treated as an exchange, E & P are reduced in an amount that may not exceed the ratable share of accumulated E & P attributable to the redeemed stock. The distributing corporation generally may not currently deduct expenses paid in connection with the redemption or reacquisition of its own stock.

E. Redemptions Through Use of Related Corporations

1. Introduction

Section 304 is designed to prevent a bailout when one or more controlling shareholders sell the stock of one corporation to another commonly controlled corporation, or when any shareholder of a parent corporation sells stock of the parent to a subsidiary. Section 304 tests these transactions for dividend equivalency by applying § 302 to determine whether the shareholder has sufficiently reduced his interest in the corporation whose stock is acquired.

2. Brother–Sister Acquisitions

If one or more persons in control of each of two corporations sell stock of one corporation (the "issuing corporation") to the other (the "acquiring corporation") in return for property, the property is treated as a distribution in redemption of the acquiring corporation's stock and is tested for dividend equivalence under § 302 by reference to the stock of the issuing corporation. If the constructive redemption is not treated as an exchange, it is a dividend to the extent of the E & P of the issuing and acquiring corporations.

3. Parent–Subsidiary Acquisitions

If a subsidiary (the "acquiring corporation") acquires stock of its parent (the "issuing corporation") from a shareholder of the parent in return for property, the property is treated as having been distributed in redemption of the parent's stock and is tested for dividend equivalency by reference to that stock. If the constructive redemption is not treated as an exchange, it is a dividend to the extent of the E & P of the issuing and acquiring corporations.

4. Relationship of § 304 to Other Code Sections

Section 304 generally overrides § 351 when the two sections overlap.

F. Redemptions to Pay Death Taxes

Even if a redemption does not qualify as an exchange under § 302, it still may qualify under § 303 if the redeemed stock was included in the decedent's gross estate for federal tax purposes and the value of the stock exceeds 35% of the gross estate less debts and expenses. Exchange treatment is available under § 303 only to the extent that the distribution does not exceed the sum of death taxes and funeral and administrative expenses.

G. Redemptions and Related Transactions

1. Redemptions and Sales

If a redemption and sale are part of an integrated disposition of a shareholder's entire interest in a corporation, the redemption will qualify as a complete termination of the shareholder's interest whether it occurs before or after the sale.

2. Redemptions Pursuant to Buy–Sell Agreements

Constructive dividend issues may be raised when a continuing shareholder is personally and unconditionally obligated to purchase stock pursuant to a buy-sell agreement and that obligation is assumed by the corporation. But a mere assignment of a continuing shareholder's contractual obligation to purchase stock from a retiring shareholder does not result in a constructive dividend. Constructive dividend issues also may be raised when a corporation redeems stock in connection with a divorce. Under proposed regulations, a divorce-related redemption results in a constructive dividend to the nontransferor spouse and § 1041 nonrecognition to the spouse whose stock is redeemed only when the redemption satisfies a primary and unconditional obligation of the nontransferor spouse or when the parties jointly elect such treatment.

3. Charitable Contribution Followed by Redemption

If a shareholder of a closely held corporation contributes stock to a charity, and the corporation later redeems the charity's stock, the transaction will not be classified as a constructive dividend to the shareholder if the charity was not legally bound to surrender the shares for redemption.

VIII. STOCK DISTRIBUTIONS AND § 306 STOCK

A. Stock Distributions

1. Introduction

A stock distribution is a distribution by a corporation of its own stock to some or all of its shareholders.

2. Nontaxable Stock Distributions

Stock distributions are generally not includible in gross income unless an exception in § 305(b) applies. The shareholder's basis in the stock held prior to a nontaxable stock distribution is allocated between the old stock and the new stock received in proportion to the relative fair market values of each on the date of the distribution. The distributing corporation recognizes no gain and it may not reduce its E & P.

3. Taxable Stock Distributions

Stock distributions are taxable in the following situations:

a. Distributions payable either in stock of the distributing corporation or in cash or other property, at the shareholder's election.

b. Distributions that result in some shareholders receiving property while others increase their proportionate interest in the earnings or assets of the corporation.

c. Distributions where some shareholders receive common stock while others receive preferred stock.

d. Distributions on preferred stock, other than an increase in a conversion ratio made to take account of a stock dividend or split.

e. Distributions of convertible preferred stock.

f. Other transactions (e.g., a change in conversion ratios; periodic redemption plans) that have the effect of increasing the proportionate interests of one group of shareholders while others receive cash or other property.

4. Distributions of Stock Rights

Distributions of stock rights are generally not taxable unless they have one of the effects described in § 305(b). If rights received in a nontaxable distribution are later exercised or sold, the shareholder must allocate his stock basis in the underlying stock between the stock and the rights unless a de minimis rule applies. Taxable rights distributions are dividends to the extent of E & P.

B. § 306 Stock

1. The Preferred Stock Bailout

Section 306 was enacted to prevent the "preferred stock bailout," which was a device to bail out earnings at capital gains rates through a tax-free distribution and later sale of preferred stock.

2. Definition of § 306 Stock

Section 306 stock includes:

a. Preferred stock received as a tax-free distribution under § 305(a) unless the distributing corporation had no current or accumulated E & P.

b. Stock which has a transferred or substituted basis determined by reference to § 306 stock (e.g., § 306 stock received by gift).

c. Certain stock received in a tax-free corporate reorganization or division, or a § 351 exchange.

3. **Dispositions of § 306 Stock**
    a. If § 306 stock is redeemed, the amount realized is taxable as a dividend to the extent of the corporation's current or accumulated E & P at the time of the redemption, and the balance of the amount realized is treated as a reduction of basis or capital gain.

    b. On a sale or other disposition of § 306 stock, the amount realized is treated as ordinary income to the extent of the dividend that would have resulted at the time of the distribution if cash rather than stock had been distributed. The remaining amount realized first reduces basis of the § 306 stock and then is capital gain.

    c. Dispositions of § 306 stock that are exempt from the punitive general rule include complete terminations of the shareholder's interest and partial liquidations, complete liquidations, dispositions that qualify for nonrecognition treatment and certain transactions that are found by the Service to not be made pursuant to a tax avoidance plan.

IX. COMPLETE LIQUIDATIONS AND TAXABLE CORPORATE ACQUISITIONS

A. Complete Liquidation Defined

A complete liquidation occurs when a corporation ceases to be a going concern and its activities are merely for the purpose of winding up its affairs, paying its debts and distributing any remaining balance to its shareholders. A complete liquidation usually is evidenced by a formal written plan, but informal plans may be found to exist if the corporation's shareholders or directors manifest an intent to liquidate.

B. Complete Liquidations Under § 331
1. **Consequences to the Shareholders**
    a. Amounts distributed to a shareholder in a complete liquidation, less liabilities assumed by the shareholder, are treated as in full payment in exchange for the shareholder's stock. A shareholder thus recognizes capital gain or loss under general tax principles. Gain or loss is computed separately for separate blocks of stock with different bases or acquisition dates.

    b. If the value of a distributed asset is in dispute, uncertain or contingent, a shareholder may be able to defer reporting gain attributable to those assets.

    c. If a closely held liquidating corporation makes an installment sale of its assets and distributes the installment obligations to its shareholders within 12 months after adoption of the liquidation plan, the shareholders may report their § 331(a) gain on the installment method.

    d. The basis of property received by a shareholder on a complete liquidation is the fair market value of the property on the date of the distribution.

2. Consequences to the Distributing Corporation

a. The *General Utilities* doctrine no longer applies to distributions of appreciated property by a liquidating corporation. As a result, a corporation generally recognizes gain or loss on a liquidating distribution as if it had sold the property for its fair market value.

b. A liquidating corporation may not recognize loss on the distribution of property to a § 267 related person (e.g., a more than 50% shareholder) if the distribution is not pro rata among the shareholders or is of "disqualified property." "Disqualified property" is any property acquired by the corporation in a § 351 transaction or as a contribution to capital during the 5–year period ending on the date of the distribution.

c. A liquidating corporation may not recognize certain losses on sales, exchanges or distributions of property acquired by the corporation in a § 351 transaction or as a contribution to capital as part of a plan the principal purpose of which was to recognize loss in connection with the liquidation. If there is no clear and substantial relationship between the contributed property and the conduct of the corporation's business, it is generally presumed that property acquired by the corporation after a date that is two years before the adoption of the liquidation plan, or after the adoption of that plan, was acquired as part of a plan to recognize loss. Only the loss that accrued prior to the corporation's acquisition of the property is disallowed.

C. Liquidation of a Subsidiary

1. Introduction

Because a liquidation of an 80% or more subsidiary is viewed as a mere change in form, neither the parent shareholder nor the liquidating subsidiary recognizes gain or loss. In keeping with this policy, the subsidiary's asset bases and other tax attributes transfer to the parent.

2. Consequences to the Shareholders

a. A parent corporation ("P") does not recognize gain on the receipt of distributions in complete liquidation of a subsidiary ("S") if the following conditions are met:

1) S distributes its assets to P in complete cancellation or redemption of its stock pursuant to a complete liquidation plan.

2) P owns at least 80% of the total voting power and 80% of the total value of S's stock from the date the liquidation plan is adopted until the liquidation is complete.

3) The liquidation occurs within certain time limits.

b. The courts sometimes have allowed corporations to intentionally avoid § 332 (e.g., to recognize a loss) by violating one of these requirements.

c.   If P does not meet the 80% control test, it may be able to "back in" to control by causing S to redeem stock held by its minority shareholders shortly before the liquidation plan is adopted.

d.   P takes a transferred basis and a tacked holding period in the assets received from S in a § 332 liquidation. P's basis in its S stock disappears.

e.   Even if a liquidation qualifies under § 332, minority shareholders of S recognize gain or loss under the general rule in § 331 and take a fair market value basis in any distributed property under § 334(a).

3.   Consequences to the Liquidating Subsidiary

S does not recognize gain or loss on distributions of property to P in a § 332 liquidation. S also does not recognize gain or loss on transfers of property to satisfy preexisting debts to P. S recognizes gain but not loss on distributions of property to minority shareholders and on certain distributions to tax-exempt and foreign parents.

D.   Taxable Acquisitions of a Corporate Business
1.   Introduction

Taxable acquisitions of a corporate business may be structured as asset or stock acquisitions. The corporation whose assets or stock is acquired is often referred to as the "target," or "T," and the purchasing corporation is referred to as "P."

2.   Asset Acquisitions

T generally recognizes gain or loss on a sale of its assets, and P takes a cost basis in the assets it acquires. If T liquidates after its assets are acquired, T's shareholders recognize gain or loss under § 331(a) unless T is an 80% subsidiary of another corporation. If T does not liquidate, its shareholders do not recognize gain or loss, but T is likely to be classified as a personal holding company that will be subject to a penalty tax if it does not annually distribute its net income. The parties to an asset acquisition must allocate the aggregate consideration paid and received for the assets under the "residual method" prescribed by the regulations. After subtracting out cash and cash equivalents, the consideration is then allocated to government and marketable securities and then to tangible and most intangible assets to the extent of their fair market values, and any residue is allocated to goodwill and going concern value.

3.   Stock Acquisitions

a.   T's shareholders recognize gain or loss on the sale of their stock to P.

b.   T generally does not recognize gain when P acquires its stock unless P purchases 80% or more of T's stock within a 12–month period and makes a § 338 election to treat the transaction as an asset acquisition. In that event, T is treated as having sold all of its assets for their fair market value to a new corporation ("new T") in a taxable transaction. Under a formula prescribed by the regulations, the sale price of T's assets generally equals P's cost for the T stock plus T's liabilities, including any liabilities resulting from the deemed sale.

c. New T generally takes an aggregate basis in its assets that equals the price paid by P for the T stock plus T's liabilities, including any liabilities resulting from the deemed sale. That basis is then allocated among new T's assets using the residual method prescribed by the regulations.

d. If P acquires an asset from T during a "consistency period" that generally begins one year before the stock purchase and ends one year after the purchase, and if T is a subsidiary of another corporation ("S") and T and S file a consolidated return, P generally must take a carryover basis in any T assets acquired during the consistency period.

4. Sales and Distributions of Stock of a Subsidiary
If T is a subsidiary of another corporation ("S") and S sells 80% or more of its T stock to P, the parties may jointly elect under § 338(h)(10) to treat T as if it had sold all of its assets for fair market value to "new T" and then distributed the sales proceeds to S in a tax-free liquidation under § 332. S thus recognizes no gain on the sale of its T stock, and T's gain or loss on the deemed sale of its assets is included on the consolidated tax return filed by S and its affiliates. This election avoids two levels of corporate tax and permits S to deduct its own net operating losses against income recognized by T on the deemed asset sale.

5. Comparison of Acquisition Methods
From a tax standpoint, the preferred method for a taxable acquisition is a stock purchase without a § 338 election. A § 338 election may be desirable, however, where T has net operating losses or where T is a subsidiary and the parties jointly make a § 338(h)(10) election.

X. ANTI–AVOIDANCE PROVISIONS

A. Introduction
Taxpayers historically have pursued strategies to avoid the corporate double tax. Among the anti-avoidance provisions created by Congress to combat these strategies are the accumulated earnings tax, the personal holding company tax and the collapsible corporation rules.

B. Accumulated Earnings Tax
1. Introduction
Because individual income tax rates historically were significantly higher than corporate tax rates, corporations were attractive vehicles to accumulate income. The accumulated earnings tax was enacted to combat accumulation strategies. In recent years, the maximum corporate tax rate is only slightly lower than the top individual rate, and the importance of this tax has diminished.

2. **The Prohibited Tax Avoidance Purpose**

The accumulated earnings tax applies to corporations formed or availed of to avoid the individual income tax by accumulating, rather than distributing, the corporation's earnings and profits. The tax is paid in addition to other taxes paid by the corporation. The existence of a prohibited tax avoidance purpose depends upon the facts and circumstances of each case.

3. **Reasonable Needs of the Business**

A rebuttable presumption of a tax avoidance purpose arises if a corporation accumulates its earnings and profits beyond the reasonable needs of its business. A determination of the reasonable needs of the business also depends on the circumstances of each case. The regulations provide guidance in making this determination.

4. **Calculating Accumulated Taxable Income**

The accumulated earnings tax is determined by applying the highest individual marginal income tax rate to a corporation's "accumulated taxable income." Accumulated taxable income is taxable income, with adjustments to arrive at a more accurate measure of the corporation's economic performance, less a dividends paid deduction and an accumulated earnings credit.

C. **Personal Holding Company Tax**
   1. **Introduction**

The personal holding company tax is designed to prevent the "incorporated pocketbooks," "incorporated talents," and "incorporated properties" tax avoidance strategies. A tax at the highest individual marginal income tax rate is imposed on the "undistributed personal holding company income" of every personal holding company. The tax is imposed in addition to other taxes paid by the corporation.

   2. **Definition of a Personal Holding Company**

A personal holding company is a company which meets both a stock ownership requirement and an income requirement. More than 50% in value of the corporation's stock must be owned, directly or indirectly at any time during the last half of the taxable year by five or fewer individuals. In addition, at least 60% of the corporation's "adjusted ordinary gross income" must be "personal holding company income."

   3. **Undistributed Personal Holding Company Income**

"Undistributed personal holding company income" is equal to the corporation's taxable income adjusted so it is a more accurate measure of economic performance, less the dividends paid deduction.

D. **Collapsible Corporations**
   1. **Background**

Prior to 1986, the combination of preferential capital gains rates and the *General Utilities* doctrine permitted taxpayers to convert ordinary income into capital gain through the use of a "collapsible corporation." The collapsible corporation rules combat this strategy by providing that certain sales or exchanges and distributions by a "collapsible corporation" which would otherwise produce capital gain instead produce ordinary income. The viability of the collapsible corporation tax avoidance strategy has been virtually eliminated since the repeal of the *General Utilities* doctrine.

2. Definition of a Collapsible Corporation

A collapsible corporation is a corporation which is formed or availed of principally for the manufacture, construction, or production of property or the purchase of certain property. The corporation must be formed with a "view" to either a sale or exchange of its stock by its shareholders or the realization by the shareholders of gain attributable to such property before the corporation realizes two-thirds of the taxable income to be derived from such property. The sale or exchange of stock may be in a liquidation or otherwise.

A corporation is presumed to be collapsible if the fair market value of its § 341 assets exceeds 50% of the adjusted basis of certain assets and 120% of those assets.

3. Exceptions to Collapsibility

Under any of the following exceptions to the collapsible corporation rules, the gain recognized by a shareholder on a disposition of stock of a collapsible corporation is not converted to ordinary income:

a. The shareholder owns 5% or less of the stock of the corporation;

b. Less than 70% of the shareholder's gain is recognized more than three years after the completion of the manufacture, construction, production or purchase of the collapsible property;

c. The unrealized appreciation in the corporation's ordinary assets is small in relation to its net worth under very specific tests; or

d. The corporation consents to recognize its gain on any disposition of certain assets.

XI. TAX–FREE REORGANIZATIONS

A. Introduction

1. Policy

Transactions that qualify as "reorganizations" under § 368 are wholly or partially tax free to the participating corporations and their shareholders. The rationale for nonrecognition is that a reorganization is merely a readjustment of a continuing corporate enterprise that results in a continuity of investment.

2. Types of Corporate Reorganizations

Corporate reorganizations include acquisitions, nondivisive nonacquisitive transactions (such as recapitalizations), and divisive transactions.

3. **Guide to Analyzing a Reorganization**
    A student first should determine whether a transaction qualifies as a reorganization under § 368. If so, the next step is to determine the specific tax consequences to the corporations and their shareholders under various "operative" provisions that are triggered once reorganization status is achieved. Some reorganizations may be wholly tax-free, while others (e.g., where permissible boot is used) may result in partial nonrecognition of gain.

4. **Judicial Requirements**
    a. The continuity of shareholder proprietary interest doctrine requires that the target's shareholders retain a continuing proprietary interest in the acquiring corporation. The acquiring corporation must provide consideration that represents a proprietary interest in its affairs, and that consideration must be a substantial part of the property transferred to the target's shareholders.

    b. The continuity of business enterprise doctrine requires that the acquiring corporation must either continue the target's historic business or continue to use a significant portion of the target's historic business assets in a business.

    c. The business purpose doctrine requires a reorganization to be motivated by a bona fide corporate business purpose apart from tax avoidance.

5. **Advance Ruling Guidelines**
    The Service historically issued guidelines for parties who desired an advance ruling on the tax-free status of a reorganization. Although the Service no longer issues "comfort rulings" in routine transactions, its guidelines continue to offer safe harbors that sometimes are stricter than the case law.

B. **Acquisitive Reorganizations**
    1. **Type A (Statutory Merger or Reorganization)**
        A Type A reorganization is a merger or consolidation under local law. All cash mergers and divisive mergers do not qualify as reorganizations. A merger of a corporate-owned LLC into another corporation does not qualify, but a merger of a corporation into a single-member LLC may qualify as a Type A reorganization. The most important qualification requirement is that the shareholders of the target corporation ("T") maintain continuity of proprietary interest by owning stock in the acquiring corporation ("P"). For ruling purposes, the Service requires that at least 50% of the consideration paid by P to acquire T must consist of P stock, which need not be common or voting stock. Sales and other dispositions of stock by T shareholders before or after a merger generally are not considered in applying the continuity of interest test even if they were made pursuant to a preexisting binding commitment.

    2. **Type B (Stock-for-Stock Acquisition)**
        A Type B reorganization is P's acquisition of T's stock solely in exchange for P voting stock where P has control (i.e., 80%) of T immediately after the

acquisition. No boot may be used in a Type B reorganization. Creeping acquisitions are permitted as long as P's earlier cash purchases of T stock are unrelated to the final stock-for-stock acquisition.

3. **Type C (Stock-for-Assets Acquisition)**

A Type C reorganization is P's acquisition of substantially all of T's assets solely in exchange for P voting stock followed by the liquidation of T. In applying the solely for voting stock requirement, P's assumption of T's liabilities is disregarded. Under a boot relaxation rule, P's use of consideration other than voting stock is permitted provided that P acquires at least 80% of the value of all of T's assets solely for voting stock. For purposes of this rule, liabilities assumed by P are treated as cash consideration. Under the regulations, P's previous acquisition of more than 20% of T's stock followed by an acquisition of T's assets solely in exchange for P voting stock (or up to 20% boot) will not by itself prevent the transaction from qualifying as a Type C reorganization.

4. **Forward Triangular Mergers**

A merger of T into a subsidiary of P will qualify as a tax-free forward triangular merger if:

a. S acquires substantially all of the properties of T.

b. No stock of S is used as consideration in the merger.

c. The transaction would have qualified as a Type A reorganization if T had merged directly into P. For ruling purposes, this means that the T shareholders collectively must receive at least 50% P stock in the merger.

5. **Reverse Triangular Mergers**

A merger of S (P's subsidiary) into T will qualify as a tax-free reverse triangular merger if:

a. After the merger, T holds substantially all of its properties and the properties of S (other than P stock and boot distributed to T shareholders).

b. In the merger, P acquires control (80%) of T in exchange for P voting stock.

6. **Multi–Step Acquisitions: Special Problems**

The IRS sometimes treats multiple steps as a single integrated transaction in order to qualify the overall acquisition as a tax-free reorganization even if the first step, in isolation, would not qualify. In deference to the policy of § 338, however, the step transaction doctrine will not be applied when the first step is a qualified stock purchase under § 338 and the integrated transaction would not qualify as a reorganization.

7. **Treatment of the Parties to an Acquisitive Reorganization**

a. If a transaction qualifies as a reorganization, the tax consequences to T's shareholders and all corporate parties to the reorganization are determined by various operative provisions.

    b.   T's shareholders generally do not recognize gain or loss on an exchange of their T stock solely for P stock, or an exchange of T securities solely for P securities. Realized gain must be recognized to the extent that the shareholder receives boot. That gain is a dividend to the extent of T's earnings and profits if the exchange has the effect of the distribution of a dividend. Dividend equivalence is tested using § 302 principles. The basis of P stock received by T shareholders is the same as their T stock, decreased by the cash and the fair market value of any other boot received, and increased by the shareholder's recognized gain. If preferred stock received in a reorganization may facilitate a later bailout, it will be classified as § 306 stock.

    c.   T generally does not recognize gain on a transfer of its assets to P pursuant to a reorganization plan. T also does not recognize gain or loss when it distributes P's stock or debt obligations to the T shareholders or creditors, but it may recognize gain on a distribution of appreciated T assets not acquired in the reorganization or appreciated boot.

    d.   P does not recognize gain on the issuance of its stock or debt obligations in an acquisitive reorganization but generally does recognize gain on a transfer of other appreciated boot property. P takes a transferred basis in T's assets. P's basis in T stock acquired in a Type B reorganization is the same as the aggregate basis of the former T shareholders. P's basis in T stock acquired in a reverse triangular merger is generally the same as T's net basis in its assets.

8. Failed Reorganizations

An acquisition that fails to qualify under § 368 is treated as a taxable acquisition of T's assets or stock.

C. Nonacquisitive, Nondivisive Reorganizations

1. Nondivisive Type D (Transfer to Controlled Corporation)

A nondivisive Type D reorganization is a transfer by one corporation of all or substantially all of its assets to a corporation controlled immediately after the transfer by the transferor or its shareholders provided that the stock, securities and other properties received by the transferor are distributed, along with its other properties, to its shareholders pursuant to a reorganization plan.

2. Type E (Recapitalizations)

Type E reorganizations are recapitalizations of a single corporation. The continuity of interest requirement does not apply to a recapitalization. Among the types of exchanges that qualify as Type E reorganizations are exchanges of stock for stock, bonds for bonds, and old bonds for new stock. An exchange of old stock for new bonds, or a combination of stock or bonds, is taxable to the extent of the boot received and may give rise to dividend treatment.

3. Type F (Change in Form)

Type F reorganizations are limited to a mere change in the identity, form or place of organization of a corporation. An example is when a corporation changes its state of incorporation.

4. **Type G (Insolvency)**

   A Type G reorganization is a transfer by a corporation of all or part of its assets to another corporation in a bankruptcy proceeding or similar case if, pursuant to a plan, stock or securities of the transferee corporation are distributed in a transaction which qualifies under § 354, § 355, or § 356.

D. **Special Problems**
   1. **Liquidation–Reincorporation Doctrine**

      Taxpayers once used the liquidation-reincorporation strategy to bail out corporate earnings at capital gains rates without paying a corporate-level tax. The Service often attacked this strategy by contending that the transaction was a nondivisive D reorganization in which the shareholders received a boot dividend. This controversy has abated because the technique is rarely viable under current law.

   2. **Dispositions of Unwanted Assets**

      A target corporation may wish to make a tax-free distribution of an unwanted business prior to being acquired in a reorganization. This topic is discussed in Chapter XII.

XII. CORPORATE DIVISIONS

A. **Introduction**

   A corporate division is a transaction in which a single corporate enterprise is divided into two or more separate corporations that remain under the same ownership. If certain statutory and judicial requirements are met, a distribution by the parent corporation ("P") of stock in one or more subsidiaries ("S") is tax free to P and its shareholders.

   1. **Types of Corporate Divisions**
      a. A spin-off, which resembles a dividend, is a pro rata distribution of S stock by P to its shareholders.

      b. A split-off, which resembles a redemption, is a distribution of S stock by P to some of its shareholders in exchange for all or part of their P stock.

      c. A split-up, which resembles a complete liquidation, is a liquidating distribution by P of stock in two or more subsidiaries (S–1, S–2, etc.).

   2. **Type D Reorganization Preceding a Division**

      P may distribute the stock of an existing or newly formed subsidiary in a corporate division. If S is newly formed, P's transfer of assets to S in exchange for S stock is a tax-free Type D reorganization if the subsequent distribution of S stock meets the requirements of § 355.

   3. **Summary of Requirements for Tax–Free Division**

      P's distribution of S stock qualifies as tax free under § 355 if the following statutory and judicial requirements are met:

a. P controls S immediately before the distribution; an 80% test is applied to measure control.

b. P either distributes all of S's stock or securities or distributes "control" and establishes that the retention of stock or securities is not motivated by tax avoidance.

c. Immediately after the distribution, both P and S are engaged in a trade or business that has been actively conducted for the five-year period preceding the distribution, was not acquired within the five-year period in a taxable transaction, and was not conducted by a corporation the control of which was acquired by P or any corporate distributee shareholder of P within the five-year period in a taxable transaction.

d. The transaction is not used as a device for distributing earnings and profits of P, S or both.

e. The division is carried out for a bona fide corporate business purpose.

f. P's shareholders maintain continuity of proprietary interest in both P and S after the distribution.

g. The anti-avoidance rules in §§ 355(d) and 355(e) are not violated; if they are, P (but not its shareholders) may recognize gain on the distribution of S stock.

B. Active Trade or Business
1. Trade or Business
A trade or business is a specific group of activities carried on with a profit motive.

2. Active Conduct
Active conduct requires the performance of active and substantial management and operational functions. A passive investment activity does not qualify.

3. Divisions of a Single Integrated Business
The active business test is met if P vertically divides an integrated business. The test is not necessarily violated by distributing certain distinct functions of a single business.

4. Five–Year Business History Rule
The active post-distribution trade or business must have been actively conducted throughout the five-year period preceding the distribution and may not have been acquired by P or a distributee corporation in a taxable transaction during that period. If P expands a preexisting trade or business during the five-year period, the new branches or locations are considered part of that older business.

5. Disposition of a Recently Acquired Business

P's distribution of S stock will fail the active business test if a controlling interest in P was acquired by a corporate shareholder within the five years preceding the distribution.

C. Device Limitation

1. Introduction

The purpose of the device limitation is to prevent bailouts of corporate earnings at capital gains rates. The importance of the limitation is diminished whenever there is no significant capital gains preference. The determination of whether a transaction was used principally as a device is often factual and turns on the presence of certain device and nondevice factors specified in the regulations.

2. Device Factors

The presence of any of the following factors is evidence of a device:

a. A pro rata distribution of S stock (i.e., a spin-off).

b. A sale or exchange of P or S stock after the distribution. A subsequent sale that was prearranged is substantial evidence of a device, while other sales are only evidence.

c. The nature and use of certain assets, such as where either P or S holds excessive liquid assets not related to its business, or where the business of P or S principally services the business of the other corporation and could be sold without adversely affecting the business it serves.

3. Nondevice Factors

The presence of any of the following factors is evidence of a nondevice:

a. A corporate business purpose. The stronger the evidence of device, the stronger the corporate business purpose must be to outweigh the device factors.

b. The fact that P is publicly traded and widely held.

c. The fact that the S stock is distributed to a domestic corporate shareholder which would be entitled to claim a dividends received deduction in the absence of § 355.

4. Presumptive Nondevice Transactions

The following types of distributions "ordinarily" are not treated as a device:

a. A distribution in which P and S have neither accumulated nor current E & P.

b. The fact that, absent § 355, the distribution would qualify as an exchange redemption under § 302 or a redemption to pay death taxes under § 303.

D. Distribution of Control Requirement
P must distribute either all the S stock or securities or an amount of S stock constituting "control" (80%) and satisfy the Service that the retention of S stock or securities is not motivated by tax avoidance.

E. Business Purpose
The business purpose test requires the distribution to be motivated by a bona fide corporate business purpose. A shareholder purpose will not suffice. The test is not met if P's goals could have been achieved without having to distribute the stock of S. The business purpose for a transaction is used as evidence in determining whether the transaction was used principally as a device for the distribution of E & P. The IRS has provided numerous examples of valid and invalid corporate business purposes.

F. Continuity of Interest
After P's distribution of S stock, one or more of P's historic predistribution shareholders must maintain, in the aggregate, continuity of interest in both P and S. For this purpose, the Service uses a 50% (by value) benchmark in testing for continuity.

G. Tax Treatment of the Parties to a Corporate Division
    1. Shareholders and Security Holders
        a. P's shareholders and security holders generally do not recognize gain on their receipt of S stock unless they receive boot in the distribution. Boot includes cash, nonsecurity debt of P, and P securities to the extent their principal amount exceeds the principal amount of any P securities surrendered.

        b. In a spin-off, the receipt of boot is treated as a § 301 distribution and is a dividend to the extent of P's E & P. In a split-off or split-up, a shareholder recognizes gain to the extent of the boot received. If the receipt of boot has the effect of a dividend, the shareholder's recognized gain is a dividend to the extent of P's E & P. In no event may loss be recognized.

        c. If no boot is received, a P shareholder allocates her old basis in the P stock between the P and S stock (or S–1 and S–2 stock in a split-up) in proportion to their relative fair market values. If boot is received, the aggregate basis of the P and S stock (or S–1 and S–2 stock in a split-up) equals the basis of the old P stock, less the cash and the fair market value of any boot received, plus any gain recognized on the distribution. That amount is then allocated between the distributed and retained stock in proportion to their relative fair market values. Boot property takes a fair market value basis.

    2. The Distributing Corporation
    Whether or not the distribution is preceded by a reorganization, P generally does not recognize gain on the distribution of S stock or securities to the P

shareholders. P recognizes gain on any distribution of appreciated boot. In no event may P recognize loss. In some situations, P may recognize gain on a distribution of S stock when the distribution is treated as a disguised sale under the "anti-avoidance" rules in §§ 355(d) and 355(e).

H. Corporate Division Combined with Tax–Free Reorganization
1. Historical Opportunities and Pitfalls

Prior to the enactment of § 355(e), P's spin-off of a trade or business with a five-year history followed by the acquisition of P's assets or stock in a Type A or Type B reorganization qualified as tax-free under § 355. If a spin-off of unwanted assets was followed by an attempted Type C reorganization, however, neither transaction qualified as tax-free. If P retained unwanted assets and spun off a wanted business by distributing the stock of a newly formed subsidiary which was then acquired in an attempted reorganization, neither the spin-off nor the acquisitive reorganization qualified as tax-free unless P was a public company, S was not a newly formed subsidiary, and no negotiations with respect to the acquisition took place prior to the spin-off.

3. Section 355(e)

A distributing corporation (but not the distributee shareholders) must recognize gain in an otherwise qualified § 355 transaction if, as part of a "plan," one or more persons acquires a 50% or greater interest in either the distributing or controlled corporations within two years before or after the distribution. The gain is determined by treating the distributing corporation as if it had sold the stock of the distributed controlled subsidiary for its fair market value on the date of the distribution. The existence of a "plan" is determined by all the facts and circumstances. Although a plan is presumed if the acquisition occurs two years before or after the distributions, the regulations provide numerous safe harbors and other factors that may be invoked by the taxpayer to rebut the presumption and avoid gain recognition under § 355(e).

XIII. CARRYOVERS OF CORPORATE TAX ATTRIBUTES

A. Introduction

The Code includes a comprehensive set of rules governing the carryover of corporate tax attributes, such as earnings and profits and net operating losses, on reorganizations and other major corporate transactions.

B. Operation of § 381
1. In General

In an acquisition of a target corporation's assets in a § 332 liquidation or certain reorganizations, the acquiring corporation succeeds to and takes into account certain tax attributes of the target corporation.

2. § 381 Limitations on Carryovers

Certain limitations on the carryover of the target corporation's tax attributes may be imposed when the target has an E & P deficit or NOLs.

3. Carryovers in Divisive Reorganizations

The carryover rules of § 381 do not apply to divisive reorganizations. Unless otherwise provided, the tax attributes of the distributing corporation in a divisive reorganization are not altered by the transaction. The E & P of the distributing corporation, however, may have to be allocated or reduced as a result of a divisive reorganization.

C. Limitations on Carryovers of Corporate Tax Attributes

1. Introduction

The principal limitations on the general § 381 carryover rules are contained in § 382.

2. Limitation on Net Operating Loss Carryforwards: § 382

a. Section 382 limits the use of a corporation's NOL carryforwards if there is a substantial change in ownership of the loss corporation. An ownership change occurs if the percentage of stock of a loss corporation owned by one or more "5–percent shareholders" increases by more than 50% over the lowest percentage of stock owned by such shareholders during the "testing period". An ownership change may result from an "owner shift involving a 5–percent shareholder", an "equity structure shift", or a combination of the two. Modified § 318 attribution rules are applied to determine stock ownership.

b. If an ownership change has occurred, all NOLs are disallowed if the new loss corporation does not continue the business enterprise of the old loss corporation at all times during the two-year period following the date of the ownership change. If the business is continued, a loss corporation's NOLs are limited to an amount equal to the value of the old loss corporation multiplied by the long-term tax-exempt rate.

c. Special rules exist when a loss corporation has a "net unrealized built-in gain". The § 382 limitation is increased by any recognized built-in gains during the five-year period following the ownership change. This rule applies only if the corporation's net unrealized built-in gain exceeds either 15% of the fair market value of its assets (less cash and certain cash equivalents) or $10 million.

d. If a loss corporation has a "net unrealized built-in loss", its recognized built-in losses during the five-year period following the ownership change are subject to the § 382 limitations as if they were a NOL carryover. This rule applies only if the corporation's net unrealized built-in loss exceeds either 15% of the fair market value of its assets (less cash and certain cash equivalents) or $10 million.

3. Special Limitations on Other Tax Attributes: § 383

Section 383 applies § 382 limitation principles with respect to carryovers of the general business credit, minimum tax credit, foreign tax credit, and capital losses of a loss corporation after an ownership change.

4. **Limitation on Use of Preacquisition Losses to Offset Built–In Gains: § 384**

Section 384 prevents a loss corporation from using its preacquisition NOLs to offset built-in gains of an acquired corporation during the five-year period following the acquisition. Section 384 applies if a corporation acquires either control (generally 80% ownership) of another corporation or the assets of another corporation in a Type A, C, or D reorganization and either corporation has a net unrealized built-in gain.

5. **Acquisitions Made to Evade or Avoid Income Tax: § 269**

Under § 269, the Service may disallow a deduction, credit, or other allowance following certain corporate acquisitions if the principal purpose of the acquisition was the evasion or avoidance of income tax.

6. **Consolidated Return Rules**

All the statutory limitations on carryovers of tax attributes apply to corporations filing a consolidated tax return. In addition, the consolidated return regulations contain special rules which apply to a "separate return limitation year" situation.

XIV. AFFILIATED CORPORATIONS

A. Introduction

The theory that each corporation is a separate taxpayer is limited in certain situations when corporations are "affiliated".

B. Restrictions on Multiple Tax Benefits

Section 1561 prevents "component members of a controlled group" from obtaining multiple tax benefits, such as the benefit of the lower marginal tax rates in § 11(b). Other Code sections contain specific limitations on multiple tax benefits for affiliated corporations. Under § 269, the Service may disallow a tax benefit of a person or persons who acquire "control" (at least 50% of total vote or value) of a corporation and the principal purpose of the acquisition is avoidance of income tax by securing a tax benefit which would be otherwise unavailable.

C. Transactions Involving Related Corporations and Other Taxpayers

The Code has a number of provisions designed to prevent tax avoidance in transactions between controlled and commonly owned corporations. Under § 482, the Service may apportion or allocate tax items between or among enterprises which are owned or controlled by the same interests in order to prevent evasion of taxes or to clearly reflect income.

D. Consolidated Returns

Commonly controlled corporations meeting certain requirements (an "affiliated group of corporations") may elect to compute and pay tax on their consolidated taxable income. Because the members of the group are treated as a single taxpayer, special rules are applied to intercompany distributions and intercompany transactions.

XV. S CORPORATIONS

A. Introduction
A Subchapter S election allows a "small business corporation" to avoid almost all corporate-level taxes. The shareholders of an S corporation are taxed directly on corporate-level profits, thereby avoiding the corporate double tax.

B. Eligibility for S Corporation Status
The special tax provisions of Subchapter S are available only to "small business corporations" making an election under § 1362(a). "Small business corporations" must meet all of the following requirements:

1. Ineligible Corporations
Ineligible corporations, as defined by § 1361(b)(2), do not qualify as small business corporations. The category includes certain types of banks and insurance companies. Beginning in 1998, a corporation is not "ineligible" if it has a subsidiary.

2. 75–Shareholder Limit
A small business corporation may not have more than 75 shareholders. Spouses and their estates are considered one shareholder for purposes of the 75–shareholder limit.

3. Restrictions on Types of Shareholders
Small business corporations may not have shareholders who are not individuals except for certain estates and trusts. Nonresident aliens are not eligible shareholders.

4. One Class of Stock Requirement
A small business corporation may not have more than one class of stock. Differences in rights to profits or assets on liquidation create a second class of stock. Differences in voting rights are disregarded when determining whether a corporation has more than one class of stock. Except in abuse cases, buy-sell and redemption agreements, and stock transfer restrictions also are disregarded. Debt that complies with a "straight debt safe harbor" rule will not be considered a second class of stock.

C. Election, Revocation and Termination of Subchapter S Status
1. Electing S Corporation Status
The shareholders of a small business corporation must make a unanimous election to be an S corporation. Elections made up to the 15th day of the third month of the taxable year are effective for that taxable year and all succeeding years until terminated.

2. Revocation and Termination of S Corporation Status
An S corporation election may be revoked with the consent of more than 50% of the shares of stock of the corporation. An election is terminated if the

corporation ceases to meet the definition of a small business corporation. An election also may be terminated if the corporation violates the "passive income limitations" of § 1362(d)(3). Revocations and terminations generally will preclude the corporation from reelecting S corporation status for five years. If a corporation inadvertently terminates its S status, the Treasury has the option to disregard the termination and allow the corporation to continue as an S corporation.

D. Tax Treatment of S Corporation Shareholders

1. Introduction

In general, an S corporation is not a taxable entity. Its income, loss, deductions, and credits are passed through to its shareholders.

2. Corporate Level Determination of Tax Results

An S corporation calculates its gross income and taxable income to determine the tax results to be passed through to its shareholders. An S corporation is allowed to select its own accounting method subject to certain limitations. The taxable year of the S corporation can be either a calendar year or an accounting year for which it establishes a business purpose. Legislative history, revenue rulings, and revenue procedures have established criteria by which the business purpose standard is evaluated.

An S corporation computes its taxable income in the same manner as an individual except that certain deductions unique to individuals are not allowed. Items of income, deductions, losses, and credits which could affect the tax liability of the shareholder if treated separately must be separately reported by the S corporation. Tax elections are made by the S corporation and not its shareholders.

3. Tax Consequences to Shareholders

Shareholders of an S corporation must account for their pro rata share (on a per share, per day basis) of the corporation's separately stated items and nonseparately computed income or loss in the taxable year in which the S corporation's taxable year ends.

A shareholder's share of an S corporation's losses is limited to the shareholder's adjusted basis in the stock of the corporation and the indebtedness of the corporation to the shareholder. Losses which pass through to the shareholder also may be limited by the § 465 at-risk limitations and the § 469 passive loss limitations.

The shareholder's share of the S corporation's income and losses which are passed through to the shareholder will increase and decrease, respectively, the shareholder's basis in the S corporation stock.

The regulations apply a partial look-through rule to characterize gain or loss on the sale of S corporation stock. In general, gain or loss on the sale of stock held for more than one year is long-term capital gain. If an S corporation owns appreciated collectibles, some of the shareholder's gain may be treated as collectibles gain taxable at a maximum rate of 28%.

E. Distributions to Shareholders

Since S corporation shareholders are taxed directly on their share of the corporation's taxable income, subsequent distributions of this income by the corporation are generally not taxed to the shareholder.

1. S Corporations Without E & P

If an S corporation has no E & P, a distribution is tax free to the extent of the shareholder's basis in the corporation's stock. Any excess of the distribution over the stockholder's adjusted basis is treated as a gain from the sale or exchange of the stock. The shareholder's adjusted basis is reduced by the amount of any distribution that is not included in the shareholder's taxable income.

2. S Corporations With E & P

If an S corporation has E & P, distributions are first treated as recovery of stock basis and then as stock gain to the extent of corporation's accumulated adjustments account ("AAA"). Any remaining distribution is first treated as a dividend to the extent of the corporation's accumulated E & P and then as recovery of stock basis or gain.

3. Distributions of Property

An S corporation recognizes gain on the distribution of appreciated property. The gain passes through and is taxed to the shareholders in the same manner as other income.

The amount of the property distribution to the shareholder is the fair market value of the property. The shareholder takes a fair market value basis in the property received. The shareholder reduces her adjusted basis in the corporation's stock by the fair market value of the distributed property.

4. Ordering of Basis Adjustments

An S corporation shareholder's stock basis is first increased by her pro rata share of income and gain items for the year before making downward adjustments for distributions. Adjustments for distributions are made before any basis reductions for losses.

5. Distributions Following Termination of S Corporation Status

Shareholders receiving distributions during a "post-termination transition period" (at least one year after the last day of the corporation's last taxable year as an S corporation) can be applied against the shareholder's stock basis to the extent of the AAA.

F. Taxation of the S Corporation

S corporations generally are relieved of paying all corporate-level taxes except for the taxes in § 1374 and § 1375.

1. **§ 1374 Tax on Built–In Gains**
   Section 1374 applies to S corporations which were once C corporations. Gain in appreciated assets held by the corporation at the time of its S election may be taxed at the highest corporate rate if the S corporation sells the asset at a gain within 10 years of making an S election. The amount of built-in gain that may be taxed under this provision is limited to the total net gain inherent in all of the corporation's assets at the time of the election.

2. **§ 1375 Tax on Excessive Passive Investment Income**
   An S corporation with E & P from Subchapter C operations is subject to tax (at the highest corporate rate) on its "excess net passive income" if its gross receipts are more than 25% "passive investment income".

G. **Coordination of Subchapter S With Subchapter C and Other Tax Provisions**
   1. **Coordination With Subchapter C**
      S corporations can engage in the wide range of corporate-shareholder transactions available to C corporations. The provisions of Subchapter C generally apply to an S corporation and its shareholders unless such treatment would be inconsistent with Subchapter S.

   2. **Coordination With Other Tax Provisions**
      Tax principles applicable to individuals generally apply to S corporations.

   3. **Application of Social Security and Employment Taxes**
      Shareholder attempts to avoid FICA and FUTA taxes by paying no salaries have not been successful. Courts have been willing to recharacterize S corporation distributions as "wages" subject to employment tax.

PART THREE: PARTNERSHIP TAXATION

XVI. FORMATION OF A PARTNERSHIP

A. **Introduction**
   Section 721 provides that no gain or loss is recognized by a partnership or any of its partners on a contribution of property to the partnership in exchange for a partnership interest.

B. **Contributions of Property**
   1. **General Rules**
      For purposes of § 721, "property" includes cash, inventory, accounts receivable, patents, installment obligations and goodwill.

   2. **Related Issues**
      Section 721 overrides the recapture provisions and also overrides § 453B so that gain is not recognized when installment obligations are contributed in exchange for a partnership interest.

3. Basis and Holding Period

A partner's "outside" basis in his partnership interest is equal to the sum of money and the adjusted basis of property contributed to the partnership. The partnership's "inside" basis in contributed property is equal to the property's basis in the hands of the contributing partner.

The holding period for the partner's partnership interest is tacked when capital or § 1231 assets are contributed and begins on the day of the exchange when any other property is contributed. A partner may have a split holding period when a combination of assets is contributed to a partnership. The partnership tacks the partner's holding period for all contributed property.

C. Treatment of Liabilities

1. Impact on Partner's Outside Basis

If a partner's share of partnership liabilities increases, that increase is treated as a contribution of money which increases the partner's outside basis. § 752(a). Partners share recourse liabilities according to which partner bears the economic burden of discharging the liability if the partnership is unable to do so. Partners generally share nonrecourse liabilities in proportion to their shares of partnership profits.

2. Contributions of Property Encumbered by Recourse Liabilities

If property subject to a liability is contributed to a partnership, the partnership is considered to have assumed the liability to the extent the liability does not exceed the property's fair market value. The partners' shares of recourse liabilities are determined under the economic risk of loss rules. A decrease in a partner's share of partnership liabilities is treated as a distribution of money which decreases a partner's outside basis. § 752(b).

D. Contributions of Services

1. Introduction

A partner who receives a partnership interest in exchange for services is being compensated for those services and is taxable under § 61 and § 83.

2. Receipt of a Capital Interest for Services

A partner who receives a capital interest in a partnership in exchange for services has gross income when the interest is transferable or is no longer subject to a substantial risk of forfeiture. If the services are not capital in nature, the partnership is entitled to a deduction for the services when the partner recognizes income.

3. Receipt of a Profits Interest for Services

A partner who receives a profits interest in a partnership in exchange for services generally is not taxable on receipt of the interest. But a service partner is taxable on the receipt of a profits interest when:

a. the profits interest relates to a substantially certain and predictable stream of income from partnership assets,

      b.   the partner disposes of the profits interest within two years, or

      c.   the interest is in a publicly traded limited partnership.

E. Organization and Syndication Expenses

Generally, no deduction is allowed for amounts paid or incurred to organize a partnership or to promote the sale of partnership interests. Certain expenses incurred to organize a partnership may be amortized ratably over 60 or more months. Qualifying expenditures are those which (1) are incident to the creation of the partnership, (2) are chargeable to a capital account, and (3) are of a type which would be amortized over the life of a partnership having an ascertainable life.

XVII. OPERATIONS OF A PARTNERSHIP

A. Aggregate and Entity Theories of Partnership Taxation

Depending on the circumstances, a partnership is treated as an aggregate of its partners or as an entity separate and apart from its partners.

B. Taxing Partnership Operations
1. Partnership Level Determination of Tax Results

Even though a partnership is not a taxable entity, a partnership must calculate its gross income and taxable income to determine tax results to its partners. The partnership elects its own accounting method and taxable year.

2. Tax Consequences to the Partners

Partners are required to take into account their distributive share of partnership items in the taxable year in which the partnership's taxable year ends. A partner's distributive share of loss is limited to the partner's outside basis at the end of the partnership year in which the loss occurred. A partner's share of loss also is limited by the at-risk and passive activity loss limitations. Disallowed losses are carried over indefinitely.

A partner must increase his outside basis by his distributive share of partnership income and tax-exempt income and decrease it (but not below zero) by partnership distributions as provided in § 733 and his distributive share of partnership losses and expenditures which are neither deductible nor chargeable to a capital account.

A simplified reporting regime is available for electing large partnerships.

C. Partnership Allocations
1. Introduction

Each partner is required to take into account his distributive share (determined under the partnership agreement) of separately stated items and nonseparately computed income or loss.

2. Special Allocations of Partnership Items

In order to be recognized as valid, the regulations require partnership allocations to have "substantial economic effect." Partnership capital accounts are used to test that requirement.

To have economic effect, an allocation must be consistent with the underlying economic arrangement of the partners, and the economic benefit or burden must be borne by the partner receiving the allocation. This requirement can be met by satisfying any of the three tests set forth in the regulations: "The Big Three," the Alternate Test for Economic Effect, or the Economic Equivalence Test.

In order to be respected, the economic effect of an allocation must be "substantial," which requires that there be a reasonable possibility that the allocation will affect substantially the dollar amounts to be received by the partners from the partnership, independent of tax consequences. An allocation is not substantial if, at the time the allocation becomes part of the partnership agreement, (1) the after-tax consequences of at least one partner may be enhanced compared to the after-tax consequences if the allocation were not contained in the partnership agreement, and (2) there is a strong likelihood that the after-tax consequences of no partner will be substantially diminished compared to the after-tax consequences if the allocation were not contained in the partnership agreement.

If either the partnership agreement is silent or the partnership allocations lack substantial economic effect, a partner's distributive share of partnership items is determined in accordance with the partner's interest in the partnership.

3. Contributed Property

Section 704(c)(1)(A) provides that income, gain, loss and deduction with respect to property contributed by a partner to a partnership shall be allocated among the partners so as to take account of the variation between the inside basis of the property and its fair market value at the time of contribution. For example, the difference between the partnership's tax and book gain or loss on the disposition of a contributed asset is allocated to the contributing partner and any additional book gain or loss is allocated in accordance with the partnership agreement. Under a "ceiling rule," the total income or loss allocated to a partner under § 704(c) may not exceed the partnership's total income or loss with respect to the contributed property for the taxable year.

The regulations authorize three § 704(c) allocation methods: the traditional method, the traditional method with curative allocations and the remedial method. The latter two methods are designed to correct distortions resulting from the ceiling rule.

The characterization of partnership gains and losses is generally determined at the partnership level. Section 724, however, provides different rules for contributed unrealized receivables, inventory items, and capital loss property.

4.   Tax Treatment of Nonrecourse Liabilities

A liability is nonrecourse to the extent that no partner bears the economic risk of loss for the liability. In order to be respected, allocations attributable to nonrecourse liabilities generally must correspond to any later gain attributable to such debt under a four-part test. A partner's share of nonrecourse liabilities is equal to the sum of:

a.   the partner's share of "partnership minimum gain"; and

b.   the amount of any taxable gain that would be allocated to the partner under § 704(c) if the partnership disposed of the property subject to nonrecourse liabilities for relief of such liabilities and no other consideration.

Any remaining partnership nonrecourse liabilities generally are shared by the partners in accordance with their shares in partnership profits.

5.   Allocations Where Partners' Interests Vary During the Year

If there are changes during the year in any partner's interest in the partnership (e.g. by entry of a new partner or partial liquidation of the partner's interest), each partner's distributive share of partnership items must be determined by taking into account the partner's varying ownership interests in the partnership during the year. Where there is a change in a partner's capital interest in the partnership, the partners' distributive shares can be determined by either (1) prorating the partnership items over the year, or (2) through an interim closing of the partnership's books.

D.   Transactions Between Partners and Their Partnerships

1.   Transactions Involving Services or the Use of Property

Section 707(a)(1) generally adopts an entity theory for determining the tax consequences of transactions between a partner and a partnership by providing that if a partner engages in a transaction with a partnership "other than in his capacity as a member of such partnership," the transaction is to be taxed as if it occurred between the partnership and a nonpartner unless a Code section provides otherwise.

2.   Disguised Payments for Services or Property: § 707(a)(2)(A)

Section 707(a)(2)(A) provides that a direct or indirect allocation and distribution received by a partner for services or property will be treated as a § 707(a)(1) payment if the performance of services (or transfer of property) and the allocation and distribution, when viewed together, are properly characterized as a transaction between the partnership and a nonpartner.

3.   Guaranteed Payments

Fixed payments to a partner for services performed as a partner or as a return on contributed capital are guaranteed payments taxable under § 707(c). A guaranteed payment is ordinary income under § 61 to the partner and is potentially deductible under § 162 by the partnership, subject to the capitalization requirement of § 263.

4. Sales and Exchanges Between Partners and Partnerships
A sale of property between a partner and a partnership generally is treated in the same manner as a sale between the partnership and a nonpartner. Section 707(a)(2)(B) prevents sales of property between a partner and partnership from being structured as nontaxable contributions and distributions under § 721 and § 731.

E. The Family Partnership Rules
Section 704(e) prevents the shifting of income among partners who might not be dealing at arms length, such as family members. A safe harbor is provided for establishing the existence of a partnership and partner status.

XVIII. SALES AND EXCHANGES OF PARTNERSHIP INTERESTS

A. Introduction
When a partner disposes of some or all of her partnership interest, she must determine the recognized gain or loss with reference to her amount realized and the adjusted basis of her partnership interest, and the gain or loss must be characterized. The buying partner ordinarily obtains a cost basis in the acquired interest.

B. Tax Consequences to the Selling Partner

1. Computation of Gain or Loss
A partner's amount realized on the disposition of a partnership interest includes the cash and the fair market value of any property received for the interest, and any decrease in the selling partner's share of partnership liabilities. The partner's adjusted basis includes his distributive share of partnership items for the taxable year of the sale. The partnership's taxable year only closes with respect to a partner who sells or exchanges his entire partnership interest.

2. Characterization of Gain or Loss
Section 751 provides that consideration received by a partner in exchange for his interest in unrealized receivables and inventory items shall be considered as realized from property producing ordinary income. The remainder of the transaction is treated under § 741 as gain or loss from the sale of a partnership interest and is a capital gain or loss. The regulations apply a capital gains look-through rule to characterize long-term capital gain. The partner's holding period for the partnership interest determines whether capital gain is long-term or short-term.

3. Related Issues
If a partner sells a partnership interest under the installment method, gain attributable to certain assets may not be deferred. An exchange of partnership interests cannot qualify for nonrecognition as a like-kind exchange.

C. Tax Consequences to the Buying Partner
1. Introduction
A buying partner will take a cost basis in the partnership interest, receiving full credit for the share of partnership liabilities attributable to the interest. The sale of a partnership interest generally has no impact on the bases of partnership property. § 743(a). But a partnership may elect to adjust the bases of its assets with respect to the buying partner under § 754.

2. Operation of § 743(b)
If the partnership has a § 754 election in effect, § 743(b) requires that if there is a sale or exchange of a partnership interest the partnership shall adjust its inside basis by the difference between the buying partner's share of inside basis and his basis in his partnership interest. The process for allocating the § 743(b) adjustment among the partnership assets is prescribed by § 755.

XIX. NONLIQUIDATING DISTRIBUTIONS

A. Consequences to the Partner
1. Cash Distributions
Under § 731(a) a partner generally does not recognize gain or loss on the receipt of a cash distribution from a partnership. But if the money distributed exceeds the partner's outside basis, the excess must be recognized as gain from the sale or exchange of the partner's partnership interest. For purposes of this rule, marketable securities are considered as money to the extent of their fair market value on the date of distribution.

2. Property Distributions
When a partnership distributes property to a partner in a nonliquidating distribution, generally neither the partner nor the partnership recognizes gain or loss. Under the general rule, a partner takes a transferred basis in property distributed by a partnership and the partner's outside basis is reduced by the basis of the distributed property.

3. Dispositions of Distributed Property
Under § 735(a), any subsequent gain or loss recognized with respect to distributed "unrealized receivables" is characterized as ordinary and any subsequent gain or loss recognized with respect to "inventory items" within five years after the distribution is characterized as ordinary income.

B. Consequences to the Partnership
1. Nonrecognition of Gain or Loss
Under § 731(b), no gain or loss generally is recognized by a partnership when it distributes property (including money) to a partner. The principal exception is a distribution which is treated as a sale or exchange under § 751(b).

2. Impact on Inside Basis
Under § 734(a) the inside basis of the partnership's assets is not adjusted as a result of a property distribution by the partnership unless it has a § 754 election in effect.

3. Adjustments to Capital Accounts

A partner's capital account is reduced by the fair market value of property received in a distribution from the partnership.

C. Mixing Bowl Transactions

1. Introduction

Subchapter K includes two provisions to combat "mixing bowl transactions," a technique used in the partnership setting to shift or defer recognition of precontribution gain on contributed property.

2. Distributions of Contributed Property to Another Partner

Under § 704(b)(1)(B), if property contributed by a partner is distributed to another partner within seven years of the contribution, the contributing partner must recognize gain or loss from the sale or exchange of the property in an amount equal to the § 704(c)(1)(A) gain that would have been allocated to that partner if the partnership had sold the property for its fair market value. To prevent double taxation, appropriate adjustments are made to the contributing partner's outside basis and the partnership's inside basis in the distributed property.

Exceptions are provided for distributions of contributed property back to the contributing partner and certain distributions of like-kind property within prescribed time limits.

3. Distributions of Other Property to the Contributing Partner

Under § 737, a contributing partner must recognize gain if she contributes appreciated property to a partnership and within seven years of the contribution the partnership distributes property other than money to that partner. In general, the amount of gain recognized is the value of the distributed property less the contributing partner's outside basis before the distribution, but in no event may the gain exceed the net precontribution gain on all property contributed to the partnership by that partner. Section 737 does not apply to the extent that § 751(b) applies.

D. Distributions That Shift the Partners' Interests in § 751 Assets: § 751(b)

1. Operation of § 751(b)

Section 751(b) applies to both liquidating and nonliquidating distributions that shift the partners' interests in unrealized receivables and substantially appreciated inventory items. Section 751(b) is designed to prevent shifts of ordinary income and capital gain among partners through property distributions.

2. Criticisms of § 751(b)

Despite its complexity, § 751(b) does not reach all shifts in income among partners. Because of its many deficiencies, the American Law Institute and other commentators have called for the repeal of § 751(b).

XX. LIQUIDATING DISTRIBUTIONS

A. Liquidation of a Partner's Interest

1. Introduction

Section 736 classifies payments received in a liquidation of a partner's interest in a partnership into two broad categories. The tax treatment of the payments is determined under other provisions of Subchapter K.

2. § 736(b) Payments

Under § 736(b), payments for a partner's interest in partnership property generally are treated as property distributions. Excluded from this treatment are payments for a general partnership interest in a partnership where capital is not a material income-producing factor if the payments are attributable to § 751(c) unrealized receivables and unstated goodwill. If a partner's interest in partnership property is determined in an arm's length agreement, that allocation generally is accepted. Section 736(b) payments may trigger § 751(b) because they are treated as partnership distributions. But § 736(b) does not apply to the distributee partner's share of unrealized receivables and unstated goodwill, two types of property which normally would have to be analyzed in applying § 751(b), when those payments are for a general partner's interest in a services partnership.

3. § 736(a) Payments

Section 736(a) payments are for three types of partnership property:

a. § 751(c) unrealized receivables (excluding recapture items) and goodwill (unless the partnership agreement expressly provides for payment of goodwill), but only when the payments are for a general partnership interest in a partnership where capital is not a material income-producing factor; and

b. amounts paid in addition to the partner's share of partnership property which are in the nature of a premium or mutual insurance.

Section 736(a) payments produce ordinary income to the distributee partner and a reduction in the income of the other partners via either reduced distributive shares or a partnership deduction.

4. Allocation and Timing of § 736 Payments

Payments made each year must be allocated between the § 736(b) portion and the § 736(a) portion. The regulations permit the distributee partner and partnership to agree on an allocation. If there is no agreement and the payments are fixed in amount and paid over a fixed number of years, the § 736(b) portion each year is equal to the agreed fixed payment for the year multiplied by a ratio of the total fixed payments under § 736(b) divided by the total fixed payments under § 736(a) and (b). If the payments are not fixed in amount they are first treated as § 736(b) payments to the extent of the partner's interest in partnership property and, thereafter, § 736(a) payments.

Section 736(a) payments which are considered a distributive share are included in income in the taxable year in which the partnership's taxable year ends. Section 736(a) payments which are considered a guaranteed payment are included in the year in which the partnership is entitled to a deduction.

5.   **§ 736 Payments Versus Sale of the Partnership Interest**
The key difference between § 736 payments and the sale of a partnership interest is that § 736(a) liquidating distributions generally produce ordinary income to retiring partners and reduce the income reportable by the continuing partners, while a sale of an interest to the partners produces capital gain to the retiring partner and the continuing partners must capitalize the purchase price as part of their outside bases.

B.   Liquidation of the Entire Partnership
1.   **Voluntary Liquidation**
Section 736 does not apply to the liquidation of an entire partnership because that section contemplates payments by an ongoing partnership. Instead, the rules in § 731, § 732, § 735 and § 751(b) apply to distributions in complete liquidation of a partnership.

2.   **Termination Forced by Statute**
Under § 708(b)(1)(B) a partnership is considered to have terminated if within a 12–month period there is a sale or exchange of 50% or more of the total interests in partnership capital and profits. The partnership is then deemed to contribute its assets and liabilities to a new partnership in exchange for a partnership interest and then liquidate by distributing the partnership interest to the purchaser and other partners.

XXI.   DEATH OF A PARTNER

A.   Introduction
When a partner dies, three things may happen to his partnership interest:

1.   the interest may pass to the partner's successor in interest who continues as a partner;

2.   the interest may be sold at the partner's death pursuant to a preexisting buy-sell agreement; or

3.   the interest may be liquidated pursuant to a preexisting agreement among the partners.

B.   The Deceased Partner's Distributive Share in the Year of Death
When a partner dies, the partnership's taxable year closes with respect to the partner and the deceased partner's final return will include his distributive share of partnership income or loss for the short taxable year.

C. Estate Tax, Income in Respect of a Decedent, and Basis Consequences

1. Federal Estate Tax

The fair market value of the deceased partner's partnership interest, including any distributive shares earned prior to death, is includible in the partner's gross estate for federal estate tax purposes.

2. Income in Respect of a Decedent

In general, "income in respect of a decedent" is a right to income which was earned by the decedent but not previously taxed. The amount of § 736(a) payments (payments for a general partnership interest in a services partnership for unrealized receivables and unstated goodwill as well as premium payments made to liquidate any partner) are income in respect of a decedent. Payments attributable to depreciation recapture are not within § 736(a) and are not income in respect of a decedent. The courts also have held that an aggregate approach is used to determine whether items are income in respect of a decedent so a deceased partner's share of a cash method partnership's accounts receivable is income in respect of a decedent.

3. Basis Consequences

The basis of a partnership interest acquired from a decedent is the fair market value of the interest at the date of her death or at the alternate valuation date, increased by the successor's share of partnership liabilities and reduced by the value of items considered income in respect of a decedent. Section 743 cannot be applied to give the successor the benefit of an inside basis adjustment in items which are income in respect of a decedent.

XXII. PARTNERSHIP ANTI–ABUSE RULES

A. Introduction

The partnership anti-abuse regulations contain two main provisions. The first allows the IRS to recast a transaction as appropriate to achieve tax results consistent with the intent of Subchapter K. The second rule permits the IRS to treat a partnership as an aggregate of its partners as appropriate to carry out the purposes of the Code or regulations. In addition, the regulations under § 704(c)(1)(B) and § 737 have anti-abuse provisions.

B. Abuse of Subchapter K Rules

The partnership anti-abuse regulations generally require that partnership transactions must satisfy business purpose, substance over form, and clear reflection of income requirements. The regulations also provide that if a partnership is formed or availed of in connection with a transaction a principal purpose of which is to reduce substantially the present value of the partners' aggregate federal tax liability in a manner inconsistent with Subchapter K, the IRS can recast the transaction to achieve appropriate tax results. The regulations employ an all facts and circumstances test to determine whether a partnership is formed or availed of for an impermissible purpose and illustrate the rule with several examples.

C. Abuse of Partnership Entity

Under the second anti-abuse rule, the Commissioner can treat a partnership as an aggregate of its partners in whole or in part as appropriate to carry out the purpose of any Code or regulation provision.

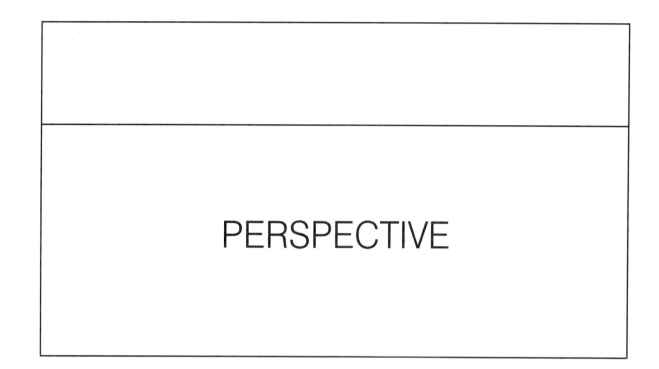

PERSPECTIVE

Analysis

A. *The Subject in General*
B. *Preparing for Examinations*
C. *Other Sources*
D. *Acknowledgements*

A. THE SUBJECT IN GENERAL

This outline has been written for students enrolled in basic courses in Corporate or Partnership Tax or in a combined course on Business Enterprise Taxation. It also may be useful for some of the topics covered in more advanced tax courses and business planning.

Whatever the format, corporate and partnership tax are regarded as among the most challenging subjects in the law school curriculum. This reputation is well deserved. Quite apart from the intricacies of the Internal Revenue Code, the underlying transactions are complex and often unfamiliar even to students with some business or accounting background. The goal of this outline is to make the rules more accessible to students by presenting them in a structured and intelligible format that includes definitions, examples, cross references and practice questions. Although the outline is generally organized to follow the life cycle of a corporation and partnership from formation to termination (the so-called "cradle to grave" approach), it should be easily adapted to whatever organization your instructor uses. We reiterate what your instructor no doubt has already preached at the first class—a study aid is no substitute for a careful reading of the primary materials assigned in your course. This outline is intended to support but not replace your armed combat with the Code and regulations.

Students quickly will become aware that the corporate and partnership tax courses devote very little time to the determination of the entity's taxable income. Those concepts should have been mastered in the basic income tax class. For students who may have suffered some memory loss, we recommend generally reviewing the concepts of gross income, deductions, timing and characterization, focusing particularly on the issues raised by the *Crane* and *Tufts* cases, the basic workings of a nonrecognition provision (such as § 1031), and some fundamental timing rules (such as installment sale reporting under § 453).

The vast majority of time in corporate tax is devoted to studying transactions between corporations and their shareholders and taxable and nontaxable dispositions of a corporate business. The study of S corporations and partnerships also revolves, to a large degree, around transactions between the entity and its owners. A particularly challenging segment of the partnership tax course involves the treatment of partnership liabilities and the ability of partners to allocate income and deductions in their partnership agreement. Your study of all these topics will be enhanced by an understanding of "the big picture"—the basic models for taxing a business enterprise and the way in which those models influence taxpayer behavior. For some additional perspective, we recommend a careful reading of Chapter I of this outline.

B.   PREPARING FOR EXAMINATIONS

As in any law school course, preparing for an examination requires a student to connect with the instructor's wave length. Some tax teachers emphasize statutory construction and problem solving. Their exams are likely to parallel the coverage during the semester but may require you to understand the relationships of concepts covered at different points in the course.

If your instructor uses the problem method, it is likely that the exam will ask you to analyze the tax consequences of hypothetical fact situations. Other instructors may spend more time on cases, tax policy, and less quantifiable issues, and their essay questions may reflect this approach. Many of these instructors, however, still require students to analyze discrete fact patterns on the exam—in both short answer and essay questions—if only because it is easier to grade a more "objective" exam. In short, it is a safe bet that virtually all corporate and partnership tax exams will be rather specific and require a mastery of many statutory details along with the broad concepts.

As with any law school exam, it is essential that you not merely write a mini-treatise on the law in general but relate the applicable rules to the facts presented in the question. Even in tax, there may not be a right answer for the essay questions. Where the law is uncertain, it is best to discuss the possibilities and reach a reasoned conclusion (perhaps one that is consistent with what the instructor may have described in class as "the better view.")

C. OTHER SOURCES

So much additional reading is available on corporate and partnership tax that students will need to protect themselves against "information overload." Among the treatises in the area are *Federal Income Taxation of Corporations and Shareholders* by Bittker and Eustice; *Mergers, Acquisitions and Buyouts* by Ginsburg and Levin; *Federal Taxation of Partnerships and Partners* by McKee, Nelson and Whitmire; *Partnership Taxation* by Willis, Pennell and Postlewaite (all available in student editions with annual supplements); and *Federal Income Taxation of S Corporations* by Eustice and Kuntz. Although these are all superb texts, keep in mind that they are not written principally for law students and they often prove to be overwhelming in their level of sophistication and detail. It may be best to confine your reading to the assigned materials and a study aid (such as this outline) specifically designed for students.

D. ACKNOWLEDGEMENTS

We are grateful for the hard work and thoughtful advice of the three student research assistants who worked on the first edition, Ray Kawasaki, Terri Murray and Mitch Salamon, and to Bruce McGovern, Marc Yassinger, Jessica Speiser and Matthew Rowan for their help on later editions. Special thanks are due to our colleague, Steve Lind, for his many helpful comments and suggestions on the manuscript of the partnership tax materials and to Cecilia Bruno for her excellent word processing skills. And none of this would have been possible without the continuing patience and support of Bev Lathrope.

*

PART ONE

GENERAL CONSIDERATIONS

Analysis

*

I

INTRODUCTION TO TAXATION OF BUSINESS ORGANIZATIONS

Analysis

A. Forms of Business Organizations
   1. Sole Proprietorship
   2. Corporation
   3. Partnership
   4. Limited Liability Company
B. Conceptual Taxation Models
   1. Aggregate Concept
   2. Entity Concept
   3. Hybrid Concepts
C. Overview of Taxing Regimes Under the Code
   1. Subchapter C
   2. Subchapter K
   3. Subchapter S
   4. Specialized Tax Regimes
D. Influential Policies
   1. The Double Tax
   2. Rate Structure
   3. Preferential Capital Gains Rates

A. Forms Of Business Organizations

The permissible forms for business enterprises in the United States are governed principally by the laws of the various states. The most common forms in which a business may be conducted are sole proprietorships, corporations, partnerships and limited liability companies.

1. Sole Proprietorship

A sole proprietorship is owned and operated by a single individual. Sole proprietors take into account the income and expenses of their businesses on their individual tax returns.

2. Corporation

A corporation is a fictitious legal entity that is the most commonly used form for operating a large, publicly held business. The corporate form is also used by closely held businesses where the owners wish to insulate themselves from personal liability for debts of the enterprise.

3. Partnership

A partnership is a business owned by two or more persons as co-owners.

a. General Partnership

In a general partnership, the partners have unlimited liability and generally are bound by the acts of the other partners. General partners ordinarily are personally liable for partnership debts.

b. Limited Partnership

A limited partnership has both a general partner (or partners) and limited partners. The general partner has unlimited liability, but the limited partners are not personally liable for partnership debts except to the extent of their capital contributions and they generally do not participate in the management of the enterprise.

c. Limited Liability Partnership

Some states authorize limited liability partnerships (LLPs). A partner of an LLP is protected, in varying degrees depending on state law, from vicarious liability for acts of the other partners. A few states authorize limited liability limited partnerships, which extend personal immunity from liability to the general partners.

d. Joint Venture

A joint venture is an arrangement between two parties to share the profits of a particular project. Many tax and nontax rules applicable to partnerships also apply to joint ventures.

4. Limited Liability Company

The limited liability company ("LLC") is a form of noncorporate entity that is now permitted under the laws of every state. All of an LLC's owners, known as "members," have limited liability for the entity's debts and claims. LLCs also may have "managers," who are analogous to general partners. The organizing document of an LLC is known as an "operating agreement." Virtually every state permits single-member LLCs. For income tax purposes, LLCs with more than one member are treated as partnerships and single-member LLCs are treated as disregarded entities unless the LLC elects corporate status. See II.C.2.b., at page 75, *infra*.

B. Conceptual Taxation Models

The appropriate tax treatment of a business enterprise initially depends on a policy decision as to the nature of the organization. The two principal views are the "aggregate" and "entity" concepts.

1. Aggregate Concept

Under the aggregate concept, a business organization is viewed as an aggregation of its owners, each of whom holds a direct undivided interest in the assets and operations of the enterprise. The organization itself is not treated as a separate taxable entity under this theory. Rather, each of the owners takes into account his or her respective share of income and expenses. Contributions to or distributions from the entity generally are ignored for tax purposes, and sales of an owner's interest are treated as sales of undivided interests in each of the organization's assets.

2. Entity Concept

Under the entity concept, a business organization is viewed as an entity that is separate and distinct from its owners. As such, the entity is subject to tax on its taxable income, and transactions between the owners and the entity are taxable events. This is sometimes referred to as "a double tax regime."

3. Hybrid Concepts

As will become apparent in studying the taxation of partnerships and "S corporations," it is possible to adopt a hybrid taxing model that treats an organization as a separate entity for some purposes (e.g., determination of income, filing of tax returns) and as an aggregate for other purposes (e.g., by passing through income and expenses to the owners and by treating a sale of an interest in the organization as a sale of the owner's proportionate share of each asset).

C. Overview of Taxing Regimes Under the Code

The Internal Revenue Code ("the Code") has adopted three principal taxing models for business organizations. These three "regimes" are found in Subchapters C, S and K.

1. **Subchapter C**

   All corporations other than "S" corporations (see I.C.3. at page 63, *infra*) are "C" corporations. § 1361(a)(2). Subchapter C (§§ 301–385) adopts an entity concept by treating C corporations as separate taxpaying entities. The taxable income of a C corporation is subject to tax at the graduated rates in § 11. Subchapter C governs the following categories of transactions between corporations and their shareholders:

   a. Nonliquidating distributions of cash, property or stock (§§ 301–317).

   b. Complete liquidations (§§ 331–346).

   c. Corporate organizations (including formations) and reorganizations (e.g., mergers, recapitalizations, insolvencies), and carryover of tax attributes following a corporate acquisition (§§ 351–384).

   d. Classification of corporate interests as stock or debt (§ 385).

   The taxation of C corporations is covered in Chapters III–XIV of this outline.

2. **Subchapter K**

   Under Subchapter K (§§ 701–761), partnerships and limited liability companies are not treated as separate taxpaying entities. Partnership income and deductions pass through to the individual partners and are taxed at the partner level. A partnership, however, is treated as an accounting entity for purposes of determining its income, and it must file an informational tax return showing how all the partnership's tax items have been allocated among the partners. A partnership and its partners also are taxed under an entity or modified-entity approach in several substantive contexts, such as formation and termination, transactions between partners and partnerships, and sales of partnership interests. The rules in Subchapter K fall into four principal categories:

   a. Determination of tax liability resulting from partnership operations (§§ 701–709).

   b. Contributions of property to the partnership (§§ 721–724).

   c. Partnership distributions (§§ 731–736).

   d. Transfers of partnership interests (§§ 741–743).

   The remaining provisions of Subchapter K (§§ 751 et seq.) include rules common to all the previous subparts (e.g., § 752, which relates to the treatment of partnership liabilities) and definitions.

   The taxation of partnerships is covered in Chapters XVI–XXII of this outline.

3. **Subchapter S**

   Subchapter S (§§ 1361–1379) is a hybrid model that governs the tax treatment of "S corporations" and their shareholders. It was enacted to minimize the influence of taxes on the choice of form for smaller, closely held businesses. Like partnerships, S corporations are treated as pass-through entities that generally are not subject to tax. S corporation status is limited to eligible corporations that make an election. In general, S corporations can have only one class of stock and no more than 75 shareholders, all of whom must be individual U.S. citizens or residents, or certain qualified trusts and tax-exempt organizations.

S corporations are covered in Chapter XV of this outline.

4. Specialized Tax Regimes

The Code also includes taxing regimes tailored for particular industries. Examples include Subchapter F (tax-exempt organizations and cooperatives), Subchapter H (banks), Subchapter L (insurance companies), and Subchapter M (mutual funds and real estate investment trusts). Because these specialized regimes are rarely covered in law school corporate and partnership tax courses, they are not discussed in this outline.

D. Influential Policies

Our system of taxing corporations and partnerships has been shaped by at least four broad tax policy decisions. The relationship of these policies influences taxpayer behavior, both as to the choice of form in which to conduct a business and the tax avoidance opportunities within each form. Tax legislation enacted over the last 20 years has radically altered some of these policies and introduced an instability into the system. As a result, some cases and Code sections that traditionally were studied in corporate and partnership courses (and still are included in many casebooks) are obsolete or less significant. The following discussion is a greatly simplified overview of the most influential policies and their past and present impact on taxation of business organizations.

1. The Double Tax

Earnings of C corporations are taxed once at the corporate level when earned and again when distributed as dividends to shareholders. In the Tax Reform Act of 1986, Congress significantly strengthened the double tax by providing that a C corporation generally recognizes gain on all distributions of appreciated property to its shareholders. Under a prior rule known as "the *General Utilities* doctrine," such distributions often were nontaxable events. Partnerships and S corporations, as pass-through entities, are generally not subject to an entity-level tax on either operating income or asset appreciation. These developments, along with changes in the rate structure discussed below, have increased the costs of operating as a C corporation and provided an incentive for taxpayers to use partnerships, S corporations or limited liability companies to conduct many closely held business and investment activities.

2. Rate Structure

For most of our tax history, the maximum individual tax rates were considerably higher than the top corporate rate. Despite the double tax, this rate advantage motivated taxpayers to operate profitable businesses as C corporations. The typical strategy was to distribute profits to owner-employees in the form of tax-deductible compensation or interest and accumulate what was left in the corporation. Accumulated profits would compound at a lower rate of tax and often were later withdrawn at highly preferential capital gains rates when the business was sold, or tax-free when an owner died. Congress enacted several anti-avoidance provisions, such as the accumulated earnings and personal holding company taxes, to curtail these strategies.

For a brief time between 1987 and 1992, the maximum corporate rate (then 34%) exceeded the highest marginal individual rate. The pendulum shifted back slightly in 1993, when individual rates were increased. Under current law, the highest individual income tax rate only slightly exceeds the top corporate rate. The interrelationship of corporate and individual rates often influences the choice of legal form for a business or investment entity. See II.D. at page 77, *supra*.

3. Preferential Capital Gains Rates

Historically, the policy decision to tax long-term capital gains at substantially lower rates than ordinary income motivated C corporations and their shareholders to structure transactions designed to "bail out" earnings at preferential capital gains rates. Many of the Code sections studied in Subchapter C were enacted to curtail these conversion devices. Similar attempts by partnerships to convert ordinary income into capital gain have contributed to much of the development of Subchapter K.

After a brief period during which there was little or no capital gains preference, Congress shifted back to the historical policy by providing a significant rate reduction for long-term capital gains of individual taxpayers. In addition, noncorporate investors who are original issuees may exclude 50% of their capital gain on the sale or exchange of stock in certain qualified small businesses (generally, C corporations that actively conduct a trade or business and have gross assets of $50 million or less) acquired after August 10, 1993, if the stock has been held for more than five years. § 1202. As a result, the conversion and bailout strategies described above remain on the planning agendas of high income taxpayers.

4. Nonrecognition

The nonrecognition concept has always played an important role in the taxation of corporations and partnerships. In general, all realized gains or losses must be recognized unless the Code provides otherwise. § 1001(c). Transactions typically qualify for "nonrecognition" treatment if they are mere changes in form which result in a continuity of investment. To ensure that realized gain or loss is only deferred, a nonrecognition provision is coupled with transferred and exchanged basis rules that preserve the gain or loss for recognition at a later time. Many corporate and partnership transactions, ranging from simple formations to complex liquidation and acquisitions, will qualify for nonrecognition treatment.

E. Pervasive Judicial Doctrines

Corporate and partnership tax issues usually can be resolved by a careful application of the statute and regulations to the transaction in question. To protect the integrity of the system, however, the courts have gone beyond the literal language of the statute and formulated "common law" doctrines that may affect the tax treatment of a transaction that literally complies with the Code but is incompatible with its purpose. Despite years of litigation, the judicial doctrines are imprecise and often are applied interchangeably. The purpose of this summary is to introduce some of the most familiar terminology.

1. Substance Over Form

In one of the earliest articulations of the "substance over form" doctrine, the Supreme Court stated that "[t]he incidence of taxation depends upon the substance of a transaction. . . . To permit the true nature of a transaction to be disguised by mere formalisms, which exist solely to alter tax liabilities, would seriously impair the effective administration of the tax policies of Congress." *Comm'r v. Court Holding Co.*, 324 U.S. 331, 65 S.Ct. 707 (1945). It is difficult to generalize as to when and how the doctrine is applied. Some illustrative controversies that are discussed later in this outline include:

a. Is a corporate instrument labelled as "debt" in reality "equity?" See V.B., at page 119, *infra*.

b. Is a payment to a shareholder-employee really "compensation" or is it a disguised dividend? See VI.E., at page 138, *infra*.

c. Is a distribution a dividend or part of the purchase price for the business? See VI.F.6., at page 141, *infra*.

d. Was a sale of assets made by the corporation or its shareholders? See IX.B.2.a., at page 193, *infra*.

Despite the substance over form doctrine, the parties to a transaction often can dictate a tax result by utilizing a particular form. This will become particularly apparent in the area of taxable and tax-free corporate acquisitions. See IX.D, at pages 200–211, *infra* and XI.B., at pages 238–260, *infra*. However, the Service has issued regulations to curb certain perceived abuses of the partnership form. See Reg. § 1.701–2, discussed in XXII., at page 482, *infra*.

2. Step Transactions

The substance of a transaction is often determined by application of the step transaction doctrine, under which the separate "steps" of formally distinct transactions are combined into a single integrated transaction for tax purposes. The courts disagree on when and how to apply the step transaction doctrine. Three principal formulations have emerged.

a. The Binding Commitment Test

A series of transactions is combined if, when the first step was taken, there was a binding commitment to undertake the later steps. This is the narrowest formulation of the doctrine and usually is the most favorable to taxpayers, who often can demonstrate that the parties were not legally obligated to engage in the later steps.

b. The End Result Test

Separate steps are combined if it is determined that they were prearranged components of a single transaction in which the parties intended from the outset to reach a particular end result. This is the broadest and least precise articulation of the doctrine because it requires a determination of the "intent" of the parties.

c. The Interdependence Test

This is a variation of the end result test which looks to whether the separate steps are so interdependent that the legal relations created by one transaction would have been fruitless without completion of the later steps. The court must determine whether the steps had independent legal significance or were merely part of the larger transaction.

Courts have resisted applying the step transaction doctrine when the Service does not simply combine steps but invents new ones which never took place in order to reach a particular result adverse to the taxpayer. See, e.g., *Esmark, Inc. v. Comm'r*, 90 T.C. 171 (1988).

3. Business Purpose

The business purpose doctrine sometimes is applied to deny tax benefits (e.g., nonrecognition of gain on a corporate acquisition) when a transaction has no substance, purpose or utility apart from tax avoidance. The doctrine is most frequently applied in connection with tax-free corporate divisions, and it has been extended through regulations to patrol certain abusive partnership transactions. See XII.E. at pages 278–279, *infra*, and XXII., at pages 482–486, *infra*. The IRS also has invoked business purpose and other judicial doctrines in its attack on a wide variety of transactions known as corporate tax shelters. The courts have held that a transaction should be respected for tax purposes if it creates a genuine legal obligation enforceable by an unrelated party. See, e.g., *United Parcel Service of America, Inc. v. Comm'r*, 254 F.3d 1014 (11th Cir. 2001). Under this broader view, a transaction does not lack a business purpose because it is principally motivated by tax planning considerations. Other courts take a narrower view, finding that a transaction should not be respected, even if it may create genuine legal obligations, if its sole motive is tax avoidance. See, e.g, *Kirchman v. Comm'r*, 862 F.2d 1486 (11th Cir. 1989).

4. Sham Transaction

A "sham" transaction will not be respected for tax purposes. This is often another way of saying that the transaction is devoid of substance or was not motivated by a bona fide business purpose. The term "sham" may include a transaction that never in fact occurred and, in that context, it connotes fraudulent conduct.

*

II

CLASSIFICATION

Analysis

A. Introduction

1. **Impact of Classification**
    The classification of a business relationship may have profound tax consequences. Entities classified as "corporations" are subject to the double tax regime of Subchapter C while income realized by a "partnership" is taxed directly to the partners under the pass-through taxing scheme of Subchapter K. If a business arrangement is classified as a "partnership," a partnership tax return must be filed and tax elections generally must be made at the partnership level. §§ 703(b), 6031. The timing and character of the income realized by the owners also may be affected if a business activity is classified as a partnership. §§ 702(b), 706(a).

    The operation of many Code sections also varies depending on whether the taxpayer is an individual, a partnership, a corporation or some other type of entity. For example, under § 179 a taxpayer may elect to currently deduct a certain amount of the cost of "§ 179 property" each year. In the case of a partnership, the dollar limit is applied at both the partnership and partner levels. § 179(d)(8). Thus, if two individuals enter into a business relationship which is not classified as a partnership, each taxpayer will be eligible to expense up to the § 179 cost limit, but if the activity is classified as a partnership the benefits of § 179 will be restricted to one limit for the partnership.

    The stakes in the classification area have changed in response to provisions in the Internal Revenue Code that, at different times, have offered incentives to classify entities as partnerships or corporations. See II.C.1. at page 74, *infra*. Under current law, however, the taxpayer's classification of the vast majority of business entities is respected.

2. **The Role of State Law**
    The classification of entities for federal tax purposes is a matter of federal law and depends on standards in the Internal Revenue Code. Reg. § 301.7701–1(a)(1). Thus, the classification or label placed on an organization under state law will not control its classification under the Code.

3. **Principal Classification Issues**
    Tax classification issues generally arise in two settings. In the first, the issue is whether an unincorporated business relationship is an entity separate from its owners, or rather is some other form of arrangement, such as co-ownership of property, employer-employee, principal-agent, debtor-creditor, etc. On this end of the spectrum, the question is whether the business relationship among the parties is such that a separate entity is recognized for tax purposes. If a separate entity is recognized, it generally will be classified as a partnership for federal tax purposes.

    In the other setting, the question is whether or not an entity should be classified as a corporation for federal tax purposes. On this end of the spectrum, the issue generally narrows to whether a limited partnership, limited liability company or trust will be classified as a corporation under the Code.

B. Existence of a Separate Entity

1. In General

The regulations provide that a joint venture or other contractual arrangement may create a separate entity for federal tax purposes if the participants carry on a trade, business, financial operation, or venture and divide the profits therefrom. Reg. 301.7701–1(a)(2). If a separate entity is created, its classification for federal tax purposes will be determined under the regulations. Generally, the separate entity will be classified as a partnership. See II.C.2.b. at page 75, *infra*. The determination of whether an organization is an entity separate from its owners for federal tax purposes is a matter of federal law and does not depend on whether the organization is recognized as an entity under local law. Reg. § 301.7701–1(a).

The regulations definition of a separate entity for federal tax purposes is derived from § 761(a) and cases that distinguished partnerships from less formal relationships. In *Comm'r v. Culbertson*, 337 U.S. 733, 742, 69 S.Ct. 1210, 1214 (1949), the Supreme Court held that a critical factor in determining whether a partnership exists is whether "the parties in good faith and acting with a business purpose intended to join together in the present conduct of the enterprise." When determining the intent of the parties, the courts typically have listed a number of elements which must be considered. A critical factor is whether the parties have a *joint* profit motive, that is, whether they are acting as co-owners or co-proprietors seeking a joint profit from the enterprise. This aspect of the case law is incorporated and emphasized in the regulations, which require that the participants "carry on a trade, business, financial operation, or venture" for a separate entity to exist.

2. Joint Profit Motive

The existence of a joint profit motive may be difficult to determine in certain circumstances. In *Allison v. Comm'r*, 35 T.C.M. 1069 (1976), Acceptance, a financing corporation, agreed to arrange for a loan to aid in the purchase and subdivision of real property. In exchange for those services, Acceptance received 75 of the subdivided lots, which it sold in a subsequent year. The arrangement between Acceptance and the developer was labeled a "joint venture" and Acceptance took the position that its receipt of the lots was a tax-free partnership distribution. See § 731(a)(1). The Service argued that no partnership existed and that receipt of the lots was ordinary income as compensation for the services provided by Acceptance. In holding that no partnership existed, the court relied largely on the fact that there were no joint sales of lots. Since each party received its share of the subdivided lots and disposed of them separately, there was no joint profit motive. The court also noted that partnership books were not kept and partnership tax returns were not filed.

In *Madison Gas & Electric Co. v. Comm'r,* 72 T.C. 521 (1979), *aff'd,* 633 F.2d 512 (7th Cir.1980), three electric companies agreed to jointly construct a nuclear power facility, own the facility as tenants-in-common, and share the electricity produced at the facility. Each company paid a share of the facility's expenses and resold its share of the electricity produced at the plant. Madison Gas & Electric argued that its expenses in the venture were currently deductible under § 162 as expenses of its existing business. The Service took the position that the expenses were nondeductible start-up costs of a new venture rather than currently deductible expenses of the taxpayer's preexisting business. The court found that the nuclear power facility constituted a partnership and that the joint profit motive requirement was satisfied by the partnership's distribution of its profits (the electricity produced at the plant) in kind. The court reasoned that partners need not realize a cash profit for a partnership to exist. A possible (but questionable) distinction between *Madison Gas & Electric.* and *Allison* is the continuing nature of the business arrangement in *Madison Gas & Electric.*

3. **Separate Entity vs. Co–Ownership of Property**
    a. **In General**

    The regulations provide that "mere co-ownership" of property which is maintained, kept in repair, and rented or leased does not constitute a separate entity for federal tax purposes. Reg. § 301.7701–1(a)(2).

    > ***Example:*** If two individuals jointly purchase a parcel of real property to hold as an investment, no separate entity is formed. But if they purchase the parcel to subdivide and develop the parcel with the intention of selling lots, a separate entity does exist because they are actively carrying on a trade or business and dividing a joint profit.

    In the area of property rental, a separate entity exists if co-owners lease space and in addition provide services to the tenants either directly or through an agent. Id. In Rev.Rul. 75–374, 1975–2 C.B. 261, the Service held that providing "customary tenant services" (heat, air conditioning, hot and cold water, unattended parking, normal repairs, trash removal and cleaning of public area) did not transform a co-ownership relationship into a partnership. The ruling states that providing "additional services" to tenants (such as attendant parking, cabanas, gas and electric or other utilities) will render a co-ownership a partnership if furnished by the owners or their agent, but not if the additional services are rendered by an independent contractor.

    b. **Fractional Interests in Rental Real Property**

    The IRS has specified the conditions under which it will rule that an undivided fractional interest in rental real property is not an interest in a business entity so that the arrangement is not treated as a partnership for tax purposes. Rev. Proc. 2002–22, 2002–14 I.R.B. 733. The determination may be significant on a disposition intended to qualify as a § 1031 like-kind exchange because otherwise eligible property held by tenants-in-common qualifies for like-kind exchange treatment while exchanges of partnership interests do not. Rev. Proc. 2002–22 lists numerous conditions that must be satisfied in order to obtain a favorable ruling.

c. Section 761(a) Election

Section 761(a) permits an unincorporated organization to elect to be excluded from Subchapter K if it is availed of (1) for investment purposes only and not for the active conduct of a business, (2) for the joint production, extraction, or use of property, but not for the purpose of selling services or property produced or extracted, or (3) by dealers in securities for the purposes of underwriting, selling, or distributing a particular issue of securities. In all cases, the participants must be able to determine their income adequately without computing partnership taxable income. A § 761(a) election may be used to assure that the organization is not subject to Subchapter K. The election also permits the members to make inconsistent tax elections (e.g., different accounting elections). See § 703(b). Note that a § 761(a) election only excludes the organization from the application of Subchapter K. The organization still may be considered a partnership for purposes of other Code provisions.

4. Separate Entity vs. Expense Sharing, Employment, Loan and Other Relationships

Because the existence of a separate entity depends on a joint profit motive, the regulations provide that an expense sharing arrangement does not constitute a partnership. Reg. § 301.7701–1(a)(2).

> ***Example:***   If Doctor A and Doctor B agree to share office and support expenses but each will retain her own clients, a separate entity is not created because there is no joint profit being produced. If the doctors agree to combine practices and divide profits from their joint activity, a separate entity does exist.

In situations where one person supplies services or capital to a business venture, the determination of whether a separate entity exists generally depends on whether the parties are sharing a joint profit as co-owners or co-proprietors. Thus, if a person supplies services or capital for a share of profits, the classification issue will be affected by the authority of that person over business affairs.

The cases in this area turn on their particular facts. For example, in *Wheeler v. Comm'r,* 37 T.C.M. 883 (1978), Wheeler and Perrault entered into an agreement to acquire and develop real estate. Perrault supplied the money needed for the purchase and Wheeler the "know how." Perrault bore all losses from the venture and was to recoup those losses plus 6% interest. Any additional profits were to be divided 75% to Perrault and 25% to Wheeler. The properties were developed and Wheeler reported his gains as capital gains. The Service took the position that the arrangement was an employer-employee relationship and Wheeler realized ordinary income. In concluding that the arrangement between Wheeler and Perrault was a partnership, the court emphasized Wheeler's authority over day-to-day operations of the venture. The business was also operated under joint names, separate books were kept for the partnership and the parties reported their tax results as if it were a partnership. Factors against a finding of a partnership were that title to the real property was kept in Perrault's name, and Wheeler did not have authority to borrow or lend money. The court concluded, that these restrictions were designed to protect Perrault and noted that Perrault was restricted in his authority to deal with the venture's assets.

C. Classification of Business Entities

1. Introduction

The Code defines a corporation as including "associations, joint-stock companies, and insurance companies". § 7701(a)(3). Thus, certain unincorporated entities— "associations"—potentially are treated as corporations for federal tax purposes, as are corporations routinely organized under state law.

"Associations" historically have been defined in terms of their corporate characteristics. In *Morrissey v. Comm'r*, 296 U.S. 344, 56 S.Ct. 289 (1935), the Supreme Court upheld the Service's classification of a business trust as an association taxable as a corporation. The Court identified four characteristics common to corporations which form the basis of the current association regulations: (1) continuity of life, (2) centralization of management, (3) limited liability of investors, and (4) free transferability of interests.

The classification regulations have a long history. The pre–1997 regulations had an anti-association bias. The regulations were adopted at a time when professionals (doctors, lawyers, accountants, etc.) were prohibited by state law from incorporating but wished to achieve corporate status in order to obtain tax benefits from qualified retirement plans and other employee fringe benefits. Although incorporation was no longer necessary to obtain most of these benefits, the regulations continued to reflect a bias against achieving corporate status.

Beginning in the 1960's, taxpayer battles in this area shifted to the tax shelter front, where investors sought partnership rather than corporate status. Limited partnerships became the preferred vehicle for tax shelters because they permitted losses to pass through to investors and provided protection for the limited partners against personal liability for debts of the enterprise. The Service found itself arguing that limited partnerships should be classified as associations under its regulations, which have a bias in favor of partnership status. The Treasury's efforts to recharacterize limited partnerships as associations were unsuccessful. See *Larson v. Comm'r*, 66 T.C. 159 (1976). The restrictions on tax shelter investments that were enacted in the Tax Reform Act of 1986 reduced but did not eliminate the importance of the association versus limited partnership classification issue.

After 1986, corporate classification battles frequently were motivated by attempts to avoid the double tax imposed on profits of C corporations. By 1996, the Treasury concluded that state law developments, such as the popularity of limited liability companies, had largely blurred the classic distinctions between corporations and unincorporated entities. In response, new regulations were proposed to make classification for tax purposes essentially elective for unincorporated entities. Those "check the box" regulations were finalized and became effective in 1997. Under the regulations, new unincorporated entities generally are automatically classified as partnerships unless they elect to be taxed as C corporations.

2. The Classification Regulations
a. Pre–1997 Regulations

The pre–1997 regulations set forth six characteristics of a "pure corporation" which distinguish it from other business organizations: (1) associates, (2) an objective to carry on a business and divide the profits, (3) continuity of life, (4) centralization of management, (5) liability for debts limited to corporate property, and (6) free transferability of interests. The determination of whether an organization was classified as an association was made by taking into account these and any other relevant factors. Reg. § 301.7701–2(a)(1) (pre–1997).

Except in the case of a corporation owned by a single shareholder, the absence of either of the first two characteristics (associates and business objective) prevented an organization from being classified as an association. When distinguishing between associations and partnerships or associations and trusts, characteristics common to corporations and those entities were disregarded and only the remaining characteristics were considered. Reg. § 301.7701–2(a)(2), (3) (pre–1997). All of the characteristics were weighted equally, and an organization was classified as an association only if it had three of the four remaining corporate characteristics. Reg. § 301.7701–2(a)(3) (pre–1997).

The pre–1997 regulations provided considerable detail on the last four corporate characteristics and the Service had an extensive and restrictive policy on issuance of advance rulings on classification issues. The regulations and Service guidance made classification issues very complex. Nevertheless, well-advised taxpayers generally could achieve their desired tax objectives by properly structuring their business ventures under those rules.

b. Current Classification Regulations
1) Introduction

The current classification regulations were effective beginning in 1997. Reg. § 301.7701–1(f). Under the regulations, if a separate entity is not a trust, it is a "business entity." Reg. § 301.7701–2(a). See II.C.4 at page 77, *infra*, regarding classification of trusts. Certain business entities are automatically classified as corporations for federal tax purposes. These include a business entity organized under a federal or state statute if the statute describes or refers to the entity as "incorporated or as a corporation, body corporate, or body politic." Reg. § 301.7701–2(b)(1). Thus, corporations routinely organized under state corporation statutes are automatically considered corporations for federal tax purposes. A business entity that is taxable as a corporation under some other provision of the Code, such as a publicly traded partnership, also is classified as a corporation for federal tax purposes. Reg. § 301.7701–2(b)(7).

2) Entities with Two or More Members
A business entity with two or more members that is not automatically classified as a corporation is classified as a partnership for federal tax purposes, unless an election is made for the entity to be classified as a corporation. Reg. §§ 301.7701–2(c)(1), –3(a), –3(b)(1)(i). Consequently, an unincorporated entity, such as a limited liability company or limited partnership, with two or more members will automatically be classified as a partnership unless such an election is made.

3) Business Entities with One Owner
A business entity with only one owner that is not automatically classified as a corporation is disregarded for federal tax purposes, unless an election is made for the entity to be classified as a corporation. Thus, if such an election is not made for the entity, it will be treated like a sole proprietorship, branch, or division of the owner. Reg. §§ 301.7701–2(a), –2(c)(2), –3(a), –3(b)(1)(ii).

4) Foreign Entities
The regulations list certain entities formed under foreign laws that will be automatically classified as a corporation (e.g., an Aktiengesellschaft formed in Germany). Reg. § 301.7701–2(b)(8). Unless a contrary election is made, a foreign entity that is not a corporation is classified as (1) a partnership if it has two or more members and at least one member does not have limited liability, (2) a corporation if all members have limited liability, or (3) disregarded as an entity if it has a single owner that does not have limited liability. Reg. § 301.7701–3(b)(2)(i).

5) Election
An entity which wishes to change its classification under the regulations must file an election. The election may be effective up to 75 days before or twelve months after it is filed. Reg. § 301.7701–3(c)(1)(iii). An election must be signed by (1) each member of the entity, including prior members affected by a retroactive election, or (2) an officer, manager, or member authorized to make the election. Reg. § 301.7701–3(c)(2). If an entity makes a classification election, it may not make another election to change its classification for 60 months unless the Service permits the change and 50% of the entity's ownership interests are owned by persons who did not own any interests when the first election was made. Reg. § 301.7701–3(c)(1)(iv).

6) **Existing Entities**

In the absence of an election, an entity in existence before 1997 generally retains the same classification that it had under the prior association regulations. An exception is made for an entity with a single owner that claimed to be a partnership. Such an entity will be disregarded as an entity separate from its owner. Reg. § 301.7701–3(b)(3)(i).

3. Publicly Traded Partnerships

"Publicly traded partnerships" are generally classified as corporations. § 7704(a). A "publicly traded partnership" is a partnership whose interests are traded on an established securities market or are readily tradable on a secondary market (or the substantial equivalent thereof). § 7704(b). Section 7704(c) provides an exception for publicly traded partnerships in which 90% or more of the gross income consists of various types of passive investment income.

4. Trusts

The regulations distinguish between "ordinary trusts"—arrangements created by will or inter vivos declaration under which trustees take title to property in order to protect and conserve it for beneficiaries—and "business trusts." Business trusts are formed to carry on a profit-making business rather than for the protection and conservation of property. Reg. § 301.7701–4(a), (b). The fact that a business is cast in trust form will not prevent it from being classified as a business entity. Reg. § 301.7701–4(b). The critical question in determining whether a trust will be classified as a business entity is whether a business objective is present or the trust was established merely to protect and conserve trust property. If a trust is a business entity, it will be classified as a partnership if it has two or more owners or members, unless an election is made for it to be classified as a corporation.

D. Choice of Entity Considerations

With the highest marginal individual income tax rates now only slightly higher than the top corporate rate, there is an incentive for business entities to select a tax regime where only one level of tax is imposed on the enterprise. This result is available in Subchapter K and Subchapter S. S corporations, however, are subject to various restrictions as to ownership (e.g., no more than 75 shareholders and only one class of stock), and Subchapter K generally is more flexible and beneficial than Subchapter S (e.g., availability of special allocations, basis credit for entity-level debt, and inside basis adjustments on the sale of an interest). Thus, partnership classification is often the preferred result from a federal tax perspective. A limited liability company ("LLC") with more than one member will be taxed as a partnership if no election is made to tax it as a corporation. Additionally, all members of the LLC have limited liability for its debts and claims. These tax and state-law benefits have fueled the increasing popularity of LLCs for the conduct of business ventures, but in many cases the LLC may not be the entity of choice. State tax considerations (e.g., LLCs are taxed as corporations in some states), familiarity with the corporate form, and individual circumstances may make a limited partnership or S corporation the preferred vehicle for a venture.

In the case of a business venture already operating in a C corporation, an S corporation election often is a good alternative for moving to a single-tax regime. Subchapter S, however, has rules that prevent the easy avoidance of the double tax on built-in gains attributable to the period when the corporation was taxed under Subchapter C. See XV.F.1, at page 336, *infra*. Converting the C corporation to a partnership or LLC will require liquidating the corporation which may produce a significant tax liability. See Chapter IX, *infra* for the taxation of corporate liquidations.

For corporations intending to reinvest their earnings for the reasonable growth needs of the business, a C corporation may be more attractive for closely held companies because of the somewhat lower corporate rates. With rare exceptions, publicly traded companies operate as C corporations.

E.   Review Questions

1. X and Y agree to build an irrigation system to drain surface water from their properties. Are X and Y partners?

2. If A and B form a limited liability company or limited partnership to conduct their business venture, how will the entity be classified for federal tax purposes? What if A alone forms a limited liability company to operate a business?

PART TWO

CORPORATE TAXATION

Analysis

*

III

THE C CORPORATION AS A TAXABLE ENTITY

Analysis

81

A. The Corporate Income Tax

1. Introduction

A C corporation is a separate taxable entity. It selects its own taxable year and accounting methods, computes its taxable income under general tax principles, files a corporate income tax return (Form 1120) and pays tax at the rates specified in § 11.

2. Rates

a. Graduated Rates

Section 11(b) provides the following four-step graduated rate structure for C corporations:

Taxable Income	Rate
Up to $50,000	15%
$50,001 to $75,000	25%
$75,001 to $10,000,000	34%
Over $10,000,000	35%

b. Phase–Out of Lower Graduated Rates

A 5% surtax is imposed on taxable income between $100,000 and $335,000, and a 3% surtax is imposed on taxable income between $15,000,000 and $18,333,333. The purpose of these surtaxes is to phase-out the tax savings from the lower brackets for corporations with substantial taxable income. A corporation with taxable income over $335,000 but not over $10,000,000 is taxed at a flat 34% rate on all of its income. A corporation with more than $18,333,333 of taxable income is taxed at a flat 35% rate on all of its income. § 11(b)(1).

Example: X Corp. has taxable income of $200,000. X's corporate income tax is computed as follows:

$$
\begin{array}{rl}
15\% \times \$50,000 & = \$\ 7,500 \\
25\% \times \$25,000 & =\quad 6,250 \\
34\% \times \$125,000 & =\quad 42,500 \\
5\% \times \$100,000 & =\quad \underline{5,000} \\
\S\ 11(b)\ \text{Tax} & = \$61,250
\end{array}
$$

c. Qualified Personal Service Corporations

A "qualified personal service corporation" is not eligible for the lower graduated rates and thus is taxable at 35% on all its income. § 11(b)(2). A qualified personal service corporation is a corporation substantially engaged in the performance of services in the fields of health, law, engineering, architecture, accounting, actuarial science, performing arts, or consulting, if substantially all of the corporation's stock is held by employees performing services for the corporation, retired employees, or their estates. § 448(d)(2).

3. Determination of Taxable Income

The taxable income of a C corporation is its gross income minus allowable deductions. § 63(a). Corporations are not required to determine adjusted gross income and are not entitled to any "standard deduction." Income and deductions are determined under general tax principles, with the exceptions and special problems discussed below.

a. Deductions: In General

Corporations are not entitled to certain personal deductions, such as the personal and dependency exemptions, medical and moving expenses, alimony, etc. Section 212, which allows a deduction for expenses incurred for the production of income, does not apply to corporations. Virtually all of a corporation's routine expenses are deductible either as business expenses under § 162, losses under § 165 or depreciation under § 168. Some other deduction rules applicable to corporations are:

1) Business losses, including casualty losses, are deductible without limitation. § 165(a).

2) All bad debts are fully deductible as business bad debts. § 166(a).

3) Charitable contributions generally must be paid within the taxable year, and a corporation's charitable deduction is limited to 10% of taxable income (determined before the dividends received deduction or the net operating loss deduction). § 170(b)(2). A corporation on the accrual method of accounting may deduct a contribution authorized by its board of directors during the taxable year if the contribution is made by the 15th day of the third month after the close of the prior year. § 170(a)(2).

4) The § 465 at-risk limitations apply only to "closely-held C corporations" as defined in § 542(a)(2)—i.e., corporations where five or fewer individuals own directly or indirectly (through attribution rules) more than 50% of the stock (by value) at any time during the last half of the taxable year. § 465(a)(1)(B).

5) The § 469 passive loss limitations apply only to "closely-held C corporations" (see definition above) and personal service corporations. § 469(a)(2). A closely-held C corporation (other than a personal service corporation) may deduct passive losses against net active business income but not against portfolio income (such as dividends, interest and capital gains). § 469(e)(2).

b. The Dividends Received Deduction

Corporate shareholders may deduct 70% of dividends received from other domestic corporations. § 243(a)(1). This deduction reduces the effective corporate tax rate on dividends from 34% to 10.2% (34% x the 30% includible portion) or from 35% to 10.5% (35% x the 30% includible portion). A corporate shareholder may deduct 80% of dividends received if it owns 20% or more of the stock (by vote and value) of the payor corporation. § 243(c). Dividends paid by one corporation to another member of its "affiliated group" (see VI.F.1., at page 139, *infra*) qualify for a 100% dividends received deduction. § 243(a)(3), (b).

c. Capital Gains and Losses

Corporate capital gains are taxed at the same rate as ordinary income. Corporations may deduct capital losses only to the extent of capital gains. Any excess may be carried back for three years and carried forward for five years. §§ 1211(a); 1212(a). Corporate shareholders are not eligible for the § 1202 exclusion for capital gains from certain small business stock. § 1202(a).

4. Taxable Year

a. In General

Subject to a few limitations discussed below, C corporations generally may adopt either a calendar year or a fiscal year. § 441.

b. Personal Service Corporations

"Personal service corporations" must use a calendar year unless they can show a business purpose for using a fiscal year. § 441(i)(1). A "personal service corporation" is a corporation whose principal activity is the performance of services that are substantially performed by "employee-owners" who collectively own more than 10% (by value) of the corporation's stock. §§ 269A(b)(1); 441(i)(2).

c. Fiscal Year Election for Personal Service Corporations

A personal service corporation that otherwise would be required to use a calendar year may elect under § 444 to adopt a fiscal year having a "deferral period" of not more than three months (i.e., a fiscal year ending September 30, October 31 or November 30) provided the corporation makes certain minimum distributions (e.g., of compensation) to employee-owners during the portion of the employee's fiscal year that ends on December 31. § 280H. If these minimum distributions are not made, some deductions must be deferred. Id.

d. S Corporations

See XV.D.2.b., at page 323, *infra*.

5. Accounting Method

C corporations generally must use the accrual method of accounting. § 448(a). The cash method is available, however, to corporations engaged in the farming business, "qualified personal service corporations" (see III.A.2.c., at page 83, *supra*), and other C corporations whose average annual gross receipts for a three-year measuring period do not exceed $5 million. § 448(b).

6. Loss Disallowance Rules

Losses from sales or exchanges of property between a shareholder and a more-than–50%-owned corporation may not be deducted. § 267(a)(1), (b)(2). Ownership for this purpose is determined after application of attribution rules in § 267(c).

7. Forced Matching Rules

An accrual method corporation may not deduct payments (e.g., compensation, interest or rent) made to a cash method owner-employee until the recipient includes the amount in income. § 267(a)(2). For this purpose, an "owner-employee" is a person who owns directly or indirectly 50% or more of the payor corporation except that, in the case of personal service corporations, the forced matching rules apply to payments to any owner-employee, regardless of percentage ownership. Id.

8. Credits

Corporations qualify for a variety of tax credits, including the foreign tax credit, the rehabilitation and energy credit, the work opportunity credit, and the credits for research expenditures. §§ 27; 41; 46–48; 51.

B. The Corporate Alternative Minimum Tax

1. Introduction

a. In General

C corporations generally are subject to the alternative minimum tax ("AMT"). The AMT is payable only to the extent that it exceeds a corporation's regular tax liability. § 55(a). Put differently, a corporation pays its regular tax or alternative minimum tax, whichever is higher. The corporate AMT is 20% of the amount by which a corporation's alternative minimum taxable income ("AMTI") exceeds an "exemption amount."

b. Small Corporation Exemption

Since 1998, certain "small" corporations are exempt from the corporate AMT. To qualify for the exemption, a corporation's average annual gross receipts must be $7.5 million or less for all preceding three-taxable-year periods (taking into account only taxable years beginning after 1993). § 55(e)(1)(A). The $7.5 million limit is reduced to $5 million for the first three-taxable-year period taken into account. § 55(e)(1)(B).

c. First Year Exemption

In its first year of existence, a C corporation is exempt from the corporate AMT regardless of its gross receipts. § 55(e)(1)(C).

2. Alternative Minimum Taxable Income

AMTI is the corporation's taxable income, with certain timing and other adjustments prescribed by §§ 56 and 58, increased by "tax preference items" listed in § 57. Some of the most common adjustments and preference items are described below.

a. Depreciation

In computing AMTI, a corporation must depreciate tangible property placed in service after 1986 under a modified version of the "alternative depreciation system" in § 168(g). § 56(a)(1). Depreciation on machinery and equipment is limited to the 150% declining balance method. Tangible personal property placed in service after 1986 but before 1999 also must be depreciated using the longer class lives prescribed by the alternative depreciation system in § 168(g). § 56(a)(1)(A)(i). Real estate must be depreciated using the straight line method over a 40–year recovery period. § 56(a)(1)(A). The special depreciation allowance for property acquired after September 10, 2001 and before September 11, 2004, is allowed for purposes of computing AMTI. § 168(k)(2)(F).

Example: In year 1 (after 1999), X Corp. places in service 5–year property which has a 7–year class life. X's cost basis is $28,000. ACRS depreciation (using the 200% declining balance method, 5–year recovery period and half-year convention) is $5,600. AMT depreciation (using the 150% declining balance method, 5–year recovery period and half-year convention) is $4,200. In determining AMTI, X must increase taxable income by the $1,400 difference between ACRS and AMT depreciation. Note that in the later years of the asset's recovery period, AMT depreciation will exceed ACRS depreciation, permitting a decrease to taxable income in determining AMTI.

b. Net Operating Losses

A corporation must compute a special AMT net operating loss which may not offset more than 90% of a corporation's AMTI, determined without regard to the net operating loss deduction. § 56(a)(4), (d).

c. Adjusted Current Earnings Adjustment

A corporation must increase AMTI by 75% of the amount by which its "adjusted current earnings" ("ACE") exceed AMTI determined without regard to this adjustment or the AMT net operating loss ("pre-ACE AMTI"). § 56(g)(1). If pre-ACE AMTI exceeds ACE, a negative adjustment is made for 75% of the excess. § 56(g)(2). ACE is determined by making various adjustments to pre-ACE AMTI. The most basic ACE adjustments are:

1) Depreciation

For property placed in service after 1989 and before 1994, ACE depreciation is determined under the alternative depreciation method in

§ 168(g)—i.e., the straight line method using longer recovery periods than under ACRS. § 56(g)(4)(A). For property placed in service after 1993, there is no ACE depreciation adjustment.

2) Earnings and Profits
Certain amounts not included in pre-ACE AMTI but taken into account in determining a corporation's "earnings and profits" (see VI.B., at pages 132–134, *infra*) must be taken into account in determining ACE. § 56(g)(4)(B)(i). An example is tax-exempt interest. Items disallowed as deductions in computing earnings and profits also must be included in determining ACE. § 56(g)(4)(C). An example is the 70% dividends received deduction. Id.

d. Tax Preference Items
In determining AMTI, taxable income is increased by the "tax preference items" listed in § 57. Some examples of tax preference items are:

1) the excess of percentage depletion over cost depletion (§ 57(a)(1));

2) excess intangible drilling costs (§ 57(a)(2)); and

3) tax-exempt interest on certain private activity municipal bonds (§ 57(a)(5)).

3. The Exemption Amount
AMTI is reduced by an "exemption amount" of $40,000. § 55(d)(2). The exemption amount is reduced by 25% of AMTI in excess of $150,000. § 55(d)(3). The exemption is fully phased out when a corporation's AMTI reaches $310,000.

Example: X Corp. has AMTI of $200,000. It must reduce its $40,000 exemption amount by $12,500 (25% × $50,000). If X had AMTI of $310,000, it must reduce its exemption amount by $40,000 (25% × $160,000) to zero.

4. Credits
a. Credits Against AMT
The AMT may be reduced by the AMT foreign tax credit. §§ 55(b)(1)(B); 59.

b. Minimum Tax Credit Against Regular Tax
A minimum tax credit for AMT paid in prior years is allowed against a corporation's regular tax liability to the extent that it exceeds its tentative AMT for the taxable year. § 53. Unlike the AMT credit applicable to individual taxpayers, the corporate AMT minimum tax credit is allowed for all of a corporation's AMT rather than merely the portion of AMT attributable to timing adjustments and preferences such as depreciation. § 53(d)(1)(B)(iv).

C. Disregard of the Corporate Entity

1. Introduction

Taxpayers sometimes argue that an entity formed as a corporation under state law should not be taxed as a corporation. Such corporations are often formed for the sole purpose of obtaining loans at rates that would violate state usury laws if the loan had been made to an individual. The taxpayer may wish to avoid the separate corporate income tax and attribute income or losses of the entity to the shareholders or some other taxpayer. Most cases reject attempts by taxpayers to disregard the corporate entity unless the corporation is clearly shown to be a mere dummy or agent.

2. The Business Activity Test

A corporation generally will be recognized as a taxable entity distinct from its shareholders if it engages in any business activity even if it has only one shareholder who exercises total control over its affairs. *Moline Properties v. Comm'r*, 319 U.S. 436, 63 S.Ct. 1132 (1943).

3. The *National Carbide* Factors

In *National Carbide Corp. v. Comm'r*, 336 U.S. 422, 69 S.Ct. 726 (1949), the Supreme Court enunciated six factors to be considered in deciding whether a corporate entity could be ignored because it was merely an agent:

a. Whether the corporation operates in the name and for the account of the principal.

b. Whether the corporation binds the principal by its actions.

c. Whether the corporation transmits money received to the principal.

d. Whether receipt of income is attributable to the services of employees of the principal and to assets belonging to the principal.

e. If the corporation is a true agent, whether its relations with its principal are dependent upon the fact that it is owned by the principal.

f. Whether the corporation's business purpose is the carrying on of the normal duties of an agent.

The corporations involved in *National Carbide* were held not to be agents because they represented to outsiders that they manufactured and sold products and they had substantial assets and many employees. Subsequent cases often relied on the fifth *National Carbide* factor in holding that a corporation which is not compensated and is owned by one or more of its principals was not a true agent. See, e.g., *Frink v. Comm'r*, 798 F.2d 106 (4th Cir.1986), vac'd, 485 U.S. 973, 108 S.Ct. 1264 (1988).

4. The *Bollinger* Factors

In *Comm'r v. Bollinger*, 485 U.S. 340, 108 S.Ct. 1173 (1988), the Supreme Court placed less importance on the *National Carbide* factors in holding that a corporation which held record title to real property as an agent for its shareholders was not the true owner of the property for tax purposes. The Court rejected the Service's contention that *National Carbide* required a corporation to have an arm's-length relationship with its shareholders before it could be recognized as their agent for tax purposes. It concluded that an agency relationship could be found if:

a. The relationship with respect to a particular asset (e.g., real estate) is set forth in a written agreement at the time the asset is acquired.

b. The corporation functions as an agent with respect to the asset for all purposes.

c. The corporation's agency status is disclosed in all dealings with third parties relating to the asset.

D.   Review Question

1. X Corp., an accrual basis taxpayer, had the following results for 2002, its first year of business:

Gross Income from Operations	$230,000
Operating Expenses	85,000
Long–Term Capital Loss	40,000
§ 1231 Gain—Sale of Land	30,000
Bad Debt	10,000
Dividend from 100% Subsidiary	20,000
Dividend from IBM Corp.	5,000
ACRS Depreciation	45,000
(§ 56(a)(1) AMT Depreciation—$ 30,000)	
Municipal Bond Interest:	
State General Obligation Bond	15,000
Private Activity Bond	22,500

Determine X Corp.'s:

(a) Taxable income for the year.

(b) Regular tax liability.

(c) Alternative minimum taxable income.

(d) Alternative minimum tax liability.

IV

FORMATION OF A CORPORATION

Analysis

A. Introduction

Without a nonrecognition provision, a taxpayer who transfers property to a newly formed corporation in exchange for stock would recognize gain or loss measured by the difference between the fair market value of the stock received and the taxpayer's adjusted basis in the transferred property. § 1001(a), (c). In theory, a corporation also might realize and recognize gain on the issuance of its stock in exchange for property. At the shareholder level, § 351 overrides these general tax principles by providing that shareholders do not recognize gain or loss on certain transfers of property to a controlled (i.e., 80% owned) corporation. Section 351 applies to transfers to newly formed C and S corporations (including the creation of corporate subsidiaries) and transfers of property to preexisting corporations by their controlling shareholders. At the corporate level, § 1032(a) provides that a corporation does not recognize gain or loss when it receives money or property in exchange for its stock. The rationale is that these transactions are mere changes in the form of the shareholders' investment and are thus inappropriate taxable events. Like other nonrecognition provisions, § 351 is accompanied by rules that preserve any unrecognized gain or loss in the shareholder's stock basis (§ 358) and in the corporation's basis in the transferred property (§ 362).

B. Requirements for Nonrecognition Under § 351

The requirements for complete nonrecognition of gain or loss under § 351(a) are: (1) one or more persons (including individuals, corporations, partnerships and other entities) must transfer "property" to a corporation; (2) the property must be transferred solely in exchange for "stock" of the transferee corporation; and (3) the transferors, as a group, must be in "control" (as defined in § 368(c)) of the corporation "immediately after the exchange." For convenience, the transferee corporation will be referred to as "Newco" throughout this chapter.

1. "Property"
"Property" includes cash, inventory, accounts receivable, patents and other intangibles such as goodwill and industrial know-how. Stock issued for past, present or future services rendered to Newco will not be treated as having been issued in return for property. § 351(d)(1); Reg. § 1.351–1(a)(1)(i). The performance of services may result in the creation of an intangible right (e.g., a contract to develop real estate) that qualifies as § 351 property. See IV.B.6.a., at pages 96–98, *infra,* for special problems involving the receipt of stock for services.

2. "Transfer"
All substantial rights in the property must be transferred to Newco. A limited license of property (e.g., a nonexclusive license to use technology) does not satisfy the "transfer" requirement, and any Newco stock received for the license is considered royalty income. One court has held that the "transfer" requirement is met if stock is issued for a perpetual nonexclusive license. *E.I. Du Pont de Nemours & Co. v. U.S.,* 471 F.2d 1211 (Ct.Cl.1973).

3. Solely in Exchange for "Stock"

a. In General

"Stock" represents an equity ownership interest in a corporation; it does not include stock rights, warrants, or convertible debt securities. Reg. § 1.351–1(a)(1). Section 351(a) once applied to transfers of property solely in exchange for stock or certain debt securities of a corporation, but the term "securities" was deleted in 1989. Any corporate interest received by a transferor of property from Newco that is not "stock" is treated as "other property"—"boot" in tax jargon. For the treatment of boot under § 351, see IV.C., at pages 100–104, *infra*.

b. Nonqualified Preferred Stock

"Nonqualified preferred stock" is treated as "other property" (i.e., boot) rather than stock for purposes of § 351. § 351(g)(1). "Nonqualified preferred stock" is preferred stock (i.e., stock that is limited and preferred as to dividends and does not participate in corporate growth to any significant extent) with any of the following debt-like characteristics:

(1) The shareholder has the right to require the issuing corporation or a "related person" (e.g., certain family members or controlled entities) to redeem or purchase the stock;

(2) The corporate issuer (or a related affiliate) is required to redeem or purchase the stock;

(3) The issuer (or a related affiliate) has the right to redeem or purchase the stock and, as of the issue date, it is more likely than not that such right will be exercised; or

(4) the stock's dividend rate is variable—e.g., set by reference to market interest rates, commodity prices or similar indices.

§ 351(g)(2)(A). The first three of the above characteristics apply only if the right or obligation to redeem or purchase may be exercised within the 20–year period beginning on the issue date of the stock and such right or obligation is not subject to a contingency which, as of the issue date, makes remote the likelihood of the redemption or purchase. § 351(g)(2)(B).

Although nonqualified preferred stock is treated as boot for gain recognition purposes, the legislative history of § 351(g) states that it is still treated as stock for purposes of the § 351(a) control test until regulations are issued that provide otherwise. H.R.Rep. No. 105–220, 105th Cong., 2d Sess. 561 (1997).

4. "Control"

To be in "control" of Newco, the transferors of property collectively must own at least 80% of the total combined voting power of all classes of stock entitled to vote and at least 80% of each class of nonvoting stock. § 368(c). Some transferors may receive voting stock while others receive nonvoting stock as long as all the transferors of property, as a group, own at least 80% of each class of stock immediately after the exchange. Simultaneous exchanges are not required where the rights of the parties have been "previously defined" and the agreement proceeds with an "expedition consistent with orderly procedure." Reg. § 1.351–1(a) (1).

Example (1): of Newco, A, B and C each transfer appreciated property. A receives 50 shares of voting common stock, B receives 50 shares of nonvoting common stock and C receives 50 shares of nonvoting preferred stock that is not nonqualified preferred stock. The control test is satisfied because the property transferors, as a group, own at least 80% of each class of Newco stock.

Example (2): Same facts as Example (1), except that C receives her nonvoting preferred stock solely in exchange for services rendered to Newco. C is not a transferor of property and may not be counted in testing for control. Because transferors of property do not own 80% or more of *each* class of nonvoting stock, the transaction does not qualify under § 351(a). A and B must recognize gain or loss on their property transfers. C recognizes ordinary income on her receipt of stock for services.

5. "Immediately After the Exchange"

The transferors of property must have control of Newco "immediately after the exchange." When a member of the transferor control group disposes of stock shortly after an incorporation exchange, an issue arises as to whether the control test should be applied before or after the disposition. Resolution of this issue is often imprecise because it requires application of the judicially created step transaction doctrine (see I.E.2., at page 66, *supra*).

a. Binding Agreements to Dispose of Stock

If a shareholder disposes of stock received in exchange for property pursuant to a prearranged binding agreement entered into prior to an incorporation exchange, the control test is applied after the stock disposition. A disposition of more than 20% of voting power or more than 20% of any class of nonvoting stock will cause a loss of control because the person ultimately acquiring the stock was not a transferor of property to Newco.

Example: On the formation of Newco, A transfers land with a basis of $10,000 and a value of $60,000, in exchange for 60 shares (60%) of Newco common stock, and B transfers equipment with a basis and value of $40,000, in exchange for 40 shares (40%). Two months later, pursuant to a prearranged binding agreement, B transfers all her Newco stock to C for $40,000 cash. The control test is applied after the transfer to C. Since C was not a transferor of property to Newco, her ownership of Newco stock will not be counted in testing for control. A only owns 60% of Newco stock immediately after the exchange and thus the 80% control test is not satisfied. A must recognize $50,000 gain on the transfer of the land. See *Intermountain Lumber Co. v. Comm'r,* 65 T.C. 1025 (1976); Rev.Rul. 79–70, 1979–1 C.B. 144. If B's disposition had not been pursuant to a preexisting binding commitment, a loss of § 351 control normally would not result unless the original transfers to Newco and the subsequent disposition of Newco stock were mutually interdependent—i.e., the legal relations created by the first step would have been fruitless without completion of all the steps. See *American Bantam Car Co. v. Comm'r,* 11 T.C. 397 (1948), aff'd per curiam, 177 F.2d 513 (3d Cir.1949), cert. denied, 339 U.S. 920, 70 S.Ct. 622 (1950).

b. Voluntary Donative Dispositions of Stock

A voluntary disposition of stock—e.g., a gift—after an otherwise qualified § 351 transfer will not cause the transaction to fail the control requirement. See *Wilgard Realty Co. v. Comm'r,* 127 F.2d 514 (2d Cir.1942), cert. denied, 317 U.S. 655, 63 S.Ct. 52 (1942). The result is likely the same even if Newco issues the stock directly to the transferor's donee. *D'Angelo Associates, Inc. v. Comm'r,* 70 T.C. 121 (1978).

> *Example:* On the formation of Newco, A and B each transfer appreciated property in exchange for 50 shares of Newco common stock. Two days later, B gives 25 shares to his daughter, C. The transfers qualify for nonrecognition under § 351(a) because control is determined immediately after the incorporation transfers and before the gift to C.

c. Corporate Transferors

In determining "control," the fact that a corporate transferor distributes part or all of the Newco stock that it receives to its shareholders is not taken into account. § 351(c).

6. Special Problems

a. Stock for Services

  1) Taxation of the Service Provider

  Stock issued for services is not considered as issued in return for property. § 351(d)(1); Reg. § 1.351–1(a)(1)(i). A service provider recognizes ordinary income under § 61 on the value of any stock received from Newco for past, present or future services. The timing of the income is determined under § 83. If the stock is subject to a substantial risk of forfeiture or is not transferable, the service provider is taxed on the fair market value of the stock at the time the restrictions lapse less the amount (if any) paid for the stock. § 83(a). The service provider, however, may elect under § 83(b) to be taxed on the fair market value of the stock at the time of transfer less any amount paid. In that event, no additional income is recognized when the restrictions lapse, and no loss (except for any amount paid) is allowed if the stock is forfeited. Reg. § 1.83–2(a)(1). In either case, the service provider's basis for the stock is the amount paid plus any amount included in income. Reg. § 1.83–4(b)(1).

Example: On the formation of Newco in Year 1, Executive receives 200 shares of Newco stock (value–$50,000) in exchange for $1,000 cash and future services. The stock is subject to a substantial risk of forfeiture and will not vest until Year 5. Assume that the stock will be worth $200,000 in Year 5. Under § 83(a), Executive has no income in Year 1 and $199,000 ordinary income (the value of the stock less the $1,000 paid by Executive in Year 1) in Year 5, and his basis in the stock is $200,000. If Executive makes the § 83(b) election, he has $49,000 ordinary income in Year 1, his basis in the stock is $50,000, and he has no additional income when the restrictions lapse in Year 5. If Executive sells the stock in Year 5 after having made an election under § 83(b), he recognizes $150,000 long-term capital gain. If he forfeits the stock in Year 3, Executive may only deduct the amount he paid ($1,000) as a long-term capital loss.

2) Deduction to Corporation
If a corporation issues stock for services rendered to the corporation, it may deduct as a § 162(a) business expense the amount of ordinary income that is taxable to the service provider at the time that income is recognized unless the nature of the services requires the corporation to amortize (e.g., organizational services) or capitalize (e.g., services related to the construction or acquisition of an asset) the expense. § 83(h); Reg. § 1.83–6.

3) Service Provider Not a Transferor of Property
A shareholder who receives stock solely for services is not considered a transferor of property. If more than 20% of any class of stock is issued to a service provider, the entire transaction fails to qualify under § 351 because transferors of property do not have control immediately after the exchange. As a result, even shareholders who receive solely stock in exchange for appreciated property must recognize gain and shareholders who receive stock for property with a built-in loss may recognize that loss.

4) Stock Received for Services and Property
A person who receives stock in exchange for both property and services recognizes ordinary income to the extent of the stock received for services

but generally is still considered as a transferor of property and may count all the stock received for purposes of the 80% control requirement—unless the value of the property transferred is of relatively small value relative to the stock received for services and the primary purpose of the property transfer is to qualify the exchanges of other transferors for nonrecognition. Reg. 1.351–1(a)(1)(ii). Under the Service's ruling guidelines, property is not considered to be "of relatively small value" if it equals at least 10% of the value of stock received for services. Rev.Proc. 77–37, 1977–2 C.B. 568.

Example (1):   On the formation of Newco, A receives 70 shares of Newco common stock (value–$70,000) in exchange for land (value–$70,000; basis–$20,000), and B receives 30 shares (value–$30,000) in exchange for $1,000 cash and services. The stock received by B for cash is of relatively small value compared to the stock received for services, and thus B is not a transferor of property. The only transferor of property is A, who is not in "control." The transaction does not qualify under § 351.

Example (2):   Same facts as Example (1), except B receives 5 shares (value–$5,000) in exchange for $5,000 cash and 25 shares (value–$25,000) in exchange for services. Because the cash transferred ($5,000) exceeds 10% of the value of the stock received for services (10% × $25,000, or $2,500), the cash is not considered to be of relatively small value. B is thus treated as a transferor of property, and all 30 shares received by B are counted in testing for control. The transaction qualifies under § 351(a), but B still recognizes ordinary income on the stock received for services.

b. Disproportionate Transfers

Section 351 does not require shareholders to receive Newco stock in proportion to the value of the property they transfer. In disproportionate transfer situations, the shareholders are first treated as having received stock in proportion to the value of the transferred property and then as having retransferred the stock among themselves. The tax consequences of the entire transaction are determined in accordance with its "true nature"—e.g., as a gift, payment of compensation or satisfaction of a debt. Reg. § 1.351–1(b)(1), (b)(2) Example (1).

Example: On the formation of Newco, A transfers appreciated property worth $6,000 in exchange for 40 shares of stock and B transfers appreciated property worth $4,000 in exchange for 60 shares. The transaction qualifies under § 351. A and B are first treated as having received 60 and 40 shares, respectively, and then A is treated as having transferred 20 shares to B. If A and B are related, it is likely that A will be treated as having made a gift to B. If B had rendered past services to A, the transfer of 20 shares may be treated as the payment of compensation from A to B; B is taxed on the value of the 20 shares received as compensation and takes a fair market value basis for those shares, and A realizes gain on the transfer of the 20 shares to satisfy his obligation to B.

c. Recapture Provisions

Section 351(a) overrides the recapture of depreciation provisions. See, e.g., § 1245(b)(3). The potential recapture gain is preserved in Newco's basis in the asset. A transferor who receives boot (i.e., property other than stock in the controlled corporation) must recapture depreciation to the extent of any recognized gain. See IV.C.1., at page 100, *infra*.

d. Installment Obligations

Section 453B(a) generally requires a taxpayer to recognize gain on any disposition of an installment obligation. If an installment obligation (e.g., a note received by a taxpayer on an installment sale of property) is transferred to the controlled corporation in a § 351(a) transaction, however, no gain is recognized. Reg. § 1.453–9(c)(2).

e. Investment Companies

Transfers to an "investment company" do not qualify for nonrecognition. § 351(e). The purpose of this rule is to prevent unrelated taxpayers from achieving tax-free diversification by transferring appreciated portfolio securities in exchange for stock of a newly formed pooled investment vehicle. For details on this exception, see Reg. § 1.351–1(c).

7. Basis and Holding Period
a. Shareholder's Basis in Newco Stock

If property is transferred in a § 351 transaction solely in exchange for Newco stock, the transferor's basis in the stock received will equal his basis in the transferred property immediately prior to the exchange. § 358(a)(1). (This is known in tax jargon as an "exchanged" or "substituted" basis.) If a transferor receives more than one class of Newco stock, the aggregate basis determined under § 358(a)(1) is allocated among all classes of stock received in proportion to the fair market values of each class. § 358(b); Reg. § 1.358–2(a)(2).

b. Shareholder's Holding Period in Newco Stock

A transferor's holding period for Newco stock received in a § 351 transaction in exchange for a capital or § 1231 asset includes the holding period of transferred property. § 1223(1). (This is known as "tacking.") The holding period of stock received in exchange for an ordinary income asset (or for services rendered) begins on the date of the exchange. If stock is received for a combination of capital and ordinary income assets, each share of Newco stock takes a split holding period allocated in proportion to the fair market values of the transferred assets. Rev.Rul. 85–164, 1985–2 C.B. 117.

c. Corporation's Basis and Holding Period in Transferred Assets

Newco's basis in the assets transferred in a § 351 transaction is the same as the transferor's basis. § 362(a). (This is known as a "transferred" or "carryover" basis.) Newco's holding period for the transferred property includes the transferor's holding period, without regard to whether the property was a capital or § 1231 asset in the transferor's hands. § 1223(2).

> **Example (1):** On the formation of Newco, A transfers land (a § 1231 asset) held long-term with a basis of $10,000 and a value of $60,000, and inventory with a basis of $30,000 and a value of $40,000, in exchange for 100 shares of Newco common stock with a value of $100,000. The transaction qualifies under § 351(a). A's basis in the Newco stock is $40,000, which is the sum of A's bases in the land and inventory. § 358(a). Because A received the Newco stock in exchange for a § 1231 asset and an ordinary income asset, each share takes a split holding period: 60% includes A's holding period in the land and 40% commences as of the date of the exchange. If A were to sell all the stock on the next day for $100,000, A would recognize $36,000 long-term capital gain and $24,000 short-term capital gain. Newco takes a $10,000 basis in the land and a $30,000 basis in the inventory under § 362(a) and a tacked holding period in each asset under § 1223(2).

> **Example (2):** Assume the same facts as in Example (1), except A receives 80 shares of Newco common stock and 20 shares of Newco preferred stock. A's aggregate basis in both classes of stock is $40,000, which is allocated in proportion to the fair market value of each class: $32,000 (80%) to the common and $8,000 (20%) to the preferred. Each share of common and preferred stock has a split holding period, 60% tacked from the land and 40% commencing on the date of the exchange.

C. Treatment of Boot

1. In General

If a transferor receives property other than stock—e.g., cash, corporate debt securities, nonqualified preferred stock, or other property (collectively known as "boot")—in a § 351 transaction, § 351(b) provides that the transferor's realized gain is recognized to the extent of the cash and the fair market value of any other boot received. Even if a transferor receives boot, however, no loss may be recognized. § 351(b)(2). The character of any gain recognized is determined by reference to the character of the transferred asset to which the gain is attributable, taking into account the depreciation recapture provisions (e.g. § 1245) and other applicable characterization rules (e.g. § 1239). As explained below (see IV.C.4., at page 103, *infra*), gain triggered by the receipt of boot results in increases to the shareholder's basis in the stock received and the corporation's basis in the transferred property.

Example (1): On the formation of Newco, A transfers $50,000 cash in exchange for 50 shares of Newco stock, and B transfers investment land with a basis of $10,000 and a fair market value of $50,000 in exchange for 40 shares of stock and $10,000 cash. The cash received by B is boot. B's realized gain on the land is $40,000, of which $10,000 must be recognized as capital gain under § 351(b).

Example (2): Assume the same facts as Example (1), except B receives 5 shares of Newco stock and $45,000 cash. Although B receives $45,000 of boot, B's recognized gain is limited to the $40,000 gain realized on the land.

2. Allocation of Boot

When several assets are transferred in exchange for a combination of stock and boot, the boot is allocated among the transferred assets in proportion to their relative fair market values. Realized gain on a transferred asset is recognized to the extent of the boot allocable to that asset, but no realized losses may be recognized under § 351(b). Rev.Rul. 68–55, 1968–1 C.B. 140. Thus, boot allocated to a loss asset will not cause recognition of gain or loss.

Example (1): On the formation of Newco, A transfers $50,000 cash in exchange for $50,000 of stock, and B transfers a capital asset with a basis of $5,000 and a value of $30,000, and equipment with a basis of $5,000 and a value of $20,000 (and $10,000 of potential § 1245 recapture), in exchange for $40,000 of stock and $10,000 cash. As to B, the $10,000 of cash boot is allocated between the capital asset and the equipment in proportion to the relative fair market values of those assets—i.e., $6,000 (60%) to the capital asset and $4,000 (40%) to the equipment. B recognizes $6,000 of capital gain on the capital asset and $4,000 of ordinary income on the equipment.

Example (2): Assume the same facts as in Example (1), except that B's basis in the $30,000 capital asset is $40,000 rather than $5,000. The $10,000 cash boot is still allocated $6,000 to the capital asset and $4,000 to the equipment. B recognizes $4,000 of ordinary income on the equipment but may not recognize any of the realized loss on the capital asset.

3. Installment Boot

A transferor who receives boot in the form of a Newco debt instrument may be allowed to defer recognition of any § 351(b) gain under § 453. Application of the installment sale rules to a § 351 transaction requires bifurcating the exchange into two parts: a § 351(a) nonrecognition exchange to the extent of the stock ("permitted property") received by the transferor and a taxable installment sale to the extent of the boot received. The basis of the transferred property is first allocated to the nonrecognition exchange, and any remaining basis (known as "excess basis") is allocated to the installment sale. Cf. § 453(f)(6); Prop.Reg. § 1.453–1(f)(1), (3)(ii). Recapture gain and gain attributable to dispositions of dealer property do not qualify for deferral. §§ 453(b)(2), (i), (*l*).

Example (1):   A, the sole shareholder of Newco, transfers Gainacre (value– $100,000; basis–$10,000) in exchange for 80 shares of Newco stock (value–$80,000), $5,000 cash and a $15,000 Newco note providing for market rate interest and a single principal payment in five years. A recognizes $20,000 gain under § 351(b); the timing of that gain is determined under § 453. Under the regulations, A is treated as having exchanged $80,000 of Gainacre for Newco stock; A's entire $10,000 basis in Gainacre is allocated to this nonrecognition transaction. The remaining $20,000 of Gainacre (with a zero basis) is treated as having been exchanged for $5,000 cash and the $15,000 note in a § 453 installment sale. For § 453 purposes, the "selling price," "total contract price" and "gross profit" are all $20,000, and the gross profit fraction is 100%. (The fraction always will be 100% if the boot received is less than the realized gain.) Payments in the year of sale are limited to the $5,000 cash. A recognizes $5,000 gain in year one and the remaining $15,000 gain when the note is paid in year five.

Example (2):   Assume the same facts as in Example (1), except that A's basis in Gainacre is $90,000 rather than $10,000. A's realized gain is $10,000. Although A receives $20,000 of boot, his recognized gain is limited to $10,000. A is treated as having exchanged $80,000 of Gainacre in exchange for Newco stock; $80,000 of his $90,000 basis in Gainacre is allocated to this nonrecognition transaction. The remaining $10,000—A's "excess basis" in Gainacre is allocated to the installment sale. For § 453 purposes, the selling price and total contract price are $20,000, the gross profit is $10,000, and the gross profit percentage is 50%. A recognizes $2,500 gain in year one ($5,000 cash × 50%) and $7,500 gain (15,000 × 50%) when the $15,000 note is paid in year five.

Example (3):   Assume the same facts as in Example (1), except Gainacre is depreciable equipment and the entire realized gain would be recaptured as ordinary income under § 1245. None of the recognized gain may be deferred under § 453.

4. **Basis and Holding Period**
   a. **Shareholder's Basis**

   1) A transferor who receives Newco stock and boot in a § 351 transaction determines his basis in the Newco stock according to the following formula: (1) transferor's basis in property transferred, minus (2) amount of cash and fair market value of boot (Newco debt and other nonstock property) received, plus (3) gain recognized by transferor. § 358(a)(1). If the transferor receives more than one class of Newco stock, the aggregate basis determined above is allocated among the various classes in proportion to the fair market value of each class. § 358(b); Reg. § 1.358–2(a)(2).

   2) The increase for gain recognized by the transferor is made at the time of transfer even though the gain may be deferred under the § 453 installment method. Prop.Reg. § 1.453–1(f)(3)(ii).

   3) In general, the basis of boot received by a transferor is its fair market value. § 358(a)(2). If a transferor who receives installment debt boot (e.g., a corporate note) reports the gain recognized under the installment method, the basis of the debt obligation is its face value less the amount of income that will be taxable to the transferor if the obligation is satisfied in full. § 453B(b).

   b. **Corporation's Basis**

   1) If the transferor recognizes gain because of the receipt of boot, the corporation's basis in the property received is the transferor's basis plus any gain recognized. § 362(a).

   2) If the transferor defers any gain recognized under the § 453 installment method, the corporation may increase its basis under § 362(a) only when that gain is recognized. Prop.Reg. § 1.453–1(f)(3)(ii).

   3) If a transferor recognizes gain when several assets are transferred in exchange for a combination of Newco stock and boot, no published authority indicates how the § 362(a) basis increase for gain recognized is to be allocated among the assets. Based on the Service's approach to boot allocation (see IV.C.2., at page ___, *supra*), it is logical for the corporation's basis in each asset to be the same as the transferor's basis increased by any gain recognized that is attributable to that asset.

   > ***Example:*** On the formation of Newco, A transfers Gainacre, with a value of $100,000 and a basis of $10,000, in exchange for Newco stock with a value of $80,000, $5,000 cash and a $15,000 Newco five-year note. A recognizes $20,000 gain, $15,000 of which may be deferred until year five. A's basis in the Newco stock is: $10,000 (basis of Gainacre), less $20,000 (value of boot received), plus $20,000 (gain recognized and to

be recognized by A), or $10,000. Since the stock is worth $80,000, this preserves $70,000 of gain that went unrecognized on the transfer of Gainacre. Newco's initial basis in Gainacre is: $10,000 (A's basis), plus $5,000 (gain recognized by A in year one), or $15,000. Newco's basis increases to $30,000 when Newco pays off the $15,000 note to A. If Newco sells Gainacre for $100,000 before the note is paid off, it will recognize $85,000 gain, but it may deduct $15,000 as a capital loss when the note is paid off in year five. Prop.Reg. § 1.453–1(f)(3)(iii) Example (1).

4) For a special limitation on any basis increase under § 362(a) attributable to Newco's assumption of a liability, see IV.D.5., at page 108, *infra*.

5. Transfer of Appreciated Boot

If a corporation transfers stock and appreciated boot property (other than its own debt obligations) to a shareholder in a transaction that otherwise qualifies under § 351 but is not a tax-free reorganization under § 368, the corporation must recognize gain as if it had distributed the property in a transaction governed by § 311(b). § 351(f). This is an unlikely result on an incorporation but could occur on a § 351 transfer by a controlling shareholder to an existing corporation. See VI.D.1., at page 136, *infra*.

Example: A, the sole shareholder of X Corp., transfers to X property with a fair market value of $20,000 in exchange for $15,000 of X stock and other property (boot) with a fair market value of $5,000 and an adjusted basis to X of $1,000. Even though the transaction generally qualifies under § 351, X must recognize $4,000 gain.

D. Assumption of Liabilities

1. In General

If, as part of an otherwise qualified § 351 exchange, Newco assumes a liability of the transferor shareholder, the assumption is not treated as boot received by the transferor. § 357(a). But to preserve any gain that otherwise would have been recognized, the liability is treated as boot for purposes of determining the transferor's basis in the Newco stock. § 358(d). These rules are subject to two exceptions, described at IV.D.2. and IV.D.3., below.

Example: On the formation of Newco, A transfers land with a basis of $20,000, a value of $60,000, and subject to a $10,000 liability, in exchange for Newco common stock worth $50,000. A recognizes no gain on the transfer because relief of the $10,000 liability is not treated as boot. A's basis in the Newco stock is: $20,000 (basis of property transferred), minus $10,000 (liability is treated as boot for basis purposes), or $10,000. This basis preserves A's $40,000 gain on the land in the Newco stock.

2. Determination of Amount of Liabilities Assumed

The determination of the amount of liabilities assumed by Newco for purposes of § 357 (and certain other provisions of the Code discussed later) depends on whether the liability is "recourse" (the transferor has personal liability on the debt) or "nonrecourse" (the liability is limited to the value of the property securing the debt).

a. Recourse Liability

A recourse liability is treated as having been assumed to the extent that, based on all the facts and circumstances, the transferee (Newco) has agreed and is expected to satisfy the liability, whether or not the transferor-shareholder has been relieved of it. § 357(d)(1)(A).

b. Nonrecourse Liability

In general, a nonrecourse liability is treated as having been assumed when an asset is transferred to Newco subject to the liability. § 357(d)(1)(B). But in situations where more than one asset secures a nonrecourse liability, the amount of the liability treated as assumed must be reduced by the lesser of:

1) The amount of that portion of the liability which an owner of other assets not transferred to Newco and also subject to the liability has agreed to and is expected to satisfy; or

2) The fair market value of the other assets to which the liability is subject.

§ 357(d)(2). The purpose of this somewhat mysterious rule is to foreclose an abusive result by preventing the liability from being counted more than once in making upward basis adjustments under § 362. For the corresponding basis rules, see IV.D.5., at page 108, *infra*.

3. Tax Avoidance Transactions

The assumption of a liability is treated as boot if the taxpayer's principal purpose in transferring the liability was the avoidance of federal income taxes or was not a bona fide corporate business purpose. § 357(b). If this exception applies, *all* the relieved liabilities, not just the abusive debts, are treated as boot. Reg. § 1.357–1(c). The taxpayer has the burden of proving the absence of an improper purpose by "the clear preponderance of the evidence." § 357(b)(2). Encumbering property for personal reasons shortly before a § 351 transfer or causing Newco to assume a transferor's personal debts are examples of improper or tax avoidance purposes.

Example: On the formation of Newco, A transfers land with a basis of $20,000, a value of $60,000 and subject to a $10,000 liability, in exchange for Newco stock worth $50,000. A encumbered the land shortly before the transfer in order to raise funds to pay personal expenses. It is likely that the transfer of the land subject to the liability was not motivated by a bona fide business purpose, and thus the $10,000 debt relief is treated as boot. A recognizes $10,000 gain under § 351(b); A's basis in the Newco stock is: $20,000 (basis of land), less $10,000 (debt relief), plus $10,000 (gain recognized), or $20,000.

4. Liabilities in Excess of Basis
a. In General

If the sum of the liabilities assumed by Newco in a § 351 transaction exceed the aggregate adjusted basis of the properties transferred by a particular transferor, the excess is treated as gain from the sale or exchange of property. § 357(c)(1). This rule is applied separately to each transferor of property. The likely purpose of the rule is to prevent a transferor from having a negative basis in the Newco stock. If § 357(b) and § 357(c) both apply to a transfer, § 357(b) takes precedence. § 357(c)(2)(A).

Example: On the formation of Newco, A transfers land with a basis of $30,000, a value of $100,000 and subject to a $55,000 liability, in exchange for Newco stock worth $45,000. If § 357(a) applied, without more, A would recognize no gain, but A's basis in the Newco stock would be: $30,000 (basis of land), less $55,000 (debt relief), or negative $25,000. Under § 357(c), however, A must recognize $25,000 gain (the excess of the $55,000 liability over A's $30,000 basis in the land). A's basis in the Newco stock is: $30,000 (basis of land), less $55,000 (debt relief), plus $25,000 (gain recognized), or zero. The transferor's basis in the Newco stock always is zero if § 357(c) applies.

b. Transferor Remains Liable to Creditor

A transferor does not avoid § 357(c) gain by remaining personally liable for debts encumbering property transferred to Newco in a § 351 transaction. *Owen v. Comm'r,* 881 F.2d 832 (9th Cir.1989), cert. denied, 493 U.S. 1070, 110 S.Ct. 1113 (1990).

c. Avoiding § 357(c) by Transfer of Note
1) The *Lessinger* Case

The Second Circuit held in *Lessinger v. Comm'r,* 872 F.2d 519 (2d Cir.1989), that a taxpayer who transfers his own enforceable note to a controlled corporation in a § 351 transaction may avoid recognizing gain under § 357(c). The court concluded that since the corporation took the note with a basis equal to its face value, the taxpayer should not be required to recognize any § 357(c) gain. This rationale is not supported by the statute.

2) The *Peracchi* Case

Applying somewhat different reasoning, the Ninth Circuit reached a similar result in *Peracchi v. Comm'r,* 143 F.3d 487 (9th Cir. 1998).

The court concluded that the taxpayer had a basis equal to face value in his own note transferred to a wholly owned corporation because the note was a corporate asset subject to the claims of creditors in the event of a bankruptcy. It thus represented a real and substantial increase in the taxpayer's corporate investment. This reasoning is limited to notes that have economic substance and have a fair market value roughly equal to face value. The court observed that contributing a promissory note did not differ economically from other transactions that would avoid § 357(c) gain, such as borrowing from an outside lender and contributing the cash to the corporation.

3) Synthesis of § 357(c) Cases
    Lessinger and *Peracchi* enable the transferor to avoid recognizing § 357(c) gain. The Service and several other courts have held, however, that a taxpayer has a zero basis in his own note for § 357(c) purposes. See, e.g., *Alderman v. Comm'r,* 55 T.C. 662 (1971). The law remains unsettled.

    Example: On the formation of Newco, A transfers land subject to a $20,000 mortgage and having a basis of $10,000 and a value of $50,000, in exchange for Newco stock worth $30,000. Under *Lessinger* and *Peracchi*, A could avoid what otherwise would be $10,000 of § 357(c) gain by transferring his own personal note for $10,000. Other courts have held that A has no basis in his note and must recognize $10,000 of gain.

d. **Character of § 357(c) Gain**
    According to the regulations, the character of any § 357(c) gain is determined by allocating the gain among the transferred assets in proportion to their respective fair market values. Reg. § 1.357–2(a). Under this sometimes anomalous approach, § 357(c) gain may be characterized by reference to an asset that has no built-in gain.

    Example: On the formation of Newco, A transfers inventory with a basis and value of $10,000 and a capital asset subject to a $25,000 liability with a basis of $5,000 and a value of $30,000. A recognizes $10,000 of gain under § 357(c) (excess of $25,000 liability over $15,000 aggregate basis of two assets transferred). Of the gross asset value of $40,000 transferred by A, 25% is attributable to the inventory and 75% is attributable to the capital asset. Under the regulations, $2,500 (25%) of the gain is ordinary income and $7,500 (75%) is capital gain even though A had no built-in realized gain on the inventory.

e. **Excluded Liabilities**
    Liabilities assumed by Newco that have not yet been taken into account by the transferor for tax purposes (either by the transferor's taking a current § 162

deduction or increasing the basis of property) are not treated as "liabilities" for purposes of determining gain recognized under § 357(c)(1) or basis under § 358. §§ 357(c)(3); 358(d)(2). Examples of such excluded liabilities are cash basis accounts payable and contingent liabilities.

Example (1):   On the formation of Newco, A, a cash method taxpayer, transfers $50,000 cash and $200,000 accounts receivable (with a zero basis) in exchange for $150,000 of Newco stock and Newco's assumption of $100,000 of A's accounts payable which would have been deductible under § 162(a) if paid by A. Under § 357(c)(1), without more, A would recognize $50,000 gain (the excess of the $100,000 accounts payable over the $50,000 cash transferred by A). Under § 357(c)(3), however, the accounts payable are not treated as "liabilities." A thus recognizes no gain. A's basis in the Newco stock is $50,000 (cash transferred); it is not reduced by the accounts payable assumed by Newco.

Example (2):   On the formation of Newco in Year 1, B, an accrual basis taxpayer, transfers contaminated land with associated contingent environmental liabilities in exchange for all of Newco's stock. B neither deducted nor capitalized any amount with respect to the liabilities. The liabilities assumed by Newco in the exchange are not "liabilities" for purposes of § 357(c)(1) and § 358(d) because they were never deducted by B and they did not create or increase the basis of any property prior to the transfer. Rev. Rul. 95–74, 1995–2 C.B. 36.

5.   Limit on Basis Increase Attributable to Liability Assumption

a.   In General

When gain is recognized by a transferor as a result of the assumption by Newco of a liability (e.g., when § 357(b) or § 357(c) applies), in no event may the basis of the property transferred to Newco be increased above the fair market value of the property. § 362(d)(1).

b.   Recognized Gain on Liability Assumption Not Taxable

A special rule applies when: (1) a transferor of property recognizes gain as a result of the assumption of a nonrecourse liability by Newco, (2) that liability also is secured by assets not transferred to Newco, and (3) no person is taxable on the recognized gain (e.g., because the transferor is a foreign person not subject to U.S. tax). Under this special rule, for purposes of § 362 basis adjustments, the transferor's gain recognized as a result of the assumption is determined as if the liability assumed by Newco equalled Newco's ratable portion of the liability as determined on the basis of the relative fair market values of all assets subject to the liability. § 362(d)(2).

E. Incorporation of a Going Business

1. Assignment of Income Doctrine

In general, the assignment of income doctrine does not apply to a transfer to Newco of accounts receivable by a cash basis taxpayer unless the taxpayer has a tax avoidance purpose. *Hempt Brothers, Inc. v. U.S.*, 490 F.2d 1172 (3d Cir.1974), cert. denied, 419 U.S. 826, 95 S.Ct. 44 (1974); Rev.Rul. 80–198, 1980–2 C.B. 113.

> *Example:*   On the formation of Newco, A transfers the assets of her cash method sole proprietorship, including zero basis accounts receivable, in exchange for Newco stock. Although A "earned" the income, she is not taxed on the transfer; Newco takes over A's zero basis and recognizes income when it collects the receivables. If A is an accrual basis taxpayer, she has a basis in the receivables equal to the amount already included in income; Newco takes that same basis and recognizes no additional income when it collects the receivables.

2. Accounts Payable and Contingent Liabilities

Accounts payable transferred to Newco by a cash basis taxpayer or contingent liabilities for which the transferor has not received any tax benefit are not treated as "liabilities" for purposes of § 357(c)(1) (see IV.D.4.e., at page 107, *supra*). Although some older cases (e.g., *Holdcroft Transp. Co. v. Comm'r*, 153 F.2d 323 (8th Cir.1946)) would treat Newco's assumption of these obligations as a nondeductible capital expenditure, the Service generally permits Newco to deduct the payables when they are paid if they would have been currently deductible by the transferor or to treat them as capital expenditures as appropriate under Newco's method of accounting. See Rev.Rul. 80–198, 1980–2 C.B. 113; Rev. Rul. 95–74, 1995–2 C.B. 36.

3. Tax Benefit Rule

The tax benefit rule requires a taxpayer who derives a tax benefit, such as a deduction, in one year to recognize income in a subsequent year on the occurrence of an event, such as a recovery of the amount deducted, that is inconsistent with the earlier deduction. It is unsettled whether the tax benefit rule overrides § 351. In *Nash v. U.S.*, 398 U.S. 1, 90 S.Ct. 1550 (1970), the Supreme Court held that the tax benefit rule did not require an accrual basis taxpayer to recognize income on the transfer of accounts receivable in a § 351 transaction when the taxpayer had previously deducted some of the receivables as uncollectible by creating a bad debt reserve. The Court held that there was no "recovery" because the taxpayer received Newco stock equal to the value of the receivables less the previously deducted bad debt reserve. The specific result in *Nash* is no longer important because accrual method taxpayers generally may not deduct bad debt reserves. As a policy matter, § 351 should override the tax benefit rule in situations where the tax benefit can be preserved and later "recaptured" through a transferred basis. Cf. § 1245(b)(3).

4. Depreciation Methods

If Newco acquires depreciable property in a § 351(a) exchange, it continues to use the transferor's depreciation method and remaining recovery period. § 168(i)(7). If the transferor recognizes § 351(b) gain allocable to a depreciable asset, Newco's § 362(a) basis increase for gain recognized may be depreciated under § 168 as if it were a separate newly acquired asset. Prop. Reg. § 1.168–5(b)(7).

F. Contributions to Capital

1. Capital Contribution Defined

When a shareholder transfers property to a corporation but does not receive stock or other consideration in exchange, the transaction is a contribution to capital and is not governed by § 351. If, however, a *sole* shareholder transfers property or all shareholders transfer property in the same proportion as their holdings, the issuance of new stock has no economic significance. Several cases have held that § 351 applies to these latter types of transfers because the issuance of stock would be "a meaningless gesture." See, e.g., *Lessinger v. Comm'r,* 85 T.C. 824 (1985), aff'd, 872 F.2d 519 (2d Cir.1989).

2. Treatment of the Contributor

A shareholder does not recognize gain or loss on a contribution of property to capital. The shareholder may increase his basis in the corporation's stock by the amount of cash and the adjusted basis of any contributed property. Reg. § 1.118–1.

3. Treatment of the Corporation

Contributions to capital are not taxable to the transferee corporation. § 118(a); Reg. § 1.118–1. An example of a contribution to capital by a nonshareholder would be a transfer of property by a municipality to encourage the corporation to build a facility there. The corporation's basis in property received as a nontaxable contribution to capital by a shareholder is the same as the transferor's basis. § 362(a)(2). The corporation's basis in property (other than cash) contributed by a nonshareholder is zero. § 362(c)(1). If cash is contributed to capital by a nonshareholder, the corporation must reduce its basis in any property acquired within 12 months of the contribution by the amount of the contributed cash, and the excess of the contribution over the reduction of basis of newly acquired property must be applied to reduce the basis of any other property held by the corporation. § 362(c)(2).

4. Non Pro Rata Surrender of Stock

A majority shareholder of a financially distressed corporation may surrender stock on a non pro rata basis in order to improve the company's credit rating. After many years of controversy, the Supreme Court has held that a controlling shareholder does not realize a deductible ordinary loss when he surrenders part of his stock without receiving cash or property in return and continues to retain voting control over the corporation after the surrender. *Comm'r v. Fink,* 483 U.S. 89, 107 S.Ct. 2729 (1987). Analogizing this transaction to a shareholder's voluntary forgiveness of a debt owed to him by the corporation, the Court held that a stock surrender is a contribution to capital. The shareholder must reallocate his basis in the surrendered shares to the shares that he retains.

G. Collateral Issues

1. Avoidance of § 351
a. Incentive to Avoid Qualification
Although § 351 is not elective, taxpayers sometimes may wish to avoid qualification in order to accelerate recognition of a loss or to recognize gain on an asset and step-up its basis for depreciation in the hands of the corporation. Taxpayers also may wish to recognize capital gain on the transfer of an appreciated asset in situations where the asset will become ordinary income (dealer) property in the hands of the corporation.

b. Avoidance Techniques
Techniques to avoid § 351 include failing the "immediately after the exchange" requirement by a prearranged disposition of stock, or structuring a transfer as a taxable "sale" rather than a tax-free § 351 transfer. These issues raise factual questions that are not susceptible to precise generalization.

> ***Example:*** A owns undeveloped land with a basis of $50,000 and a value of $200,000. A intends to subdivide the land and sell homes at an anticipated aggregate sale price of $500,000. If A develops the land, he would recognize $450,000 ordinary income. A might wish to transfer the land to a controlled corporation in order to recognize $150,000 of predevelopment capital gain that is taxable at a maximum rate of 28%, step-up the basis of the land to $200,000 and limit the anticipated ordinary income to $300,000. A may attempt to avoid § 351 by transferring the land to Newco in exchange for a small amount of stock and Newco debt. Some cases (e.g., *Burr Oaks Corp. v. Comm'r,* 365 F.2d 24 (7th Cir.1966), cert. denied, 385 U.S. 1007, 87 S.Ct. 713 (1967)) would reclassify the debt as stock and hold that A recognizes no gain under § 351, while others (e.g., *Bradshaw v. U.S.,* 683 F.2d 365 (Ct.Cl.1982)) would respect the taxpayer's form and treat the transaction as a taxable sale.

2. Relationship to Other Code Sections
a. Reorganization Provisions
A § 351 exchange may be part of a larger transaction known as a tax-free reorganization. For an example of the overlap between § 351 and a Type D reorganization, see XII.A.2., at page 270, *infra.*

b. Dividend Provisions
An existing corporation may engage in a § 351 transaction that, in part, has the effect of the distribution of a taxable dividend. Reg. § 1.351–2(d). See Chapter VI, *infra.*

Example: A, the sole shareholder of X Corp. transfers property with a value of $20,000 in exchange for $20,000 of X stock and $2,000 cash. The $2,000 excess value may be classified as a taxable dividend.

c. Section 482

Section 482 permits the Service to reallocate income between two or more commonly controlled trades or businesses if necessary to prevent tax evasion or clearly reflect the income of the taxpayers. See XIV.C.2., at page 307, *infra.* In situations where §§ 351 and 482 overlap, the courts have held that § 482 takes precedence and permits the Service to reallocate income or expenses from the transferee corporation back to a transferor of property if the purpose of the transfer was to avoid taxes. See, e.g., *Foster v. Comm'r,* 756 F.2d 1430 (9th Cir.1985); Reg. § 1.482–1(d)(5).

H. Organizational Expenses

1. Amortization

Expenses of forming a corporation are nondeductible capital expenditures. Section 248 permits a corporation to amortize its organizational expenses over a period of 60 months or more beginning with the month in which the corporation commences business.

2. Organizational Expenses Defined

"Organizational expenditures" are defined by § 248(b) as expenditures which are: (1) incident to the creation of the corporation, (2) chargeable to capital account, and (3) of a character which, if expended to create a corporation having a limited life, would be amortizable over that life. Examples include legal fees for drafting the articles of incorporation and bylaws, state filing fees and necessary accounting services. Reg. § 1.248–1(b)(2). Costs of issuing or selling stock are not organizational expenses and must be capitalized. Reg. § 1.248–1(b)(3)(i). Expenses related to the transfer of particular assets also are not amortizable, but the corporation may add these expenses to its basis in the asset.

I. Review Questions

1. A and B incorporate a house painting business ("Newco"). A transfers a van (value–$11,000, basis–$15,000, subject to outstanding debt–$8,000) in exchange for 3,000 shares of Newco common stock. B transfers $7,000 cash in exchange for 7,000 shares of Newco common stock.

   (a) Does the incorporation qualify for nonrecognition under § 351(a)?

   (b) Determine A and B's bases and holding periods in their respective shares of Newco common stock, and Newco's basis and holding period in the van.

(c) If B gives her shares to her favorite nephew shortly after the incorporation, will the transaction still qualify for nonrecognition under § 351?

(d) Assume that A's adjusted basis in the van was only $7,000, and A had taken $8,000 of depreciation on the van as a sole proprietor. What result to A on the incorporation?

(e) How might A have avoided any gain recognized in (d), above?

2. A and B form a development company ("Newco"). A transfers land (value–$50,000, basis–$30,000) in exchange for 45,000 shares of Newco common stock (value–$45,000) and $5,000 cash. In consideration of B's past and future promotional and management services, Newco issues to B 5,000 shares of Newco common stock (value–$5,000) on the condition that if B resigns his position with Newco within two years he must return 2,500 shares to Newco.

(a) Does the transaction qualify for nonrecognition under § 351?

(b) Determine A's recognized gain and A's basis in the Newco stock.

(c) Determine the tax consequences of the transaction to B in the year of transfer, assuming first that § 83(a) applies and then that B made the § 83(b) election.

(d) If B makes the § 83(b) election and then leaves Newco at the beginning of year 2, how much loss, if any, may B recognize on the forfeiture of his 2,500 shares?

3. On an incorporation of Newco that qualifies under § 351, A transfers Gainacre (value–$40,000, basis–$8,000) and Lossacre (value–$10,000, basis–$15,000) in exchange for 4,000 shares of Newco stock (value–$40,000) and $10,000 of cash.

(a) How much gain, if any, must A recognize?

(b) Determine A's basis in the Newco stock and Newco's basis in Gainacre and Lossacre.

4. On an incorporation of Newco that qualifies under § 351, A transfers Gainacre (value–$50,000, basis–$5,000) in exchange for 3,000 shares of Newco common stock (value–$30,000), $5,000 cash and a $15,000 Newco note to be paid in five equal annual installments (with market rate interest) beginning in the year after the incorporation.

(a) Determine the tax consequences (gain recognized, basis in Newco stock) to A in the year of the incorporation and as payments are received on the Newco note.

(b) Determine Newco's basis in Gainacre.

*

V

CAPITAL STRUCTURE

Analysis

A. Introduction

1. Sources of Corporate Capital

The sources of corporate capital fall into two broad categories: "debt" and "equity." The combination of debt and equity used by a corporation to finance its operations is known as the corporation's "capital structure."

a. Equity Capital

Equity capital is contributed to a corporation in exchange for an ownership interest evidenced by shares of stock.

1) Preferred Stock

Preferred shareholders have limited financial rights that are preferred over the rights of common shareholders. Conventional preferred stock has fixed dividend and liquidation preferences. Other types of preferred stock have more of the characteristics of debt, such as a variable dividend rate (e.g., based on an index) or a mandatory redemption feature. Preferred stock can be voting or nonvoting. It often is subject to repurchase ("redemption") at a stated price at the option of the corporation. A corporation may have several different classes of preferred stock.

Example: Newco issues $8.00 nonvoting preferred stock with a liquidation preference of $100 per share. A holder of the stock is entitled to a dividend of $8 per share before Newco may pay dividends to common shareholders, and to a distribution of $100 per share (after payment of all corporate debts) if Newco should liquidate.

2) Common Stock

Common stock is the most basic form of corporate ownership. Common shareholders are not entitled to receive dividends or assets on liquidation until the rights of creditors and preferred shareholders have been satisfied. Common stock represents "residual" ownership because the interests of common shareholders are not fixed or limited, enabling them to benefit from the growth of a corporation's earnings and assets. At least one class of common stock must have voting rights. Most states also permit a corporation to issue nonvoting common stock or different classes of common stock with variations as to voting power, dividends and liquidation rights.

3) Convertible Stock

Stock is "convertible" if it can be converted from one class into another— e.g., preferred stock may be convertible into common at a ratio or price stated at the time of issuance.

> *Example:* Newco issues a class of convertible preferred stock with a value and liquidation preference of $100 per share. The preferred is convertible into common stock at a rate of 2 shares of common for each share of convertible preferred. A preferred shareholder would not be economically motivated to convert until the value of the common equals or exceeds $50 per share.

b. Debt Capital

Corporate debt securities include bonds, debentures, notes and more complex variations. Debt also may be in the form of advances to the corporation that are not evidenced by a formal instrument. Debt usually is evidenced by a written unconditional obligation of the corporation to pay a specified amount on demand or on a certain date. Debt differs from preferred stock in that interest on debt is an unconditional obligation of the corporation while dividends on preferred stock, even if fixed in amount, are discretionary with the board and normally may not be paid unless the corporation has sufficient earnings. Holders of debt also have priority over preferred shareholders on liquidation.

1) Bonds and Debentures

Bonds and debentures are usually evidenced by a written unconditional obligation to pay a specific amount at a future date. They may be registered in the name of the holder or in "bearer" form with interest coupons attached. "Registered" means that the debt instrument is made payable to a specific payee whose name is registered with the corporation. Interest and principal at maturity on bearer debt are payable to whomever has physical possession of the coupons and the certificate. Bonds are secured debts; debentures are unsecured.

2) Notes

Notes are negotiable written instruments evidencing an unconditional promise to pay. Notes may be secured or unsecured. Notes usually have a shorter term than bonds or debentures.

3) Convertible Debt

Some debt may be convertible into equity—e.g., a debenture may be convertible into common stock at a ratio stated at the time the debt is issued.

c. Hybrid Instruments

Many tax classification controversies involve hybrid instruments (including convertible debt) which have characteristics common to both debt and equity. The investment community has exploited the lack of clear guidance in this area by designing financial products that seek "best of both worlds" treatment—i.e., debt for tax purposes and equity for regulatory, financial rating, and accounting purposes. The Service has threatened to reclassify and treat as equity debt instruments with long maturities or provisions permitting repayment of principal with corporate stock. See, e.g., IRS Notice 94–47, 1994–1 C.B. 357; IRS Notice 94–48, 1994–1 C.B. 357. Despite these warnings, many hybrid securities continue to be designed and marketed by large financial institutions. An example is the now well-accepted "trust preferred security," which typically has a maturity of from 20 to 30 years, a fixed interest rate, and a right on the part of the issuer to defer interest payments for up to five years at a time.

2. Tax Differences Between Debt And Equity
a. Tax Advantages of Debt

In the case of C corporations, the federal tax laws create a bias in favor of debt. These tax advantages are influential when a corporation is formed and later when additional capital is needed. In reviewing the advantages listed below, keep in mind that the shareholders and principal creditors of a closely held corporation may be the same persons.

1) Interest Deduction

The principal tax advantage of debt is avoidance of the "double tax" on corporate profits. A corporation can deduct interest paid on its debt under § 163 but may not deduct dividends.

2) Repayment of Principal

The repayment of principal on corporate debt is a tax-free return of capital to the lender. If the amount repaid exceeds the lender's basis in the debt, the excess generally is treated as a capital gain. See § 1271. By contrast, when a corporation redeems (i.e., buys back) its stock from a shareholder, the entire amount received may be a dividend if the redeemed shareholder or related persons continue to own stock. See Chapter VII, *infra*.

3) Defense Against Accumulated Earnings Tax

The existence of debt may permit a corporation to accumulate earnings to retire the debt and thus provide a defense against imposition of the accumulated earnings tax. A comparable accumulation to redeem stock normally is not regarded as reasonable for purposes of the accumulated earnings tax. See X.B.3., at page 215, *infra*.

b. Tax Advantages of Equity

The tax advantages of equity are limited to special transactions and situations.

1) § 351 Nonrecognition

A transfer of property to a controlled corporation qualifies for complete nonrecognition under § 351(a) only if it is solely in exchange for stock.

Debt securities received in a § 351 transaction are boot which may result in the recognition of gain under § 351(b). See IV.C., at page 100, *supra*.

2) Character of Loss on Worthlessness

If a shareholder loans money to a corporation and is not repaid, the loss usually is a capital loss. See V.C.2., at page 123, *infra*. If stock becomes worthless, the loss also is generally a capital loss, except that § 1244 provides limited ordinary loss treatment on the sale or worthlessness of stock issued by certain small, closely held corporations. See V.C.3., at page 124, *infra*.

3) Corporate Shareholders

Equity may be preferable to debt for corporate shareholders because interest income is fully taxable but dividends qualify for the 70% (or sometimes 80% or 100%) dividends received deduction. § 243. See VI.F.1., at page 139, *infra*.

4) Qualified Small Business Stock

In limited situations, a noncorporate shareholder may exclude from gross income 50% of the eligible gain from a sale or exchange of "qualified small business stock." § 1202(a). Generally, the gross assets of the business must not exceed $50 million, and the shareholder must be an original issuee who has held the stock for more than five years prior to the disposition. § 1202(b), (c).

B.   Distinguishing Between Debt And Equity

The Service may seek to reclassify nominal debt instruments as equity for tax purposes. These controversies typically involve closely held corporations that are capitalized with an excessive amount of shareholder debt.

1.   § 385
a.   Delegation to Treasury

Section 385(a) authorizes the Treasury to promulgate regulations "as may be necessary or appropriate" to determine for all tax purposes whether an interest in a corporation is to be treated as stock or debt. Section 385 also permits the regulations to characterize an instrument "as part stock and in part indebtedness." § 385(a).

b.   § 385 Factors

Section 385(b) lists five factors that may be taken into account under the regulations in determining whether an interest in a corporation is debt or equity:

(1) Form—i.e., whether the instrument pays a fixed rate of interest and is evidenced by a written unconditional promise to pay a sum certain on demand or on a specific date in return for an adequate consideration.

(2) Subordination—i.e., whether the debt under scrutiny is subordinated to or has preference over any other indebtedness of the corporation.

(3) The debt/equity ratio of the corporation. Section 385 is silent as to how the ratio is computed or when it is excessive, but see V.B.2., at page 120, *infra,* for the approach of the courts.

(4) Convertibility—i.e., whether the interest is convertible into stock.

(5) Proportionality—i.e., the relationship between the holdings of stock in the corporation and holdings of the debt under scrutiny.

c. Obligation of Consistency
The issuing corporation's classification of an interest as stock or debt at the time of issuance is binding on the issuer and all holders of the interest, but not the Service. This obligation of consistency does not apply to holders who disclose on their tax returns that they are treating the interest in a manner inconsistent with the issuing corporation's characterization. § 385(c).

d. The § 385 Regulations
Eleven years after § 385 was enacted, the Treasury promulgated proposed regulations, which were amended several times before being withdrawn. It is unlikely that any new regulations will be forthcoming in the immediate future, but Congress has admonished the Treasury to increase the issuance of published revenue rulings on debt vs. equity questions. Until regulations under § 385 are promulgated, debt vs. equity questions must be resolved by applying the case law.

2. Case Law
The courts treat debt vs. equity classification issues as factual questions to be resolved by applying a list of factors. The numerous decisions are impossible to synthesize. Some courts list as many as 16 separate factors to consider but emphasize that no single factor is conclusive. The ultimate question is often framed as whether the investment, analyzed in terms of its economic reality, constitutes risk capital or a strict debtor-creditor relationship, viewing the transaction as if it were with an outside lender. See, e.g., *Scriptomatic, Inc. v. United States,* 555 F.2d 364 (3d Cir. 1977). The principal factors are summarized below.

a. Form of the Obligation
To be classified as debt, an instrument should have the formal indicia of a debt obligation—e.g., an unconditional promise to pay, a specific term, and a stated

rate of interest payable in all events. Hybrid instruments that have voting rights or make interest payments contingent on earnings are likely to be treated as equity.

b. Proportionality

Debt held by shareholders in the same proportion as their stock is subject to special scrutiny. The rationale is that if debt is held in the same proportion as stock, the shareholders have no economic incentive to act like creditors by setting or enforcing the terms of the purported debt.

Example: A, B and C are equal shareholders of Newco. They each contribute $10,000 cash in exchange for 100 shares of common stock and each loan Newco $50,000 in exchange for a 5–year Newco note. The nominal debt may be reclassified as equity.

c. Debt/Equity Ratio

The ratio between a corporation's debt and its equity capital is known as the "debt/equity ratio." A corporation with a high debt/equity ratio is often said to be "thinly capitalized," making it more likely that the Service will reclassify the debt as equity on the theory that the purported debt is really at risk in the venture because no rational creditor would loan money to a thinly capitalized corporation. The cases are not consistent as to how the debt/equity ratio is computed or when a ratio is excessive.

1) Debt

In computing the ratio, "debt" includes all loans from shareholders. The ratio of shareholder debt to equity is sometimes called the "inside debt/equity ratio." Some courts also include other long-term liabilities but exclude short-term accounts payable. The ratio of all long-term liabilities to equity is sometimes called the "outside debt/equity ratio."

2) Equity

"Equity" is the shareholders' ownership interest in the corporation—i.e., the difference between the corporation's assets and liabilities. Courts disagree as to whether to reflect assets at their adjusted basis for tax purposes or current fair market value. The proposed § 385 regulations provided that assets were to be reflected at their adjusted basis, but current value may be a more accurate measure in some situations. The cases also conflict over whether intangible assets, such as goodwill, should be taken into account in determining equity.

3) When Is Debt/Equity Ratio Excessive?

Generalizations are perilous here, but an inside debt/equity ratio of 3:1 or lower is normally not excessive. Whether or not a ratio is excessive may depend on norms for the particular business in which the corporation is engaged. The withdrawn § 385 regulations included two safe harbors: a corporation's debt was not "excessive" if its outside debt/equity ratio did not exceed 10:1 and its inside debt/equity ratio did not exceed 3:1. See Prop.Reg. § 1.385–6(g)(3) (withdrawn in 1983).

d. Intent

Some cases turn on whether the parties "intended" to create a debtor-creditor relationship. Intent may be measured by objective criteria such as a lender's reasonable expectation, evaluated in light of the financial condition of the corporation and its ability to pay principal and interest. Often the inquiry is whether an outside lender would have loaned money to the corporation under the same terms. See, e.g., *Fin Hay Realty Co. v. U.S.,* 398 F.2d 694 (3d Cir.1968). Adherence to certain formalities (such as treatment of the interest on the corporate books, and payment of interest and principal when due) may be relevant in determining intent. One appeals court has framed the "intent" question in terms of whether the transaction was "in substance" a loan or whether it was "a mere sham or subterfuge set up solely or principally for tax-avoidance purposes." *J.S. Biritz Construction Co. v. Comm'r,* 387 F.2d 451 (8th Cir.1967).

e. Subordination

Subordination of shareholder debt to claims of outside lenders and trade creditors is sometimes regarded as evidence that the shareholder debt should be reclassified as equity. But because many lenders typically require shareholder loans to be subordinated, this factor alone is not controlling.

f. All or Nothing Approach

The case law rarely, if ever, treats a single instrument as part debt and part equity. If debt is reclassified, it usually is treated as equity in its entirety. Since 1989, however, § 385(a) has authorized the Treasury to issue regulations treating an instrument as part debt and part equity.

3. Consequences of Reclassification

If debt is reclassified as equity, payments labeled as "interest" are recharacterized as constructive dividends to the extent of the corporation's earnings and profits. Repayment of the principal of reclassified debt is treated as if stock were redeemed by the corporation and may result in a dividend to the shareholder rather than a tax-free return of capital. See VII.C., at page 149, *infra*.

4. Shareholder Guaranteed Debt

Instead of making direct loans, shareholders may guarantee repayment of corporate loans from outside lenders. The Service sometimes argues that, in substance, shareholder guaranteed debt is equivalent to a loan from the outside lender to the shareholders followed by a contribution to capital. Under this reclassification, an "interest" payment from the corporation to the lender is treated as a constructive dividend to the shareholders followed by a transfer of the same amount by the shareholders to the lender as interest. See *Casco Bank & Trust Co. v. U.S.*, 544 F.2d 528 (1st Cir.1976), cert. denied, 430 U.S. 907, 97 S.Ct. 1176 (1977); *Plantation Patterns, Inc. v. Commissioner*, 462 F.2d 712 (5th Cir.1972), cert. denied, 409 U.S. 1076, 93 S.Ct. 683 (1972).

Example: On the formation of Newco, A, B and C each transfer $20,000 cash in exchange for 100 shares of Newco common stock. Newco also borrows $600,000 from Bank at market rate interest, and Bank requires A, B and C to personally guarantee the loan. Newco pays $30,000 to Bank at the end of year one and deducts that amount as "interest." Because Newco may be thinly capitalized (it has a debt/equity ratio of 10:1) and the bank debt is guaranteed by the shareholders in proportion to their stock holdings, the Service may treat the transaction as if the shareholders borrowed $600,000 from Bank and contributed that amount to Newco's capital. In that event, Newco's $30,000 "interest" payment will be treated as a nondeductible dividend. A, B and C each realize $10,000 dividend income and, logically, they each should be treated as paying $10,000 interest to Bank, which should be deductible as investment interest subject to the limitations in § 163(d).

C. Character of Loss on Corporate Investment

1. In General

Stock and debt instruments (unless held by a dealer) are almost always capital assets, and thus any loss on their sale or exchange is treated as a capital loss. Special problems may arise when stock or debt becomes worthless.

2. Loss on Worthlessness of Debt

The tax treatment of a worthless corporate debt investment depends on whether the instrument is a "security," as defined in § 165(g)(2) and, if not, whether the debt is a business or nonbusiness bad debt.

a. Debt Evidenced by Security

If a "security" which is a capital asset becomes worthless during the taxable year, the holder's resulting loss is treated as a loss from the sale or exchange of a capital asset as of the last day of the taxable year. § 165(g)(1). For this purpose, the term "security" includes bonds, debentures, notes or other corporate debt instruments with interest coupons or in registered form. A loss by a corporation on the worthlessness of securities in an "affiliated corporation" is an ordinary loss. A corporation is "affiliated" if the corporate holder owns at least 80% of its voting power and value and more than 90% of its gross receipts are from sources other than passive investment income. § 165(g)(3).

> *Example:* In year one, A loans Newco, Inc. $50,000 and receives a Newco bond with a face amount of $50,000. Two years later, Newco is unable to repay the principal of the bond, which is a capital asset in A's hands. The bond is a § 165(g)(2) "security," and A recognizes a $50,000 long-term capital loss as of the last day of the year in which the bond becomes worthless.

b. Debt Not Evidenced by Security

Losses on corporate debts that are not evidenced by a security are characterized by the bad debt provisions in § 166. Losses from wholly or partially worthless business bad debts are ordinary. § 166(a). Losses of noncorporate lenders from a wholly worthless nonbusiness bad debt are treated as a short-term capital loss. § 166(d). Losses from partially worthless nonbusiness bad debts are not deductible.

1) Business vs. Nonbusiness Bad Debt

A nonbusiness bad debt is a debt other than (1) a debt created or acquired in connection with the taxpayer's trade or business or (2) a debt the loss from the worthlessness of which is incurred in the taxpayer's trade or business. § 166(d)(2).

2) Shareholder–Employees

If a shareholder who also is an employee loans money to a closely held corporation, any resulting loss usually is treated as a nonbusiness bad debt on the theory that the loan was made in the taxpayer's capacity as an investor. To be deductible as a business bad debt, a taxpayer must show that his dominant motivation for making the loan was related to his trade or business. *U.S. v. Generes,* 405 U.S. 93, 92 S.Ct. 827 (1972).

> *Example:* A is the president and majority shareholder of X, Inc. A's salary is $90,000 per year and her stock is worth $500,000. To assist X in meeting working capital requirements, A advanced $150,000 in open account loans. X subsequently went bankrupt and was unable to pay back the $150,000 to A. If, as is likely, the dominant motivation for A's loan was to protect her investment in X rather than her job as president, her loss is from a nonbusiness bad debt and is treated as a short-term capital loss.

3. Loss on Worthlessness of Equity
a. In General

A loss incurred by a noncorporate shareholder on the sale of stock is treated as a capital loss if, as is likely, the stock is a capital asset. Because stock is a "security," as defined by § 165(g)(2), a loss on the worthlessness of stock held as a capital asset is treated as a capital loss on the last day of the taxable year in which the loss is incurred. § 165(g)(1).

b. **§ 1244 Stock**

A loss incurred by an individual shareholder on the sale or worthlessness of "§ 1244 stock" is deductible as an ordinary loss, subject to various requirements and limitations described below.

1) Qualifying Shareholders

Only individual taxpayers and partnerships who were original issuees of § 1244 stock are eligible for ordinary loss treatment. § 1244(a). Trusts, estates and corporate shareholders do not qualify. Partners qualify only if they were partners when the partnership acquired the stock. Reg. § 1.1244(a)–1(b)(2).

2) Qualifying Stock

Section 1244 applies to common or preferred stock that has been issued by a domestic corporation for money or property. § 1244(c)(1). Stock issued for services does not qualify. Reg. § 1.1244(c)–1(d).

3) Small Business Corporation Status

An issuer of § 1244 stock must be a "small business corporation" when the stock is issued. That status is attained if the aggregate amount of money and other property received by the corporation for stock, as a capital contribution and as paid-in surplus does not exceed $1 million. § 1244(c)(3). For this purpose, property is valued at its adjusted basis, less encumbering liabilities, at the time it is contributed. § 1244(c)(3)(B). The $1 million cap applies to amounts received for the shares seeking to qualify as § 1244 stock and all previously issued stock. If the $1 million cap is exceeded in the same taxable year, the corporation may designate which shares are to be treated as § 1244 stock. Reg. § 1.1244(c)–2(b).

Example: On the formation of Newco, A contributes $100,000 cash and B contributes land with a value of $100,000 and an adjusted basis of $50,000, each in exchange for 100 shares of Newco common stock. In the following taxable year, C contributes $1,000,000 cash in exchange for 1,000 shares of Newco common stock. The aggregate amount of money and property received by Newco when it issues stock to A and B is $150,000 (valuing the land at its adjusted basis), and all 200 shares qualify as § 1244 stock. After Newco issues the 1,000 shares to C, the aggregate amount of money and property received is $1,150,000. Because the $1 million threshold is exceeded, only 850 ($850,000) of the 1,000 shares qualifies as § 1244 stock. If the shares had all been issued in the same taxable year, Newco could designate the shares to be treated as § 1244 stock.

4)   Gross Receipts Test When Loss Sustained
     Even if stock qualified under § 1244 when it was issued, ordinary loss
     treatment is denied unless the corporation derived more than 50% of its
     aggregate gross receipts from sources other than certain passive income
     items (e.g., dividends, interest, royalties, rents, and gains from the sale or
     exchange of stock or securities) for the five taxable years ending before the
     year in which the loss was sustained (or the period of the corporation's
     existence, if shorter). § 1244(c)(1)(C).

5)   Limit on Amount of Ordinary Loss
     The maximum amount that a taxpayer may treat as an ordinary loss
     under § 1244 for any one taxable year may not exceed $50,000 ($100,000
     on a joint return). § 1244(b). In the case of a partnership, the loss ceiling
     is determined separately as to each partner. Reg. § 1.1244(b)–1(a).

6)   Reduction of Ordinary Loss
     In computing any § 1244 ordinary loss, a taxpayer who has a transferred
     basis in § 1244 stock received in exchange for "loss property" (i.e., property
     with a basis in excess of its value) must reduce his stock basis by the
     built-in loss in the contributed property. § 1244(d)(1)(A). Any ordinary loss
     disallowed under this provision is treated as a capital loss. The purpose of
     this rule is to prevent a taxpayer from converting the character of a loss
     from capital to ordinary.

     Example: In a transaction that qualifies under § 351(a), A transfers a
                  capital asset with a value of $10,000 and a basis of $15,000 in
                  exchange for 100 shares of Newco stock. A takes a $15,000
                  transferred basis in the stock, which qualifies as § 1244
                  stock. Five years later, the stock becomes worthless, and A
                  recognizes a $15,000 loss. A's § 1244 ordinary loss is limited
                  to $10,000; the remaining $5,000 is a long-term capital loss.

D.   Special Problems of Excessive Corporate Debt

Debt/equity classification issues historically were confined to closely held corporations
with excessive shareholder debt. During the 1980's, however, a wave of corporate
takeovers and restructurings was fueled by an increased use of debt financing, and that
trend has continued. In response, Congress enacted several narrow provisions aimed at
curbing perceived abuses of debt financing. This outline will merely describe the
problems and the general approach of the legislation.

1.   Junk Bonds
a.   "Junk Bond" Defined
     A "junk bond" is an unsecured high-yield corporate debt obligation that a bond
     rating service would classify as below investment grade because of its high

risk. Junk bonds often are issued in debt-financed corporate acquisitions, such as leveraged buyouts. Although some junk bonds pay interest currently, many are issued as "zero coupon" obligations with an issue price that is significantly lower than the stated redemption price at maturity. A variation, known as a "pay in kind" bond, pays interest in the form of additional debt securities or preferred stock rather than cash. Issuers of junk bonds often deducted interest as it accrued even if actual payment was deferred for many years.

b. Applicable High Yield Discount Obligations

1) Definition

An "applicable high yield discount obligation" is an instrument with (a) more than a five-year maturity, (b) a yield to maturity that is five percentage points or more than the applicable federal rate in effect under § 1274(d) for the month in which the obligation is issued, and (c) "significant" original issue discount, as defined by § 163(i)(2). § 163(i)(1).

2) Tax Treatment

A corporation that issues an applicable high yield discount obligation must defer any interest deduction until it makes actual payments in cash or property other than its own stock or debt. § 163(i)(3). If an instrument with significant original issue discount, as defined, has a yield that is more than six percentage points over an indexed cap, a portion of the interest deduction is disallowed. § 163(e)(5)(C).

2. Earnings Stripping

"Earnings stripping" is a device where a corporate borrower pays tax-deductible interest to an economically related lender, such as a foreign subsidiary, that is effectively exempt from U.S. tax. Section 163(j) disallows a deduction for any interest paid or accrued by a corporation to certain related entities which are exempt from U.S. taxation. The disallowance applies only if the payor corporation has:

a. a debt-equity ratio that exceeds 1:5 to 1;

b. interest expense for the taxable year that exceeds 50% of the corporation's taxable income, computed without regard to its net interest expense (interest expense less interest income) or net operating losses.

3. Limitation on Net Operating Losses

Section 172(m) limits the ability of a corporation to carry back net operating losses which are created by interest deductions attributable to various debt-financed transactions.

E. Review Questions

1. Identify four important factors that the courts utilize in determining whether to reclassify "debt" as "equity."

2. X Corp. has the following balance sheet:

Assets	Adj. Basis	F. Mkt. Value
Cash	$100,000	$ 100,000
Inventory	20,000	100,000
Land	380,000	600,000
Goodwill	0	200,000
Total	$500,000	$1,000,000
Liabilities and Capital		
Bank Loan	100,000	100,000
Shareholder Loans	300,000	300,000
Capital Stock	100,000	600,000
Total	$500,000	$1,000,000

What is X Corp's debt/equity ratio? If the shareholder loans are pro rata, what is the risk of those loans being reclassified as capital contributions?

3. A is the sole shareholder and principal employee of X Corp. A's adjusted basis in her X stock is $50,000. A also has loaned $100,000 to X Corp.; the debt is evidenced by an X Corp. promissory note that is not in registered form. X goes bankrupt and A's stock and note are both worthless. What is the character of A's losses?

VI

NONLIQUIDATING DISTRIBUTIONS

Analysis

A. Introduction

1. Distribution vs. Dividend

For purposes of Subchapter C, a "distribution" is any kind of payment by a corporation to its shareholders with respect to their stock. A "dividend" is a distribution out of the current or accumulated "earnings and profits" of a corporation. Payments to shareholders that are unrelated to their ownership of stock (e.g., salary, interest, rent, etc.) are neither distributions nor dividends. "Nonliquidating" (sometimes called "operating") distributions are made by an ongoing corporation. "Liquidating" distributions are made by a corporation that is dissolving under state law. This chapter covers nonliquidating distributions of cash or property other than stock of the distributing corporation. Later chapters examine distributions by a corporation to buy back (redeem) its own stock (see Chapter VII, *infra*), distributions of stock (see Chapter VIII, *infra*) and distributions in partial or complete liquidation of a corporation (see Chapters VII and IX, *infra*).

2. Dividends Under Corporate Law

The term "dividend" under corporate law ordinarily is used in state statutes restricting the power of corporations to make distributions that invade or reduce their permanent capital. These rules have no bearing on whether a distribution is a dividend for federal tax purposes.

3. Distributions And Dividends Under The Code
a. Statutory Roadmap

The order of analysis in evaluating whether a distribution is a dividend in the tax sense is to determine: (1) the amount of the distribution under § 301(b), (2) how much of that amount is a "dividend" as defined in § 316, and (3) the specific tax treatment of these amounts as provided in § 301(c).

b. Amount of the Distribution

The amount of a distribution is the amount of cash received by the shareholder plus the fair market value (determined as of the date of the distribution) of any other property received, reduced by any liabilities assumed by the shareholder in connection with the distribution or liabilities to which the property is subject before and after the distribution. § 301(b).

c. Amount of the Dividend

A distribution is a dividend to the extent it is made out of the "earnings and profits" (see VI.B., at page 132, *infra*) for the taxable year in which the distribution is made ("current E & P"), or, if current E & P are insufficient, out of earnings and profits accumulated by the corporation since February 28, 1913 ("accumulated E & P"). § 316(a).

d. Tax Treatment of Distributions

A dividend is includible in the gross income of the distributee shareholder. §§ 61(a)(7); 301(c)(1). The portion of a distribution that is not a dividend (because it exceeds both current and accumulated E & P) is first treated as a tax-free return of capital that reduces the shareholder's basis in the stock. § 301(c)(2). Any amount in excess of basis is treated as a gain from a sale or exchange of stock—generally capital gain if the shareholder holds the stock as a capital asset. § 301(c)(3). For additional rules applicable to corporate shareholders, see VI.F., at page 139, *infra*.

> ***Example:*** X Corp. has $5,000 of current E & P and no accumulated E & P. X distributes $12,000 cash to A, its sole shareholder, who has an $8,000 basis in her X stock (held long-term). Of the $12,000 distribution, $5,000 is taxable as a dividend, and the remaining $7,000 reduces A's stock basis to $1,000. If A's basis had only been $6,000, she would reduce her basis to zero and the remaining $1,000 of the distribution would be long-term capital gain.

B. Earnings and Profits

1. The Concept

The principal function of earnings and profits is to measure the extent to which a distribution is made from a corporation's economic income. "Taxable income" is an inaccurate measure for this purpose because it excludes many economic receipts and outlays. "Retained earnings," an accounting concept, also is inadequate because it can be eliminated on a corporation's financial statement without any actual economic outlay (e.g., by an accounting transfer to paid-in capital resulting from a stock dividend).

2. Determination of Earnings and Profits

The term "earnings and profits" is not defined in the Code or the regulations, but § 312 describes the effect of various transactions on E & P. It is well settled that E & P are determined by starting with taxable income and making certain additions, subtractions, and adjustments, as described below. Remember that E & P represent a tax accounting concept, not a particular corporate bank account or fund.

a. Add Back Items Excluded From Taxable Income

Certain items that are excluded from taxable income are added back to taxable income in determining E & P. Examples include tax-exempt municipal bond interest, life insurance proceeds and federal tax refunds. Reg. § 1.312–6(b). Examples of excludable items that are not added back are contributions to capital and realized gains that are not recognized for tax purposes. § 312(f)(1).

b. Add Back Certain Tax–Deductible Items

Tax-deductible items that do not represent actual economic outlays are added back to taxable income for E & P purposes. A common example is the § 243 dividends received deduction. Because net operating losses and capital losses are taken into account for E & P purposes in the year incurred, any carryover amounts deducted in computing taxable income must be added back.

c. Subtract Nondeductible Items

Some nondeductible items represent actual outlays that must be subtracted from taxable income in computing E & P. Examples include federal income taxes, expenses related to tax-exempt income, losses between related taxpayers and charitable contributions in excess of the percentage limitations. Excess corporate capital losses and net operating losses, although not currently deductible, reduce E & P in the year incurred.

d. Add Back or Subtract Timing Adjustments

To ensure that E & P represent a corporation's true economic gain or loss, various adjustments are required to override rules that permit a corporation to defer income artificially or accelerate deductions in computing taxable income. Some examples include:

1) Depreciation

   For E & P purposes, a corporation must depreciate tangible property under the alternative depreciation system in § 168(g) rather than the accelerated cost recovery system (ACRS). § 312(k)(3). (This rule is stated as an "exception" in the Code; the "general rule" in § 312(k)(1) applies to intangible property and older tangible assets not depreciated under § 168 and rarely applies.) Machinery and equipment that would be "5–year property" under ACRS generally must be depreciated on the straight line method over a seven-year recovery period using a half-year convention. Real estate generally must be depreciated over a forty-year recovery period. See § 168(g)(2).

2) Gain or Loss on Sale of Depreciable Asset

   As a result of the E & P depreciation adjustments described above, an asset's E & P adjusted basis will differ from its taxable income adjusted basis. An appropriate E & P adjustment to taxable gain or loss is required when the asset is sold.

3) § 179 Deduction

   A corporation that elects to expense the cost of depreciable property under § 179 must amortize that expense ratably over five years in determining E & P. § 312(k)(3)(B).

4) Installment Sale Reporting

   Realized gains that are deferred under the installment sale method of accounting must be included in E & P in the year of sale. § 312(n)(5).

5)   Inventory Accounting

Profits on the sale of inventory that have been reported under the last-in-first-out (LIFO) method must be reported for E & P purposes under the first-in-first-out (FIFO) method. § 312(h)(4).

e.   Accounting for Earnings and Profits

A corporation determines its E & P under the same accounting method (e.g., cash or accrual) that it uses to compute taxable income. Reg. § 1.312–6(a).

C.   Cash Distributions

1.   In General

Cash distributions are dividends to the extent they are made out of current or accumulated E & P. The source of a cash distribution is determined by first looking to current E & P, as of the end of the taxable year without reduction by distributions made during the year, and then (if necessary) looking to the most recently accumulated E & P. § 316(a); Reg. § 1.316–2(a).

2.   Current E & P Exceed Distributions

If current E & P exceed cash distributions made during the taxable year, then each distribution is a taxable dividend out of current E & P. Any remaining current E & P are added to the accumulated E & P account. Reg. § 1.316–2(b).

Example: At the beginning of the taxable (calendar) year, X Corp. has $10,000 of accumulated E & P. X has $30,000 of current E & P, all realized during the last six months of the year. On July 1, X distributes $20,000 to its shareholders. The entire distribution is a dividend out of current E & P. X's accumulated E & P at the end of the year are $20,000 ($10,000 current E & P remaining after reduction for the distribution plus $10,000 accumulated E & P from prior years). The entire distribution is a dividend even if X has an accumulated E & P deficit at the beginning of the year.

3.   Distributions Exceed Current E & P

If cash distributions exceed current E & P, the portion of each distribution that is treated as coming from current E & P is determined by the following formula in Reg. § 1.316–2(b):

$$\text{Amount of Each Distribution} \times \frac{\text{Current E \& P}}{\text{Total Current Distributions}}$$

The remainder of each distribution is a dividend to the extent of the accumulated E & P available on the date of the distribution. In this situation, "accumulated" means E & P accumulated through the end of the taxable year preceding the distribution, less any distributions made earlier in the current year out of accumulated E & P.

Example: At the beginning of the taxable (calendar) year, X Corp. has $5,000 of accumulated E & P. X has $12,000 of current E & P and distributes $20,000 cash to A, its sole shareholder—$10,000 on April 1 and 10,000 on October 1. Applying the formula in Reg. § 1.316–2(b), 60% of each $10,000 distribution, or $6,000, is treated as a dividend paid out of current E & P. X has $5,000 of accumulated E & P available as of the April 1 distribution; thus, the $4,000 balance of that distribution is a dividend, leaving $1,000 accumulated earnings and profits available as of October 1. Of the $4,000 balance of the October 1 distribution, $1,000 is a dividend and $3,000 is a reduction of A's basis in the X stock. The separate tax treatment of the April and October distributions would be more important if A sold X stock on a date between the two distributions.

4. Accumulated E & P But Current Deficit

If a corporation has accumulated E & P at the beginning of the year and a current deficit, the tax treatment of a distribution depends on the accumulated E & P available at the date of distribution. For this purpose, accumulated E & P as of the beginning of the current year are reduced by that portion of the current deficit allocable to the period prior to the distribution. Unless the corporation can trace the deficit to a particular time of the year, it must be prorated on a daily basis to the date of distribution. Reg. § 1.316–2(b); Rev.Rul. 74–164, 1974–1 C.B. 74 (but the Ruling does not consider the possibility of tracing the deficit).

Example: At the beginning of the taxable (calendar) year, X Corp. has $12,000 of accumulated E & P. X has a $10,000 current deficit and makes cash distributions of $20,000 to A, its sole shareholder—$10,000 on April 1 and $10,000 on October 1. A has a $40,000 basis in his X stock. If X is unable to show when the deficit was incurred, it must prorate the deficit over the year ($2,500 per calendar quarter) in determining the accumulated E & P available at the date of the distributions. On April 1, accumulated E & P are $9,500 ($12,000 less $2,500 current deficit prorated to March 31). Of the $10,000 April 1 distribution, $9,500 is a dividend and $500 is a reduction of basis. No further accumulated E & P are available at the time of the October 1 distribution, and thus the entire $10,000 is a reduction of A's basis. X's accumulated E & P deficit as of the beginning of year two is $7,500. See Rev.Rul. 74–164, *supra.* If X were able to show that it incurred its $10,000 deficit in the first quarter of the year and broke even for the remaining nine months, the deficit would eliminate $10,000 of accumulated E & P as of the April 1 distribution, and only $2,000 of the distribution would be a dividend.

D. Property Distributions

1. Consequences to the Distributing Corporation

  a. Background

In *General Utilities & Operating Co. v. Helvering,* 296 U.S. 200, 56 S.Ct. 185 (1935), the Supreme Court held that a corporation did not recognize gain on a distribution of appreciated property to a shareholder even though the shareholder took a fair market value basis in the distributed asset. This rule—known as "the *General Utilities* doctrine"—is codified in § 311(a). Congress gradually concluded, however, that the *General Utilities* doctrine was inconsistent with the double tax regime of Subchapter C. Although § 311(a) remains in the Code as a "general rule," it now applies only to nonliquidating distributions of "loss" property. Section 311(b) applies to nonliquidating distributions of appreciated property. Liquidating distributions are governed by § 336, which is discussed in Chapter IX, *infra.*

  b. Appreciated Property

  1) General Rule

A corporation recognizes gain on a nonliquidating distribution of appreciated property (other than its own debt obligations) in an amount equal to the difference between the fair market value of the property and its adjusted basis. § 311(b)(1).

Example: X Corp. distributes Gainacre ($30,000 value, $10,000 adjusted basis) to its sole shareholder, A. X recognizes $20,000 gain on the distribution. As discussed below (see VI.D.1.e., at page 137, *infra*), the distribution also increases X's current E & P by $20,000.

  2) Treatment of Liabilities

If distributed property is subject to a liability or if a shareholder assumes a liability of the distributing corporation in connection with the distribution, the fair market value of the distributed property is treated as not less than the amount of liability. §§ 311(b)(2); 336(b).

  c. Loss Property

A corporation may not recognize loss on the distribution of property with an adjusted basis that exceeds its fair market value. § 311(a).

Example: X Corp. distributes Lossacre ($10,000 value, $30,000 adjusted basis) to its sole shareholder, A. X may not recognize its $20,000 loss. X should have sold Lossacre, recognized the $20,000 loss (which would have reduced current E & P by $20,000) and distributed the $10,000 cash proceeds to A.

d.   Distribution of Corporation's Own Debt Obligations

The general gain recognition rule in § 311(b) does not apply to distributions of a corporation's own debt obligations. As a result, § 311(a) applies, and no gain or loss is recognized by the distributing corporation.

e.   Effect of Distributions on Earnings and Profits

1)   In General

Current E & P are determined as of the end of the taxable year without regard to distributions made during the year. Consequently, although a distribution may be a dividend "out of" current E & P, it does not reduce current E & P. Technically speaking, to determine accumulated E & P at the beginning of the following year, accumulated E & P as of the beginning of the year are increased by current E & P of the prior year and then reduced by the amount of the distribution. A distribution may not, however, create a deficit in accumulated E & P. § 312(a).

2)   Appreciated Property

On a distribution of appreciated property, the distributing corporation first increases its *current* E & P by the gain recognized under § 311(b). § 312(b)(1). (The Code does not distinguish between the effect of a distribution on current and accumulated E & P but the rules outlined here are generally accepted.) *Accumulated* E & P are reduced by the fair market value of the distributed property. § 312(a)(3), (b). If a shareholder assumes liabilities encumbering the distributed property or takes the property subject to liabilities, the decrease in E & P resulting from the distribution is reduced by the amount of the liabilities. § 312(c); Reg. § 1.312–3. (In other words, liability relief *increases* E & P.) This treatment is equivalent to the result if the corporation had first sold the appreciated property and then distributed the net cash proceeds.

Example: Before any distributions, X Corp. has $35,000 of accumulated E & P and no current E & P. X distributes Gainacre ($50,000 value, $30,000 adjusted basis) to its sole shareholder, A, who takes the property subject to a $10,000 mortgage. X recognizes $20,000 gain under § 311(b), and the distribution generates $20,000 of current E & P. The amount of the distribution is $40,000, all of which is a dividend—$20,000 out of current E & P and $20,000 out of accumulated E & P. Accumulated E & P at the beginning of the next year are $15,000, calculated: $35,000 (balance at beginning of year 1), plus $20,000 (current E & P), minus $50,000 (value of distributed Gainacre), plus $10,000 (mortgage relief). The result would be the same if X had sold Gainacre for $50,000 and distributed the $40,000 net proceeds to A.

3) Loss Property
Current E & P are unaffected by a distribution of loss property, and the corporation reduces accumulated E & P by the adjusted basis of the distributed property. § 312(a)(3).

4) Corporation's Own Obligations
A corporation that distributes its own debt obligations reduces accumulated E & P by the principal amount of those obligations. If a corporation distributes a debt obligation with a fair market value that is less than its face amount (because, for example, the obligations have a stated interest rate that is below prevailing market rates), it reduces accumulated E & P by the "issue price" of the obligations (determined under the original issue discount rules) at the time of the distribution.

2. Consequences to Shareholders
The amount of a property distribution is the fair market value of the distributed property on the date of the distribution reduced by any liabilities to which the property is subject. § 301(b). The portion of the distribution that is a dividend is determined under the same rules applicable to cash distributions. See VI.C., at page 134, *supra*. The shareholder's basis in the distributed property is its fair market value on the date of the distribution without any reduction for liabilities. § 301(d).

E. Constructive Dividends

1. In General
A corporation may attempt to avoid the double tax by providing economic benefits to its shareholders (or close relatives of shareholders) in transactions that are not formally labeled as dividends. The Service may reclassify these transactions as "constructive dividends." Whether or not a payment or economic benefit is a constructive dividend ordinarily is a factual question. Some illustrative controversies are described below. Note that in all cases, a constructive distribution is not a dividend under § 316 unless the corporation has sufficient E & P.

2. Examples of Constructive Dividends
a. Unreasonable Compensation
A payment of unreasonable compensation (see § 162(a)(1)) to shareholder-employees or their relatives is income to the shareholder in all events (unless it is an excludable fringe benefit), but the corporation may not deduct excessive compensation that is reclassified as a dividend. Although the failure of a closely held corporation to pay dividends is a significant factor in determining whether compensation paid to shareholder-employees is reasonable, compensation will not automatically be reclassified as a dividend solely because the corporation has not paid more than an insubstantial portion of its earnings as dividends. Rev.Rul. 79–8, 1979–1 Cum.Bull. 92.

b. Low Interest Loans

Section 7872 treats the "foregone" interest on a genuine corporate-shareholder demand loan as a dividend to the shareholder followed by a retransfer of the same amount as interest back to the corporation.

c. Loans Without Expectation of Repayment

If a corporation loans money to a shareholder without any expectation of repayment, the constructive dividend is the entire amount loaned, not just the foregone interest.

d. Payments on Debt Reclassified as Equity

Interest or principal payments by a corporation on purported shareholder debt that is reclassified as equity (see V.B.3., at page 122, *supra*) are treated as constructive dividends.

e. Bargain Sales or Leases to Shareholders

On a bargain sale, the dividend is the difference between the amount paid by the shareholder and the value of the property or, in the case of a lease, the spread between rent paid, if any, and fair market rent. See Reg. § 1.301–1(j).

f. Excessive Payments to Shareholders for Purchase or Rental of Property

This is the flip side of a bargain sale or lease. The dividend is the excessive purchase price or rent paid by the corporation to the shareholder.

g. Personal Benefits to Shareholder

Corporate payments of expenses (e.g., for meals, travel and entertainment) that provide only an incidental benefit to the business and are primarily for the personal benefit of a shareholder or his family may be classified as constructive dividends. See, e.g., *Nicholls, North, Buse Co. v. Comm'r*, 56 T.C. 1225 (1971) (75% personal use of corporate yacht was constructive dividend to extent of 75% of yacht's fair rental value); *Ireland v. United States*, 621 F.2d 731 (5th Cir. 1980) (personal use of corporate aircraft; value determined by comparable charter air flights).

h. Transfers Between Commonly Controlled Corporations

Transfers of funds or the use of property from one corporation to another corporation controlled by the same shareholders may be treated as a dividend from the payor corporation to the controlling shareholders followed by a capital contribution to the payee corporation.

F. Special Problems of Corporate Shareholders

1. The Dividends Received Deduction

To alleviate multiple taxation at the corporate level, corporate shareholders generally may deduct 70% of dividends received from other domestic corporations.

§ 243(a)(1). This deduction results in an effective corporate tax rate of 10.5% on dividends received (35% maximum corporate rate × 30% includible portion of dividend = 10.5%). The deduction is increased to 80% for certain corporations that own 20% or more of the distributing corporation's stock, or to 100% if the shareholder and distributing corporations are members of the same electing "affiliated group" (see XIV.D.2., at page 309, *infra*).

2. Holding Period Requirements

The lower effective corporate rate on dividends may motivate a corporate shareholder to convert capital gain (taxed at a maximum rate of 35%) into partially excludable dividend income by acquiring stock shortly before a dividend is paid, collecting the dividend, and then realizing a short-term capital loss on sale of the stock for its lower post-dividend value. Section 246(c) blocks this technique by disallowing the dividends received deduction on any share of stock which is held by the taxpayer for 45 days or less during the 90–day period beginning on the date on which the taxpayer becomes entitled to receive the dividend (the "ex-dividend date"). § 246A(c)(1)(A). For certain preferred stock, the required holding period is 90 days before the ex-dividend date. § 246(c)(2). The 45 or 90–day period is tolled whenever the corporate shareholder diminishes its risk of loss in any one of several manners specified in § 246(c)(4).

3. Extraordinary Dividends: Basis Reduction

To prevent an opportunity for tax arbitrage, a corporate shareholder that receives an "extraordinary dividend" must reduce its basis in the underlying stock (but not below zero) by the "nontaxed portion" of the dividend (i.e., the amount not includible in gross income after the dividends received deduction) if the shareholder has not held the stock for more than two years before the earliest of the date at which the distributing corporation declares, announces or agrees to pay the dividend. § 1059(a)(1), (b), (d)(5). The required basis reduction generally occurs immediately before any sale or disposition of the stock. § 1059(d)(1)(A). If the nontaxed portion of an extraordinary dividend exceeds the shareholder's adjusted basis in the stock, the excess is treated as gain from the sale or exchange of property in the taxable year in which the extraordinary dividend is received. § 1059(a)(2). A dividend is "extraordinary" if it exceeds 5% of the shareholder's adjusted basis in preferred stock or 10% of its adjusted basis in the case of any other stock. § 1059(c)(1), (2). These rules do not apply to dividends that qualify for the 100% dividends received deduction and in certain other specialized situations. § 1059(e)(2), (3). For special rules applicable to distributions in partial liquidations and non-pro rata redemptions, see § 1059(e)(1) and VII.D.1.d., at page 159, *infra*.

4. Debt–Financed Portfolio Stock

To prevent another type of arbitrage opportunity, the dividends received deduction is reduced to the extent that the dividend is attributable to debt-financed portfolio stock. § 246A. "Portfolio stock" is all stock held by a corporation unless the corporate shareholder owns either 50% of the total voting power and value, or at least 20% of the total voting power and value and five or fewer shareholders own at least 50% of the voting power and value (excluding preferred stock) of the distributing corporation. § 246A(c)(2). Portfolio stock is "debt-financed" if it is encumbered by any indebtedness directly attributable to the investment in the stock (e.g., all or part of the stock was acquired with borrowed funds). § 246A(d)(3)(A).

5. Earnings and Profits Adjustments

Section 312(n) requires certain adjustments to E & P to more accurately reflect economic gain and loss. See VI.B.2.d., at page 133, *supra*. For example, if a corporation reports gain on the installment method in computing taxable income, E & P must be computed as if the corporation did not use the installment method, resulting in an increase to E & P in the year of sale and decreases in later years. § 312(n)(5). For purposes of determining the taxable income of (and the adjusted basis in any stock held by) a corporate shareholder that owns (directly or indirectly through attribution rules) at least 20% of the voting power or value of another corporation's stock, § 301(e) provides that the § 312(n) adjustments shall not be made to the E & P of the distributing corporation. This rule has the effect of reducing the distributing corporation's E & P—but only for purposes of determining the tax consequences of distributions to 20% corporate shareholders.

6. Preacquisition Dividend Strips

A parent corporation that is about to sell the stock of a subsidiary in a taxable transaction may attempt to convert capital gain on the sale to dividend income by causing the subsidiary to make a large distribution shortly prior to the acquisition. Under the case law, the success of this technique depends primarily on the timing of the distribution and the source of the distributed money or property.

Example: X, Inc. owns all the stock of T, Inc., which has a value of $1,000,000. X's basis in the T stock is $200,000. T has ample E & P. P, Inc. wishes to purchase the T, Inc. stock. If X sells its T stock to P for $1,000,000 cash, X realizes $800,000 of gain taxable at 35%. If X causes T to distribute $800,000 to X and the entire amount is a dividend, X may deduct 100% under § 243(a), and it realizes no further gain on the sale of the T stock for $200,000. If, after negotiations began for the sale of T, the distribution were paid in the form of a T promissory note that was later paid off with funds supplied by P, it likely will be reclassified as a payment of the purchase price. But if T distributed its own excess liquid assets, the dividend likely will not be reclassified even if the buyer infuses T with liquid assets shortly after the purchase. Compare *Waterman Steamship Corp. v. Comm'r*, 430 F.2d 1185 (5th Cir.1970), with *TSN Liquidating Corp. v. U.S.*, 624 F.2d 1328 (5th Cir.1980) and *Litton Industries, Inc. v. Comm'r*, 89 T.C. 1086 (1987).

Caveat: This strategy may not be viable if X and T file a consolidated return or if the distribution to X is an "extraordinary dividend" under § 1059.

G. Review Questions

1. The concept of "earnings and profits" is identical to "taxable income." True or False?

2. Able Corp. properly elected to expense the cost of depreciable property under § 179. Must Able make any adjustment with respect to this item for E & P purposes?

3. What is the principal function of E & P? Are E & P relevant when a corporation makes no distributions during the taxable year?

4. Baxter Corp. distributes $10,000 cash to its shareholders on July 1 of the current year. At the close of the year, Baxter has $10,000 of current E & P, but it had only $2,000 of current E & P on July 1. Baxter has no accumulated E & P. What are the tax consequences of the distribution?

5. Calder Corp. distributed to its sole shareholder, A, property with a fair market value of $50,000 and an adjusted basis of $40,000. Does Calder recognize gain on the distribution? What is the effect of the distribution on current and accumulated earnings and profits? What is the amount of the distribution to A and A's basis in the distributed property?

6. Would the result in question 5, above, be different if the adjusted basis of the distributed property were $60,000?

7. Name five different situations in which a shareholder may be deemed to have received a constructive dividend.

VII

STOCK REDEMPTIONS AND PARTIAL LIQUIDATIONS

Analysis

A. Introduction

1. Redemption Defined

A redemption is a repurchase of a corporate security by its issuer. This chapter is concerned with redemptions of stock. For tax purposes, a redemption is defined as an acquisition by a corporation of its stock from a shareholder in exchange for cash, debt securities or other property, whether or not the acquired stock is cancelled, retired or held as treasury stock. § 317(a). Some redemptions are known as "partial liquidations." See VII.C.4., at page 155, *infra*.

2. Overview of Tax Consequences

a. Consequences to Distributee Shareholder

The shareholder-level tax consequences of a redemption depend on whether the distribution more resembles a dividend or a sale. If a corporation distributes money or property in exchange for its own stock and the distributee shareholder's equity interest in the corporation is essentially unchanged, the distribution resembles a dividend and should be taxed as such. If a redemption significantly reduces a shareholder's equity interest, however, it is more akin to a sale or exchange of stock. Consistent with these policies, a redemption is taxed as a distribution under § 301 (i.e., a dividend to the extent of E & P) unless it qualifies for "exchange" treatment under one of four tests in § 302(b). Three of these exceptions (§ 302(b)(1)–(3)) measure whether the redemption significantly reduces the shareholder's interest in the corporation. The exception for partial liquidations (§ 302(b)(4)) looks to whether the redemption results in a meaningful contraction of the corporation's business activities.

b. Consequences to Distributing Corporation

As in the case of nonliquidating distributions, the distributing corporation recognizes gain on a distribution of appreciated property in redemption, but it may not recognize loss on a distribution of property that has declined in value. § 311(a), (b). For the details and the effect of a redemption on earnings and profits, see VII.D.2., at page 159, *infra*.

3. Tax Stakes to Shareholders

Noncorporate shareholders generally prefer a redemption to be treated as an exchange. Exchange treatment results in immediate recovery of the shareholder's basis in the redeemed stock, and recognition of capital gain or loss in the usual case where the redeemed stock is a capital asset. Corporate shareholders may prefer dividend treatment if the distribution qualifies for the § 243 dividends received deduction (and is not an "extraordinary dividend" under § 1059) or if the consolidated return rules apply.

B. Constructive Ownership Of Stock

1. In General

In determining stock ownership for purposes of § 302, an individual or entity is treated as owning stock owned by certain related family members, corporations, partnerships, estates and trusts under the attribution rules in § 318. § 302(e)(1). The rules arbitrarily assume that these related individuals and entities have a unity of economic interest. Section 318 is most directly relevant to redemptions, but it also may apply to other transactions described elsewhere in this outline.

2. Family Attribution

An individual is treated as owning stock owned by her spouse, children (including legally adopted children), grandchildren and parents, but not her siblings or in-laws. Grandchildren are not considered to own stock owned by their grandparents. § 318(a)(1). Stock constructively owned by one family member may not be reattributed to another family member—e.g., no attribution is permitted from parent to child and then to child's spouse. § 318(a)(5)(B).

Example: X Corp.'s 100 outstanding shares are owned by Husband (10), his Wife (20), their Child (20), Wife's Father (30) and Wife's Sister (20). The actual and constructive ownership of X Corp.'s shares is:

Shareholder	Actual	Constructive
Husband	10%	40%
Wife	20%	60%
Child	20%	30%
Wife's Father	30%	60%
Wife's Sister	20%	30%

Husband constructively owns shares from Wife and Child but not from Wife's Father or Sister. Wife owns shares from her Husband, Child and Father, but not from her Sister. Child owns her parents' shares, but no shares from her grandfather or aunt. Father owns shares from his children and grandchild, but not from Wife's Husband. Sister is deemed to own only her Father's shares.

3. Entity to Beneficiary (or Owner) Attribution
a. From Partnerships or Estates

Stock owned by or for a partnership or estate is considered as owned by the partners or beneficiaries with present interests (e.g., life estates) in proportion to their beneficial interests. § 318(a)(2)(A). A person ceases to be a beneficiary of an estate when he receives all property to which he is entitled (e.g., a specific bequest) and the possibility that the person must return the property to satisfy claims is remote. Reg. § 1.318–3(a).

Example (1):   A, B and C are equal partners in the ABC general partnership. The partnership owns 120 shares of X Corp. stock. A, B and C each are considered to own 40 shares of X.

Example (2):   D dies, leaving a $50,000 specific bequest to E, and his residuary estate to F. E is no longer a beneficiary for

attribution purposes after she receives her bequest, but F
remains a beneficiary until the estate is closed.

b. From Trusts

Stock owned by a trust (other than a qualified employee retirement plan) is
considered as owned by its beneficiaries in proportion to their actuarial
interests in the trust, however small or remote. § 318(a)(2)(B)(i). Stock owned
by a grantor trust is considered as owned by the person who is taxable on the
income of the trust. § 318(a)(2)(B)(ii).

Example: Trust owns 100 shares of X Corp. A is the income beneficiary of
              Trust and B is the remainderperson. A and B's actuarial interests
              are 60% and 40%, respectively. A and B are considered to own 60
              and 40 shares of X Corp., respectively.

c. From Corporations

Stock owned by a corporation is considered as owned proportionately (by
reference to value) by a shareholder who owns, actually or constructively, 50
percent or more in value of the corporation's stock. § 318(a)(2)(C).

Example: A owns 60% (by value) of the stock of X Corp. X Corp. owns 100
              shares of Y Corp. A is considered to own 60 shares of Y Corp. If A
              owned only 40% of X, A would not be considered as owning any
              shares of Y through X. If A owned 40% of X Corp. actually and
              another 20% constructively (e.g. from a family member), A would
              be a 50% or more shareholder and thus would constructively own
              60 shares of Y through X.

4. Beneficiary (or Owner) to Entity Attribution
a. To Partnerships or Estates

All stock owned actually or constructively by partners or beneficiaries of an
estate is considered as owned by the partnership or estate. § 318(a)(3)(A).

Example: A, B and C are equal partners of the ABC general partnership. A
              owns 60 shares of X Corp. actually and is considered as owning 40
              shares from his Wife, W. ABC is considered to own 100 shares of
              X Corp. from A, as well as any shares owned actually and
              constructively by B and C.

b. To Trusts

All stock owned by a trust beneficiary is attributed to the trust unless the
beneficiary's interest is both remote and contingent. A beneficiary's contingent
interest is remote if its actuarial value is 5% or less of the value of the trust
property, assuming the trustee will exercise maximum discretion in favor of the

beneficiary. § 318(a)(3)(B)(i). Grantor trusts are considered as owning stock owned by the grantor or other person taxable on the trust's income. § 318(a)(3)(B)(ii).

> *Example:*   A is the income beneficiary of Trust. A owns 100 shares of X Corp., all of which are considered owned by Trust. If A had only a contingent remainder interest in Trust that was worth 5% or less than the value of the trust property, none of A's shares would be attributed to Trust.

c. To Corporations

All stock owned by a shareholder who actually and constructively owns 50% or more of a corporation's stock is attributed to the corporation. § 318(a)(3)(C).

> *Example:*   A owns 60% (by value) of X Corp. stock. A owns 100 shares of Y Corp. X Corp. is considered to own 100 shares of Y Corp. from A. If A owned less than 50% of X, however, none of A's shares in Y would be attributed to X.

5. Option Attribution

A person holding an option to acquire stock is considered as owning that stock. § 318(a)(4). If stock may be considered as owned by an individual under either family attribution or option attribution, the option attribution rules take precedence. § 318(a)(5)(E). This may permit reattribution of the optioned stock to another family member despite the no double family attribution rule.

> *Example:*   Husband has an option to acquire 100 shares of X Corp. stock owned by Child. Husband is considered to own Child's 100 shares under the option attribution rules. As a result, these shares may be reattributed to Husband's parents, grandparents and other children. If Husband did not hold the option, he still would be considered as owning Child's shares under the family attribution rules, but the shares could not be reattributed to another family member.

6. Other Operating Rules
a. Reattribution

With exceptions noted below, stock constructively owned by a person under § 318 is considered as actually owned for purposes of reattributing that stock to another person. § 318(a)(5)(A).

> *Example:*   A and B (who are unrelated) each own 50 of the 100 outstanding shares of X Corp. X Corp. owns 100 shares of Y Corp. A is a 50% partner in the AC Partnership. B is the sole beneficiary of Trust. A and B each is considered as owning 50 shares of Y through X. A's shares of Y are reattributed to the AC Partnership, and B's

shares of Y are reattributed to Trust. In addition, the Partnership and Trust each is deemed to own 50 shares of X directly from A and B, respectively.

b. No Double Family Attribution

As noted earlier (see VII.B.2., at page 146, *supra*), stock constructively owned under the family attribution rules in § 318(a)(1) may not be reattributed to another family member. § 318(a)(5)(B).

c. No "Sidewise" Attribution

Stock owned by a beneficiary, partner or shareholder that is attributed to an entity may not be reattributed from the entity to another beneficiary, partner or shareholder. § 318(a)(5)(C).

> *Example:* A and B, who are unrelated, are equal partners in the AB general partnership. A owns 100 shares of X Corp. stock. The partnership is considered to own A's 100 shares of X Corp. under § 318(a)(3)(A), but those shares may not be reattributed to B from the partnership under § 318(a)(2)(A).

d. S Corporation Treated as Partnership

For purposes of § 318, an S corporation is treated as a partnership, and shareholders of an S corporation are treated like partners. § 318(a)(5)(E). This rule applies for purposes of attributing stock to and from the S corporation, but not for determining constructive ownership of stock in the S corporation.

> *Example:* A, B and C (unrelated) are equal shareholders in S Corp., which owns 120 shares of X Corp. A's wife, W, owns 100 shares of Y Corp. (X and Y are C corporations.) A, B and C each is deemed to own 40 shares of X from S Corp. because S Corp. is treated as a partnership for this purpose. If S were not treated as a partnership, none of S's shares of X would be attributed to its shareholders because neither A, B nor C is a 50% or more shareholder of S. A is deemed to own W's 100 shares of Y, and all these shares are reattributed to S.

C. Redemptions Treated as Exchanges

A redemption that is described in § 302(b)(1)–(4) is treated as an exchange. § 302(a). Otherwise, it is treated as a distribution to which § 301 applies. § 302(d).

1. Substantially Disproportionate Redemptions
a. Requirements

A distribution in redemption is treated as an exchange if it is "substantially disproportionate" with respect to the shareholder. § 302(b)(2). A distribution is "substantially disproportionate" if it meets three mechanical requirements:

1) Immediately after the redemption, the shareholder must own less than 50% of the total combined voting power of all classes of stock entitled to vote.

2) The percentage of voting stock owned by the shareholder immediately after the redemption must be less than 80% of the percentage of voting stock owned by that shareholder immediately before the redemption.

3) The percentage of common stock (whether or not voting) owned by the shareholder immediately after the redemption must be less than 80% of the percentage of common stock owned immediately before the redemption. If there is more than one class of common stock outstanding, this test is applied in the aggregate by reference to fair market value. Rev.Rul. 87–88, 1987–2 C.B. 81.

The § 318 attribution rules fully apply in determining ownership.

Example: A owns 60 out of the 100 outstanding shares (60%) of X Corp. X redeems 20 of A's shares so that, after the redemption, A owns 40 out of the 80 X Corp. shares (50%) still outstanding. The redemption is not substantially disproportionate because A does not own less than 50% of X's voting power and A's percentage ownership after the redemption is not less than 80% of her ownership before. If X redeemed 25 of A's shares, A would own 35 out of the 75 X shares still outstanding after the redemption. The redemption would be substantially disproportionate because A owns less than 50% of X's voting power, and her percentage ownership after the redemption (46.7%) is less than 80% of her ownership before—i.e., 46.7% is less than 48% (80% × 60%).

b. Series of Redemptions
A redemption is not substantially disproportionate if it is made pursuant to a plan which has the purpose or effect of a series of redemptions that, taken together, result in distributions that are not substantially disproportionate. § 302(b)(2)(D). Whether or not such a plan exists is determined from all the facts and circumstances. Reg. § 1.302–3(a). The Service has ruled that a plan exists if a series of redemptions are "causally related" even if they are not part of a joint plan or arrangement. Rev.Rul. 85–14, 1985–1 C.B. 83.

Example: A and B each own 50 out of the 100 outstanding shares of X Corp. On January 1 of the current year, X redeems 20 shares from A. Six months later, X redeems 20 shares from B. In isolation, A's redemption would be substantially disproportionate because her interest drops from 50% (50/100) to 37.5% (30/80). Taken together, the two redemptions result in pro rata distributions because before and after the series of distributions, each shareholder owns 50% of X.

c. "Piggyback" Redemptions

Redemptions of nonvoting stock are not within § 302(b)(2) because the shareholder does not reduce voting power. If a corporation redeems sufficient voting stock from a shareholder to meet § 302(b)(2), however, a redemption of nonvoting preferred stock which is not § 306 stock (see VIII.B.2., at page 181, *infra*) in the same transaction also qualifies as an exchange. Reg. § 1.302–3(a).

2. Complete Terminations of a Shareholder's Interest

a. In General

A redemption that completely terminates a shareholder's actual and constructive stock interest in the corporation is treated as an exchange under § 302(b)(3). If the corporation distributes its debt obligations in exchange for the redeemed stock and the shareholder may recover the stock if the corporation defaults, the Service may contend that the shareholder has not terminated her equity interest.

b. Waiver of Family Attribution

A redemption that completely terminates a shareholder's *actual* interest in a corporation will be treated as an exchange even if the shareholder (called the "distributee" in § 302(c)) constructively owns stock of a family member under § 318(a)(1), provided the following requirements for waiver of family attribution in § 302(c)(2) are met.

1) All Interests Terminated

The distributee must have no interest in the corporation as a shareholder, officer, director or employee immediately after the distribution. § 302(c)(2)(A)(i). In *Lynch v. Comm'r,* 801 F.2d 1176 (9th Cir.1986), the court held that a taxpayer who performs post-redemption services for the corporation as an independent contractor retains a prohibited interest. The Tax Court has been more lenient, looking to the degree of managerial control or financial stake retained by the taxpayer. See, e.g., *Estate of Lennard v. Comm'r,* 61 T.C. 554 (1974). The retention or acquisition of an interest as a creditor is permitted. A person is considered to be a creditor only if her rights are not greater or broader in scope than necessary for enforcement of the claim. Reg. § 1.302–4(d).

2) Ten–Year–Look–Forward Rule

The distributee may not acquire any of the forbidden interests (other than stock acquired by bequest or inheritance) during the 10–year period beginning on the date of the distribution in redemption. § 302(c)(2)(A)(ii). A distributee who remains a creditor of the corporation after a redemption is not considered as acquiring a prohibited interest by acquiring corporate assets to enforce her rights as a creditor, but an acquisition of stock is prohibited. Reg. § 1.302–4(e).

3) Procedural Requirement

The distributee must attach a statement to her income tax return for the year of the redemption reciting that she has not acquired any prohibited interest since the distribution and agreeing to notify the Service of any such acquisition within 30 days after it occurs during the 10–year-look-forward period and to extend the statute of limitations for assessing and collecting a tax with respect to the distribution to one year after the notice. § 302(c)(2)(A)(iii). The Service may grant extensions for filing the agreement if the taxpayer shows "reasonable cause" for a late filing. Reg. § 1.302–4(a)(2).

4) Ten–Year–Look–Back Rule

This rule has two tests and a liberal exception. First, the distributee must not have acquired any portion of the redeemed stock within the 10–year period preceding the distribution from a person whose stock is attributable to the distributee under the family attribution rules in § 318(a)(1). Second, at the time of the distribution no person may own stock which is attributable to the distributee under the family attribution rules if that related family member acquired *any* stock in the corporation from the distributee within the 10–year-look-back period. Neither rule applies, however, if the acquisition or disposition by the distributee during the 10–year-look-back period was not principally motivated by a tax avoidance purpose. § 302(c)(2)(B). A gift of stock is not principally motivated by tax avoidance merely because the donee is in a lower income tax bracket. Reg. § 1.302–4(g).

> ***Example:*** Parent and Child each own 50 of the 100 outstanding shares of X Corp. Parent, who wishes to retire and shift control of X to Child, makes a gift of 20 shares to Child and X Corp. redeems Parent's other 30 shares, leaving Child as the sole shareholder. Parent retains no other interest in X Corp. Tax avoidance was not one of the principal purposes of the transfer to Child, and the 10–year-look-back rule will not prevent the redemption from qualifying for waiver of family attribution under § 302(c). See Rev.Rul. 77–293, 1977–2 C.B. 91.

c. **Waiver of Family Attribution by Entities**

Section 302(c)(2)(C) permits an entity to waive the family attribution rules. A waiver may be useful when a redemption terminates an entity's actual stock ownership but the entity still owns stock that is attributed from one family member to another "related person" and is then reattributed to the entity. This rule applies only to waive *family* attribution under § 318(a)(1); it does not waive direct beneficiary (or owner) to entity attribution under § 318(a)(3).

1) Entity Defined

For this purpose, an entity means a partnership, estate, trust or corporation. § 302(c)(2)(C)(ii)(I).

2) Related Person Defined

A "related person" is any person to whom ownership of stock in the corporation is (at the time of the distribution) attributable under the family attribution rules if the stock is further attributable to the entity. § 302(c)(2)(C)(ii)(II).

Example (1): A and Estate each own 50 of the 100 outstanding shares of X Corp. The sole beneficiary of Estate is A's son, S. A's shares are attributed to S under § 318(a)(1) and are further attributable from S to Estate under § 318(a)(3). S is a "related person." If S actually owned 50 shares, he would not be a related person.

3) Conditions for Entity Waiver

An entity may waive family attribution if the entity and each "related person" meet the usual requirements for a waiver under § 302(c) (i.e., the 10–year-look-back and forward rules and the notice requirement described above), and each related person agrees to be jointly and severally liable for any tax deficiency that may result if an interest is acquired in the 10–year-look-forward period. § 302(c)(2)(C)(i).

Example (2): Assume in Example (1) that X Corp. redeems Estate's 50 shares. Estate has terminated its actual ownership in X but continues to own 50 shares from A through beneficiary S. Assuming no 10–year-look-back rule problems, Estate can waive family attribution and break the chain from A to S if Estate and S jointly agree not to acquire a prohibited interest for 10 years and agree to notify the Service if an interest is so acquired. S also must agree to be jointly and severally liable for any tax deficiency resulting from such an acquisition. If S actually owned 50 shares of X, S's shares would be directly attributed to Estate, and the entity waiver rules would not allow Estate to terminate its interest under § 302(b)(3).

3. Redemptions Not Essentially Equivalent To A Dividend
a. The Meaningful Reduction Standard

If a redemption does not satisfy one of the specific § 302 safe harbors, it still is treated as an exchange under § 302(b)(1) if it is not "essentially equivalent to a dividend." The Supreme Court held in *U.S. v. Davis,* 397 U.S. 301, 90 S.Ct. 1041 (1970), reh. denied, 397 U.S. 1071, 90 S.Ct. 1495 (1970), that a redemption is not essentially equivalent to a dividend if it results in a "meaningful" reduction of the shareholder's proportionate interest in the corporation. Id. at 312, 90 S.Ct. at 1048. Dividend equivalence "depends upon the facts and circumstances of each case." Reg. § 1.302–2(b). The § 318 attribution rules fully apply, and a business purpose or lack of tax avoidance motive is irrelevant.

Example: On its formation in Year 1, X Corp. issues 25 shares of common stock each to Father, Mother and their two children. In Year 3, for a valid business purpose, Father contributes $25,000 to X Corp. in exchange for 100 shares of nonvoting preferred stock. In Year 5, X distributes $25,000 to Father in redemption of all his preferred stock. Under the attribution rules, Father is considered to be a 100% shareholder before and after the redemption. The redemption of the preferred stock is essentially equivalent to a dividend.

b. Examples of Meaningful Reductions

Although the *Davis* case limits the applicability of § 302(b)(1), the Service has identified several situations that do not qualify under the specific § 302(b) tests but still are not essentially equivalent to a dividend. In determining whether a reduction is "meaningful," the Service considers the three most significant shareholder rights: (1) voting, (2) participation in current earnings and corporate growth, and (3) sharing in net assets on liquidation. Rev.Rul. 81–289, 1981–2 C.B. 82. If the redeemed shareholder has a voting interest, a reduction in voting power is a key factor, together with the potential to participate in a control group with other shareholders. Rev.Rul. 85–106, 1985–2 C.B. 116.

1) **Partial Redemption of Nonvoting Preferred Stock**

    If a corporation redeems one-half of the nonvoting preferred stock of a shareholder who owns no other class of stock, the distribution ordinarily is not essentially equivalent to a dividend. Reg. § 1.302–2(a), third sentence.

2) **Significant Loss of Control**

    A reduction of voting rights from 57% to 50% (with corresponding reductions in rights to earnings and net assets on liquidation) has been ruled to be "meaningful" where the remaining shares are held by one unrelated shareholder. Rev.Rul. 75–502, 1975–2 C.B. 111.

3) **Loss of Control in Concert with Others**

    A reduction of common stock ownership from 27% to 22% is meaningful where the remaining shares are owned by three unrelated shareholders because the redeemed shareholder lost the power to control the corporation in concert with one other shareholder. Rev.Rul. 76–364, 1976–2 C.B. 91.

4) **Reduction of Ownership by Isolated Minority Shareholder**

    A reduction of common stock ownership by a minority shareholder from 30% to 24.3% is meaningful. Rev.Rul. 75–512, 1975–2 C.B. 112. Even a very minimal reduction of a shareholder's interest is meaningful if the shareholder exercises no control—e.g., a de minimis reduction resulting from a tender offer by a publicly traded corporation. Rev. Rul. 76–385,

1976–2 C.B. 92. But a pro rata redemption of stock by a public company is not a meaningful reduction even if the redeemed shareholder has a small minority interest. Rev. Rul. 81–289, 1981–2 C.B. 82.

5) Family Discord

One court has held that evidence of family discord may negate the presumption of the family attribution rules for purposes of § 302(b)(1). *Haft Trust v. Comm'r,* 510 F.2d 43 (1st Cir.1975). The Service and other courts disagree, but the Tax Court concedes that family discord may be a relevant "fact and circumstance" under § 302(b)(1) *after* the family attribution rules have been applied. See, e.g., *David Metzger Trust v. Comm'r,* 693 F.2d 459 (5th Cir.1982), cert. denied, 463 U.S. 1207, 103 S.Ct. 3537 (1983); *Cerone v. Comm'r,* 87 T.C. 1 (1986).

> ***Example:*** X Corp. has 100 shares of stock outstanding, 50 of which are owned by Mother and the other 50 by her Daughter. Mother and Daughter have been estranged for many years. X Corp. redeems 10 shares from Mother. If the attribution rules apply, the redemption is essentially equivalent to a dividend because Mother is a 100% shareholder before and after the distribution. The courts disagree over whether only Mother's actual ownership of shares should be considered because of the hostile relationship with Daughter.

4. Partial Liquidations

a. The Concept

A partial liquidation occurs when a corporation significantly contracts its business and makes a related distribution (of assets or their sale or insurance proceeds) to its shareholders in redemption of all or part of their stock. Congress concluded that when a distribution in redemption results from such a "corporate contraction," the transaction is more like a sale than a dividend. Section 302(b)(4) reflects this policy by providing exchange treatment for distributions in redemption of stock held by noncorporate shareholders if the transaction is a "partial liquidation" (as defined in § 302(e)) of the distributing corporation. Unlike the three other tests for exchange treatment, which look to the effect of a redemption on the distributee shareholder, qualification under § 302(b)(4) turns on the nature of the assets distributed and the corporation's reason for making the distribution.

b. Only Noncorporate Shareholders Qualify

Only noncorporate shareholders qualify for partial liquidation treatment. § 302(b)(4). S corporations in their capacities as shareholders of other corporations are treated as individuals for this purpose and thus also should qualify. Stock held by a partnership, estate or trust is treated as if held proportionately by its partners or beneficiaries. § 302(e)(5).

c. Partial Liquidation Defined
A distribution is treated as in partial liquidation if: (1) it is not essentially equivalent to a dividend, (2) the distribution is pursuant to a "plan" (a simple corporate resolution will suffice), and (3) the distribution occurs within the taxable year in which the plan is adopted or the succeeding taxable year. § 302(e)(1).

d. Not Essentially Equivalent to a Dividend
Whether a distribution is not essentially equivalent to a dividend is determined at the corporate rather than shareholder level. The requirement is met by satisfying the amorphous "corporate contraction" doctrine (a product of case law), or a more precise "termination of business" safe harbor in § 302(e)(2).

e. Corporate Contraction Doctrine
Under the case law, a distribution in partial liquidation is not essentially equivalent to a dividend if it results from a contraction of the corporation's business. Examples include:

1) Involuntary Events
After a fire damages a manufacturer's factory, the company distributes the insurance proceeds and contracts its business operations. *Imler v. Comm'r,* 11 T.C. 836 (1948); Reg. § 1.346–1(a).

2) Change in Nature of Business
A corporation distributes working capital that is no longer needed because of a change in the scale of its operations.

3) Reserve for Expansion
A corporation no longer needs funds that had been accumulated for expansion. Some older cases hold this is a legitimate contraction, but the Service has ruled to the contrary. See Rev.Rul. 78–55, 1978–1 C.B. 88; Reg. § 1.346–1(a).

The corporate contraction standard is amorphous and can not be relied upon with any assurance for planning purposes.

f. Termination of Business Safe Harbor
A distribution will not be essentially equivalent to a dividend if: (1) it is attributable to the termination of a "qualified trade or business," and (2) immediately after the distribution, the corporation continues to be engaged in the conduct of another qualified trade or business. § 302(e)(2).

1) Qualified Trade or Business
A qualified trade or business is any trade or business that was actively conducted throughout the five–year period ending on the date of the

distribution and was not acquired (by the distributing corporation) in a taxable transaction during that five–year period. § 302(e)(3). Raw land held for investment or a securities portfolio is not an active trade or business. See Reg. § 1.355–3(b)(2)(iv), which applies to the similar active trade or business requirement under § 355. See XII.B., at page 271, *infra*.

2) Distribution of Assets or Proceeds of Sale
The terminated business must be operated directly by the distributing corporation. The distribution must be of the assets of that business, or the proceeds of sale of those assets. The distribution of the stock of a subsidiary, or the proceeds of sale of such stock, will not qualify as a partial liquidation. Rev.Rul. 79–184, 1979–1 C.B. 143. A distribution of stock, however, may qualify as a tax-free corporate division. See § 355 and Chapter XII, *infra*.

3) Pro Rata Redemptions
Qualification as a partial liquidation under the termination of business safe harbor is determined without regard to whether the redemption is pro rata to the shareholders. § 302(e)(4).

g. **No Surrender of Stock Required**
Although a partial liquidation is a redemption in form, the Service has ruled that an actual surrender of shares is not required if it would be a "meaningless gesture," such as on a pro rata distribution. In that case, each shareholder is deemed to have surrendered shares with a value equal to the amount of the distribution, and an appropriate portion of the shareholder's stock basis is allocated to the shares deemed surrendered. See Rev.Rul. 90–13, 1990–1 C.B. 65.

Example: A, B and C each own 100 shares of X Corp. with a basis of $15,000 and a value of $100,000. X Corp. distributes $40,000 cash pro rata to each shareholder in a transaction that qualifies as a partial liquidation, but the shareholders do not surrender any stock. Each shareholder is deemed to have surrendered 40 shares of X Corp. stock with a basis of $6,000 (40% of $15,000) in exchange for the $40,000 distribution, and each recognizes a $34,000 long–term capital gain.

D. Specific Tax Consequences of Redemptions

1. Consequences to Shareholders
   a. Redemption Treated as Exchange
   If a redemption is treated as an exchange, the distributee shareholder computes gain or loss as if the redeemed stock had been sold to an outsider. In

the case of losses, however, § 267(a)(1) disallows a deduction if the redeemed shareholder owns (directly or indirectly) more than 50% of the corporation's stock. A shareholder who holds more than one block of stock with different bases may designate the shares to be redeemed.

Example: A owns 100 shares of X Corp. stock held long-term with an adjusted basis of $50,000. X Corp. distributes $90,000 to A in a redemption of 60 shares that qualifies as substantially disproportionate under § 302(b)(2). A allocates $30,000 (60% of her overall basis) to the redeemed stock and recognizes a $60,000 long-term capital gain on the redemption. If A's basis in the 100 shares had been $200,000, A would allocate $120,000 to the redeemed stock and recognize a $30,000 long-term capital loss.

b.   Redemption Treated as § 301 Distribution

If a redemption is not treated as an exchange, it is subject to the general distribution rules in § 301. § 302(d). See VI.C., at pages 134–135, *supra*. The distribution is a dividend to the extent of the distributing corporation's E & P, and the balance is a reduction of basis or capital gain. § 301(c). If a distribution in redemption is a dividend, the shareholder may not offset her basis in the redeemed stock. In that event, the basis does not disappear but is added to the basis of any remaining shares held by the distributee or, if no shares are retained, to the basis of shares held by a § 318 related shareholder. Reg. § 1.302–2(c).

Example (1):   A, the sole shareholder of X Corp., owns 100 shares with a basis of $50,000. X, which has ample E & P, distributes $80,000 in redemption of 40 shares. The distribution is a dividend. The basis of the redeemed shares ($20,000) is added to the basis of the shares retained by A.

Example (2):   Same facts as in Example (1), except A owned 40 shares with a basis of $20,000; his son, S, owned the other 60 shares with a basis of $30,000; and X redeemed A's shares in a transaction that does not qualify for waiver of family attribution. The entire distribution is a dividend, and A's $20,000 basis would be reassigned to S, who then would hold his 60 shares with a basis of $50,000. Reg. § 1.302–2(c) Example (2).

c.   Basis of Distributed Property

If a shareholder receives property (other than cash) in a redemption treated as a § 301 distribution, the shareholder's basis is the fair market value of the property on the date of the distribution. § 301(d). The result should be the same in the case of a redemption treated as an exchange, although the only applicable authority is the general "cost basis" rule of § 1012. "Cost" for this purpose is the fair market value of the redeemed stock, which ordinarily will be the same as the value of the distributed property.

d. Corporate Shareholders

If a redemption is treated as an exchange, the tax consequences to a corporate shareholder are the same as described above. If a redemption is treated as a dividend, the dividend generally qualifies for the § 243 dividends received deduction, except that a dividend resulting from a redemption which is part of a partial liquidation, or which is not pro rata to all shareholders, is treated as an "extraordinary dividend" under § 1059 without regard to the corporate shareholder's holding period in the stock. § 1059(e)(1). A corporation receiving an "extraordinary dividend" must reduce its basis in the stock of the distributing corporation by the portion of the dividend that was not taxed because of the dividends received deduction. If the nontaxed portion of the extraordinary dividend exceeds the corporate shareholder's stock basis, the excess is treated as gain from the sale or exchange of stock for the taxable year in which the extraordinary dividend is received. § 1059(a). See VI.F.3., at page 140, *supra.*

2. Consequences to Distributing Corporation

a. Recognition of Gain or Loss

The distributing corporation recognizes gain on a distribution of appreciated property in redemption of its stock, but it may not recognize loss on a distribution of property that has declined in value. § 311(a), (b). The rules are the same whether or not the redemption is treated as an exchange to the shareholders.

b. Effect on Earnings and Profits

1) Distribution of Appreciated Property

   The distributing corporation increases its current earnings and profits by the gain recognized on a distribution of appreciated property. § 312(b). If the basis of the property for E & P purposes is different from its basis for taxable income purposes, the increase is the E & P gain, not the taxable gain.

2) Redemption Treated as § 301 Distribution

   If a redemption is treated as a § 301 distribution, the effect on E & P is the same as on any other ordinary distribution. Accumulated E & P are reduced by the amount of money, the fair market value of any appreciated property distributed, the E & P adjusted basis of any loss property distributed, and the principal amount of debt obligations. § 312(a), (b).

3) Redemption Treated as Exchange

   If a redemption is treated as an exchange, E & P are reduced in an amount that may not exceed the ratable share of accumulated E & P attributable to the redeemed stock. § 312(n)(7). In no event may the E & P reduction exceed the amount of the distribution. If the corporation has only one class of stock outstanding, the E & P attributable to the redeemed stock are determined by multiplying accumulated E & P by the ratio of redeemed shares over total outstanding shares. More complex computations are required if a corporation has more than one class of stock outstanding.

> **Example:** X Corp. has 1,000 shares of common stock outstanding (its only class), owned equally by A and B. X has $160,000 of accumulated E & P and no current E & P. In a redemption treated as an exchange, X distributes $100,000 in redemption of A's 500 shares. Since the redeemed stock is 50% of the total number of shares outstanding, X may reduce E & P by $160,000 × 50%, or $80,000. If X had accumulated E & P of $240,000, the reduction would be limited to $100,000 (the amount of the distribution).

c. Stock Reacquisition Expenses

A corporation generally may not currently deduct any expenses paid in connection with the reacquisition (including redemption) of its own stock. Rather, such expenses are nondeductible, nonamortizable capital expenditure. § 162(k)(1). This deduction disallowance rule does not apply to the allocable costs of borrowing to finance a stock redemption. Those costs may be amortized over the term of the indebtedness. § 162(k)(2)(ii). The policy for this exception is that the borrowing transaction is separate from the redemption. Other corporate payments made contemporaneously with a reacquisition (e.g., payments to employees to discharge a contractual obligation under an employment agreement) are not subject to the disallowance rule in § 162(k).

E. Redemptions Through Use of Related Corporations

1. Introduction
a. Policy

Section 304 prevents a shareholder from selling stock of one corporation to another related corporation in order to withdraw ("bail out") earnings while treating the transaction as a sale rather than a dividend. Section 304 applies when one or more controlling shareholders sell stock of one corporation to another controlled corporation (a "brother-sister acquisition"), or when any shareholder of a parent corporation sells stock of the parent to a subsidiary (a "parent-subsidiary acquisition"). Section 304 tests these transactions for dividend equivalency by applying § 302 to determine whether the shareholder has sufficiently reduced his interest in the corporation whose stock has been transferred.

> **Example:** A owns all the stock of both X Corp. and Y Corp., each of which have ample E & P. If either corporation were to redeem shares held by A, the distribution would be a dividend. If A sells all or part of her X stock to Y, the effect of the transaction is the same

as a dividend because A has withdrawn funds from Y without reducing her 100% control of both corporations. The same would be true if A owned all the stock of X Corp. which in turn owned all the stock of Y Corp., and A sold all or part of her X stock to Y for cash. Section 304 treats these transactions as constructive redemptions and tests them for dividend equivalency under § 302.

b. Section 304 Glossary

Familiarity with several statutory terms of art is essential to an understanding of § 304.

1) Property

Section 304 applies only to acquisitions of stock in return for "property." For this purpose, "property" includes money, securities and other property but not stock in the corporation making the acquisition. § 317(a). See *Bhada v. Comm'r*, 89 T.C. 959 (1987), *aff'd sub nom., Caamano v. Comm'r*, 879 F.2d 156 (5th Cir.1989).

2) Acquiring Corporation

The "acquiring corporation" is the corporation that acquires stock from a shareholder of another related corporation in return for property. In a parent-subsidiary acquisition, the acquiring corporation always is the subsidiary.

3) Issuing Corporation

The "issuing corporation" is the corporation whose stock has been transferred. In a parent-subsidiary acquisition, the issuing corporation is always the parent.

4) Control

For purposes of § 304, "control" means the ownership of stock possessing at least 50% of the total combined voting power of all classes of stock entitled to vote, *or* at least 50% of the total value of shares of all classes of stock. § 304(c)(1). This is not the same as the 80% "control" test in § 368(c) that is used for certain other corporate-shareholder transactions, such as corporate formations and reorganizations. In determining control, the attribution rules in § 318 apply except that stock may be attributed between a corporation and a 5% or more (instead of 50% or more) shareholder. § 304(c)(3). In the case of a corporation with more than one class of stock, the value prong of the "control" test is applied to the aggregate value of all classes of stock, not class-by-class. Rev.Rul. 89–57, 1989–1 C.B. 90. Thus, a shareholder who owns 50% or more of the value of all the corporation's stock has "control" even if she owns less than 50% of a particular class. If a person or persons are in "control" of one corporation which in turn owns at least 50% of either the total combined voting power or stock value of a second corporation, then that person or persons are treated as in "control" of the second corporation. § 304(c)(1).

c. Mode of Analysis

In analyzing § 304 issues, the following four-step process may be helpful:

1) Determine if § 304 applies—i.e., is the sale either a "brother-sister" or "parent-subsidiary" acquisition. If so, the transaction is treated as a constructive redemption.

2) If § 304 applies, determine whether the constructive redemption qualifies for exchange treatment under § 302(b) by comparing the shareholder's actual and constructive ownership in the issuing corporation's stock before and after the transaction. In so doing, remember that all or part of the transferred stock is still outstanding and may be attributed back from the acquiring corporation to the shareholder.

3) If the constructive redemption is treated as a § 301 distribution, determine the amount and source of any dividend by looking first to the E & P of the acquiring corporation and then to the E & P of the issuing corporation. § 304(b)(2).

4) Finally, determine the collateral consequences of the transaction—e.g., effect on basis and earnings and profits.

2. Brother–Sister Acquisitions: § 304(a)(1)
a. The Constructive Redemption

If one or more persons are in "control" of each of two corporations and sell stock of one corporation (the "issuing corporation") to the other (the "acquiring corporation") in return for property, the property is treated for purposes of §§ 302 and 303 as a distribution in redemption of the stock of the acquiring corporation. § 304(a)(1). Note that § 304(a)(1) applies when two or more unrelated shareholders who in the aggregate control each of two corporations sell stock of one corporation to the other in related transactions even if no single shareholder has control. § 304(a)(1)(B). The constructive redemption is then tested for dividend equivalence under § 302 by reference to the stock of the issuing corporation. § 304(b)(1).

b. Tax Consequences
1) § 301 Distribution

If the constructive redemption is treated as a § 301 distribution, the amount and source of any dividend is determined first by reference to the E & P of the acquiring corporation and then, if necessary, to the E & P of the issuing corporation. § 304(b)(2). The controlling shareholder is treated as having transferred the stock of the issuing corporation to the acquiring corporation in exchange for acquiring corporation stock in a tax-free transaction to which § 351(a) applies. Then, the acquiring corporation is treated as if it had redeemed the stock that it was treated as issuing in the hypothetical § 351 exchange. § 304(a)(1). The acquiring corporation thus takes a transferred basis from the shareholder in the acquired stock. § 362(a). The shareholder's basis in the stock of the acquiring corporation is then increased by the basis of the issuing corporation stock that the shareholder is treated as having transferred in the hypothetical § 351 transaction and is decreased only if part of the distribution is treated as a reduction of basis under § 301(c)(2). Reg. § 1.304–2(a). Such a basis reduction would occur, for example, if all or part of the distribution were not a dividend because of insufficient earnings and profits.

2) Exchange

If the transaction is treated as an exchange, the shareholder recognizes gain or loss measured by the difference between the amount realized and the adjusted basis in the transferred stock. (Allowance of losses may be limited by § 267). The shareholder's basis in the stock of the acquiring corporation remains unchanged, and the acquiring corporation takes a § 1012 cost basis in the issuing corporation's stock. Reg. § 1.304–2(a). Any E & P reduction is limited by § 312(n)(7) to an amount not in excess of the redeemed stock's ratable share of E & P (see VII.D.2., at page 159, *supra*), but it is unclear which corporation's E & P will be affected. A reasonable answer is that the required E & P reduction should be made first to the acquiring corporation's E & P and then, if necessary, to the issuing corporation's E & P.

Example (1): A and B (unrelated) each own 100 of the 200 outstanding shares of X Corp. and Y Corp., respectively. X has $70,000 of E & P, and Y has $40,000 of E & P. A sells 30 shares of X Corp. stock (having an adjusted basis to A of $10,000) to Y for $100,000. X is the "issuing corporation" and Y is the "acquiring corporation." Because A is in control of both corporations (he owns at least 50% of each) and sells X stock to Y in exchange for cash, § 304(a)(1) applies.

The transaction is treated as a constructive redemption of Y stock which is tested for dividend equivalence by reference to A's stock holdings in X. Before the sale, A owns 50% (100 shares) of X. After the sale, A owns 42.5% of X (70 shares actually and 15 shares constructively from Y Corp.). Since A's percentage ownership of X stock after the sale is not less than 80% of his percentage ownership before the sale, the redemption does not qualify as substantially disproportionate under § 302(b)(2).

If § 302(b)(1) does not apply, the entire $100,000 received by A is a dividend—$40,000 from Y's E & P and $60,000 from X's E & P. A is treated as having transferred 30 shares of X Corp. to Y Corp. in exchange for Y Corp. stock of equivalent value in a tax-free § 351 transaction, and then Y Corp. is treated as if it redeemed the Y Corp. shares that it issued in that hypothetical transaction. Y Corp. takes a $10,000 transferred basis in the 30 shares of X Corp. stock. A adds $10,000 to the basis of his Y stock. If § 302(b)(1) applies, the transaction is treated as a sale, A recognizes $90,000 long-term capital gain, and Y takes a $100,000 cost basis in the 30 shares of X stock.

Example (2): Same as Example (1), except A owns only 40% of the stock of X Corp. and Y Corp., and B owns 60%. If only A transfers X stock to Y, § 304 does not apply because the X stock has not been acquired from a person or persons in "control" of both corporations.

Example (3): Same as Example (2), except A is B's father. Applying the § 318 attribution rules, A is in control of both X and Y, and § 304(a)(1) applies.

3. Parent–Subsidiary Acquisitions: § 304(a)(2)

a. The Constructive Redemption

If a subsidiary (the "acquiring corporation") acquires stock of its parent (the "issuing corporation") from a shareholder of the parent in return for property, the property is treated as a distribution in redemption of the issuing corporation's (i.e. parent's) stock. § 304(a)(2). The constructive redemption is tested for dividend equivalency by reference to the stock of the parent. § 304(b)(1). For this purpose, the parent-subsidiary relationship is determined by the 50% control test in § 304(c). Reg. § 1.304–3(a). See VII.E.1.b.4., at page 161, *supra*.

b. Tax Consequences

1) § 301 Distribution

If the constructive redemption is treated as a § 301 distribution, the amount and source of the dividend is determined first by reference to the E & P of the acquiring corporation and then, if necessary, by the E & P of the issuing corporation. § 304(b)(2). The regulations do not specifically address the basis consequences in this situation, but it is logical to add the shareholder's basis in the transferred parent stock to the basis in his remaining parent stock. Cf. Reg. § 1.304–3(a). The subsidiary likely takes a cost basis in the stock of the parent that it acquires in the transaction. See *Broadview Lumber Co. v. U.S.*, 561 F.2d 698 (7th Cir.1977). Logically, the acquiring (subsidiary) corporation's E & P are reduced to the extent they are the source of the dividend and then the issuing (parent) corporation's E & P are reduced to the extent they were the source.

2) Sale

If the constructive redemption is treated as a sale or exchange, the selling shareholder recognizes gain or loss under normal tax principles, and the subsidiary takes a cost basis in the parent stock that it acquires. The impact on E & P under § 312(n)(7) is unsettled, leaving taxpayers the leeway to use any reasonable approach.

Example: A owns 60 of the 100 outstanding shares of X Corp., which owns 80 of the 100 outstanding shares of Y Corp. and thus "controls" Y. A sells 20 shares of X (basis–$20,000) to Y in exchange for $80,000. The transaction is treated by § 304(a)(2) as a distribution in redemption of X Corp. stock. Before the sale, A owns 60% (60 out of 100 shares) of X. After the sale, A owns 40 shares actually and 6.4 shares constructively (80% of the 20 shares of X owned by Y, or 16 shares, are attributed to X, and 40% of those 16 shares, or 6.4 shares, are reattributed to A), for a total of 46.4%. A's ownership of X is reduced from 60% to 46.4%, qualifying the redemption for substantially disproportionate exchange treatment under § 302(b)(2). A thus recognizes $60,000 LTCG and Y takes an $80,000 cost basis in the Y stock.

c. Overlap Situations

If a transaction is both a brother-sister and a parent-subsidiary acquisition, the parent-subsidiary rules in § 304(a)(2) take precedence. § 304(a)(1). But because the attribution rules transform virtually all actual brother-sister relationships into parent-subsidiary, an actual brother-sister acquisition is subject to § 304(a)(1) even if it also may be a constructive parent-subsidiary acquisition. Reg. § 1.304–2(c) Example (1).

4. Relationship of § 304 to Other Code Sections
a. Coordination With § 351

In overlap situations, § 304(b)(3)(A) provides that § 351 will not apply to any "property" received in a § 304(a) distribution, except that § 304 will not apply to any debt incurred or assumed in connection with the acquisition of the transferred stock. § 304(b)(3)(B). Keep in mind that stock of the acquiring corporation is not "property" (§ 317(a)), and thus a transaction may be bifurcated into a § 351 nonrecognition exchange and a § 304 distribution.

Example (1): A owns 80 out of the 100 outstanding shares of X Corp., and Y Corp., respectively. Both corporations have ample E & P. The remaining stock is owned by unrelated shareholders. A sells

20 shares of X (basis–$4,000; value–$20,000) to Y in exchange for 15 newly issued shares of Y (value–$15,000) and $5,000 cash. The transfer qualifies under § 351, which applies to the exchange of X stock for Y stock (§ 304 does not apply because the Y stock is not "property"), but § 304 applies to the exchange of X stock for $5,000 cash.

Example (2):   Same as Example (1), except A transfers 20 shares of X to Y in exchange for 15 shares of Y, and Y takes the stock subject to a $5,000 liability incurred by A when he acquired the X stock. A recognizes no gain on the transaction under §§ 351 and 357; § 304 does not apply to Y's assumption of the $5,000 liability.

b. Relationship to Partial Liquidation Rules

If a § 304 transaction also qualifies as a partial liquidation under § 302(b)(4), it may qualify for exchange treatment. In testing the transaction, the courts have looked to the contraction in the acquiring corporation's business. See *Blaschka v. U.S.,* 393 F.2d 983 (Ct.Cl.1968).

F. Redemptions to Pay Death Taxes

1. Policy

Section 303 treats certain redemptions as exchanges even if the transaction would not have qualified for exchange treatment under § 302. The redeemed stock must have been included in the gross estate of a decedent for federal estate tax purposes. The policy of § 303 is to facilitate redemptions of closely held stock by estates (or, in some cases, beneficiaries) who may need to raise funds to pay death taxes and other estate administration expenses. Since the stock ordinarily has a date-of-death basis under § 1014, a redemption qualifying under § 303 usually results in recognition of little or no gain or loss.

2. Requirements and Limitations
a. Stock Included in Decedent's Gross Estate

The redeemed stock must have been included in the decedent's gross estate for federal estate tax purposes (§ 303(a)), or the stock must take its basis from stock that was included in the decedent's gross estate and the "old stock" must have qualified for § 303(a) exchange treatment (§ 303(c)).

b. Relationship of Stock to Decedent's Estate
1) 35% Rule

The value of the distributing corporation's stock that is included in the decedent's gross estate must exceed 35% of the value of the gross estate less debts, claims and administrative expenses allowable as deductions under §§ 2053 and 2054. § 303(b)(2)(A).

2) Two or More Corporations Aggregation Rule

The stock of two or more corporations may be aggregated for purposes of the 35% rule if 20% or more in value of each corporation's total outstanding stock is included in the decedent's gross estate. For purposes of the 20% requirement, stock held by the decedent's surviving spouse as community property, or held with the decedent in joint tenancy, tenancy-by-the-entirety or tenancy-in-common is treated as if it were included in determining the value of the decedent's gross estate. § 303(b)(2)(B).

> ***Example:*** D died with a gross estate less deductible debts and expenses of $2,000,000. Included in D's gross estate were 1,000 shares of X Corp. (value–$600,000) held by D as separate property and constituting 25% of X's outstanding stock, and 500 shares of Y Corp. (value–$200,000), constituting 12% of Y's outstanding stock, and representing D's 50% interest in 1,000 shares held by D and his surviving spouse, S, as tenants-in-common. Since the value of the X and Y stock included in D's gross estate constitute 20% or more in value of the total outstanding stock of those corporations (treating S's interest in the Y Corp. stock as having been included in determining the value of D's gross estate for this purpose), the X and Y stock are treated as stock of a single corporation, with a value of $800,000, allowing D's estate to satisfy the 35% test.

c. Dollar Limitations

Section 303 exchange treatment is available only to the extent that the distribution does not exceed the sum of: (1) death taxes imposed because of the decedent's death, and (2) funeral and administrative expenses allowed as estate tax deductions under § 2053.

d. Timing of Redemption

A § 303 redemption generally must occur within 90 days after the expiration of the statute of limitations for assessment of federal estate taxes (usually three years). The period is extended if a petition for redetermination of an estate tax deficiency is filed in the Tax Court or if the estate is eligible and elects to pay estate taxes in installments under § 6166. § 303(b)(1). Additional limitations are imposed for distributions made more than four years after the decedent's death. § 303(b)(4).

e. Shareholder Must Bear Burden of Estate Tax

Stock redeemed under § 303 ordinarily is held by the decedent's estate. Beneficiaries of stock included in the decedent's gross estate also may qualify to the extent that their interests are reduced by an obligation to pay death taxes or administrative expenses. § 303(b)(3).

3. Consequences to Distributing Corporation

A corporation that distributes property in a § 303 redemption must recognize gain under § 311(b) but may not recognize loss under § 311(a). The effect of a § 303 redemption on the distributing corporation's E & P is determined under § 312(n)(7). See VII.D.2.b.3. at page 159, *supra*.

G. Redemptions and Related Transactions

1. Redemptions and Sales

If a redemption and sale are part of an integrated transaction to dispose of a shareholder's entire interest in the corporation, the redemption will qualify as a complete termination under § 302(b)(3) whether it occurs before or after the sale. *Zenz v. Quinlivan*, 213 F.2d 914 (6th Cir.1954). This technique is often used by individual shareholders to remove liquid assets from a corporation and sell the remaining stock at a reduced price in a transaction known as a "bootstrap acquisition." A sale and redemption also may be combined to qualify the redemption as "substantially disproportionate" under § 302(b)(2). Rev.Rul. 75–447, 1975–2 C.B. 113.

> ***Example (1):*** A owns all 100 outstanding shares of X Corp. The value of X Corp. is $100,000, including $20,000 in cash and $80,000 of operating assets. X Corp. has $50,000 of E & P. B wishes to acquire X Corp. (without the cash) for $80,000. X first distributes $20,000 to A in redemption of 20 shares, and A then sells her remaining 80 shares to B for $80,000. If the redemption and sale are part of an integrated plan, A is considered to have completely terminated her interest in X and the redemption qualifies for exchange treatment under § 302(b)(3).

> ***Example (2):*** A and B, who are unrelated, each own 50 of X Corp.'s 100 outstanding shares. To bring C (also unrelated) into the business and rearrange control, X issues 25 new common shares to C and, pursuant to the same plan, X redeems 25 shares of its stock from A and B, respectively. Viewing the transactions as a whole, A and B's interests were reduced from 50% (50/100 shares) to 33⅓% (25/75 shares), and the redemptions qualify as substantially disproportionate under § 302(b)(2).

2. Redemptions Pursuant to Buy–Sell Agreements
a. Buy–Sell Agreements

Closely held corporations frequently use buy-sell stock purchase agreements to provide for the continuity of a business, to satisfy economic and tax goals when a shareholder dies or retires, and to resolve shareholder disputes. Under a "cross-purchase" agreement, the departing shareholder or his estate sells the stock to the continuing shareholders. Under an "entity-purchase" agreement, the corporation redeems the departing shareholder's stock. The obligation to buy (or sell) may be mandatory or optional, as the parties agree. Buy-sell agreements also typically include other restrictions on the transfer of shares and provisions to determine the value of any stock purchased pursuant to the agreement.

b. Constructive Dividend Issues

Constructive dividend issues may arise when a continuing shareholder is personally and unconditionally obligated to purchase stock pursuant to a buy-sell agreement and that obligation is assumed by the corporation. See, e.g., *Wall v. U.S.*, 164 F.2d 462 (4th Cir.1947); *Sullivan v. U.S.*, 363 F.2d 724 (8th Cir.1966), *cert. denied*, 387 U.S. 905, 87 S.Ct. 1683 (1967). A mere assignment to the corporation of an option (or other contractual right) to purchase stock from another shareholder does not result in a constructive dividend. *Holsey v. Comm'r*, 258 F.2d 865 (3d Cir.1958).

Example (1):   A and B, who are unrelated, own all 100 shares of X Corp. They agree that upon the death of either shareholder, the survivor will be unconditionally obligated to purchase the decedent's X stock from his estate. After B dies, A causes the corporation to assume his obligation and redeem the stock from B's estate. The redemption results in a constructive distribution to A. Rev. Rul. 69–608, 1969–2 C.B. 42, Situations 1 & 2.

Example (2):   Same as Example (1), except that the agreement provides that upon the death of either shareholder, X Corp. has an option to purchase the decedent's stock. If X chooses not to exercise the option, the surviving shareholder is obligated to purchase any unredeemed shares. If B dies and X redeems all of B's stock, the redemption is not a constructive distribution to A because A was not primarily obligated to buy the stock. Rev. Rul. 69–608, *supra*, Situation 5.

Example (3):   Same as Example (1), except that the agreement provides that either shareholder has an option to purchase the stock of the other on the occurrence of certain events but is free to assign the option to others. At B's retirement, A assigns his option to X Corp., which redeems all of B's stock. The redemption is not a constructive distribution to A because A had no unconditional obligation to buy the stock. Rev. Rul. 69–608, *supra*, Situation 4.

c. Redemptions Incident to Divorce

1) The Problem

Constructive dividend issues also may arise when a closely held corporation redeems stock in connection with a divorce settlement. Assume, for example, that H and W each own 50% each of the highly appreciated stock of X Corp., and H agrees to buy W's 50% interest upon their divorce. If H buys W's stock for cash, the transfer is governed by § 1041; W does not recognize gain, and H takes a transferred basis in the stock. But what if H's (unconditional?) obligation is fulfilled by a redemption of W's stock by

X, Corp., leaving H as the sole shareholder? Is that transaction still governed by § 1041; does H (or W) have a constructive dividend; or is neither party taxable? The law on these questions is unsettled.

2) Case Law
The Ninth Circuit has held that when Husband ("H") and Wife ("W") each own 50% of the stock of Corporation, and Corporation redeems W's stock pursuant to a divorce settlement, the transaction should be treated as a tax-free § 1041 transfer of W's stock to H (see Reg. § 1.1041–1T(c), Q & A 9, treating such a transfer as made by W "on behalf of" H), followed by a redemption from H. In so holding, the court suggested that the subsequent redemption of half of H's stock results in a § 301 distribution and possible dividend to H. *Arnes v. U.S.*, 981 F.2d 456 (9th Cir.1992). See also *Hayes v. Comm'r*, 101 T.C. 593 (1993). In a related case, the Tax Court, addressing the same transaction, held that H did not have a constructive dividend because he was not unconditionally obligated to buy W's stock. *Arnes v. Comm'r*, 102 T.C. 522 (1994). In a later case, the Tax Court held (on similar facts where the agreement allowed H to buy W's stock or cause the corporation to do so in a redemption) that § 1041 applied to W's transfer because it was made "on behalf of" H and suggested that, as a result, H had a constructive dividend. *Read v. Comm'r*, 114 T.C. 14 (2000).

3) Proposed Regulations
The Service has issued proposed regulations to clarify this area and harmonize the "primary and unconditional" standard for constructive dividends with the policy of § 1041. Under the proposed regulations, if a divorce-related redemption results in a constructive distribution to the nontransferor spouse under "applicable tax law" (applying the primary and unconditional standard), the redeemed stock is treated as if it were transferred by the transferor spouse in a tax-free § 1041 transaction (if all the § 1041 requirements are met) and then retransferred by the nontransferor spouse to the corporation in a redemption. Prop. Reg. § 1.1041–2(a)(1), (b)(1). If the redemption does not satisfy a primary and unconditional obligation of the nontransferor spouse, the form of the transaction is respected—i.e., the corporation is treated as directly redeeming the transferor spouse's stock and § 1041 does not apply. Id. Under a special rule, the spouses may depart from "applicable tax law" and elect to treat a divorce-related redemption as a constructive distribution to the transferor spouse (even without a primary and unconditional obligation) and a tax-free § 1041 transfer. Prop. Reg. § 1.1041–2(c).

Example (1):   H and W each own 50 shares of X Corp. which has ample E & P. Pursuant to a divorce agreement, H is unconditionally obligated to purchase W's stock for cash. H is short of funds, however, and causes X Corp. to fulfill his obligation by redeeming W's stock for cash. Under the proposed regulations, the transaction is treated as a tax-free § 1041 transfer of W's stock from W to H followed by a redemption that results in a constructive dividend to H.

Example (2): Same as Example (1), except the agreement gave H the option to purchase W's stock or to request X Corp. to redeem the stock. Since H did not have a primary and unconditional obligation to buy W's stock, the form of the transaction is respected for tax purposes under the proposed regulations. Because the redemption terminates W's interest in X Corp. (and there is no family attribution after their divorce), the redemption likely qualifies as an exchange to W under § 302(b)(3), and H is not taxable.

Example (3): Same as Example (2), except H and W agree in writing to treat the redemption as a constructive dividend to H and a tax-free § 1041 transfer by W. Under the proposed regulations, the tax results are the same as in Example (1).

3. Charitable Contribution Followed By Redemption

A shareholder of a closely held corporation may indirectly withdraw earnings but avoid dividend treatment by contributing stock to a charity and causing the corporation to redeem the stock from the charitable donee. The Service was unsuccessful in reclassifying this type of transaction as a constructive dividend followed by a charitable gift of cash. See *Grove v. Comm'r,* 490 F.2d 241 (2d Cir.1973). It subsequently ruled that a contribution of stock followed by a redemption shall be treated as a dividend to the donor only if the charitable donee is legally bound or can be compelled by the corporation to surrender the shares for redemption. Rev.Rul. 78–197, 1978–1 C.B. 83.

H. Review Questions

1. X Corp. has 1,000 shares of stock outstanding which are owned as follows:

Husband ("H")	200 shares
Wife ("W")	100 shares
Trust for H and W's children	100 shares
HYZ Partnership	300 shares
Y (W's Father)	300 shares

H and W are married. The equal general partners of the HYZ Partnership are H, Y (W's Father) and Z (unrelated). How many shares of X Corp. are constructively owned by: H, H and W's children, Z, and Y?

2. Incorporate the facts of question 1, above, and assume that X Corp. redeems all 100 shares from the Trust. X Corp. has ample E & P. What are the tax consequences of the redemption to the Trust?

3. Individuals A, B and C are unrelated equal shareholders of X Corp. X has operated a nationwide restaurant chain for the past 10 years. Three years ago, it opened a restaurant division in the State of Depression but, because of adverse economic conditions, X has decided to sell the Depression division and distribute the proceeds pro rata to its shareholders. X has ample earnings and profits. What are the tax consequences of the distribution to the shareholders? What if shareholder A were a corporation?

4. A owns 700 shares of X Corp.'s 1,000 shares of common stock in which A has a $700 basis. A also owns 500 shares of Y Corp.'s 1,000 shares of common stock in which A has a $500 basis. X has $10,000 of E & P and Y has $15,000 of E & P. A sells 300 shares of X to Y for $30,000. What are the tax consequences of this transaction to A, X and Y?

VIII

STOCK DISTRIBUTIONS AND § 306 STOCK

Analysis

173

A. Stock Distributions

1. Introduction

a. Types of Stock Distributions

A corporation makes a stock distribution when it distributes its own stock to some or all of its shareholders. Stock distributions include "stock dividends" and "stock splits." Under corporate law and accounting practice, a stock dividend may differ from a "split." Stock splits result in an increase in the number of outstanding shares of the same class. Stock dividends usually are smaller in degree than splits and may be of another class of stock—e.g., preferred stock distributed to common shareholders.

> ***Example (1):*** X Corp. has 1,000 shares of common stock outstanding. A owns 200 shares. X declares a 10% common stock dividend. Each shareholder will receive one new share of common stock for each 10 shares held. Thus, A will receive 20 shares. Cash normally will be distributed in lieu of fractional shares.

> ***Example (2):*** Same as Example (1), except X declares a 2–for–1 stock split and issues one new common share for each share held. After the split, X has 2,000 shares of common stock outstanding, and A owns 400 shares.

b. History of Taxation of Stock Distributions

In *Eisner v. Macomber,* 252 U.S. 189, 40 S.Ct. 189 (1920), the Supreme Court held that a "common on common" stock dividend was not taxable because it did not constitute gross income within the meaning of the Sixteenth Amendment to the Constitution. In a later case, the Court held that a "common on preferred" stock dividend was taxable because the shareholder received an interest different from her former stock holdings. *Koshland v. Helvering,* 298 U.S. 441, 56 S.Ct. 767 (1936). From these and other cases, a test evolved under which a stock dividend was taxable only if it increased a shareholder's proportionate ownership interest in the corporation. When Congress and the Treasury abandoned this approach in 1954, tax advisors devised methods that offered shareholders a choice between receiving taxable cash dividends or increasing their proportionate interests in the corporation through nontaxable distributions. Section 305, enacted in 1969 and accompanied by detailed regulations, represents Congress's response.

c. Policy of Section 305

Section 305 has two underlying policies. A stock dividend generally is not taxable if it does not increase a shareholder's proportionate ownership interest in the corporation. If a stock distribution increases the interests of some shareholders, however, or results in some shareholders receiving cash or property while others increase their proportionate interests, the distribution is usually taxable.

2. Nontaxable Stock Distributions
a. General Rule
Section 305(a) provides that stock distributions are not includible in gross income unless an exception in § 305(b) applies. Examples of nontaxable stock dividends include: "common on common" and "preferred on common" stock dividends where no other classes of stock are outstanding.

b. Allocation of Basis
If a stock distribution ("new stock") is not taxable, the shareholder's basis in the stock held prior to the distribution ("old stock") is allocated between the old and new stock in proportion to the relative fair market values of each on the date of the distribution. § 307(a).

Example (1): A owns 100 shares of X Corp. common stock with a basis of $12,000 ($120 per share). As a result of a 2–for–1 split, A receives 100 additional shares of X common stock. The stock distribution is not taxable, and A allocates his $12,000 basis between the old and new shares, leaving him with a basis of $60 per common and preferred share after the distribution.

Example (2): A owns 100 shares of X Corp. common stock with a basis of $12,000 ($120 per share). X declares a preferred stock dividend on its common stock, and A receives 25 preferred shares with a value of $25,000. The value of A's common stock after the distribution is $75,000. A allocates his $12,000 basis in the common between the common and preferred based on their relative fair market values (75% common, 25% preferred), and thus takes a $9,000 basis ($90 per share) in the common stock and a $3,000 basis ($120 per share) in the preferred stock.

c. Holding Period
The holding period of the new stock includes the holding period of the old stock. § 1223(5).

d. Consequences to Distributing Corporation
The distributing corporation recognizes no gain or loss on a nontaxable stock distribution (§ 311(a)(1)), and it may not reduce its E & P (§ 312(d)(1)(B)).

3. Taxable Stock Distributions
Stock distributions described in § 305(b) are treated as distributions to which § 301 applies and thus are dividends to the extent of the distributing corporation's

available E & P. The amount of the distribution is the fair market value of the distributed stock. Reg. § 1.305–1(b)(1). Stock distributions are taxable in the situations described below.

a.   Election of Stock or Property

If a stock distribution is, at *any* shareholder's election, payable either in stock of the distributing corporation or in cash or other property, the stock distribution is taxable to all shareholders regardless of whether any shareholder exercises the election. § 305(b)(1).

Shareholders who participate in stock reinvestment plans by acquiring stock in lieu of cash dividends are taxable under § 305(b)(1) on the fair market value of the stock received. Rev.Rul. 78–375, 1978–2 C.B. 130.

Example: X Corp. has only common stock outstanding. X declares a cash dividend of $10 per share, or a shareholder may elect to receive additional common stock with a value of $10 per share for each share held. Shareholders who elect to receive stock are treated as receiving a § 301 distribution of $10 per share, even if all shareholders elect stock. Reg. § 1.305–2(a).

b.   Disproportionate Distributions

If the result of a distribution (or series of distributions) is that some shareholders receive cash or other property while others increase their proportionate interest in the earnings or assets of the corporation, those who increase their proportionate interest are taxed on the value of the increased interest. § 305(b)(2). Cash and stock distributions can have a disproportionate effect even if they are not pursuant to a plan and are unrelated. If distributions are separated by more than 36 months, however, they are presumed to be beyond the reach of § 305(b)(2) unless they are made pursuant to an integrated plan. Reg. § 1.305–3(b)(2), (4).

Example (1):   X Corp. has two classes of common stock outstanding: Class A and Class B. Each class has equal rights. X pays a cash dividend of $10 per share on the Class A stock and a dividend on the Class B stock payable in additional shares of Class B stock with a value of $10 per share. The stock distribution is taxable because the Class B shareholders increase their proportionate interest in earnings and assets of X while the Class A shareholders receive cash. Reg. § 1.305–3(e) Example (1).

Example (2):   X Corp. has two classes of stock outstanding: common and preferred. X declares a dividend on the common payable in additional common stock and pays a cash dividend on the preferred stock. The cash dividend is taxable, but the common on common stock dividend is not because it does not increase the proportionate interests of the common shareholders as a class. Reg. § 1.305–3(e) Example (2).

Example (3): Same facts as Example (2) except that X Corp. declares a dividend on the common stock payable in shares of the preferred. Since the interests of the common shareholders in the assets and earnings of the corporation have increased (they have new rights and preferences as preferred shareholders), the preferred stock dividend is taxable. If the dividend had been payable in a new class of preferred stock that was subordinated in all respects to the old preferred, however, the distribution would not be taxable because it would not increase the proportionate interests of the common shareholders. The issuance of the junior preferred stock does not give the common shareholders more than they had before the distribution. Reg. § 1.305–3(e) Example (3).

c. Distributions of Common and Preferred Stock

If a distribution (or series of distributions) has the result of some common shareholders receiving preferred stock and others receiving common stock, all the distributions are taxable. § 305(b)(3). The rationale is that the shareholders who receive common stock increase their proportionate interest in earnings and assets while the other shareholders receive a relatively fixed interest akin to cash.

Example: X Corp. has two classes of common stock outstanding: Class A and Class B. Each class has equal rights. X declares a dividend on Class A stock payable in additional shares of Class A and a dividend on Class B stock payable in a new issue of preferred stock. Both stock distributions are taxable. Reg. § 1.305–4(b) Example (1).

d. Distributions on Preferred Stock

All distributions on preferred stock are taxable except for an increase in the conversion ratio of convertible preferred stock that is made solely to take account of a stock dividend or split. § 305(b)(4). For this purpose, "preferred stock" is any stock which does not participate in corporate growth to any significant extent and has limited rights and privileges. Reg. § 1.305–5(a).

Example (1): X Corp. has two classes of stock outstanding: common and nonconvertible preferred. X declares a dividend on both the common and preferred, in each case payable in additional shares of the common. The distribution is taxable to the preferred shareholders but not to the common shareholders.

Example (2): X Corp. has two classes of stock outstanding: common and preferred. Each share of preferred is convertible into two shares of common. X pays a dividend of one share of common stock for each common share held and doubles the conversion ratio of the preferred. Neither the common stock distribution nor the doubling of the conversion ratio is taxable.

e. Distributions of Convertible Preferred

A distribution of convertible preferred stock is taxable unless the taxpayer establishes to the satisfaction of the Service that it will not have the result of a disproportionate distribution. § 305(b)(5). A distribution of convertible preferred is likely to have a disproportionate effect if the right to convert must be exercised within a relatively short period and it is likely that some shareholders will convert and others will not, taking into account factors such as the dividend rate and market conditions. If the right may be exercised over many years and the extent of conversion cannot be predicted, the corporation probably can establish that the distribution will not have a disproportionate effect. Reg. § 1.305–6(a)(2).

> **Example:**   X Corp. has only common stock outstanding. It declares a convertible dividend payable in a new issue of preferred stock convertible into common for a period of 20 years. If the corporation can show that it is impossible to predict the extent to which the preferred will be converted, the distribution will not be taxable. If, however, the preferred were convertible over a short period of time and, on the facts, it was likely that some shareholders would convert while others would sell their stock, the distribution is taxable because it results in the receipt of cash by some shareholders and an increase in the proportionate interests of others. Reg. § 1.305–6(b) Examples (1), (2).

f. Deemed Stock Distributions

1) In General

Many transactions that are not distributions in form have the effect of increasing the proportionate interests of one group of shareholders while other shareholders are receiving cash or other property. Because these transactions may have the same effect as the taxable stock distributions described in § 305(b), § 305(c) and the regulations treat them as § 301 distributions to the shareholders whose equity interests have been increased. A few basic deemed distributions are illustrated below.

2) Change in Conversion Ratio

A "conversion ratio" is the rate at which a security may be converted into a security of another class. Most convertible securities have an "antidilution provision" which prevents the dilution that otherwise would result from stock dividends or splits on the security into which the convertible security may be converted. Changes in a conversion ratio to prevent dilution are not deemed stock distributions under § 305(c), but a conversion ratio adjustment that has the effect of increasing the proportionate interest of a class of shareholders will be treated as a taxable stock distribution.

> **Example:** X Corp. has two classes of common stock outstanding: Class A and Class B. Both classes have the same rights to earnings and assets. Each share of Class B stock is convertible into one share of Class A stock. If cash dividends are paid on Class A stock, the Class B conversion ratio is increased. X declares a cash dividend of $10 per share on the Class A stock and simultaneously increases the Class B conversion ratio so that each share of Class B stock is convertible into 1.05 shares of Class A. The increase in conversion ratio of the Class B stock is a § 305(c) deemed distribution to the Class B shareholders because their proportionate interest in the corporation has been increased while the Class A shareholders receive cash. Reg. § 1.305–3(e) Example (7).

3) **Dividend Equivalent Periodic Redemption Plans**
    If a redemption pursuant to an ongoing plan is treated as a § 301 distribution and has the effect of increasing the proportionate interests of other shareholders, the corporation is deemed to have made a stock distribution to the shareholders whose interests have been increased. Reg. § 1.305–7(a). An "isolated" redemption, however, even if it is treated as a dividend, will not cause § 305 to apply to those shareholders who have increased their proportionate interests. Reg. § 1.305–3(b)(3).

    > **Example (1):** X Corp. has one class of common stock outstanding, owned by five equal related shareholders. X adopts an annual redemption plan that enables shareholders to sell a limited amount of their stock back to the company. Pursuant to the plan, X distributes cash in redemption of a portion of the stock held by two shareholders. The redemptions are treated as § 301 distributions. The three shareholders whose stock is not redeemed increase their proportionate interests in X as a result of the redemptions of the others. The nonredeemed shareholders are treated as having received stock distributions to which § 305(b)(2) and § 301 apply. Rev.Rul. 78–60, 1978–1 C.B. 81. For the method of computing the amount of the deemed distribution, see Reg. § 1.305–3(e) Examples (8) and (9).

    > **Example (2):** Same facts as Example (1), except the redemptions are not pursuant to a periodic plan but rather are made to shift control from older to younger shareholders. Because this is an "isolated" redemption, § 305(b)(2) does not apply to the shareholders whose proportionate interests have increased.

g. **Basis and Holding Period**

The basis to a shareholder who receives a taxable stock dividend is the fair market value of the distributed stock. § 301(d). The holding period of the stock commences as of the date of the distribution.

h. **Consequences to the Distributing Corporation**

The distributing corporation recognizes no gain or loss on a taxable stock distribution. § 311(a)(1). The corporation may reduce its E & P by the fair market value of the distributed stock. Reg. § 1.312–1(d).

4. **Distributions of Stock Rights**
   a. **"Rights" Defined**

   "Rights" are options to purchase shares from an issuing corporation at a fixed price during a relatively short period of time.

   b. **Nontaxable Rights**
      1) In General

         A distribution by a corporation of rights to acquire its stock is generally not includible in gross income unless the distribution has one of the effects described in § 305(b)—e.g., some shareholders get cash while others receive rights that have the effect of increasing their proportionate interest in earnings and assets.

      2) Allocation of Basis

         If a distribution of rights is nontaxable and the rights are later exercised or sold, § 307(a) requires an allocation of basis between the underlying stock and the rights in proportion to their relative fair market values on the date of distribution. If the rights are exercised, the basis allocated to the rights is added to the cost of the new stock acquired. If the rights lapse, no loss may be recognized and the underlying stock retains its same basis. Reg. § 1.307–1(a).

      3) De Minimis Rule

         Rights take a zero basis if their fair market value is less than 15% of the stock with respect to which they were distributed unless the shareholder elects to use the allocation method prescribed by § 307(a). § 307(b).

      4) Holding Period

         The holding period of nontaxable rights includes the holding period of the underlying stock. § 1223(5).

   c. **Taxable Rights**

      Taxable rights are treated as § 301 distributions. § 305(b). As such, assuming they have a value, they are taxed as dividends to the extent of the distributing corporation's E & P. The basis of taxable rights is their fair market value on the date of the distribution, and the shareholder's holding period begins as of that date. A lapse of taxable rights results in a deductible loss.

B.   Section 306 Stock

1.   The Preferred Stock Bailout

a.   Background

The "preferred stock bailout" was a device used by shareholders prior to 1954 to withdraw corporate earnings at then very favorable long-term capital gains rates. A profitable corporation would make a tax-free distribution of preferred stock to its common shareholders. The shareholders then sold the preferred stock to an investor, reporting a long-term capital gain. In computing the gain, a portion of the shareholder's basis in the common was allocated to the preferred. The corporation later redeemed the preferred stock from the investor. The net effect was that the shareholders received cash without reducing their proportionate interest in the corporation—the essence of a dividend. The Service contended that the preferred stock dividend was taxable on these facts, but its argument was rejected in *Chamberlin v. Comm'r,* 207 F.2d 462 (6th Cir.1953), cert. denied, 347 U.S. 918, 74 S.Ct. 516 (1954). Congress responded by enacting § 306.

b.   Overview of § 306

Congress decided not to tax the receipt of a preferred stock dividend but rather to identify stock with bailout potential, label it as "§ 306 stock," and generally require a shareholder to recognize ordinary income rather than capital gain on a sale, redemption or other disposition of the stock. Another disadvantage of § 306 treatment is that a shareholder may not offset her stock basis against the amount realized on a disposition of § 306 stock. Exceptions are provided for dispositions, such as a complete termination of a shareholder's interest in the corporation, that do not have bailout potential.

2.   Definition of § 306 Stock

a.   In General

The principal category of § 306 stock is preferred stock distributed to a shareholder as a tax-free stock dividend under § 305(a). Common stock is not included because it participates in corporate growth and thus lacks bailout potential. § 306(c)(1)(A). If stock has either a limited right to dividends or a limited right to assets upon liquidation, it is not "common" stock for this purpose. Rev.Rul. 79–163, 1979–1 C.B. 131. Voting common stock that is subject to the issuing corporation's right of first refusal at net book value is "common" stock. Rev.Rul. 76–386, 1976–2 C.B. 95.

b.   No Earnings and Profits

Section 306 stock does not include stock distributed by a corporation with no current or accumulated E & P for the year of the distribution. The test is whether no part of a tax-free stock distribution would have been a dividend if cash had been distributed instead of stock. § 306(c)(2). If even a small part of a cash distribution would have been a dividend, then all the stock is § 306 stock.

> **Example:**   X Corp., a calendar year taxpayer, makes a tax-free distribution of preferred stock with a value of $25,000 to its common shareholders on July 1. X has no accumulated E & P. On July 1, X has $10,000 current E & P, but by the end of the year it has a $1,000 current E & P deficit. The preferred stock is not § 306 stock because a distribution of cash in lieu of the stock would not have been a dividend. If X had ended the year with $20 of current E & P, however, all the preferred stock would be § 306 stock.

c.   **Stock With Transferred or Substituted Basis**
Section 306 stock includes stock which has a transferred or exchanged basis determined by reference to the basis of § 306 stock. § 306(c)(1)(C). Examples include stock received as a gift (with a § 1015 transferred basis from the donor), or stock (of whatever class) received in exchange for § 306 stock in a tax-free § 351 transaction. The § 306 taint is removed on the death of a shareholder, however, because the stock will take a date-of-death basis under § 1014.

> **Example (1):**   Parent gives 100 shares of X Corp. preferred stock, which is § 306 stock to Child. The stock remains § 306 stock in Child's hands. If Parent were to die and bequeath the stock to Child, it would no longer be § 306 stock.

> **Example (2):**   A transfers 100 shares of X Corp. preferred stock, which is § 306 stock, to Y Corp. in exchange for 100 shares of Y Corp. common stock in a transaction that qualifies as tax-free under § 351(a). The X Corp. preferred stock (which has a § 362(a) transferred basis) and the Y Corp. common stock (which has a substituted basis determined by reference to the Y Corp. stock under § 358(a)) are each § 306 stock.

d.   **Stock Received in a Reorganization or Division**
Stock other than common stock which is received in a tax-free corporate reorganization or division is § 306 stock if the effect of the transaction is substantially the same as receipt of a stock dividend, or if the stock was received in exchange for § 306 stock. § 306(c)(1)(B). This aspect of § 306 is discussed in the context of reorganizations (see XI.B.7.b.4, at page 257, *infra*) and divisions (see Chapter XII, *infra*).

e.   **Certain Stock Acquired in § 351 Exchange**
Preferred stock acquired in a § 351 exchange is § 306 stock if the receipt of money instead of the stock would have been treated as a dividend to any

extent. § 306(c)(3). In determining whether the receipt of money would have been equivalent to a dividend, rules similar to those in § 304 (dealing with redemptions through the use of related corporations) are applied. See § 304(b)(3), discussed at VII.E.4.a., at page 165, *supra*. This exception is intended to prevent shareholders from avoiding § 306 by contributing common stock of a profitable company to a newly organized holding company (with no E & P) in a § 351 transaction in exchange for common and preferred stock of the holding company. Such preferred stock has bailout potential but, without a special rule, it would not be § 306 stock because the holding company has no E & P.

> ***Example:*** A is the sole common shareholder of X Corp., which has ample E & P. A transfers her X common stock to newly formed Y Corp. in exchange for Y common and preferred stock. The Y preferred stock will be § 306 stock because a transfer of cash to A in lieu of the preferred stock would have been treated as a dividend under § 304(a)(1). In applying § 304, recall that even if the acquiring corporation (Y) has no E & P, the E & P of the issuing corporation (X) may result in dividend treatment. § 304(b)(2)(B). See VII.E., at page 160, *supra*.

3. Dispositions of § 306 Stock
a. Redemptions

If § 306 stock is redeemed, the amount realized by the redeemed shareholder is treated as a distribution to which § 301 applies and thus is taxable as a dividend to the extent of the corporation's current or accumulated E & P at the time of the redemption. § 306(a)(2). The balance, if any, of the amount realized is first treated as a reduction of basis and then, if necessary, as capital gain under the rules generally applicable to distributions. See VI.A.3.d., at page 132, *supra*.

> ***Example:*** X Corp. makes a tax-free distribution of preferred stock with a value of $20,000 to its sole common shareholder, A. X has $5,000 of E & P at the time of the distribution. A's allocable basis in the preferred stock (which is § 306 stock) is $10,000. Two years later, X redeems A's preferred stock for $20,000, at a time when X has $30,000 of E & P. A continues to own 100% of X's common stock. The entire $20,000 amount realized on the redemption is a dividend. A's basis in the preferred stock probably is added back to the basis of A's common stock. If X had no E & P at the time of the redemption, the entire $20,000 would be a return of capital under § 301(c)(2). A probably could reduce his basis in both the preferred and the common stock before recognizing any gain under § 301(c)(3).

b. Sales and Other Dispositions

On a sale or other disposition of § 306 stock, the amount realized is first treated as ordinary income to the extent of the stock's "ratable share" of the amount that would have been a dividend at the time of the distribution if cash rather than stock had been distributed. The ordinary income is not considered a dividend, and thus corporate shareholders are not allowed a § 243 dividends received deduction, and the corporation may not reduce its E & P. Reg. § 1.306–1(b)(1). The balance, if any, of the amount realized first reduces the basis of the § 306 stock, and any excess is treated as gain from the sale or exchange of the stock. § 306(a)(1)(B). No loss may be recognized on a disposition of § 306 stock, but any unrecovered basis is allocated back to the stock with respect to which the § 306 stock was distributed. § 306(a)(1)(C); Reg. § 1.306–1(b)(2) Examples (2), (3).

Example (1):   X Corp. makes a tax-free distribution of preferred stock with a value of $20,000 to its sole common shareholder, A. X has $50,000 of E & P at the time of the distribution. A's allocable basis in the preferred stock (which is § 306 stock) is $2,000. Two years later, at a time when X has no E & P, A sells the § 306 stock for $24,000. Of this amount, $20,000 is treated as ordinary income; this is the amount that would have been a taxable dividend if cash rather than stock had been distributed at the time of the distribution. Of the balance, $2,000 is a reduction of A's basis in the preferred stock, and $2,000 is treated as gain from a sale of the stock.

Example (2):   If X's E & P in Example (1) had been $8,000 at the time of the distribution, only $8,000 of A's amount realized on the sale of the § 306 stock is ordinary income; $2,000 is a reduction of basis; and $14,000 is treated as gain from a sale of the stock.

Example (3):   Same facts as Example (1), except A sells the § 306 stock for $21,000. Of this amount, $20,000 is treated as ordinary income and $1,000 is a reduction of A's $2,000 basis in the preferred stock. No loss will be allowed. A may add the remaining $1,000 basis in the preferred back to his basis in the X common stock. Reg. § 1.306–1(b)(2) Example (2).

c. Exempt Dispositions
Four types of dispositions are exempted from the punitive general rule of § 306(a) because they do not present any opportunity for a bailout.

1) Complete Terminations and Partial Liquidations
A disposition of § 306 stock in a transaction (other than a redemption) that terminates the shareholder's entire stock interest in the corporation is exempt if the shareholder does not transfer the stock to a § 318 related person or entity. § 306(b)(1)(A)(i), (ii). In determining whether the shareholder has completely terminated her interest, the § 318 attribution rules apply. § 306(b)(1)(A)(iii). Redemptions of § 306 stock that result in a

complete termination of the shareholder's interest under § 302(b)(3) or qualify as a partial liquidation under § 302(b)(4) also are exempt. § 306(b)(1)(B).

> ***Example:***   A owns 500 shares of X Corp. common stock and 250 shares of X Corp. preferred stock, which is § 306 stock. She owns no X stock constructively. A sells all of her common and preferred stock to an unrelated person. A's sale of the preferred stock is not subject to § 306(a) because she completely terminates her interest in the corporation.

2) Complete Liquidations

Section 306(a) does not apply to a redemption of § 306 stock in a complete liquidation. § 306(b)(2).

3) Nonrecognition Transactions

Dispositions that qualify for nonrecognition treatment, such as § 351 transfers, contributions to capital and tax-free exchanges of stock under § 1036, are exempt. § 306(b)(3). Any stock received in a tax-free exchange, however, becomes § 306 stock. § 306(c)(1)(C).

4) Transactions Not in Avoidance of Tax

Section 306(a) does not apply if the taxpayer satisfies the Service that either: (a) the distribution and the subsequent disposition or redemption of § 306 stock, or (b) in the case of a prior or simultaneous disposition (or redemption) of the underlying stock with respect to which the § 306 stock was issued, the disposition or redemption of the § 306 stock was not made pursuant to a plan having federal tax avoidance as one of its principal purposes. § 306(b)(4). The Service has ruled that § 306(b)(4) relief is not automatically available on dispositions of preferred stock of widely held corporations. Rev. Rul. 89–63, 1989–1 C.B. 90.

> ***Example (1):***   Minority Shareholder, who holds both common and preferred (§ 306) stock in X Corp., sells her § 306 stock in an isolated transaction. The sale qualifies for relief under § 306(b)(4)(A) unless (unlikely on these facts) the distribution of the § 306 stock and Minority Shareholder's sale were pursuant to a tax avoidance plan. Reg. § 1.306–2(b)(3).

> ***Example (2):***   In year 1, A receives a distribution of 100 shares of preferred (§ 306) stock with respect to her holding of 100 shares of common stock of X Corp. In year 3, A sells all her common stock. In year 4, A sells all her § 306 stock but continues to own X Corp. common stock by § 318

attribution. A's disposition of her § 306 stock ordinarily is not considered a tax avoidance transaction because she previously disposed of the common stock that allowed her to participate in the ownership and growth of the business. § 306(b)(4)(B); Reg. § 1.306–2(b)(3).

Example (3):   Same as Example (2), above, except A only sold 50 shares of her common stock in year 3 and, although she substantially reduced her proportionate interest in the common stock, A retained effective control pursuant to X Corp.'s bylaws. A is not entitled to relief on the disposition of her § 306 stock because she retained effective control of the corporation. *Fireoved v. U.S*, 462 F.2d 1281 (3d Cir. 1972).

Example (4):   Same as Example (2), above, except A simultaneously sold 50 shares of her common stock and 50 shares of her § 306 stock in year 3, and she did not retain effective control of the corporation. Absent any facts indicating a tax avoidance plan, A's sale of the § 306 stock should qualify for relief under § 306(b)(4)(B). But see Rev. Rul. 75–247, 1975–1 C.B. 104, holding that a similar simultaneous disposition did not, in itself, establish the requisite non-tax avoidance purpose.

C.   Review Questions

1. Why do "common on common" and "preferred on common" stock distributions made by a corporation with no other classes of stock outstanding qualify as tax-free distributions?

2. X Corp. distributes one share of nonconvertible $10 preferred stock for every 10 shares of common held by its shareholders. X has 1,000 shares of common stock outstanding. A owns 100 shares of common with a basis of $1,000 and receives 10 shares of preferred with a value of $100 after the distribution. The value of A's common stock after the distribution is $1,900. X has $100,000 of current and no accumulated E & P at the end of the year in which the distribution takes place. What are the tax consequences of the distribution to A and X Corp.?

3. Assume the same facts as in question 2, above, except that the shareholders have the option of taking cash in lieu of the preferred stock. If none of the X shareholders exercise this option, what are the tax consequences of the distribution to A?

4. Assume the same facts as in question 2, above, except that some of the X shareholders receive common stock and others receive preferred stock. Assume that

A receives preferred stock. In general, what are the tax consequences of the distribution to A?

5. Using the same facts as in question 2, above, assume that A sells all of her preferred stock for $250 one year after the distribution. What are the tax consequences of the sale to A?

6. Same facts as question 5, above, except that A sells all the preferred stock for $80.

7. Same facts as question 5, above, except that A previously sold all of her common stock and now sells all her preferred for $250.

*

IX

COMPLETE LIQUIDATIONS AND TAXABLE CORPORATE ACQUISITIONS

Analysis

A. Complete Liquidation Defined

On a complete liquidation, a corporation distributes all of its assets (or the proceeds of their sale), subject to any liabilities, to its shareholders in exchange for all their stock. The corporation then dissolves under state law. A corporation liquidates for tax purposes when it ceases to be a going concern and its activities are merely for the purpose of winding up its affairs, paying its debts and distributing any remaining balance to its shareholders. Cf. Reg. § 1.332–2(c). Legal dissolution under state law is not required for a liquidation to be complete, and the corporation may retain a nominal amount of assets to pay remaining debts and preserve its legal existence. Rev.Rul. 54–518, 1954–2 C.B. 142.

A complete liquidation typically is evidenced by a formal "plan," which may be nothing more than a shareholders' or directors' resolution stating the corporation's intention to liquidate. Even in the absence of a formal written plan, an informal plan of liquidation may be found to exist when the shareholders or directors manifest their intent to liquidate the corporation.

B. Complete Liquidations Under § 331

1. Consequences to the Shareholders
a. Recognition of Gain or Loss
1) General Rule
Amounts distributed to a shareholder in complete liquidation are treated as in full payment in exchange for the shareholder's stock. § 331(a). The difference between the amount realized and the shareholder's adjusted basis in the stock is treated as capital gain or loss in the usual case where the stock is a capital asset. The shareholder's amount realized is the amount of money and the fair market value of all other property received from the liquidating corporation, less any liabilities assumed by the shareholder or encumbering the distributed property.

2) Different Blocks of Stock
A shareholder who holds several blocks of stock with different bases and acquisition dates determines his gain or loss separately for each block rather than on an aggregate basis. Reg. § 1.331–1(e).

Example: A holds 40 shares of X Corp. stock short-term with a $50,000 basis and 60 shares long-term with a $30,000 basis. X distributes $100,000 to A in complete liquidation. A allocates the $100,000 distribution pro rata between the two blocks of stock and recognizes $10,000 of short-term capital loss ($50,000 basis less $40,000 amount realized) on the 40 shares and $30,000 of long-term capital gain ($60,000 amount realized less $30,000 basis) on the 60 shares.

3) Series of Distributions

A distribution in complete liquidation includes one of a series of distributions in redemption of all the stock of a corporation pursuant to a plan. § 346(a). If liquidating distributions are made in two or more taxable years, the Service permits the shareholders first to recover their basis before recognizing any gain or loss. Rev.Rul. 85–48, 1985–1 C.B. 126. If a distribution is made before liquidation status exists, it will be treated as a nonliquidating distribution (and thus potentially a dividend) under § 301. This risk is eliminated by adopting a formal plan of liquidation before making the first of a series of liquidating distributions.

Example: A has a $30,000 basis in 100 shares of X Corp., which adopts a plan of complete liquidation in Year 1. X distributes $30,000 in Year 1 and $20,000 in Year 2. A may recover her entire $30,000 basis before reporting any gain. She thus has no gain in Year 1 and $20,000 long-term capital gain in Year 2. If X did not adopt a plan of liquidation in Year 1, there is a risk that the Year 1 distribution will be classified as a § 301 distribution.

4) Distribution of Disputed and Contingent Claims

If a liquidating corporation distributes disputed or contingent claims that do not have a readily ascertainable fair market value, the shareholder may be able to treat the liquidation as an "open transaction" and defer including these assets in the amount realized until their value is ascertainable. Open transaction treatment is limited, however, to "rare and extraordinary" cases. Rev.Rul. 58–402, 1958–2 C.B. 15; see also Reg. § 15A.453–1(d)(2)(iii). Treating the transaction as open rather than closed affects both the timing and character of the shareholder's gain or loss.

Example (1):   Pursuant to a plan of complete liquidation in Year 1, X Corp. distributes to its sole shareholder, A, $20,000 cash, $50,000 in tangible assets, and a disputed claim against B in the amount of $50,000 but with an uncertain value. A has an $80,000 basis in his X stock. Under the open transaction method, A has no gain in Year 1 because the $70,000 of distributed cash and property does not exceed A's basis in the stock. The claim is not included in A's amount realized until it is collected or has an ascertainable value. If A collects $40,000 on the claim in Year 3, he would recognize $30,000 LTCG ($110,000 total distributions less $80,000 basis) at that time.

Example (2):   Same as Example (1), except the disputed claim is valued at $25,000 when it is distributed to A in Year 1, but A collects the full $40,000 in Year 3. The transaction must be closed in Year 1 because the claim has an ascertainable value. A recognizes $15,000 LTCG ($95,000 total distributions less $80,000 basis) on the liquidation, and takes a $25,000 basis in the claim under § 334(a). A recognizes $15,000 ($40,000 received less $25,000 basis) on collection of the claim; the gain is ordinary income because a collection is not a sale or exchange.

5) Installment Sale Reporting

If a liquidating corporation sells assets on the installment method to a person who is not "related" within the meaning of § 1239(b) and then distributes the installment obligations to its shareholders, the shareholders may report their § 331(a) gain on the installment method. Installment sale reporting is accomplished by treating the shareholders' receipt of payments on the installment obligations as if they were payments in exchange for their stock. § 453(h)(1)(A). The installment obligations must have been acquired by the corporation in respect of a sale or exchange of property during the 12 months beginning on the date of adoption of a plan of complete liquidation, and the liquidation must be completed within that 12–month period. Installment obligations arising from the sale of inventory do not qualify for deferral unless substantially all of the inventory is sold to one person in one transaction. § 453(h)(1)(B). Installment sale treatment is not available, however, on a liquidation of a publicly traded corporation (§ 453(k)(2)) or if the shareholder elects out of § 453 (§ 453(d)).

Example: A is the sole shareholder of X Corp. and has a $20,000 basis in his X stock (held long-term). X's only asset is undeveloped land with a value of $50,000. In Year 1, X adopts a liquidation plan and sells the land to an unrelated buyer for $10,000 cash and a $40,000 installment note payable in Year 4. Within 12 months of the adoption of the plan, X distributes the $10,000 cash and $40,000 note to A in complete liquidation. (Ignore any corporate tax liability that X may have incurred.) A's $30,000 gain may be reported on the installment method. A's gross profit is $30,000, the total contract price is $50,000, and thus ⅗, or 60%, of each payment is long-term capital gain. § 453(c). A recognizes $6,000 gain in Year 1 and the remaining $24,000 in Year 4 when the note is paid.

b. **Basis of Distributed Property**

The basis of property received by a shareholder on a § 331 complete liquidation is the fair market value of the property on the date of distribution, without reduction for any liabilities to which the property is subject. § 334(a).

2. Consequences to the Distributing Corporation
a. Background

1) *General Utilities* Doctrine

Under the *General Utilities* doctrine, a corporation did not recognize gain or loss on a nonliquidating distribution of property even though the shareholder took a fair market value basis in the distributed property. See VI.D.1.a., at page 136, *supra*. This doctrine, which also applied to liquidating distributions, was once codified in § 336(a). Prior to 1954, however, *sales* of assets by a liquidating corporation were fully taxable.

2) *Court Holding* Doctrine

Because of the disparate tax treatment of liquidating distributions (nontaxable) and sales (taxable) prior to 1954, *corporate*-level gain on the sale of a business could be avoided by a tax-free distribution in kind to the shareholders, who would take the assets with a fair market value basis and then sell them to the buyer without recognizing gain on the sale. In contrast, a corporation recognized gain when it sold an asset and then distributed the proceeds in complete liquidation. (In either case, the shareholders would recognize gain or loss on their stock.) If the sale were negotiated by the corporation but formally consummated by the shareholders, controversies arose over whether in substance the sale had been made by the corporation or the shareholders. Compare *Comm'r v. Court Holding Co.,* 324 U.S. 331, 65 S.Ct. 707 (1945) (sale attributed to corporation under step transaction doctrine) with *U.S. v. Cumberland Public Service Co.,* 338 U.S. 451, 70 S.Ct. 280 (1950) (sale made by shareholders rather than corporation).

3) Former §§ 336 and 337

In response to the disparate results under the pre–1954 law, Congress enacted former § 337, which extended the *General Utilities* doctrine to most liquidating sales and made it unnecessary to determine whether the corporation or the shareholders made the sale. Under former §§ 336 and 337, a corporation generally did not recognize gain on either a distribution of property in complete liquidation or a sale pursuant to a complete liquidation plan. Exceptions were provided for recapture income, certain sales of inventory and tax benefit items.

4) *General Utilities* Repeal

After chipping away at the *General Utilities* doctrine over many years, Congress rejected it completely in 1986 by repealing old §§ 336 and 337.

b. Recognition of Gain or Loss

Under current law, a corporation recognizes gain or loss when it distributes property in complete liquidation as if it had sold the property to the distributee for its fair market value. § 336(a). Gain or loss is determined separately on each asset. If the distributed property is subject to a liability or a shareholder assumes a corporate liability in connection with the distribution, the fair market value of the property is treated as not less than the amount of the liability. § 336(b).

Example (1):   A is the sole shareholder of X Corp., whose only asset is land with an adjusted basis of $40,000 and a fair market value of $100,000. X recognizes $60,000 gain if it distributes the land to A in complete liquidation.

Example (2):   Same as Example (1), except the fair market value of the land is only $80,000 but it is subject to a $100,000 mortgage. For purposes of determining the gain under § 336(a), the land is treated as having a fair market value of not less than the $100,000 liability. X thus recognizes $60,000 gain on a distribution of the land in complete liquidation.

c. Limitations on Recognition of Loss

Losses on transactions between related taxpayers generally are disallowed under § 267(a)(1), but § 267 does not apply to any loss realized by a distributing corporation (or distributee shareholder) on a distribution in complete liquidation. Section 336(d), however, limits the recognition of loss by the distributing corporation in the three situations described below.

1) Distributions to Related Persons

A liquidating corporation may not recognize loss on the distribution of any property to a § 267 "related person" if the distribution is not pro rata or is of "disqualified property" as defined in § 336(d)(1)(B).

a) Related Person

An individual shareholder is "related" to a corporation under § 267(b)(2) if the shareholder owns directly or indirectly (through attribution rules in § 267(c)) more than 50% in value of the corporation's outstanding stock.

b) Non Pro Rata

A distribution of loss property is non pro rata for purposes of § 336(d)(1)(A)(i) if it is not distributed to the shareholders in the same proportion as their stock ownership in the corporation.

c) Disqualified Property

"Disqualified property" is any property acquired by the liquidating corporation in a § 351 transaction or as a contribution to capital during the 5–year period ending on the date of the distribution. § 336(d)(1)(B).

Example (1): X Corp. has 100 outstanding shares, of which A owns 60 and B owns 40. A and B are unrelated. X's only assets are Gainacre (basis–$10,000; value–$40,000), Lossacre (basis–$80,000; value $40,000), and $20,000 cash. Both parcels were acquired by X more than five years ago and thus neither is "disqualified property." X adopts a plan of complete liquidation and distributes 60% of each asset to A and 40% of each asset to B. Because the distribution is pro rata, § 336(d)(1) does not apply, and X recognizes $30,000 gain on Gainacre and $40,000 loss on Lossacre.

Example (2): Same as Example (1), except X distributes Lossacre and the cash to A and Gainacre to B. X recognizes $30,000 gain on Gainacre, but it may not recognize the $40,000 loss because Lossacre was distributed to A, a related person, and the distribution was not pro rata.

Example (3): Same as Example (1), except X distributes Gainacre and the cash to A and Lossacre to B. X recognizes $30,000 gain on Gainacre and $40,000 loss on Lossacre. Although Lossacre is not distributed pro rata, B is not a related person and thus § 336(d)(1)(A) does not apply.

Example (4): Same as Example (1), except that X acquired Lossacre three years ago in a § 351 transaction at a time when the fair market value of Lossacre exceeded its basis. Although the distribution is pro rata, Lossacre is "disqualified property" and X may not recognize the $24,000 loss on the 60% interest in Lossacre that it distributes to A, a related person. X may recognize the $16,000 loss on the distribution of the 40% interest to B because B is not a related person. It is irrelevant under § 336(d)(1) that Lossacre had no built-in loss when it was contributed to X.

2) Property Acquired for Tax Avoidance Purpose
   a) General Rule
      Section 336(d)(2) limits recognition of loss if property distributed, sold or exchanged by a liquidating corporation was acquired in a § 351 transaction or as a contribution to capital as part of a plan the principal purpose of which was to recognize loss by the liquidating corporation in connection with the liquidation. Section 336(d)(2) only disallows the loss that accrued before the corporation acquired the

property. This is accomplished by a rule that requires the corporation to reduce its basis for determining loss (but not below zero) by the precontribution built-in loss—i.e., the excess of the adjusted basis of the property when it was acquired over the fair market value of the property at that time.

b) **Plans to Recognize Loss**

Except as provided by regulations, any property acquired by the liquidating corporation after a date that is two years before the adoption of the liquidation plan (or after the adoption of that plan) is treated as acquired as part of a plan to recognize loss. § 336(d)(2)(B)(ii). No regulations have yet been issued, but Congress indicated in the legislative history that this presumption will be limited to cases where there is no clear and substantial relationship between the contributed property and the conduct of the corporation's current or future business. Only in "rare and unusual cases" will a tax avoidance plan be found if the property is contributed more than two years before the adoption of the liquidation plan. See H.R.Rep. No. 99–841, 99th Cong., 2d Sess. II–200–201 (1986).

c) **Recapture in Lieu of Disallowance**

Section 336(d)(2) is broad enough to apply to a disposition of property in a taxable year ending prior to the year in which the liquidation plan is adopted. If the corporation deducted the loss in the prior year and it is later disallowed, the Service may permit the corporation to "recapture" the disallowed loss by treating it as income in the later year in lieu of filing an amended return for the year the loss was reported. § 336(d)(2)(C).

d) **Overlap with Section 336(d)(1)**

If both §§ 336(d)(1) and (2) apply to the same transaction, § 336(d)(1) takes precedence.

> ***Example (1):*** X Corp. has 100 outstanding shares, of which A owns 60 and B owns 40. X's only assets are Gainacre (basis–$10,000; value–$40,000), Lossacre (basis–$70,000; value–$40,000), and $20,000 cash. Lossacre, which has no relationship to X's business, was contributed to X in a § 351 transaction one year ago when it had a value of $60,000 and a basis of $70,000. X adopts a plan of complete liquidation and distributes Gainacre and the cash to A and Lossacre to B. Because Lossacre was contributed to X less than two years prior to the adoption of the liquidation plan and has no relationship to X's business, it is

presumed to have been contributed in a plan to recognize loss. X must reduce its adjusted basis by $10,000 (the built-in loss when X acquired Lossacre) and recognizes only a $20,000 loss ($60,000 basis less $40,000 value) on the distribution. Section 336(d)(1) does not apply because the distribution was not made to a related person.

Example (2):   Same as Example (1), except X planned to subdivide the land as part of its business. If X can show there was a clear and substantial relationship between Lossacre and its business, § 336(d)(2) will not apply and X may recognize the entire $30,000 loss on the distribution to B.

3)   Distributions in § 332 Liquidations
A liquidating corporation may not recognize loss on a distribution to a minority shareholder on a § 332 liquidation of a subsidiary and in certain other specialized situations. See IX.C.3., at page 199, *infra.*

d.   Distributions Pursuant to Reorganization Plan
Section 336 does not apply to liquidating distributions made pursuant to a tax-free reorganization plan under § 368. §§ 336(c), 361(c)(4). See XI.B.7.c., at page 257, *infra.*

C.   Liquidation of a Subsidiary

1.   Introduction
Congress views the liquidation of a subsidiary as a mere change in form. As a result, §§ 332 and 337 generally provide that neither the parent shareholder nor the liquidating subsidiary recognizes gain or loss. In keeping with the policy of nonrecognition provisions, the subsidiary's asset bases and other tax attributes (such as earnings and profits) transfer to the parent.

2.   Consequences to the Shareholders
a.   Requirements for Nonrecognition Under Section 332
A parent corporation does not recognize gain on the receipt of distributions in complete liquidation of a subsidiary if the following requirements under § 332(b) are met. § 332(a).

1)   Cancellation of Stock Pursuant to Plan
The subsidiary must distribute property to its parent in complete cancellation or redemption of its stock pursuant to a plan of liquidation. §§ 332(b)(2), (3).

2) Control

The parent must own at least 80% of the total voting power and 80% of the total value of all outstanding stock of the subsidiary on the date of the adoption of the plan of complete liquidation and at all times thereafter until the liquidation is completed. §§ 332(b)(1); 1504(a)(2). Certain nonvoting preferred stock is ignored for purposes of these 80% tests.

3) Timing

The distributions must occur within one taxable year (even if it is not the same year that the liquidation plan is adopted), in which case the plan need not specify when the liquidation will be complete. § 332(b)(2). Alternatively, in the case of a series of distributions, the plan must provide that all the subsidiary's property will be distributed to the parent within three years after the close of the taxable year of the subsidiary in which the first distribution is made. Failure to meet the 3–year deadline will retroactively disqualify the liquidation under § 332. § 332(b)(3). If the parties rely on the 3–year timing rule, the parent must file a waiver of the statute of limitations and may be required to post a bond. § 332(b).

4) Parent's Gain or Loss on Stock Eliminated

Section 332 has the effect of permanently eliminating the parent's "outside" gain or loss on its subsidiary's stock. The parent inherits the subsidiary's "inside" gain or loss on its assets and other tax attributes under §§ 334(b)(1) and 381.

5) Intentionally Avoiding § 332

On rare occasions, such as where the parent wishes to recognize a current loss on its stock in the subsidiary or avoid inheriting the subsidiary's E & P, the parties may attempt to avoid § 332 by intentionally violating one of its requirements. One avoidance technique that has been upheld by the courts is the sale of sufficient stock after the adoption of a liquidation plan to bring the parent's ownership below 80%. *Comm'r v. Day & Zimmermann, Inc.*, 151 F.2d 517 (3d Cir.1945).

6) Backing Into Control

A controlling corporation that does not meet the 80% control test may seek to qualify under § 332 by acquiring more stock or by causing the subsidiary to redeem stock held by minority shareholders shortly before a liquidation. If the sale or redemption occurs prior to the adoption of a liquidation plan, this technique has been upheld. See *George L. Riggs, Inc. v. Comm'r*, 64 T.C. 474 (1975); Rev.Rul. 75–521, 1975–2 C.B. 120. A possible risk is that the Service may determine that control is lacking because the acquisition or redemption was part of an integrated liquidation plan that was adopted before the parent had 80% control. See Rev.Rul. 70–106, 1970–1 C.B. 70.

7) Subsidiary Insolvent

If a liquidating subsidiary is insolvent and the parent receives nothing in exchange for its common stock, § 332 does not apply. In that case, the parent shareholder may take a worthless security deduction on its common stock under § 165(g)(2) unless the stock became worthless in a prior year. Because the corporations are "affiliated," the deduction likely is an ordinary loss. § 165(g)(3). *H.K. Porter Co., Inc. v. Comm'r,* 87 T.C. 689 (1986).

b. Basis and Holding Period of Distributed Property

The parent corporation takes a transferred basis and a tacked holding period in any property received from the subsidiary in a § 332 liquidation. § 334(b)(1).

c. Treatment of Minority Shareholders

Even if a liquidation qualifies under § 332, minority shareholders recognize gain or loss under the general rule in § 331(a) and take a fair market value basis in any distributed property under § 334(a).

Example: P Corp. owns 90% of the stock of S Corp. and has a $20,000 basis in its S stock. The remaining 10% of S is owned by individual ("I"), who has a $3,000 basis in her S stock. S's only assets are $10,000 cash and Gainacre (value–$90,000, basis–$40,000). S adopts a plan of complete liquidation and distributes Gainacre to P and the cash to I. P recognizes no gain on the liquidation, but I recognizes $7,000 LTCG. P takes a $40,000 transferred basis in Gainacre. P's basis in its S stock disappears, and its $70,000 realized gain on its S stock is never recognized.

d. Carryover of Tax Attributes

On a § 332 liquidation, the liquidating subsidiary's tax attributes (e.g., earnings and profits, net operating loss carryovers) carry over to the parent subject to certain limitations in § 381. See Chapter XIII, *infra*.

3. Consequences to the Liquidating Subsidiary

a. Distributions to Parent

A liquidating subsidiary does not recognize gain or loss on distributions of property to its parent (referred to in the Code as "the 80% distributee") in a complete liquidation to which § 332 applies. § 337(a).

b. Distributions to Minority Shareholders

The subsidiary recognizes gain but not loss on a distribution of property to a minority shareholder (i.e., a shareholder other than "the 80% distributee") in a § 332 liquidation. §§ 336(a), (d)(3).

c. Distributions to Satisfy Debt of Subsidiary to Parent

If a subsidiary owes a debt to its parent on the date of the adoption of a § 332 liquidation plan, any transfer of property by the subsidiary to satisfy the debt is treated as a distribution subject to the general nonrecognition rule of § 337(a). § 337(b)(1).

Example (1): P Corp. owns 90% of the stock of S Corp. and has a $20,000 basis in its S stock. The remaining 10% of S is owned by individual ("I"), who has a $3,000 basis in her S stock. S owes $10,000 to P. S's only assets are $10,000 cash, Gainacre (value–$90,000, basis–$30,000), and Lossacre (value–$10,000, basis–$40,000). Pursuant to a plan of complete liquidation, S distributes Gainacre to P, Lossacre to I, and S uses the $10,000 cash to satisfy its debt to P. Under § 337(a), S does not recognize gain on the distribution of Gainacre, and P takes a $30,000 transferred basis under § 334(b)(1). Under § 336(d)(3), S may not recognize loss on the distribution of Lossacre, and I takes a $10,000 fair market value basis under § 334(a). Distribution of a loss asset to a minority shareholder thus results in permanent elimination of the loss.

Example (2): Same as Example (1), except S distributes the $10,000 cash to I and distributes Lossacre to P in satisfaction of the $10,000 debt. S recognizes neither gain nor loss on the distribution of Gainacre and Lossacre, and P takes a transferred basis in each asset.

d. Distributions to Tax–Exempt and Foreign Parents

To prevent the nonrecognition provided by § 337 from becoming a permanent exemption from corporate-level tax, § 337(b)(2) provides (with specialized exceptions) that a liquidating subsidiary recognizes gain or loss on distributions of property to certain tax-exempt or foreign parent corporations. In that event, the parent takes a fair market value basis in the distributed property. § 334(b)(1).

D. Taxable Acquisitions of a Corporate Business

1. Introduction

When a corporate business is acquired, the transaction may be structured as a purchase of either the corporation's assets or the shareholder's stock. For the remainder of this chapter, a corporation whose assets or stock are acquired will be referred to as the "target," or "T," and the purchaser (usually another corporation) will be referred to as "P." This chapter discusses *taxable* acquisitions; tax-free acquisitions (known as "reorganizations") are discussed in Chapter XI, *infra*.

2. Asset Acquisitions

Asset acquisitions include T's direct sale of its assets to P or a "cash merger" of T into P (or a P subsidiary), where T's assets are automatically transferred to P (or a

P subsidiary) under state law and T's shareholders receive cash or a combination of cash and P debt obligations, and T disappears.

a. Tax Consequences to T

T recognizes gain or loss on the sale of its assets under general tax principles whether or not the sale is followed by a complete liquidation of T. P's assumption of T's liabilities is included in T's amount realized. Section 336(d)(2) may disallow precontribution built-in loss on a liquidating sale of property acquired by T in a § 351 transaction or as a contribution to capital if the property was acquired as part of a tax-avoidance plan. See IX.B.2.c., at page 194, *supra*.

b. Tax Consequences to the T Shareholders

1) T Liquidates

If T liquidates after selling its assets, T's shareholders recognize capital gain or loss on their stock under § 331(a) (see IX.B.1.a. at page 190, *supra*) unless T is an 80% or more subsidiary of another corporation (the "parent") in which case the liquidation is tax-free to the parent under § 332 and taxable to any minority shareholders under § 331(a) (see IX.C., at page 197, *supra*). In a taxable liquidation, the shareholders may defer all or part of their gain on the § 453 installment method to the extent that T sold its assets for installment obligations of the buyer and distributed those obligations to the shareholders in the liquidation. See § 453(h) and IX.B.1.a.5, at page 192, *supra*.

2) T Does Not Liquidate

If T does not liquidate after its assets are acquired, its shareholders do not recognize any gain or loss. They can avoid any shareholder-level gain by holding the stock until death, when their estate will take a stepped-up basis in the stock under § 1014. A C corporation that remains in existence as an investment company, however, is likely to be classified as a "personal holding company" and will be subject to a penalty tax if it does not distribute its net income to its shareholders. See §§ 541 et seq. and X.C., at page 219, *infra*. In view of the ongoing problem of the double tax, staying alive may be more expensive than liquidating.

c. Tax Consequences to P

P takes a § 1012 cost basis in assets that it purchases in a taxable acquisition. P's cost includes the price paid for the assets (in cash or notes) plus any T liabilities transferred to P and acquisition expenses.

d. Allocation of Purchase Price and Basis

1) In General

A sale of assets of a going business for a lump sum is treated for tax purposes as a sale of each individual asset of the business. The parties must allocate the aggregate purchase price among the assets sold. Under § 1060, which applies to any "applicable asset acquisition" including taxable corporate asset acquisitions, this allocation of total "consideration" is made using the "residual method." Reg. § 1.1060–1(a)(1). Consideration received is the seller's aggregate amount realized from the sale of its assets determined under general tax principles. Consideration paid is the buyer's aggregate cost of purchasing the assets that is properly taken into account in determining basis. Reg. § 1.1060–1(c)(1). Aggregate consideration is then allocated by assigning all "acquisition date assets" among seven classes and allocating the consideration among those classes in a prescribed order. Reg. § 1.1060–1(c)(2), incorporating by reference Reg. § 1.338–6. No asset in any class (except the final "residual" category) is allocated more than its fair market value. Reg. § 1.338–6(c)(1).

2)   Applying the Residual Method of Allocation

In applying the residual method of allocation, the "consideration" is first reduced by cash and cash equivalents (known as "Class I acquisition date assets") transferred by the seller. Reg. § 1.338–6(b)(1). The remaining consideration then is allocated first to highly liquid assets, such as certificates of deposit, U.S. Government and other marketable securities ("Class II assets") in proportion to their gross fair market values, then to accounts receivable, mortgages and credit card receivables (Class III), then to inventory and other dealer-type property (Class IV), then to all assets other than those in the preceding categories (Class V, which includes most tangible assets such as equipment and real estate), then to § 197 intangibles, excluding goodwill and going concern value (Class VI) to the extent of their fair market values, and finally any remaining consideration is allocated to goodwill and going concern value (Class VII). Reg. § 1.338–6(b)(2).

Example: On July 1 of the current year, P purchases all of T's assets for $300,000. T's assets include: $20,000 cash; marketable securities (value–$50,000); land and building (value–$100,000); and a § 197 intangible asset (value–$40,000). Total consideration of $300,000 is first reduced by the $20,000 cash to $280,000 and then allocated $50,000 to Class II assets (the securities), $100,000 to Class III assets (land and building), $40,000 to Class VI assets (the § 197 intangible), and the $90,000 "residue" to Class VII (goodwill and going concern value).

3.   Stock Acquisitions

Stock acquisitions include P's purchase of T stock directly from T's shareholders or a "reverse cash merger" in which T merges into a subsidiary of P and T's shareholders receive cash or a combination of cash and P notes.

a. Background

An acquisition of T stock for cash or notes of P is a taxable event to the selling T shareholders, who recognize capital gain or loss. P takes a cost basis in the acquired T stock. The difficult conceptual questions are whether T also should recognize corporate-level gain or loss and whether the basis of T's assets should remain unchanged or be determined by reference to the amount paid by P for the T stock. If the form of the transaction is respected, T would not recognize gain, and its asset bases and other tax attributes would not change.

1) *Kimbell–Diamond* Case

Prior to 1954, the courts held that when P acquires the stock of T with the intent of obtaining T's assets by a prompt liquidation, P should be treated as having made a direct purchase of those assets, resulting in an asset basis equal to the amount paid by P for the stock. *Kimbell–Diamond Milling Co. v. Comm'r*, 14 T.C. 74 (1950), *aff'd per curiam*, 187 F.2d 718 (5th Cir.1951), cert. denied, 342 U.S. 827, 72 S.Ct. 50 (1951).

2) Former § 334(b)(2)

The *Kimbell–Diamond* concept was refined and codified in 1954 Code § 334(b)(2), which treated P's purchase of 80% or more of T's stock within a 12–month period as a purchase of assets if T were liquidated within two years after completion of the stock purchase. This mandatory rule enabled P to obtain a cost basis for T's assets and to avoid inheriting T's E & P and other tax attributes, but only if P liquidated T. If T stayed alive, it retained its old asset bases and other tax attributes.

3) Enactment of § 338

Congress enacted § 338 to further refine the original *Kimbell–Diamond* concept, eliminate subjective determinations of a purchaser's "intent," and provide greater parity between stock and asset acquisitions. Section 338 generally applies only to an electing corporate purchaser of at least 80% of T's stock within a 12–month period. If elected, it treats T as having sold all of its assets in a single transaction for their fair market value to a hypothetical "new" T, which takes an aggregate basis in those assets in an amount generally equal to what P paid for T's stock. There is no requirement that T be liquidated. Prior to the Tax Reform Act of 1986, a § 338 election was attractive because T generally did not recognize gain or loss on the deemed sale of its assets under "old" § 337. See IX.B.2.a., at page 193, *supra*. With the repeal of the *General Utilities* doctrine, however, T recognizes gain or loss on the deemed sale, just as it would on an actual sale of assets. See IX.B.2.b., at page 193, *supra*. This change makes a § 338 election far less desirable in most cases.

b. Operation of § 338: Basic Requirements

1) Qualified Stock Purchase Requirement

The § 338 election is available only when P makes a "qualified stock purchase" of the stock of T.

a) A "qualified stock purchase" is a transaction or series of transactions in which P acquires by "purchase" at least 80% of the total voting power and value of T during a 12–month "acquisition period." § 338(d)(3). Nonvoting preferred stock is generally ignored in applying the 80% tests. § 1504(a)(4).

b) A "purchase" is generally an acquisition from an unrelated person in a transaction where P takes a cost rather than a transferred basis in the acquired stock—e.g., an acquisition for cash or notes of P from a person whose stock is not attributable to P under § 318. § 338(h)(3).

c) The first day that the "qualified stock purchase" requirement is met is known as the "acquisition date." § 338(h)(2). P must acquire 80% of T during the 12–month "acquisition period." Stock acquired during this period and held on the acquisition date is "recently purchased stock." § 338(b)(6)(A). Stock purchased prior to the 12–month period does not count in meeting the 80% test and is "nonrecently purchased stock." § 338(b)(6)(B).

> *Example (1):*   T has 100 shares of common stock outstanding. On January 1 of the current year, P purchases 90 shares for cash. Individual A continues to own the other 10 shares. P has made a qualified stock purchase and is eligible to make the § 338 election.

> *Example (2):*   Same as Example (1), except P purchases 40 shares on February 1 of Year 1, 30 shares on August 1, and 20 shares on January 1 of Year 2. P has made a qualified stock purchase because it acquired at least 80% of T stock by purchase during a 12–month period. The acquisition date is January 1 of Year 2.

> *Example (3):*   Same as Example (1), except P purchased 20 shares five years ago and 80 shares on January 1 of the current year. P has made a qualified stock purchase, but the 20 shares purchased five years ago are "nonrecently purchased stock."

> *Example (4):*   Same as Example (3), except P purchased only 70 shares on January 1 of the current year and the remaining 10 shares on February 1 of Year 2. P has not made a qualified stock purchase.

2) The § 338 Election

P must make the § 338 election no later than the 15th day of the ninth month beginning after the month in which the "acquisition date" occurs.

§ 338(g)(1). Once P has acquired the requisite 80% interest within a 12–month period, it may not create a new acquisition date and thus extend the election deadline by acquiring additional stock. Once made, a § 338 election is irrevocable. § 338(g)(3).

Example: P Corp. purchases 10% of T Corp. stock on February 1 of the current year, 60% on July 1, 10% on August 1 and 20% on November 1. The 12–month acquisition period begins on February 1; the acquisition date (the date within the acquisition period on which the 80% qualified stock purchase is completed) is August 1. The § 338 election must be made no later than May 15 of the following year.

c. The Deemed Sale of T's Assets

If P makes a valid § 338 election, T is treated as having sold all of its assets at the close of the acquisition date for their fair market value in a single transaction to a new corporation ("new T"). § 338(a)(1). The deemed sale has tax consequences to both "old T" and "new T."

1) Consequences to Old T
a) Determination of Aggregate Deemed Sale Price

Old T recognizes gain or loss on the deemed sale, just as if it actually had sold its assets. Old T is deemed to have sold *all* its assets even if P acquires less than 100% of the T stock. The regulations treat T as selling its assets for their "aggregate deemed sales price" ("ADSP"), which is the sum of: (1) the grossed-up amount realized on the sale to P of P's recently purchased T stock, and (2) old T's liabilities, including any tax liabilities resulting from the deemed sale. Reg. § 1.338–4(b). The grossed-up amount realized on the sale of P's recently purchased stock is an amount equal to the amount realized on the sale to P of P's recently purchased T stock (without regard to costs of sale), divided by the percentage of T stock (by value, determined on the acquisition date) attributable to that recently purchased stock, less any selling costs (e.g., brokerage commissions) incurred by the selling T shareholders. Reg. § 1.338–4(c).

In the simple case where P purchases 100% of T's stock during the 12–month acquisition period, the ADSP is P's cost for the stock plus liabilities of old T. The gain or loss from the deemed § 338 sale is reported on old T's tax return and may not be included in any consolidated return filed by P and its other subsidiaries. § 338(h)(9). But the economic burden of old T's tax liability ordinarily is borne by P, which will take it into account in determining the price paid for the T stock. Old T's E & P and other tax attributes terminate after the deemed asset sale.

b)   Liabilities of Old T: Special Problems
As discussed above, the ADSP includes the liabilities of old T,
determined as of the beginning of the day after the acquisition date,
and including tax liabilities arising from the deemed asset sale. Reg.
§ 1.338–4(d)(1). A T liability must be one that is properly taken into
account under general principles. (In some cases, this may require
inclusion of contingent liabilities at the time of sale.) The inclusion of
tax liabilities from the deemed sale in determining the ADSP causes a
potentially circular calculation because T's tax liability depends on the
ADSP, and vice versa. The regulations resolve this dilemma by
providing the following (simpler than it seems) formula, where G is the
grossed-up amount realized on the sale to P of P's recently purchased
T stock, L is T's liabilities (other than deemed sale tax liabilities), T_r is
the applicable corporate tax rate, and B is the adjusted basis of the
assets deemed sold:

$$ADSP = G + L + T_r \, (ADSP—B)$$

Reg. § 1.338–4(g) Examples.

2)   Consequences to New T
a)   Adjusted Grossed–Up Basis
New T is treated as having purchased old T's assets as of the
beginning of the day after the "acquisition date." New T's aggregate
basis in the acquired assets is the "adjusted grossed-up basis"
("AGUB"), which is defined as the sum of: (1) "the grossed-up basis" of
P's recently purchased stock, (2) P's basis in its nonrecently purchased
T stock, and (3) the liabilities of new T. Reg. § 1.338–5(a), (b). The
grossed-up basis of P's recently purchased T stock is generally P's cost
basis in that stock multiplied by a fraction the numerator of which is
100% minus the percentage attributable to P's nonrecently purchased
stock, and the denominator of which is P's percentage ownership of
recently purchased stock. Reg. § 1.338–5(c). AGUB is similar but not
identical to ADSP. The principal difference arises from the fact that,
although the AGUB calculation grosses up the basis of T stock not
owned by P, it does not "gross up" the basis of P's *nonrecently*
purchased stock. P, however, may elect to recognize the gain on its
nonrecently purchased stock as if it had sold that stock for the average
price paid by P for the recently purchased T stock. In that case, P may
increase the AGUB of T's assets by the amount of such recognized
gain. § 338(b)(3); Reg. § 1.338–5(d). If P holds only recently purchased
T stock, the AGUB and the ADSP are usually the same.

b)   Allocation of AGUB
New T's aggregate AGUB is allocated among its assets using the
residual method prescribed by Reg. § 1.338–6. See IX.D.2.d., *supra*, at
page 201.

3) Examples

In the following examples, assume that the applicable corporate income tax rate for any ordinary income or capital gain arising from T's deemed asset sale is 35%.

Example (1): T has 1,000 shares of common stock outstanding. T's only asset is Gainacre (basis–$50,000, value–$300,000). P buys all of T's stock for $212,500 and makes a § 338 election. All the T stock acquired by P is recently purchased, and thus the grossed-up amount realized is $212,500. The ADSP is $212,500 plus T's tax liability on the deemed sale. Under the formula in the regulations, where G is the grossed-up amount realized ($212,500), L is liabilities other than the deemed sale tax liability (0), T_r is the corporate tax rate (.35), and B is the adjusted basis of T's assets deemed sold ($50,000), ADSP is determined as follows:

$$ADSP = G + L + T_r \, (ADSP—B)$$

$$ADSP = \$212,500 + 0 + .35 \, (ADSP—\$50,000)$$

$$ADSP = \$212,500 + .35 \, ADSP—\$17,500$$

$$.65 \, ADSP = \$195,000$$

$$ADSP = \$300,000$$

T thus recognizes $250,000 gain on the sale of Gainacre, and T's tax liability is $87,500 (35% x $250,000).

New T's adjusted grossed-up basis ("AGUB") is the $212,500 paid for all of T's stock plus the $87,500 tax liability on the deemed sale, for a total of $300,000 all of which is allocated to Gainacre.

Example (2): Same as Example (1), except P buys only 900 shares of T stock for $191,250. The remaining 100 shares are owned by Individual ("I"). T's grossed-up amount realized on the sale to P of the 900 shares of recently purchased T stock is the $191,250 amount realized divided by .90 (the percentage of total T stock attributable to recently purchased stock), or $212,500. The analysis is then identical to Example 1, above.

Example (3): Same as Example (1), except P purchased 100 shares of T five years ago for $10,000 and 900 shares in the current year for $191,250. As in Examples 1 and 2, above, T's grossed-up amount realized on the sale to P of the 900 shares of recently purchased T stock is $212,500, P's ADSP is $300,000, and the gain on the deemed sale of Gainacre is $250,000, resulting in a $87,500 tax liability.

New T's AGUB is the sum of: (1) the cost basis to P of its 900 shares of recently purchased stock ($191,250), which is not grossed-up in this case since P owns 100% of T, (2) the basis of P's nonrecently purchased stock ($10,000), and (3) T's tax liability on the deemed sale ($87,500), for a total AGUB of $287,750. T could increase its basis to $300,000 if it elected to recognize gain under § 338(b)(3) on a hypothetical sale of the nonrecently purchased stock for the average price paid for the recently purchased stock ($212.50 per share). This election would cause P to recognize $11,250 gain ($21,250 amount realized less $10,000 basis).

d. The Consistency Period Requirements

The consistency period requirements were originally designed to prevent P from selectively (and opportunistically) obtaining disparate favorable tax treatment for different assets acquired from the same corporate enterprise— e.g., a cost basis for some of T's assets and a transferred basis for others. These rules are far less significant after the repeal of the *General Utilities* doctrine. As currently interpreted by the Service in regulations, the consistency period rules now apply only where T is a member of a group of affiliated corporations that file a consolidated return and in a few other very specialized situations. See Reg. § 1.338–8.

1) The Consistency Period

The consistency period generally begins one year before the first purchase of T stock that is included in a "qualified stock purchase" and ends one year after the "acquisition date." § 338(h)(4)(A). The Service may extend the period to prevent plans to circumvent its restrictions. § 338(h)(4)(B).

Example (1): P buys 80% of T's stock on July 1, 2002 (which is the "acquisition date") and the remaining 20% on September 1, 2002. The consistency period begins on July 1, 2001 and ends on June 30, 2003.

Example (2): Same as Example (1), except P buys 40% of T's stock on July 1, 2002, 20% on August 1, 2002, and the remaining 40% on October 1, 2002 (which is the "acquisition date"). The consistency period begins on July 1, 2001 and ends on September 30, 2003.

2) Asset Acquisition Consistency Rules

Under the regulations, the asset acquisition consistency rules generally apply only if: (1) P acquires an asset directly from T during the consistency period, (2) T is a subsidiary of another corporation ("S"), and (3) T and S file a consolidated corporate tax return. Reg. § 1.338–8(a)(2). In this situation, unless a § 338 election is made, P generally takes a carryover (rather than cost) basis in any asset purchased from T during the consistency period. The purpose of the rule is to prevent P from exploiting the consolidated return investment basis adjustment rules by acquiring assets from T with a stepped-up cost basis and then acquiring T stock from S at no additional tax cost to the S consolidated group. See XIV.D.3.a., at page 309, *infra*. The mandatory carryover basis rule does not apply, however, if T sold the asset in the ordinary course of its business and in certain other narrow situations. Reg. § 1.338–8(d)(2).

> ***Example:*** S and T, S's 100% subsidiary, file a consolidated return. S has a $100 basis in its T stock, which has a fair market value of $180. On January 1, 2002, T sells Asset (basis–$20, value–$100) to P and recognizes $80 of gain. Under the consolidated return regulations, S may increase its T stock basis from $100 to $180. On March 1, 2002, S sells the T stock to P for $180 and recognizes no gain or loss. Because P acquired Asset from T during the consistency period and T's gain is reflected in S's basis in its T stock, P must take an $80 carryover basis for Asset.

3) Stock Acquisition Consistency Rules

The stock acquisition consistency rules in § 338(f) have become virtually irrelevant and are now applied only when necessary to prevent avoidance of the asset consistency rules. Reg. § 1.338–8(a)(6).

4. Sales and Distributions of Stock of a Subsidiary
a. The § 338(h)(10) Election

If T is a subsidiary of another corporation ("S"), whether or not T and S file a consolidated tax return (they normally would) and P wishes to acquire T, S can avoid recognizing gain on its T stock if T sells its assets directly to P and then distributes the sales proceeds to S in a tax-free § 332 liquidation, or if T first liquidates, distributes its assets to S and then S sells the assets to P. A corporate parent and its subsidiary-target can achieve the same result on a sale of T stock to P by making a joint election with P under §§ 338 and 338(h)(10) to treat T as if it sold all of its assets for fair market value to "new T" while a member of the S consolidated group and then T distributed the sales proceeds to S in a tax-free § 332 liquidation. S does not recognize gain or loss on the sale of its stock, S inherits T's tax attributes (e.g., earnings and profits), T is treated as having sold its assets for fair market value in a taxable transaction with any gain or loss included in the consolidated tax return filed by S and its affiliates, and new T is treated as having acquired old T's assets for an amount equal to their adjusted grossed-up basis as determined by a formula prescribed in the regulations. Reg. § 1.338(h)(10)–1(d). Like §§ 332 and 337, the purpose of § 338(h)(10) is to prevent the imposition of two tiers of corporate-level tax.

Situations in which a § 338(h)(10) election may be desirable include: (1) when S's "outside" gain on its stock exceeds T's "inside" gain on its assets (the election eliminates the outside gain); and (2) S's consolidated group has losses that can be used to offset any gain recognized by T on the deemed sale of its assets.

Example: S, Inc. owns all 100 outstanding shares of T, Inc. stock and has a $20,000 basis in its T stock. S and T file a consolidated return. T's only asset is Gainacre (basis–$40,000, value–$100,000). P purchases the T stock for $100,000 cash, and the parties jointly make the § 338 and § 338(h)(10) elections. T is treated as having sold Gainacre for $100,000 and recognizes $60,000 gain, which is includible on S and T's consolidated return. S recognizes no gain on the sale of its T stock. P takes a $100,000 basis in the T stock, and "new T" takes a $100,000 basis in Gainacre.

b.   The § 336(e) Election

Section 336(e) is similar in effect to § 338(h)(10). It permits an 80% or more parent corporation to elect to treat a sale, exchange or distribution of a subsidiary's stock as a disposition of the subsidiary's assets and to ignore any gain or loss on the actual disposition of the stock. Like § 338(h)(10), § 336(e) equates the sale of a subsidiary's stock with an actual sale of the subsidiary's assets followed by a distribution of the sales proceeds in a tax-free § 332 liquidation. Unlike § 338(h)(10), § 336(e) applies to *distributions* (liquidating and, apparently, nonliquidating) as well as sales, and to sales of a subsidiary's stock to an individual buyer, and it only requires the seller to make the election.

Example (1):   Individual A owns all the stock of P Corp., which owns all the stock of S Corp. A has a $10,000 basis in her P stock and P has a $10,000 basis in its S stock. S owns one asset, Gainacre (basis–$10,000, value–$30,000). P liquidates and distributes the S stock to A. Under § 336(a), P recognizes $20,000 gain on the distribution of the S stock to A, and A recognizes $20,000 gain (less tax paid by P on its gain) on the liquidation under § 331(a). Although A takes a $30,000 basis in the S stock, S still has a built-in gain of $20,000 on Gainacre. Section 336(e) permits P to elect to treat the distribution of S stock as a disposition of S's assets and to ignore any gain or loss on the distribution of the S stock. Under a § 336(e) election, S recognizes $20,000 gain on the constructive disposition and takes a $30,000 basis in Gainacre. P recognizes no gain or loss on the distribution of the S stock. A recognizes $20,000 gain on receipt of the S stock in the liquidation and takes a fair market value basis in the S stock.

Example (2):   Same as Example (1), except P sells the S stock to B, an individual, in anticipation of the liquidation. Section 338(h)(10) does not apply because the buyer, B, is not a corporation. Under § 336(e), P may elect to treat the sale of S stock as a disposition by S of Gainacre and ignore the gain on the actual sale of S stock. S recognizes $20,000 gain and "new S" takes a $30,000 fair market value basis in Gainacre. P must pay the tax on S's gain.

5.   Comparison of Acquisition Methods

From a tax standpoint, the preferred method for a taxable acquisition of a profitable company is a stock purchase with no § 338 election because T may defer any gain inherent in its assets. An asset purchase, or a stock purchase coupled with a § 338 election, results in gain at both the corporate and shareholder levels. On a stock purchase, a § 338 election may be desirable, however, when T has net operating loss carryovers that will offset the gain recognized on T's deemed asset sale, or where T is a subsidiary and the parties also jointly make a § 338(h)(10) election.

E.   Review Questions

1. X Corp. has 100 shares of common stock outstanding, of which 80 shares are owned by individual A (stock basis–$300,000) and 20 shares are owned by individual B (stock basis–$600,000). X's only assets are:

Asset	Adj. Basis	F. Mkt. Value
Gainacre	$100,000	$500,000
Lossacre	800,000	500,000

Both assets were transferred to X 18 months ago in a § 351 transaction. At that time, Lossacre had an adjusted basis of $800,000 and a fair market value of $900,000. In the current year, before taking into account any of the transactions below, X had accumulated E & P of $100,000 and no current E & P.

(a) Pursuant to a plan of complete liquidation, X distributes each asset pro rata to its shareholders. What are the tax consequences to X, A and B?

(b) Same as (a), above, except Lossacre had an $800,000 adjusted basis and a $700,000 fair market value at the time it was transferred to X in a § 351 transaction.

(c) Same as (a), above, except the § 351 transfers occurred six years prior to the liquidation.

(d) Same as (a), above, except that shareholder A is a corporation which has held its X stock continuously for the past three years.

2. S Corp. has 100 shares of common stock outstanding, of which 90 shares are owned by P Corp. (stock basis–$50,000) and 10 shares are owned by individual B (stock basis–$2,000). Pursuant to a plan of complete liquidation, S distributes Gainacre, its only asset (adjusted basis–$70,000; fair market value–$100,000), pro rata to its shareholders. What are the tax consequences to S, P and B?

3. Target Corporation ("T") has 100 shares of common stock outstanding, of which 80 shares are owned by Mr. S (stock basis–$100,000) and 20 shares are owned by Ms. I (stock basis–$50,000). T owns the following assets subject to no liabilities:

Asset	Adj. Basis	Fair Mkt. Value
Cash	$120,000	$120,000
Inventory	$ 30,000	50,000
Land	100,000	300,000
Goodwill	0	30,000
Total	$250,000	$500,000

P Corporation ("P") wishes to acquire T's business for cash.

(a) Identify three principal methods for structuring P's acquisition of T.

(b) In general, what are the tax consequences of each of the principal acquisition methods?

(c) What is the most desirable acquisition method from a tax standpoint?

(d) Would your answer to (c), above, change if S were a corporation that filed a consolidated tax return with T, and S had $2,000,000 of unexpired net operating loss carryforwards? Assume that T is a wholly-owned subsidiary of S.

X

ANTI–AVOIDANCE PROVISIONS

Analysis

A.   Introduction

The structure of Subchapter C is based upon the double taxation of corporate profits. Corporate income is taxed once when earned by the corporation and again when distributed as dividends to the corporation's shareholders. Historically, taxpayers have pursued strategies to lessen the full impact of the double tax and Congress has responded with anti-avoidance provisions to combat those strategies. This chapter examines three of those anti-avoidance provisions: the accumulated earnings tax, the personal holding company tax and the collapsible corporation rules.

B.   Accumulated Earnings Tax

1.   Introduction

For most of the period prior to 1987, the rates applied to the taxable income of individuals were significantly higher than the corporate rates. The lower rates on corporate taxable income made corporations attractive vehicles for accumulating income. High-bracket shareholders could allow corporate income to accumulate and compound at lower rates in corporate solution. The accumulation strategy also had the benefit of deferring imposition of a second level of tax on corporate distributions. Shareholders needing to realize corporate profits could sell stock and recognize capital gains while shareholders not needing cash could wait and leave the stock to their heirs, who would take a stepped-up § 1014 basis.

The accumulated earnings tax was enacted to combat the accumulation strategy. It applies to corporations formed or availed of to avoid the individual income tax rather than distributing the corporation's earnings and profits. § 532(a). The current rate structure, which taxes high-income individuals at rates only slightly higher than corporations (38.6% in 2002 and 2003, phasing down to 35% in later years, compared to a 35% or 34% corporate rate), reduces the importance of the accumulated earnings tax, but it still may be applied to combat accumulation strategies designed to avoid the double tax of Subchapter C.

The accumulated earnings tax is paid in addition to other taxes paid by the corporation and generally applies to every corporation formed or availed of for the purpose of avoiding the individual income tax by accumulating rather than distributing earnings and profits. §§ 531, 532(a). Publicly held, as well as closely held, corporations are subject to the tax. § 532(c). The tax is currently determined by applying the highest marginal individual income tax rate under § 1(c) to a C corporation's "accumulated taxable income." § 531. Personal holding companies, foreign personal holding companies, tax-exempt corporations and passive foreign investment companies are not subject to the tax. § 532(b).

2.   The Prohibited Tax Avoidance Purpose

The accumulated earnings tax only applies to a corporation that is formed or availed of for a tax avoidance purpose. The statutory standard is met if tax avoidance is one of several factors which motivated corporate accumulations. *U.S. v. Donruss Co.,* 393 U.S. 297, 89 S.Ct. 501 (1969). The existence of a tax avoidance purpose depends upon the particular circumstances of each case, including (1) dealings between the corporation and its shareholders, such as personal loans to the shareholders or expenditures by the corporation for the personal benefit of the shareholders, (2) investments having no reasonable relationship to the corporation's business, and (3) the extent to which the corporation distributes its earnings and profits. § 1.533–1(a)(2).

The fact that a corporation accumulates its earnings and profits "beyond the reasonable needs of the business" establishes a presumption of tax avoidance purpose unless the corporation rebuts the presumption by a preponderance of the evidence. § 533(a). This presumption adds still more weight to the general presumption of correctness that attaches to a determination of tax liability by the Service. § 1.533–1(b). A taxpayer may shift the burden of proof on the reasonableness of its accumulations to the Service in a Tax Court proceeding if, in response to the Service's notice proposing an accumulated earnings tax deficiency, it submits a statement and alleges facts sufficient to show that the accumulation was reasonable. §§ 534(a)(2), (c). Under § 533(b), the fact that a corporation is a "mere holding or investment company" is prima facie evidence of a tax avoidance purpose.

3. Reasonable Needs of the Business
a. In General
If a corporation permits its earnings and profits to accumulate beyond the reasonable needs of its business, that fact establishes a tax avoidance purpose unless the corporation proves it does not have such a purpose by a preponderance of the evidence. § 533(a). While it is possible for a corporation with unreasonable accumulations to rebut the presumption of a tax avoidance purpose, that situation rarely occurs. Thus, the critical question in accumulated earnings cases usually is whether corporate accumulations are beyond the reasonable needs of the business.

The regulations provide that the question of whether there is an accumulation beyond the reasonable needs of the business depends on the circumstances of each case. Thus, the issue is essentially factual in nature and the corporation normally will put forward several business needs which it claims justified its accumulation of profits. Courts typically are reluctant to question the business judgment of corporate management if the plans for an accumulation have substance and are not a facade for retaining corporate earnings. See generally, *Myron's Enterprises v. U.S.,* 548 F.2d 331 (9th Cir.1977), in which accumulations for the purchase and improvement of business property were justified as being for the reasonable needs of the business.

b. Examples of Reasonable Business Needs
The regulations provide the following list of grounds which, if supported by sufficient facts, may indicate that earnings and profits have been accumulated for the reasonable needs of the business. Reg. § 1.537–2(b).

1) To provide for bona fide expansion of business or replacement of plant;

2) To acquire a business enterprise through a stock or assets purchase;

3) To provide for retirement of bona fide business indebtedness;

4) To provide necessary business working capital;

5) To provide for investments or loans to suppliers or customers in order to maintain the corporation's business; and

6) To provide for payment of reasonably anticipated product liability losses.

c. Examples of Unreasonable Accumulations

Accumulations for the following nonexclusive list of objectives may indicate that earnings and profits are being accumulated beyond the reasonable needs of the business. Reg. § 1.537–2(c).

1) Loans to shareholders or the expenditure of corporate funds for the personal benefit of the shareholders;

2) Loans to relatives or friends of shareholders, or to other persons, having no reasonable relation to the conduct of the business;

3) Loans to another corporation engaged in a different business which is controlled by the controlling shareholders of the corporation;

4) Investments in properties or securities unrelated to the corporation's business; and

5) Retention of earnings and profits to provide against unrealistic hazards.

d. Anticipated Needs of the Business

Section 537(a)(1) provides that the reasonable needs of the business include the "reasonably anticipated" needs of the business. The regulations state that to justify an accumulation for anticipated needs, a corporation must show a business need for the accumulation and it must have "specific, definite, and feasible plans for the use of such accumulation." The accumulation does not have to be for immediate use or even use within a short period so long as it will be used within a reasonable time depending on all the facts and circumstances relating to the future needs of the business. § 1.537–1(b)(1). Because reasonably anticipated needs of the business are determined at year end, subsequent events are not used to show that retention of profits was unreasonable at the close of the taxable year. Subsequent events, however, may be considered to determine whether the taxpayer actually intended to consummate or has actually consummated the plan for which earnings and profits were accumulated. If an accumulation justified for future needs is never consummated, the amount of the accumulation is considered in determining the reasonableness of subsequent accumulations. § 1.537–1(b)(2).

e. The "Business" of the Corporation

The business of a corporation is not merely the one it has previously carried on but includes, in general, "any line of business it may undertake." Reg. § 1.537–3(a). Thus, reasonable needs include expansions of existing businesses and acquisition of related businesses. Accumulations to acquire entirely unrelated businesses run the risk of being labeled "investments in properties, or securities which are unrelated to the activities of the business of the taxpayer," which may indicate the accumulation is beyond the reasonable needs of the business. Reg. § 1.537–2(c)(4). In the case of investments in a subsidiary corporation, reasonable needs of the parent include the needs of an 80% or more subsidiary. Otherwise, the determination of whether the subsidiary's business needs are attributed to the parent depends on the particular circumstances. Reg. § 1.537–3(b).

f. Working Capital Needs of the Corporation

Accumulations to provide necessary business working capital may indicate that accumulations are for the reasonable needs of the business. Reg. § 1.537–2(b)(4). The courts have approached this question by attempting to determine the capital requirements of the corporation for one operating cycle, which in general is the time it takes to purchase raw materials, make finished goods, sell the product, and collect any outstanding receivables so the process may be repeated. The analysis, which is called the *Bardahl* formula after *Bardahl Manufacturing Corp. v. Comm'r*, 24 T.C.M. 1030 (1965), provides an approximation of the corporation's working capital needs.

g. Stock Redemptions

Section 537(a)(2) provides that accumulations designed to meet the reasonably anticipated needs of the corporation for § 303 redemptions to pay death taxes which are made in the year a shareholder dies or any taxable year thereafter are for the reasonable needs of the business. See § 537(b)(1). The treatment of accumulations for other types of non pro rata redemptions varies. In theory, the tax treatment of the accumulation should depend upon whether the redemption is motivated by *corporate* purposes or personal needs of the shareholders. Thus, accumulations to redeem the stock of dissenting minority shareholders or to prevent stock from falling into the hands of antagonistic shareholders have been determined to be for the reasonable needs of the business. For example, in *Gazette Publishing Co. v. Self*, 103 F.Supp. 779 (E.D.Ark.1952), the court determined that the redemption of a shareholder's voting stock in a newspaper publisher to prevent the stock from being owned by special interests who might oppose the paper's editorial policy was a reasonable need of the business.

4. **Accumulated Taxable Income**
   a. **In General**
      A corporation subject to the accumulated earnings tax must pay a tax
      determined by applying the highest marginal individual income tax rate under
      § 1(c) to the corporation's "accumulated taxable income." Accumulated taxable
      income is taxable income adjusted under § 535(b), minus the § 561 dividends
      paid deduction and the § 535(c) accumulated earnings credit. § 535(a).

   b. **§ 535(b) Adjustments to Taxable Income**
      The corporation's taxable income is adjusted under § 535(b) to arrive at a more
      accurate determination of the corporation's economic success. Thus, certain
      nondeductible taxes and charitable contributions in excess of the 10%
      limitation are permitted as reductions to taxable income. § 535(b)(1), (2). The
      dividends received deduction and net operating loss deduction are not allowed
      and must be added back to taxable income in arriving at accumulated taxable
      income. § 535(b)(3), (4).

      Net capital gain, less attributable taxes, is deducted from taxable income.
      § 535(b)(6). For purposes of determining net capital gain, net capital loss from
      prior taxable years is treated as short-term capital loss. § 535(b)(7)(A). A
      corporation also may deduct its net capital loss for the year but the deduction
      is limited to the lesser of the "nonrecaptured capital gains deduction" (as
      defined in § 535(b)(5)(C)) or the corporation's accumulated earnings and profits
      at the end of the year. § 535(b)(5)(A), (B).

   c. **§ 561 Dividends Paid Deduction**
      A corporation may reduce its accumulated taxable income by the amount of the
      dividends it pays during the year and the amount of the "consent dividends" for
      the year. §§ 535(a); 561(a)(1), (2); 562(a). For this purpose, the amount of a
      dividend paid in property other than money is the corporation's adjusted basis
      in the property. Reg. § 1.562–1(a); *Fulman v. U.S.*, 434 U.S. 528, 98 S.Ct. 841
      (1978). To be eligible for the dividends paid deduction, the distribution
      generally must be pro rata among the shareholders. § 562(c). A portion of a
      liquidating distribution or a distribution in redemption of stock also may
      qualify for the dividends paid deduction. § 562(b)(1). Dividends paid on or
      before the 15th day of the third month following the taxable year are
      considered as paid in such year for purposes of the accumulated earnings tax.
      § 563(a).

      "Consent dividends" are amounts which the shareholders agree to consider to
      have been distributed even though there was no actual distribution. Consent
      dividends must be pro rata in order to be deductible and must be for amounts
      which would have been dividends if actually distributed. § 565(b). Under
      § 565(c), consent dividends are considered to be distributed in money to the
      shareholder on the last day of the corporation's taxable year, thereby producing
      a dividend, and recontributed to the corporation on the same day.

d. § 535(c) Accumulated Earnings Credit

Under § 535(c)(1), a corporation, other than a mere holding or investment company, is entitled to a deduction equal to the portion of its earnings and profits retained for the reasonable needs of its business less the deduction for net capital gains. Under § 535(c)(2), the amount of this deduction can not be less than the amount by which $250,000 ($150,000 for service corporations in certain businesses) exceeds the accumulated earnings and profits at the close of the year. This provision, in effect, permits every corporation to accumulate $250,000, regardless of the purpose for the accumulation.

C. Personal Holding Company Tax

1. Introduction

The accumulated earnings tax has certain limitations. Its application is based on determining the purpose for accumulations, and the accumulated earnings credit permits taxpayers to accumulate substantial amounts of corporate earnings. Congress enacted the personal holding company tax, in part, to respond to these deficiencies in the accumulated earnings tax.

The original targets of the personal holding company tax were the so-called "incorporated pocketbooks," "incorporated talents," and "incorporated properties" strategies. Incorporated pocketbooks involved the transfer of investment assets (stocks, bonds, etc.) to a corporation which was taxed at rates significantly lower than the rates paid by individual taxpayers. Passive investment income could be earned and compounded subject only to the lower corporate tax rates, and dividends received by the corporation would be eligible for the dividends received deduction. The shareholders could defer recognition of income until needed, at which time it could be realized in transactions producing capital gain. Alternatively, the shareholders could leave the stock to their heirs who would take a stepped-up § 1014 basis. In the "incorporated talents" strategy, a highly compensated individual would form a corporation which would then contract out the services of its owner. The shareholder could receive enough salary to meet personal needs and allow the remainder of the income to accumulate in the corporation at lower corporate tax rates. The "incorporated properties" strategy involved the transfer of a nonbusiness asset, such as a yacht or home, to a corporation which would then rent the property back to the shareholder. The goal was to deduct depreciation on the nonbusiness asset to offset the rent payment and other corporate income.

Section 541 attacks these tax avoidance devices by imposing a tax determined by applying the highest marginal individual income tax rate under § 1(c) to the undistributed personal holding company income of every personal holding company. The tax is imposed in addition to other taxes paid by the corporation. Certain corporations subject to special tax rules are not subject to the personal holding company tax.

2. Definition of Personal Holding Company

Under § 542(a), a "personal holding company" is a company which meets both a stock ownership requirement and an income requirement.

a. Stock Ownership Requirement

More than 50% in value of a corporation's stock must be owned, directly or indirectly, at any time during the last half of the taxable year by five or fewer individuals. § 542(a)(2). Attribution rules are applied to test stock ownership. Stock owned by a corporation, partnership, estate or trust is considered owned proportionately by its shareholders, partners or beneficiaries. § 544(a)(1). An individual also is considered to own stock owned by or for her family (brothers, sisters, ancestors and lineal descendants) or by or for her partner. § 544(a)(2). Stock subject to an option to purchase is considered to be owned by the option holder. § 544(a)(3). Securities convertible into stock are considered stock for purposes of the stock ownership test if the effect of such inclusion is to make the corporation a personal holding company. § 544(b)(1).

b. Income Requirement

At least 60% of a corporation's adjusted ordinary gross income ("AOGI") for the taxable year must be personal holding company income. § 542(a)(1). AOGI is equal to the corporation's ordinary gross income ("OGI") with certain adjustments. OGI is equal to the corporation's gross income less its gains from the sale or other disposition of capital assets and § 1231(b) property. § 543(b)(1). The adjustments to OGI in arriving at AOGI are designed to take into account the costs of earning certain forms of gross income so corporations can not easily generate gross receipts to avoid the personal holding company tax. Thus, AOGI includes the corporation's income from rents and mineral, oil and gas royalties after adjustments for cost recovery, property taxes, interest and rents. § 543(b)(2)(A), (B). Copyright royalties, produced film rents, and active business computer software royalties, however, are not adjusted in determining AOGI. § 543(b)(2)(A), (3). Interest on U.S. obligations held by dealers and interest on condemnation awards, judgments and tax refunds are excluded from AOGI. § 543(b)(2)(C).

c. Definition of Personal Holding Company Income

Section 543(a) defines "personal holding company income" as the portion of AOGI consisting of specified types of income. The definition of personal holding company income focuses on passive investment income and income from personal services contracts. Section 543(a) is extremely complex because it contains a number of statutory tests which, in general, are designed to distinguish between passive forms of income and income earned in pursuit of the corporation's business.

1) Passive Investment Income

Dividends, interest, and royalties (other than mineral, oil or gas royalties or copyright royalties) included in AOGI are personal holding company income. § 543(a)(1). Active computer software royalties (as defined) also are excluded from the general passive income category. § 543(a)(1)(C). But royalties from patents, secret processes and formulas, goodwill, trademarks, trade brands, franchises and comparable properties are included in personal holding company income. Reg. § 1.543–1(b)(3).

2) Rents

Under § 543(a)(2), rents are personal holding company income unless the adjusted income from rents (as defined in § 543(b)(3)) constitutes 50% or more of AOGI. § 543(a)(2)(A). The theory of this test is that where rental income represents the major activity of the corporation that activity is more likely to be of an active rather than passive nature. In general, a corporation with adjusted gross income from rents equal to 50% or more of its AOGI may have its rents classified as personal holding company income if it has large amounts of other forms of personal holding company income which it does not distribute to its shareholders. § 543(a)(2)(B).

3) Mineral, Oil and Gas Royalties

The adjusted income from mineral, oil, and gas royalties (as defined in § 543(b)(4)) is personal holding company income unless (1) it constitutes 50% or more of AOGI, (2) certain other types of personal holding company income are not more than 10% of OGI, and (3) the corporation's § 162 trade or business deductions (other than for shareholder provided services and deductions allowable under other sections) are 15% or more of AOGI. § 543(a)(3).

4) Copyright Royalties

Under § 543(a)(4), copyright royalties are personal holding company income unless (1) they constitute 50% or more of OGI, (2) certain other personal holding company income is not more than 10% of OGI, and (3) the corporation's § 162 trade or business deductions allocable to such royalties (other than for shareholder provided services, amounts paid or incurred for royalties, and deductions allowable under other sections) equals or exceeds 25% of OGI less the sum of the royalties paid or accrued and the amounts allowed under § 167 as depreciation for copyright royalties.

5) Produced Film Rents

"Produced film rents" (as defined in § 543(a)(5)(B)) are personal holding company income unless they constitute 50% or more of OGI. § 543(a)(5)(A).

6) Use of Corporate Property by Shareholder

Under certain conditions, rents received from 25% or more shareholders (by value) are personal holding company income. § 543(a)(6). This provision is designed to attack the "incorporated properties" strategy.

7) Personal Service Contracts

Amounts received by a corporation under a contract for personal services, or a sale of the contract, are personal holding company income under

§ 543(a)(7) if some person other than the corporation has the right to designate by name or description the individual who performs such services or the individual who will perform the services is designated in the contract. This provision only applies to amounts received for services if a 25% or more shareholder (by value) is the individual who has performed, is to perform, or may be designated to perform the services. Section 543(a)(7) is the provision which deals with the "incorporated talents" strategy.

In Revenue Ruling 75–67, 1975–1 C.B. 169, the Service applied § 543(a)(7) to a professional service corporation which was 80% owned by a doctor who was the only doctor employed by the corporation. Typically, a physician-patient relationship arises from a general agreement of treatment between a physician and patient. Either party generally may terminate the relationship at will and a physician who is unable to treat the patient when services are needed may provide a qualified and competent substitute physician to render the services. Because of the special nature of the physician-patient relationship, Rev.Rul. 75–67 concluded that the establishment of the relationship does not constitute a designation under § 543(a)(7). But if the physician contracts to provide particular services with no right of substitution, or if the nature of the physician's services are so unique as to preclude substitution, there is a designation for purposes of § 543(a)(7).

8) Amounts Received From Estates and Trusts
Amounts included in a corporation's taxable income as a result of it being a beneficiary of an estate or trust are personal holding company income. § 543(a)(8).

9) Active Computer Software Royalties
Personal holding company income does not include "active computer software royalties." § 543(a)(1)(C), (4). "Active computer software royalties" are defined as royalties received in connection with the licensing of computer software, if: (1) the royalties are received by a corporation engaged in the active conduct of the trade or business of developing, manufacturing, or producing computer software and are attributable to software developed, manufactured, or produced in connection with the business or directly related to such business; (2) the royalties must constitute at least 50% of OGI; (3) the corporation's expenses under § 162 (other than compensation paid to certain shareholders and expenses allowable under other sections), § 174, and § 195 for the year properly allocable to the software business must be equal to at least 25% of OGI or the average of such deductions for the past five years (or the life of the corporation if shorter) must be at least 25% of the average OGI for such period; and (4) the dividends paid during the year (including dividends considered paid on the last day under § 563 and consent dividends under

§ 565) must equal or exceed the corporation's other personal holding company income (with adjustments) less 10% of OGI. § 543(d).

3. Undistributed Personal Holding Company Income

The personal holding company tax is determined by applying the highest marginal individual income tax rate under § 1(c) to the corporation's "undistributed personal holding company income" ("UPHCI"). § 541. UPHCI is defined in § 545(a) as taxable income with adjustments minus the § 561 dividends paid deduction.

a. Adjustments to Taxable Income

In calculating UPHCI, several adjustments are required to reach a more accurate measure of the corporation's economic performance. A deduction for certain nondeductible items, such as federal income taxes and excess charitable contributions, is allowed. § 545(b)(1), (2). The dividends received deduction is not allowed and there are special rules for net operating losses. § 545(b)(3), (4). In order to eliminate capital gains from the base of the personal holding company tax, a deduction equal to the corporation's net capital gain minus allocable taxes is allowed in computing UPHCI. § 545(b)(5). In the case of property leased by the corporation, § 162 and § 167 deductions allocable to the operation and maintenance of such property are allowed only to the extent of the rent or compensation generated by the property unless the taxpayer establishes that (1) the rent or other compensation was the highest obtainable, (2) the property was held in the course of a business carried on bona fide for profit, and (3) either there was a reasonable expectation of profit from the operation of the property or the property was necessary to the conduct of the business. § 545(b)(6).

b. § 561 Dividends Paid Deduction

1) In General

A corporation may reduce its UPHCI by the amount of the dividends it pays during the year, the consent dividends for the year under § 565, and the dividend carryover in § 564. §§ 545(a), 561(a). To be eligible for the dividends paid deduction, the distribution generally must be pro rata among the shareholders. § 562(c). The amount of any dividend paid in property other than money is the corporation's adjusted basis in the distributed property. Reg. § 1.562–1(a); *Fulman v. U.S.,* 434 U.S. 528, 98 S.Ct. 841 (1978).

Generally, operating distributions and distributions characterized as § 301 distributions (e.g., certain redemptions and stock dividends) produce dividends to the extent of the corporation's earnings and profits. In addition, under § 316(b)(2) any distribution by a personal holding company is a dividend to the extent of its UPHCI for the year. This rule also applies to distributions which are considered made in the year under § 563(b) and deficiency dividends under § 547.

2)   § 563(b) Election
In the case of dividends paid on or before the 15th day of the third month following the taxable year, the corporation may elect to have the dividend be considered as paid during the year. § 563(b). This election is limited to an amount of dividends which does not exceed either the corporation's UPHCI for the year or 20% of the dividends otherwise paid during the year.

3)   Consent Dividends
"Consent dividends" are amounts which the shareholders agree to consider to have been distributed even though there was no actual distribution. Consent dividends must be pro rata in order to be deductible and must be for amounts which would have been dividends if actually distributed. § 565(b)(1). Under § 565(c), consent dividends are considered to be distributed in money on the last day of the corporation's taxable year thereby producing a dividend, and then to be recontributed to the corporation on the same day.

4)   § 564 Dividend Carryover
Corporations also are potentially eligible for a dividend carryover from the preceding two years which will reduce UPHCI. The amount of the dividend carryover from each of those years is the excess of the dividends paid deduction (without carryovers) for the year over taxable income computed with the adjustments provided in § 545. If there is such an excess in the earlier of the two years, that excess is offset by the excess, if any, of taxable income over the dividends paid deduction (without carryovers) in the later year. § 564(b)(4), (5).

5)   Liquidating Distributions
Under § 562(b)(2), liquidating distributions to corporate distributees within 24 months of the adoption of a plan of liquidation are treated as dividends paid to the extent of the corporate distributee's allocable share of UPHCI for the year. Under § 316(b)(2)(B), distributions in complete liquidation to noncorporate shareholders may be designated as dividend distributions to the extent of the distributee's allocable share of UPHCI. If a payment to a noncorporate shareholder is so designated, the shareholder must treat that portion of the distribution as a dividend.

6)   § 547 Deficiency Dividends
If a determination is made that a corporation is liable for the personal holding company tax, § 547 permits a deduction for "deficiency deductions" for purposes of determining UPHCI and tax liability, but not interest and penalties. "Deficiency dividends" are dividends paid within 90 days of a determination of liability for personal holding company tax which would have been included in the § 561 dividends paid deduction in the year to

which the liability exists if distributed in that year. § 547(d)(1). A claim for a deficiency dividend deduction must be filed within 120 days after the determination of liability for personal holding company tax. § 547(e).

D. Collapsible Corporations

1. Background

Historically, capital gains were taxed at rates substantially below the rates on ordinary income. Prior to 1987, the *General Utilities* doctrine generally permitted a corporation to escape recognition of gain or loss on distributions in complete liquidation or sales of assets in contemplation of liquidation. The combination of highly preferential capital gain rates and the *General Utilities* doctrine encouraged taxpayers to convert ordinary income into capital gain through the use of a "collapsible corporation." The prototype transaction involved a group of individuals coming together to complete a single project, such as production of a movie or development of a parcel of real estate. A corporation would be formed and the individuals involved in the project took stock in lieu of compensation for their efforts. The corporation would develop the project and then liquidate, avoiding recognition of gain under pre–1987 law. The individual shareholders who worked on the project could sell their stock or receive the assets of the project in a liquidating distribution from the corporation. In either case, they would recognize capital gain. Section 341 combats this strategy by providing that gain from (1) the sale or exchange of stock of a collapsible corporation, (2) a distribution in complete or partial liquidation of a collapsible corporation, or (3) a distribution by a collapsible corporation which is treated as a sale or exchange of property under § 301(c)(3)(A), which would otherwise be capital gain, is considered ordinary income. § 341(a).

Despite the survival of a significant capital gains rate preference for individuals, the repeal of the *General Utilities* doctrine has eliminated the viability of the collapsible corporation strategy. Since a corporation must fully recognize its gain on liquidating distributions and sales, the classic collapsible corporation plan is no longer opportunistic, and § 341 has become virtually obsolete. Congress nonetheless has retained § 341 in the Code. Although most corporate tax instructors no longer cover collapsible corporations, a general description of § 341 is provided below for students enrolled in corporate tax history courses or whose instructors are suffering from dementia.

2. Definition of a "Collapsible Corporation"
a. In General

Section 341(b)(1) defines a collapsible corporation as a corporation formed or availed of principally for the manufacture, construction, or production of property or for the purchase of "§ 341 assets," with a view to: (1) the sale or exchange of its stock by its shareholders (in a liquidation or otherwise) or a distribution to its shareholders before the corporation realizes two-thirds of the taxable income to be derived from the property, and (2) the realization by the shareholders of gain attributable to such property.

Both new and preexisting corporations may be collapsible. Under § 341(b)(2), a corporation is deemed to have manufactured, constructed, produced, or purchased property if it (1) engages in those activities "to any extent," (2) holds such property with a transferred basis, or (3) holds property with an exchanged basis determined by reference to property manufactured, constructed, produced, or purchased by the corporation.

"Section 341 assets" are defined as property held for less than three years which is stock in trade, inventory, property held primarily for sale to customers, unrealized receivables or fees, or § 1231(b) property which is not used in the manufacture, construction, production or sale of stock in trade, inventory or dealer property. The determination of whether property is § 1231(b) property is made without regard to the holding period requirement in that section. The three-year holding period requirement for any § 341 asset is determined after taking into account the § 1223 rules of "tacking" holding periods. § 341(b)(3).

b. The Required "View"

To be collapsible, a corporation must be formed or availed of with a view to a collapse event (a shareholder stock sale, liquidation or distribution) before realization by the corporation of two-thirds of the taxable income to be derived from its manufactured, produced, etc. property. The required view is present if a collapse of the corporation "was contemplated by those persons in a position to determine the policies of the corporation, whether by reason of their owning a majority of the voting stock or otherwise." This requirement is satisfied if a collapse was merely recognized as a possibility during the manufacture, production, construction or purchase required in § 341. Reg. § 1.341–2(a)(2), (3). Moreover, if the persons with corporate control have the required view, the corporation is collapsible as to all shareholders. Reg. § 1.341–2(a)(2). If the collapse event is attributable solely to circumstances arising after manufacture, production, etc., of the property which could not be reasonably anticipated, the required view is not present. Reg. § 1.341–2(a)(3).

If the corporation realizes two-thirds of the taxable income from its manufactured, produced, etc. property prior to a shareholder stock sale, liquidation or distribution, the required view cannot be present and the corporation is not collapsible. The courts have interpreted this rule to require corporate *recognition* of the income. *Manassas Airport Industrial Park, Inc. v. Comm'r*, 66 T.C. 566 (1976), aff'd per curiam, 557 F.2d 1113 (4th Cir.1977). The regulations take the position that the two-thirds recognition requirement applies to each separate property which has substantial unrealized taxable income. But integrated projects which consist of several properties similar in kind are considered a single property for purposes of the two-thirds recognition requirement. Reg. §§ 1.341–2(a)(4); –5(b)(5), (c)(2). The regulations include examples in which two office buildings built in separate years are treated as two projects and movies are treated as separate projects. Reg. § 1.341–5(d)

Examples (2) and (4). In the case of stock in trade, inventory and dealer property, the regulations provide that, ordinarily, a corporation will not be collapsible if the amount of such property on hand is not in excess of the amount which is normal either (1) for purposes of its business and it has a substantial prior business history and continues in business, or (2) for purposes of an orderly liquidation and it has a substantial prior business history and is in the process of liquidation. Reg. § 1.341–5(c)(1).

> ***Example:*** X Corp. manufactures two properties. Property One has a fair market value of $100,000 and a basis of $60,000. Property Two has a fair market value of $50,000 and a basis of $30,000. Assume that a collapse event was contemplated by the majority shareholders of X during the manufacture of the properties. If X sells Property One for $100,000 it will recognize $40,000 of the $60,000 of total taxable income in both of its properties. If Property One and Property Two are considered to be one integrated project, X will have recognized two-thirds of the total taxable income to be derived from its assets and will no longer be collapsible. If, however, Property One and Property Two are separate properties, after the sale of Property One X will not have recognized two-thirds of the taxable income in each of its properties and it will still be collapsible. If the two properties are separate, X also would have to recognize two-thirds of the $20,000 of potential income in Property Two to avoid collapsibility.

c. § 341(c) Presumption
Under § 341(c), a corporation is presumed to be collapsible if the fair market value of its § 341 assets is (1) 50% or more of the adjusted basis of its total assets (less cash, debt obligations which are held as capital assets and stock in other corporations), and (2) 120% or more of the adjusted basis of such § 341 assets. The § 341(c) presumption is rebuttable and failure to meet these valuation tests does not create a presumption against collapsibility.

3. Exceptions to Collapsibility
a. § 341(d) Exceptions
Section 341(d) provides three exceptions under which the gain recognized by a shareholder on stock of a collapsible corporation is not converted to ordinary income.

1) De Minimis Rule
Section 341(a) does not apply to any shareholder who owns 5% or less of the stock of the corporation (including stock owned through attribution) from the time manufacture, construction, production, or purchase of collapsible property begins and thereafter. § 341(d)(1). This exception is intended to protect shareholders who are not likely to have corporate control and did not have the required view.

2) 70:30 Rule

Section 341(a) does not apply to a shareholder's gain unless more than 70% of that gain is attributable to collapsible property. The regulations apply the 70% rule by analyzing the amount of gain the shareholder would have recognized if the corporation had no collapsible property at the time of the collapse event. § 1.341–4(c)(2). Thus, a shareholder will recognize capital gain on a sale or exchange of stock if 30% of the gain is attributable to noncollapsible property such as capital assets or manufactured, produced, etc. properties on which two-thirds of the income has been recognized.

Example: Z Co. has developed a real estate tract with homes. The tract has a $2 million fair market value and a $1.5 million basis. In addition, Z owns an investment asset which has a $200,000 fair market value and a $100,000 basis. Assume Z is a collapsible corporation because it constructed the real estate improvements at a time when its controlling shareholders had a view to a collapse event. If Z were to sell $400,000 of the real estate with a $300,000 proportionate share of basis, it would recognize $100,000 of gain. Even though Z would still be a collapsible corporation, § 341(a) will not treat any shareholder's gain on a stock sale as ordinary income because under § 341(d)(2) 70% or less of the gain would be attributable to collapsible property. The remaining real estate would have a value of $1.6 million and a basis of $1.2 million and the gain inherent in collapsible property would be $400,000. There is $100,000 of gain inherent in the investment asset and $100,000 of any shareholder's gain would be attributable to the portion of the real estate tract already sold. Thus, $400,000 of the $600,000 of total appreciation in the corporation is attributable to collapsible property and under § 341(d)(2) the shareholders would be entitled to capital gain on a sale of stock.

3) Three–Year Rule

Section 341(a) does not apply to gain recognized more than three years following the completion of the manufacture, construction, production or purchase of property. If some properties have been sufficiently "aged" and others have not, the regulations provide that § 341(a) does not apply to the portion of the gain attributable to the aged properties. Reg. § 1.341–4(d).

b. **§ 341(e) Exceptions**

The theory of § 341(e) is that a shareholder's capital gain should not be converted to ordinary income if the unrealized appreciation in the corporation's ordinary income assets is small in relation to its net worth. Section 341(e)(1)(A) begins with a rule that a corporation is not considered collapsible with respect to a sale or exchange of stock by a shareholder if the net unrealized appreciation in the corporation's "subsection (e) assets" does not exceed 15% of its net worth. The exception does not apply to sales to either the issuing corporation or certain related persons.

"Subsection (e) assets" are defined so as to prevent easy avoidance of this test. In general, subsection (e) assets are: (1) property (other than § 1231(b) property) which if sold by the corporation or a more than 20% shareholder (including ownership by attribution) would produce ordinary income, other than certain types of recapture income; (2) § 1231(b) property, if the unrealized depreciation in such property exceeds the unrealized appreciation, that is, such property would, if sold, produce ordinary income and losses; (3) if there is net unrealized appreciation in § 1231(b) property, any § 1231(b) property which if sold by a more than 20% shareholder (including ownership by attribution) would produce ordinary income, other than certain types of recapture income (e.g., a 20% or more shareholder is a dealer in such property); and (4) copyrights, literary, musical or artistic compositions, letters or memoranda, or similar material if the property was created or prepared in whole or part by the personal efforts of a 5% or more owner. § 341(e)(5), (6), (10), (12). For purposes of this definition, the status of § 1231(b) property is determined without regard to holding period. § 341(e)(9). The net worth of the corporation generally is the fair market value of all of its assets less its liabilities. Transfers to the corporation for stock or as contributions to capital within one year which increase its net worth are disregarded if the transfer was not for a substantial bona fide business purpose. § 341(e)(7).

Section 341(e)(1) modifies the basic test for shareholders with certain levels of stock ownership. If a shareholder owns more than 5% of a corporation, the net unrealized appreciation in assets which would be subsection (e) assets if the shareholder were a 20% shareholder is added to the net unrealized appreciation in subsection (e) assets for purposes of the 15% test. § 341(e)(1)(B). If a shareholder owns more than 20% of the stock of a corporation, the basic "subsection (e) asset" definition applies. In addition, if a 20% shareholder also owns more than 20% of another corporation (the "second corporation") sales or exchanges of property by the second corporation are attributed to the shareholder for purposes of determining whether the shareholder is a dealer in applying the basic subsection (e) asset definition. § 341(e)(1)(C)(ii).

Example: Assume Y Co. owns depreciable plant and equipment with a fair market value of $1 million and a basis of $800,000. In addition, Y Co. owns inventory with a fair market value of $300,000 and a basis of $150,000. Assume Y Co. is a collapsible corporation because the inventory was manufactured or purchased with a view to a collapse event and is in excess of the amount which would be normal for purposes of Y's business. Under § 341(e)(1)(A), however, Y Co. will not be considered collapsible because the net unrealized appreciation in subsection (e) assets (the $150,000 of appreciation in the inventory) does not exceed 15% of its net worth ($1.3 million). If a more than 20% shareholder were a dealer in the plant and equipment, those assets would be subsection (e) assets under § 341(e)(5)(A)(iii) and the net appreciation in Y's subsection (e) assets ($350,000) would exceed 15% of its net worth. Thus, no shareholder would be protected by § 341(e). If a 5% to 20% shareholder were a dealer in the plant and equipment, those assets would not be subsection (e) assets but they would be counted in testing the corporation's assets under § 341(e) for that shareholder. § 341(e)(1)(B). Thus, all shareholders other than the 5% to 20% shareholder would be protected by § 341(e).

c. § 341(f)

Under § 341(f), § 341(a) does not apply to a sale of stock (other than to the issuing corporation) if the corporation consents to recognize its gain on any disposition of a "subsection (f) asset." A "subsection (f) asset" is defined as any property which on the date of the stock sale is not a capital asset and is owned, or subject to an option to purchase, by the corporation. § 341(f)(4)(A). All land interests (including improvements but not security interests), plus unrealized receivables and fees are considered to not be capital assets. § 341(f)(4)(A), (C).

Once made, a § 341(f) consent applies to stock sales made during the next six months. § 341(f)(1). A corporation can file more than one § 341(f) consent. A shareholder, however, may not take advantage of § 341(f) on stock sales in different corporations within a five-year period. § 341(f)(5). The only exceptions to the corporate recognition rule are for certain intercorporate transactions such as § 332 liquidations, § 351 transfers, and reorganizations. § 341(f)(3). For these exceptions to apply, the transferee must agree to recognize any gain on its disposition of the transferred subsection (f) asset. § 341(f)(3)(B).

With the repeal of the *General Utilities* doctrine, liquidating distributions and sales in contemplation of liquidation are fully taxable events and § 341(f) provides a relatively painless way in which to avoid § 341(a). The principal cost of a § 341(f) consent is that the corporation is unable to use nonrecognition provisions such as § 1031 (like-kind exchanges) and § 1033 (involuntary conversions).

E.   Review Questions

1. If a corporation permits its earnings and profits to accumulate beyond the reasonable needs of its business, it is conclusively presumed to have been formed for a tax avoidance purpose. True or False?

2. What requirements must be met for a corporation to be classified as a "personal holding company"?

3. What is the definition of a "collapsible corporation"?

4. What exceptions to collapsibility are provided by the Code?

*

XI

TAX–FREE REORGANIZATIONS

Analysis

A. Introduction

1. Policy

The term "reorganization" is used in the Internal Revenue Code to describe a variety of transactions that result in a fundamental change in the ownership or structure of one or more corporations. Transactions that qualify as reorganizations under § 368 are wholly or partially tax free to the corporations and their shareholders. The rationale for nonrecognition is that a reorganization is merely a readjustment of a continuing corporate enterprise, resulting in a continuity of investment. See Reg. § 1.368–1(b). In keeping with nonrecognition principles, the gain or loss of the corporate parties to a reorganization and their shareholders is not permanently forgiven but merely deferred through transferred and exchanged bases for the corporation's assets and the shareholders' stock.

2. Types of Corporate Reorganizations

Corporate reorganizations fall into three broad categories:

a. Acquisitive Reorganizations

Acquisitive reorganizations are transactions where one corporation (the "acquiring corporation," hereafter referred to as "P") acquires the assets or stock of another corporation ("the target corporation," hereafter "T"). Included in this category are statutory mergers or consolidations (Type A), stock-for-stock acquisitions (Type B), stock-for-assets acquisitions (Type C), and variations, known as "triangular reorganizations," which involve the use of a subsidiary.

b. Nonacquisitive, Nondivisive Reorganizations

Nonacquisitive, nondivisive reorganizations are adjustments to the corporate structure of a single, continuing corporate enterprise. This category includes recapitalizations (Type E); changes in the identity, form or place of incorporation (Type F); certain transfers of substantially all of the assets of one corporation to another commonly controlled corporation followed by a liquidation of the first corporation (nondivisive Type D); and transfers of a corporation's assets to another corporation in connection with a bankruptcy reorganization plan (Type G).

c. Divisive Reorganizations

Divisive reorganizations are divisions of a single corporation into two or more separate corporate entities. Corporate divisions are covered in Chapter XII, *infra*.

3. Guide to Analyzing a Reorganization

A student should first determine if a transaction qualifies as a reorganization. To qualify, a transaction must satisfy both the literal statutory requirements for one of the reorganization "types" in § 368 and also meet the applicable judicial requirements (continuity of proprietary interest, continuity of business enterprise and business purpose) that are now incorporated in the regulations. Reg. § 1.368–1(b). See XI.A.4., at pages 236–237, *infra*. Depending on the facts, other judicial doctrines, such as substance over form and the step transaction doctrine, also may be applied by the Service and the courts in analyzing a reorganization. Reg. § 1.368–1(c). See I.E., at pages 66–67, *supra*. If a transaction qualifies as a reorganization, the specific tax consequences to the parties are determined by "operative provisions" that govern recognition of gain or loss, treatment of liabilities, basis, and carryover of tax attributes (e.g., earnings and profits and net operating losses). See XI.B.7., at pages 254–260, *infra*. If a transaction fails to qualify as a reorganization, the tax consequences are determined under general Subchapter C principles. See XI.B.8., at page 260, *infra*.

4. Judicial Requirements
a. Continuity of Shareholder Proprietary Interest

The purpose of the continuity of interest doctrine is to prevent transactions that resemble sales from qualifying as tax-free reorganizations. Continuity of interest requires that a substantial part of the proprietary interest in T be preserved through an equity interest in P. Reg. § 1.368–1(e)(1). Put differently, P must acquire T by using consideration that represents a proprietary interest in P's affairs—i.e., stock—and that stock must be a substantial part of the value of the consideration used in the reorganization. Reg. § 1.368–2(e)(1)(i). Debt instruments, including convertible debt, do not confer the requisite proprietary interest. Id. The continuity of interest requirement has been incorporated into most of the statutory definitions in § 368. For example, the only permissible consideration in a Type B reorganization is voting stock. Where the statutory definition is imprecise as to consideration, as with Type A reorganizations, satisfying the judicial requirement becomes critical. See XI.B.1.b., at page 238, *infra*, for specific applications.

b. Continuity of Business Enterprise

To qualify as an acquisitive reorganization, the regulations require "continuity of business enterprise" under the modified corporate form. Reg. § 1.368–1(b). P either must continue T's historic business or continue to use a "significant portion" of T's "historic business assets" in a business. Reg. § 1.368–1(d)(1). The fact that P and T are in the same line of business tends to establish the requisite continuity but is not alone sufficient. If T has more than one business, P only must continue a "significant" line of T's business. Reg. § 1.368–1(d)(2)(ii). T's "historic business assets" are the assets used in its historic business. All the facts and circumstances are considered in evaluating whether a line of business is "significant". In general, the portion of those assets that are considered "significant" is based on their relative importance to the operation of the business. Reg. § 1.368–1(d)(2)(iii), (iv), –1(d)(3)(iii). The continuity of business enterprise requirement does not apply to the business or business assets of P prior to the reorganization. Rev.Rul. 81–25, 1981–1 C.B.

132. The regulations include extensive guidance on whether the continuation of T's historic business in tiered entities and through partnerships satisfies continuity of business enterprise. See Reg. § 1.368–1(d)(5) Examples (7)-(12).

Caveat: Some older cases, decided prior to the current regulations, have held that P need not continue T's historic business or use its business assets but merely must engage in some type of business activity. See, e.g., *Bentsen v. Phinney,* 199 F.Supp. 363 (S.D.Tex.1961).

Example (1): T conducts three separate lines of business which are of equal value. T disposes of two of the businesses for cash and, six months later, T merges into P, with T shareholders receiving P stock. If P continues T's remaining business, the continuity of business enterprise test is met because P is continuing a "significant line" of T's business. Reg. § 1.368–1(d)(5) Example (1).

Example (2): T is a manufacturer and P operates a lumber mill. T merges into P, which disposes of T's assets immediately after the merger and does not continue T's manufacturing business. Continuity of business enterprise is lacking because T neither continues T's historic business nor uses its historic business assets. Reg. 1.368–1(d)(5) Example (5).

Example (3): Same as Example (2), except after the merger P sells its lumber mill and uses the proceeds to expand the manufacturing business formerly conducted by T. The continuity of business enterprise requirement is met because P continues T's historic business. It is irrelevant that P sold the business it conducted prior to the merger. Rev.Rul. 81–25, 1981–1 C.B. 132.

c. Business Purpose

A transaction will not qualify as a reorganization unless it is motivated by a business or corporate purpose apart from tax avoidance. Reg. § 1.368–1(c). This requirement is most significant in connection with divisive reorganizations and will be discussed in detail in Chapter XII, *infra.*

5. Ruling Guidelines

Historically, most tax-free reorganizations would not be consummated unless the parties first received a favorable advance ruling from the Internal Revenue Service. Many transactions were planned in reliance on the Service's extensive advance ruling guidelines. More recently, the Service has announced that it will not grant "comfort" rulings on straightforward transactions, but it will continue to rule on transactions presenting a "significant issue." See, e.g., Rev. Proc. 2002–3,

§ 3.01(30), 2002–1 I.R.B. 117, 119. The Service's ruling guidelines remain an influential source of law, and they will be noted below when relevant to a specific transaction.

B. Acquisitive Reorganizations

1. **Type A Reorganizations (Statutory Merger or Consolidation)**
   a. **Merger and Consolidation Defined**
      1) In General
         A Type A reorganization is a merger or consolidation that meets the requirements of applicable state corporate law. In a typical merger, the assets and liabilities of T are transferred to P, and T dissolves by operation of law. The consideration received by T's shareholders is determined by the merger agreement. A consolidation is a transfer of assets and liabilities of two or more existing corporations to a newly created corporation. The transferor corporations dissolve by operation of law and their shareholders own stock of the new company.

      2) Divisive Mergers
         A "divisive" merger is a transaction that is a merger under state law where a corporation's assets are divided among two or more corporations. A divisive merger where only some of T's assets are transferred and T remains in existence does not qualify as a Type A reorganization. Rev. Rul. 2000–5, 2000–1 C.B. 436 (Situation 1). Similarly, T's transfer of assets and liabilities to two acquiring corporations followed by T's dissolution, with T's shareholders receiving stock of both acquiring corporations, does not qualify. Id. (Situation 2).

      3) Mergers Involving Disregarded Entities
         A single-member limited liability company ("SMLLC") is a disregarded entity for tax purposes and thus is treated as a division of its corporate owner unless it elects to be taxed as a separate corporation. Reg. § 301.7701–2(a). A merger of an SMLLC owned by a corporation ("X") into another corporation ("P") in exchange for P stock does not qualify as a Type A reorganization because it results in X's assets and liabilities being divided between X and P. Prop. Reg. § 1.368–2(b)(1)(iv) Example 5. But a merger of a corporation ("T") into an SMLLC may qualify if the continuity of interest and business enterprise requirements are met and T's legal existence terminates. Prop. Reg. § 1.368–2(b)(1)(iv) Example 2.

   b. **Continuity of Shareholder Proprietary Interest Requirement**
      Section 368(a)(1)(A) does not expressly limit the permissible consideration in a merger or consolidation. It is settled, however, that a transaction will not qualify as a Type A reorganization unless the continuity of shareholder

proprietary interest requirement is met. See *Southwest Natural Gas Co. v. Comm'r,* 189 F.2d 332 (5th Cir.1951). The test focuses on the quality of consideration received by T's shareholders (stock maintains continuity, debt or cash does not) and the percentage (by value) of equity consideration paid by P in the reorganization relative to the total consideration. For ruling purposes, the Service requires that at least 50% of the consideration paid by P must consist of P stock, which may be common or preferred and need not be voting stock. Rev.Proc. 77–37, 1977–2 C.B. 568. Some older cases have held that the continuity of interest requirement is met by lesser percentages. See, e.g., *John A. Nelson Co. v. Helvering,* 296 U.S. 374, 56 S.Ct. 273 (1935) (38% preferred stock sufficient). The test is met even if some T shareholders receive only cash or P debt as long as the T shareholders as a group maintain continuity of interest. Rev.Rul. 66–224, 1966–2 C.B. 114.

Example (1): T merges into P under state law. T shareholders receive a combination of cash and short-term P notes. The merger fails to qualify as a Type A reorganization because there is no continuity of interest. Such a cash merger is treated as a taxable sale of T's assets followed by a complete liquidation of T.

Example (2): Same as Example (1), except T shareholders receive P nonvoting preferred stock. There is 100% continuity and the merger qualifies as a Type A reorganization.

Example (3): Same as Example (1), except each T shareholder receives 50% P preferred stock and 50% cash. There is 50% continuity and the merger qualifies, but the T shareholders must recognize their realized gain to the extent of the cash received.

Example (4): Same as Example (1), except shareholders owning 60% of T stock receive P preferred stock and the remaining T shareholders receive cash. Even though some T shareholders only receive cash, the shareholders as a group have 60% continuity, and thus the transaction qualifies as a Type A reorganization. But the T shareholders who receive only cash will recognize gain. See XI.B.7.b. at page 255, *infra.*

c. Postacquisition Continuity
1) Prior Law

T's shareholders have never been required to maintain continuity of interest in P for any particular period of time after a Type A reorganization. But in determining if the continuity of interest requirement has been met, the Service historically considered sales and other dispositions of stock occurring subsequent to a merger which are part of the same overall "plan." Rev.Proc. 77–37, 1977–2 C.B. 568. For example, where the former T shareholders sold P stock pursuant to a binding commitment made prior to the merger, the merger and sale have been treated as one integrated transaction that may fail the continuity of interest test. The courts have disagreed over whether a pre-merger intent to sell (without any binding commitment) will defeat continuity of interest. See, e.g., *McDonald's Restaurants of Illinois, Inc. v. Comm'r,* 688 F.2d 520 (7th Cir.1982), rev'g, 76 T.C. 972 (1981), where the Tax Court treated a post-merger sale as a separate transaction because the former T shareholders were not contractually bound to sell, but the Seventh Circuit reversed, holding that a binding commitment was not required for application of the step transaction doctrine.

> *Example:* T merges into P, and T's sole shareholder, A, receives 1,000 shares of P stock. If A sells 700 of his P shares after the merger pursuant to a binding commitment, the continuity of interest test was not met under the historical case law. Some courts would reach the same result if A intended from the outset to sell more than 50% of his P stock or if the merger would not have been consummated unless A had been guaranteed the opportunity to make the sale.

2) Current Regulations

Regulations issued in 1998 change the rules discussed above by providing that subsequent dispositions of P stock by former T shareholders generally are not considered in determining whether the continuity of shareholder interest requirement is met, even if the dispositions are pursuant to a preexisting binding contract. Reg. § 1.368–1(e)(1)(i). If the facts demonstrate that T shareholders have sold their P stock for cash to P or a related party (e.g., a P subsidiary) before the transaction, the continuity of interest requirement may not be satisfied. Reg. § 1.368–1(e)(1)(ii), –1(e)(2). But if, after a reorganization, P initiates an open market stock repurchase program that was not previously negotiated with T or its shareholders, and some former T shareholders sell their P stock to P for cash in the open market, the sales will not be treated as "in connection with" the merger and thus will not have a negative effect on continuity of interest. Rev. Rul. 99–58, 1999–2 C.B. 701.

> *Example (1):* T merges into P, and T's sole shareholder, A, receives $50,000 cash and $50,000 of P common stock. One month later, pursuant to a preexisting binding contract negotiated by A, A sells all the P stock received in the merger to B, a party unrelated to P. The merger satisfies the continuity of interest requirement because, in the merger, A received stock of P representing a substantial part of the value of the total consideration transferred in the acquisition. Reg. § 1.368–1(e)(6) Example 1(i). As a

result of the merger and subsequent sale, A would be fully taxable on the disposition of his T stock, but T would not recognize gain on the transfer of its assets, and P would take a transferred basis in those assets. §§ 361(a); 362(b).

Example (2):   Same as Example (1) except one month after the merger S, a P subsidiary, buys the P stock received by A for cash. On these facts, the cash is treated as furnished by P, and the merger does not satisfy the continuity of interest requirement. Reg. § 1.368–1(e)(6) Example 4(iii).

d.   Preacquisition Continuity by Historic T Shareholders
1)   In General
     At one time, the continuity of interest doctrine required that a substantial part of the consideration paid by P in a potential reorganization must have consisted of P stock paid to "historic" shareholders of T. In tax jargon, a "historic shareholder" was a person whose T stock was "old and cold" when acquired by P. Historic shareholders generally must have held their T stock prior to the time P commenced its efforts to acquire control of T in a reorganization. Identification of historic shareholders often was problematic in the case of acquisitions of publicly traded companies because of numerous open market transactions that occur after a merger is announced but before it is consummated.

2)   Erosion of Historic Shareholder Concept
     The importance of the historic shareholder concept diminished, at least in the context of publicly traded corporations, after the Tax Court's decision in *J.E. Seagram Corp. v. Comm'r*, 104 T.C. 75 (1995). The fact pattern and holding are illustrated in the example below.

Example: X Corp. wishes to acquire T Corp. but is unable to negotiate a friendly takeover. P Corp. also wishes to acquire T. X, P, and T are all publicly traded companies. On January 1 of Year 1, X commences a cash tender offer to T shareholders. On January 15, P commences a competing tender offer to acquire all of T's stock for a combination of cash and P stock. As of March 1, X acquires 32% of T's stock for cash, and P acquires 46% of T's stock for cash. P emerges as the successful bidder and negotiates a merger with T's board of directors. On April 1, P acquires in the merger the 54% of T stock that it did not own (including the 32% acquired by X in its tender offer) in exchange for P stock. X realizes a loss on the exchange of its T stock for P stock, and it seeks to deduct the loss on the theory that the merger was not a tax-free reorganization because 78% of the "historic" T shareholders received cash for their T stock. In *J.E. Seagram Corp., supra*, the Tax Court denied X's loss, holding that the merger satisfied the continuity of interest doctrine and thus qualified as a tax-free reorganization. Noting that X's purchase of 32% of T stock for cash was independent of P's competing offer, the court suggested that X had become a "historic" shareholder of T. The opinion also can be read as holding that the continuity of interest test should be applied by focusing on the extent of equity consideration used by P without the necessity of identifying historic T shareholders. The court also noted that it was difficult to apply the historic shareholder concept in cases involving public companies because of frequent market transactions (e.g., arbitrage activity) after a takeover bid is announced. Thus, *J.E. Seagram* may be a narrow holding only applicable to transactions involving widely-held companies.

3) Current Regulations
    Regulations issued in 1998 eliminate the relevance of historic shareholders in acquisitive reorganizations except in limited situations. They provide that a "mere disposition" of T stock prior to a potential reorganization to buyers unrelated to T or P is disregarded in applying the continuity of interest doctrine. Reg. § 1.368–1(e)(1)(i).

    Example (1):   A owns 100% of the stock of T, Inc. (value–$100,000), which has negotiated a merger with P. Shortly before the merger is consummated, B, who is unrelated to T or P, purchases all of A's T stock for $100,000. Then, in the merger, B receives $50,000 cash and $50,000 P stock in exchange for her T stock. Continuity of interest is satisfied because B's T stock was exchanged for a sufficient amount of P stock (50% of total consideration) to preserve a substantial part of the value of the proprietary interest in T. The fact that B was not a "historic" T shareholder is irrelevant. Reg. § 1.368–1(e)(6) Example 1(ii).

    Example (2):   A owns 60% and B owns 40% of the stock of T, which has negotiated a merger with P. Because A does not wish to own P stock, T redeems all of A's T shares in exchange for cash, none of which is provided by P. T then merges into P, and B receives solely P stock. T's prereorganization redemption is not considered in determining if continuity of interest is preserved. The merger qualifies as a Type A reorganization because B's proprietary interest is preserved. Reg. § 1.368–1(e)(6) Example (9).

e. **Relationship to Taxable Stock Acquisitions**
    When P acquires 80% or more of T stock for cash or notes within a 12–month period and no § 338 election is made, the regulations treat P as owning the T

stock for continuity of interest purposes if T later transfers its assets to P or a P subsidiary in a transaction (e.g., a merger) that otherwise qualifies as a tax-free reorganization. See Reg. § 1.338–3(d), reversing the result in *Yoc Heating Corp. v. Comm'r*, 61 T.C. 168 (1973). In other words, P's exchange of T stock for a direct interest in T is treated as preserving continuity of interest for purposes of determining the *corporate-level* consequences of the merger. Some older case law provides that P may not be treated as a historic T shareholder in determining the tax consequences to minority shareholders who receive P stock when T merges into P (or a P subsidiary). *Kass v. Comm'r*, 60 T.C. 218 (1973), aff'd without opinion, 491 F.2d 749 (3d Cir.1974). The current regulations continue to follow this case law. Reg. § 1.368–3(d). The purpose of these confusing regulations is to reinforce the policy of § 338 by ensuring that P may not obtain a *Kimbell-Diamond* type cost basis in T's assets after a qualified stock purchase unless a § 338 election is made.

> ***Example:*** P acquires 90 of T's 100 outstanding shares for cash on January 1 and does not make a § 338 election. On July 1 of the same year, T merges into S, a subsidiary of P. In the July 1 merger, T's minority shareholder, A, receives P stock in exchange for her 10 shares of T stock. As to P and T, the merger qualifies as a tax-free reorganization because the T stock acquired by P for cash may be counted for continuity of interest purposes. Thus, T does not recognize gain or loss on the transfer of its assets, P does not recognize gain or loss on the exchange, and the assets take a transferred basis in S's hands. Reg. § 1.338–3(d)(5) Example (i)-(iv). The merger does not qualify as a Type A reorganization as to A, however, because continuity of interest is tested by reference to T's "historic" shareholders prior to P's acquisition of 90 shares. A thus must recognize gain or loss on her T stock. Reg. § 1.368–3(d)(5) Example (v).

f. Drop Downs

A transaction otherwise qualifying as a Type A reorganization is not disqualified if P transfers all or part of the T assets that it acquires to a controlled subsidiary of P. § 368(a)(2)(C).

2. Type B Reorganizations (Stock–for–Stock Acquisition)
a. Definition

A Type B reorganization is P's acquisition of T stock solely in exchange for P voting stock (or voting stock of P's parent) provided that P is in "control" of T immediately after the acquisition. § 368(a)(1)(B). For this purpose, "control" is ownership of 80% or more of T's voting power and 80% or more of the total shares of each class of T's nonvoting stock. § 368(c). T remains alive as a subsidiary of P after a Type B reorganization.

> ***Example (1):*** P transfers its voting stock to all of T's shareholders in exchange for their T stock. The acquisition qualifies as a Type B reorganization.

Example (2):   Same as Example (1), except that P only acquires 90% of the T stock. Because P is in "control" of T immediately after the exchange, the transaction qualifies as a Type B reorganization.

b. Solely for Voting Stock Requirement

Voting stock is the only permissible consideration in a Type B reorganization. With some minor exceptions noted below, even an insignificant amount of boot (including any nonvoting stock) will disqualify the exchange. To qualify as voting stock, shareholders must have an unconditional right to vote on routine corporate matters, not merely extraordinary events such as mergers and liquidations. Cf. Reg. § 1.302–3(a).

1) Fractional Shares
    The payment of cash in lieu of fractional shares in an otherwise qualifying stock-for-stock exchange will not violate the solely for voting stock requirement. Rev.Rul. 66–365, 1966–2 C.B. 116.

2) P's Payment of Expenses
    P may pay T's expenses (e.g., legal and accounting fees, registration fees) related to the reorganization without violating the solely for voting stock requirement, but P's payment of expenses of T's shareholders is impermissible consideration and will disqualify the exchange. Rev.Rul. 73–54, 1973–1 C.B. 187.

3) Buyouts of Dissenting Minority Shareholders
    If shareholders of T object to a stock-for-stock exchange, T may redeem their shares for cash prior to the exchange with P without violating the solely for voting stock requirement provided that the consideration is not provided by P. Rev.Rul. 55–440, 1955–2 C.B. 226. Alternatively, other T shareholders may purchase shares from dissenters for cash prior to a Type B reorganization. If a shareholder participates in the exchange and her new P voting stock is then redeemed by P for cash, the post-exchange redemption may disqualify the entire transaction if P was obligated to redeem the stock from the outset.

c. Creeping Acquisitions

To satisfy the "control" requirement in § 368(a)(1)(B), P must be in control after the stock-for-stock exchange, but P is not required to acquire 80% or more of T's stock in a Type B reorganization. The final step of a "creeping" acquisition thus may qualify as a Type B reorganization if P uses solely voting stock and any earlier cash acquisitions of voting stock are "old and cold." Whether or not an earlier cash acquisition is "old and cold" is usually a factual question, but the regulations assume acquisitions are related if they take place over a relatively short time span (e.g., 12 months) but not if they are separated by a very long interval (e.g., 16 years). Reg. § 1.368–2(c).

Example (1):   P acquired 60% of the stock of T for cash in 1980. P acquired an additional 30% of T stock in 1995 solely for P voting stock. Assuming, as is likely, that the cash acquisition is old and cold, the stock-for-stock exchange qualifies as a Type B reorganization because P has control of T after the transaction.

Example (2):   Same as Example (1), except P acquired 60% of T for cash in 1994 as a first step to acquiring control of T. It is likely that the cash and stock acquisitions will be integrated and, if so, the stock-for-stock exchange does not qualify as a Type B reorganization.

Example (3):   Same as Example (2), except P acquired only 10% of T for cash and, one year later, pursuant to the same overall plan, P acquired the remaining 90% solely for P voting stock. The stock-for-stock exchange does not qualify as a Type B reorganization even though more than 80% of T was acquired for voting stock. But if the 10% cash acquisition had been unrelated ("old and cold"), the later acquisition of 90% for stock would qualify. See *Chapman v. Comm'r*, 618 F.2d 856 (1st Cir.1980).

Example (4):   Same as Example (3), except P sold its 10% interest in T to an unrelated buyer and then acquired 100% of the T stock solely for P voting stock. If the earlier sale was unconditional, the stock-for-stock acquisition qualifies as a Type B reorganization. Rev.Rul. 72–354, 1972–2 C.B. 216.

d. Contingent Consideration

A Type B reorganization will not lose its tax-free status if, as part of the plan, P agrees to transfer additional P voting stock to the former T shareholders based on future earnings or other subsequent events. Contingent consideration will not disqualify the transaction if the additional stock is not evidenced by a negotiable instrument and certain other detailed requirements imposed by the Service are met. See Rev.Proc. 84–42, 1984–1 C.B. 521, § 3.03. Alternatively, P may place some of its stock in escrow on the condition that it be transferred to the T shareholders only if certain conditions (e.g., T's attaining specified earnings) are met. Id. at § 3.06.

e. Drop Downs

A transaction otherwise qualifying as a Type B reorganization is not disqualified if P transfers all or part of the T stock it acquires to a controlled subsidiary of P. § 368(a)(2)(C).

f. Subsequent Liquidation of T

If P acquires T stock in a stock-for-stock acquisition that qualifies as a Type B reorganization and then liquidates T pursuant to the same plan, the transaction is treated as an asset acquisition and is tested under the rules applicable to Type C reorganizations. Rev.Rul. 67–274, 1967–2 C.B. 141. See XI.B.3.h., at page 249, *infra*.

3. Type C Reorganizations (Stock–for–Assets Acquisition)
a. Definition

With a few exceptions described below, a Type C reorganization generally is P's acquisition of substantially all of T's assets solely in exchange for P voting stock (or voting stock of P's parent). A Type C stock-for-assets acquisition differs from a merger in that T's assets and liabilities are not automatically transferred to P by operation of law, and T does not immediately dissolve but must distribute the consideration it receives from P (and any assets it retains) to its shareholders in a complete liquidation.

b. "Substantially All of the Properties" Requirement

P must acquire substantially all of the properties of T. For advance ruling purposes, the Service has required a transfer of assets representing at least 90% of the fair market value of T's "net assets" (i.e., assets less liabilities) and at least 70% of the fair market value of the gross assets held by T immediately prior to the transfer. Rev.Proc. 77–37, 1977–2 C.B. 568. For this purpose, assets distributed by T to redeem stock held by dissenting and other minority shareholders and unwanted assets sold by T to other buyers are considered as assets held by T if the distributions are part of the reorganization plan. Id. The ruling policy is merely a safe harbor, not operative law. Some authorities interpret this requirement more flexibly by stating that no particular percentage is controlling and by looking to the type of assets retained by T and the purpose for the retention. For example, it may be permissible for T to retain nonoperating liquid assets (e.g., cash) to pay liabilities. Rev.Rul. 57–518, 1957–2 C.B. 253. If T sells 50% of its historic assets to unrelated parties for cash and then transfers all its assets (including the sales proceeds) to P, the "substantially all" requirement is met because T transfers all its assets and the effect of the transaction was not divisive. Rev. Rul. 88–48, 1988–1 C.B. 117.

Example (1):   T has $100,000 of assets and $20,000 of liabilities. T's gross assets are $100,000 (70% = $70,000) and its net assets are $80,000 (90% = $72,000). To satisfy the "substantially all" requirement under the Service's ruling guidelines, P must acquire at least $72,000 of T's assets.

Example (2):   T has $100,000 of assets, consisting of $70,000 of operating assets and $30,000 cash, and no liabilities. It distributes the cash to A, a 30% shareholder, in redemption of A's T stock. P then acquires the operating assets from T solely in exchange for P voting stock. If the pre-exchange redemption is part of the reorganization plan, the cash is considered a T asset for purposes of the "substantially all" test, and the acquisition fails the Service's guidelines because P has not acquired 90% ($90,000) of T's net assets. Under the case law, however, the transaction may qualify as a Type C reorganization because T has not retained operating assets.

c. Assumption of Liabilities

In applying the solely for voting stock requirement in § 368(a)(1)(C), P's assumption of T's liabilities, or taking of property subject to liabilities, is disregarded.

Example: T has $100,000 of assets and $20,000 of liabilities. P acquires all of T's assets and assumes its liabilities in exchange for $80,000 of P voting stock. The exchange qualifies as a Type C reorganization.

d. Boot Relaxation Rule

P's use of consideration other than its voting stock will not disqualify an exchange provided that P acquires at least 80% of the fair market value of *all* of T's assets solely for voting stock. For this purpose, T liabilities assumed (or taken subject to) by P are treated as cash consideration. § 368(a)(2)(B). As a result, a combination of liabilities assumed and other boot likely will disqualify an exchange.

Example (1): T has $100,000 of assets and no liabilities. P acquires all of T's assets in exchange for $80,000 of P voting stock and $20,000 cash. The transaction qualifies because P has acquired at least 80% of T's assets solely for P voting stock.

Example (2): Same as Example (1), except P acquires $90,000 of T's assets for $75,000 of P voting stock and $15,000 cash, and T retains $10,000 of its assets. The transaction does not satisfy the boot relaxation rule because P only acquires 75% of T's assets for P voting stock.

Example (3): Same as Example (1), except that T has $100,000 of assets and $20,000 of liabilities, and P acquires all of T's assets in exchange for $79,000 of P voting stock, $1,000 cash, and the assumption of all $20,000 of T's liabilities. The transaction does not satisfy the boot relaxation rule because the liability assumption is treated as cash consideration and thus P only acquires 79% of T's assets for P voting stock.

e. Liquidation Requirement

In a Type C reorganization, T must distribute all of the stock or securities it receives from P and all of its other assets pursuant to the reorganization plan unless the Service agrees to waive this requirement. § 368(a)(2)(G). As a practical matter, this means that T must completely liquidate after its exchange with P. In the rare case where the Service waives the distribution requirement, T is treated for tax purposes as if it had distributed its assets and recontributed them to the capital of a new corporation. H.R.Rep. No. 98–861, 98th Cong., 2d Sess. 845–846 (1984).

f. Creeping Acquisitions

If P previously acquired more than 20% of T's stock (even in an unrelated transaction) and then acquires all of T's assets solely in exchange for P voting stock, and T distributes the P voting stock to its shareholders (other than P) in complete liquidation, one old case held that the transaction failed to qualify as a Type C reorganization. *Bausch & Lomb Optical Co. v. Comm'r,* 267 F.2d 75 (2d Cir.1959), cert. denied, 361 U.S. 835, 80 S.Ct. 88 (1959). The questionable rationale was that P acquired more than 20% of T's assets in the liquidation of T in exchange for the *T* stock that P previously owned. The Service followed *Bausch & Lomb* for many years, but ultimately rejected its rationale. The regulations now provide that P's prior ownership of some T stock does not by itself prevent the "solely for voting stock" requirement from being met. The theory is that a transaction in which P converts an indirect interest in T's assets (through ownership of T stock) to a direct interest does not necessarily resemble a taxable sale of T's assets. Reg. § 1.368–2(d)(4)(i). But if the § 368(a)(2)(B) boot relaxation rule applies to the final step of a creeping C reorganization, the sum of: (1) the boot distributed to T's shareholders other than P and to T's creditors, and (2) the liabilities of T assumed by P, may not exceed 20% of the value of all of T's assets. Id. Finally, if in connection with potential C reorganization, P acquires T *stock* for cash or other boot from a T shareholder or T itself, that consideration is treated as boot exchanged by P for T's assets. As a result, the overall transaction will not qualify as a Type C reorganization unless at least 80% of the consideration consists of P voting stock. Id.

Example (1): Several years ago, in an unrelated transaction, P acquired 60% of T's stock for cash. The other 40% of T stock is owned by A. T has assets with a fair market value of $110,000 and a $10,000 liability. T transfers all of its assets to P in exchange for $30,000 of P voting stock and $10,000 cash. T then distributes the P voting stock and cash to A and liquidates. Applying the boot relaxation rule, the transaction qualifies as a Type C reorganization because the $10,000 cash and $10,000 liability assumption does not exceed $22,000 (20% of the value of T's assets). P's prior ownership of 60% of T stock does not adversely affect qualification. Reg. § 1.368–2(d)(4)(ii) Example (1).

Example (2): Same as Example (1), except P purchased its 60% stock interest in T for $60,000 cash as the first step in an overall plan to acquire T's assets—i.e., the 60% stock acquisition was not "unrelated" to the subsequent asset acquisition. The asset acquisition does not qualify as a Type C reorganization because P is treated as having acquired all of T's assets for consideration consisting of $70,000 cash ($60,000 for T stock and $10,000 in the later asset acquisition), $10,000 of liability assumption, and $30,000 of P voting stock. Reg. § 1.368–2(d)(4)(ii) Example (2).

g. Drop Downs

A transaction otherwise qualifying as a Type C reorganization is not disqualified if P transfers all or part of the T assets it acquires to a controlled subsidiary of P. § 368(a)(2)(C).

h. Overlap Issues

To prevent the use of Type C reorganizations to accomplish a tax-free corporate division without satisfying § 355 (see Chapter XII, *infra*), a transaction that qualifies as both a Type C and Type D reorganization is treated (and tested) as a Type D. § 368(a)(2)(A). If P acquires T stock in a stock-for-stock event acquisition that qualifies as a Type B reorganization and then liquidates T pursuant to the same plan, the transaction is treated as an asset acquisition and is tested under the rules applicable to Type C reorganizations. Rev.Rul. 67–274, 1967–2 C.B. 141.

4. Forward Triangular Mergers
a. Background

If P wishes to acquire T's assets in a tax-free acquisitive reorganization, it may be unwilling to incur the risk of T's unknown or contingent liabilities. This risk might continue even if P drops down T's assets and liabilities to a P subsidiary after a merger of T into P. P also may not wish to incur the expense and delay of securing formal approval of its shareholders to a merger or direct asset acquisition. The "forward triangular merger" solves many of these nontax problems. In its simplest form, a forward triangular merger consists of the following steps:

1) P forms a new subsidiary, S, by transferring P stock (and perhaps other consideration) for S stock in an exchange that is tax free under § 351.

2) T is merged into S under state law. T shareholders receive P stock and any other consideration provided by the merger agreement. P ordinarily does not need to secure approval from its shareholders because S is the party to the merger and P is the only shareholder of S. All of T's assets and liabilities are automatically transferred to S, which remains a wholly owned subsidiary of P.

b. Qualification Requirements

A forward triangular merger qualifies as a tax-free reorganization under § 368(a)(2)(D) if the following requirements are met:

1) S must acquire substantially all of the properties of T. This is the same requirement imposed on Type C reorganizations, and similar standards are applied. See XI.B.3.b., at page 246, *supra*.

2) No stock of S may be used as consideration in the merger. Use of S debt securities is not prohibited.

3) The transaction must have qualified as a Type A reorganization if T had merged directly into P. This means that the transaction must satisfy the judicial continuity of interest requirement—i.e., under the Service's ruling guidelines, P must acquire T using at least 50% P stock (voting or nonvoting).

> *Example (1):* T merges into S, a wholly owned subsidiary of P. Under the merger agreement, T shareholders as a group receive $100,000 of P nonvoting stock and $100,000 of P notes. The transaction qualifies as a forward triangular merger.

> *Example (2):* Same as Example (1), except the T shareholders receive $100,000 of P nonvoting stock and $100,000 of S voting stock. The transaction does not qualify because stock of S was used as consideration.

> *Example (3):* Same as Example (1), except prior to the merger T distributes 35% of its operating assets to shareholder A in redemption of all of A's T stock. T then merges into S, and the remaining T shareholders receive solely P voting stock. If the redemption was part of the reorganization plan, the transaction will not qualify because it fails the "substantially all of the properties" test.

c. **Subsequent Transfers of S Stock to P Subsidiary**

If, after a valid forward triangular merger in which T merges into S (a P subsidiary), P tranfers its S stock to S–1 as part of an overall reorganization plan, the transfer will not cause P to be treated as not in "control" of S (now a second-tier subsidiary) for purposes of § 368(a)(2)(D), and thus the transaction continues to qualify as a reorganization. Rev. Rul. 2001–24, 2001–22 I.R.B. 1290. Note that if the transaction were recast under the step transaction doctrine, T's assets would be treated as having been acquired by a second-tier P subsidiary (S) and the transaction would not qualify under § 368(a)(2)(D) because P would not directly "control" S (S–1 would control S).

5. **Reverse Triangular Mergers**
   a. **Background**

   P may wish to acquire the stock of T in a tax-free reorganization and keep T alive as a subsidiary in order to preserve certain rights under state law or valuable assets (e.g., a lease or franchise) that might be lost if T liquidated. A Type B reorganization may not be feasible, however, if P wishes to use consideration other than its voting stock. The "reverse triangular merger" was developed to accommodate these objectives. It consists of the following steps:

1) P forms a new subsidiary, S, by transferring P voting stock and other consideration for S stock in an exchange that is tax free under § 351. (Alternatively, P could make the transfer to an existing subsidiary.)

2) S merges into T under state law. T shareholders receive P voting stock and any other consideration provided by the merger agreement. P exchanges its S stock for T stock. S disappears and T survives as a wholly owned subsidiary of P. The end result is similar to a Type B reorganization.

b. Qualification Requirements

A reverse triangular merger qualifies as a tax-free reorganization under § 368(a)(2)(E) if the following requirements are met:

1) After the merger, T must hold substantially all of its properties and the properties of S (other than the stock of P distributed in the transaction and any boot used by S to acquire shares of minority shareholders). If, as is likely, S is a transitory subsidiary, it will not have any properties other than the consideration used to acquire T.

2) In the merger transaction, P must acquire 80% "control" of T in exchange for P voting stock. The remaining 20% of T may be acquired for cash or other boot. Note that 80% of T stock must be acquired for P voting stock in a single merger transaction; prior T stock held by P will not help to meet this requirement. Thus, the permissible consideration in a reverse triangular merger is more restrictive than in a forward triangular merger, and creeping acquisitions will not qualify.

Example (1): S, a wholly owned subsidiary of P, has no assets other than P voting stock and cash. P owns no stock of T. S merges into T. In the merger, T shareholders owning 90% of T stock receive P voting stock and holders of the remaining 10% of T stock receive cash. T continues to hold all of its own assets. The transaction qualifies as a reverse triangular merger.

Example (2): Same as Example (1), except P had acquired 21% of T five years ago in an unrelated transaction. In the merger of S into T, shareholders holding the remaining 79% of T stock receive P voting stock in exchange for their T stock. P does not acquire "control" of T in one transaction in exchange for P voting stock, and thus the transaction does not qualify as a reverse triangular merger. If S is a transitory corporation formed solely to effectuate the merger, the transaction will qualify as a Type B reorganization where, as here, the sole consideration used is P voting stock. See Reg. § 1.368–2(j)(7) Example (4).

c. Payments to Dissenting Shareholders

For purposes of the "control" requirement, T stock that is redeemed for cash or T property prior to a reverse merger is not treated as outstanding prior to the reorganization even if the redemption is related to the merger. Reg. § 1.368–2(j)(3)(i). But cash and property of T used to redeem stock of dissenting shareholders is taken into account in applying the "substantially all of the properties" requirement. Reg. § 1.368–2(j)(3)(iii).

Example: T has 1,000 shares of common stock outstanding, of which 800 shares are owned by A and 200 by B. S, a wholly owned subsidiary of P, merges into T. In a related transaction prior to the merger, T distributed cash in redemption of B's 200 shares. In the merger, P acquired 640 of A's shares for P voting stock and the remaining 160 shares for cash. Since B's shares are not treated as outstanding for purposes of determining whether P has acquired "control" of T with P voting stock, the acquisition satisfies the control requirement. But the cash used by T to redeem B's stock is treated as a T asset in applying the "substantially all of the properties" test. Reg. § 1.368–2(j)(7) Example (3).

d. Subsequent Sale of T Assets

If, following a qualified reverse triangular merger and as part of an overall acquisition plan, T sells 50% of its operating assets to an unrelated buyer and retains the cash proceeds, the asset sale will not cause the transaction to fail the requirement in § 368(a)(2)(E) that the surviving corporation "holds" substantially all of its properties. Rev. Rul. 2001–25, 2001–22 I.R.B. 1291. Compare Rev. Rul. 88–48, 1988–1 C.B. 117 ("substantially all" requirement met for Type C reorganization where T sells for cash one of two historic businesses representing 50% of its operating assets and then transfers cash and remaining assets to P in exchange for P voting stock and assumption of liabilities). The policy underlying these rulings is that the sale of 50% of T's assets to an unrelated buyer for cash, even if part of the overall plan, did not effect a divisive reorganization where former T shareholders sold part of T for cash and part for P stock.

6. Multi–Step Acquisitions: Special Problems

For nontax and strategical reasons, the parties to a corporate acquisition may desire to employ a multi-step structure. As discussed above, the tax consequences of multi-step ("creeping") acquisitions often turn on whether or not the various steps are analyzed separately or are treated as one integrated transaction. The Service has shown an increasing inclination to apply the step transaction doctrine to qualify multi-step acquisitions as reorganizations except when doing so violates a clear statutory policy (e.g., § 338). This complex area is best explained through a series of examples based on selected cases, regulations, and published rulings.

Example (1):   As part of an integrated acquisition plan where P intends to acquire T's assets, P first acquires all of T's stock from T's shareholders for consideration consisting of 51% P stock and 49% cash. T then promptly merges into P. Viewed in isolation, the first step does not qualify as a Type B reorganization because it fails the "solely for voting stock" requirement. Applying the step transaction doctrine, however, the overall acquisition qualifies as a Type A reorganization because at least 50% of the total consideration consists of P stock. *King Enterprises v. United States*, 418 F.2d 511 (Ct. Cl. 1969).

Example (2):   As a first step in a plan to acquire T, P initiates a tender offer for at least 51% of T stock, to be acquired solely for P voting stock. After acquiring the requisite 51% of T stock, P then forms S, and S merges into T. In the merger, T's remaining shareholders (holding 49% of T stock) exchange their T stock for a combination of consideration consisting of 2/3 P voting stock and 1/3 cash. Overall, T's shareholders have received 83.7% P stock and 16.3% cash for their T stock, and P owns 100% of T. If all the other requirements are met, the two steps will be integrated and will qualify as a § 368(a)(2)(E) reverse triangular merger even though neither step, viewed separately, qualifies as a reorganization. Rev. Rul. 2001–26, 2001–23 I.R.B. 1297. Note that the Service will apply the step transaction doctrine to these facts only if there is a factual basis to do so—e.g., the first step tender and the second step merger are announced as a package.

Example (3):   Pursuant to an integrated plan to acquire T's assets, P first forms a subsidiary, S, and S merges into T. In the merger, T shareholders receive solely cash. Shortly thereafter, T merges into T. The Service treats these steps as, first, P's "qualified stock purchase" of T (as defined in § 338(d)(3)) followed by a tax-free § 332 liquidation of T. As a result, if no § 338 election is made, P takes a transferred (rather than cost) basis in T's assets. Even though the step transaction properly could be applied here to disregard the existence of transitory S and treat the transaction as a direct taxable acquisition of T's assets, the Service respects the form of the two steps in deference to Congress's intent to replace the *Kimbell-Diamond* doctrine (treating a stock purchase followed by an upstream merger or liquidation of T as an asset purchase) with a more precise statutory regime (§ 338) which allows P to elect the tax treatment of the transaction at the corporate level. Rev. Rul. 90–95, 1990–2 C.B. 67. See IX.D.3., at pages 202–209, *supra*.

Example (4):   Same as Example (3), except in the first step (the reverse merger) T shareholders exchange their T stock for consideration consisting of 70% P stock and 30% cash. Shortly thereafter, T merges into P. Viewed in isolation, the first step (the merger of S into T) does not qualify as a § 368(a)(2)(E) reverse triangular merger because too much cash (more than 20%) was used as consideration. If, however, the two steps are treated as an integrated transaction— i.e., a single statutory merger of P into T—the overall acquisition qualifies as a Type A reorganization because the 30% cash does not violate continuity of interest. Rev. Rul. 2001–46, 2001–42 I.R.B. 1. Note that application of the step transaction doctrine to these facts does not violate the policy underlying § 338 because the integrated transaction qualifies as a reorganization in which P acquires T's assets with a transferred basis under § 362. As a result, the Service has ruled that a unilateral § 338 election may not be made in such a situation.

Example (5):   T Corp. is a wholly owned subsidiary of S Corp. P wishes to acquire T. As a first step, S sells all of its T stock to P for 50% P stock and 50% cash, and the parties jointly make a § 338(h)(10) election. Pursuant to a preconceived plan, T then merges upstream into P. As of mid–2002, the Service was considering whether to respect the form of the separate steps and the validity of the § 338(h)(10) election, which would permit the parties to treat P's acquisition of T as a taxable sale of T's assets. If the two steps were integrated as in Example (4), above, the transaction would qualify as a Type A reorganization, and P would take a transferred basis in T's assets. A reasonable approach would be to respect the separate steps and permit the § 338(h)(10) election where both parties have agreed to this treatment as part of their negotiations. The result would be that T would recognize gain or loss on a deemed sale of its assets, and P would take a fair market value ("cost") basis in T's assets.

7.   Treatment of the Parties to an Acquisitive Reorganization

If a transaction qualifies as a reorganization under § 368, the tax consequences to T's shareholders and any corporation that is a "party to a reorganization" are governed by the various operative provisions discussed below. Carryover of tax attributes (other than basis) in a reorganization is discussed in Chapter XIII, *infra*.

a.   Operative Provisions Glossary

1)   The operative provisions apply only if "stock or securities" are issued by a "party to a reorganization." A "party" includes the acquiring and target

corporations, the controlling parent corporation in a triangular reorganization, and the surviving corporation in a consolidation. § 368(b).

2) "Stock" is an equity interest in the corporation but does not include rights, warrants or options to purchase stock. Reg. § 1.354–1(e). Debt convertible into stock is treated as debt until the holder actually converts.

3) "Securities" are debt obligations that represent a degree of continuing participation in the corporation that falls short of an equity interest but is greater than an interest held by a short-term creditor. See *Camp Wolters Enterprises, Inc. v. Comm'r*, 22 T.C. 737 (1954), aff'd, 230 F.2d 555 (5th Cir.1956), cert. denied, 352 U.S. 826, 77 S.Ct. 39 (1956). Long-term bonds (10 years or more) generally qualify as securities but short-term notes (5 years or less) do not.

4) "Boot" is tax jargon for cash, short-term notes, the excess of securities received over securities surrendered by the taxpayer, and other property that does not qualify for nonrecognition. It often is referred to in the Code as "other property."

5) "Nonqualified preferred stock" is preferred stock with certain debt-like characteristics specified in § 351(g). See IV.B.3.b., at page 94, *supra*. Nonqualified preferred stock is treated as boot except to the extent it is exchanged for other nonqualified preferred stock. §§ 354(a)(2)(C)(i); 356(e).

b. Consequences to T Shareholders and Security Holders

The rules described in this section generally apply to all types of acquisitive reorganizations.

1) Recognition of Gain or Loss

T shareholders do not recognize gain or loss on an exchange of their T stock solely for P stock. § 354(a)(1). Realized gain must be recognized, however, to the extent that a T shareholder receives boot. § 356(a). A security holder of T does not recognize gain on the receipt of P securities in at least the same principal amount as the securities surrendered by the holder. But if the principal amount of P debt securities received exceeds the principal amount of T debt securities surrendered, the fair market value of the excess is treated as boot, and the security holder's realized gain is recognized to the extent of that boot. § 354(a)(2). In all events, a T shareholder or security holder who receives boot may not recognize any realized loss. § 356(c).

2) Character of Gain

Gain recognized by a T shareholder on an acquisitive reorganization is treated as a dividend if the exchange "has the effect of the distribution of a dividend" to the extent of the shareholder's ratable share of post–1913 earnings and profits "of the corporation." § 356(a)(2). In determining dividend equivalency, the principles of § 302 (see VII.C, at pages 149–157, *supra*) and the § 318 attribution rules apply. For this purpose, each T shareholder is treated as having initially received only P stock, a portion of which is then considered to be redeemed by P for an amount equal to the boot received. *Comm'r v. Clark,* 489 U.S. 726, 109 S.Ct. 1455 (1989); Rev.Rul. 93–61, 1993–2 C.B. 118. If this hypothetical redemption meets any of the tests for exchange treatment in § 302(b), the receipt of boot does not have the effect of a dividend and the shareholder recognizes capital gain. If the hypothetical redemption does not qualify for exchange treatment, the amount of recognized gain is a dividend to the extent of the shareholder's "ratable share" of "the corporation's" accumulated earnings and profits, and any remaining gain is capital gain. Although the statute is unclear, the majority view seems to be that the dividend determination is made by looking to T's earnings and profits. Any capital gain attributable to installment boot (e.g., a P note or bond that is not readily tradable) may be reported on the § 453 installment method unless the T stock surrendered was publicly traded. § 453(f)(6), (k)(2). See Prop.Reg. § 1.453–1(f)(2).

Example: A, an individual, is the sole shareholder of T Corp., which has $150,000 of accumulated E & P. A has a $60,000 basis in her T stock. P Corp. has 100,000 shares of common stock outstanding with a fair market value of $10 per share. T merges into P in a Type A reorganization. A receives 20,000 shares of P stock (value–$200,000) and $100,000 cash. A realizes $240,000 gain ($300,000 amount realized less A's $60,000 basis). A must recognize $100,000 of that gain under § 356(a)(1) (to the extent of the $100,000 cash boot). In determining dividend equivalency, A is treated as having received 30,000 shares of P stock (value–$300,000), of which 10,000 shares are redeemed by P in exchange for $100,000 cash. Before this hypothetical redemption, A is treated as owning 30,000 out of P's 130,000 outstanding shares (23.1%). After the redemption, A actually owned 20,000 out of P's 120,000 outstanding shares (16.67%). The redemption thus qualifies as substantially disproportionate under § 302(b)(2) (A's percentage ownership after the redemption is less than 80% of her ownership before), and A's $100,000 gain is capital gain because it does not have the effect of a dividend.

3) Basis and Holding Period
The basis of "nonrecognition property"—i.e., stock or nonboot securities received by former T shareholders—is the same as the T stock or securities surrendered, decreased by the cash and the fair market value of any other

boot received, and increased by the amount treated as a dividend and any other gain recognized. § 358(a)(1). Nonrecognition property takes a tacked holding period. § 1223(1). If different types of nonrecognition property are received (e.g., two classes of P stock), the aggregate § 358(a)(1) exchanged basis is allocated in proportion to their relative fair market values on the date of the exchange. Reg. § 1.358–2. Any boot received takes a fair market value basis and its holding period begins as of the date of the exchange. § 358(a)(2).

4) § 306 Stock

Preferred stock received in a reorganization may be § 306 stock if: (a) it is received in exchange for § 306 stock, or (b) the effect of the transaction was substantially the same as the receipt of a stock dividend and the taxpayer would have realized dividend income under § 356(a)(2) if cash, rather than preferred stock, had been received. § 306(c)(1)(B), (c)(2); Reg. § 1.306–3(d). See VIII.B.3., at page 183, *supra*. In view of the decision in the *Clark* case, it is less likely that cash received in an acquisitive reorganization will be equivalent to a dividend and, as a result, preferred stock is unlikely to constitute § 306 stock. The Service nonetheless has ruled that where shareholders of publicly traded T receive both common and preferred stock of publicly traded P, the preferred stock is § 306 stock and the § 306(b)(4) no tax avoidance exception does not apply. Rev.Rul. 89–63, 1989–1 C.B. 90. Preferred stock is not § 306 stock if the shareholder surrenders preferred stock that was not § 306 stock and the stock received and surrendered are of equal value and have comparable terms.

c. Consequences to T

The rules described below apply to T's transfer of its assets in a Type A or Type C reorganization or a forward triangular merger, and to T's distribution to its shareholders of the consideration it receives from P, along with any assets that it retains, in a complete liquidation pursuant to the reorganization plan.

1) Treatment of the Reorganization Exchange

T recognizes no gain or loss on an exchange of property, pursuant to a reorganization plan, solely for stock or securities of P. § 361(a). P's assumption of T liabilities is not treated as boot and does not prevent the exchange from qualifying as tax-free to T except in the rare case where the liability assumption is motivated by tax avoidance or lacks a business purpose. § 357(a), (b). If T receives boot, it must recognize its realized gain (but may not recognize loss) to the extent of the cash and the fair market value of any boot that T does not distribute to its shareholders or creditors pursuant to the reorganization plan. § 361(b), (c). Since any boot passes directly to the T shareholders in a merger and must be distributed to the T shareholders in a Type C reorganization, T will rarely recognize gain or loss on a reorganization exchange.

2) **Treatment of Distributions by T**

T does not recognize gain or loss when it distributes "qualified property" to its shareholders pursuant to a reorganization plan. § 361(c). In this context, "qualified property" includes P stock or debt obligations received by T in the reorganization exchange. A transfer of "qualified property" directly to creditors to satisfy T liabilities is treated as a "distribution" for this purpose. § 361(c)(3). If T distributes an asset other than qualified property, such as unwanted T assets not acquired by P in the reorganization, or boot received from P that appreciates between its receipt and later distribution, T recognizes gain (but not loss) as if the property had been sold for its fair market value. § 361(c)(1), (2).

3) **Sales Prior to Liquidation of T**

After a reorganization exchange with P but prior to liquidating, T may sell some of the P stock or securities it receives to third parties. These sales are fully taxable events even if they were necessary to raise funds to pay off creditors. If T transfers the stock or securities directly to creditors, however, no gain is recognized because the transfer is treated as a "distribution" of "qualified property" under § 361(c).

4) **Basis and Holding Period**

T is generally unconcerned with the basis and holding period of the P stock or securities received in an acquisitive reorganization because those properties ordinarily will be distributed tax free under § 361(c) to T's shareholders, who will determine their basis and holding period by reference to their former T stock under §§ 358 and 1223. See XI.B.7.b.3., at page 256, *supra*. Even in a Type C reorganization where the Commissioner waives the distribution requirement, T is deemed to have distributed its assets to its shareholders, who are then treated as having recontributed the property to a "new" corporation which takes over the shareholders' basis and holding period. T takes a fair market value basis in any boot received from P. § 358(a)(2).

Example (1): In a Type C reorganization, T transfers assets worth $100,000 with an aggregate adjusted basis of $65,000 to P in exchange for $100,000 of P voting stock. T immediately distributes the P stock to its shareholders in complete liquidation of T. T recognizes no gain on either the transfer of its assets or the distribution of the P stock.

Example (2): Same as Example (1), except T receives $90,000 of P voting stock and $10,000 cash in exchange for its assets, and T immediately distributes the P stock and cash to its shareholders. T recognizes no gain on either the transfer of its assets or the distribution. The result is the same if T uses the cash to pay debts not assumed by P.

Example (3): Same as Example (1), except T receives $90,000 of P voting stock and a $10,000 parcel of land (Gainacre) in exchange for its assets, and Gainacre is worth $12,000 when T distributes it along with the P stock to its shareholders. T recognizes no gain on the transfer of its assets to P. T recognizes no gain on the distribution of the P voting stock but recognizes $2,000 gain ($12,000 value less $10,000 § 358(a)(2) basis) on the distribution of Gainacre.

Example (4): Same as Example (1), except that T transfers $10,000 of the P stock received in exchange for its assets to a T creditor in full satisfaction of a $10,000 T debt that P did not assume. T recognizes no gain because a transfer of "qualified property" (the P stock) directly to a creditor is treated as a tax-free distribution under § 361(c). T would recognize gain if it sold the P stock and used the proceeds to pay the debt.

d. Consequences to P

1) Recognition of Gain or Loss

P does not recognize gain or loss on the issuance of its stock (or the stock of its parent) in an acquisitive reorganization. § 1032(a). P recognizes no gain if it issues securities or other debt consideration because the issuance is treated as a purchase. Reg. § 1.61–12(c)(1). If P transfers other "boot" property in connection with a reorganization exchange, it recognizes gain or loss under general tax principles. Rev.Rul. 72–327, 1972–2 C.B. 197. In a triangular reorganization, a subsidiary does not recognize gain on the acquisition of property in exchange for the stock of its parent. Rev.Rul. 57–278, 1957–1 C.B. 124.

2) Basis and Holding Period of T Assets Received

P's basis in T assets received in a Type A or Type C reorganization or a forward triangular merger is the same as T's basis in those assets increased by any gain recognized by T on the reorganization exchange. § 362(b). Since T rarely recognizes gain (see XI.B.7.c., at page 257, *supra*), P almost always takes a transferred basis. P takes a tacked holding period for capital and § 1231 assets that it receives from T. § 1223(2). In a Type B reorganization or reverse triangular merger, the bases of T's assets are unaffected.

3) Basis and Holding Period of T Stock Received

In a Type B reorganization, P's basis in the T stock equals the aggregate bases of the former T shareholders. §§ 362(b); 1223(2). In a forward triangular merger in which T merges into S (a P subsidiary), P may increase its basis in its S stock (usually zero, if S is newly formed) by the "net basis" (aggregate basis of assets less liabilities assumed) of T's assets. Reg. § 1.358–6(c)(1). In a reverse triangular merger, where S, a subsidiary of P, merges into T, P's basis in the T stock that it holds after the merger is generally the same as T's "net basis" in its assets increased by P's basis, if any, in its S stock. If S is a transitory subsidiary formed solely to carry out the merger, P likely will not have any basis in its S stock. Reg. § 1.358–6(c)(2).

8. Failed Reorganizations

An acquisition that fails to qualify as a reorganization under § 368 is treated as a taxable acquisition of T's assets or stock. See IX.D., at pages 200–211, *supra*. In the case of a failed Type A or C reorganization or a forward triangular merger, T recognizes gain or loss on the transfer of its assets and T's shareholders are treated as receiving a distribution in complete liquidation that is taxable under § 331. P obtains a cost basis in T's assets. In the case of a failed Type B reorganization or reverse triangular merger, T's shareholders recognize gain or loss on the sale of their stock. T does not recognize gain and retains its same asset bases unless P makes a § 338 election.

C. Nonacquisitive, Nondivisive Reorganizations

1. Nondivisive Type D Reorganizations (Transfer To Controlled Corporation)

A nondivisive Type D reorganization is a transfer by one corporation ("T" for transferor) of all or part of its assets to a corporation ("P") controlled immediately after the transfer by T or its shareholders (or any combination) provided that the stock or securities of P are distributed in a transaction that qualifies under § 354.

a. Control

For purposes of nondivisive D reorganizations, the definition of "control" is borrowed from § 304(c)—i.e. 50% of voting power and value. § 368(a)(2)(H).

b. Distribution Requirement

Section 354(b) requires that T must transfer "substantially all" of its assets to P and must distribute all of its properties (including the P stock and securities) to its shareholders.

c. Application

Taxpayers rarely seek to qualify a transaction as a nondivisive D reorganization. The Service historically has used the nondivisive D provisions to attack the now outmoded liquidation-reincorporation strategy. See XI.D.1., at page 264, *infra*.

2. Type E Reorganizations (Recapitalizations)
a. Introduction

A Type E reorganization is a recapitalization. "Recapitalization" is not defined in the Code but has been described by the Supreme Court as a "reshuffling of a capital structure within the framework of an existing corporation." *Helvering v. Southwest Consolidated Corp.,* 315 U.S. 194, 202, 62 S.Ct. 546, 551 (1942). In a recapitalization, a corporation's shareholders or creditors exchange their interests for other equity or debt interests. The assets of the corporation generally remain unchanged.

b. Judicial Requirements
Because a recapitalization involves only a single corporation, the Service has ruled that neither continuity of proprietary interest nor continuity of business enterprise is required for a recapitalization to qualify as a Type E reorganization. Rev.Rul. 77–415, 1977–2 C.B. 311; Rev.Rul. 82–34, 1982–1 C.B. 59. A recapitalization still must serve some corporate business purpose to qualify for nonrecognition. Reg. § 1.368–1(b).

c. Stock for Stock
Virtually all stock-for-stock exchanges, including preferred for common and common for preferred, will qualify as Type E reorganizations if they are carried out pursuant to a plan. Reg. § 1.368–2(e)(2)–(4). A stock-for-stock exchange also may qualify as tax-free under § 1036.

1) Receipt of Boot
   A shareholder does not recognize gain on a Type E stock-for-stock recapitalization unless boot is received. In that event, realized gain is recognized to the extent of the boot. See §§ 354; 356; and XI.B.7.b., at pages 255–257, *supra.* The gain is capital gain unless the transaction has the effect of the distribution of a dividend, in which case the dividend income is limited by both the shareholder's recognized gain and his ratable share of the corporation's E & P. § 356(a)(2). As with acquisitive reorganizations, § 302 principles are used in determining dividend equivalence. See XI.C.2.f., at page 262, *infra,* for additional issues raised when a shareholder receives a combination of stock and bonds for stock.

2) § 305 Aspects
   A recapitalization may result in a deemed stock distribution under § 305(c) (see VIII.A.3.f., at pages 178–179, *supra)* if it is: (a) pursuant to a plan to periodically increase a shareholder's proportionate interest in the assets or earnings and profits of the corporation, or (b) is with respect to preferred stock with dividend arrearages and the preferred shareholder increases his proportionate interest in the corporation as a result of the exchange. Reg. § 1.305–7(c). In these cases, the dividend (assuming sufficient E & P) is the amount of the increase in the shareholder's liquidation preference or the amount of the dividend arrearages that were eliminated. Reg. § 1.368–2(e)(5).

3) § 306 Aspects
   Stock received in a recapitalization will constitute § 306 stock if: (a) it is not common stock, (b) it was received pursuant to a plan of reorganization,

(c) no gain or loss was recognized on its receipt under §§ 354 and 356, and (d) the effect of the transaction was substantially the same as the receipt of a stock dividend or the stock was received in exchange for § 306 stock. § 306(c)(1)(B). Dividend equivalence results if cash received in lieu of the preferred stock received in a recapitalization would have been a dividend under § 356(a)(2). See Reg. § 1.306–3(d).

4) Nonqualified Preferred Stock

Although nonqualified preferred stock is generally treated as boot for purposes of § 368 reorganizations (see XI.B.7.a., at page 255, *supra*), it is not so treated in the case of an otherwise qualified recapitalization of certain "family-owned" corporations. § 354(a)(2)(C)(ii).

d. Bonds for Bonds

A creditor's exchange of outstanding bonds for newly issued bonds of the same corporation qualifies as a Type E reorganization. Rev.Rul. 77–415, 1977–2 C.B. 311. The creditor may recognize income, however, insofar as the bonds received are attributable to accrued or unpaid interest or the principal amount of the bonds received in the exchange exceeds the principal amount of the bonds surrendered. §§ 354(a)(2); 356(d). In some cases, a bonds-for-bonds recapitalization may result in discharge of indebtedness income to the corporation. The new bonds also may give rise to original issue discount.

e. Bonds Exchanged for Stock

When a creditor of a corporation exchanges old bonds for new stock in the debtor corporation, the exchange generally qualifies as a tax-free Type E reorganization. Reg. § 1.368–2(e)(1). Such exchanges commonly occur when a financially distressed corporation pays off outstanding bonds by transferring preferred or common stock to the creditor. If the principal amount of the surrendered bonds exceeds the fair market value of the stock, the corporation may recognize discharge of indebtedness income.

f. Stock Exchanged for Bonds or Stock and Bonds

A shareholder who surrenders old stock in exchange for new bonds, or a combination of new stock and bonds, has fundamentally altered his investment to the extent that new debt replaces old equity.

1) Stock for Bonds

An exchange of old stock solely for new bonds is treated as a redemption and is tested for dividend equivalency under §§ 301 and 302 whether or not the overall transaction is a Type E reorganization. See Reg. §§ 1.354–1(d) Example (3); 1.301–1(l).

2) Stock for Stock and Bonds

An exchange of old stock for new stock and bonds may qualify as a Type E reorganization. If so, the bonds constitute boot, and the shareholder's realized gain is recognized to the extent of the fair market value of the bonds received. § 354(a)(2)(A)(ii), (d). If the bonds are issued pro rata to all the shareholders, this gain likely will be characterized as a dividend under § 356(a)(2) to the extent of each shareholder's ratable share of E & P. If the bonds are not issued pro rata, the gain is more likely to be capital gain.

3) Securities Bailouts

In *Bazley v. Comm'r*, 331 U.S. 737, 67 S.Ct. 1489 (1947), the Supreme Court held that an exchange of old stock for a combination of new stock and bonds was not a recapitalization and that the shareholders realized dividend income (to the extent of E & P) under § 301 in an amount equal to the fair market value of the bonds received. *Bazley* was decided prior to enactment of the rule in § 354(a)(2)(A), which treats securities received in a recapitalization as boot if no securities are surrendered. The difference between the result in *Bazley* and the current statutory scheme is that under *Bazley* the entire value of the bonds is a dividend (even if the shareholder has no recognized gain), while under §§ 354 and 356 the dividend is limited to the shareholder's recognized gain on the stock. The extent to which *Bazley* still applies to a recapitalization is unsettled.

3. Type F Reorganizations (Change In Form)

A Type F reorganization is a mere change in identity, form, or place of organization of one corporation, however effected. § 368(a)(1)(F). Some courts once held that an F reorganization could include a combination of two or more active corporations. Although these transactions also qualified as Type A reorganizations, Type F status was preferable because postacquisition net operating losses of the new corporation could be carried back to offset profits earned by the previous corporation that conducted the same business. § 381(b). Congress eventually amended the Code to make it clear that F reorganizations are limited to transactions involving only a single operating corporation.

Example (1): X Corp., which is incorporated in California, wishes to change its state of incorporation to Delaware. To that end, X merges into newly formed Y Corp., a Delaware corporation. Pursuant to the merger, the X shareholders receive Y stock and X dissolves by operation of law. The merger qualifies as an F reorganization.

4. Type G Reorganizations (Insolvency)

A Type G reorganization is a transfer by one corporation of all or part of its assets to another corporation in a bankruptcy proceeding under Title 11 of the U.S. Code or a similar proceeding (e.g., receivership, foreclosure) in federal or state court, provided that the stock or securities of the transferee corporation are distributed pursuant to a plan of reorganization in a transaction that qualifies under §§ 354, 355 or 356. § 368(a)(1)(G). In overlap situations, the Type G rules take precedence. § 368(a)(3)(C).

D. Special Problems

1. Liquidation–Reincorporation

a. Background

The classic liquidation-reincorporation strategy was used by taxpayers to bail out corporate earnings at capital gains rates without paying corporate-level tax. A corporation with liquid and operating assets would distribute all its assets to its shareholders in complete liquidation and then recontribute the operating assets to a new corporation that would continue to operate the same business. If the strategy worked, the corporation would not recognize gain on the liquidation, and the shareholders would recognize capital gain under § 331. The new corporation would obtain a fair market value basis in the recontributed operating assets. This technique has largely been rendered obsolete by repeal of the *General Utilities* doctrine.

b. Attacks by the Service

The Service's principal line of attack was to apply the step transaction doctrine and classify the distribution of liquid assets as a dividend to the shareholders. To reach this result, it often argued that liquidation-reincorporation transactions were nondivisive Type D reorganizations (see XI.C.1., at page 260, *supra*). The Service generally was successful when the new corporation acquired substantially all of the old corporation's assets, as required by § 354(b). In applying the "substantially all" test for this purpose, the courts tended to focus on operating assets and ignore nonessential liquid assets. See, e.g., *Smothers v. U.S.*, 642 F.2d 894 (5th Cir.1981). The Service sometimes argued that a liquidation-reincorporation was really an F reorganization in which the shareholders realized a "boot dividend" to the extent of the liquid assets received on the "liquidation."

c. Current Viability of Strategy

Liquidation-reincorporation transactions are rarely desirable under current law because the liquidation will trigger corporate-level gain under § 336. In most cases, any benefits from this strategy will be outweighed by the acceleration of the corporate-level gain.

2. Dispositions of Unwanted Assets

A target corporation may wish to dispose of certain unwanted assets before being acquired in a tax-free reorganization. For the techniques and pitfalls of such preacquisition dispositions, see XII.H., at pages 284–287, *infra*.

E. Review Questions

1. Determine whether or not the transactions described below qualify as a reorganization under § 368:

(a) T, Inc. has 200 shares of common stock outstanding, owned 81% by A and 19% by B. In a single transaction, P, Inc. acquires all the stock of T in a stock-for-stock exchange in which A receives P voting stock and B receives P nonvoting preferred stock that is not nonqualified preferred stock.

(b) Same as (a), above, except that P liquidates T one week after acquiring the T stock.

(c) Same as (a), above, except that P acquired 21% of the T stock for cash 15 years ago and acquired the remaining 79% upon the merger of S, a transitory subsidiary of P formed to effect the transaction, into T. In the merger, T's shareholders (other than P) received P voting stock for their T stock.

(d) T, Inc., a computer software manufacturer, merges into P, Inc., a book publisher. T shareholders receive P voting stock (75% of the consideration) and P long-term bonds (25% of the consideration). One month after the merger, P sells T's assets and uses the proceeds to expand its book publishing business.

(e) T, Inc. owns operating assets with a fair market value of $200,000 subject to liabilities of $50,000. P, Inc. acquires the assets of T (subject to $25,000 of liabilities) in exchange for P voting stock worth $150,000 and $25,000 cash. T uses the cash to pay off its remaining liabilities and then liquidates, distributing the P voting stock to its shareholders.

2. T, Inc. is a closely held corporation with 100 shares of common stock outstanding, owned 50 shares by A (basis–$200,000) and 50 shares by B (basis–$400,000). T has the following assets:

	Adj. Basis	Fair Mkt. Value
Operating Assets	$600,000	$1,000,000
Liquid Assets	100,000	200,000
Total	$700,000	$1,200,000

T has $200,000 of liabilities and $300,000 of accumulated earnings and profits.

Determine the tax consequences to all relevant parties if P, Inc., a publicly traded company with 2 million shares of common stock outstanding, acquires T's assets, in the following alternative transactions:

(a) T merges into P. A and B each receive $500,000 of P nonvoting preferred stock that is not nonqualified preferred stock.

(b) Same as (a), above, except P acquires all of T's assets subject to its liabilities in exchange for $1,000,000 of P nonvoting preferred stock, and T promptly liquidates, distributing the P stock pro rata to A and B.

(c) Same as (a), above, except A and B each receive $300,000 of P voting stock and $200,000 of P long-term bonds.

(d) P acquires T's operating assets in exchange for $1,000,000 of P voting stock. T transfers $200,000 of the P voting stock to its creditors to pay off its liabilities, and then liquidates, distributing $800,000 of P voting stock and its $200,000 of liquid assets to its shareholders.

(e) P forms a new subsidiary, S, and S merges into T. In the merger, A and B receive only cash and P notes. Shortly thereafter, as part of the same overall plan, T merges into P. No § 338 election is made.

(f) Same as (e), above, except in the initial merger, A and B each receive consideration consisting of 60% P stock and 40% cash.

CORPORATE DIVISIONS

Analysis

A. Introduction

Corporate divisions are transactions in which a single corporate enterprise is divided into two or more separate corporations that remain under the same ownership. A division is accomplished when a parent corporation—known as "the distributing corporation"—distributes to its shareholders stock or securities of one or more controlled subsidiaries. If various judicial and statutory requirements are met, the transaction is tax free to the distributing corporation and its shareholders. The rationale is that a corporate division is merely a change in the form of businesses which continue to be owned and operated by the same shareholders. As with other nonrecognition provisions, gain or loss is preserved through transferred and exchanged bases. In this chapter, the parent distributing corporation will be referred to as "P" and the controlled subsidiary corporations will be referred to as "S," "S–1," "S–2," etc. P shareholders receiving S stock sometimes will be referred to as "distributees."

1. Types of Corporate Divisions
a. Spin–Offs
A spin-off is a pro rata distribution of S stock by P to its shareholders. S may be a preexisting subsidiary or a corporation that was formed by P immediately prior to the distribution. A spin-off resembles a dividend.

Example: P operates hotel and restaurant chains as separate divisions. P transfers the assets of the hotel division to a newly formed subsidiary, S, and distributes the S stock pro rata to its shareholders. After the distribution, the P shareholders own all the stock of both P and S.

b. Split–Offs
A split-off is a non pro rata distribution of S stock by P to some of its shareholders in exchange for all or part of their P stock. A split-off resembles a redemption.

Example: A and B are two equal shareholders of P, which operates hotel and restaurant chains as separate divisions. P transfers the hotel division assets to a newly formed subsidiary, S, and distributes the S stock to A in redemption of all of her P stock. After the distribution, A owns all the stock of S, and B owns all the stock of P.

c. Split–Ups
A split-up is a distribution of S–1 and S–2 stock, either pro rata or non pro rata, by P (which owns no other assets) to all of its shareholders. A split-up resembles a complete liquidation.

>***Example:*** A and B are two equal shareholders of P, which operates hotel and restaurant chains as separate divisions. P transfers the hotel division assets to a newly formed subsidiary, S–1, and the restaurant division assets to a newly formed subsidiary, S–2. P distributes the S–1 stock to A and the S–2 stock to B in complete liquidation. Alternatively, P might distribute the S–1 and S–2 stock pro rata to A and B. In either case, the transaction would be a split-up.

2. Type D Reorganization Preceding A Division

As illustrated above, the first step in a corporate division may involve P's transfer of the assets of a distinct trade or business to a controlled subsidiary, S, in exchange for S stock followed by P's distribution of the S stock in a spin-off, split-off or split-up. This first step qualifies as a divisive Type D reorganization if (as is likely) immediately after the transfer P or one or more of its shareholders or any combination thereof is in "control" of S and the subsequent distribution of S stock meets the requirements of § 355. § 368(a)(1)(D). In testing for "control," the fact that the shareholders of the distributing corporation dispose of part or all of the distributed stock, or the fact that the corporation whose stock was distributed issues additional stock, shall not be taken into account. § 368(a)(2)(H)(ii). The resulting tax consequences of a divisive Type D reorganization are:

a.   P recognizes no gain or loss on the transfer of assets to newly formed S. § 361(a).

b.   P's basis in its S stock is the same as the aggregate basis in the P assets transferred to S. § 358(a).

c.   S takes a transferred basis in the assets contributed to it by P. § 362(b).

Note that the same tax consequences generally would result on the formation of S under §§ 351, 358 and 362(a). See Chapter IV, *supra*. In a divisive Type D reorganization, however, the earnings and profits of P are allocated between P and S, and there are some other minor differences on collateral matters. See Reg. § 1.312–10 and XII.G.2.e., at page 283, *infra*.

3. Summary of Requirements for Tax–Free Division

P's distribution of S stock to P's shareholders will be tax free to P and its shareholders if the following statutory and judicial requirements are satisfied:

a.   P must control S immediately before the distribution—i.e., P must own at least 80% of S's voting power and 80% of each class of outstanding S nonvoting stock. §§ 355(a)(1)(A); 368(c).

b.   P must distribute either all of its S stock or securities held by P immediately before the distribution or distribute an amount of stock representing "control" of S and establish to the Service's satisfaction that the retention of S stock or securities was not part of a tax avoidance plan. § 355(a)(1)(D).

c. Immediately after a spin-off or split-off distribution, both P and S must be engaged in the active conduct of a trade or business. In a split-up, P must own no assets other than stock or securities of two or more subsidiaries immediately prior to the distribution, and each of those subsidiaries must engage in the active conduct of a trade or business after the distribution. § 355(b)(1)(B).

d. Each postdistribution trade or business must have been actively conducted throughout the five-year period preceding the distribution, must not have been acquired during that period in a taxable transaction, and must not have been conducted by a corporation the control of which was acquired by P, or by any corporate distributee shareholder of P, in a taxable transaction during the five-year predistribution period. § 355(b)(2)(D).

e. P's distribution of S stock and securities must not have been used principally as a "device" for the distribution of earnings and profits of P or S, or both. § 355(a)(1)(B).

f. The division must be carried out for a bona fide corporate business purpose. Reg. § 1.355–2(b).

g. The shareholders of P prior to the distribution must maintain sufficient continuity of proprietary interest in both P and S following the distribution. Reg. § 1.355–2(c).

h. The anti-avoidance rules in §§ 355(d) and 355(e) must not be violated; if they are, P (but not its shareholders) may recognize gain on the distribution.

B. Active Trade or Business

To qualify as a tax-free corporate division, P and S (or, in a split-up, S–1 and S–2) each must be engaged in the active conduct of a trade or business immediately after the distribution. These trades or businesses must have been actively conducted throughout the five-year period preceding the distribution and generally must not have been acquired by P or S in a taxable transaction within that five-year period.

1. Trade or Business
A "trade or business" is a specific group of activities carried on by the corporation for the purpose of earning income or profit. The activities must include every operation that forms a part of the process of earning income, including the collection of income and payment of expenses. Reg. § 1.355–3(b)(2)(ii).

2. Active Conduct
"Active conduct" of a trade or business requires the corporation to perform "active and substantial management and operational functions." Reg. § 1.355–3(b)(2)(iii).

Activities performed by outsiders, such as independent contractors, are not considered as performed by the corporation. Id. "Active conduct" does not include the holding of stock, securities, raw land or other purely passive investments, or the ownership (including leasing) of real or personal property used in a trade or business unless the owner performs significant services with respect to the operation and management of the property. Reg. § 1.355–3(b)(2)(iv).

Example (1):   P has discovered oil on land which it uses in a ranching business. If P has not engaged in any significant development activities with respect to its mineral rights, the holding of those rights is not an active business. Reg. § 1.355–3(c) Example (3).

Example (2):   P owns real estate that it leases to others. P performs no services with respect to the property apart from collection of rent. P's rental activities do not constitute the active conduct of a trade or business. See, e.g., *Rafferty v. Comm'r,* 452 F.2d 767 (1st Cir.1971).

Example (3):   Same as Example (2), except that P actively manages and maintains its rental properties. The activity is an active trade or business because P performs significant services with respect to the property. Reg. § 1.355–3(c) Example (12).

3.   Divisions of a Single Integrated Business
a.   Vertical Divisions
Section 355 does not require two distinct predistribution businesses. The active business test is met if P vertically divides an integrated business by transferring a portion of its assets and liabilities to S and then distributing the S stock to one or more of P's shareholders.

Example: A and B each own 50% of the stock of P. For more than five years, P has engaged in a construction business. P transfers one of its two major construction contracts, along with cash and equipment, to a new subsidiary, S, and distributes the S stock to A in redemption of A's P stock. After the distribution, P (now wholly owned by B) owns the other construction contract and the remaining equipment and cash. The distribution satisfies the active business requirement even though P conducted only one predistribution trade or business. *Comm'r v. Coady,* 289 F.2d 490 (6th Cir.1961); Reg. § 1.355–3(c) Example (4).

b.   Horizontal (or Functional) Divisions
The active business test is not necessarily violated on a distribution of certain distinct functions of a single business enterprise—e.g., the separation of manufacturing and research departments. A functional division, however, may present evidence of a device. Reg. § 1.355–2(d)(2)(iv)(C).

Example: For more than five years, P has engaged in a manufacturing business and maintained a research department in connection with its manufacturing activities. P transfers the assets of the research department to a new subsidiary, S, and distributes the S stock pro rata to P's shareholders. After the distribution, S continues its research activities, furnishing services only to P. The division satisfies the active business test. The result is the same if S performed services for P and outsiders after the distribution. Reg. § 1.355–3(c) Example (9). Even though the active business test is met, the distribution may be evidence of a device if S serves only P. See XII.C.2.c., at page 276, *infra*.

4. Five–Year Business History Rule

The postdistribution trades or businesses must have been actively conducted throughout the five-year period preceding the distribution. The assets of the business must not have been acquired within that period in a transaction that is taxable to the seller and the business must not have been conducted by a corporation the control (i.e., 80% of the stock) of which was acquired by P or a distributee corporation in a taxable transaction. § 355(b)(2)(B)–(D). These rules have engendered controversies over whether a particular activity is a separate business requiring its own five-year history or is simply part of an integrated business which has been actively conducted for more than five years.

a. Expansion of Existing Trade or Business

If P has engaged in a trade or business for more than five years and expands that business to other geographical locations within the five-year predistribution period, each location is considered part of an integrated trade or business with a more-than-five-year history. Even if P acquired the assets of a new branch within the five-year predistribution period in a taxable transaction, the new branch will be treated as an expansion of P's original business unless the acquisition effects such a change in character that it constitutes the acquisition of a new or different business. Reg. § 1.355–3(b)(3)(ii); *Lockwood's Estate v. Comm'r*, 350 F.2d 712 (8th Cir.1965).

Example (1): P has been engaged in the operation of a department store in City for more than five years. Two years ago, it opened a second store in Suburb. P transfers the assets of the suburban store to a new subsidiary, S, and distributes the S stock pro rata to P's shareholders. Both P and S are considered to satisfy the five-year business history rule. Reg. § 1.355–3(c) Example (7).

Example (2): P has been engaged in the manufacture of farm machinery in Nebraska for more than five years. Two years ago, it acquired the assets of a similar manufacturing plant in Maine, where P had not previously conducted business. P transfers the assets of the Maine facility to a new subsidiary, S, and distributes the S stock pro rata to P's shareholders. Both P and S satisfy the five-year business history rule because the acquisition of the Maine plant was an expansion of an existing trade or business rather than an acquisition of a new business. Reg. § 1.355–3(c) Example (8).

b. **Acquisition of a New Trade or Business**
The active business test is violated if P acquired the assets (§ 355(b)(2)(C)) or if P or a distributee corporation acquired a controlling stock interest (§ 355(b)(2)(D)) in the business in a taxable transaction within the five years preceding the distribution. A "taxable" transaction is one in which gain or loss was recognized to the seller in whole or in part—i.e., almost any acquisition other than a wholly tax-free reorganization under § 368 or a liquidation of a subsidiary under § 332. Reg. § 1.355–3(b)(4)(i).

Example (1): P has been engaged in the apparel business for more than five years. Two years ago, it acquired for cash all the assets of a hardware business. P transfers the hardware assets to a newly formed subsidiary, S, and distributes the S stock pro rata to the P shareholders. The distribution fails the active business test because P acquired the hardware assets in a taxable transaction within five years prior to the distribution.

Example (2): Same as Example (1), except P acquired the hardware assets two years ago in a Type A reorganization in which some of the former shareholders of the hardware business recognized gain because they received boot. The distribution would not qualify because the hardware assets were acquired in a partially taxable transaction.

Example (3): Same as Example (1), except that two years ago P acquired 100% of the stock of S, which has operated the hardware business for more than five years, in a transaction that was taxable to the former S shareholders. The distribution fails the active business test because P acquired control of S in a taxable transaction within the five-year predistribution period.

Example (4): Same as Example (3), except P acquired 100% of the S stock in a tax-free Type B reorganization. The distribution would qualify under the active business test because S has been engaged in the hardware business for more than five years and P did not acquire S in a taxable transaction.

5. **Disposition of a Recently Acquired Business**
A distribution will fail the active business test if a controlling interest in P was acquired by a corporate distributee (i.e., a corporate shareholder of P) in a taxable transaction within the five-year predistribution period. § 355(b)(2)(D). The purpose

of this requirement is to prevent a corporation from using § 355 to dispose of a recently acquired subsidiary without paying a corporate-level tax.

Example: P and its wholly owned subsidiary, S, each have been engaged in the active conduct of a trade or business for more than five years. Two years ago, X Inc. purchased 100% of the stock of P and did not make a § 338 election. X wishes to sell the business operated by S without recognizing gain. Even if the other § 355 requirements are met, P's distribution of its S stock to X will not satisfy the active business test because X acquired control of P in a taxable transaction within the five years preceding the distribution. (In any event, it is doubtful whether this transaction would satisfy the business purpose or continuity of interest requirements.)

C. Device Limitation

A distribution does not qualify as tax-free under § 355 if it is used principally as a device for the distribution of the earnings and profits of P, S, or both corporations. § 355(a)(1)(B).

1. Introduction

The primary purpose of the device limitation is to prevent bailouts of corporate earnings at preferential capital gains rates where P distributed its S stock pro rata to the P shareholders, who then sold the P or S stock. In the absence of a significant capital gains preference, the limitation also serves to prevent tax avoidance through a recovery of basis. Reg. § 1.355–2(d)(1). The regulations provide that the determination of whether a transaction was used principally as a device is a factual question, and they identify certain factors that constitute evidence of a device or a nondevice. Reg. § 1.355–2(d)(1). Section 355(a)(1)(B) provides that the "mere fact" that stock or securities of either P or S are sold subsequent to the distribution shall not be construed to mean that the distribution was used principally as a device unless the sale was negotiated or agreed upon prior to the distribution. The regulations nonetheless emphasize that subsequent sales of P or S stock may be evidence of a device. Reg. § 1.355–2(d)(2)(iii). See XII.C.2.b., below.

2. Device Factors

The presence of any of the following factors is evidence of a device, the strength of which depends on the facts and circumstances. Reg. § 1.355–2(d)(2)(i).

a. Pro Rata Distribution

Because a pro rata or substantially pro rata distribution of S stock presents the greatest potential for a bailout, pro rata distributions (e.g., spin-offs) are evidence of a device. Reg. § 1.355–2(d)(2)(ii).

b. Subsequent Sale or Exchange of P or S Stock

A sale or exchange of either P or S stock after the distribution is evidence of a device. The strength of the evidence increases as more stock of P or S is sold and decreases as more time passes between the distribution and subsequent sale. Reg. § 1.355–2(d)(2)(iii)(A). The strength of the evidence also depends upon whether the sale or exchange is pursuant to an arrangement negotiated or agreed upon before the distribution—i.e., if enforceable rights to buy or sell existed before the distribution or if the sale was discussed by the parties and was reasonably to be anticipated before the distribution. Reg. § 1.355–2(d)(2)(iii)(D). A subsequent sale that was prearranged is *substantial* evidence of a device, while other subsequent sales are only evidence. A subsequent exchange of P or S stock in a wholly tax-free reorganization, or a reorganization where only an insubstantial amount of gain is recognized, is not treated as a subsequent sale or exchange. Reg. § 1.355–2(d)(2)(iii)(E).

c. **Nature and Use of Assets**
Evidence of a device exists if either P or S holds assets, such as cash or portfolio securities, that are not used in or related to the reasonable needs of the qualifying active business. The strength of this evidence depends on all the facts and circumstances, including the ratio for P and S of the nonbusiness assets to the value of the active businesses. Reg. § 1.355–2(d)(2)(iv)(B). Evidence of a device also exists if the business of P or S is a "secondary business" that principally services the business of the other corporation and which can be sold without adversely affecting the business that it serves. Reg. § 1.355–2(d)(2)(iv)(C).

Example (1): P and its wholly owned subsidiary, S, each engage in the active conduct of a trade or business. P distributes its S stock pro rata to the P shareholders. Prior to the distribution, P transferred to S excess cash not reasonably related to the conduct of either business. The result of this transfer is that the percentage of unrelated liquid assets is substantially greater for S than for P. The transfer of cash by P to S in connection with the distribution is relatively strong evidence of a device. Reg. § 1.355–2(d)(4) Example (3). If P and S held liquid assets in amounts proportional to the values of their businesses after a transfer of cash by P to S, the transaction would be relatively weak evidence of device. Reg. § 1.355–2(d)(4) Example (2).

Example (2): P engages in the manufacture and sale of steel. Its wholly owned subsidiary, S, operates a coal mine solely to supply P's needs for coal. If P distributes the S stock pro rata to the P shareholders and S continues to supply coal exclusively to P, the relationship of P and S after the distribution constitutes evidence of a device if it can be demonstrated that the coal mine could be sold without adversely affecting P's steel business. Reg. § 1.355–2(d)(2)(iv)(C).

3. **Nondevice Factors**
The presence of any of the following factors is evidence of a "nondevice," the strength of which depends on the facts and circumstances. Reg. § 1.355–3(d)(3)(i).

a. Corporate Business Purpose

The corporate business purpose for P's distribution is evidence of a nondevice, the strength of which depends on all the facts and circumstances, including but not limited to:

1) The importance of achieving the purpose to the success of the business.

2) The extent to which the transaction is prompted by a person not having a proprietary interest in either corporation, or by other outside factors beyond the control of P.

3) The immediacy of the conditions prompting the transaction. Reg. § 1.355–2(d)(3)(ii).

The stronger the evidence of device, the stronger the corporate business purpose must be to prevent the distribution from failing the device test. Id.

b. P is Publicly Traded and Widely Held

The fact that P is publicly traded and has no shareholder that directly or indirectly owns more than 5% of any class of P stock is evidence of nondevice. Reg. § 1.355–2(d)(3)(iii).

c. Distributions to Domestic Corporate Shareholders

The fact that the stock of S is distributed to a domestic corporate distributee which, without § 355, would be entitled to an 80% or 100% dividends received deduction under § 243, is evidence of nondevice. Reg. § 1.355–3(d)(3)(iv). Note that distributions to corporate shareholders that would be entitled to only the 70% dividends received deduction are not evidence of nondevice.

4. Presumptive Nondevice Transactions

The following types of distributions "ordinarily" are not treated as a device notwithstanding the presence or absence of any device factors. Reg. § 1.355–2(d)(5)(i).

a. Absence of Earnings and Profits

A distribution in which P and S have neither accumulated nor current E & P as of the date of the distribution, taking into account the possibility that a distribution by P would create E & P if § 355 did not apply. Reg. § 1.355–2(d)(5)(ii).

b. Section 302 or 303 Exchange Redemption

In the absence of § 355, the distribution would qualify, with respect to each distributee shareholder, as an exchange redemption under § 302(a) (see VII.C., at pages 149–157, *supra*) or a redemption to pay death taxes under § 303 (see

VII.F., at pages 166–168, *supra*). Reg. § 1.355–2(d)(5)(iii), (iv). This nondevice presumption does not apply, however, if P distributes the stock of two or more subsidiaries and the distribution facilitates avoidance of the dividend provisions through the subsequent sale of stock of one subsidiary and the retention of stock of another. Reg. § 1.355–2(d)(5)(i).

D. Distribution of Control Requirement

P must distribute either all the S stock or securities that it holds immediately before the distribution or an amount of S stock constituting "control," as defined in § 368(c) (i.e., 80% of voting power and total shares of each class of nonvoting stock) and establish to the satisfaction of the Service that the retention of S stock or securities is not part of a plan having tax avoidance as one of its principal purposes. § 355(a)(1)(D). For this purpose, "stock" does not include "rights" to acquire stock. Reg. § 1.355–1(b). The stock does not have to be distributed pro rata among the shareholders to satisfy this requirement. § 355(a)(2)(A). Ordinarily, the business purpose for the division will require P to distribute all of the S stock or securities. Reg. § 1.355–2(e)(2). A series of distributions of S stock over several years will not meet this requirement unless P was under a binding commitment to distribute all the S stock or securities from the outset. *Comm'r v. Gordon,* 391 U.S. 83, 88 S.Ct. 1517 (1968).

E. Business Purpose

To qualify as tax free under § 355, a corporate division must be motivated by a "real and substantial non-Federal tax purpose" germane to the business of P or S. Reg. § 1.355–2(b)(1)–(2). The business purpose limitation is a judicially created requirement that is set forth in the regulations and extensive IRS ruling guidelines. It is independent of the other requirements under § 355.

1. Background
The business purpose requirement is generally applicable to tax-free reorganizations but assumes its greatest significance when applied to corporate divisions. It originated in the case of *Gregory v. Helvering,* 293 U.S. 465, 55 S.Ct. 266 (1935), where the Supreme Court held that a transaction that literally satisfied the requirements for tax-free treatment did not qualify as a reorganization because it had "no business or corporate purpose" and was a "mere device" to bail out earnings at capital gains rates. *Gregory* also was one of the first articulations of the substance over form doctrine. See I.E.1., at page 66, *supra.*

2. Corporate Business Purpose
A § 355 distribution must be motivated by a corporate rather than a shareholder business purpose. In cases where a shareholder purpose is so nearly coextensive with a corporate business purpose as to preclude any distinction between them, the requirement will be satisfied. Reg. § 1.355–2(b)(2). For advance ruling purposes,

the Service requires a detailed explanation of the corporate business purposes motivating a proposed § 355 transaction and why they cannot be achieved through a transaction that does not involve a distribution of stock. Rev. Proc. 96–30, App. A, 1996–1 C.B. 696. Examples of valid corporate business purposes include:

a. To comply with a law or court decree requiring a division of P's businesses— e.g., an antitrust decree. Reg. § 1.355–2(b)(5) Example (1).

b. A split-up to resolve a shareholder dispute or to enable shareholders with different expertise to devote their undivided attention to separate parts of the business. Reg. § 1.355–2(b)(5) Example (2).

c. To enable a key employee to acquire an equity interest in either P or S. Reg. § 1.355–2(b)(5) Example (8); Rev.Rul. 88–34, 1988–1 C.B. 115.

d. To dispose of a business that is unwanted by a corporation seeking to acquire P. See, e.g., Rev.Rul. 70–434, 1970–2 C.B. 83.

e. To reduce state or local taxes provided that the transaction does not also result in a comparable or greater reduction of Federal taxes. Reg. §§ 1.355–2(b)(2), –2(b)(5) Examples (6) and (7).

f. To help P secure needed additional debt capital. Rev.Rul. 85–122, 1985–2 C.B. 118.

g. To resolve administrative, management, systemic, or other problems resulting from the operation of two or more businesses by a single corporation. Rev. Proc. 96–30, App. A, § 2.05, 1996–1 C.B. 696.

3. Business Purpose For Distribution

The business purpose requirement is not satisfied if P's goals could have been achieved through a nontaxable transaction that: (a) would not have required the distribution of S stock and (b) was neither impractical nor unduly expensive. Reg. § 1.355–2(b)(3).

Example: P actively conducts a candy business and a toy business. To protect the candy business from the risks of the toy business, P transfers the toy assets to a newly formed subsidiary, S, and distributes the S stock to the P shareholders. The business purpose requirement is not met because P could have achieved its purposes simply by transferring the toy assets to S. Reg. § 1.355–2(b)(5) Example (3).

4. Relationship to Device Limitation

The corporate business purpose for a transaction is used as evidence in determining whether the transaction was used principally as a device for the distribution of E & P. See XII.C.3.a., at page 277, *supra*.

F.   Continuity of Interest

The § 355 regulations incorporate the judicial continuity of interest requirement by providing that, after P's distribution of S stock, one or more of the historic predistribution P shareholders must maintain, in the aggregate, continuity of interest in both P and S. Reg. § 1.355–2(c)(1). The regulations indicate that this requirement is met if one or more of the predistribution P shareholders own at least 50% (by value) of both P and S after the division. Some historic shareholders may own P stock and others may own S stock provided that, in the aggregate, the historic P shareholders maintain continuity in both P and S. Reg. § 1.355–2(c)(2) Examples (2) and (4). See also Rev.Proc. 96–30, § 4.06, 1996–1 C.B. 696.

Example (1):   A and B each own 50% of the stock of P. P and its wholly owned subsidiary, S, each conduct an active business. P and S are equal in value. For a valid corporate business purpose, P distributes the S stock to B in exchange for all of his P stock, and A continues as the sole shareholder of P. The continuity of interest requirement is met because the prior owners of P (A and B), in the aggregate, retain sufficient continuity in P and S after the distribution. Reg. § 1.355–2(c) Example (1).

Example (2):   Same as Example (1), except that pursuant to a plan to acquire a stock interest in P, unrelated individual C purchases all of A's stock in P before the distribution. After the distribution, C owns 100% of P and B owns 100% of S. The continuity of interest requirement is not met. Even though historic P shareholders (i.e., B) own 50% of the overall enterprise, they have not maintained a 50% interest in P. C is not considered an historic P shareholder because he acquired his P stock shortly before and in anticipation of the distribution. Reg. § 1.355–2(c) Example (3).

G.   Tax Treatment of the Parties To A Corporate Division

1.   Shareholders and Security Holders
a.   No Boot Received
With exceptions noted below, P's shareholders and security holders generally do not recognize gain or loss on the receipt of S stock or securities if the requirements of § 355 are met. The shareholders allocate their old basis in the P stock between the P and S stock in proportion to their relative fair market values, and they may tack the holding period of their P stock to the S stock received from P. Shareholders who receive S stock in exchange for all their P stock (e.g., in a split-up) take a basis in the new S stock equal to the basis in their old P stock. §§ 358(a); 1223(1).

Example: A is the sole shareholder of P and has a $12,000 basis in her P stock. P distributes all the stock of its 100% subsidiary, S, to A in a spin-off that qualifies under § 355. After the distribution, the fair market values of A's P and S stock were $40,000 and $20,000, respectively. A allocates her $12,000 basis as follows: ⅔ ($8,000) to the P stock and ⅓ ($4,000) to the S stock.

b. Boot Received

1) Boot Defined

For purposes of § 355 transactions, boot includes any property other than S stock or securities (e.g., cash, short-term debt obligations, stock rights or warrants), S securities (e.g., debt obligations with a longer term) to the extent that their principal amount exceeds the principal amount of any securities surrendered, and any stock of S that was acquired by P (or a subsidiary of P) in a taxable transaction within the five-year period preceding the distribution. §§ 355(a)(3)(B); 356(a), (b), (d)(2)(C). Boot also may include nonqualified preferred stock, as defined in § 351(g). See IV.B.3.b., at page 94, *supra*. Thus, if P had owned 90% of S for many years and acquired the remaining 10% six months prior to the distribution, the newly acquired stock will be treated as boot. Reg. § 1.355–2(g). See *Dunn Trust v. Comm'r,* 86 T.C. 745 (1986).

2) Spin–Offs

In a spin-off, the receipt of boot is treated as a § 301 distribution (without regard to the shareholder's realized gain) and is thus a dividend to the extent of P's E & P. Any remaining portion of the distribution first reduces the shareholder's basis in his P stock and then is treated as capital gain under the rules in § 301(c). § 356(b).

3) Split–Offs and Split–Ups

A P shareholder who receives boot in a split-off or split-up recognizes her realized gain to the extent of the boot. § 356(a)(1). If the exchange has "the effect of the distribution of a dividend," the recognized gain is a dividend to the extent of the shareholder's ratable share of P's accumulated E & P. § 356(a)(2). Any remaining recognized gain is gain from an exchange of property—usually capital gain. Reg. § 1.356–1(b)(2). Dividend equivalence is tested by applying § 302 principles (reduction of proportionate interest) prior to the exchange by treating the recipient shareholder as having received the boot in redemption of an amount of P stock equal to the value of the boot and by then comparing the shareholder's interest in P before the exchange with the interest the shareholder would have retained if she had surrendered only an amount of P stock equal in value to the boot. Rev.Rul. 93–62, 1993–2 C.B. 118. In no event may loss be recognized. § 356(c).

Example: A owns 100 shares of P stock with a fair market value of $1,000 ($10 per share) and a basis of $200 ($2 per share). P has 1,000 shares of stock outstanding. In a split-off that qualifies under § 355, P distributes all the stock in its 100% subsidiary, S (value–$500) and $250 cash in redemption of 75 shares of A's P stock. A recognizes $250 of gain on the distribution. To determine if that gain is a dividend, it is assumed that P only distributed $250 to A in redemption of 25 P shares. Under this analysis, A owned 10% of P ($^{100}/_{1000}$ shares) before and 7.7% ($^{75}/_{975}$ shares) after the redemption. The hypothetical redemption qualifies as substantially disproportionate under § 302(b)(2) and A's $250 gain is capital gain.

4) Basis and Holding Period

The aggregate basis of the P and S stock (or, in a split-up, the S–1 and S–2 stock) after a corporate division is the same as the basis of the shareholder's P stock (prior to the exchange), reduced by the cash and the fair market value of any boot property received, and increased by the shareholder's recognized gain (including any dividend income). That amount is then allocated between the P and S stock (or, in a split-up, the S–1 and S–2 stock) in proportion to their relative fair market values. §§ 358(b)(2), (c); Reg. § 1.358–2. The S stock takes a tacked holding period. § 1223(1). The boot received takes a fair market value basis, and its holding period begins on the date of the exchange. § 358(a)(2).

2. The Distributing Corporation
a. Distribution Preceded by Reorganization

If a § 355 distribution is pursuant to a Type D reorganization plan (see XII.A.2., at page 270, *supra*), P does not recognize gain when it distributes S stock or S debt obligations ("qualified property") to the P shareholders. § 361(c)(1), (2). P recognizes gain, however, on a distribution of appreciated boot in a § 355 transaction. § 361(c)(2). In no event may P recognize loss.

b. Distribution Not Preceded by Reorganization

If a § 355 distribution is not preceded by a reorganization—e.g., where S is not a newly formed subsidiary of P—P recognizes no gain or loss on a distribution of S stock or securities ("qualified property") to the P shareholders. P recognizes gain on a distribution of property other than S stock or securities. § 355(c).

c. Certain Disqualified Distributions

The nonrecognition rules of §§ 355(c) and 361(c) do not apply to a "disqualified distribution" of S stock or securities. § 355(d)(1). This rule is designed to prevent the use of § 355 to facilitate a tax-free sale of part of a business following a corporate takeover.

1) Disqualified Distribution

A distribution is "disqualified" if, immediately after the distribution, any person holds "disqualified stock" in either P or any controlled subsidiary of

P that constitutes a 50% or greater interest (measured by voting power or value) in that corporation. § 355(d)(2). Aggregation rules are used in applying the 50% ownership test. § 355(d)(7), (8). For example, two or more otherwise unrelated persons who act pursuant to a plan to acquire P or S stock are treated as a single person for purposes of § 355(d). § 355(d)(7)(B). The § 318 attribution rules also apply, as modified to provide that stock is attributed from a corporation to 10% (rather than 50%) shareholders. § 355(d)(8).

2) Disqualified Stock

"Disqualified stock" is any stock in either P or any controlled subsidiary of P that is acquired by purchase after October 9, 1990, during the five-year period preceding the distribution. A "purchase" is a transaction where the acquirer takes a cost basis in the stock of P or P's subsidiary. Stock with a § 1014 date-of-death basis or a transferred basis is generally not acquired by purchase. § 355(d)(5)(A). The five-year holding period is suspended whenever the holder's risk of loss is substantially diminished (e.g., by an option or special class of stock). § 355(d)(6).

> ***Example:***   T Corp. has actively conducted four distinct businesses (of equal size) for more than five years through wholly owned subsidiaries. A, B, C and D are four unrelated corporations, each of which wishes to acquire one of the T subsidiaries. After October 9, 1990, A, B, C and D each acquires 25% of T's stock and, after waiting a sufficient time to establish their status as historic T shareholders for continuity of interest purposes, T distributes 100% of the stock of a subsidiary to A, B, C and D, respectively, in exchange for their T stock. The distribution is "disqualified" because the distributees each hold "disqualified stock" representing a 100% interest in the distributed subsidiary. Although the split-up may qualify as tax-free to the distributee shareholders, T recognizes gain on the distribution of the stock of its subsidiaries.

d. Section 355 Distributions Related to Acquisition Plan

The nonrecognition rules of §§ 355(c) and 361(c) do not apply to certain distributions of S stock or securities that are made in connection with related acquisitions of one or more businesses controlled by P. § 355(e). See XII.H.2, at pages 284–285, *infra*.

e. Tax Attributes

All of P's tax attributes, except E & P, stay with P following a § 355 distribution even if the division is pursuant to a reorganization plan. Section 381 does not apply to divisive Type D reorganizations. (See XIII.B.3., at page 292, *infra*). All of P's tax attributes thus disappear when P liquidates following a split-up. If a § 355 distribution is part of a Type D reorganization, P's E & P are allocated between P and S in proportion to the relative fair market value of the assets held by each corporation after the distribution. Reg. § 1.312–10(a). Different rules may apply if P and S file a consolidated return.

H. Corporate Division Combined With Tax–Free Reorganization

1. Background

Corporate divisions historically have been used to facilitate an acquisition of one of several corporate businesses in a tax efficient manner. For example, one corporation ("P") operating two separate businesses as divisions would contribute the assets of the unwanted business to a newly created subsidiary ("S") and spin off the stock of S prior to a tax-free acquisition of P's remaining business. Or P would retain direct ownership of the unwanted business, transfer the wanted assets to S, and spin off the S stock to the P shareholders to set the stage for X's acquisition of S in a reorganization. The tax consequences of these transactions often depended on the form used by the parties. Under current law, § 355 distributions made in conjunction with an attempted tax-free acquisition of part of P's business may cause P (but not necessarily its shareholders) to recognize gain under § 355(e). It is possible that the same transaction may be subject to both § 355(d) and § 355(e). If so, § 355(d) takes precedence. § 355(e)(2)(D). Section 355(e) was enacted to prevent avoidance of corporate-level gain on the sale of part of a business. Its reach is very broad and it may extend to transactions that previously were viewed as appropriate for tax-free treatment. The Service, however, has issued temporary regulations narrowing the scope of § 355(e).

2. Historical Opportunities and Pitfalls

a. The *Morris Trust* Technique

Prior to enactment of § 355(e), the preferred planning technique was to spin-off the unwanted business and then transfer the wanted business in a tax-free Type A or Type B reorganization. If both businesses satisfied the active trade or business test and the other requirements of §§ 355 and 368 were met, the spin-off was tax-free to the distributing corporation and its shareholders under § 355, and the acquisition qualified as tax-free under § 368. *Comm'r v. Morris Trust,* 367 F.2d 794 (4th Cir.1966); Rev.Rul. 70–434, 1970–2 C.B. 83.

b. Historical Pitfalls

A spin-off of unwanted assets followed by a Type C reorganization or triangular merger was likely to be treated as an integrated transaction, with the result that the unwanted assets were considered in determining whether P transferred substantially all of its assets. If the unwanted assets were a substantial part of P's business, the acquisition did not qualify as a reorganization, and the spin-off probably was not tax-free under § 355. *Helvering v. Elkhorn Coal Co.,* 95 F.2d 732 (4th Cir.1937), cert. denied, 305

U.S. 605, 59 S.Ct. 65 (1938). If the transaction was structured as a spin-off of the wanted business followed by an attempted tax-free acquisition of that business and the steps were prearranged, the Service historically took the position that neither the spin-off nor the reorganization qualified for tax-free treatment. Rev. Rul. 70–225, 1970–1 C.B. 80. In taking that position, the Service applied the step transaction doctrine and treated the transaction as if the distributing corporation exchanged the stock of the controlled subsidiary for stock of the acquiring corporation and then distributed the acquiring corporation stock to its shareholders. This "recasting" caused the distribution to fail to qualify under § 355 because the distributing corporation was not in "control" of the acquiring corporation at the time of the deemed distribution. Rev. Rul. 96–30, 1996–1 C.B. 36.

c. IRS Change of Position

In a significant about face, the Service retreated from its application of the step transaction doctrine to deny § 355 treatment because of postdistribution "restructurings" or acquisitions of the controlled subsidiary. Rev. Rul. 98–27, 1998–1 C.B. 1159. It now will patrol any abuse from these transactions through the device limitation (at the shareholder level) and § 355(e) (at the corporate level).

3. Corporate–Level Gain Recognition: § 355(e)
a. Recognition of Gain by Distributing Corporation

Section 355(e) requires recognition of gain by the distributing corporation (but not the distributee shareholder) on a distribution of appreciated stock or securities in a transaction that otherwise qualifies as a tax-free corporate division. Specifically, the distributing (parent) corporation must recognize gain as if it had sold the stock of the distributed controlled subsidiary for its fair market value on the date of the distribution if, as part of a "plan" or series of related transactions, one or more persons acquires (directly or indirectly) a 50% or greater interest in either the distributing or controlled corporation within two years before or after the distribution. § 355(e)(1), (2). Technically, this result is achieved by excluding the stock or securities in the distributed controlled subsidiary from the definition of "qualified property" for purposes of § 355(c)(2) or § 361(c)(2), causing gain to be recognized under § 311(b). Neither the distributing nor controlled corporations may adjust the basis of their assets or stock to reflect the recognition of gain under § 355(e).

b. Plan Requirement

Section 355(e) applies only if the transaction is part of a "plan" or series of related transactions to acquire 50% or more of the target corporation. Whether or not a "plan" exists is based on all the facts and circumstances, subject to the safe harbors and factors summarized below. Reg. § 1.355–7T(b)(1). In general, in the case of an acquisition not involving a public offering after a distribution, the distribution will be treated as part of a "plan" only if there was an agreement, understanding, arrangement, or substantial negotiations regarding the acquisition (collectively referred to below as "talks") at some time during the two–year period ending on the date of the distribution. Reg. § 1.355–7T(b)(2). If the distribution is motivated in whole or substantial part by a corporate business purpose other than to facilitate the acquisition and it would have occurred at approximately the same time and in a similar form regardless of whether the acquisition was effected, the taxpayer has a better chance of establishing that a "plan" does not exist. Id.

c. Two–Year Presumption

If one or more persons directly or indirectly acquire a 50% or greater interest in the distributing corporation or any controlled corporation during the four-year period beginning two years before the distribution, the acquisition is presumed to be pursuant to a plan unless the taxpayer establishes that such a plan did not exist. § 355(e)(2)(B).

d. Rebutting the Presumption

1) Plan and Nonplan Factors

In the absence of a safe harbor, the regulations contain an extensive non-exclusive list of plan and nonplan factors to consider in making the facts and circumstances determination. Examples of "plan factors" include "talks" during the two–year period ending on the date of the distribution and a business purpose to facilitate the acquisition. Reg. § 1.355–7T(b)(3). Examples of "nonplan factors" include unexpected changes in market or business conditions occurring after the distribution that influenced the acquisition and the absence of talks with the acquiring corporation during the two–year period ending on the date of the distribution.

2) Safe Harbors

If any one of seven safe harbors in the regulations is met, the existence of a plan is negated without further inquiry. A key factor under most of the safe harbors is whether there were "talks" concerning an acquisition during a specified time period. See Reg. § 1.355–7T(d).

e. Examples

Example (1): T Corp. manufactures video games. Its wholly owned subsidiary, S Corp., manufactures parts for wireless phones. T Corp. is relatively small in its industry. T wants to combine with P Corp., a large video game company. T and P begin negotiating for P to acquire T, but P is not interested in acquiring S. To facilitate its acquisition, T agrees to distribute all of its S stock pro rata to its shareholders before the acquisition. Prior to this distribution, T and P enter into a contract for T to merge into P. One month thereafter, T distributes the S stock and, the next day, T's merger into P is completed, with T shareholders receiving T stock (representing less than 50% of T's outstanding stock) in the merger. Under the regulations, the agreement between T and P regarding the acquisition and the fact that the distribution was motivated by a business purpose to facilitate the merger are "plan factors." Since there are no "nonplan factors," the distribution of S and the merger of T into P are considered part of a plan. As a result, T will recognize gain on the distribution of its S stock. Reg. § 1.355–7T(j) Example 1. If the requirements of §§ 355 and 368 are met, however, T's shareholders will not recognize gain on the spin-off or the merger.

Example (2):   Same as Example (1), except after the merger of T into P, T's former shareholders own more than 50% of P. Section 355(e) would not apply to this fact pattern because a 50% interest in T or S was not acquired in the transaction.

Example (3):   Same as Example (1), except T's spin-off of S was motivated by a corporate business purpose unrelated to the acquisition of T, and the acquisition occurred more than six months after the distribution, and there were no "talks" concerning the acquisition of T during the one–year period before and six–month period after the distribution. This fact pattern would be covered by Safe Harbor I in the regulations and thus the distribution and acquisition will not be considered part of a plan. Reg. § 1.355–7T(d)(1).

I. Review Questions

1. A tax-free corporate division under § 355 must be pursuant to a Type D reorganization plan. True or False?

2. P Corp. has been engaged in two separate businesses as divisions for more than five years. It wishes to separate the assets of one business from the risks and liabilities of the other. Will this constitute a sufficient corporate business purpose for a spin-off under § 355?

3. Consider whether the following distributions qualify under the active business test:

   (a) P Corp. has been engaged in a manufacturing business for six years. It distributes the stock of its 100% subsidiary, S Corp., which has owned investment securities for seven years.

   (b) P Corp. has been engaged in the business of manufacturing mens' pants for 20 years. It wishes to distribute the stock of a hat business that it started two years ago.

(c) P Corp. has been engaged in the newspaper business for 10 years. Three years ago, in a Type B reorganization, it acquired the stock of a corporation that has operated a radio station for 15 years.

4. Federal law requires that P Corp., a television station, divest itself of its 100% subsidiary, S Corp., which publishes a newspaper. Under what circumstances will a spin-off of S Corp., followed by a sale of the S Corp. stock by its new shareholders constitute a forbidden bailout device for purposes of § 355?

5. A is the sole shareholder of P Corp. and has a $100,000 basis in his P stock. P Corp. has a $40,000 basis in the stock of its 100% subsidiary, S Corp. In a spin-off that qualifies under § 355, P Corp. distributes the stock of S Corp. to A. After the distribution, the fair market value of the P stock is $600,000 and the fair market value of the S stock is $200,000. What are the tax consequences of the transaction to both corporations and to A?

6. P Corporation has 1,000 shares of common stock (its only class) outstanding. Each share has a fair market value of $1. A, one of P's five unrelated individual shareholders, owns 400 shares of P stock. P owns all the outstanding stock of S. The S stock has a total fair market value of $200. P distributes all the S stock plus $200 cash to A in exchange for all of A's P stock. But for the receipt of the cash, the exchange satisfies the requirements of § 355. What are the tax consequences of the exchange to A?

XIII

CARRYOVERS OF CORPORATE TAX ATTRIBUTES

A.   Introduction

The Code contains a comprehensive set of rules governing the impact of various corporate transactions, such as reorganizations, on the tax attributes (earnings and profits, net operating losses, etc.) of a target corporation. In general, § 381(a) provides that in an acquisition of a target's assets by another corporation in a liquidation under § 332 or in a reorganization (other than a Type B or E reorganization), the acquiring corporation "shall succeed to and take into account" the target's tax attributes.

Carryovers of the target's tax attributes are limited by rules in § 381 and by the provisions of § 382, § 383, § 384, § 269 and the rules governing consolidated tax returns. The purpose of these limitations is to prevent profitable corporations from acquiring loss corporations in order to use the loss corporation's earnings and profits deficit and net operating losses to offset its positive earnings and profits account and future taxable income.

B.   Operation of § 381

1.   In General

Section 381(a) provides for the carryover of 26 corporate tax attributes specified in § 381(c) on a liquidation of a controlled subsidiary under § 332 and on Type A, Type C and Type F reorganizations and nondivisive Type D and Type G reorganizations. These tax attributes are transferred to the parent or acquiring corporation as of the close of the day of distribution or transfer of assets. The principal carryover items are earnings and profits and net operating losses. Other items specified in § 381(c) include capital loss carryovers, accounting methods, inventories and depreciation methods. The list of items specified in § 381(c) is not exclusive, and some items not listed may carry over under principles developed in the case law.

The general § 381 carryover rules do not apply to Type B and Type E reorganizations (and presumably reverse triangular reorganizations) because in those transactions the target or recapitalized corporation remains in existence and retains all of its tax attributes. In other triangular reorganizations, the "acquiring corporation" is the corporation which, pursuant to the plan of reorganization, ultimately acquires the target's assets.

Example: S Corp. is a wholly owned subsidiary of P Corp. S acquires all of the assets of T Corp. solely in exchange for P voting stock. S is the acquiring corporation for purposes of § 381. Alternatively, if P acquired all of T's assets in a Type C reorganization and dropped down T's assets to S under § 368(a)(2)(C), S is the acquiring corporation for purposes of § 381.

2. **§ 381 Limitations On Carryovers**

a. **Earnings and Profits (E & P) Deficits**

Section 381(c)(2)(B) provides that if the acquiring corporation or the target has an E & P deficit, the deficit only may offset E & P accumulated after the transfer and not preacquisition E & P. For purposes of this rule, the E & P of the acquiring corporation in the year of the acquisition are deemed to accumulate pro rata over the year.

Example (1):   P acquires T on December 31, 2002, in a Type C reorganization. At the time of the acquisition, P has $10,000 of accumulated E & P and T has a $30,000 E & P deficit.

Assume that in 2003 the combined P has $5,000 of current E & P and it distributes $5,000 to its shareholders. The $5,000 distribution is a dividend since it is out of current E & P. § 316(a)(2). The distribution would eliminate P's $5,000 of current E & P and it would begin 2004 with $10,000 of accumulated E & P and T's $30,000 preacquisition deficit.

Assume that in 2003 the combined P has $5,000 of current E & P and makes no distributions to its shareholders. In that case, T's preacquisition deficit may offset the $5,000 of postacquisition accumulated E & P. Beginning in 2004, P would have $10,000 of accumulated E & P and $25,000 of T's preacquisition deficit.

Example (2):   T merges into P midway through the current year. For the year of the merger, T has a $20,000 E & P deficit and P has $30,000 of current E & P. Under § 381(b)(2)(B), P has $15,000 of preacquisition accumulated E & P and $15,000 of postacquisition E & P. T's deficit can be used to eliminate the $15,000 of postacquisition E & P and the combined P will begin the next year with $15,000 of preacquisition accumulated E & P and $5,000 of T's preacquisition deficit.

b. **Net Operating Losses**

Under § 172, a corporation's net operating losses ("NOLs") generally may be used to offset taxable income by being carried back three years and forward for fifteen years. § 172(b)(1). Under § 381(c)(1), a target's NOLs carry over to an acquiring corporation, but only to taxable years ending after the acquisition date. In the year of the acquisition, the acquiring corporation may deduct an NOL inherited from the target only against the portion of its income (determined on a per day basis) attributable to the post-acquisition period. Note that while § 381 may permit the carryover of a target's NOLs to an acquiring corporation, other Code sections (primarily § 382) may limit the acquiring corporation's use of those NOLs.

If a loss corporation with NOLs acquires a profitable corporation, § 381 and other Code sections may limit the loss corporation's ability to use pre-acquisition NOLs against taxable income generated by the profitable business. Section 381(b)(3) provides that, except in the case of Type B, E and F reorganizations, an acquiring corporation cannot carry back an NOL incurred after the acquisition to a taxable year of the profitable target. The concern behind this rule is to avoid the complex accounting problems involved in allocating a post-reorganization loss to the entities which existed prior to the acquisition. Because the allocation problems do not exist in a § 332 liquidation or Type E and F reorganizations, this limitation does not apply in those situations. The Ninth Circuit has held that § 381(b)(3) does not limit the carryback of an NOL to a pre-acquisition year of a corporation which merges in a forward triangular reorganization into a shell corporation. *Bercy Industries, Inc. v. Comm'r,* 640 F.2d 1058 (9th Cir.1981).

Example: P acquires all of T's assets in a statutory merger on December 31 of the current year. Assume that next year, P sustains a $50,000 operating loss. Section 381(b)(3) prohibits the carryback of the loss to a preacquisition year of T but the loss may be carried back to a preacquisition year of P or forward to offset future income of P. Section 172(b)(3) permits P to waive the carryback of the loss.

3. Carryovers in Divisive Reorganizations

Section 381 does not apply to divisive reorganizations. In general, the tax attributes of the distributing corporation are not altered by the transaction except in the case of a split-up, where the tax attributes of the distributing corporation do not survive its liquidation. See XII.G.2.e., at page 283, *supra,* for further details.

C. Limitations on Carryovers of Corporate Tax Attributes

1. Introduction

Without restrictions, § 381 would allow any acquiring corporation to use a target corporation's NOLs to offset its future income. Congress has long sought to prevent the "trafficking in loss corporations" which would result from unlimited carryforward of a target's NOLs. The principal limitation is in § 382, which restricts the use of NOL carryforwards. Other sections also potentially limit the carryforward of capital losses, deductions, credits, and other tax allowances. See, e.g., § 383.

2. Limitation on Net Operating Loss Carryforwards: § 382

Section 382 limits the use of a loss corporation's NOL carryforwards if there is a substantial change in ownership of the corporation. If the new corporation does not continue the business enterprise of the old loss corporation for at least two years after an "ownership change," the preacquisition NOLs are disallowed. § 382(c). If the continuity of business requirement is met, the taxable income permitted to be offset by preacquisition NOLs is limited to the value of the loss corporation multiplied by the "long-term tax-exempt rate." § 382(b). The theory of this limitation is that after a substantial ownership change the preacquisition NOLs should only be permitted to offset the future income of the business which generated the losses. That income figure is arbitrarily determined by multiplying the fair market value of the old loss business by an assumed rate of return that is periodically adjusted.

a. Ownership Change Requirement

1) In General

The § 382 limitation is triggered only after an "ownership change" occurs with respect to a corporation that has net operating loss carryovers. § 382(a), (g), (k)(3). An "ownership change" takes place if, immediately after any "owner shift involving a 5–percent shareholder" or an "equity structure shift," the percentage of stock of a loss corporation owned by one or more "5–percent shareholders" increases by more than 50% over the lowest percentage of stock in the corporation owned by such shareholders during the "testing period" (generally the prior three years if the corporation has NOL carryovers). § 382(g)(1), (i). The percentage of stock held by a person is determined on the basis of the stock's fair market value, and nonvoting, nonconvertible preferred stock is not counted. § 382(k)(5), (6).

2) Owner Shifts Involving 5% Shareholders

An owner shift involving a 5% shareholder is any change in stock ownership of a corporation which affects the percentage ownership of a person who is a 5% shareholder before or after the change. § 382(g)(2). Examples include stock purchases, redemptions, § 351 transfers and recapitalizations. A few special rules apply. All less than 5% shareholders are treated as one 5% shareholder for purposes of determining whether an ownership shift has occurred. § 382(g)(4)(A). Gifts, transfers at death and transfers between spouses are disregarded and the transferee is treated as having owned the stock during the period it was owned by the transferor. § 382(l)(3)(B). Changes in proportionate ownership attributable solely to fluctuations in value of different classes of stock also are disregarded, except as provided in regulations. § 382(l)(3)(C).

Example (1):   Loss Co. has a large NOL which it can carry forward to future years. If Buyer purchases 51% of Loss Co. she will be a 5% shareholder and an owner shift involving a 5% shareholder has occurred. The owner shift increases Buyer's percentage ownership in Loss Co. by more than 50%, producing an "ownership change" which triggers the § 382 limitation. The result is the same if Buyer acquires 51% of Loss Co. in a series of transactions stretching over the three-year testing period. These transactions could include the redemption of stock from other Loss Co. shareholders which have the result of increasing Buyer's ownership interest above the 50% threshold.

Example (2):   Buyer purchases 40% of Loss Co. and, within the three-year testing period, Other Buyer purchases 15% of Loss Co. In that situation, both Buyer and Other Buyer are 5% shareholders. An ownership change has occurred which triggers § 382 since the percentage ownership of one or more 5% shareholders has increased by more than 50% during the testing period.

Example (3):   Loss Co. is publicly traded and has a large NOL which it can carry over to future years. No single shareholder owns 5% or more of Loss Co. If more than 50% of Loss Co. is traded to other less than 5% shareholders during the testing period, the § 382 limitations are not triggered. Since all less than 5% shareholders are treated as one 5% shareholder, that single hypothetical shareholder has continued to own 100% of Loss Co. at all times and no ownership change has taken place.

Example (4):   A, an individual, owns 100% of Loss Co. If A sells 2% of Loss Co. to each of 50 buyers during the testing period, there will be an ownership change that triggers the § 382 limitation. The 50 buyers will be treated as a single 5% shareholder whose interest in Loss Co. has increased from zero percent to 100%.

3)   Equity Structure Shifts

An "equity structure" shift is defined as any reorganization other than a Type F reorganization or Type D and Type G reorganizations which are divisive. The term also includes taxable reorganization-type transactions and public offerings. § 382(g)(3)(B). In determining the change of ownership in a reorganization involving a loss corporation, the prereorganization ownership of the loss corporation is compared with the postreorganization ownership of the surviving corporation. § 382(k)(1), (3). In a reorganization setting the less than 5% shareholders of each corporation are treated as one 5% shareholder in that corporation. § 382(g)(4)(B)(i). In virtually all cases, an equity structure shift also will be an owner shift involving a 5% shareholder and, apart from specialized transitional rules, the distinction appears to have no substantive significance.

Example: Loss Co. is owned 20% by A, 30% by B and 50% by the public. Profit Co. is publicly owned. If Loss Co. merges into Profit Co.

with the Loss Co. shareholders receiving 40% of the outstanding Profit Co. stock, an equity structure shift and ownership change will occur and the § 382 limitation will apply. The ownership of the Profit Co. shareholders in Loss Co. before the merger (zero percent) is compared with their ownership interest in the surviving corporation, Profit Co. (60%) which is now the "loss corporation." § 382(k)(1), (3). Thus, the percentage ownership of one or more 5% shareholders has increased by more than 50% during the testing period. If, instead, Profit Co. merged into Loss Co. and received 60% of the outstanding stock of Loss Co., an equity structure and an ownership change again would result. The ownership of the Profit Co. shareholders in Loss Co. (zero percent) is compared with their ownership interest in Loss Co. after the reorganization (60%).

In both situations, the less than 5% shareholders in Loss Co. and Profit Co. are treated as a single more than 5% shareholder in their respective corporations. The two groups are not aggregated into a single more than 5% shareholder. § 382(g)(4)(B)(i).

4) Attribution Rules
In testing stock ownership to determine whether an ownership change has occurred, § 382(*l*)(3) applies modified § 318 attribution rules. In general, these rules provide that: (1) an individual and all members of his family (as described in § 318(a)(1)) are treated as one individual, (2) stock owned by a partnership, trust, estate or corporation is treated as owned proportionately by the beneficial owners and the entity's actual ownership is disregarded, and (3) attribution to entities is disregarded. The impact of these rules is to disregard transfers within a family and to focus the § 382 ownership test on corporate ownership by individuals.

b. **Effect of an Ownership Change**
1) Continuity of Business Enterprise Requirement
If an ownership change takes place, § 382(c) provides that all NOLs are disallowed if the new loss corporation does not continue the business enterprise of the old loss corporation at all times during the two-year period following the date of the ownership change. § 382(c)(1), (j). This provision requires the new loss corporation to either continue the business of the loss corporation or use a significant portion of its historic business assets in one of its businesses for the two-year period. Reg. § 1.368–1(d)(2). See XI.A.4.b., at page 236, *supra*.

2) The § 382 Limitation
a) In General
If there is an ownership change and the continuity of business enterprise requirement is satisfied, the new loss corporation may use

NOLs in any "post-change year" (a year after the ownership change) only in an amount equal to the value of the old loss corporation multiplied by the long-term tax-exempt rate. § 382(a), (b)(1). If the amount of this limitation exceeds the taxable income of the new loss corporation for the year, the excess carries over and increases the next year's limitation. § 382(b)(2). If an ownership change takes place mid-year and the § 382 limitation applies, the limit is prorated over the year by time. § 382(b)(3)(B).

Example: Assume Loss Co. has a value of $1,000,000 and losses of $300,000. If Loss Co. is subject to § 382 and the long-term tax exempt rate is 5%, it may use its loss carryforwards only to the extent of $50,000 ($1,000,000 multiplied by 5%). If it only had $40,000 of taxable income in the year, the $10,000 excess of the limitation over its taxable income carries over and increases the § 382 limitation in the next year. If the ownership change triggering § 382 did not occur on the first day of the loss corporation's taxable year, the § 382 limitation would have to be prorated over the year of the ownership change. For example, if the § 382 limitation for the full year were $50,000 and the ownership change took place three-fourths of the way through the year, the § 382 limitation for the remainder of the year would be $12,500. The § 382 limitation does not apply to the portion of the taxable year prior to the ownership change and taxable income during the year of the ownership change is allocated ratably to each day in the year. § 382(b)(3)(A).

b) Long–Term Tax–Exempt Rate
    The § 382 limitation is determined by multiplying the long-term tax-exempt rate by the value of the company. § 382(b)(1). The long-term tax-exempt rate is the highest federal long-term rate under § 1274(d) in effect for any month in the three-month period ending with the calendar month in which the ownership change occurs, adjusted for the differences between long-term taxable and tax-exempt rates. § 382(f).

c) Value of the Company
    The value of the old loss corporation is the value of its stock, including preferred stock, immediately before the ownership change. § 382(e)(1), (k)(6)(A). Section 382 has rules to prevent manipulation of the value either before or after the ownership change. If a redemption or corporate contraction takes place in connection with an ownership change, the loss corporation's value is determined after taking the

redemption or contraction into account. § 382(e)(2). Any contribution to the loss corporation as part of a plan to avoid or increase the § 382 limitation is ignored in determining the corporation's value, and a contribution made within two years before the date of the ownership change is treated as part of such a plan, unless it is exempted by the regulations. § 382(*l*)(1). This later rule prevents preownership-change "stuffing" contributions designed to increase the corporation's value and its § 382 limitation. In certain instances the value of a corporation also may be reduced by a portion of its nonbusiness, i.e., investment, assets. If at least one-third of a loss corporation's assets are nonbusiness assets, its value is reduced by the percentage of its net value represented by the fair market value of nonbusiness assets, less a proportionate amount of corporate indebtedness. § 382(*l*)(4).

> ***Example (1):*** P Corp. purchases 80% of the stock of Loss Corp. when the Loss stock is worth $20 million. As part of the acquisition plan, the other 20% of the Loss stock is later redeemed for $4 million. Under § 382(e)(2), the redemption is taken into account in determining the value of Loss for purposes of the § 382 limitation. Thus, the value of Loss is $16 million for § 382 purposes, not $20 million.

> ***Example (2):*** In anticipation of an ownership change, the shareholders of Loss Corp. make a $1,000,000 capital contribution to the corporation. The value of Loss Corp. for purposes of the § 382 limitation will be determined without regard to the additional stock value attributable to the contribution. If the contribution were made within two years of the ownership change, it is presumed to be part of a prohibited plan.

3) Special Rules for Built–In Gains and Losses

If a loss corporation has a "net unrealized built-in gain"—that is, on the date of the ownership change the fair market value of its assets (other than cash and certain cash equivalents) exceeds their aggregate adjusted basis—the § 382 limitation is increased by any *recognized* built-in gain during the five-year period after the ownership change. § 382(h)(1)(A)(i). This rule applies only if the corporation's net unrealized gain exceeds either 15% of the fair market value of its assets (other than cash and certain cash equivalents) or $10 million. § 382(h)(3)(B). The total amount of recognized built-in gain eligible for this preferred treatment is limited to the amount of net unrealized built-in gain. § 382(h)(1)(A)(ii). The corporation has the burden of showing that a recognized built-in gain accrued before the ownership change. § 382(h)(2)(A). If applicable, this rule permits a corporation to increase its § 382 limitation so it is able to deduct losses against built-in gains from asset sales or deemed asset sales resulting from a § 338 election.

If a loss corporation has a "net unrealized built-in loss"—that is, on the date of the ownership change the aggregate basis of its assets (other than cash and certain cash equivalents) exceeds their fair market value—the corporation's recognized built-in loss during the five-year period after the ownership change is subject to the § 382 limitation in the same manner as if it were a carryover NOL. § 382(h)(1)(B)(i). This rule applies only if the corporation's net unrealized built-in loss exceeds either 15% of the fair market value of its assets (other than cash and certain cash equivalents) or $10 million. § 382(h)(3)(B). The total amount of recognized built-in loss subject to this rule is limited to the amount of the net unrealized built-in loss. § 382(h)(1)(B)(ii). The corporation has the burden of showing that a loss recognized during the five-year period is not a built-in loss by establishing that the asset disposed of was not held by the loss company immediately before the change date or that the loss exceeds the loss which had accrued at the time of the ownership change. Depreciation or other cost recovery during the five-year period attributable to the excess of an asset's adjusted basis over its fair market value on the change date is considered a recognized built-in loss and subject to the limitation. § 382(h)(2)(B).

Example (1):   Loss Co., a calendar year taxpayer, has $2 million of loss carryforwards. On January 1 of the current year, P Co. acquired all of Loss's assets for $5 million of P Co. stock in a Type C reorganization and Loss liquidated. After the reorganization, the Loss shareholders own 20% of the P Co. stock. The Loss assets, other than cash and cash equivalents, had a $4.5 million aggregate fair market value and a $3 million basis at the time of P's acquisition. Loss had held all of its assets for more than two years. A parcel of real estate owned by Loss at that time had a fair market value of $300,000 and a basis of $200,000. The long-term tax-exempt rate is 5%. P Co. sells the real estate for $300,000 in September of this year.

There has been an ownership change since before the acquisition the P Co. shareholders owned no Loss stock and after they own 80% of P Co., the surviving corporation. § 382(g)(1), (3). Since Loss Co. is worth $5 million on the change date, its loss carryforwards can be deducted to the extent of 5% of $5 million, or $250,000.

There is net unrealized built-in gain in the Loss Co. assets since the fair market value of the assets, less cash and cash equivalents, exceeds their aggregate basis. The net unrealized built-in gain is $1.5 million which exceeds 15% of their fair market value. Under § 382(h)(1)(A), when P Co. recognizes its $100,000 gain on the sale of the real estate, its § 382 limitation for the year will be increased by that gain to $350,000. If P Co. sold the land for more than $300,000, its increase in the § 382 limitation would still be limited to $100,000, the appreciation in the parcel of real estate on the change date. § 382(h)(2)(A)(ii).

Example (2):   Assume the same facts as in Example (1) except that Loss's assets had an aggregate basis of $6 million and the parcel of real estate had a basis of $400,000. In that case, there is a net unrealized built-in loss in the Loss Co. assets since the aggregate basis of the assets, less cash and cash equivalents, exceeds their fair market value. The net unrealized built-in loss is $1.5 million which again exceeds the 15% threshold. Under § 382(h)(1)(B), the $100,000 loss on the sale of the real estate is treated as a loss carryforward and is subject to the § 382 limitation. If the real estate were sold for less than $300,000, the loss in excess of the $100,000 loss on the change date is not subject to this limitation and would be fully deductible.

3. Special Limitations on Other Tax Attributes: § 383

Under the authority of § 383, the Treasury has issued regulations which will apply the principles of § 382 following an ownership change to the general business credit under § 39, the minimum tax credit under § 53, the foreign tax credit carryover under § 904, and capital losses. Thus, a change of ownership under § 382 will result in a limitation in these tax attributes as well as NOLs. Section 383(b) requires that the § 382 limitation be further reduced by any net capital loss permitted to be deducted under § 383.

4. Limitation on Use of Preacquisition Losses To Offset Built–In Gains: § 384

Section 384 prevents a loss corporation from applying its preacquisition losses against recognized built-in gains of another corporation. The section, which employs many of the definitions developed in § 382, applies if: (1) a corporation acquires directly or through other corporations "control" (defined as 80% ownership under the affiliated corporation rules in § 1504(a)(2)) of another corporation or the assets of another corporation in a Type A, C or D reorganization, and (2) either corporation is a "gain corporation," that is, a corporation with a net unrealized built-in gain as defined in § 382(h)(3). § 384(a), (c)(4). If those requirements are met, income attributable to recognized built-in gains of one of the corporations may not be offset by a pre-acquisition loss of the other corporation during the five-year period following the acquisition. § 384(a). The limitation does not apply to the preacquisition loss of a corporation if it and the gain corporation were members of the same controlled group (generally, more than 50% common ownership by vote and value) for five years prior to the acquisition. § 384(b)(1). Section 384 also applies to certain other tax attributes. § 384(d).

> ***Example:*** Loss Co. has substantial NOL carryovers. In the current year, Loss acquires all of the assets of Profit Co. in a Type C reorganization. After the reorganization, the preacquisition Loss Co. shareholders still own 60% of the Loss Co. stock. Thus, § 382 will not apply to Loss Co. But if Profit Co. had a net unrealized built-in gain, i.e., it is a "gain corporation," the combined corporation will not be able to use Loss's preacquisition NOLs to offset any recognized built-in gains attributable to the acquired Profit assets during the five-year period after the acquisition.

5. Acquisitions to Evade or Avoid Income Tax: § 269

Section 269(a) permits the Service to disallow a deduction, credit or other allowance following a corporate acquisition if the principal purpose of the acquisition was the evasion or avoidance of federal income tax by having the acquiring party secure a tax benefit which would not otherwise have been enjoyed. § 269(a). The provision applies to acquisitions in which either (1) a person or persons acquire, directly or indirectly, control of a corporation, or (2) a corporation acquires, directly or indirectly, property with a transferred basis from a corporation which is not controlled. "Control" is defined as ownership of stock which has either 50% of the total voting power or 50% of the total value of the corporation. Thus, § 269(a) potentially applies to the various types of acquisitive reorganizations, provided the transaction is motivated by a prohibited purpose. Under § 269(b) the Service's power to disallow tax benefits is extended to liquidations motivated by a prohibited tax purpose if the liquidation occurs within two years of a qualified stock purchase in which no § 338 election was made.

Because § 269 employs a subjective tax avoidance standard, its principal role in the area of corporate tax attribute carryovers is to act as a backstop to the various other statutory limitations, such as §§ 382 and 383, which may come into play. For example, the Service might invoke § 269 in a situation where there is a shift in corporate ownership which impacts control but which is not sufficient to trigger § 382. Section 269, however, is not limited to the carryover area; it can apply in a much wider range of settings.

6. Consolidated Return Rules

Because the consolidated return rules permit an affiliated group to combine the separate taxable income or loss figures of its members for purposes of determining the group's tax obligation, the potential exists for the improper deduction of losses of one member against the post-affiliation income of another. See XIV.D.3., at page 309, *infra*. To prevent that abuse, all of the various limitations on the carryover of tax attributes apply to corporations filing a consolidated return. See Reg. § 1.1502–

90 through Reg. § 1.1502–99. The consolidated return regulations contain an additional restriction on the use of a member's preaffiliation NOLs: the separate return limitation year ("SRLY") limitation.

A separate return limitation year ("SRLY") of a member of an affiliated group is a year in which the member filed its taxes separately or as a member of another affiliated group. § 1.1502–1(e), (f). Under the consolidated return rules, the NOLs of a member of an affiliated group from a SRLY generally may be carried over and deducted only against the income of that member. § 1.1502–21(c).

Example: If Profit Co. acquires Loss Co. and the two file a consolidated tax return, Loss's NOLs from separate return limitation years can not be carried over to post-affiliation years and be deducted against Profit's income.

In general, the SRLY limitation does not apply when a corporation becomes a member of a consolidated group (where the limitation otherwise applies) within six months of the change date of a § 382(g) change of ownership. As a result, in many acquisitions the SRLY limitation relinquishes jurisdiction over NOLs as well as recognized built-in losses to § 382. Reg. §§ 1.1502–15(g), –21(g)(1) & (2).

D. Review Questions

1. In what ways does § 382 limit the carryover of a target's tax attributes following a reorganization?

2. P Co. is considering acquiring an interest in T Co., which has substantial NOLs. Which of the following acquisitions will be an ownership change which triggers the § 382 limitation?

   (a) P Co. acquires 80% of the T Co. stock pursuant to a cash tender offer for T shares.

   (b) Same as (a), except P Co. acquires 50% of the T Co. stock.

   (c) T Co. merges into P Co. in exchange for P Co. stock and following the merger the T Co. shareholders own 60% of P Co.

*

XIV

AFFILIATED CORPORATIONS

Analysis

A. Introduction

A corporation generally determines its taxable income or loss without reference to the taxable income or loss of its shareholders or other entities. The theory that each corporation is a separate taxpayer is limited, however, in certain situations in which corporations are "affiliated" (i.e., subject to common control or joined through interlocking ownership). In the case of affiliated corporations, Code restrictions limit the ability to obtain multiple tax benefits and to manipulate intercompany transactions to reduce tax liability. The Code also recognizes that the identities of affiliated corporations may merge at certain very high levels of common control. For tax purposes, it is permissible to treat the corporations as a single entity in which intercompany transactions are disregarded. For example, intercompany dividends may be eligible for a 100% dividends received deduction and an "affiliated group" of corporations, as defined in § 1504, is permitted to file a consolidated tax return in which it is treated as a single entity for tax purposes.

B. Restrictions on Multiple Tax Benefits

1. In General

Without restrictions, taxpayers would have an incentive to multiply the number of corporations employed in operating a business to take advantage of certain tax benefits. For example, absent a limitation, a business could be organized in several corporations with each corporation eligible to: (1) take advantage of the lower marginal tax rates in § 11(b), (2) obtain a $40,000 exemption amount in computing the alternative minimum tax, (3) obtain a $250,000 accumulated earnings tax credit, and (4) expense depreciable business property under § 179, etc. Section 1561 contains restrictions on certain multiple tax benefits for affiliated corporations and many Code sections which authorize a deduction or credit contain similar limitations.

2. § 1561
a. Tax Benefits Restricted

Under § 1561(a), the "component members of a controlled group" are limited to: (1) the benefits of the lower marginal tax rates in § 11(b) only to the extent of the maximum amount in each bracket, (2) one $250,000 (or $150,000 if any member is a "personal service corporation") minimum accumulated earnings tax credit, (3) one $40,000 exemption amount in computing the minimum tax, and (4) one $2 million exemption amount for purposes of computing the § 59A environmental tax. These benefits generally are divided equally among the component members of the group on December 31. In certain cases the members may consent to an unequal allocation. However, the taxable income of all component members is taken into account in applying the additional taxes levied under § 11(b) on C corporations with taxable income in excess of $100,000 or $15,000,000. See III.A.2.b., at page 83, *supra*.

b. Component Members of a Controlled Group of Corporations

Under § 1563(a), a "controlled group of corporations" may be either a "parent-subsidiary" controlled group or a "brother-sister" controlled group. Combinations of parent-subsidiary and brother-sister groups also are possible. § 1563(a)(3).

1) Parent–Subsidiary Controlled Group

A parent-subsidiary controlled group exists if one or more chains of corporations are connected through stock ownership with a common parent and (1) each corporation (other than the parent) is at least 80% owned (by voting power or value) by one or more of the other corporations and (2) the parent directly owns at least 80% (by voting power or value) of at least one of the other corporations. § 1563(a)(1).

Example: P Co. owns 80% of the only class of stock of S Co. and T Co. S Co. owns 30% of the only class of stock of V Co. and T Co. owns 50% of the V Co. stock. P Co. is the common parent of a parent-subsidiary controlled group consisting of P Co., S Co., T Co. and V Co.

2) Brother–Sister Controlled Group

A brother-sister controlled group is two or more corporations having five or fewer persons who are individuals, estates, or trusts that own (1) at least 80% (by voting power or value) of each corporation, and (2) more than 50% (by voting power or value) of each corporation taking into account the stock ownership of each person only to the extent it is identical, or overlapping, in each corporation. § 1563(a)(2). In *U.S. v. Vogel Fertilizer Co.,* 455 U.S. 16, 102 S.Ct. 821 (1982), the Supreme Court held that only persons owning stock in each corporation of the group may be counted in applying these tests. See Reg. § 1.1563–1(a)(3)(b).

Example: A (an individual) owns 75% of the only class of stock of X Co. and 90% of the only class of stock of Y Co. B (an individual) owns 25% of X Co. Under these facts, X Co. and Y Co. are not a brother-sister controlled group. For purposes of making that determination, B's stock ownership in X Co. is ignored since B does not own stock in Y Co. Without B's stock, the 80% test is not satisfied since A only owns 75% of X Co. If, however, B owned 1% of Y Co.'s stock, the two corporations would be a brother-sister controlled group. See Reg. § 1.1563–1(a)(3)(b)(ii) Example (1).

3) Other Rules

Nonvoting preferred stock, treasury stock and "excluded stock" (as defined) are not considered in applying the parent-subsidiary and brother-sister ownership tests. § 1563(c). Various constructive ownership rules also are applied to test stock ownership. § 1563(d), (e), (f). In general, every member of a controlled group of corporations on December 31 is a "component member" of the group. Special rules apply to corporations which are not members of the group for the full year and corporations taxed under other statutory schemes, such as tax-exempt and foreign corporations, are excluded from the group. § 1563(b).

3. Other Restrictions

Several other Code sections contain specific limitations on multiple tax benefits for affiliated corporations. Some examples are:

a.   A controlled group, as defined in § 1563(a), is limited to one $25,000 amount for purposes of computing the general business credit limitation. § 38(c)(4)(B).

b.   All component members of a controlled group are treated as one taxpayer for purposes of expensing the cost of § 179 property. § 179(d)(6), (7).

c.   Section 269 gives the Service the discretion to disallow various tax benefits if any person or persons acquire, directly or indirectly, control of a corporation and the principal purpose for the acquisition is tax avoidance. "Control" is defined for this purpose as 50% of voting power and value. Although § 269 is more commonly applied to limit the use of pre-acquisition losses following a corporate acquisition (see XIII.C.5., at page 300, *supra*), the fact that a person or persons organize two or more corporations to secure the benefits of the lower graduated rates in § 11 or multiple accumulated earnings tax credits indicates a tax avoidance purpose. Reg. § 1.269–3(b)(2).

d.   The Service may disallow under § 1551 all or part of the benefits of the lower § 11(b) rates or the accumulated earnings tax credit if:

1)   a corporation or five or fewer individuals transfer property (other than money) to a transferee corporation which either was created for the purpose of acquiring such property or is not actively engaged in business at the time of the acquisition; and

2)   the transferors are in "control" of the transferee during any part of the taxable year.

The Service may not disallow these benefits, however, if the transferee corporation establishes by a clear preponderance of the evidence that securing either of the benefits was not a major purpose of the transfer. Note that in comparison to §§ 1561 and 269, § 1551 permits the Service to disallow two specific tax benefits and employs a shifting burden of proof with respect to motivation.

C.   Transactions Involving Related Corporations And Other Taxpayers

1. In General

Without some limitations, commonly controlled business organizations could engage in transactions designed to reduce their overall tax liability. Income shifting and recognition of losses in transactions between controlled entities are the most obvious avoidance strategies. The Code has a number of provisions designed to prevent tax avoidance in transactions between related taxpayers and many of those provisions apply to controlled and commonly owned corporations. For example, the loss disallowance and matching of income and deduction rules in § 267(a) apply to corporations which are members of the same controlled group as defined in § 267(f). § 267(b)(3). See III.A.7., at page 86, *supra*. Another example is the application of the related-party resale rules in § 453(e) which also apply to controlled groups defined in § 267(f). § 453(e), (f)(1)(B). In addition to the various statutory limitations applicable to specific transactions, § 482 empowers the Serviced to prevent tax evasion in transactions between controlled businesses.

2. Allocations of Income and Deductions: § 482

a. Purpose of § 482

Under § 482, the Service may distribute, apportion, or allocate tax items between or among organizations, trades, or businesses which are owned or controlled, directly or indirectly, by the same interests when the reallocation of the items is necessary to prevent evasion of taxes or clearly to reflect the income of any of the businesses. To illustrate the type of manipulation at which § 482 is directed, assume that one commonly controlled business is very profitable and another has sustained large losses. Transactions between the two businesses involving services, the leasing of property, transfers or use of intangible property, or sales of goods could be structured so as to shift income from the profitable business to the one with losses. Section 482 is frequently applied to transactions between a domestic corporation and a commonly controlled foreign corporation which are structured to shift income to more lightly taxed foreign jurisdictions. In these situations, § 482 is the Service's principal weapon for preventing abuse. The regulations state that the purpose of the section is to place a controlled taxpayer on a parity with an uncontrolled taxpayer by determining the controlled taxpayer's true taxable income using the standard of an uncontrolled taxpayer. Reg. § 1.482–1(b)(1).

b. Commonly Controlled Trades or Businesses

Section 482 applies to transactions involving two or more "organizations, trades, or businesses," regardless of whether they are incorporated, domestic or foreign, or file consolidated returns. "Organization" is defined expansively and includes sole proprietorships, partnerships, trusts, estates, associations and corporations. Reg. § 1.482–1(i)(1). Two or more organizations, trades or businesses are considered "controlled" for § 482 purposes if there is control of any kind, direct or indirect, whether legally enforceable or not. The regulations state that the "reality of the control" is the key question, "not its form or the mode of its exercise." Further, a presumption of control is created if income or deductions are arbitrarily shifted between two entities. Reg. § 1.482–1(i)(4).

c. The Arm's Length Standard

Transactions between controlled taxpayers are subjected to special scrutiny under § 482 and the Service has the authority to make adjustments in cases involving inadvertence as well as those motivated by tax avoidance considerations. Reg. § 1.482–1(f)(1)(i). In testing transactions under § 482, the standard applied is that of an uncontrolled taxpayer dealing at arm's length with another uncontrolled taxpayer. Reg. § 1.482–1(b)(1).

Whether a controlled transaction produces an arm's length result is generally evaluated by comparing the results of that transaction to those realized by uncontrolled taxpayers engaged in comparable transactions under comparable circumstances. The comparability of transactions and circumstances must be evaluated considering all factors that could affect prices or profits in arm's length dealings, including functions, contractual terms, risks, economic conditions, and property or services. Reg. § 1.482–1(d)(1). To be considered comparable to a controlled transaction, an uncontrolled transaction does not have to be identical to a controlled transaction, but it must be sufficiently similar that it provides a reliable measure of an arm's length result. Reg. § 1.482–1(d)(2). When an adjustment is made to the income of one member of a group of controlled taxpayers under this standard, an appropriate correlative adjustment must be made to other members involved in the adjustment. Reg. §§ 1.482–1(g)(1), (g)(2). The § 482 regulations provide guidance for the application of the arm's length standard in specific situations, such as loans and advances, performance of services, use of tangible property, sales of tangible property, and sales or use of intangible property. Reg. §§ 1.482–2(a) through (c), –3, –4.

> **Example:** Assume services are provided by a profitable controlled business to an unprofitable controlled business at a price below that which would have been paid in an arm's length arrangement. When additional income is allocated under § 482 to the profitable business, a correlative deduction must be provided to the unprofitable business, assuming payment for the services is currently deductible. Note that the deduction may simply increase the unprofitable business' losses and not provide a current tax benefit.

D. Consolidated Returns

1. Introduction

The Code permits commonly controlled corporations meeting certain requirements (i.e., an "affiliated group of corporations") to be treated as a single entity for tax purposes. The theory is that at very high levels of common ownership a family of corporations may be viewed as a single economic unit which should be eligible to compute joint, or "consolidated," tax liability. The principal advantages of filing a consolidated return are: (1) losses of one member of the group may be used to offset income of other members; (2) intercompany dividend distributions are eliminated from income; and (3) income from intercompany transactions is deferred. A principal disadvantage is that an election to file a consolidated return may not be revoked without the Service's approval. Other possible disadvantages include the fact that losses on intercompany transactions also are deferred.

2. Eligibility to File a Consolidated Return

Under § 1501, an "affiliated group of corporations" is eligible to file a consolidated return in lieu of separate returns. All corporations who are members of the group must consent to application of all of the consolidated return regulations, which are issued by the Service under the authority granted it in § 1502.

An "affiliated group" is one or more chains of "includible corporations" in which a parent corporation owns directly at least 80% (by vote and value) of at least one includible corporation and at least 80% (by vote and value) of each includible corporation is owned directly by one or more other includible corporations. § 1504(a)(1), (2). For purposes of the ownership tests, nonconvertible preferred stock which has redemption and liquidation rights limited to its issue price is disregarded. § 1504(a)(4). "Includible corporations" generally are all corporations except those subject to certain special taxing schemes.

> *Example:* P Corp. owns 90% of X Co.'s only class of stock. X Co. owns 80% of the only class of stock of Y Co. and 60% of the only class of stock of Z Co. Y Co. owns the other 40% of Z Co.'s stock. Z Co. owns 75% of the class of stock of T Co. and 100% of Foreign Co., a corporation formed in Germany. The remaining 25% of T Co.'s stock is publicly traded. On these facts, P Corp., X Co., Y Co., and Z Co. are an affiliated group eligible to file a consolidated return. Foreign Co. is not an includible corporation and cannot be part of the affiliated group. If another 5% of the T Co. stock were owned by other members of the group, T Co. would then be part of the affiliated group. If filing a consolidated return were advantageous, each corporation in the group would have to consent to all the consolidated return regulations.

3. Computing Consolidated Taxable Income
a. In General

The consolidated taxable income for a consolidated group generally is determined by combining the separate taxable income or loss of each member of the group. § 1.1502–11(a)(1). In computing its separate taxable income, each member of the group uses the common parent's taxable year and its own accounting method. § 1.1502–17(a), –76(a). The separate taxable incomes of the members are aggregated and combined with certain items that must be determined on a consolidated basis, and tax liability is computed based upon consolidated taxable income. § 1.1502–2.

"Investment adjustments" are required to be made at the end of each consolidated return year to the basis of each member's stock in a subsidiary member of the group. In general, upward adjustments are made to stock to reflect undistributed earnings and profits of the subsidiaries and downward adjustments are made to reflect earnings and profits deficits. § 1.1502–32. The regulations permit these adjustments to result in a negative basis in the stock. § 1.1502–32(a)(3)(ii), –19(a)(2). These stock basis adjustments are designed to prevent double recognition of gain or loss on a disposition of the subsidiary's stock.

b. Intercompany Distributions

Since a consolidated group is considered a single tax entity, intercompany distributions generally are eliminated from the computation of consolidated taxable income. § 1.1502–13(f)(2)(ii). Intercompany dividends are reflected by a downward investment adjustment in the subsidiary's stock. § 1.1502–32(b)(2)(iv).

c. Intercompany Transactions

The consolidated return regulations have extensive and detailed rules for the taxation of intercompany transactions. Under the regulations, the selling member in a transaction is referred to as "S," and its items of income, gain, deduction, and loss from an intercompany transaction are referred to as "intercompany items." Reg. § 1.1502–13(b)(2)(i). The buying member in a transaction is referred to as "B" and its tax items from an intercompany transaction are referred to as "corresponding items." Reg. § 1.1502–13(b)(3)(i). A "recomputed corresponding item" is the corresponding item that B would take into account if S and B were divisions of a single corporation and the intercompany transaction were between those divisions. Reg. § 1.1502–13(b)(4). The following examples illustrate how the regulations employ these definitions in routine intercompany transactions.

Example (1): S and B are members of an affiliated group that files a consolidated return. S sells property with a $70 basis to B for $100 in year 1. In year 3, B sells the property to X for $110. S's gain on its sale to B is its intercompany item. B's $10 gain from its sale to X is its corresponding item. For each consolidated return year, S takes its intercompany item into account under a matching rule to reflect the difference for the year between B's corresponding item taken into account and the recomputed corresponding item. If S and B were divisions in the same corporation, B would have taken S's $70 basis and would have a $40 gain on the sale to X in year 3, instead of $10. Thus, S takes no gain into account in years 1 and 2 and takes the entire $30 gain into account in year 3, to reflect the $30 difference in that year between the $10 gain B takes into account and the $40 recomputed corresponding item. Reg. § 1.1502–13(c)(7) Example (1).

Example (2): Assume again that S and B are members of an affiliated group that files a consolidated return. S leases land to B for year 1 in exchange for a $100 rent payment that is deductible to B under its separate accounting method. S takes its $100 of rental income into account in year 1 to reflect the difference between B's rental deduction and the $0 recomputed rental deduction (the rental deduction if S and B were divisions of a single corporation). See Reg. § 1.1502–13(c)(7) Example (8).

E. Review Questions

1. The outstanding stock of W Co., X Co., Y Co. and Z Co. are owned as follows:

   A, an individual, owns 35% of W Co. and 25% of Y Co.

   B, an individual, owns 50% of X Co. and 35% of Z Co.

   C, an individual, owns 47% of W Co., 25% of X Co., 60% of Y Co. and 10% of Z Co.

   Twenty other unrelated individuals own the remaining shares in W Co., X Co., Y Co. and Z Co. A, B and C are not related to one another.

   Which, if any, of the corporations form a brother-sister controlled group under § 1563(a)(2)?

2. Under what circumstances will the Service most likely challenge intercompany transactions and what is its authority?

*

XV

S CORPORATIONS

Analysis

A.   Introduction

Corporate profits distributed to shareholders in the form of dividends generally are subject to tax at both the corporate and shareholder levels. A corporation is subject to the tax under § 11 on its taxable income at rates of 15% to 35%. When the after-tax profits are distributed, individual shareholders must include any dividends in their taxable income and pay tax at rates (in 2003) ranging from 10% to 38.6%. §§ 1(a)–(d), 61(a)(7) and 301. In contrast, a partnership is generally treated as an aggregate of its partners rather than a taxable entity. § 701. The partners are taxed directly on the income from the enterprise, and partnership distributions generally do not produce additional taxable income. §§ 702; 731.

In 1958, Congress created a simple method for avoiding the double tax by enacting Subchapter S, which allows the shareholders of a "small business corporation" to elect to be taxed directly on corporate-level profits. The S corporation taxing scheme was substantially improved by the Subchapter S Revision Act of 1982, which adopted a simplified pass-through approach for the taxation of S corporations. As a result, the taxation of small business corporations and their shareholders became similar, but not identical, to the taxation of partnerships and their partners, and S corporations became a more attractive legal form for operating a business enterprise. Subsequent legislation has liberalized the eligibility requirements and made S corporations more flexible vehicles for operating a closely held business.

B.   Eligibility for S Corporation Status

The special tax provisions in Subchapter S are available only to an "S corporation," which is defined as a "small business corporation" which has an election under § 1362(a) in effect for the year. § 1361(a)(1). Any corporation which is not an S corporation is referred to as a "C corporation." § 1361(a)(2). A "small business corporation" is defined as a domestic corporation which meets the following requirements set forth in § 1361.

1.   Ineligible Corporations and Subsidiaries
a.   In General
Ineligible corporations do not qualify as small business corporations. § 1361(b)(1). The "ineligible corporation" category includes four specialized types of corporations (such as banks and insurance companies) that are subject to their own taxing regimes under the Code. § 1361(b)(2). At one time, a corporation was "ineligible" if it was a member of an affiliated group—e.g., a parent with an 80% subsidiary.

b.   Wholly Owned Subsidiaries
S corporations may have 80% or more subsidiaries under certain conditions.

1)   C corporation subsidiaries are generally permitted, but the S corporation parent and the C corporation subsidiary may not file a consolidated return. § 1504(b)(8).

2) Parent-subsidiary relationships between two S corporations are permitted if the parent elects to treat the subsidiary as a "qualified subchapter S subsidiary" ("QSSS"). § 1361(b)(3)(A). To be "qualified," the subsidiary must not be an ineligible corporation (see above) and must otherwise have been eligible for S status if all of its stock were held by shareholders of the parent. § 1361(b)(3)(B). If this election is made, all the assets, liabilities, income, deductions, and credits are treated as belonging to the S parent. § 1361(b)(3)(A). In effect, even though the subsidiary is a separate corporation, it is treated as a division of its parent for tax purposes. The regulations provide detailed rules for making or revoking a QSSS election. See Reg. § 1.1361–3, –4, –5.

2. 75–Shareholder Limit

An S corporation may not have more than 75 shareholders. § 1361(b)(1)(A). A husband and wife (and their estates) are considered as one shareholder for purposes of the 75–shareholder limit. § 1361(c)(1). If stock is owned (other than by a husband and wife) by tenants in common or joint tenants, each owner is considered to be a shareholder of the corporation. Reg. § 1.1361–1(e)(2). Stock held by a nominee, guardian, custodian or agent is considered to be held by the beneficial owner of the stock. Reg. § 1.1361–1(e)(1).

Example (1): Assume 99 of 100 outstanding shares of stock in X Corp. are owned by 74 individuals. If the remaining share is owned in joint tenancy by Herman and Wanda, who are husband and wife, X is considered to have 75 shareholders and may qualify as a small business corporation. If Herman and Wanda were brother and sister, X would have 76 shareholders and could not elect S status.

Example (2): Assume again that Herman and Wanda in Example (1) are husband and wife. If Herman dies, Wanda and his estate will continue to be considered as one shareholder until distribution of the stock by the estate to a beneficiary other than Wanda. If the stock were distributed by Herman's estate to another beneficiary, X would have 76 shareholders and would no longer qualify as an S corporation. § 1362(d)(2)(A). If Herman and Wanda get divorced, X will have 76 shareholders and will cease to qualify as a small business corporation.

3. Restrictions on Types of Shareholders
a. In General

An S corporation may not have as a shareholder a person (other than an estate and certain trusts) who is not an individual or a § 501(c)(3) tax-exempt charitable organization or qualified pension trust. § 1361(b)(1)(B). For this purpose, the term "estate" includes the bankruptcy estate of an individual. § 1361(c)(3). Thus, an S corporation cannot have another corporation or a partnership as a shareholder. Reg. § 1.1361–1(f).

b. Nonresident Alien Restriction

An S corporation may not have a nonresident alien as a shareholder.
§ 1361(b)(1)(C).

c. Trusts as Eligible Shareholders

The following types of domestic trusts are eligible S corporation shareholders:

1) Grantor trusts—i.e., domestic trusts treated for income tax purposes as owned by an individual who is a U.S. citizen or resident. § 1361(c)(2)(A)(i). The deemed owner of the trust is treated as the shareholder. § 1361(c)(2)(B)(i). If the deemed owner of a grantor trust dies and the trust continues in existence as a testamentary trust, it continues to be a permissible shareholder for the 2–year period following the deemed owner's death. § 1361(c)(2)(A)(ii). The estate of the deemed owner is considered to be the owner of the stock. § 1361(c)(2)(B)(ii).

2) Testamentary trusts to which stock has been transferred pursuant to a will, but only for the 2–year period beginning on the day of transfer. § 1361(c)(2)(A)(iii). The testator's estate is treated as the shareholder during this period. § 1361(c)(2)(B)(iii).

3) Voting trusts—i.e., trusts created to exercise the voting power of stock. Each beneficial owner is treated as a separate shareholder. § 1361(c)(2)(A)(iv); 1361(c)(2)(B)(iv).

> *Example:* Assume 90 of 100 outstanding shares of stock in Y Corp. are owned by 70 individuals. If the remaining 10 shares are owned by a voting trust, Y may qualify as a small business corporation as long as the trust does not have more than 5 beneficial owners.

4) Qualified Subchapter S Trusts and Electing Small Business Trusts, discussed below.

d. Qualified Subchapter S Trusts

Section 1361(d)(1) permits the beneficiary of a "qualified Subchapter S trust" to elect to have the trust treated as a qualified shareholder for Subchapter S purposes and to be treated as the owner of the portion of the trust consisting of S corporation stock. A "qualified Subchapter S trust" is a trust the terms of which require that:

1) during the life of the current income beneficiary, the trust shall have only one income beneficiary;

2) any corpus distributed during the life of the current income beneficiary may be distributed only to that beneficiary;

3) the income interest of the current income beneficiary shall terminate on the earlier of the beneficiary's death or the termination of the trust;

4) upon the termination of the trust during the life of the current income beneficiary, the trust shall distribute all of its assets to such beneficiary; and

5) all of the income is or must be distributed currently to one individual who is a U.S. citizen or resident. § 1361(d)(3).

e. Electing Small Business Trusts

The electing small business trust ("ESBT") was added as an eligible shareholder to provide more flexibility in estate planning for businesses operated as S corporations. An ESBT, for example, may have more than one current income beneficiary, and the trustee may have discretion over distributions of income and corpus. The requirements for an ESBT are (§ 1361(e)(1)):

1) All the beneficiaries must be individuals, estates, or tax-exempt organizations that are eligible S corporation shareholders, or charitable organizations holding contingent remainder interests;

2) No interests in the trust may have been acquired by purchase; and

3) The trustee must elect ESBT status.

Each current income beneficiary of an ESBT is treated as a shareholder for purposes of the 75–shareholder limit. § 1361(c)(2)(B)(v). An ESBT's pro rata share of S corporation income is taxable to the trust at the highest marginal § 1(e) rates, whether or not the income is distributed. § 641(d).

4. One–Class–Of–Stock Requirement

a. In General

An S corporation may not have more than one class of stock. § 1361(b)(1)(D). The purpose of this rule is to simplify the allocation of income and deductions among an S corporation's shareholders. An S corporation generally is treated as having one class of stock if all of its outstanding shares confer identical rights to distribution and liquidation proceeds. Differences in voting rights are disregarded. Thus, an S corporation may issue both voting and nonvoting common stock. Reg. § 1.1361–1(*l*)(1). Distributions that take into account varying interests in stock during the taxable year do not violate the "identical rights" requirement. Reg. § 1.1361–1(*l*)(2)(iv). For purposes of this requirement, outstanding stock does not include § 83 restricted stock that is not substantially vested unless the holder made a § 83(b) election. Reg. § 1.1361–1(*l*)(1)(4)(i).

b. Buy–Sell and Redemption Agreements

Buy-sell agreements among shareholders, stock transfer restriction agreements, and redemption agreements generally are disregarded in determining whether a corporation has more than one class of stock unless a principal purpose of the agreement is to circumvent the one-class-of-stock requirement and the agreement establishes a purchase price that, at the time the agreement is entered into, is significantly higher or lower than the fair market value of the stock. Reg. § 1.1361–1(*l*)(2)(iii).

c. Obligations Treated as Equity Under General Principles

Unless the § 1361(c)(5) straight debt safe harbor applies (see XV.B.4.d., below), S corporation debt instruments or obligations treated as equity under general tax principles are treated as a second class of stock if the principal purpose of issuing the instrument is to circumvent the identical-rights-to-distributions and liquidation-proceeds rule or the shareholder-limitation rules. Reg. § 1.1361–1(*l*)(4)(ii)(A).

d. Straight Debt Safe Harbor

1) Background

At one time, S corporations with debt instruments (e.g., bonds) outstanding risked losing their S status if their debt was reclassified as equity under general debt/equity principles because the Service argued that the corporation had more than one class of stock. That threat has diminished with the enactment of the § 1361(c)(5) "straight debt safe harbor" under which "straight debt" will not be treated as a second class of stock.

2) Straight Debt Defined

"Straight debt" is any written, unconditional obligation, whether or not embodied in a formal note, to pay a sum certain on demand or on a specified date, if:

a) the interest rate and payment dates are not contingent on profits, the borrower's discretion, the payment of dividends on common stock, or similar factors;

b) the instrument is not convertible (directly or indirectly) into stock; and

c) the creditor is an individual, estate or a trust that would be a permissible S corporation shareholder.

Reg. § 1.1361–1(*l*)(5)(i). The fact that an obligation is subordinated to other debt of the corporation does not prevent it from qualifying as straight debt. Reg. § 1.1361–1(*l*)(5)(ii).

3) Treatment of Straight Debt for Other Purposes

An obligation of an S corporation that satisfies the straight debt safe harbor will not be treated as a second class of stock even if it is considered equity under general tax principles. Straight debt generally will be treated as debt for other purposes of the Code (e.g., the interest deduction). But if a straight debt obligation bears an unreasonably high rate of interest, an appropriate portion of that interest may be recharacterized as a payment that is not interest. Reg. § 1.1361–1(*l*)(5)(iv). Such a recharacterization, however, does not result in a second class of stock. Id.

4) Treatment of Converted C Corporation Debt
   If a C corporation has outstanding debt obligations that satisfy the straight debt safe harbor but might be classified as equity under general tax principles, the safe harbor ensures that the obligation will not be treated as a second class of stock if the C corporation elects to convert to S status. The conversion and change of status also is not treated as a taxable exchange of the debt instrument for stock. Reg. § 1.1361–1(*l*)(5)(v).

C. Election, Revocation and Termination Of Subchapter S Status

1. Electing S Corporation Status
a. In General
In order to be an S corporation, a small business corporation must make an election to which all of its shareholders consent. § 1362(a). An S election is effective for the taxable year for which it is made and for all succeeding taxable years of the corporation until it is terminated. § 1362(c). The Service may waive the effect of an inadvertent invalid election (e.g., failure to obtain all necessary shareholder consents) under certain circumstances. § 1362(f).

b. Timing and Effective Date of Election
An S election may be made for a taxable year at any time during the preceding taxable year or on or before the fifteenth day of the third month of the taxable year. § 1362(b)(1).

> ***Example (1):*** Assume Z Corp. qualifies as a small business corporation under § 1361(b). If the shareholders of Z wish to elect S corporation status for calendar year 2003, they must make the election either during 2002 or before March 16, 2003.

An election made after the 15th day of the third month of the taxable year and before the same day in the following year is generally treated as made for the following year. § 1362(b)(3). If an election is made during a taxable year and on or before the 15th day of the third month of the year, but either (1) the corporation was not a small business corporation on one or more days before the election was made, or (2) one or more persons who held stock in the corporation prior to the time the election was made does not consent, then the election is treated as made for the following year. § 1362(b)(2). The Service, however, has the authority to treat a late election as timely for reasonable cause. § 1362(b)(5).

Example (2):   Assume Z Corp. in Example (1) makes an election to be an S corporation on March 10, 2003. If Z had a shareholder which was a partnership during January, 2003, it could not elect S status for the 2003 taxable year, because it had an ineligible shareholder during the period of the taxable year prior to the election. The election would be treated as made for Z's 2004 taxable year.

Example (3):   Assume that on January 1, 2003, W Co., which is a C corporation, had 10 shareholders. On January 15, 2003, one of W's shareholders, A, who is an individual, sells her W stock to B, who also is an individual. On March 5, 2003, W files an election to be an S corporation for its 2003 taxable year. Assuming W qualifies as a small business corporation, its election will be effective only if all of the shareholders as of March 5, 2003, as well as former shareholder A, consent to the election. If W's election were to be effective for its 2004 taxable year, A would not have to consent to the election.

2. Revocation and Termination of S Corporation Status
a. Revocation

An S election may be revoked with the consent of more than one-half of the shares of the stock (including nonvoting stock) of the corporation on the day the revocation is made. § 1362(d)(1)(B); Reg. § 1.1362–2(a)(1). The corporation may specify any effective date on or after the day of the revocation. If an effective date is not selected, a revocation is effective: (1) on the first day of the taxable year if made before the sixteenth day of the third month of such year, or (2) on the first day of the next taxable year if it is made after the fifteenth day of the third month of the year. § 1362(d)(1)(C), (D).

b. Termination
1) Ceasing to Be a Small Business Corporation

An S corporation election terminates whenever the corporation ceases to be a small business corporation. The termination is effective on and after the day of the event that terminated its small business corporation status. § 1362(d)(2). Reg. § 1.1362–2(b).

Example: If an S corporation exceeds the 75–shareholder limit, has an impermissible shareholder, issues a second class of stock, or otherwise ceases to be a small business corporation, its Subchapter S election will terminate as of the day of the disqualifying event.

2) Passive Income Limitation for Certain S Corporations

An S corporation's election will terminate if it has Subchapter C accumulated earnings and profits (i.e., E & P from its pre-Subchapter S existence) at the close of three consecutive taxable years and more than 25% of its gross receipts for each of those years consists of passive investment income. The termination is effective on the first day of the taxable year beginning after the three-year measuring period. § 1362(d)(3)(A)(i), (ii). An S corporation which has never been a C corporation or which was a C corporation but has no E & P from that period would not be concerned about a termination under this provision. "Passive investment income" generally includes gross receipts from royalties, rents, dividends, interest, annuities and sales or exchanges of stock or securities. § 1362(d)(3)(D)(i). Gross receipts from sales or exchanges of stock or securities are taken into account only to the extent of gains. Gross receipts from dispositions of capital assets other than stock or securities are taken into account only to the extent that capital gains from such dispositions exceed capital losses. § 1362(d)(3)(C). See also Reg. § 1.1362–2(c).

c.   S Termination Year

If an S corporation's election is revoked or terminated, the corporation has an "S termination year," which consists of an S short year and a C short year. § 1362(e)(1), (4). In general, the tax results for the S termination year are assigned to the two short years on a pro rata basis unless all persons who were shareholders during the S short year and all of the shareholders on the first day of the C short year elect to make the allocation on the basis of normal tax accounting rules. § 1362(e)(2), (3). Since the C short year is subject to the full sting of the double tax on corporate profits, the corporation will be motivated to select the method which allocates the most income to the S short year. The pro rata method may not be used if there is a sale or exchange of 50% or more of the stock in the corporation during the year. § 1362(e)(6)(D). Once the allocation between the short years is made, the tax liability for the C short year is computed on an annualized basis. § 1362(e)(5). See Reg. § 1.1362–3.

d.   Inadvertent Terminations

If an S corporation's election is revoked or terminated, the corporation generally is not eligible to reelect S corporation status for five years unless it receives the Treasury's consent to an earlier election. § 1362(g). Section 1362(f) provides relief for terminations that occur when the corporation ceases to be a small business corporation or violates the passive income limitation. If (1) the Treasury determines that the termination was inadvertent, (2) the corporation takes steps to rectify the problem within a reasonable period of time after discovery, and (3) the corporation and all of the persons who were shareholders during the relevant period agree to make certain adjustments required by the Treasury, then the corporation will retain its S corporation status. The fact that the terminating event was not reasonably within the control of the corporation and took place despite its due diligence tends to establish that a termination was inadvertent. Reg. § 1.1362–4(b).

Example: X Corporation, in good faith, determined that it had no earnings and profits, but the Service later determined on audit that X's S election terminated because X violated the passive income test for three consecutive years by having accumulated earnings and profits. If the shareholders were to agree to treat the earnings as distributed and include the dividends in income, it may be appropriate to waive the terminating event, so X's election is treated as if it never terminated.

D. Tax Treatment of S Corporation Shareholders

1. Introduction

Except in a few situations discussed later in this chapter (See XV.F., at pages 336–339, *infra*), an S corporation is not a taxable entity. § 1363(a). Instead, the corporation's income, loss, deductions, and credits are taxed directly to its shareholders. § 1366(a). Even though aggregate principles are employed for the taxation of an S corporation's income or loss, entity principles generally are used for its computation.

2. Corporate Level Determination Of Tax Results

An S corporation is required to calculate its gross income and taxable income in order to determine the tax results which pass through to the shareholders. §§ 1366(c); 1363(b). An S corporation also must file its own tax return (Form 1120S) and is subject to audit and examination by the Internal Revenue Service. §§ 6037 and 6241–45.

a. Accounting Method

An S corporation generally is free to select its own accounting method. But if an S corporation is a "tax shelter" as defined in § 448, it may not use the cash method of accounting, and under § 267 the corporation is, in effect, required to use the cash method for purposes of taking deductions on payments to persons who own stock in the corporation either directly or by way of attribution. § 267(a)(2), (e).

b. Taxable Year
1) In General

The shareholders of an S corporation are required to include in income their pro rata share of S corporation income in the taxable year in which the S corporation's taxable year ends. § 1366(a). The calendar year shareholders of a profitable S corporation would prefer the corporation to adopt a January 31 taxable year so that they could wait 14½ months (until April 15 of the following year) to pay tax on the corporation's income. To preclude this type of deferral, § 1378 requires an S corporation's taxable year to be a "permitted year," which is defined as a calendar year or an accounting year for which the corporation establishes a business purpose. Deferral of income to the shareholders is not treated as a business purpose. § 1378(b). The legislative history provides that: (1) the use of a particular year for regulatory or financial accounting purposes, (2) hiring patterns of a business, (3) administrative considerations, such as compensation or retirement arrangements with staff or shareholders, and (4) the fact that the business uses price lists, model years, etc., which change on an annual basis, ordinarily are not sufficient to satisfy the business purpose requirement. H.R.Rep. No. 99–841, 99th Cong.2d Sess. II–319 (1986).

> ***Example:*** Assume W Corp. is an S corporation and its principal business is selling new automobiles. The fact that W's new model cars come out in late summer or fall ordinarily is not sufficient to establish a business purpose for it to use a taxable year ending at that time.

2) Natural Business Year

The business purpose standard is satisfied if the taxable year of an S corporation coincides with a "natural business year." The Service has quantified the natural-business-year concept by providing that a corporation will be deemed to have adopted a natural business year if in each of the prior three years its gross receipts for the last two months of the requested taxable year equalled or exceeded 25% of the gross receipts for the full requested year. Rev.Proc. 87–32, 1987–2 C.B. 396. An S corporation unable to satisfy this standard still may demonstrate that a particular taxable year satisfies the business purpose standard under a facts and circumstances test. The Service, however, considers the tax consequences (i.e., deferral) of the year selected to be a fact and circumstance relevant to the question. Rev.Rul. 87–57, 1987–2 C.B. 117.

> ***Example:*** Y Co. desires to use a May 31 tax year. Y's reason for the requested tax year is that due to weather conditions its business is operational only during the period of September 1 through May 1. For its 10–year business history, Y has had insignificant gross receipts for the period of June 1 through August 31. Y's facility is not used for any other purpose during those months. Despite the fact that Y was unable to satisfy the mechanical "natural business year" test, the Service ruled in Revenue Ruling 87–57 that Y established a business purpose for a May 31 tax year.

3) § 444 Fiscal Year Election

Section 444 alleviates some of the harshness of the permitted year requirement. It permits an S corporation to adopt a taxable year other than the calendar year normally required by § 1378, provided the year selected results in no more than three months of tax deferral. As a cost for this relief, the corporation must make "required payments" under § 7519 which are designed to offset the financial benefits of the tax deferral provided by § 444. A § 444 election and § 7519 payments, however, are not required if an S corporation can establish a business purpose for the taxable year it selects. § 444(e).

Example: Assume T Corp. is an S corporation which cannot establish a business purpose for using a taxable year other than a calendar year. T may elect under § 444 to select a fiscal year ending on September 30, October 31, or November 30. If it makes a § 444 election, T will have to make § 7519 required payments to, in effect, "pay back" the benefits of its shareholders being able to defer inclusion of its income for an additional one to three months. Section 7519 has a de minimis provision which would relieve T of this burden if its required payment for a taxable year is $500 or less. If T establishes a business purpose for adopting a taxable year other than a calendar year, it may adopt such a year without electing under § 444 and making § 7519 payments.

c. S Corporation Taxable Income

An S corporation is required to compute its taxable income in the same manner as an individual except that it is not permitted certain deductions allowed only to individuals, such as personal exemptions, medical expenses, alimony and expenses for the production or collection of income under § 212. §§ 1363(b)(2); 703(a)(2)(A), (E). Because an S corporation's losses pass through to its shareholders, the corporation is not permitted a net operating loss deduction. §§ 1363(b)(2); 703(a)(2)(D). Net operating losses from years in which the corporation was a C corporation also may not be carried over to a taxable year in which it is an S corporation. § 1371(b)(1).

In order to preserve their unique character as they pass through to the shareholders, the corporation must separately report any item of income (including tax-exempt income) loss, deduction or credit the separate treatment of which could affect the tax liability of any shareholder. These are known as "separately stated" items. § 1363(b)(1). The characterization of items is determined at the corporate level. § 1366(b). Certain separately stated items, such as charitable contributions, foreign taxes, and depletion, are not deductible by the corporation in computing its taxable income, but they still pass through to the shareholders. §§ 1363(b)(2); 703(a)(2)(B), (C), (F). Examples of other separately stated items include: (1) capital gains and losses, so that the § 1211 limitation on capital losses may be applied at the shareholder level after consideration of each shareholder's other capital gains and losses; (2) § 1231 transactions, so the provisions of § 1231 are applied at the shareholder level taking into account all of the shareholder's § 1231 transactions; and (3) investment interest, so the § 163(d) investment interest limit is applied after taking into account each shareholder's personal tax situation.

Example: T corporation, which has an S election in effect, makes a charitable contribution during the year. Since T is not allowed a charitable deduction in computing taxable income, the special 10% limitation on corporate charitable deductions in § 170(b)(2) does not apply. Instead, the charitable contribution is a separately stated item which passes through to the shareholders who each combine their share of the deduction with their personal charitable deductions before applying the § 170 limits on charitable contributions by individuals.

Because an S corporation generally must compute its taxable income as if it were an individual, it is not allowed deductions granted only to corporations such as the § 243 dividends received deduction. An S corporation, however, is allowed to amortize its organizational expenses over 60 months under § 248. § 1363(b)(3).

d. Tax Elections

Elections affecting the determination of taxable income generally are made by the S corporation rather than its shareholders. § 1363(c)(1).

Example: An election to amortize organizational expenditures under § 248 must be made by the S corporation, not on a shareholder-by-shareholder basis. An election to expense the cost of § 179 property must be made by the S corporation and the dollar limitations in § 179(b) apply at both the S corporation and shareholder levels. § 179(d)(8).

3. Tax Consequences to Shareholders
a. Timing and Character of Pass Through Items

S corporation shareholders are required to take into account their respective pro rata shares of the corporation's separately stated items and nonseparately computed income or loss (i.e., the net total of the items which are not separately stated) in the taxable year in which the S corporation's taxable year ends. § 1366(a). The separately stated items retain their character when reported by the shareholders. § 1366(b).

Example: Assume S Corp. (which is an S corporation) has properly adopted a November 30 taxable year and during its current year has the following income and expenses:

Business Income	$100,000
Salary Expense	$ 40,000
Depreciation	$ 10,000
Taxes	$ 5,000
§ 1245 gain	$ 25,000
§ 1231 gain	$ 20,000

LTCG from stock sale	$ 15,000
LTCL from stock sale	$ 4,000
STCL from stock sale	$ 6,000

Of these items, the § 1231 gain and capital gain and losses are separately stated items because their separate treatment could affect the tax liability of a particular shareholder depending on the results of the shareholder's other asset dispositions during the year. The analogous partnership regulations permit separate netting of long- and short-term capital gain transactions. Reg. § 1.702–1(a)(1), (2). Thus, S's separately stated items will be: § 1231 gain—$20,000; LTCG—$11,000 ($15,000 of gain and $4,000 of loss); and STCL—$6,000. These items will retain their character when they are reported by the shareholders. S's nonseparately computed income will be $70,000 ($100,000 business income plus $25,000 § 1245 gain less $55,000 of deductions (salary, depreciation and taxes)). Because the § 1245 gain is ordinary income, its tax treatment cannot vary among shareholders so it is not a separately reported item. Each shareholder will have to take into account his or her pro rata share of the § 1231 gain, LTCG, STCL, and $70,000 of nonseparately computed income in the taxable year in which S's November 30 taxable year ends. Calendar year shareholders would report their pro rata shares of these items on April 15 of the following year.

b. Determining Each Shareholder's Pro Rata Share

1) In General

Each shareholder's pro rata share of S corporation tax items is determined on a per share, per day basis. § 1377(a)(1).

Example: Assume Z Co. is an S corporation and has 100 shares of stock outstanding. If shareholder A owns 30 shares of Z for the full year, he will be allocated 30% of each of Z's separately stated items and its nonseparately computed income or loss. If A sells 10 of his shares to D midway through the year, he would be allocated 25% of Z's separately stated items and nonseparately computed income or loss (30% for one-half the year, or 15%, plus 20% for one-half the year, or 10%, for a 25% total).

2) Special Rule for Termination of a Shareholder's Interest

If a shareholder's interest in the corporation is terminated, all shareholders during the year may agree to elect to treat the year as if it consisted of two taxable years with the first year ending on the day of termination. § 1377(a)(2).

Example: Assume X Corp. is an S corporation and has 100 shares of stock outstanding. During the year X earns $50,000 of nonseparately computed income and under its accounting method, $40,000 of the $50,000 was earned in the first half of the year. Assume shareholder B sells all 40 of her X shares midway through the year. Under the per share, per day method of allocation, B will report $10,000 of the nonseparately computed income (40% for one-half the year, or 20% of the $50,000). Alternatively, if all of the shareholders in the corporation agree, X's books can be treated as closing as of the day of B's sale and she will report $16,000 (40% of the $40,000 earned in the first half of X's year). Presumably, B will agree to this arrangement only if she has other losses or deductions to offset the additional income or she has some other reason (maybe a family relationship?) to help the other shareholders save taxes.

3)   Special Rule for a Family Group
In order to prevent tax avoidance within a family group through the use of an S corporation, § 1366(e) authorizes the Service to reallocate an S corporation's income if an individual who is a member of the "family" (defined as including a spouse, ancestors and lineal descendants) of an S corporation shareholder renders services or provides capital to the corporation and does not receive reasonable compensation. Note that the service or capital provider need not be a shareholder of the S corporation. The statute only requires that a family member of the service or capital provider be a shareholder. In applying § 1366(e), the courts look to what would be paid to obtain comparable services or capital from an unrelated party. See Reg. § 1.1375–3(a) (interpreting the pre–1982 version of § 1366(e)); *Davis v. Comm'r,* 64 T.C. 1034 (1975).

Example: Assume W Co. is an S corporation with 100 shares of stock outstanding which are owned 20 shares by Dad, 40 shares by Daughter, and 40 shares by Son. If Dad performs $20,000 of deductible services without charge for W, the Service can step in and allocate $20,000 of W's income to Dad. The allocation would produce a $20,000 deduction for W which would reduce the income (or increase the loss) otherwise allocable to Daughter and Son.

c.   **Limitations on Losses**
1)   § 1366(d) Basis Limit
A shareholder's share of S corporation losses and deductions is limited to the shareholder's adjusted basis in the (1) stock of the corporation, and (2) indebtedness of the corporation to the shareholder. § 1366(d)(1). Losses or deductions disallowed under this rule carry over indefinitely and may be

used when the shareholder obtains additional stock or debt basis by, for example, contributing or loaning additional funds to the corporation or buying more stock. § 1366(d)(2).

Example (1):   C is a shareholder in an S corporation and has a $5,000 basis in her stock. C also loaned the corporation $4,000 in exchange for a corporate note. If C's share of the corporation's nonseparately computed loss for the year is $12,000, she will be limited to a $9,000 deduction (her combined basis in the stock and note) and will have $3,000 of suspended loss which will carry over until she obtains additional basis.

If the basis limitation is exceeded by a combination of different types of losses, the limit consists of a proportionate amount of each type of loss. See Reg. § 1.704–1(d)(2), which uses this approach in the analogous partnership setting.

Example (2):   D is a shareholder in an S corporation and has a $3,000 basis in his stock. D's share for the year of the corporation's long-term capital loss is $6,000 and his share of nonseparately computed operating loss is $3,000. Under § 1366(d)(1), D will be allowed a $3,000 loss deduction for the year which will be made up as follows:

$$\frac{6000}{9000} \times 3000 = 2000 \text{ LTCL}$$

$$\frac{3000}{9000} \times 3000 = 1000 \text{ OL}$$

D would have a $4,000 long-term capital loss carryover and a $2,000 operating loss carryover going into the next year.

2)   Basis Credit for Shareholder Guarantee of S Corporation Debt

Most courts agree that an S corporation shareholder does not obtain basis credit for a guarantee of a loan made by a lender directly to the corporation. The taxpayer's argument, accepted only by the Eleventh Circuit, is that since the lender is ultimately looking to the shareholder for repayment, the transaction should be treated as a loan to the shareholder followed by a capital contribution (or loan) to the corporation. *Selfe v. U.S.,* 778 F.2d 769 (11th Cir.1985). The issue is important because of the § 1366(d) limitation on pass through of losses. All other courts require the shareholder to perform under his guaranty in order to receive a basis increase. See, e.g. *Estate of Leavitt v. Comm'r,* 875 F.2d 420 (4th Cir.1989), *cert. denied,* 493 U.S. 958, 110 S.Ct. 376 (1989) (holding that an economic outlay is required to increase the basis of S corporation stock and that until the guarantee is performed it is a mere promise to pay); *Harris v. U.S.,* 902 F.2d 439 (5th Cir.1990) (the court declined to recast a shareholder guarantee of a corporate loan as a capital contribution concluding that, as structured, the transaction had substance and the shareholder had never made an economic outlay); and *Uri v. Comm'r,* 949 F.2d 371 (10th Cir.1991).

3) **Use of Suspended Losses After Termination of S Corporation Status**
    If a shareholder's losses or deductions are disallowed because of inadequate stock basis and the corporation's status as an S corporation terminates, the loss is treated as incurred at the end of the "post-termination transition period" (a period defined in § 1377(b) as extending at least one year after the last day of the corporation's last taxable year as an S corporation). § 1366(d)(3)(A). Thus, if the shareholder has adequate stock basis (debt basis is not considered) at that time by virtue of having made an additional contribution to the corporation, the suspended loss will pass through and reduce the shareholder's personal tax liability. § 1366(d)(3)(B). A corresponding reduction is required in the basis of the stock. § 1366(d)(3)(C).

4) **Related Provisions**
    Losses that pass through to the shareholders also may be disallowed by the at-risk rules in § 465 and the passive activity limitations in § 469. The at-risk rules are applied to an S corporation on an activity-by-activity basis, except that all activities constituting a trade or business are treated as one activity if the taxpayer actively participates in the management of the trade or business, or 65% or more of the losses are allocable to persons who actively participate in management of the trade or business. § 465(c)(3)(B). Under the passive loss limitations, if an S corporation shareholder does not materially participate in an activity, his losses from the activity will only be deductible against income from passive activities. § 469(a), (c)(1), (d)(1). Any disallowed passive activity loss may be carried forward to the next taxable year. § 469(b).

d. Basis Adjustments

The basis of each shareholder's stock in an S corporation is first increased by the shareholder's share of both separately and nonseparately computed income items and decreased, but not below zero, by distributions to the shareholder and then decreased by the shareholder's share of separately and nonseparately computed losses, deductions, and expenses which are not deductible and not capital expenditures. § 1367(a). For the rules providing that basis adjustments for distributions are made before applying the § 1366(d) loss limitation for the year, see §§ 1366(d)(1)(A); 1368(d), last sentence. If losses and deductions exceed the shareholder's stock basis, they may be applied against and reduce (but not below zero) the shareholder's basis in any S corporation debt. § 1367(b)(2)(A). If debt basis is reduced under this provision, later net increases are first applied to restore that basis before being applied to increase the basis of the shareholder's stock. § 1367(b)(2)(B). Basis adjustments are made at the end of the corporation's taxable year unless during the year the shareholder disposes of the stock or the debt is wholly or partially repaid in which case the adjustments are effective immediately before the disposition or repayment. Reg. § 1.1367–1(d)(1), –2(d)(1).

Example: C is a shareholder in an S corporation who paid $5,000 for her stock and loaned the corporation $1,000 in exchange for a corporate note. During the corporation's first taxable year (Year 1), C's share of the corporation's tax items is:

LTCG	$2,000
Operating Income	$4,000
STCL	$1,000

C will report and pay tax on these items in her taxable year in which the corporate taxable year ends. At the end of Year 1 her stock basis is adjusted as follows:

$ 5,000	Original Stock Basis
+ 2,000	§ 1367(a)(1)(A)
+ 4,000	§ 1367(a)(1)(B)
– 1,000	§ 1367(a)(2)(B)
$10,000	New Stock Basis

C's basis in the corporate note remains $1,000.

In Year 2, C's share of the corporation's tax items consists of $12,000 of operating loss. Under § 1366(d), C can only deduct $11,000 of the loss (the total of her stock and debt basis in the corporation). The remaining $1,000 of loss will be suspended and carry over to Year 3. C's basis in her stock and debt will be reduced to zero under § 1367(a)(2)(C) and § 1367(b)(2)(A).

In Year 3, the corporation's business improves and C's share of the corporation's tax items consists of $5,000 of operating income. C will include the $5,000 of income in her personal tax return and will be allowed to deduct the $1,000 loss from the prior year. For basis purposes, the $5,000 increase attributable to the income will be reduced by the $1,000 loss. The remaining $4,000 of basis will first be allocated to the debt to restore it to its original $1,000 basis. § 1367(b)(2)(B).

At the end of Year 3, C's stock basis is adjusted as follows:

$　　0	Beginning Basis
+ 5,000	Income
− 1,000	Suspended Loss Deductible This Year
− 1,000	Restoration of Debt Basis
$3,000	New Stock Basis

e.　Sale of S Corporation Stock

S corporation stock is a capital asset and historically has been treated as such for purposes of characterizing gain or loss to a selling shareholder. More recently, the regulations apply a partial and fairly narrow "look-through" rule for sales and exchanges of S corporation stock. Reg. § 1.1(h)–1. Shareholders who sell S corporation stock held for more than one year may recognize either collectibles gain (taxable at a maximum rate of 28%) or residual capital gain (taxable at a maximum rate of 20%) or loss. A selling shareholder's share of collectibles gain is the amount of "net collectibles gain" (but not loss) that would be allocated to that shareholder if the S corporation sold all of its collectibles in a fully taxable transaction immediately before the sale of the stock. The "residual" capital gain (or loss) is the amount of long-term capital gain or loss that the shareholder would recognize on the sale of the stock ("pre-look-through capital gain or loss") less the shareholder's share of collectibles gain. Reg. § 1.1(h)–1(c). It is possible for a selling shareholder who has a pre-look-through gain to end up with a collectibles gain and a residual capital loss. These look-through rules do not extend to ordinary income assets or to the 25% "unrecaptured section 1250 gain" that may be realized on the sale of depreciable real estate.

Example:　　A, B and C are equal shareholders in S Corp., an S corporation that invests in antique collectibles. A, who has held her S Corp. stock for more than one year and has an adjusted basis of $1,000, sells her stock to P for $1,500, recognizing $500 of pre-look-through long-term capital gain. S Corp. owned antiques which, if sold for their fair market value, would result in $3,000 of collectibles gain, of which $1,000 would be allocable to A. Therefore, on the sale of her stock, A recognizes $1,000 of collectibles gain and $500 of residual long-term capital loss. Reg. § 1.1(h)–1(f) Example 4.

E.　Distributions to Shareholders

Because the shareholders of an S corporation are taxed directly on their share of the corporation's income, whether actually received or not, distributions of that income should not be taxed again. Section 1368 accomplishes that result in straightforward fashion for corporations that do not have E & P. Distributions by S corporations with E & P (for example, from prior operation as a C corporation or acquisition of a C corporation) present some additional complications.

1. S Corporations Without E & P

Distributions by S corporations with no E & P are tax free to the extent of the shareholder's adjusted basis in stock of the corporation. § 1368(b)(1). If the distribution exceeds the shareholder's stock basis, the excess is treated as gain from the sale or exchange of the stock, normally capital gain if the stock is a capital asset. § 1368(b)(2). Finally, the shareholder's stock basis is reduced by the amount of any distribution which is not includible in income by reason of the distribution rules. § 1367(a)(2)(A).

> *Example:* D is a shareholder in an S corporation and has a $5,000 basis in his stock. If the corporation distributes $8,000 of cash to D he will be permitted to receive $5,000 tax free and $3,000 will be treated as gain from the sale or exchange of D's stock. D's stock basis will be reduced to zero as a result of the distribution.

2. S Corporations With E & P
a. In General

In order to determine the tax consequences of a distribution by an S corporation with E & P, a concept is needed to separate the results of the corporation's operations as an S corporation from its prior C corporation existence. The concept adopted for this purpose is the accumulated adjustments account (the "AAA"). To the extent of the AAA, distributions are treated in the same fashion as distributions by S corporations without E & P—first as a tax-free recovery of stock basis, then as gain from the sale or exchange of stock. If distributions during the year exceed the AAA, the AAA is proportionately allocated based on the amount of each distribution. Amounts distributed in excess of the AAA are first treated as a dividend to the extent of the corporation's E & P and then as a recovery of any remaining stock basis and gain from the sale or exchange of stock. § 1368(c). Alternatively, all shareholders receiving distributions during the year may jointly elect to have all distributions first treated as dividends to the extent of available E & P. § 1368(e)(3); Reg. § 1.1368–1(e)(2).

b. The Accumulated Adjustments Account

The AAA is an account of the corporation which is adjusted for the period since the corporation has been an S corporation (beginning in 1983) in the same general manner as adjustments are made to a shareholder's basis. § 1368(e)(1)(A). The AAA is a corporate account and is not apportioned among the shareholders. Reg. § 1.1368–2(a). The AAA is best understood as a running total of the undistributed earnings of the corporation which have been taxed to the shareholders since it has been an S corporation.

Example: On January 1, 2003, T Corporation elected to be an S corporation. Prior to 2003, T operated as a C corporation and at the time of its S election it had $6,000 of accumulated E & P. During 2003, T had $30,000 of operating income from its business and made no distributions to its shareholders. During 2004, T had a $10,000 LTCG, $20,000 of operating loss from its business and made no distributions. During 2005, T broke even in its business and distributed $20,000 to each of its two equal shareholders, A and B. Assume A's basis in her T stock at the beginning of 2005 is $12,000 and B's basis in his T stock is $8,000.

T's AAA is $20,000 for purposes of characterizing the distributions to A and B:

$30,000	1998 operating income
+10,000	1999 LTCG
−20,000	1999 operating loss
$20,000	AAA

Thus, the first $10,000 of each distribution will be treated as recovery of stock basis (to the extent thereof) and gain from the sale or exchange of stock. The next $3,000 of each distribution will be a dividend as a result of T's accumulated E & P. The final $7,000 of each distribution will be recovery of any remaining stock basis and gain. In summary, the results to A and B are:

A		**B**
$10,000	§ 1368(c)(1), (b)(1)	$8,000
	§ 1368(c)(1), (b)(2), (b)(1)	$2,000
$ 3,000	§ 1368(c)(2)	$3,000
$ 2,000	§ 1368(c)(3), (b)(1)	
$ 5,000	§ 1368(c)(3), (b)(2)	$7,000

As a result of the distributions, both A's and B's stock bases will be zero at the end of the year. § 1367(a)(2)(A). T's AAA will also be reduced to zero because it is allowed a $20,000 reduction for the amount of the distribution received by A and B tax free. §§ 1368(e)(1)(A); 1367(a)(2)(A). T's E & P will be zero at the end of the year. §§ 312(a)(1); 1371(c)(3). Since T no longer has E & P, it will be able to operate in the future without having to worry about its AAA unless it later obtains E & P—e.g., through an acquisition of a C corporation. Finally, it would not have mattered on these facts, but if the distributions had been smaller (e.g.,

$3,000 to each shareholder) A and B could have considered a joint election to treat the distribution as a dividend. The benefit of such an election would be to eliminate T's E & P and the need for the AAA. Elimination of E & P also would remove the threat of a termination or corporate-level tax as a result of passive investment income. See §§ 1362(d)(3) and 1375.

3. Distributions of Property

The rules in § 1368 do not distinguish between cash and property distributions at the shareholder level. The amount of a property distribution will be the fair market value of the property and a shareholder will take a fair market value basis in distributed property. § 301(b)(1), (d). The shareholder's stock basis also will be reduced by the fair market value of the distributed property. §§ 1367(a)(2)(A) and 1368.

At the corporate level, a distribution of appreciated property to a shareholder will require recognition of gain as if the property were sold. §§ 311(b)(1), 1368(a) and 1371(a)(1). The gain will be taxed directly to the shareholders like any other gain recognized by the corporation.

Example: Assume W Co. (an S corporation) has no E & P, breaks even in business during the year, and distributes appreciated land (a capital asset held long-term with a $50,000 fair market value and $20,000 adjusted basis) to C, one of its two equal shareholders. Also, assume C's basis in her W stock is $70,000 and W makes a simultaneous $50,000 cash distribution to D, its other shareholder. W will recognize $30,000 of LTCG, $15,000 of which will be taxed to each shareholder. C will receive a $50,000 tax-free distribution, and her stock basis beginning the next year will be:

$70,000 Stock Basis
+15,000 §§ 1366(a)(1)(A), 1367(a)(1)(A)
−50,000 §§ 1368(b)(1), 1367(a)(2)(A)
$35,000

4. Ordering of Basis Adjustments

A shareholder's basis is first increased by his pro rata share of income and gain for the year and then decreased (but not below zero) by distributions before any further reduction for losses. § 1368(d), last sentence. Thus, downward basis adjustments for distributions are made before applying the § 1366(d) loss limitation for the year. § 1366(d)(1)(A). This is similar to the ordering rules used by partnerships. Reg. § 1.704–1(d)(2).

Example: A is the sole shareholder of X Corp., an S corporation with no accumulated E & P. On January 1 of the current year, A's adjusted basis in her X stock is $1,000, and A holds no X debt. During the year, X recognizes a $200 LTCG, sustains an operating loss of $900, and distributes $700 cash to A. A's adjusted basis in her X stock is first increased by $200, to $1,200, to reflect the $200 LTCG. A's basis is then reduced by the distribution to $500 ($1,200 less the $700 distribution) before applying the § 1366(d)(1) loss limitation. A may deduct $500 of X's operating loss and reduces her adjusted stock basis to zero. The remaining $400 of loss may be carried forward under § 1366(d)(2).

5. Distributions Following Termination Of S Corporation Status
Following termination of a corporation's S status, cash distributions during a "post-termination transition period" (a period defined in § 1377(b) as extending at least one year after the last day of the corporation's last taxable year as an S corporation) are applied against stock basis to the extent of the AAA. § 1371(e)(1). All shareholders receiving distributions during the post-termination transition period may elect to not have this rule apply. § 1371(e)(2).

F. Taxation of the S Corporation

The principal benefit of a corporation making an S election is relief from paying all corporate-level taxes. Thus, an S corporation is not subject to the § 11 tax on corporate taxable income, the corporate alternative minimum tax, and various penalty taxes such as the § 531 accumulated earnings tax and the § 541 personal holding company tax. S corporations with a prior C corporation history, however, are subject to taxation in certain limited circumstances.

1. § 1374 Tax on Built–In Gains
  a. Policy of Built-in Gains Tax
  When Congress repealed the remaining remnants of the *General Utilities* doctrine, it was concerned that Subchapter S might be used to avoid tax on corporate-level gain. The fear was that a C corporation seeking to liquidate or distribute a highly appreciated asset to its shareholders could make an S election prior to the contemplated distribution. Although corporate-level gain would be recognized, it would pass through to the shareholders and no corporate-level tax would be paid. The shareholders possibly would be required to recognize gain on the liquidation but only after an upward adjustment in their stock basis as a result of taking the gain into income. If permitted, this technique would reduce or eliminate the full burden of the double tax.

  To curtail this strategy, Congress enacted § 1374, which applies to S corporations making an election after 1986. In keeping with its narrow purpose, § 1374 does not apply to corporations that have always been S corporations. § 1374(c)(1).

  b. Operation of § 1374
  Section 1374 imposes a tax (generally at the highest § 11(b) rates) on an S corporation's net recognized built-in gain for any taxable year during a 10–year

"recognition period" beginning with the first day it became an S corporation. § 1374(a), (b)(1), (d)(7). An S corporation's recognized built-in gain is any gain recognized during the relevant 10–year period unless the corporation establishes that it did not hold the asset when it made its S election or the gain recognized exceeded the gain inherent in the asset at the time of the S election. § 1374(d)(3). Built-in gains subject to § 1374 include not only gains from sales or exchanges of property but also other income items, such as cash basis accounts receivable, that were earned (but not collected) when the corporation was a C corporation. § 1374(c)(5)(A). The base for the tax, "net recognized built-in gain," is the lesser of the corporation's recognized built-in gains and losses for the year or the corporation's taxable income (computed with various modifications). § 1374(d)(2). The net recognized built-in gain, however, cannot exceed the excess of the total net unrealized gain in the corporation's assets at the time of its S election over the net recognized built-in gain for prior years in the 10–year period. § 1374(c)(2).

Example: Assume S Co. was formed in 1980 and made an S election effective as of the beginning of the current year, when it had no E & P and the following assets:

Asset	Adjusted Basis	F.M.V.
Asset # 1	$40,000	$20,000
Asset # 2	$25,000	$50,000
Asset # 3	$ 5,000	$15,000
Total	$70,000	$85,000

If S sells Asset #3 for $20,000 in the year after its S election, it has a $15,000 gain ($20,000 amount realized less $5,000 adjusted basis). Its recognized built-in gain, however, is $10,000 ($15,000 FMV less $5,000 adjusted basis), assuming it can establish the $15,000 fair market value of the asset at the time of its S election. Assuming S's taxable income (computed with the relevant modifications) is greater than $10,000, its net recognized built-in gain will be $10,000 and its § 1374 tax is $3,500 (the top § 11(b) rate of 35% times $10,000). If S's taxable income for the year were less than $10,000, the § 1374 tax would be 35% of the lesser amount. In that event, the difference between $10,000 and S's taxable income would be treated as a recognized built-in gain in S's next taxable year. § 1374(d)(2)(B).

If S sells Asset #2 for $50,000 in its next year as an S corporation, it will have a $25,000 gain ($50,000 amount realized less $25,000 adjusted basis). It also appears to have a $25,000 net recognized built-in gain. Section 1374(c)(2), however, limits the net recognized built-in gain for the year to the $15,000 of total gain potential in S's assets at the time of its election ($85,000 FMV less $70,000 adjusted basis) less the $10,000 of net recognized built-in gain in its first year. Thus, S's net recognized built-in gain for its second year is $5,000 and its § 1374(b) tax will be $1,750 (35% of $5,000), assuming its taxable income for the year is not less than $5,000.

c. Treatment of Substituted Basis Properties

An S corporation may dispose of or acquire assets in a wide variety of nontaxable transactions. Section 1374(d)(6) and (8) describe the impact of these transactions under the § 1374 tax. Under § 1374(d)(6), if property held by an S corporation ("new property") has a basis determined by reference to the basis of property held by the corporation at the time of its S election ("old property"), the new property is treated as held by the corporation as of the time of the election, and if it is sold the recognized built-in gain or loss is determined with reference to the basis and value of the old property at the time of the election.

Example: If an S corporation exchanges property it held at the time of its S election ("old property") for property of like kind ("new property") in a nontaxable (or partially nontaxable) transaction under § 1031, any built-in gain in the old property will be recognized under § 1374 if the new property is disposed of in a taxable transaction during the recognition period.

Section 1374(d)(8) contains a similar rule for assets acquired by an S corporation from a C corporation in a tax-free reorganization. In that situation, the 10–year recognition period with respect to such property begins on the day the S corporation acquires the assets, not the day of its S election. § 1374(d)(8)(B)(i). The exclusion from § 1374 for corporations that have always been an S corporation does not apply if a corporation acquires assets from a C corporation in a tax-free reorganization. § 1374(d)(8)(B)(ii).

d. Installment Sales and § 1374

If an S corporation disposes of an asset with a built-in gain during the recognition period for deferred payments due after the recognition period, § 1374 continues to apply to the payments received after the recognition period. The gain in later years will be taxed to the extent it would have been taxed under § 1374 if the corporation had elected to recognize the gain in the year of sale under § 453(d). Reg. § 1.1374–4(g).

2. § 1375 Tax on Excessive Passive Investment Income

If an S corporation has E & P from Subchapter C operations and more than 25% of its gross receipts consist of "passive investment income," it is subject to a 35% tax (the highest § 11(b) rate) on its "excess net passive income." An S corporation with no E & P is not subject to § 1375. "Passive investment income" generally consists of the classic forms of investment income (dividends, interest, rents, etc.) and § 1375 borrows the definitions employed in § 1362(d)(3) relating to termination of an S election for excessive passive investment income. § 1375(b)(3); see XV.C.2.b.2, at page 321, *supra*.

The regulations define "rents" as amounts received for the use of, or right to use property. But if significant services are also provided, the amounts received are not considered rents. Reg. § 1.1362–2(c)(5)(ii)(B)(2). For example, payments made to a parking lot where an attendant parks the car are not rents. Rev.Rul. 65–91, 1965–1 C.B. 431. But rents received in a mobile home community are "rents" because the services provided (utilities, garbage collection, etc.) are of the type generally provided by a landlord and, hence, not "significant." *Stover v. Comm'r*, 781 F.2d 137 (8th Cir.1986).

"Excess net passive income," the base for the tax, is a portion of the corporation's net passive income, which is generally defined as passive income less directly connected deductions for the year. § 1375(b)(1). This amount is determined by a ratio. The numerator of the ratio is the amount by which the corporation's passive investment income exceeds 25% of its gross receipts for the year and the denominator is passive investment income. Excess net passive income, however, cannot exceed the corporation's taxable income (computed with certain changes). § 1375(b)(1)(B).

The Service may waive the § 1375 tax if the S corporation establishes that it determined in good faith that it had no E & P and within a reasonable time after discovering that it did have E & P it distributed the E & P to its shareholders. § 1375(d).

Example: S Corp. (which is an S corporation) has Subchapter C E & P. During the current year, it has $150,000 of gross receipts, $50,000 of which are passive investment income. S also has $10,000 of expenses directly connected to the production of the passive investment income. S is subject to the § 1375 tax because it has E & P and its passive investment income is at least 25% of its gross receipts ($50,000 passive investment income/$150,000 gross receipts equals 33%). S's net passive income is $40,000 ($50,000 gross receipts less $10,000 of directly connected expenses). Its excess net passive income will be $40,000 (net passive income) multiplied by a ratio having $12,500 as its numerator ($50,000 of passive investment income less 25% of gross receipts) and $50,000 as the denominator (passive investment income). Thus, S's excess net passive income is $10,000 and its § 1375 tax will be $3,500 ($10,000 × 35%). This assumes that S's taxable income as computed under § 1375(b)(1)(B) is less than $10,000.

G. Coordination of Subchapter S With Subchapter C And Other Tax Provisions

1. Subchapter C

Even though it is not subject to the corporate income tax, an S corporation is still a corporation and can engage in a wide array of corporate-shareholder transactions. Thus, an S corporation may redeem its own stock or distribute its net assets to its shareholders in a liquidating distribution. An S corporation also may participate in potentially tax-free or taxable corporate acquisitions as the purchasing corporation or the target and it is free to rearrange its structure under § 355. Subchapter S provides limited guidance on the tax treatment of an S corporation and its shareholders in these Subchapter C transactions. Section 1371(a) states that Subchapter C applies to an S corporation and its shareholders, except as otherwise provided or to the extent inconsistent with Subchapter S. Section 1368 also provides that its distribution rules apply to all distributions to which § 301(c) would otherwise apply. Thus, if an S corporation redeems some of its stock in a transaction that does not qualify for exchange treatment under § 302, the distribution will be taxed under § 1368.

2. Other Tax Provisions

Section 1363(b) provides that with certain exceptions an S corporation computes its taxable income in the same manner as an individual. Thus, the tax principles throughout the Code which apply to individual taxpayers generally apply to S corporations. For purposes of fringe benefit provisions in the Code, § 1372 provides that an S corporation is to be treated as a partnership and any 2% shareholder (direct or through attribution) shall be treated as a partner. This provision has the effect of denying the tax advantages of fringe benefits such as group-term life insurance and medical reimbursement plans to disqualified shareholders.

3. Employment Tax Issues

S corporation shareholders sometimes attempt to avoid paying federal social security (FICA) and unemployment taxes (FUTA) by converting wages into tax-free distributions. The base for employment taxes is "wages"—remuneration paid for employment. In cases where an S corporation paid no salary to its principal employee and shareholder, the courts have concluded that all or part of the corporation's distributions were, in substance, wages subject to federal employment taxes. *Joseph Radtke, S.C. v. U.S.,* 895 F.2d 1196 (7th Cir.1990); *Spicer Accounting, Inc. v. U.S.,* 918 F.2d 90 (9th Cir.1990).

H. Review Questions

1. C Corp. has one 100% owned subsidiary which has been active for several years. In 2003, C decides to elect S corporation status. May it do so?

2. C Corp.'s 100 outstanding shares are owned as follows:

F and J (a married couple)	25 shs.
A and B (unmarried joint tenants)	25 shs.
73 individual unrelated shareholders	50 shs.

Will C qualify as a "small business corporation"?

3. Assume that in question 2 the shares owned by A and B in joint tenancy are purchased by X Partnership. Will C now qualify as a "small business corporation"?

4. S Corp. (a small business corporation) has 70 individual shareholders. One of its shareholders, M, dies and pursuant to M's will the S stock is transferred to a trust. Does M's death affect S's ability to qualify as a small business corporation?

5. C Corp. has two classes of common stock authorized. Class A is issued and outstanding. Class B has been authorized but has not been issued. Does C qualify as a small business corporation?

6. Assume that S Corp. is an S Corporation with 20 shareholders and 100 shares outstanding and that A, who owns 10 shares, wants to revoke S's status as an S corporation. How many votes are necessary for A to achieve that result?

7. In question 6, assuming revocation is achieved, when will the revocation be effective?

8. Assume that a corporation's S status has been terminated because it violates the 75 shareholder limit. On what date is the termination of S status effective?

9. Does a corporation falling under the situation in question 8 have any recourse as to the termination of its S status?

10. Assume that B, a shareholder in S Corp., an S corporation, guarantees a loan made by a lender directly to S. Will B receive a basis increase for the amount of the loan guarantee?

11. In considering the pass through of losses from an S corporation to its shareholders, what limitations besides the shareholder's basis in S stock and debt are relevant?

12. A is a shareholder in an S corporation and at the beginning of the year has a $4,000 basis in her stock. The corporation does not have any E & P. The corporation distributes $10,000 to A on July 15. A's pro rata share of the corporation's income and loss for the year is:

Nonseparately Computed Income	$8,000
Long–Term Capital Loss	$6,000

Determine the tax results to A for the year and the results of the July 15 distribution.

13. What is the "AAA"?

14. In what situations will an S corporation be concerned with the § 1374 tax on built-in gains?

PART THREE

PARTNERSHIP TAXATION

Analysis

*

XVI

FORMATION OF A PARTNERSHIP

Analysis

A. Introduction

If a taxpayer contributes property to a newly formed partnership in exchange for an interest in the partnership, the exchange arguably should be taxable to both the new partner and the partnership. The new partner might be required to recognize gain or loss equal to the difference between the fair market value of the partnership interest and the adjusted basis of the contributed property. Likewise, the partnership might have to recognize gain or loss on its receipt of the contributed property. § 1001(a), (c). Section 721 eliminates these theoretical concerns by providing that gain or loss is not recognized by either a partnership or its partners on a contribution of property to the partnership in exchange for a partnership interest. The policy is that the contribution of property to a partnership is a mere change in the form of the taxpayer's investment and not an appropriate taxable event. Consistent with its nonrecognition policy, § 721 is accompanied by Code sections which preserve the unrecognized gain or loss in the new partner's basis in the partnership interest (§ 722) and the partnership's basis in the contributed property (§ 723).

B. Contributions of Property

1. General Rules

The nonrecognition rule in § 721 applies to contributions of property to both newly formed and existing partnerships. Reg. § 1.721–1(a). The principal requirement is that the partner must receive the partnership interest in exchange for "property." "Property" is not defined in the Code, but the courts have been guided by the interpretation of the term under § 351, the counterpart of § 721 in the corporate area. "Property" includes cash, inventory, accounts receivable, patents, installment obligations, and other intangibles such as goodwill and industrial know how. "Property" does not include the performance of services for the partnership, and a partner who receives a partnership interest in exchange for services normally recognizes ordinary income under §§ 61 and 83. Reg. § 1.721–1(b)(1). See XVI.D., at page 353, *infra* for the tax treatment of a partner receiving a partnership interest in exchange for services.

Section 721 does not apply to transactions between a partnership and a partner not acting in the capacity of a partner. Reg. § 1.721–1(a). For example, if a partner sells or leases property to the partnership, the transaction is not governed by § 721. See XVII.D.4., at page 415, *infra*.

2. Related Issues
a. Recapture Provisions

Section 721 overrides the depreciation recapture provisions. See §§ 1245(b)(3); 1250(d)(3). The potential recapture income is preserved in the partnership's basis in the asset.

b. Installment Obligations

A partner does not recognize § 453B gain when an installment obligation is contributed to a partnership in exchange for a partnership interest. Reg. §§ 1.453–9(c)(2) and 1.721–1(a).

c. Investment Partnerships

Under § 721(b), transfers of property to a partnership which would be an investment company if incorporated do not qualify for nonrecognition. This rule prevents taxpayers from diversifying their investment portfolios tax free. See § 351(e)(1) and Reg. § 1.351–1(c).

3. Basis and Holding Period

a. "Outside" and "Inside" Bases

A partner's basis in her partnership interest is referred to as the "outside" basis. A partnership's basis in its assets is referred to as the "inside" basis. These terms will be used to distinguish between the partner's and the partnership's bases.

On a contribution of property in exchange for a partnership interest, a partner's outside basis under § 722 is equal to the sum of the money and the adjusted bases of property contributed to the partnership. Under § 723, the partnership's inside basis is equal to the basis the contributing partner had in the property. Both the contributing partner and the partnership obtain a basis increase if gain is recognized under the investment partnership rule in § 721(b). These basis provisions are designed to preserve the gain or loss that went unrecognized under § 721 on the contribution of the property.

In certain situations, § 724 preserves the character of the gain or loss that the property would have had in the hands of the contributing partner. Section 704(c) also requires the precontribution gain or loss in a partnership asset to be allocated to the contributing partner when the partnership disposes of the asset. See XVII.C.3., at page 387, *infra*.

b. Holding Period

A partner's holding period for her partnership interest includes the period that the partner held any contributed property that was a capital or § 1231 asset. § 1223(1). The holding period for a partnership interest received for other property (cash or ordinary income assets) begins on the date of the exchange. If a partnership interest is received for a mixture of capital, § 1231 and ordinary income assets, it takes a split holding period based on the fair market values of the contributed assets until it is sufficiently "aged" so that it has been held long-term. See Reg. § 1.1223–3(b)(1). For this purpose, recapture gain (e.g., under § 1245) is treated as a separate asset which is not a capital or Section 1231 asset. Reg. § 1.1223–3(e). A partner's holding period in contributed property carries over to the partnership. § 1223(2).

Example: Partner A contributes the following assets to the newly formed
ABC partnership in exchange for a one-third interest in the
partnership:

Asset	A.B.	F.M.V.
Accounts Receivable for Services Performed in A's Business	$ 0	$ 10,000
Capital Asset	$70,000	$ 60,000
Equipment (all § 1245 gain)	$10,000	$ 30,000
Total	$80,000	$100,000

Under § 721, neither A nor ABC recognizes gain or loss since A
transfers property in exchange for the partnership interest.
Accounts receivable for services have been held to be property
under § 351. *Hempt Brothers, Inc. v. U.S.,* 490 F.2d 1172 (3d
Cir.1974), *cert. denied,* 419 U.S. 826, 95 S.Ct. 44 (1974). The gain
on the equipment normally would be recaptured as ordinary
income under § 1245(a). Section 1245(b)(3), however, creates an
exception to the general recapture rule for certain otherwise tax-
free transactions, including § 721 exchanges, when the property
takes a transferred basis. The recapture potential remains in the
equipment and will be recognized if the equipment is sold by the
partnership. See § 1245(a)(2).

A's outside basis under § 722 will be $80,000. This is the sum of
the bases of the accounts receivable, capital asset and equipment.
A will be allowed a tacked holding period on 70% of the
partnership interest that is attributable to the fair market value
of the capital asset and the basis of the equipment. This only
matters until A actually has a long-term holding period for the
partnership interest. ABC will take a transferred basis in each of
the assets contributed by A and may tack holding periods for all of
the properties received. §§ 723; 1223(2).

C.   Treatment of Liabilities

1.   Impact on Partner's Outside Basis

a.   Introduction

Because a partnership is treated as an aggregate of its individual partners for
purposes of taxing its income, Subchapter K adopts aggregate principles to
determine the impact of partnership liabilities on the partners and their
outside bases. Under the *Crane* case, a taxpayer who acquires property subject
to a debt includes the amount of the debt in the basis of the property on the

assumption that the debt will be repaid. A taxpayer who sells property subject to a debt must include the debt relief in the amount realized on the theory that relief of debt is the same as receipt of an equivalent amount of cash.

For partners, these basic principles are incorporated in § 752, which applies to a wide array of transactions, including contributions of property. Section 752 generally applies to all partnership liabilities except those that would be deductible when paid (e.g., accounts payable of a cash basis partnership). Rev.Rul. 88–77, 1988–2 C.B. 128. Under § 752(a), an increase in a partner's share of partnership liabilities is considered a contribution of money which increases the partner's outside basis under § 722. A decrease in a partner's share of partnership liabilities is considered under § 752(b) to be a distribution of money to the partner which decreases the partner's outside basis (but not below zero) under §§ 705(a) and 733. If a decrease in a partner's share of partnership liabilities exceeds the partner's outside basis, the partner must recognize the excess as capital gain from the sale or exchange of the partnership interest. §§ 731(a)(1); 741.

b. Classification of Liabilities and Partners' Shares of Partnership Liabilities

The § 752 regulations use the concept of "economic risk of loss" both to classify partnership liabilities as recourse or nonrecourse and to determine the partners' shares of recourse liabilities. A partnership liability is classified as "recourse" only to the extent that a partner bears the economic risk of loss for the liability. Reg. § 1.752–1(a)(1). A partner's share of the recourse liabilities of a partnership equals the portion of the recourse liabilities for which the partner bears the economic risk of loss. Reg. § 1.752–2(a). A liability is "nonrecourse" to the extent that no partner bears the economic risk of loss for the liability. Reg. § 1.752–1(a)(2). The partners generally share nonrecourse liabilities in proportion to their share of partnership profits. Reg. § 1.752–3(a).

> *Example:* A, B and C each contribute $20,000 cash to form the ABC partnership and agree to share all partnership profits and losses equally. ABC purchases a parcel of investment real estate for $150,000, paying $60,000 cash and giving the seller a $90,000 purchase money note secured by the real estate. No partner is personally liable for the note. The purchase money obligation is a nonrecourse liability which will be shared equally by the partners because they have equal interests in partnership profits. A, B and C each will be treated as if they contributed $30,000 to ABC under § 752(a) to reflect the increase in their share of partnership liabilities (from zero to $30,000). As a result, each partner's outside basis will be $50,000 under § 722.

A more detailed study of the tax treatment of nonrecourse liabilities requires an examination of the Code provisions for determining the partners' shares of partnership income and profits in more complex situations. The tax treatment of nonrecourse liabilities will be revisited after those topics are covered. See XVII.C.4., at pages 398–408, *infra*. The remainder of this chapter will focus on recourse liabilities and the concept of economic risk of loss.

c. Economic Risk of Loss

A partner bears the economic risk of loss for a partnership liability to the extent that the partner would bear the economic burden of discharging the obligation represented by the liability if the partnership were unable to do so. The regulations employ a "doomsday" liquidation analysis to determine whether a partner bears the economic risk of loss for a liability. Basically, the regulations assume that all of the partnership assets are worthless, all of the partnership liabilities are due and payable and the partnership disposes of all its assets in a fully taxable transaction for no consideration. They then ask whether any partner or partners would be obligated to make a payment to a creditor or contribution to the partnership in order to pay the liability. § 1.752–2(b)(1). If a partner or partners are so obligated, the liability is a recourse liability and is shared by the partners who bear the economic risk of loss. For this purpose, guarantees, indemnifications, and other reimbursement arrangements are taken into account. Reg. § 1.752–2(b)(3)(i)–(iii), –2(b)(5). A payment obligation is disregarded if it is: (1) subject to contingencies unlikely to occur, or (2) arises at a future time after an event that is not determinable with reasonable accuracy. Reg. § 1.752–2(b)(4). It generally is assumed that a partner will actually discharge an obligation even if the partner's net worth is less than the amount of the obligation. Reg. § 1.752–2(b)(6).

Example (1): Equal partners in a general partnership ordinarily will share the economic risk of loss for any partnership recourse liability equally because they share the economic burden of that debt equally. Similarly, limited partners ordinarily do not bear the economic risk of loss for any partnership liability because they generally have no obligation to contribute additional capital to the partnership.

Example (2): C and D each contribute $500 in cash to the new CD general partnership. CD purchases property from an unrelated seller for $10,000, paying $1,000 cash and borrowing $9,000. The debt is evidenced by a note that is a general obligation of the partnership—i.e., no partner is relieved from personal liability. Under the partnership agreement, C and D agree to share partnership profits and losses 40% to C and 60% to D. The partners' shares of the $9,000 note depend on how they would bear the economic risk of loss for the liability in a constructive liquidation of the partnership. That depends on the effect of their allocation of profits and losses on their capital accounts and obligations to the partnership. Reg. § 1.752–2(f) Examples 1 and 2. That topic is covered with partnership allocations. See XVII.C.2.c.5, at page 380, *infra,* for a discussion of this issue and an example.

Example (3):   G, the general partner, and L, the limited partner, form the GL limited partnership with each contributing $10,000 cash. G and L agree to share partnership profits and losses equally. GL purchases a parcel of rental real estate for $20,000 cash and $80,000 of nonrecourse financing which is secured by the property. Under the terms of the loan the lender may only look to the rental real estate if GL defaults on the loan. In addition, G personally guarantees the loan. Under the guarantee if GL defaults on the loan, G will pay the lender the difference between the balance of the loan and the property's value. Under the doomsday liquidation analysis, if the property becomes worthless and the loan becomes due, G will be obligated to pay the lender under the guarantee. Accordingly, G bears the economic risk of loss for the full liability and it is a "recourse" liability. See Reg. § 1.752–2(f) Example 5.

Example (4):   Assume the same facts as Example (3), except that in connection with G's guarantee, G and L enter into an indemnification agreement under which L agrees to reimburse G for 50% of any payment that G is required to make under the guarantee. Under these facts, G and L each bear the economic risk of loss for 50% of GL's liability under the guarantee and indemnification agreement. The liability is a recourse liability which will be shared equally by G and L. See Rev.Rul. 83–151, 1983–2 C.B. 105.

Example (5):   G, the general partner, and L, the limited partner, form the GL limited partnership with each contributing $20,000. G and L agree to share partnership profits and losses equally. GL purchases investment real property for $40,000 cash and a recourse purchase money note for $60,000. Under the regulations, G bears the economic risk of loss for the liability because she would be legally obligated to make a contribution to GL to pay the liability in a doomsday liquidation.

Example (6):   Assume the same facts as Example (5), except that L, the limited partner, guarantees GL's liability. Under the guarantee, if GL defaults on the liability, L is obligated to pay the outstanding balance of the debt. In addition, L is subrogated to the lender's rights against GL under the loan for any payments made pursuant to the guarantee. Under the regulations, G still bears the economic risk of loss for the liability. While L may have to pay the liability under the guarantee, he is entitled to reimbursement by GL for any payments made under the guarantee pursuant to his right to subrogation. G, as general partner, is obligated to make a contribution to GL in order to pay the balance of the loan to L, as subrogee. See Reg. § 1.752–2(f) Examples 3 & 4.

d. Special Rules

1) Part Recourse and Part Nonrecourse Liabilities

The regulations provide that if a partner or partners bear the economic risk of loss for only a portion of a liability, the liability is bifurcated and treated as part recourse and part nonrecourse. Reg. § 1.752–1(i). For example, if a partner personally guarantees 50% of a nonrecourse liability, the partner bears the economic risk of loss for 50% of that liability and the liability is treated as recourse to that extent. See Rev.Rul. 84–118, 1984–2 C.B. 120.

2) Tiered Partnerships

If a partnership (the "upper-tier partnership") is a partner in another partnership (the "subsidiary partnership"), the upper-tier partnership's share of the subsidiary partnership's liabilities (other than liabilities owed to the upper-tier partnership) are treated as liabilities of the upper-tier partnership for purposes of applying § 752 to the partners of the upper-tier partnership. Reg. § 1.752–4(a); see Rev.Rul. 77–309, 1977–2 C.B. 216.

Example: The AB equal general partnership is a 30% general partner in another general partnership which has a $20,000 recourse liability outstanding. As a 30% general partner, AB's share of the $20,000 liability is $6,000 which will be treated as a liability of the AB partnership for purposes of applying the § 752 regulations to A and B. If the $6,000 were AB's only liability, it would be shared equally by its general partners, $3,000 to A and $3,000 to B.

2. Contributions of Property Encumbered By Recourse Liabilities

If property is contributed by a partner to a partnership and the property is subject to a liability, the partnership is considered to have assumed the liability to the extent it does not exceed the fair market value of the property at the time of the contribution. § 752(c); Reg. § 1.752–1(e). For a recourse liability, the partners' shares of the liability will be determined under economic risk of loss analysis. Reg. § 1.752–2(a).

Example (1):   A contributes property with a $10,000 adjusted basis to a general partnership for a 25% interest in the partnership. The property is subject to a $2,000 recourse liability and has a fair market value greater than $2,000. The partnership is considered to have assumed the liability and A's individual liabilities are considered to have decreased by $2,000. Under economic risk of loss analysis, A remains personally liable to the creditor for the debt and none of the other partners bears the economic risk of loss for the liability. This assumes that neither state law nor an agreement among the partners makes any partner other than A bear the risk of loss for the liability. Therefore, A's share of partnership liabilities increases by $2,000. Under Reg. § 1.752–1(f), if both an increase and a decrease in a partner's share of partnership liabilities (or individual liabilities) occurs in a single transaction, only the net increase or decrease is taken into account. Since there is no net change in the sum of A's individual liabilities and his share of the partnership liabilities, A's outside basis will be $10,000 (A's basis for the contributed property). See Reg. § 1.752–1(g) Example 1.

Example (2):   Assume the same facts as Example (1), above, except that the other partners agree to indemnify A for up to $1,500 of the liability. In that case, A bears the risk of loss for $500 of the $2,000 liability and A's share of partnership liabilities increases by $500. Since the net change in A's individual and partnership liabilities is a decrease of $1,500 ($2,000 decrease in personal liabilities and $500 increase in partnership liabilities), A's outside basis will be $8,500 ($10,000 basis in contributed property less $1,500).

Example (3):   Assume the same facts as Example (2), above, except that A's basis in the contributed property is $1,200. Since the net change in A's individual and partnership liabilities is a decrease of $1,500, A's outside basis will be reduced to zero and A will recognize $300 of capital gain.

D. Contributions of Services

1. Introduction

Section 721 does not provide nonrecognition for contributions of services. A partner who receives a partnership interest for services is being compensated for those services and is taxable under §§ 61 and 83.

A service partner may receive either a "capital" or "profits" interest in a partnership in exchange for services. A "capital" interest is generally defined as an interest in both the partnership's assets and its future profits, while a "profits" interest only entitles a partner to share in partnership profits. A partner possessing only a profits interest is not entitled to share in partnership assets if the partnership liquidates or the partner withdraws from the partnership. Rev.Proc. 93–27, 1993–2 C.B. 343; see Reg. § 1.704–1(e)(1)(v).

2. Receipt of a Capital Interest For Services
a. Tax Consequences to the Service Partner

A partner who receives a capital interest in a partnership in exchange for services has gross income under §§ 61 and 83(a) when the interest is either transferable or no longer subject to a substantial risk of forfeiture. The amount of income is equal to the fair market value of the capital interest when it is included in income less any amount paid by the partner. See § 83; Reg. § 1.721–1(b)(1).

Example: The AB general partnership has $90,000 of assets. A and B wish C to join the partnership because C is familiar with the partnership's business and is an excellent manager. To entice C to join the firm, A and B have offered C a one-third capital interest. If C leaves the partnership within three years, C, or any transferee of C, must forfeit the partnership interest. Assume C accepts the offer and at the end of Year 3 the partnership's assets are worth $150,000. C's partnership interest is subject to a substantial risk of forfeiture for three years because her rights to full enjoyment are conditioned on the performance of future services. § 83(c). The interest is also not transferable because a transferee of C is subject to a substantial risk of forfeiture. Under § 83(a), C has $50,000 of gross income (fair market value of the interest when the restrictions lapse) at the end of Year 3 and C's outside basis is $50,000. Alternatively, under § 83(b), C could elect to include $30,000 (the fair market value of the interest at transfer) of gross income in the year of transfer when the partnership interest is still restricted. A disadvantage of a § 83(b) election is that no deduction is allowed if the partnership interest is subsequently forfeited because C fails to work for the partnership for three years. § 83(b)(1).

b. Tax Consequences to the Partnership
1) Business Expense Deduction to the Partnership

If a capital interest is transferred in exchange for services, the partnership may take a § 162 business expense deduction for the amount of ordinary income that is includible in the service partner's income in the taxable year that the income is recognized unless the nature of the services requires the partnership to amortize (e.g., organizational expenses) or capitalize (e.g., services related to the acquisition or construction of an asset) the expense. § 83(h). See Reg. §§ 1.83–6(a)(4); 1.721–1(b)(2); 1.707–1(c). Any allowable deduction logically should be allocated to the existing partners, not the new service partner, and the partners may assure this result by a special allocation under § 704(b).

2) Taxable Event to Partnership

Under the majority view, a partnership that transfers a capital interest for services is treated as transferring an undivided interest in each of its assets to the service partner in a taxable transaction and must recognize any gain or loss inherent in the transferred portion of each asset. Reg. § 1.83–6(b); cf. *McDougal v. Comm'r,* 62 T.C. 720 (1974). The service partner is then treated as retransferring the assets back to partnership in a tax-free § 721 transaction. A few commentators believe that the transfer of a capital interest for services should not be a taxable event to the partnership. They note, by analogy, that a corporation does not recognize gain when it issues stock as compensation for services. Cf. § 1032(a).

Example: Assume that the AB partnership in the preceding example has $90,000 of assets, consisting solely of land used in AB's business which has a $60,000 adjusted basis. Assume C accepts the offer of a one-third partnership interest, does not make a § 83(b) election, and works three years for AB. At the end of the third year, the AB assets are worth $150,000 and consist of the land which is now worth $120,000 and $30,000 of cash. When the restrictions lapse, AB will be entitled to a $50,000 deduction, assuming C's services qualify as ordinary and necessary business expenses. AB will be viewed as having transferred one-third of its land ($40,000 fair market value, $20,000 adjusted basis) and cash ($10,000) to C for services and must recognize $20,000 of gain on the land. The one-third interest in the land and cash is then deemed to be transferred back to AB by C, who takes a $50,000 outside basis in her partnership interest. The land would now have an $80,000 inside basis ($40,000 in the two-thirds interest which remained in the partnership plus $40,000 in the one-third interest deemed transferred by C).

The $20,000 gain and $50,000 deduction logically should be allocated to partners A and B because the appreciation in the land took place before C became a partner and A and B paid for C's services with their partnership capital. The remaining $40,000 of gain in the land should be taxable to A and B when the land is sold since that gain represents appreciation prior to C's entry into the partnership. The partners can assure these results by creating "special allocations" for these tax items under § 704(b). See XVII.C.2., at pages 372–387, *infra.*

3. Receipt of a Profits Interest For Services
a. Tax Consequences to the Service Partner
1) Historical Approach

Prior to the *Diamond* case (see below), it was generally believed that the receipt of a profits interest in exchange for services was not a taxable event to the service partner. That position largely was based on Reg. § 1.721–1(b)(1), which provides:

> To the extent that any of the partners gives up any part of his right to be repaid his contributions (as distinguished from a share in partnership profits) in favor of another partner as compensation for services * * *, section 721 does not apply.

It was argued that the purpose of the parenthetical in the regulation was to ensure that the receipt of an interest in future partnership profits was not a currently taxable event. Dictum in one Tax Court opinion supported this position. See *Hale v. Comm'r*, 24 T.C.M. 1497, 1502 n. 3 (1965).

2)   The *Diamond* Case

In *Diamond v. Comm'r*, 492 F.2d 286 (7th Cir.1974), the Seventh Circuit affirmed the Tax Court's ruling that Sol Diamond was taxable on the receipt of a profits interest in a real estate partnership. In return for his services as a mortgage broker, Diamond received a 60% interest in future partnership profits after the other partner recovered his investment. Three weeks later, Diamond sold his interest for $40,000, claiming a short-term capital gain. This treatment was preferable to ordinary income because Diamond could offset the gain with capital losses from other transactions. The court held that Diamond realized $40,000 of ordinary income on the receipt of the profits interest for past services. The value of the interest was established by Diamond's sale. The court distinguished Reg. § 1.721–1(b)(1) as applying only to capital interests and acknowledged that the receipt of a profits interest with a more speculative value might not be taxable.

3)   Safe Harbor: Revenue Procedure 93–27

For many years after the decision in *Diamond*, the tax consequences of the receipt of a profits interest for services were unsettled. *Diamond* involved taxable years prior to the enactment of § 83, and it was unclear whether a profits interest was "property" for § 83 purposes. Some courts held that receipt of a profits interest was a taxable event under § 83 but concluded, on the facts of the case, that the interest had no value or its value was too speculative and could not be ascertained with reasonable certainty. See, e.g., *Campbell v. Comm'r*, 943 F.2d 815 (8th Cir.1991).

This area was clarified by the issuance of Rev.Proc. 93–27, 1993–2 C.B. 343, under which the Service generally will not treat the receipt of a profits interest as a taxable event when the interest is received for the provision of services to or for the benefit of a partnership by a person acting in a partner capacity or in anticipation of being a partner. See XVII.D.1., at page 410, *infra*, regarding when a partner is acting in a partner capacity. A service partner, however, is taxable under Rev.Proc. 93–27 on the receipt of a profits interest when:

a)   The profits interest relates to a substantially certain and predictable stream of income from partnership assets, such as income from high-quality debt securities or a high-quality net lease;

b) The partner disposes of the profits interest within two years of its receipt; or

c) The interest is in a publicly traded limited partnership as defined by § 7704(b).

4) Timing Issues: Revenue Procedure 2001–43

Under Rev. Proc. 2001–43, the determination of whether an interest granted to a service provider is a profits interest is tested at the time the interest is granted even if the interest is not substantially vested under § 83. Also, the Service will not treat the grant of a nontaxable profits interest, or the event that causes the interest to be substantially vested under § 83, as a taxable event. As a result, a § 83(b) election is not needed if the partnership interest is not substantially vested when it is granted. These rules apply if: (1) the partnership and the service provider treat the service provider as the owner of the interest from the date of its grant and the service provider takes into account all items associated with the interest for as long as the service provider has the interest, (2) neither the partnership not the partner deducts any amount for the fair market value of the interest either upon the grant of the interest or when it becomes substantially vested, and (3) all the other requirements of Rev. Proc. 93–27 (see above) are satisfied.

b. Tax Consequences to the Partnership

If a service partner is taxable on receipt of a profits interest under Rev.Proc. 93–27, the partnership logically should be allowed a § 162 deduction (or, at worst, an amortizable or capital expenditure) for the amount included in the service partner's income. § 83(h). In addition, the partnership may be considered as having transferred a portion of its future profits in exchange for the services performed by the partner. The disposition will be taxable to the partnership and the profits share then should be treated as if it were transferred back to the partnership, resulting in a tax cost outside basis for the service partner and a fair market value inside basis in the profits share for the partnership. The partnership's basis in the profits share should be amortized over some period of time to offset the future partnership profits it represents. The benefit of those deductions should be allocated to the service partner to prevent double taxation of the same profits. See XVII.C.2., at page 372, *infra.*

E. Organization and Syndication Expenses

1. General Rule

Neither a partnership nor any partner may currently deduct amounts paid or incurred to organize a partnership or to promote the sale (or to sell) partnership interests. § 709(a).

2. Amortization of Organization Fees

Certain expenses paid or incurred to organize a partnership may be amortized ratably over a period of not less than 60 months if the partnership so elects. § 709(b)(1). To qualify for amortization, an organizational expense must be: (1) incident to the creation of the partnership; (2) chargeable to capital account; and (3) of a character which would be amortizable over the life of a partnership having an ascertainable life. § 709(b)(2). Examples of qualifying expenses are: legal fees for negotiation and preparation of the partnership agreement, accounting services incident to organizing the partnership, and filing fees. Reg. § 1.709–2(a). Expenses incurred in connection with the acquisition of partnership assets are not organizational expenses and must be capitalized and added to the basis of the asset.

3. Syndication Expenses

"Syndication expenses"—i.e., expenses connected with issuing and marketing partnership interests—may not be deducted either over the 60–month amortization period in § 709 or once the syndication effort is abandoned. Rev.Rul. 89–11, 1989–1 C.B. 179. Syndication expenses include brokerage fees, registration fees, legal fees for securities advice and tax disclosure, accounting fees for representations in offering materials, printing costs, and other selling and promotional material. Reg. § 1.709–2(b). The Service has ruled that fees paid for the tax opinion in a partnership prospectus is a syndication expense. Rev.Rul. 88–4, 1988–1 C.B. 264. Capitalized syndication expenses may be deductible as a capital loss on the liquidation of the partnership. Cf. Rev.Rul. 87–111, 1987–2 C.B.160.

F.   Review Questions

1. A contributes the following property in exchange for a 50% interest in the AB partnership:

	A.B.	F.M.V.
Cash	$ 5,000	$ 5,000
Installment Obligations	15,000	20,000
Equipment (§ 1245 gain)	20,000	40,000
Land	30,000	10,000
	$70,000	$75,000

(a) What amount of gain or loss is recognized by A and AB when A transfers his property in exchange for the partnership interest?

(b) What is A's outside basis in his partnership interest?

(c) What is AB's inside basis in the contributed property?

2. G, the general partner, and L, the limited partner, each contribute $20,000 and form the GL limited partnership. G and L agree to allocate partnership profits and losses 80% to G and 20% to L. GL purchases land for $40,000 cash and a $60,000 recourse purchase money note.

   (a) Who bears the economic risk of loss for the liability?

   (b) What is G's outside basis?

   (c) What is L's outside basis?

3. The ABC partnership transfers to D a 25% capital interest in ABC on the condition that D must continue to work for the partnership for five years. If D should cease to perform services within the five years, he forfeits the partnership interest. When ABC transfers the partnership interest to D, ABC's assets have a fair market value of $100,000 and an adjusted basis of $40,000. At the end of five years, ABC's assets have a fair market value of $400,000.

   (a) If D does not make a § 83(b) election, when does he recognize income and how much income will he have?

   (b) How much gain or loss does ABC recognize in (a), above?

   (c) If D makes a § 83(b) election, when does he recognize income and how much will he have?

   (d) If D makes a § 83(b) election and leaves the partnership after three years, what are D's tax consequences? Assume ABC's assets have a fair market value of $200,000 at the end of year three.

   (e) What is D's outside basis in the one-quarter partnership interest in (a) and (c) above?

4. Which of the following expenses are amortizable as organizational expenses under § 709:

   (a) Legal fees for the negotiation of the partnership agreement?

   (b) Registration fees connected with issuing partnership interests?

   (c) Accounting fees for representations in offering materials?

   (d) Filing fees?

   (e) Accounting fees for services incident to organizing the partnership?

   (f) Printing costs of offering materials?

   (g) Fees for tax opinion in the partnership prospectus?

*

XVII

OPERATIONS OF A
PARTNERSHIP

Analysis

A. Aggregate and Entity Theories Of Partnership Taxation

A recurring issue throughout Subchapter K is whether a partnership is treated for tax purposes as an aggregate of its individual partners or an entity separate and apart from its partners. The Code does not exclusively use either approach. Partnerships are treated as entities for some tax purposes and aggregates for others. For example, partnership income is taxed directly to its partners under an aggregate theory. § 701. At other times, the Code blends the two theories and adopts a modified aggregate or entity approach to determine the tax results to the partners. As you study partnership operations, it is important to focus upon the particular approach that the Code employs.

B. Taxing Partnership Operations

1. Partnership Level Determination Of Tax Results

Even though a partnership is not a taxable entity, it must calculate its gross income and taxable income to determine the tax results to its partners. §§ 702(c); 703(a). A partnership also must file its own informational tax return and is subject to audit and examination by the Internal Revenue Service. §§ 6031; 6221–33.

a. Partnership Accounting Method

A partnership generally is free to elect its own accounting method, which may be different from that of its partners. § 703(b). Under § 448, however, a partnership which has a C corporation (other than "a qualified personal service corporation") as a partner or which is a "tax shelter" may not use the cash method of accounting. § 448(a), (b)(2). Partnerships in the farming business or with average annual gross receipts of less than $5 million for the prior three years are not subject to the C corporation-as-shareholder limitation. § 448(b)(1), (b)(3), (c).

b. Partnership Taxable Year
1) Mechanical Rules

A partnership has its own taxable year. § 706(b)(1)(A). In computing taxable income, a partner includes in income his distributive share of partnership items in the taxable year in which the partnership taxable year ends. § 706(a). Under § 706, a partnership generally determines its taxable year according to mechanical rules. First, a partnership is required to use the taxable year of its partners having more than a 50% interest in partnership profits and capital. § 706(b)(1)(B)(i), (4)(A). If partners owning more than a 50% interest do not have the same taxable year, the partnership must use the taxable year of all the principal partners (i.e., partners with a 5% or more interest in profits or capital) of the partnership. § 706(b)(1)(B)(ii), (3). If neither of these rules applies, the regulations require the partnership to use the taxable year that results in the least aggregate deferral of income to the partners. § 706(b)(1)(B)(iii); Reg. § 1.706–1T(a).

Example (1):   In the ABC equal partnership, A and B are calendar year taxpayers and C uses a November 30 fiscal year. ABC must use a calendar year because partners owning more than 50% of its profits and capital (A and B) use a calendar year.

Example (2):   The Acme Limited Partnership is owned by G, the general partner, who owns 10% of the partnership and uses a June 30 fiscal year, and 90 limited partners, each of whom owns 1% of the partnership. Forty of the limited partners use a calendar year, 40 use a November 30 fiscal year, and 10 use an October 31 fiscal year. Acme must use a June 30 fiscal year. No group of partners with a single taxable year owns more than 50% of Acme's profits and capital so it must use the taxable year of G, its only principal partner. If Acme had another 10% general partner who uses a September 30 fiscal year, it would have to use the taxable year which provides the least aggregate deferral of income to the partners. That calculation is based on the months of deferral for each partner and each partner's interest in profits. Reg. § 1.706–1T(a)(2).

2) Business Purpose

A partnership may avoid the mechanical rules of § 706 if it can establish to the satisfaction of the Service a business purpose for adopting a different year. § 706(b)(1)(C). Deferral of income to the partners is not treated as a business purpose. The Service, however, has ruled that the business purpose standard is satisfied if the taxable year of the partnership coincides with its "natural business year." A partnership has a "natural business year" if in each of the prior three years its gross receipts for the last two months of the requested taxable year equalled or exceeded 25% of the gross receipts for the requested year. Rev.Proc. 87–32, 1987–2 C.B. 396. A partnership unable to satisfy this standard may demonstrate that a particular taxable year satisfies the business purpose test under an all the facts and circumstances test. One of the facts the Service considers is the tax consequences (i.e., tax deferral) of the year selected. Rev.Rul. 87–57, 1987–2 C.B. 117.

3) Fiscal Year Election

Section 444 permits a partnership to adopt a taxable year other than one required by the § 706(b) mechanical rules, provided the year selected results in no more than three months of tax deferral. As a cost for this relief, the partnership must make "required payments" under § 7519 which are designed to offset the financial benefits of the tax deferral provided by § 444. A § 444 election and § 7519 payments, however, are not required if a partnership establishes a business purpose for the taxable year it selects. § 444(e).

c.   Partnership Taxable Income

A partnership computes its taxable income in the same manner as an individual except it is not permitted certain deductions, such as personal exemptions, medical expenses, alimony and expenses for the production or collection of income under § 212. § 703(a)(2)(A), (E). A partnership is not permitted a net operating loss deduction because a partnership's losses pass through to its partners. § 703(a)(2)(D).

The characterization of tax items is determined at the partnership level. § 702(b); see Rev.Rul. 68–79, 1968–1 C.B. 310 (holding period for long-term capital gain is based on the partnership's holding period for the asset). The partnership must separately state certain items to preserve their unique character as they pass through to the partners. This enables the partners to combine the passed through items with their nonpartnership tax items when computing tax liability. The tax items required to be separately stated are listed in § 702(a): short-term capital gains and losses, long-term capital gains and losses, § 1231 gains and losses, charitable contributions, dividends eligible for the dividends received deduction, and foreign taxes. § 702(a) (1)–(6). This list is expanded by the regulations to include any other tax item (e.g., § 1202 capital gain on qualified small business stock or capital gain on a collectible taxed at a 28% rate) which if separately taken into account by any partner could affect the tax liability of that partner. § 702(a)(7); Reg. § 1.702–1(a)(8)(i), (ii). Tax items specially allocated under § 704(b) or (c) also must be separately stated. Reg. § 1.702–1(a)(8)(i); see XVII.C.2, at page 372, *infra*. Once all of the separately stated items have been identified, the remaining partnership items are combined in a net taxable income or loss calculation. § 702(a)(8). This figure is sometimes referred to as "nonseparately computed" or "bottom line" income or loss.

d.   Tax Elections

Elections affecting the determination of partnership taxable income generally are made by the partnership. § 703(b); see *Demirjian v. Comm'r,* 457 F.2d 1 (3d Cir.1972) (§ 1033 election to avoid recognition of gain on an involuntary conversion is made by the partnership).

Example: An election out of the installment method under § 453(d) would be made by the partnership, not on a partner-by-partner basis. An election to amortize organization expenses under § 709 also would be made by the partnership.

2.   Tax Consequences to the Partners
a.   Timing and Character of Pass Through Items

Partners are required to take into account their distributive shares of the partnership's separately stated items and nonseparately computed income or loss in the taxable year in which the partnership's taxable year ends. §§ 702(a); 706(a). The separately stated items retain their character when reported by the partners. § 702(b).

Example: Assume the ABC cash method partnership has an October 31 fiscal year and during its current year has the following income and expenses:

Operating income	$90,000
Salary expense	$30,000
Rental expense	$20,000
Auto expense	$ 5,000
§ 179 expense	$ 9,000
Charitable contribution	$ 3,000
§ 1245 gain	$10,000
§ 1231 gain	$15,000
LTCG from stock sale	$20,000
LTCL from stock sale	$ 8,000
STCG from stock sale	$ 6,000

Of these items, the § 179 expense, the charitable contribution, the § 1231 gain, and the capital gains and losses are separately stated items because their separate treatment could affect the tax liability of a particular partner depending on the partner's personal tax results during the year. For example, the § 179 expense and the charitable contribution are separately stated so that the dollar and percentage limitations in those sections can apply at the partner level. See §§ 170(b); 179(b), (d)(8). The regulations permit the separate netting of long-and short-term capital gain transactions. Reg. § 1.702–1(a)(1), (2). Thus, ABC's separately stated items will be: § 179 expense—$9,000; charitable contribution—$3,000; § 1231 gain—$15,000; LTCG—$12,000; and STCG—$6,000. These items will retain their character when they are reported by the partners. ABC's nonseparately stated income will be $45,000 ($90,000 operating income plus $10,000 § 1245 gain less $55,000 of deductions (salary expense, rental expense and auto expense)). Because the § 1245 gain is ordinary income, its tax treatment cannot vary among the partners and thus it is not a separately stated item. Each partner in ABC must include his or her distributive share of the § 179 expense, charitable contribution, § 1231 gain, LTCG, STCG and nonseparately computed income in the taxable year in which ABC's October 31 taxable year ends. Calendar year partners would report their distributive shares of these items on their April 15th tax return the following year.

b. Basis Adjustments

Under § 702, a partner is taxed directly on his distributive share of the partnership's separately stated items and nonseparately computed income or loss. Section 705 adjusts the partner's outside basis to reflect these results. In general, a partner must increase his outside basis by his distributive share of partnership taxable income and tax-exempt income and decrease it (but not below zero) by partnership distributions, as provided in § 733, and his distributive share of partnership losses and expenditures by the partnership which are neither deductible nor chargeable to a capital account. § 705(a).

Example: Partner A has a $10,000 outside basis in her partnership interest and her distributive share of partnership items for the year is:

Long-term capital gain	$3,000
Tax-exempt interest	$2,000
Charitable contribution	$1,000
Nonseparately computed income	$5,000

Each of the items passes through to A and is reported on her personal tax return. A's share of partnership taxable income as computed under § 703(a) is $8,000 (long-term capital gain plus nonseparately computed income). Under § 705(a), her outside basis will be adjusted as follows:

+ $8,000	§ 705(a)(1)(A)
+ $2,000	§ 705(a)(1)(B)
− $1,000	§ 705(a)(2)(B)
+ $9,000	

Thus, A's outside basis will be $19,000 ($10,000 plus $9,000) beginning the next year. The charitable contribution is an expenditure which the partnership is not allowed to deduct under § 703(a)(2)(C) and it is not capitalized. If the partnership distributed $5,000 of cash to A at the end of the year, her outside basis would be reduced to $14,000 by the distribution. §§ 705(a)(2); 733.

c. Limitation on Losses

Under § 704(d), a partner's distributive share of partnership loss (including capital loss) is limited to the partner's outside basis at the end of the partnership year in which the loss occurred. See *Kingbay v. Comm'r,* 46 T.C. 147 (1966) (limited partners share of partnership losses restricted by § 704(d); corporate general partner liable for partnership liabilities was not disregarded). Losses or deductions disallowed under this rule carry over indefinitely and may be used when the partner obtains sufficient outside basis to use the suspended loss.

Example: A is a partner in the ABC partnership and has a $4,000 outside basis. If A's distributive share of nonseparately computed loss for the year is $6,000, she will be limited to a $4,000 deduction and will have $2,000 of suspended loss which will carry over until she obtains additional outside basis.

If the basis limitation is exceeded by a combination of different types of losses, the regulations provide that the currently allowable losses consist of a proportionate amount of each type of loss. Reg. § 1.704–1(d)(2).

Example: D is a partner in the DEF partnership and has a $6,000 outside basis. D's distributive share of partnership long-term capital loss is $4,000 and his distributive share of nonseparately computed loss is $8,000. Under § 704(d), D will be allowed a $6,000 loss for the year which will be characterized as follows:

$$\frac{\$\ 4,000}{\$12,000} \times \$6,000 = \$2,000 \text{ LTCL}$$

$$\frac{\$\ 8,000}{\$12,000} \times \$6,000 = \$4,000 \text{ Ordinary Loss}$$

D would have a $2,000 long-term capital loss carryover and a $4,000 nonseparately computed loss carryover at the beginning of the next year.

d. Related Provisions
The § 465 at-risk limitations and the § 469 passive loss limitations also may limit a partner's ability to deduct her distributive share of partnership losses.

1) At–Risk Limitation
   a) Introduction
      Under § 465, a partner's share of partnership losses and deductions is limited to his amount "at risk." The at-risk limitation is applied on a partner-by-partner and activity-by-activity basis. § 465(a)(1), (c)(2)(A). Aggregation rules, however, may apply to combine activities. § 465(c)(2)(B), (3)(B).

   b) At–Risk Amount
      A partner initially is considered at risk to the extent of (1) cash contributions to the partnership, (2) the adjusted basis of property contributed to the partnership, and (3) amounts borrowed for use in the activity for which the partner is personally liable or has pledged property (other than property used in the partnership) as security to the extent of the property's fair market value. § 465(b)(1), (2). Amounts borrowed from persons with an interest (other than as a creditor) in the activity or related persons generally are not considered at risk. § 465(b)(3). Recourse borrowings are not considered at risk if the taxpayer is protected against loss through guarantees, stop loss agreements, or similar arrangements. § 465(b)(4). In the case of

partnerships involved in the holding of real property, a partner's amount at risk also includes "qualified nonrecourse financing." Qualified nonrecourse financing is nonconvertible debt which is (1) borrowed from or guaranteed by a governmental body, or (2) borrowed from a person actively engaged in the business of lending money. § 465(b)(6)(B)(ii), (iv). Qualified nonrecourse financing cannot be borrowed from the seller of property or a person who receives a fee with respect to taxpayer's investment (i.e., promoters). §§ 49(a)(1)(D)(iv); 465(b)(6)(D)(i). Financing borrowed from a "related person" is qualified nonrecourse financing only if it is commercially reasonable and on substantially the same terms as a loan to unrelated persons. § 465(b)(6)(D)(ii).

Except for qualified nonrecourse financing, a partner is not considered at risk for nonrecourse borrowings of the partnership. As a result, nonrecourse debt of the partnership may produce outside basis for a partner sufficient to avoid the § 704(d) limitation, but the partner still may be denied a deduction for partnership losses and deductions because he is not sufficiently at risk in the venture. In that situation the partner's outside basis is nonetheless reduced by the distributive share of partnership loss passed through from the partnership.

> ***Example:*** A and B form the AB general partnership with each contributing $50,000. The partnership will engage in mining, which is not a "real estate" activity for purposes of the qualified nonrecourse financing exception. § 465(b)(6)(E)(ii). The AB partnership borrows $200,000 on a nonrecourse basis to finance its operations. A and B will each have a $150,000 outside basis ($50,000 contribution plus $100,000 share of nonrecourse loan) but will be considered at risk only to the extent of their $50,000 contributions.
>
> A limited partner normally is not considered at risk with respect to partnership liabilities other than qualified nonrecourse financing. If, however, a limited partner has an obligation to make additional contributions to the partnership or guarantees a partnership liability, these undertakings may be included in the partner's at-risk amount. § 465(b)(2). For example, if limited partners are personally obligated to make additional contributions to pay any deficiency on a partnership recourse liability, the limited partners will be considered at risk with respect to the liability. *Pritchett v. Comm'r,* 827 F.2d 644 (9th Cir.1987); *Abramson v. Comm'r,* 86 T.C. 360 (1986).

c) **Adjustments to Amount At Risk and Carryover of Suspended Losses**
A partner's at-risk amount is determined annually. If a partner includes a share of the partnership's loss for the year, his at-risk

amount is reduced by the amount of the allowable loss. § 465(b)(5). Losses disallowed under § 465 are allowed in subsequent years when the taxpayer is sufficiently at risk. § 465(a)(2).

> ***Example:*** Assume A is a partner in a partnership and contributed $10,000 to the venture. The partnership borrowed funds on a nonrecourse basis and those borrowings are not included in A's at-risk amount. Thus, A's at-risk amount is $10,000. In the first year of partnership operations, A's distributive share of partnership loss is $2,000. A will be allowed to deduct the loss and his at-risk amount will be $8,000 at the beginning of the partnership's second year. If A's distributive share of partnership loss is $12,000 in the second year, he will be allowed to deduct $8,000 (his remaining at-risk amount) and the $4,000 of disallowed loss will carry over and be allowed in later years when A has additional amounts at risk in the partnership.

2) Passive Activity Loss Limitation
    a) Introduction
        Under § 469(a), a taxpayer's passive activity loss and credit for the year are disallowed. The purpose of § 469 is to prevent taxpayers from using losses from passive activities to offset salary and investment income. The limitation is applied on a partner-by-partner basis, not at the partnership level. § 469(a)(2)(A). A taxpayer's "passive activity loss" is the amount by which her aggregate losses from all passive activities exceed her aggregate income from such activities. § 469(d)(1). A passive activity is defined as an activity which involves the conduct of a trade or business in which the taxpayer does not materially participate. § 469(c)(1). All rental activity is defined as being passive, with limited exceptions for individual taxpayers who (1) "actively participate" in rental real estate activities and have adjusted gross income below certain specified levels, or (2) perform more than half their personal services in real estate trades or businesses in which they materially participate and devote more than 750 hours per year to those pursuits. §§ 469(i), (c)(7). To prevent easy avoidance of the loss limitation, traditional forms of "portfolio" investment income (interest, dividends, annuities and royalties) and compensation for personal services are not considered passive activity income. § 469(e)(1), (3). A partner's share of partnership portfolio income is nonpassive even if the partner does not materially participate in the partnership's activities. The Service also is granted authority to recharacterize income or gain from a limited partnership as not passive to prevent avoidance of the limitation. § 469(*l*)(3).

    b) Material Participation
        "Material participation" is defined as involvement in the activity on a regular, continuous, and substantial basis. § 469(h)(1). The regulations

set out several specific tests for ascertaining whether a taxpayer materially participates in an activity. The material participation requirement is designed to distinguish passive investors in traditional tax shelters from taxpayers actively engaged in business and the regulation tests are consistent with that purpose. For example, an individual is considered to be materially participating in an activity if she participates for more than 500 hours, her participation constitutes substantially all of the participation for the year, or she devotes more than 100 hours to the activity during the year and no other individual participates more. Temp.Reg. § 1.469–5T(a)(1)–(3). Under these standards, a general partner who manages the partnership or devotes substantial time to its business should be able to satisfy the material participation tests.

Except as provided in regulations, limited partnership interests are considered interests in which the taxpayer does not materially participate. § 469(h)(2). Under the regulations, a limited partner is considered to be materially participating if she participates for more than 500 hours in the activity or satisfies certain tests regarding material participation in prior years. Temp.Reg. § 1.469–5T(e)(2). A limited partner who also holds a general partnership interest is not treated as holding a limited partnership interest. Thus, if a partner is treated as materially participating with respect to the general partnership interest, she also is treated as materially participating with respect to the limited partnership interest. Temp.Reg. § 1.469–5T(e)(3)(ii).

c) Definition of "Activity"
A single partnership may engage in more than one passive "activity." The identification of separate activities is important in applying the material participation test and in determining when a taxpayer has fully disposed of the activity. Each "undertaking" in which a taxpayer owns an interest is treated as a separate activity. Temp.Reg. § 1.469–4T(a)(4)(i). An "undertaking" generally consists of all business or rental activities conducted at the same location and owned by the same person. Temp.Reg. § 1.469–4T(a)(3)(ii). The regulations go into great detail defining the scope of activities for § 469 purposes. See Temp.Reg. § 1.469–4T.

d) Later Use of Suspended Losses
Losses disallowed under § 469 carry over and may be deducted in subsequent years against passive income or may be deducted in full upon a taxable disposition of the entire activity. § 469(b), (g)(1). A partner's outside basis is reduced under § 705 by the amount of an otherwise allowable loss which is disallowed under § 469.

Example: G, the general partner, and L, the limited partner, form the GL limited partnership to manufacture a new product. If GL produces tax losses in its early years of operations, both G and L will have to confront the passive loss limitation in § 469. Assuming G devotes substantial time (more than 500 hours) to managing GL, he will be considered as materially participating in the partnership and it will not be a passive activity as to him. Even if G does not spend 500 hours participating in the partnership, it is likely that he will satisfy one of the other tests for material participation. L, as a limited partner, is ordinarily deemed not to materially participate. Thus, L's interest is a passive activity and her distributive share of GL losses will be subject to § 469. In that case, if GL holds assets which produce "portfolio" income (interest, dividends, etc.), L's distributive share of that income will be separated from her share of partnership business losses and will not be considered passive income. Finally, if L also owned a general partnership interest in GL, her limited partnership interest would be ignored and her participation in the partnership would be tested with respect to her general partnership interest.

e. Electing Large Partnerships

Partners in an electing large partnership ("ELP") may utilize a simplified regime for reporting the tax results of partnership operations. §§ 771–777. The rules for ELPs are designed to reduce the reporting and audit burden by reducing the number of separately stated items that must be reported.

1) ELP Defined; ELP Election
    An ELP generally is any partnership with 100 or more partners in the preceding taxable year that makes an election to have the special rules apply. §§ 771; 775(a). If elected, the ELP rules continue to apply for all subsequent taxable years unless the election is revoked with the consent of the IRS. § 775(a)(2). Service partnerships may not make an ELP election. § 775(b).

2) Effect of ELP Election on Partners
    Each partner in an ELP takes into account his or her distributive share of (1) taxable income or loss from passive loss limitation activities, (2) taxable income or loss from other activities, (3) net capital gain or loss separated between passive loss limitation and other activities, (4) tax-exempt interest, (5) net alternative minimum tax adjustment separately computed for passive loss limitation activities and other activities, (6) several general and specialized tax credits, (7) foreign income taxes, and (8) other items to the extent the IRS determines that separate treatment is appropriate. § 772(a).

3) Taxable Income of ELP
    The taxable income of an ELP is computed in the same manner as an individual except that the items listed above must be separately stated. § 773(a)(1)(A). An ELP is not allowed a deduction for personal exemptions, net operating losses, or certain itemized deductions other than § 212 expenses. § 773(b)(1). Tax elections generally are made by the partnership. § 773(a)(2). Limitations and other provisions affecting the computation of taxable income of an ELP are applied at the partnership level, except that the § 68 limitation on itemized deductions, the at risk and passive activity loss limitations, and any other provision specified in regulations are applied at the partner level. § 773(a)(3). The IRS is given broad authority to carry out the ELP rules.

4) ELP Deductions: Special Rules
    Special rules apply to certain ELP deductions. Section 67 does not apply to the partnership but 70% of the miscellaneous itemized deductions are disallowed. § 773(b)(3). Charitable contributions are not separately stated but an ELP is subject to the 10%–of-taxable-income limitation that applies to C corporations. § 773(b)(2).

C. Partnership Allocations

1. Introduction

Under § 702(a), each partner is required to take into account his distributive share of separately stated items and nonseparately computed income or loss. Unless otherwise provided in Subchapter K, a partner's "distributive share" of these items is determined by the partnership agreement, including amendments made up to the time for filing the partnership's tax return. §§ 704(a); 761(c). If the partnership agreement is silent on the issue, the partners' distributive shares are determined in accordance with their interests in the partnership. § 704(b)(1). Thus, partners initially are given considerable flexibility to fashion their tax results. The following sections examine the Code's restrictions on the ability of partners to determine their tax results in the partnership agreement.

2. Special Allocations
a. Introduction

Under § 704(b)(2), the partners' distributive shares will be allocated in accordance with their interests in the partnership if the allocations agreed to in the partnership agreement lack substantial economic effect. The regulations originally used the "substantial economic effect" standard to determine whether the principal purpose of a partnership allocation was to avoid or evade income tax. See *Orrisch v. Comm'r,* 55 T.C. 395 (1970), aff'd per curiam (9th Cir.1973). In the Tax Reform Act of 1976, the "substantial economic effect" test became the Code's standard for testing all allocations of partnership items, including allocations of bottom line income or loss.

The "substantial economic effect" standard is amplified by extensive and detailed regulations. They require that partnership allocations be consistent with the underlying economic arrangement agreed to by the partners. Reg. § 1.704–1(b)(2)(ii)(*a*). To determine whether an allocation has substantial economic effect, the regulations apply a two-part analysis at the end of each partnership taxable year. First, the allocation must have "economic effect." Second, the economic effect must be "substantial." Reg. § 1.704–1(b)(2)(i). Partnership capital accounts are used to test those requirements.

b. Partnership Accounting: The Basics

Because the business or financial relationship among partners, as memorialized in the partnership agreement, may not directly correspond to the tax results you have studied in Subchapter K, principles of financial accounting are used to "keep score" of partnership activities. A partnership's accountants will maintain records of the partnership's assets, liabilities, and each partner's share of partnership capital. Typically, these matters are reflected in the partnership's balance sheet, with partnership assets on the left side and partnership capital and liabilities on the right side. The main rule of thumb for financial accounting is that an enterprise's assets equal its liabilities plus the owner's equity or capital. A simple example illustrates these principles. Assume A and B agree to form the AB general partnership with A contributing $20,000 of cash and B contributing an asset in which she has a $12,000 adjusted basis and which the partners agree has a $20,000 fair market value. A and B agree to be equal partners and share all partnership income or loss equally. B's outside basis will be $12,000 under § 722, and the partnership's inside basis in the asset contributed by B will be $12,000 under § 723. The partnership's financial balance sheet, however, will look like this:

Assets		Liabilities/Partners' Capital	
	Bk. Value		**Bk. Value**
Cash	$20,000	Liabilities:	none
Asset	20,000	Capital	
		A	$20,000
		B	20,000
Total	$40,000	Total	$40,000

The AB balance sheet reflects assets at their fair market value at the time of acquisition or contribution. This figure is frequently referred to as "book value" or "historical cost." Thus, B's asset is recorded at its agreed $20,000 fair market value. On the right side, A's and B's interests in partnership assets are reflected in their capital accounts which, in accordance with their agreement to be equal partners, are credited with their $20,000 contributions.

The results of operations also will be reflected in the partnership's financial records. Assume that in its first year of operations the AB partnership earns a $10,000 cash profit which is shared equally by A and B. At the end of the year,

AB would have $10,000 more of cash and the partnership balance sheet would look like this:

Assets		Liabilities/Partners' Capital	
	Bk. Value		**Bk. Value**
Cash	$30,000	Liabilities:	none
Asset	20,000	Capital	
		A	$25,000
		B	25,000
Total	$50,000	Total	$50,000

If the $10,000 cash profit were distributed to A and B, the adjustments to the balance sheet would be straightforward. The partnership would have $10,000 less cash and A's and B's capital accounts would be reduced to $20,000 to reflect their reduced interests in partnership assets.

The financial books of the partnership and the partners' capital accounts will be kept in accordance with the partnership agreement and reflect the business arrangement agreed to by the partners. Thus, on the ultimate liquidation of the AB partnership, A and B will have equal capital accounts reflecting the fact that they agreed to share partnership assets equally.

c. Economic Effect

1) Introduction

To have economic effect, an allocation must be consistent with the underlying economic arrangement of the partners. The economic benefit or burden corresponding to an allocation must be borne by the partner receiving the allocation. Reg. § 1.704–1(b)(2)(ii)(a). The regulations use a three-part test to determine whether an allocation is consistent with the underlying economic arrangement of the partners. This basic test is backed up by an alternate test and an economic effect equivalence test which, if satisfied, can validate an allocation.

2) Basic Test: "The Big Three"

The basic test to determine whether an allocation has economic effect is mechanical. Generally, an allocation has economic effect if, throughout the full term of the partnership, the partnership agreement provides:

1) That the partners' capital accounts will be determined and maintained in accordance with the rules in Reg. § 1.704–1(b)(2)(iv);

2) That upon the liquidation of the partnership (or a partner's partnership interest) liquidating distributions will be made in accordance with the positive capital account balances of the partners; and

3) That if a partner has a deficit capital account balance after all adjustments for the year, he is unconditionally obligated to restore the

deficit by the end of the partnership taxable year (or, if later, within 90 days of the liquidation) in order to pay partnership creditors or partners with positive capital account balances.

To determine whether these requirements are met, the "partnership agreement" is deemed to include all agreements among the partners or between one or more partners and the partnership. The agreements can be written or oral and need not be embodied in a document the partners call "the partnership agreement." Reg. § 1.704–1(b)(2)(ii)(*h*).

Collectively, the three requirements for economic effect will be referred to as "The Big Three." The first requirement of The Big Three (determination and maintenance of capital accounts) generally is satisfied if each partner's capital account is *increased* by (1) the amount of money contributed by the partner to the partnership; (2) the fair market value of property contributed by the partner to the partnership, net of liabilities secured by the property; and (3) allocations to the partner of partnership income or gain (including tax-exempt income); and *decreased* by (1) the amount of money distributed to the partner; (2) the fair market value of property distributed to the partner net of liabilities secured by the property; (3) allocations to the partner of partnership expenditures which are not deductible and not properly chargeable to capital account; and (4) allocations of partnership loss and deduction of other than those described in (3), above. Reg. § 1.704–1(b)(2)(iv)(*b*). These rules are quite similar to the rules for determining and adjusting a partner's outside basis. The principal difference is that property contributions and distributions of property are accounted for at the property's fair market value, rather than at its basis. When determining capital accounts, the fair market value assigned to property will be accepted if it was agreed to in arm's length negotiations among partners with sufficiently adverse interests. Reg. § 1.704–1(b)(2)(iv)(*h*). The Big Three, by linking allocations to the partners' capital accounts, requiring that the partnership liquidate in accordance with capital account balances and requiring each partner to restore any deficit in her capital account, assures that the economic benefit or burden of each allocation will correspond to the allocation.

Example (1): A and B form a general partnership with each contributing $30,000 cash. The partnership uses the $60,000 to purchase depreciable personal property. The partnership agreement provides that A and B will share partnership taxable income and loss (other than cost recovery deductions) and cash flow equally, but all cost recovery deductions will be allocated to A. A and B agree to properly maintain capital accounts but on liquidation partnership assets will be distributed equally (regardless of capital account balances) and no partner has an obligation to restore a deficit balance in her capital account. Assume for simplicity that in its first year AB breaks even (income equals expenses) except that it has a $15,000 cost recovery deduction which under the terms of the partnership agreement is all to be allocated to A. The allocation does not have economic effect. To understand the problem with the allocation, assume all the cost recovery deductions are allocated to A. A's and B's initial capital accounts were credited with $30,000. A's would decrease by $15,000 as a result of the allocation, leaving a balance of $15,000, while B's would remain at $30,000. If the depreciable personal property declined in value to $45,000, as the regulations require us to assume, and the partnership were liquidated it would have $45,000 of assets to distribute. Under the partnership agreement the assets would be distributed $22,500 each to A and B. As structured, B actually bore $7,500 of the economic burden associated with the cost recovery deduction because the partnership agreement did not require liquidation of the partnership in accordance with the partners' capital account balances. That is, B receives $22,500 while her capital account is $30,000. Consequently, the regulations require that the $15,000 of cost recovery deductions be reallocated $7,500 to A and $7,500 to B.

Example (2): Assume the same facts as Example (1), except that the partners agree to properly maintain capital accounts and to distribute partnership assets on liquidation in accordance with positive capital account balances, but no partner has an obligation to restore a deficit balance in her capital account. On these facts, The Big Three would not be satisfied because there is no unconditional obligation to restore a deficit capital account balance throughout the term of the partnership. The cost recovery deduction will be allocated in accordance with the partners' interests in the partnership. The next section demonstrates that this allocation will be respected under the alternate test for economic effect if the partnership agreement is properly structured.

Example (3): Assume the same facts as Example (1), except that the partnership agreement includes The Big Three. Assume that in each of its first three years AB breaks even (income equals expenses) except that in each year it has a $15,000 cost recovery deduction which under the partnership agreement is all to be allocated to A. Since The Big Three is satisfied, the allocation has economic effect. At the end of the third year, A's and B's capital accounts would be:

A	B
$30,000	$30,000
− $45,000 deductions	
− $15,000	

If the depreciable personal property declined in value to $15,000 ($60,000 adjusted basis less $45,000 cost recovery deductions) and the partnership were liquidated, it would have $15,000 of assets to distribute. Under the partnership agreement, the $15,000 of assets must go to B (liquidation in accordance with positive capital account balances). In addition, A must contribute $15,000 to restore her deficit capital account balance. The $15,000 contributed by A would go to B to pay her remaining positive capital account balance. On these facts it is clear that complying with The Big Three ensures that A will bear the economic burden of the cost recovery deductions. Therefore, the allocation of those deductions has economic effect.

3) Alternate Test for Economic Effect

Limited partners typically are unwilling to be obligated to restore a deficit capital account balance. If the partnership agreement satisfies the first two requirements of The Big Three but fails to include an unconditional deficit restoration obligation, the regulations provide an alternate test to establish that an allocation has economic effect. Reg. § 1.704–1(b)(2)(ii)(*d*). Under that test, an allocation will be respected to the extent it does not cause or increase a deficit in the partner's capital account. For purposes of this rule, certain limited obligations of a partner to restore capital account deficits— promissory notes given to the partnership meeting certain conditions, obligations under the partnership agreement, and obligations under state law—are recognized. Reg. § 1.704–1(b)(2)(ii)(*c*).

When determining whether the allocation causes or increases a capital account deficit, various *reasonably expected* events must be considered. The most important of these are distributions which, at the end of the year, are reasonably expected to be made to the partner. Finally, the partnership agreement must contain a "qualified income offset"—i.e., a provision which requires that if a partner has a deficit capital account balance as a result of one of the listed events occurring *unexpectedly* (e.g., an unexpected distribution) that partner will be allocated items of income or gain in an amount and manner sufficient to eliminate the deficit as quickly as possible. Reg. § 1.704–1(b)(2)(ii)(*d*).

Example (1)
(Basic Example of Alternate Test):

A and B form a general partnership with each contributing $30,000 cash. The partnership uses the $60,000 to purchase depreciable property. The partnership agreement provides that A and B will share partnership taxable income and loss (other than cost recovery deductions) and cash flow equally, but all cost recovery deductions will be allocated to A. A and B agree to properly maintain capital accounts and on liquidation of the partnership (or any partner's interest) partnership assets will be distributed in accordance with capital account balances, but no partner has an obligation to restore a deficit balance in her capital account. The partnership agreement also contains a qualified income offset. Assume that in its first year AB breaks even (income equals expenses) except that it has a $15,000 cost recovery deduction which under the terms of the partnership agreement is all to be allocated to A. Assuming future distributions are not reasonably expected to create a deficit in A's capital account, the allocation will have economic effect under the alternate test for economic effect. At the end of the year, B's capital account will be $30,000 and A's capital account will be:

$$\begin{array}{l} \$30,000 \\ -\ \underline{\$15,000} \quad \text{cost recovery deduction} \\ \$15,000 \end{array}$$

Example (2)
(Reallocation to Reflect Economic Burden):

Assume the same facts as Example (1) and assume that in its second year of operation AB again breaks even except that it has a $20,000 cost recovery deduction and future distributions are not reasonably expected to create a deficit in A's capital account. Under the alternate economic effect test, only $15,000 of the allocation would have economic effect because a greater allocation would create a deficit in A's capital account. The remaining $5,000 of cost recovery deductions will be allocated in accordance with the partners' interests in the partnership. Under the partnership agreement, if the property were sold at the end of the partnership's second taxable year for $25,000 (its adjusted basis) the $25,000 would be distributed to B (in accordance with positive capital account balances). Thus, B, who has a positive capital account balance, not A, bears the economic burden of the additional cost recovery deductions and $5,000 of those deductions will be reallocated to B. See Reg. § 1.704–1(b)(5) Example (1)(iv).

Example (3)
(Reasonably Expected Distribution):

Assume the same facts as Example (2) except that in AB's second taxable year a $3,000 cash distribution (from proceeds of a partnership loan secured by the depreciable property) is reasonably expected to be made to A. In that situation the reasonably expected distribution must be considered when determining if the allocation of cost recovery deductions will create a deficit in A's capital account. Thus, if no capital account increases are reasonably expected, only $12,000 of the allocation will have economic effect ($15,000 capital account at the beginning of year two less the $3,000 reasonably expected distribution).

Example (4)
(Partial Deficit Restoration Agreements):

Assume again that A's capital account is $15,000 at the beginning of AB's second taxable year, no distributions are reasonably expected, and AB breaks even in its second year except that it has a $20,000 cost recovery deduction which is allocated to A. If A has a $5,000 partial deficit restoration obligation because either the partnership agreement or state law requires A to restore a $5,000 deficit or A gave a $5,000 promissory note (meeting certain conditions) to the partnership, the full $20,000 allocation would have economic effect under the alternate test. It is important to remember that *partial* deficit restoration obligations are recognized under the alternate test even though they are not recognized under The Big Three.

Example (5)
(Qualified Income Offset):

Assume that at the beginning of AB's third taxable year A's capital account is zero and A has no deficit restoration obligation (unconditional or partial). If a previously unexpected distribution occurs, resulting in a deficit in A's capital account, under the qualified income offset A must be allocated items of income and gain (a pro rata portion of each partnership item, including gross income) in an amount and manner sufficient to eliminate the deficit as quickly as possible.

4) Economic Effect Equivalence
Allocations which do not have economic effect under The Big Three or the alternate economic effect test will be deemed to have economic effect if at the end of each partnership taxable year a liquidation of the partnership would produce the same economic results to the partners as The Big Three. Reg. § 1.704–1(b)(2)(ii)(*i*).

Example: Assume C and D form a partnership and agree that partnership income, gain, loss and deduction will be allocated 60% to C and 40% to D. The CD partnership agreement fails to require the maintenance of capital accounts, but under a state law right of contribution C and D are ultimately liable for 60% and 40%, respectively, of partnership debts. The partnership allocation will have economic effect under the economic effect equivalence test. See Reg. § 1.704–1(b)(5) Example (4)(ii).

5) **The Relationship Between Economic Risk of Loss and Economic Effect**
Under the § 752 regulations, a partnership liability is classified as "recourse" to the extent that one or more partners bear the economic risk of loss for the liability. Reg. § 1.752–1(a)(1). A partner's share of a recourse partnership liability equals the portion of the liability for which the partner bears the economic risk of loss. Reg. § 1.752–2(a). A partner is considered to bear the economic risk of loss for a partnership liability to the extent that, if the partnership constructively liquidated, the partner would be obligated to make a payment because that liability became due and payable. Reg. § 1.752–2(b)(1). All statutory and contractual obligations are taken into account in determining whether a partner has such an obligation, including the obligation to make a capital contribution to restore a deficit capital account on liquidation of the partnership. Reg. § 1.752–2(b)(3)(ii). See XVII.C.2.c., at page ___, *supra*. Thus, the economic risk of loss analysis used to allocate partnership liabilities under § 752 and the § 704(b) economic effect test are conceptually linked and often correspond to one another. Because of this relationship, capital account analysis frequently assists in determining which partners bear the economic risk of loss for a partnership liability in more complicated situations.

Example: A and B form a general partnership with each contributing $20,000 cash. A and B agree to share all partnership profits equally but partnership net taxable loss will be allocated 90% to A and 10% to B. A and B also agree to comply with The Big Three. The partnership purchases depreciable personal property for $40,000 in cash and a recourse purchase money note of $60,000. Under the doomsday liquidation analysis employed by the § 752 regulations, all partnership assets are deemed worthless and all partnership liabilities are deemed due and payable. If the partnership immediately liquidated after incurring the purchase money obligation, it would recognize a $100,000 tax loss on the disposition of its depreciable personal property for no consideration. Under the partnership agreement, A would be allocated $90,000 of the loss and B $10,000. Their capital accounts would be adjusted as follows:

	A	**B**
Capital Account	$20,000	$20,000
Less Loss	– $90,000	– $10,000
	– $70,000	$10,000

If the partnership were liquidated, A would be required to contribute $70,000 to restore her deficit capital account balance. The $70,000 would be used to repay the $60,000 purchase money obligation and distribute $10,000 to B. Thus, even though the lender could attempt to recover the balance on the note from either general partner, A and B have agreed, as between them, that A will bear the economic risk of loss for the loan. Therefore, the liability is allocated entirely to A. See Reg. § 1.752–2(f) Example 1.

d. Substantiality

1) General Rules

In order to be respected, the economic effect of an allocation must be "substantial," which requires that there be a reasonable possibility that the allocation will affect substantially the dollar amounts to be received by the partners from the partnership, independent of tax consequences. Reg. § 1.704–1(b)(2)(iii)(*a*). The regulations clarify this standard by providing that the economic effect of an allocation is not substantial if, at the time the allocation becomes part of the partnership agreement: (1) the after-tax economic consequences of at least one partner may, in present value terms, be enhanced compared to such consequences if the allocation were not contained in the partnership agreement, and (2) there is a strong likelihood that the after-tax economic consequences of no partner will, in present value terms, be substantially diminished compared to such consequences if the allocation were not contained in the partnership agreement. In determining the after-tax economic benefit or detriment to a partner, the interaction of the allocation with the partner's nonpartnership tax attributes is considered. *Id.* Thus, for an allocation to have *substantial* economic effect, it must have the potential to actually impact the economic relationship among the partners, apart from the tax results.

Example: A and B are equal partners in the AB partnership. Over the next several years, A expects to be taxed at the highest federal tax rate and B expects to be taxed at the lowest. There is also a strong likelihood that over the next several years AB will realize approximately equal amounts of dividend income and tax-exempt interest. The AB partnership agreement complies with The Big Three. Assume the partners allocate a disproportionate amount of the tax-exempt interest to A and a disproportionate amount of the dividends to B so as to take advantage of their respective tax rates and increase their total after-tax returns from the partnership. Such allocations would have economic effect but the economic effect will not be substantial. At the time the allocation became part of the partnership agreement, the after-tax economic consequences of A are expected to be enhanced and there is a strong likelihood that the after-tax economic consequences of neither A nor B will be substantially diminished. Put more simply, the allocation does not have the potential to actually affect the economic relationship between A and B, apart from tax results, so the dividends and tax-exempt interest will have to be reallocated in accordance with the partners' interests in the partnership. See Reg. § 1.704–1(b)(5) Example (5)(i).

2) Shifting and Transitory Allocations
   a) Shifting Allocations

   The regulations amplify the general rules regarding substantiality by focusing on what are referred to as "shifting" and "transitory" allocations. An allocation is shifting and not substantial if, at the time the allocation becomes part of the partnership agreement, there is a strong likelihood that (1) the net increases and decreases in the partners' capital accounts will not differ substantially from the net increases and decreases if the allocation was not part of the partnership agreement, and (2) the total tax liability of the partners will be reduced as a result of the allocation (taking into account the impact of the partners' nonpartnership tax items). If, at the end of a partnership's taxable year, the net increases and decreases in the partners' capital accounts do not differ substantially from the net increases and decreases if there had been no allocation, and the tax liability of the partners is reduced, it is presumed that there was a strong likelihood that those results would occur at the time the allocation became part of the partnership agreement. Reg. § 1.704–1(b)(2)(iii)(*b*). Again, the test is whether the allocation has the potential to actually change the economic relationship among the partners, disregarding the tax consequences.

   Example (1):   C and D are equal partners in the CD partnership. In the partnership agreement, C and D agree to comply with The Big Three. C expects to be taxed at the highest federal tax rate during the current year and D expects to be taxed at the lowest. During the current taxable year, C and D agree to share the first $10,000 of the partnership's tax-exempt income on a 90/10 basis (90% to C, 10% to D), and the first $10,000 of the partnership's dividend income on a

10/90 basis (10% to C, 90% to D). The allocations will have economic effect. If there is a strong likelihood that the partnership will earn more than $10,000 of both tax-exempt income and dividends, the economic effect of the allocations will not be substantial because the net increases and decreases in C's and D's capital accounts will be the same as they would have been if the allocations had not been made and the partner's total tax liability is reduced. Assuming the partnership realizes at least $10,000 of both tax-exempt income and dividends, those items will be reallocated equally between C and D.

Example (2): Assume the same facts as Example (1). If there is not a strong likelihood that the partnership will earn at least $10,000 of both tax-exempt income and dividends, and the amount of tax-exempt income and dividends will be the same, the regulations state that the economic effect of the allocations generally will be substantial. Reg. § 1.704–1(b)(5) Example (7)(iii).

b) Transitory Allocations

Transitory allocations are similar to shifting allocations except that they involve more than one taxable year. Again, the issue is whether there is a strong likelihood at the time the allocations became part of the partnership agreement that: (1) the net increases and decreases in the partners' capital accounts as a result of allocations over more than one year differ substantially from the net increases and decreases had the allocations not been made, and (2) the partners' total tax liability is reduced. If these results occur it is presumed that there was a strong likelihood of that result. But if there is a strong likelihood that an offsetting allocation (increase or decrease) will not be made within five years, the original and offsetting allocations will be considered substantial. Reg. § 1.704–1(b)(2)(iii)(*c*).

Example (1): E and F are equal partners in the EF partnership. In the partnership agreement E and F agree to comply with The Big Three. For the next three years the partnership will invest in equal amounts of tax-exempt bonds and corporate stock and over that period of time E expects to be in a higher tax bracket than F. Assume that during the three-year period the partners agree to allocate the tax-exempt interest 90% to E and 10% to F, and the dividends 10% to E and 90% to F. If there is a strong likelihood that the amount of tax-exempt interest and dividends realized will not differ substantially over the three-year period, the economic effect of the allocations will not be substantial because at the end of that period the net increases and decreases to the partners' capital accounts will be the same as they would have been without the allocations and the tax paid by the partners will be reduced. If the tax-exempt interest and dividends are the same over the three-year period, they will be reallocated equally between E and F. See Reg. § 1.704–1(b)(5) Example (7)(i).

Example (2):   Assume the same facts as Example (1). Assume further that any gain or loss on the tax-exempt bonds is allocated to E and any gain or loss on the stock is allocated to F. If at the time the allocations became part of the partnership agreement there is not a strong likelihood that the gain or loss on these assets will be substantially equal, the allocations of gain and loss will have substantial economic effect. Id.

3)   **Presumption Validating "Gain Chargeback" Provisions**
For purposes of determining whether an allocation's economic effect is substantial, the adjusted basis of property is presumed to be its fair market value and cost recovery deductions are presumed to be matched by a corresponding decrease in the property's value. Reg. § 1.704–1(b)(2)(iii)(c). Under this presumption, there cannot be a strong likelihood that the economic effect of an allocation of cost recovery deductions will be largely offset by an allocation of corresponding gain on the disposition of the property. This presumption validates so-called "gain chargeback" provisions.

Example: G and H are equal partners in the GH partnership. In the GH partnership agreement the partners agree to comply with The Big Three and all partnership cost recovery deductions are allocated to G. In addition, the partnership agreement contains a "gain chargeback" provision under which any gain on the sale of partnership depreciable property is allocated to G to the extent of the prior allocations to G of cost recovery deductions, and any additional gain is allocated equally between G and H. Even if it is likely that gain on a sale will be sufficient to offset prior cost recovery deductions, the allocation has substantial economic effect because in testing whether the economic effect of the allocation is substantial, the property is presumed to decrease in value by the amount of the cost recovery deductions.

e.   **Partner's Interest in the Partnership**
If either the partnership agreement is silent or partnership allocations lack substantial economic effect, a partner's distributive share of partnership items

is determined in accordance with the partner's interest in the partnership. § 704(b). A partner's interest in the partnership is determined by the manner in which the partners have agreed to share the economic benefit or burden corresponding to the partnership's tax items. Reg. § 1.704–1(b)(3)(i). This determination is made by taking into account all facts and circumstances, including: (1) the partner's contributions to the partnership, (2) the interests of the partners in economic profits and losses (if different from that in taxable income or loss) and cash flow, and (3) the rights of the partners to distributions of capital on liquidation of the partnership. Reg. § 1.704–1(b)(3)(ii). All partners initially are presumed to have equal interests in the partnership but this presumption may be rebutted by either the taxpayer or the Service. Reg. § 1.704–1(b)(3)(i).

If an allocation satisfies the first two requirements of The Big Three and is substantial but the partnership agreement does not have an unlimited deficit restoration provision, the regulations provide that a partner's interest in the partnership for purposes of reallocating an item is determined by comparing the manner in which distributions (and contributions) would be made if all partnership property were sold at book value and the partnership were liquidated at the end of taxable year to which the allocation relates with the results of an identical liquidation at the end of the prior taxable year. Reg. § 1.704–1(b)(3)(iii). This test may save simple allocations that failed The Big Three or the alternate test because the partnership agreement did not include all the provisions required by those tests.

Example (1): Assume A and B form the AB partnership by making equal cash contributions. The AB partnership agreement provides that A and B will have equal shares of taxable income and loss (except any cost recovery deductions) and cash flow and that all cost recovery deductions will be allocated to A. The agreement requires proper maintenance of capital accounts but, upon liquidation of the partnership, distributions will be made equally to A and B and no partner is required to restore a deficit capital account balance. The allocation of cost recovery deductions to A does not have economic effect because the partnership agreement does not comply with The Big Three, and the allocation fails the alternate test because the agreement does not include a qualified income offset provision. As a result, the cost recovery deductions will be reallocated in accordance with the partners' interests in the partnership. Since A and B made equal contributions, share equally in cash flow, and will share liquidation distributions equally, the cost recovery deductions will be reallocated equally between A and B. If the partners' interests in these items had not been equal, the regulations do not give clear guidance as to how they should be balanced to determine the partners' interests in the partnership.

Example (2):   J and K are equal partners in the JK partnership. In the JK partnership agreement the partners agree to comply with The Big Three. During the year the partnership expects to incur § 1231 losses and other ordinary losses. In the partnership agreement, the partners allocate the first $20,000 of § 1231 losses to J, who does not have any § 1231 gains, and the first $20,000 of ordinary loss to K, who does have nonpartnership § 1231 gains. These allocations have economic effect. If there is a strong likelihood that the partnership will have at least $20,000 of both § 1231 and ordinary losses, the economic effect of the allocations is not substantial because there was a strong likelihood at the time the allocations became part of the partnership agreement that the net increases and decreases in the partners' capital accounts would not differ substantially from the net increases and decreases had the allocations not been made and the partners' tax liability will be reduced. The partners' taxes are reduced because K is allocated ordinary losses from the partnership which will not impact the capital gain characterization of his nonpartnership § 1231 gains. If K had been allocated § 1231 losses from the partnership, those losses would reduce the potential tax advantages available to the nonpartnership § 1231 gains.

If in fact the partnership recognizes at least $20,000 of both § 1231 and ordinary loss, those items will be reallocated equally between J and K. If not, the § 1231 losses and ordinary losses will be reallocated in proportion to the net decreases in their capital accounts due to the allocations of those items under the partnership agreement. For example, if the partnership actually ends up recognizing $20,000 of § 1231 losses (which are allocated to J) and $10,000 of ordinary losses (which are allocated to K) for the year, the allocation will not have substantial economic effect if there was a strong likelihood the partnership would have $20,000 of both types of losses when the allocations became part of the partnership agreement. Based on these facts, the losses would be reallocated as follows:

J:	$13,333	§ 1231 loss
	$ 6,666	ordinary loss
K:	$ 6,666	§ 1231 loss
	$ 3,333	ordinary loss

See Reg. § 1.704–1(b)(5) Example (6).

f.   Allocations of Depreciation Recapture

Allocations of depreciation recapture cannot have substantial economic effect because classifying part of the gain as recapture merely changes its tax character. The identification of part of the gain taxed to a partner as ordinary or capital gain does not change the economic arrangement among the partners; instead, it simply changes their tax results. Consequently, the regulations attempt to minimize the mismatching of depreciation and recapture allocations. Reg. §§ 1.704–3(a)(11); 1.1245–1(e)(2); 1.1250–1(f). Under the regulations, a partner's share of recapture gain generally is equal to the lesser of (1) the partner's share of the total gain from the disposition of the property, or (2) the total amount of depreciation previously allocated to the partner with respect to the property. Reg. §§ 1.1245–1(e)(2)(i) & (ii); 1.1250–1(f).

g.   Allocations of Tax Credits

Allocations of tax credits and credit recapture generally are not reflected in the partners' capital accounts and cannot have economic effect. Thus, tax credits and credit recapture generally must be allocated in accordance with the partners' interests in the partnership. Reg. § 1.704–1(b)(4)(ii).

3.   Contributed Property

a.   § 704(c) Allocations: General Principles

Section 704(c)(1)(A) provides that income, gain, loss and deduction items with respect to property contributed by a partner to a partnership shall be shared among the partners so as to take account of the variation between the inside basis of the property and its fair market value at the time of the contribution. The purpose of this rule is to prevent the shifting of precontribution gains and losses among partners. Reg. § 1.704–3(a)(1). Section 704(c)(1)(A) principally applies to sales and exchanges by a partnership of contributed property and depreciation and depletion with respect to contributed property. "Contributed property" (also known as "§ 704(c) property") is property which, at the time it is contributed to a partnership, has a fair market (book) value that differs from the contributing partner's adjusted tax basis (a "book/tax disparity"). Reg. § 1.704–3(a)(3)(i). Because contributed property is recorded on the partnership's books at its fair market value, allocations of precontribution gain or loss are tax allocations that do not have economic effect. For example, if contributed property is sold by the partnership for its book value, there is no book gain and no adjustments to the partners' capital accounts.

Example: A and B form the AB equal partnership with A contributing property with a $30,000 fair market value and $18,000 adjusted basis and B contributing $30,000 cash. A and B agree to share all partnership income or loss and distributions equally and the partnership agreement includes The Big Three. Neither A nor B will recognize gain on their contributions. A's outside basis will be $18,000 and B's will be $30,000. AB's inside basis in the asset contributed by A will be $18,000. Both A and B will have a

$30,000 capital account since A's capital account is credited with the fair market value of the property she contributed. After its formation, AB's balance sheet will be as follows:

Assets			Liabilities/Partners' Capital		
	A.B.	**Bk. Value**		**A.B.**	**Bk. Value**
Cash	$30,000	$30,000	Liabilities	none	
Asset	18,000	30,000	Capital		
			A	$18,000	$30,000
			B	30,000	30,000
Total	$48,000	$60,000		$48,000	$60,000

Assume the partnership sells the asset contributed by A for its fair market value of $30,000. AB will have a $12,000 recognized gain which, absent § 704(c)(1)(A), would be allocated under the partnership agreement $6,000 to A and $6,000 to B, thereby increasing their outside bases to $24,000 and $36,000, respectively. If this result is permitted, $6,000 of A's precontribution gain in the asset will be shifted to B. The shift is not permanent since B's outside basis is increased to $36,000, and on a sale or cash liquidation of her partnership interest she will recognize $6,000 of loss. But that event may occur many years later and the character of B's loss may not be the same as the income recognized on the disposition of the asset. To prevent these distortions, § 704(c)(1)(A) requires that the $12,000 of precontribution gain inherent in the asset shall be allocated to A, which will increase her outside basis to $30,000.

b. § 704(c) Allocation Methods

    1) In General

Under the regulations, a partnership may use any reasonable method of making § 704(c) allocations that is consistent with the purpose of § 704(c). Reg. § 1.704–3(a)(1). The regulations specifically authorize three methods: the "traditional" method, the "traditional method with curative allocations," and the "remedial method." A partnership may use different allocation methods with respect to different items of contributed property, but the method used for a particular property must be consistently applied by the partnership and the partners from year to year. Reg. § 1.704–3(a)(2). In all events, the overall method or combination of methods used must be reasonable under the facts and circumstances. Id. An allocation method is not reasonable if the contribution of the property and the corresponding § 704(c) allocations with respect to it are made with a view to shifting the tax consequences of built-in gain or loss in a manner that substantially reduces the present value of the partners' aggregate tax liability. Reg. § 1.704–3(a)(10). For example, the partners may not manipulate § 704(c) to shift income over a short period of time from a partner in a high marginal tax bracket to a partner who anticipates no tax liability because of expiring net operating losses.

2) The Ceiling Rule

Under the "ceiling rule," the total income, gain, loss or deduction allocated to a partner for a taxable year with respect to any § 704(c) property may not exceed the total partnership income, gain, loss, or deduction with respect to that property for the taxable year. The ceiling rule, which has traditionally been incorporated into the regulations by the Service, has the effect of temporarily shifting precontribution gains or losses among partners or limiting tax depreciation allocated to noncontributing partners. The purpose of a curative or remedial allocation (see below) is to eliminate the distortions resulting from the ceiling rule.

3) Sales and Exchanges of Contributed Property

a) Traditional Method

Under the traditional method, if a partnership sells § 704(c) property and recognizes gain or loss, the built-in gain or loss inherent in the property at the time of its contribution is allocated for tax purposes to the contributing partner. Reg. § 1.704–3(b)(1). Any additional book gain or loss is allocated in accordance with the partnership agreement if the allocation has substantial economic effect. Reg. § 1.704–1(b)(2)(iv)(*b*), (*d*), and (*g*); –1(b)(5) Example (13)(i). Under the "ceiling rule," however, the total precontribution gain or loss allocated to the contributing partner with respect to § 704(c) property may not exceed the partnership's total tax gain or loss with respect to that property. Reg. § 1.704–3(b)(1).

Example (1):   A and B form the AB equal partnership with A contributing an asset (fair market value, $30,000; basis, $18,000) and B contributing $30,000 cash. If AB sells the asset contributed by A for $30,000, its tax gain is $12,000 ($30,000 amount realized less $18,000 adjusted basis) and its book gain is zero ($30,000 amount realized less $30,000 book value). Under the traditional method, the $12,000 difference between the tax and book gains (all of the precontribution or "built-in gain") is allocated to A and there is no additional book gain.

Example (2):   Assume that AB in Example (1) sells the asset contributed by A for $38,000. In that situation its tax gain is $20,000 ($38,000 amount realized less $18,000 adjusted basis) and its book gain is $8,000 ($38,000 less $30,000 book value).

Again, under the traditional method the $12,000 difference between the tax and book gain ($20,000 less $8,000) is allocated to A under § 704(c)(1)(A) and the $8,000 book gain is allocated $4,000 to A and $4,000 to B in accordance with the partnership agreement. A's outside basis would be increased by $16,000 to $34,000. Both A's and B's capital accounts would be increased by $4,000, their respective shares of the partnership's book gain.

Example (3):   C and D form the CD equal partnership with C contributing property with a $20,000 fair market value and $24,000 adjusted basis and D contributing $20,000 cash. C and D agree to share all partnership income or loss and distributions equally and in the CD partnership agreement they agree to comply with The Big Three. Assume CD sells the asset contributed by C for $18,000. CD's tax loss is $6,000 ($18,000 amount realized less $24,000 adjusted basis) and its book loss is $2,000 ($18,000 amount realized less $20,000 book value). The $4,000 precontribution built-in loss is allocated to C under the traditional method, and the $2,000 book loss is allocated $1,000 to C and $1,000 to D in accordance with the partnership agreement.

Example (4) (Ceiling Rule):   Assume CD in Example (3) sells the asset contributed by C for $22,000. CD's tax loss is $2,000 ($22,000 less $24,000 adjusted basis) and it has a $2,000 book gain ($22,000 amount realized less $20,000 book value). Ideally, one would like to allocate $4,000 of tax loss (the amount of the precontribution loss) to C and $1,000 of gain (one-half of the total book gain) to both C and D. The traditional method, however, contains a "ceiling" rule under which § 704(c) allocations are limited to the recognized tax gain or loss of the partnership. Thus, all of the $2,000 tax loss is allocated to C. This has the effect of not requiring D to include the $1,000 of book gain, and the disparity between the partnership's tax and capital accounts is not totally eliminated.

b)   Traditional Method With Curative Allocations

A partnership using the traditional method may make reasonable "curative allocations" to correct book/tax disparities created by the ceiling rule. A curative allocation is an allocation that differs from the partnership's allocation of the corresponding book item. Reg. § 1.704–3(c)(1). In the case of sales of § 704(c) property, a curative allocation must be made with respect to the gain or loss from the partnership's sale of other property of similar character. A curative allocation may not exceed the amount necessary to offset the effect of the ceiling rule and must be made using a tax item that would have the same effect on the partners as the tax item affected by the ceiling rule. Reg. § 1.704–3(c)(3)(i) & (iii). Curative allocations may be made to offset ceiling rule distortions from a prior taxable year if they are made over a reasonable period of time and were authorized by the partnership agreement in effect for the year of the contribution of the § 704(c) property. Reg. § 1.704–3(c)(3)(ii). Because curative allocations have only tax effect and not economic effect, they are not reflected in the partners' capital accounts.

Example: A and B form the AB equal partnership with A contributing Oldacre (value $30,000, basis $22,000) and B contributing $30,000 cash, which the partnership uses to purchase Newacre. Both properties are capital assets. At the end of its first year, AB sells Oldacre for $25,000. Under the traditional method, AB's $3,000 tax gain ($25,000 amount realized less $22,000 tax basis) is all allocated to A, while the $5,000 book loss ($30,000 book value less $25,000 amount realized) is allocated $2,500 each to A and B. The ceiling rule causes a $2,500 disparity between the partners' book and tax accounts, requiring $2,500 more tax gain to be allocated to A and $2,500 of tax loss to be allocated to B to cure the disparity. If the partnership were to sell Newacre in the same taxable year for $35,000, it would have a $5,000 tax and book gain. An allocation of the first $2,500 of tax gain on Newacre to A, with the remaining tax gain being split equally between A and B would be a reasonable curative allocation because it offsets the disparity caused by the ceiling rule.

c)   Remedial Method

Curative allocations are allocations of tax items actually realized by the partnership. Remedial allocations are tax allocations of income, gain, loss, or deduction created by the partnership that are offset by other tax allocations of income, gain, loss, or deduction created by the partnership. Reg. § 1.704–3(d)(1). Under the remedial method, if the ceiling rule results in a book allocation to a noncontributing partner that differs from the corresponding tax allocation, the partnership makes a remedial allocation to the noncontributing partner equal to the full amount of the disparity and a simultaneous offsetting remedial allocation to the contributing partner. Id. A remedial allocation must have the same effect on each partner's tax liability as the item limited by the ceiling rule—e.g., capital loss must offset capital gain. Reg. § 1.704–3(d)(3). Remedial allocations are solely for tax purposes and have no effect on the partnership's book capital accounts.

> ***Example:*** I and J form the IJ equal partnership with I contributing Blackacre (value $10,000, basis $4,000) and J contributing Whiteacre (value $10,000, basis $10,000). At the end of IJ's first taxable year, the partnership sells Blackacre for $9,000, recognizing a capital gain of $5,000 ($9,000 amount realized less $4,000 tax basis), and a book loss of $1,000 ($9,000 amount realized less $10,000 book basis). Under the ceiling rule, I would be allocated the entire $5,000 of tax gain, and the $1,000 book loss would be allocated equally to the partners, creating a $500 disparity between each partner's book and tax accounts. Under the remedial method, IJ may make an allocation of $500 capital loss to J and an offsetting remedial allocation of $500 capital gain to I. This has the same effect as allocating to I the entire $6,000 precontribution gain less I's share ($500) of postcontribution loss (for a net gain of $5,500), and of allocating to J her $500 share of postcontribution loss.

4)   Depreciation and Depletion

Section 704(c)(1)(A) also governs the allocation of depreciation and depletion with respect to contributed property. Where a partner contributes depreciable property with a built-in gain to a partnership, a general goal of § 704(c) is to allocate that gain to the contributing partner (even before the asset is sold). A related goal is to ensure that noncontributing partners do not suffer when a contributing partner contributes depreciable property with a tax basis that is less than its book value to the partnership. These goals are accomplished by allocating tax depreciation to the *noncontributing* partners in an amount equal to their share of book depreciation, and then allocating any remaining tax depreciation to the contributing partner. As explained below, the ceiling rule may frustrate these policies.

a)   Traditional Method

Under the traditional method, tax depreciation is allocated first to the noncontributing partner in an amount equal to his share of book depreciation and the balance of tax depreciation is allocated to the contributing partner. Reg. § 1.704–3(b)(1). Book and tax depreciation must be computed using the same depreciation method and useful life. Reg. § 1.704–1(b)(2)(iv)(g)(3). The ceiling rule, however, limits the tax depreciation allocated to the noncontributing partner to the partnership's total tax depreciation with respect to the contributed property.

Example (1)
(Traditional
Method):

L and M form the LM equal partnership with L
contributing depreciable equipment with a fair
market value of $10,000 and an adjusted basis of
$6,000 and M contributing $10,000 cash. The LM
partnership agreement complies with The Big Three
and provides that § 704(c) allocations shall be made
under the traditional method. The equipment has a
10–year remaining recovery period and is depreciated
using the straight-line method. The partnership's
book depreciation is $1,000 per year (10% x $10,000)
and tax depreciation is $600 (10% x $6,000). M, the
noncontributing partner, is allocated tax depreciation
in an amount up to his share of book depreciation, or
$500. The remaining $100 of tax depreciation is
allocated to E.

Example (2)
(Ceiling
Rule):

Assume that in Example (1), the equipment
contributed by L has a basis of $4,000. Book
depreciation would again be $1,000 per year, but the
partnership's tax depreciation would be only $400 per
year (10% x $4,000). Noncontributing partner M
should be entitled to $500 of tax depreciation (equal
to M's book depreciation). But under the ceiling rule,
the partnership may only allocate $400 of tax
depreciation, and it must be allocated entirely to M.
See Reg. § 1.704–3(b)(2) Example 1(ii).

b) Traditional Method With Curative Allocations
If the ceiling rule causes the noncontributing partner to be allocated
less tax depreciation than book depreciation with respect to an item of
depreciable § 704(c) property, the traditional method with curative
allocations permits the partnership to make a curative allocation to
the noncontributing partner of tax depreciation from *another item* of
partnership property to make up the difference.

Example (3)
(Curative
Allocation):

Assume the same facts as in Example (2), except that
LM uses the $10,000 cash contributed by M to
purchase inventory for resale. The partnership
agreement provides that LM will use the traditional
method with curative allocations. As in Example (2),
the partnership's annual book depreciation is $1,000
and the tax depreciation is $400, and the ceiling rule
requires that no more than $400 of tax depreciation is
allocated to M.

Finally, assume that LM sells the inventory for
$10,700 at the end of its first year, recognizing $700
of ordinary income, allocated $350 each to L and M

for book and tax purposes. Because the ceiling rule creates a $100 disparity between the partners' book and tax accounts, LM may make a curative allocation to L (and away from M) of an additional $100 of ordinary income from the sale of the inventory.

c)   Remedial Method

To eliminate ceiling rule distortions from depreciation of § 704(c) property, the remedial method allocates ordinary income to the contributing partner and additional tax depreciation to the noncontributing partner. For this purpose, the determination of book and tax depreciation differs from the traditional method. Under the remedial method, the portion of the partnership's book basis in § 704(c) property that is equal to the tax basis of the property at the time of contribution is depreciated under the same method used for tax depreciation (generally, over the property's remaining recovery period at the time of contribution). The amount by which the book basis exceeds the tax basis ("the excess book basis") is depreciated using any applicable recovery period and depreciation method available to the partnership for newly acquired property. Reg. § 1.704–3(d)(2).

> ***Example (4)***
> (Remedial Method):
>
> Assume the same facts as in Example (2) except that the partnership agreement provides that LM will make § 704(c) allocations using the remedial method and that the straight-line method will be used to recover any excess book basis. Assume that the equipment, which has a $4,000 tax basis, has 10 years remaining on its 20–year recovery period when it is contributed to LM. Tax depreciation is thus $400 per year for 10 years. Under the remedial method, LM's book depreciation for each of its first 10 years is $400 ($4,000 tax basis divided by remaining 10 years in recovery period) plus $300 ($6,000 excess of book value over tax basis divided by a new 20–year recovery period), or $700. To simplify the example, book depreciation is determined without regard to any first-year depreciation convention. L and M are each allocated $350 of book depreciation (50% of $700), M is allocated $350 of tax depreciation and L is allocated the remaining $50 of tax depreciation. No remedial allocations are yet necessary because the ceiling rule does not cause a book allocation of depreciation to the noncontributing partner that differs from the tax allocation. For years 11 through 20, however, LM has $300 of book depreciation, allocated $150 each to L and M, but no more tax

depreciation. Since M is allocated $150 of book depreciation but no tax depreciation, LM must make a remedial allocation of $150 of tax depreciation to M and an offsetting allocation of $150 of ordinary income to L for each of years 11 through 20. See Reg. § 1.704–3(d)(5) Example 1.

c. Application of § 704(c)(1)(A) Principles to the Entry of a New Partner

The entry of a new partner to an ongoing partnership raises a question as to how the preexisting gains and losses in partnership assets should be allocated among the partners. Ideally, those gains and losses should be allocated to the old partners. The new partner should share in gains and losses accruing after entry into the partnership. The regulations apply § 704(c) principles to resolve this question.

> *Example:* G and H form the GH equal partnership by each contributing $20,000 cash, and the partnership uses the $40,000 to purchase securities. In the GH partnership agreement, G and H agree to comply with The Big Three. When the securities are worth $60,000, J is permitted to join the partnership as a one-third partner for a contribution of $30,000 cash. The $20,000 of gain in the securities should be allocated to G and H, and any appreciation in the securities above $60,000 should be shared equally among the partners. If the gain is not allocated in this fashion, G and H will have transferred one-third of the $20,000 of appreciation ($6,666) to J and that transfer may be a gift or disguised compensation.

There are two ways for partners to accomplish the allocation of preexisting gains and losses. One is to specifically provide in the partnership agreement for the allocation of such gains and losses to the partners previously in the partnership. Such an allocation has substantial economic effect and will be respected. See Reg. § 1.704–1(b)(5) Example (14)(iv).

Alternatively, the regulations permit the partners to restate their capital accounts to reflect the revaluation of partnership property upon the entry of a new partner. Reg. § 1.704–1(b)(2)(iv)(*f*). Upon revaluation and restatement of the capital accounts, the difference between the partnership's tax and book gain or loss is allocated to the prior partners and any book gain or loss is allocated among all the partners (including the new partner). See Reg. § 1.704–1(b)(4)(i), –1(b)(5) Example (14)(i). These "reverse § 704(c) allocations" may be made under any reasonable method that is consistent with the § 704(c) regulations. Reg. § 1.704–3(a)(6).

> *Example:* Assume the same facts as the previous example. If the partnership agreement requires revaluation of partnership assets and restatement of capital accounts upon the entry of a new partner, the securities will be revalued at their fair market value

of $60,000 when J enters the partnership. G's and H's capital accounts will each be restated at $30,000. If the securities are later sold for $66,000, the difference between the tax gain of $26,000 ($66,000 amount realized less $40,000 basis) and the book gain of $6,000 ($66,000 amount realized less $60,000 restated book value) , or $20,000, would be allocated $10,000 each to G and H. The $6,000 book gain would be allocated $2,000 each to G, H, and J.

d. Distributions of Contributed Property Within Seven Years of Contribution

In most situations, distributions of property by a partnership to a partner do not result in gain or loss to either the partner or the partnership. § 731; see XIX.A.2.a., at page 440, *infra*. Under § 704(c)(1)(B), however, if property contributed by a partner is distributed to another partner within seven years of its contribution, the contributing partner is treated as recognizing gain or loss from the sale or exchange of the property in an amount equal to the gain or loss which would have been allocated to that partner under § 704(c)(1)(A) if the property had actually been sold for its fair market value. § 704(c)(1)(B)(i). A related anti-abuse rule applies to a partner who contributes appreciated property and receives a distribution of other property. See § 737. Because these transactions are related to the operating distribution rules, they are discussed in Chapter XIX. See XIX.C., at page 449, *infra*.

e. Characterization of Gain or Loss Upon Partnership's Disposition of Contributed Property

Section 704(c) prevents the shifting among partners of built-in gain or loss when a partnership disposes of contributed property and § 724 prevents the conversion of the character of that gain or loss. Normally, the characterization of partnership gains and losses is determined at the partnership level. § 702(b). Section 724, however, provides different rules for three categories of contributed property: "unrealized receivables," "inventory items," and "capital loss property." To prevent easy avoidance, these rules also apply to any substituted basis property (other than corporate stock received in a § 351 exchange) received in a nonrecognition transaction (or series of transactions) for contributed property subject to § 724. § 724(d)(3).

1) Unrealized Receivables

Under § 724(a) any gain or loss recognized on the disposition of a contributed unrealized receivable is characterized as ordinary income or loss. "Unrealized receivables" generally are defined as rights (contractual or otherwise) to payment not previously included in income for services or property which is not a capital asset. §§ 724(d)(1), 751(c).

Example: A contributes accounts receivable which have a $5,000 fair market value and zero basis to the ABCD partnership. If the partnership collects the receivables or sells them for $5,000, A will be taxed on $5,000 of ordinary income under § 704(c)(1)(A) and § 724. The receivables were unrealized receivables in A's hands and under § 724(a) any income on the receivables is characterized as ordinary even if the receivables might have been a capital asset in the hands of the partnership.

2) Inventory Items

Under § 724(b) any gain or loss recognized on the disposition of a contributed inventory item within five years of contribution is characterized as ordinary income or loss. "Inventory items" generally are defined as property described in § 1221(1) (stock in trade, inventory, and property held primarily for sale to customers) and any other property which if sold by the contributing partner would be considered property other than a capital asset or § 1231 property (without regard to holding period). §§ 724(d)(2), 751(d)(2).

Example: B contributes inventory which has a fair market value of $5,000 and a basis of $3,000 to the BC equal partnership. If the partnership sells the inventory within five years of contribution for $7,000, the first $2,000 of gain will be allocated to B under § 704(c)(1)(A).

The $2,000 of book gain ($7,000 amount realized less $5,000 book value) will be allocated $1,000 to B and $1,000 to C in accordance with the partnership agreement. All of the gain would be characterized as ordinary income under § 724(b). If the inventory is sold for $7,000 more than five years after B's contribution, the gain will be allocated in the same manner. The character of the gain, however, will be determined at the partnership level and would be capital gain if the inventory is a capital asset in the hands of the partnership. § 702(b).

3) Capital Loss Property

Under § 724(c) any loss recognized on the disposition of an asset which was a capital asset in the hands of the contributing partner within five years of the contribution is characterized as a capital loss to the extent that the basis of the property exceeded its fair market value at the time of contribution.

Example (1): D contributes a capital asset which has a fair market value of $12,000 and a basis of $16,000 to the DE equal partnership. Assume DE is a dealer in the type of property contributed by D. If DE sells the property contributed by D within five years of contribution for

$10,000, the first $4,000 of loss will be allocated to D under § 704(c)(1)(A). The remaining $2,000 of book loss will be allocated $1,000 to D and $1,000 to E in accordance with the partnership agreement. Under § 724(c) the first $4,000 of loss allocated to D will be capital loss and the remaining $2,000 of loss is characterized at the partnership level as ordinary loss. If the property is sold for $10,000 more than five years after D's contribution, the loss will be allocated in the same manner. The character of the loss, however, will be determined at the partnership level and will all be ordinary loss.

Example (2):   If DE in Example (1) sold the property contributed by D for $19,000, the $3,000 of gain ($19,000 amount realized less $16,000 adjusted basis) would be allocated $1,500 to both D and E. The gain would be characterized at the partnership level and will all be ordinary income.

4)   Depreciation Recapture
If a partner contributes depreciable property which has potential recapture income under § 1245 or § 1250 to a partnership, the character of that income is preserved by the definition of "recomputed basis" in § 1245(a)(2) and "depreciation adjustments" in § 1250(b)(3).

4. Nonrecourse Liabilities
a. Introduction
A liability is "nonrecourse" to the extent that no partner bears the economic risk of loss for the liability. Reg. § 1.752–1(a)(2). Because no partner bears the economic risk of loss for nonrecourse liabilities, economic risk of loss analysis cannot be used to determine the partners' shares of those liabilities. And because no partner bears the economic burden corresponding to allocations attributable to nonrecourse debt (e.g., cost recovery deductions on depreciable property acquired using nonrecourse financing), an allocation of such deductions cannot have economic effect. Reg. § 1.704–2(b)(1).

Example: The GL limited partnership is formed with G as the general partner and L as the limited partner. Assume GL purchases a $250,000 building by borrowing the full purchase price on a nonrecourse basis. No partner will bear the economic risk of loss for the liability and allocations of cost recovery deductions attributable to the building will not have economic effect because if the building declines in value below the amount of the debt, that loss will be sustained by the creditor, not G and L.

b. Allocations Attributable to Nonrecourse Liabilities
1)   Introduction
Even though partners do not bear the economic risk of loss for partnership nonrecourse liabilities, they must bear the corresponding tax burden of

including relief from those liabilities in their amount realized upon a disposition of property encumbered by the debt. *Comm'r v. Tufts,* 461 U.S. 300, 103 S.Ct. 1826 (1983), rehearing denied, 463 U.S. 1215, 103 S.Ct. 3555 (1983). The regulations provide a four-part test which basically requires that, in order to be respected, allocations attributable to nonrecourse liabilities must correspond to any later gain attributable to that debt. If the test is satisfied, the allocations are deemed to be in accordance with the partners' interests in the partnership. Reg. § 1.704–2(b)(1). The four-part test employs several very detailed definitions. The basics of the definitions are provided in the following sections.

2) "Partnership Minimum Gain"
   Partnership minimum gain with respect to a particular nonrecourse liability is defined as the amount of gain, if any, that would be realized if the partnership disposed of the partnership property subject to the liability in full satisfaction of such liability and no other consideration. Reg. § 1.704–2(d)(1). Under Reg. § 1.704–2(d)(3), partnership minimum gain is determined with reference to the book value of partnership property if book value differs from the property's adjusted tax basis. Partnership minimum gain is the aggregate of the separately computed gains. The increase or decrease in partnership minimum gain is determined by comparing the partnership minimum gain on the last day of the preceding taxable year with the partnership minimum gain on the last day of the current taxable year. Id.

3) "Nonrecourse Deductions"
   A partnership's "nonrecourse deductions" for the year generally equal the net increase in the amount of partnership minimum gain for the year. Reg. § 1.704–2(c). Increases in minimum gain generally would occur as the result of cost recovery deductions which would reduce the bases of assets encumbered by nonrecourse liabilities.

4) The Test for Respecting Allocations of Nonrecourse Deductions
   Allocations of nonrecourse deductions are deemed to be in accordance with the partners' interests in the partnership only if they meet the following requirements:

   a) During the life of the partnership the partnership agreement complies with the first two requirements of The Big Three (proper maintenance of capital accounts and liquidation of the partnership in accordance with positive capital account balances); and either: (1) the third requirement of The Big Three (deficit restoration obligation) is satisfied, or (2) the partnership agreement contains a qualified income offset;

   b) Beginning in the first taxable year in which there are nonrecourse deductions, the partnership agreement allocates such deductions in a manner reasonably consistent with allocations, which have substantial economic effect, of some other significant partnership item attributable to the property securing nonrecourse liabilities of the partnership;

c)   Beginning in the first taxable year in which there are nonrecourse deductions or a distribution of the proceeds of a nonrecourse liability that are allocable to an increase in partnership minimum gain, and thereafter, the partnership agreement must contain a provision that complies with the "minimum gain chargeback" requirement; and

d)   All other material allocations and capital account adjustments under the partnership agreement must be recognized under the § 704(b) regulations. Reg. § 1.704–2(e).

5)   Minimum Gain Chargeback Requirement

If there is a net decrease in partnership minimum gain for a partnership taxable year, the minimum gain chargeback requirement applies and generally each partner must be allocated items of income and gain for the year equal to that partner's share of the net decrease in partnership minimum gain. Reg. § 1.704–2(f)(1). A partner's share of net decrease in partnership minimum gain is generally based on the nonrecourse deductions allocated to that partner. Reg. § 1.704–2(g)(1) & (2). A partner's share of partnership minimum gain increases the limited dollar amount, if any, of a deficit capital account balance that the partner is obligated to restore under the alternate test for economic effect. Reg. § 1.704–2(g)(1).

In essence, a minimum gain chargeback forces each partner to bear the burden of his share of minimum gain if nonrecourse liabilities produce recognition of gain on the disposition of encumbered property. A net decrease in partnership minimum gain also commonly occurs when the partnership makes principal payments on nonrecourse liabilities. In that situation, partners with deficit capital account balances from nonrecourse deductions must be allocated income and gain sufficient to restore the deficit.

Example: G and L form the GL limited partnership with G, the general partner, contributing $20,000 and L, the limited partner, contributing $180,000. GL purchases a building (on leased land) for $1,000,000 paying $200,000 cash and borrowing $800,000 on a nonrecourse basis. The loan is secured by the building and no principal payments are due for ten years (only interest is payable during that period). The partnership agreement requires proper maintenance of the partners' capital accounts and liquidation of the partnership in accordance with positive capital account balances. Only G is obligated to restore a deficit in her capital account. The partnership agreement also contains a qualified income offset and a minimum gain chargeback. Except as required by the qualified income offset or minimum gain chargeback, all partnership items are allocated 10% to G and 90% to L until the partnership has recognized items of income and gain that exceed the items of loss and deduction it previously has recognized, and thereafter all additional partnership items will be allocated equally between G and L.

The partnership agreement provides that all distributions, other than in liquidation of the partnership or of a partner's interest in the partnership, will be made 90% to L and 10% to G until a total of $200,000 has been distributed and thereafter all distributions will be made equally to L and G.

Assume that in each year of operations the partnership generates $95,000 of rental income, $10,000 of operating expenses (including land lease payments), $80,000 of interest deductions, and a $90,000 depreciation deduction, for a taxable loss of $85,000. The allocations of the first two years of those losses have substantial economic effect:

	L	G
Capital Account at Formation	$180,000	$20,000
Loss in Years 1 and 2	−153,000	−17,000
Capital Account after Year 2	$ 27,000	$ 3,000

In its third taxable year, the partnership again has a loss of $85,000 and makes no distributions. The building's adjusted basis at the end of the third year would be $730,000 ($1 million less $270,000 of depreciation) and if the partnership disposed of the building in full satisfaction of the $800,000 nonrecourse liability at the end of the third year it would realize $70,000 of gain. Because the net increase in partnership minimum gain for the third year is $70,000, there are $70,000 of partnership nonrecourse deductions for that year. The nonrecourse deductions are considered to consist first of the depreciation deductions. Reg. § 1.704–2(c). Under the partnership agreement the $85,000 net taxable loss, including the $70,000 of nonrecourse deductions, is allocated 90% to L and 10% to G.

	L	G
Capital Account After Year 2	$27,000	$3,000
Year 3 Loss Without Nonrecourse Deductions	−13,500	−1,500
Year 3 Nonrecourse Deductions	−63,000	−7,000
Capital Account	$−49,500	$−5,500

The allocation of the $15,000 of taxable loss (excluding nonrecourse deductions) has substantial economic effect under the alternate test because it does not create a deficit in L's capital account. The allocation of the $70,000 of nonrecourse deductions is deemed to be made in accordance with the partners' interests in the partnership because it satisfies the four-part test in the regulations for allocations of nonrecourse deductions. The second requirement of that test is satisfied because the allocation of the nonrecourse deductions is consistent with the allocations having substantial economic effect of other significant items attributable to the building. At the end of the third year L's and G's shares of partnership minimum gain are $63,000 and $7,000, respectively. L therefore is treated as obligated to restore a $63,000 deficit capital account balance under the alternate test for economic effect. Since L's deficit capital account balance is only $49,500, 13,500 of partnership deductions and losses that are not nonrecourse deductions could be allocated to L in the next year.

If the partnership were to dispose of the building in full satisfaction of the nonrecourse liability ($800,000) at the beginning of the fourth year, partnership minimum gain would decrease by $70,000 and the minimum gain chargeback would require that L and G be allocated $63,000 and $7,000, respectively, of the gain from the disposition. See Reg. § 1.704–2(m) Example (1)(i).

The four-part test in the regulations requires that nonrecourse deductions be allocated in a manner reasonably consistent with allocations that have substantial economic effect of some other significant partnership item attributable to the property securing the nonrecourse liability. In this example all deductions (including nonrecourse deductions) were allocated 90% to L and 10% to G, so the requirement was satisfied. The § 704 regulations provide that if: (1) the nonrecourse deductions were allocated in any ratio between 90% to L/10% to G and 50% to L/50% to G, and (2) it is likely that over the partnership's life it will realize amounts of income and gain significantly in excess of amounts of loss and deduction (other than nonrecourse deductions), the reasonable consistency requirement is satisfied. But an allocation of 99% of the nonrecourse deductions to L and 1% to G does not satisfy that requirement. Reg. § 1.704–2(m) Example (1)(ii) & (iii).

6) **Refinancings and Distributions of Nonrecourse Liability Proceeds Allocable to Increase in Minimum Gain**

If a partnership incurs additional nonrecourse liabilities through refinancings or additional borrowings, there is an increase in partnership minimum gain and an increase in nonrecourse deductions. The increase in nonrecourse deductions is reduced by distributions during the year of proceeds of a nonrecourse liability that are allocable to an increase in partnership minimum gain. Reg. § 1.704–2(c).

> *Example:* Assume the ABC limited partnership satisfies the requirements in the regulations regarding allocations attributable to nonrecourse liabilities. The partnership owns real property with an adjusted basis of $200,000 which is subject to a $250,000 nonrecourse liability. Thus, there is $50,000 of partnership minimum gain. Assume the partnership obtains an additional nonrecourse loan of $100,000 on the real property, secured by a second mortgage. Partnership minimum gain increases by $100,000 to $150,000. If the proceeds of the loan are not distributed, nonrecourse deductions increase by $100,000. Under the regulations, the first $100,000 of partnership deductions for the year are treated as nonrecourse deductions, and each partner's share of partnership minimum gain is increased by that partner's allocable share of those deductions. Reg. § 1.704–2(m) Example (1)(vi).

If a partnership distributes nonrecourse liability proceeds allocable to an increase in partnership minimum gain, then nonrecourse deductions are not produced by the liability to the extent of the distribution. Reg. § 1.704–2(c). The distribution is allocable to an increase in partnership minimum gain, which means that the partners receiving the distribution can add the additional share of partnership minimum gain to their limited deficit restoration obligation under the alternate test for economic effect. Reg. § 1.704–2(g)(1), (h)(1). See XVII.C.2.c.3, at page 377, *supra*.

> *Example:* Assume the same facts as the previous Example, except that the partnership distributes the $100,000 of loan proceeds to

its partners. No nonrecourse deductions result from the new borrowings. The distributions are allocable to the increase in partnership minimum gain and will increase the deficit restoration obligation of the limited partners under the alternate test for economic effect. The deficit restoration obligation will be made up when partnership minimum gain is reduced, for example, on a disposition of the property or a repayment of the liability.

c. The Partners' Shares of Partnership Nonrecourse Liabilities

A partner's share of partnership nonrecourse liabilities is equal to the sum of: (1) the partner's share of "partnership minimum gain" and (2) the amount of any taxable gain that would be allocated to the partner under § 704(c) if the partnership disposed of its property subject to nonrecourse liabilities for relief of such liabilities and no other consideration. Reg. § 1.752–3(a)(1) & (2). Any remaining partnership nonrecourse liabilities are shared by the partners in accordance with their shares in partnership profits. Reg. § 1.752–3(a)(3). The partners' interests in partnership profits are determined by taking into account all facts and circumstances relating to the economic arrangements of the partners. The regulations also permit the partners to specify their interests in partnership profits for purposes of determining their shares of nonrecourse liabilities as long as the interests are reasonably consistent with allocations of some significant items of partnership income or gain among the partners.

Alternatively, the partners may agree to allocate any remaining nonrecourse liabilities in the manner in which it is reasonably expected that the deductions attributable to those nonrecourse liabilities will be allocated. Additionally, in the case of contributed property subject to a nonrecourse liability, the partnership may first allocate an excess nonrecourse liability to the contributing partner to the extent that Section 704(c) gain on the property is greater than the gain resulting from the liability exceeding the property's basis. The method used to allocate nonrecourse liabilities remaining after considering partnership minimum gain and § 704(c) gain may vary from year to year.

Example (1) (Allocation per Specified Interests in Profits and Minimum Gain):

G and L form the GL limited partnership with G, the general partner, contributing $20,000 and L, the limited partner, contributing $180,000. The partnership purchases a building (on leased land) for $1,000,000, paying $200,000 cash and borrowing $800,000 on a nonrecourse basis. The loan is secured by the building and no principal payments are due for ten years (only interest is payable during that period). The partnership agreement requires proper maintenance of the partners' capital accounts and liquidation of the partnership in accordance with positive capital account balances. Only G is obligated to restore a deficit in her capital account. The partnership agreement also contains a qualified income offset and a minimum gain chargeback.

Except as required by the qualified income offset or minimum gain chargeback, all partnership items are allocated 10% to G and 90% to L until the partnership has recognized items of income and gain that exceed the items of loss and deduction it previously has recognized, and thereafter all additional partnership items will be allocated equally between G and L. Finally, the partnership agreement specifies that G and L have equal interests in partnership profits for purposes of determining their share of partnership nonrecourse liabilities and at the time the partnership agreement is entered into there is a reasonable likelihood that over its life GL will recognize income and gain significantly in excess of the amount of loss and deduction it recognizes. Assume for simplicity that each year GL's business operations break even (cash income equals cash expense), except that it also has $50,000 of cost recovery deductions.

The $800,000 partnership liability is a nonrecourse liability because no partner bears the economic risk of loss. At the end of each of GL's first four years, the nonrecourse liability will be allocated equally between G and L ($400,000 to each) because the partnership agreement provision so directing is reasonably consistent with the equal division of partnership income and gain that is required once cumulative income and gain exceeds cumulative loss and deduction. See Reg. § 1.704–2(m) Example (1)(ii) & (iii).

At the end of GL's fifth year there is $50,000 of partnership minimum gain ($800,000 nonrecourse liability less property's $750,000 adjusted basis) and G's and L's shares will be $5,000 and $45,000, respectively. The $800,000 nonrecourse liability will be allocated to the partners first according to their shares of minimum gain and any excess will be allocated equally according to the provision in the partnership agreement. Thus, at the end of year five, G's and L's shares of nonrecourse liabilities are $380,000 ($5,000 share of partnership minimum gain plus $375,000 share of the excess) and $420,000 ($45,000 share of minimum gain plus $375,000 share of excess), respectively. See generally, Reg. § 1.752–3(b) Example (1).

Example (2)
(Allocation
Upon
Contribution
of Property
Encumbered
by Nonrecourse
Liability):

B and C form a general partnership to operate residential rental property. B contributes $500,000 cash to the partnership and C contributes an apartment building with a fair market value of $1,200,000 and a $520,000 adjusted basis. The apartment building contributed by C is subject to a $700,000 nonrecourse loan. It is expected that B will actively manage the partnership and B and C agree to share all partnership profits and losses equally.

The liability encumbering the apartment building will be a nonrecourse liability of the partnership because no partner bears the economic risk of loss for the liability. Under § 752(c) the partnership is considered to have assumed the liability upon C's contribution of the building to the partnership. As a result of this assumption, C's individual liabilities decrease by $700,000.

The partners' shares of nonrecourse liabilities will be determined under Reg. § 1.752–3. First, partnership minimum gain is computed using the apartment building's book value rather than its tax basis. Reg. § 1.704–2(d)(3). Thus, because the book value ($1,200,000) exceeds the amount of the nonrecourse liability ($700,000), there is no partnership minimum gain.

Under Reg. § 1.752–3(a)(2) a partner's share of the nonrecourse liabilities next includes the amount of taxable gain that would be allocated to the contributing partner under § 704(c) if the partnership, in a taxable transaction, disposed of the contributed property in full satisfaction of the nonrecourse liability and for no other consideration. If BC sold the apartment building in full satisfaction of the liability and for no other consideration it would recognize a $180,000 taxable gain ($700,000 amount of the nonrecourse liability over $520,000 adjusted basis). The hypothetical sale would also result in a $500,000 book loss to BC (excess of $1,200,000 book value over $700,000 amount of nonrecourse liability). Under the partnership agreement, the book loss would be allocated equally between B and C. Because B receives a $250,000 book loss and no corresponding tax loss, the hypothetical sale would result in a $250,000 disparity between B's book and tax allocations.

If BC used the traditional method of making § 704(c) allocations, C would be allocated a total of $180,000 of taxable gain from the hypothetical sale of the contributed property. Therefore, C would be allocated $180,000 of nonrecourse liabilities under the regulations. If BC adopted the remedial allocation method of making § 704(c) allocations, it would make a remedial allocation of $250,000 of loss to B to eliminate the $250,000 disparity between B's book and tax allocations. BC would also be required to make an offsetting remedial allocation of tax gain to C of $250,000. Thus, C would be allocated a total of $430,000 of tax gain ($180,000 of actual gain to C plus $250,000 allocation of remedial gain) from the hypothetical sale. Therefore, if BC adopts the remedial allocation method, C would be allocated $430,000 of nonrecourse liabilities immediately after the contribution. If BC uses the traditional method with curative allocations to reduce or eliminate the difference between B's book and tax allocations, the IRS takes the position that curative allocations to C are not taken into account in allocating nonrecourse liabilities because such allocations can not be determined solely from the hypothetical sale of the apartment building. Rev. Rul. 95–41, 1995–1 C.B. 132. Thus, under the traditional method with curative allocations, C would be allocated $180,000 of nonrecourse liabilities immediately after the contribution.

Finally, under the regulations, the remaining nonrecourse liabilities ($520,000 under the traditional method and the traditional method with curative allocations; $270,000 under the remedial method) are allocated between B and C in accordance with their shares in partnership profits. The partner's interests in partnership profits is determined by taking into account all facts and circumstances relating to the economic arrangement of the partners. The partnership agreement also may specify the partner's interests in profits for purposes of determining their shares of nonrecourse liabilities as long as the interests are reasonably consistent with allocations of some other significant item of partnership income or gain. Alternatively, the partners may agree to allocate the remaining nonrecourse liabilities in the manner in which it is reasonably expected that the deductions attributable to the excess nonrecourse liabilities will be allocated. Additionally, the partnership could allocate the remaining nonrecourse liabilities to C, up to the amount of built-in gain that is allocable to C in excess of the gain resulting from the liability exceeding the property's basis.

In this example, the partnership agreement provides that each partner will be allocated 50 percent of all partnership items. Assuming that those allocations have substantial economic effect, BC could choose to allocate the additional nonrecourse liabilities 50 percent to each partner. Alternatively, if the partners agreed to allocate the additional nonrecourse liabilities in the manner in which it is reasonably expected that the deductions attributable to those liabilities will be allocated, all the remaining liabilities would be allocated to B. As 50 percent partners, B and C would each be allocated $600,000 of book depreciation over the life of the apartment building. However, because the apartment building only has a $520,000 adjusted basis, the entire $520,000 of tax depreciation over the life of the property must be allocated to B. Therefore, BC must allocate all of the excess liabilities to B if it chooses to allocate the excess nonrecourse liabilities in accordance with the manner that the deductions attributable to the excess nonrecourse liabilities will be allocated. See Rev. Rul. 95–41, 1995–1 C.B. 132. The partnership also could allocate the remaining nonrecourse liabilities to C, up to the amount of built-in gain that is allocable to C in excess of the gain resulting from the liability exceeding the property's basis. There is $680,000 of total § 704(c) gain allocable to C [$680,000 tax gain ($1,200,000 amount realized less $520,000 adjusted basis) and zero book gain ($1,200,000 amount realized less $1,200,000 book value)]. Thus, there is $500,000 of total § 704(c) gain in excess of the gain resulting from the liability exceeding the property's basis ($680,000 of total § 704(c) gain less $180,000 of gain from the liability exceeding the property's basis). Up to $500,000 of the remaining nonrecourse liability could be allocated to C under this provision.

C's individual liabilities decrease by $700,000. Once C's increase in partnership liabilities is determined, the net decrease is taken into account under § 752. Reg. § 1.752–1(f). The net decrease will be treated as a distribution of money which reduces C's outside basis. See §§ 731; 733.

5. Allocations Where Partners' Interests Vary During The Year
a. Introduction

The taxable year of a partnership generally does not close as a result of shifts during the year in the partners' interests in the partnership. For example, if a partner dies, a new partner enters the partnership, or a partner disposes of part of her partnership interest through a gift or sale, the partnership's taxable year closes at its normal time and the partners include their distributive share of partnership items at that time. § 706(c)(1), (2) (B). If, however, there are changes during the year in any partner's interest in the partnership (by entry of a new partner, partial liquidation of the partner's interest, gift or otherwise),

§ 706(d)(1) requires that each partner's distributive share of partnership items be determined by taking into account the partners' varying interests in the partnership during the year. The varying interest rule in § 706(d)(1), however, applies only if there is some shift in the capital interests of the partners. If the capital interests of the partners do not shift during the year, the partners are free at year end to amend the partnership agreement and reallocate profits and losses. §§ 704(a); 761(c). When there is a change in a partner's capital interest in the partnership, the regulations permit the distributive shares of the partners to be determined by either (1) prorating partnership items over the year as if they were earned or incurred ratably, or (2) through an interim closing of the partnership's books in which the items of income and deduction are allocated to different segments of the year under the partnership's accounting method. Cf. Reg. § 1.706–1(c)(3)(ii).

Example: Assume Nupartner joins a partnership as a one-fourth partner on July 1 of the current year. Under § 706(d)(1) all of the partners' distributive shares must be determined by taking into account their varying interests during the year. Under the proration method, Nupartner would be allocated one-half of his hypothetical one-fourth share of partnership items for the full year. Under the interim closing of the books method, Nupartner would be allocated one-fourth of the partnership items properly allocated to the July 1 to December 31 period under the partnership's method of accounting.

b. § 706(d)(2): Distributive Shares of Allocable Cash Basis Items

To prevent cash method partnerships from using the interim closing of the books method to shift deductions to partners entering the partnership at or near year end, § 706(d)(2)(A) requires that, if there is a change in any partner's interest in the partnership, each partner's distributive share of any "allocable cash basis item" must be determined on a per-day, per-partner basis. This requirement effectively puts cash method partnerships on the accrual method of accounting for allocable cash basis items, which are defined as interest, taxes, payments for services or the use of property, and any other item identified in regulations by the Service. § 706(d)(2)(B).

Example: Nupartner joins a cash method partnership as a 50% partner on December 31 of the current year. Late in the afternoon of December 31, the partnership pays $100,000 of interest which is the annual payment on a partnership loan. Under the interim closing of the books method of allocation Nupartner could have been allocated one-half of the $100,000 interest deduction. Under § 706(d)(2)(A) Nupartner will be allocated one-half of 1/365th of the $100,000 interest deduction.

If an allocable cash basis item is attributable to a prior year (e.g., rental paid for property used in the preceding year), it is assigned to the first day of the taxable year in which it is paid. § 706(d)(2)(C)(i). It is then allocated among the partners who were partners in such prior year in proportion to their varying interests in the partnership for that period. Amounts which are allocable under this rule to persons who are no longer partners must be capitalized as part of the bases of partnership assets. § 706(d)(2)(D). If an allocable cash basis item is attributable to a period after the close of the taxable year (e.g., prepaid rent for the next year), it is assigned to the last day of the taxable year in which it is paid and allocated to the partners in accordance with their proportionate interests on that date. § 706(d)(2)(C)(ii).

> *Example:*   Assume the ABCD equal partnership fails to pay $40,000 of rental expense in year one. On December 31 of year one, A sells her 25% interest in the partnership to B so that beginning in year two B owns 50% of the partnership and C and D each own 25%. If the partnership pays the $40,000 of rental expense in year two, B, C and D will each be allocated $10,000 of the deduction (corresponding to their 25% interests in year one). A cannot be allocated a share of the year two expenditure since she is no longer a partner. Her $10,000 share of the rental expense will be capitalized and added to the bases of partnership assets under the rules in § 755. See XVIII.C.2.b.2., at page 433, *infra.*

c.   Tiered Partnerships

The potential exists for these rules to be avoided by using tiers of partnerships. For example, a business could be operated in a partnership (the "lower-tier" partnership) which has other partnerships ("upper-tier" partnerships) as its partners. Changes in ownership of upper-tier partnerships would not alter ownership of the lower-tier partnerships and would not be subject to § 706(d). In order to prevent easy avoidance of the varying interest and allocable cash basis item rules in § 706(d), if there is a change in any partner's interest in an upper-tier partnership then the distributive shares of the partners in the upper-tier partnership attributable to a lower-tier partnership must be determined on a per-day, per-partner basis. § 706(d)(3).

D.   Transactions Between Partners And Partnerships

1.   Transactions Involving Services Or The Use Of Property

A partner and a partnership may engage in a wide variety of transactions. One may perform services, loan funds, lease or sell property, etc., to the other. Section 707(a)(1) generally adopts an entity theory for determining the tax consequences of transactions between a partner and a partnership by providing that if a partner engages in a transaction with a partnership "other than in his capacity as a member of such partnership," the transaction is to be taxed as if it occurred between the partnership and a nonpartner unless § 707 provides otherwise. The key question under § 707(a)(1) is whether the partner is engaging in the transaction in an independent, nonpartner capacity. The regulations offer little guidance concerning how to make this determination, stating only that "the substance of the transaction will govern rather than its form." Reg. § 1.707–1(a). In the area of services, the courts have held that when partners perform "basic duties" or "services within the normal scope of their duties as general partners" pursuant to the partnership agreement, they are acting in their capacity as partners. *Pratt v. Comm'r*, 64 T.C. 203 (1975), aff'd in part, 550 F.2d 1023 (5th Cir.1977); but see *Armstrong v. Phinney*, 394 F.2d 661 (5th Cir.1968) (holding that a partner providing services may qualify as an "employee" for purposes of the § 119 exclusion for meals and lodging provided by an employer). Thus, nonpartner status is more likely to be found if the partner performs limited consultant-type services as an independent contractor, such as acting as the partnership's lawyer or accountant. Classifying a payment as being between the partnership and a nonpartner may affect the character and timing of income and deductions arising from the transaction.

Example: Assume the ABC partnership has $150,000 of bottom line income and $50,000 of long-term capital gain for the year. If A receives $50,000 for performing services for the partnership, plus one-third of any remaining partnership income, the classification of A's services will affect the tax results to A and the remaining partners. If the $50,000 is an allocation of partnership income, A will be taxed on $100,000 of partnership income ($50,000 plus one-third of the remaining $150,000 of partnership income), consisting of $75,000 of ordinary income and $25,000 of long-term capital gain, in the year in which the partnership's taxable year ends. § 706(a). The distributive shares of the remaining partners, B and C, would be proportionately reduced to $50,000 each, consisting of $37,500 of ordinary income and $12,500 of long-term capital gain. If the $50,000 paid to A is a § 707(a) payment because the services were performed in a nonpartner capacity, A would have $50,000 of ordinary income under § 61 upon receipt of the payment, assuming A is a cash method taxpayer. Assuming the partnership uses the cash method and the payment for A's services is currently deductible, A, B, and C would be taxed on their one-third distributive shares of the partnership's remaining $100,000 of net income ($150,000 less the $50,000 deduction for A's services) and $50,000 of long-term capital gain. Thus, each would include $33,333 of ordinary income and $16,666 of long-term capital gain. If the payment to A had to be capitalized by the partnership, A, B, and C would be taxed on their one-third distributive shares of $150,000 of net income and $50,000 of long-term capital gain. If the partnership uses the accrual method of accounting and A is a cash method taxpayer, no deduction would be allowed to the partnership for the services until it pays the $50,000 to A. § 267(a), (e).

2. § 707(a)(2)(A): Disguised Payments for Services or Property
a. Introduction

If a § 707(a)(1) payment made by a partnership to a partner is capital in nature (e.g., a payment to a partner for drafting the partnership agreement and other organizational documents), the partnership must treat the payment in the same manner as a capital expenditure made to a nonpartner. The expense must be capitalized and, if permitted, deducted or amortized over the applicable recovery period. A distributive share allocated to a partner, on the other hand, has the same impact as an immediate deduction on the distributive shares of the other partners. This difference in tax treatment provides an incentive for a partnership to compensate a partner who provides services or property which are capital in nature with a special allocation of partnership income rather than a § 707(a)(1) payment.

Example: Partner A plans to lease equipment to the ABC partnership for five years at an annual $10,000 rental fee. If the partnership pays A the full $50,000 five-year rental fee in the first year, A will have $50,000 of income and the partnership will have to capitalize the $50,000 expenditure and deduct it at the rate of $10,000 per year. Alternatively, if the partnership could give a $50,000 special allocation of gross income in the first year, that allocation would have the same effect as an immediate $50,000 deduction in that it would reduce the distributive shares of the other partners.

Section 707(a)(2)(A) prevents this strategy from being successful by providing that a direct or indirect allocation and distribution received by a partner for services or property will be treated as a § 707(a)(1) payment if the performance of services (or transfer of property) and the allocation and distribution, when viewed together, are properly characterized as a transaction between the partnership and a nonpartner. An allocation recharacterized under § 707(a)(2)(A) as a § 707(a)(1) payment is then analyzed to make certain that the partnership is entitled to an immediate deduction.

The legislative history makes it clear that, in enacting § 707(a)(2)(A), Congress did not intend to reverse the general rule in § 721. Partners can still contribute property to a partnership and receive a share of profits on a tax-free basis. Section 707(a)(2)(A) is targeted at a more limited category of transactions and the legislative history lists six factors which help to determine whether a partner is receiving an allocation and distribution as a partner.

b. 707(a)(2)(A) Factors

The six factors listed in the legislative history are: (1) risk as to amount of the payment to the partner; (2) transitory status of the partner; (3) closeness in time between the allocation and distribution and the performance of services or transfer of property; (4) whether the recipient of the allocation and distribution became a partner primarily to obtain tax benefits which would not have been available if he had acted in a nonpartner capacity; (5) in a service context, whether the value of the partner's continuing profits interest is small in comparison to the allocation being tested (a substantial continuing interest, however, does not suggest that the allocation should be recognized); and (6) in connection with property transfers, whether the § 704(b) capital account requirements are respected. The legislative history also invited the Treasury to describe other relevant factors.

Example: A number of individuals wish to form a limited partnership. Attorney will do the legal work for the partnership and normally charges $1,500 for such services. Attorney contributes cash for a 10% interest in the partnership and receives both a 10% distributive share of net income for the life of the partnership and an allocation of the first $1,500 of the partnership's gross income in its first year of operation. The partnership expects to have sufficient cash in its first year to distribute $1,500 to Attorney.

It is likely that the $1,500 allocation and distribution will be recharacterized under § 707(a)(2)(A) as a § 707(a)(1) payment. When recharacterized the payment will be subject to the rules relating to organization and syndication expenses in § 709. Key factors in recharacterizing the allocation and distribution are: (1) the allocation is fixed in amount and it is likely the partnership will have the gross income and cash to pay Attorney, and (2) the distribution is close in time to Attorney's performance of services.

In the legislative history, Congress specifically stated that it was concerned with allocations to pay organization or syndication expenses. If Attorney were a partner for only one year or had a very small partnership interest (e.g., 1%), those would be additional factors indicating that the allocation and distribution were not made to Attorney in a partner capacity.

3. Guaranteed Payments
a. Introduction

Fixed payments to a partner for services performed as a partner or as a return on contributed capital are guaranteed payments taxable under § 707(c).

Example: Partner A provides ongoing management services to the ABC limited partnership. The ABC partnership agreement provides that A will be paid $40,000 each year for these services. The ABC partnership agreement also provides that each limited partner annually will be paid a 10% return on the partner's capital account balance. The $40,000 payment to A and the 10% return paid to the limited partners on their capital account balances are § 707(c) guaranteed payments. These amounts are not § 707(a)(1) payments because A's services are performed as a partner and the 10% return is paid on contributed (not loaned) capital. The payments also are not distributive shares because they are "guaranteed," that is, not contingent on partnership profits.

A guaranteed payment produces § 61 ordinary income and is includible by a partner in the taxable year in which the partnership's taxable year ends. §§ 706(a); 707(c). Because a partner must include a guaranteed payment in income even if it has not been received, the partner should receive an upward adjustment in the outside basis of his partnership interest when the guaranteed payment is included and a downward adjustment when it is paid. *Gaines v. Comm'r*, 45 T.C.M. 363 (1982). On the partnership side, a guaranteed payment is potentially deductible under § 162, subject to the capitalization requirement of § 263. Thus, a guaranteed payment to a partner which is capital in nature will produce ordinary income to the partner and either no deduction or deferred deductions to the partnership. A guaranteed payment generally is treated as a distributive share for purposes of other Code provisions. The regulations, however, provide that a guaranteed payment is not considered to be an interest in partnership profits for purposes of § 706(b)(3) (partner's interests for selecting a taxable year), § 707(b) (disallowing losses and recharacterizing gains on sales of property), and § 708(b) (termination of partnership by sale or exchange of partnership interests). Reg. § 1.707–1(c).

b.   Calculation of Guaranteed Payments

Example (1):   Partner A in the AB partnership is to receive $30,000 for deductible services, plus 50% of any partnership income or loss. After deducting the $30,000 payment to A the partnership has a $20,000 loss. A will report $30,000 of ordinary income plus her $10,000 distributive share of partnership loss. If the partnership also had a $6,000 long-term capital gain, that item would be separately stated and A also would include a $3,000 distributive share of the gain.

Example (2):   Partner C in the CD partnership is to receive 40% of partnership income but not less than $25,000. If partnership income is $100,000, C will receive a $40,000 distributive share (40% of $100,000), none of which is a guaranteed payment. If partnership income were $50,000 instead of $100,000, C's distributive share would be $20,000 (40% of $50,000) and the remaining $5,000 payable to C would be a guaranteed payment.

Example (3):   Partner E in the EF partnership is to receive 40% of partnership income but not less than $90,000. For the taxable year the partnership's income before taking into account any guaranteed amount is $150,000, consisting of $110,000 of ordinary income and $40,000 of long-term capital gain. E's guaranteed payment is $30,000 ($90,000 guaranteed amount less $60,000 distributive share (40% of $150,000 of partnership income)). After taking into account E's guaranteed payment, the taxable income of the partnership is $120,000

($80,000 of ordinary income and $40,000 of long-term capital gain). E's distributive share of that income under the partnership agreement is $60,000 and F's is also $60,000. Hence, the effective profit sharing ratio is 50/50 for the year and both E and F will have distributive shares of $40,000 of partnership ordinary income and $20,000 of long-term capital gain. In addition, E will have $30,000 of ordinary income as a result of the guaranteed payment.

4. Sales and Exchanges Between Partners and Partnerships
a. General Rules

Under § 707(a)(1), a sale of property between a partner and a partnership generally is treated in the same manner as a sale between the partnership and a nonpartner. A number of provisions are designed to prevent tax avoidance through transactions between related parties. Section 707(b)(1) disallows losses on sales or exchanges of property between a partnership and a partner who owns, directly or indirectly, more than 50% of the capital or profits interests of the partnership. Losses are also disallowed on sales or exchanges between two partnerships in which the same persons own, directly or indirectly, more than 50% of the capital and profits interests. Under § 707(b)(2) and § 1239, gain on the sale or exchange of property between a partner and a controlled (i.e., more than 50% owned) partnership or between two controlled partnerships is characterized as ordinary income if the property: (1) is not a capital asset in the hands of the transferee or (2) is depreciable in the hands of the transferee. For purposes of § 707(b) and § 1239, ownership interests are tested taking into account the attribution rules in § 267(c), other than § 267(c)(3) (which would attribute each partner's interest to the other partners). §§ 707(b)(3); 1239(c)(2). To prevent manipulation of the installment sales, the second disposition rules in § 453(e) and the rules relating to sales of depreciable property in § 453(g) apply to certain partner/partnership transactions. See §§ 453(e); (f)(1); (g)(1), (3).

b. § 707(a)(2)(B): Disguised Sales Between Partners and Partnerships

Section 707(a)(2)(B) is designed to prevent sales of property between a partner and partnership from being structured as nontaxable contributions and distributions under §§ 721 and 731. The section provides that if there are direct or indirect transfers of money and property between a partner and a partnership and the transfers, when viewed together, are properly characterized as a sale or exchange of property, then the transfers are to be treated as a sale or exchange between the partner and partnership (or between two partners). Under the regulations, transfers of property and money constitute a sale if based on all the facts and circumstances the transfer of money would not have been made but for the transfer of property and, in the case of transfers that are not simultaneous, the subsequent transfer is not dependent on the entrepreneurial risks of the partnership. Reg. § 1.707–3(b)(1). The legislative history states that closeness in time between the "contribution" and "distribution" is a key factor and the regulations have adopted a presumption that contributions and distributions within two years of one another are related. Reg. § 1.707–3(c)(1). Transfers more than two years apart are presumed not to be related. Reg. § 1.707–3(d). Either presumption may be rebutted. Transfers of property by a partner and transfers of money or other consideration by the partnership to that partner within two years before or after the transfer of property must be reported to the Service if the partner does not treat the transfer as a sale. Reg. § 1.707–3(c)(2). The regulations also provide that the disguised sale rules apply to situations where the transferor partner receives the proceeds of certain loans secured by the property (such as by borrowing against the property on the eve of contribution) and responsibility for repaying the loan rests with the partnership. Reg. § 1.707–5(a)(1). Loans incurred within two years of transferring the property to the partnership generally are presumed to be in anticipation of the transfer. Reg. § 1.707–5(a)(7). The partnership's assumption of a loan incurred more than two years before the transfer of property is disregarded in determining whether the transfer is a sale. Reg. § 1.707–5(a)(5), (6). See Reg. § 1.707–5(f) Example 5.

E.   Family Partnerships

Section 704(e) largely codifies the assignment of income principles studied in individual income tax. Its purpose is to prevent the shifting of income among partners who are not dealing at arm's length, such as family members. Section 704(e)(1) provides a safe harbor for establishing the existence of a partnership and partner status by providing that any person owning a capital interest in a partnership in which capital is a material income-producing factor shall be recognized as a partner even if the interest was received as a gift. If the test in § 704(e)(1) cannot be satisfied (e.g., because capital is not a material income-producing factor), the parties may still establish the existence of a partnership by showing a bona fide intent to conduct an enterprise as partners. *Comm'r v. Culbertson,* 337 U.S. 733, 69 S.Ct. 1210 (1949). Under § 704(e)(2), when a partnership interest is created by gift (from a family member or otherwise), the donee's distributive share must be determined by adequately compensating the donor for any services and compensating the donor for contributed capital at a rate not less than the rate of return on the donee's capital. This rule also applies to partnership interests purchased from a family member. The "family" of an individual include only his spouse, ancestors, lineal descendants, and trusts for the primary benefit of such persons. § 704(e)(3).

Example: Mother owns $500,000 of securities which she contributes to a partnership in which she is an equal partner with Daughter, who provides no capital for her one-half interest in the partnership. The income from the partnership is $75,000. Under § 704(e)(1) Daughter will be recognized as a partner in the partnership and her distributive share must be determined so as to adequately compensate Mother. § 704(e)(2). If, for example, Mother provides investment services to the partnership worth $15,000, an allocation of partnership profits which did not compensate her for those services (e.g., $37,500 of profits to both Mother and Daughter) would not be respected. An allocation which did not compensate Mother for her partnership capital at the same rate as Daughter also would not be respected. The same analysis would apply if Daughter purchased her partnership interest from Mother for $250,000. § 704(e)(3).

F. Review Questions

1. The ABC equal partnership owns a swimming facility which has derived 50% of its income in July and August for the last three years. A and B use a November 30 fiscal year, while C uses a calendar year. What taxable year may the partnership adopt?

2. When computing its taxable income, which of the following items must the ABC partnership separately state? What is ABC's nonseparately computed, or bottom line, income?

Gross Business Revenue	$200,000
Salary Expense	$ 20,000
Depreciation Expense	$ 8,000
Interest Income	$ 15,000
§ 1231 Loss	$ 10,000
Gain from Sale of Machine (§ 1245)	$ 25,000
Charitable Contributions	$ 10,000
Maintenance Expense	$ 14,000

3. Elections impacting the determination of taxable income are made on a partner-by-partner basis. True or False?

4. A and B contribute $20,000 each to form the AB partnership and agree to share profits and losses 80% to A and 20% to B. AB's partnership items for the year are as follows:

Long-term Capital Gain	$20,000
Tax–Exempt Interest	$16,000
Nonseparately Computed Income	$24,000

(a) What is A's portion of partnership income for the year?

(b) What is A's outside basis at the beginning of the next year?

5. A and B form the AB partnership by contributing $10,000 each. A and B agree to share profits and losses 75% to A, 25% to B. In Year 1 of operations, AB had business revenues of $10,000, business expenses of $14,000 and a short-term capital loss of $12,000. What are the tax results to A and B?

6. A and B form the AB equal general partnership. A contributes $10,000 cash and a depreciable asset with an adjusted basis of $40,000 and a fair market value of $90,000. B contributes $50,000 cash and a parcel of land with an adjusted basis of $70,000 and a fair market value of $50,000.

   (a) What are A and B's outside bases?

   (b) What is the balance in A's and B's capital accounts at formation?

7. A and B form the AB partnership with each contributing $50,000. The partners agree to comply with The Big Three and to share profits and losses equally. At the beginning of Year 1, AB purchases a $50,000 depreciable asset. Assume the property is depreciated over five years under the straight line method. Per the partnership agreement, A is allocated all the cost recovery deductions. Assume AB breaks even each year except for $10,000 of cost recovery. If AB sells the property at the end of Year 3 for $20,000 and immediately liquidates, how must the proceeds be distributed to qualify under The Big Three?

8. Can an allocation that does not have economic effect be cured by state law?

9. A and B form the AB partnership with each contributing $50,000. A and B agree to comply with The Big Three. AB purchases $50,000 of stock and $50,000 of tax-exempt bonds and there is a strong likelihood the stock and bonds will produce approximately equal amounts of dividend income and tax-exempt interest. In Year 1, A expects to be in a higher marginal tax bracket than B. A and B agree that in Year 1 the tax-exempt interest will be allocated 90% to A, 10% to B and the dividend income will be allocated 10% to A and 90% to B.

   (a) Does this allocation have substantial economic effect?

   (b) If AB receives $10,000 of tax-exempt interest and $5,000 of dividends in Year 1, and the allocation does *not* have substantial economic effect, how will the amounts be reallocated to A and B?

10. A and B form the AB equal general partnership. A contributes $50,000 cash and a parcel of land with a fair market value of $50,000 and an adjusted basis of $20,000, while B contributes $100,000 cash. A and B agree to comply with The Big Three, to share all profits and losses equally, and to use the traditional method in making § 704(c) allocations.

    (a) If AB sells the parcel of land for $70,000, what are the tax consequences to A and B?

    (b) If AB sells the parcel of land for $40,000, what are the tax consequences to A and B?

11. A and B form the AB equal general partnership. A contributes $50,000 cash and a depreciable asset with a fair market value of $50,000 and an adjusted basis of

$20,000. Assume the property is depreciable by the partnership over five years under the straight line method. B contributes $100,000 cash. A and B agree to comply with The Big Three, to share all profits and losses equally, and to use the traditional method in making § 704(c) allocations.

(a) What is the amount of depreciation in Year 1 for book purposes and for tax purposes?

(b) How is the depreciation allocated between A and B?

(c) What are A's and B's outside bases in their partnership interests at the end of Year 1? Assume that AB breaks even except for cost recovery deductions.

(d) What are the balances in A's and B's capital accounts at the end of Year 1? Assume that AB breaks even except for cost recovery deductions.

12. If A contributes accounts receivable with a fair market value of $50,000 and zero adjusted basis to a partnership, what are the tax consequences to A in the following circumstances?

(a) The partnership sells the receivables in Year 1 for $50,000?

(b) The partnership sells the receivables in Year 6 for $50,000?

13. If A, a car dealer, contributes cars with a fair market value of $100,000 and an adjusted basis of $60,000 to the ABC partnership, what are the tax consequences to A under the following circumstances:

(a) If ABC (not in the car business) sells the cars for $100,000 in Year 1?

(b) If ABC (not in the car business) sells the cars for $100,000 in Year 6?

14. A and B form the AB equal general partnership. A contributes $100,000 of cash and B contributes property with a $160,000 fair market value, $20,000 adjusted basis and subject to a $60,000 nonrecourse loan. The AB partnership agreement complies with The Big Three, provides that the partners share profits and losses equally, and uses the traditional method to make § 704(c) allocations. What are A and B's outside bases in their partnership interests?

15. D joins the ABC partnership as a one-quarter partner on July 1. If the partnership has income of $36,000 for the year and the partners use a proration method of allocation, how will the income be allocated to A, B, C and D?

16. A, a cash method taxpayer, contributes $25,000 to the ABCD partnership for a one-quarter partnership interest. A also contributes the use of office space for five years in a building owned by A to the partnership in exchange for a special allocation of the first $30,000 of partnership gross income. How will the $30,000 allocation most likely be treated for tax purposes?

*

XVIII

SALES AND EXCHANGES OF PARTNERSHIP INTERESTS

Analysis

A. Introduction

Under general tax principles, a taxpayer's gain or loss on a sale or other disposition of property is equal to the difference between the amount realized on the sale and the taxpayer's adjusted basis for the property. § 1001. The character of gain or loss depends on the nature of the property (is it a capital asset?) and the type of disposition (is it a sale or exchange?) §§ 64; 1221; 1222. A purchaser of property generally takes a cost basis. § 1012.

These same principles generally apply to sales and exchanges of partnership interests. A partnership interest is treated as a capital asset. A selling partner's capital gain or loss is the difference between the amount realized on a sale of the interest and the partner's outside basis at the time of sale. To prevent partners from converting ordinary income into capital gain, however, Subchapter K modifies this general rule by carving up the transaction and treating a partner as having sold her share of certain "ordinary income" assets held by the partnership.

A hybrid approach also is used on the buying partner's side of the transaction. The buyer's outside basis is her cost of acquiring the interest. If the partnership makes an election, the buying partner's personal inside basis in each of the partnership's assets may be adjusted to reflect more accurately the price that she paid for her partnership interest.

This chapter examines the interaction between the Code's basic structure for taxing property dispositions and the rules in Subchapter K specifically applicable to sales and exchanges of partnership interests.

B. Tax Consequences to the Selling Partner

1. Computation of Gain or Loss

A selling partner first must determine the amount realized on a sale or exchange of his partnership interest and the adjusted basis of the interest to determine the gain or loss recognized on the transaction.

a. Amount Realized

A partner's amount realized is the sum of the cash and the fair market value of any property received for the interest. § 1001(b). In addition, § 752(d) and the principles of the *Crane* case require the selling partner to include relief from her share of any partnership liabilities in the amount realized.

b. Adjusted Basis of Partnership Interest

The selling partner's adjusted basis for her partnership interest is her outside basis determined under § 705(a) (see XVII.B.2.b., at page 365, *supra*), adjusted to reflect her share of partnership income or loss for that part of the partnership's taxable year up to the sale. Although the taxable year of a partnership generally does not close as a result of partner-level events (§ 706(c)(1)), it does close with respect to a partner who sells or exchanges her entire interest in the partnership (§ 706(c)(2)(A)(i)). In that situation, the selling partner includes in income her distributive share of partnership items for the short taxable year, and they are reflected in her outside basis. The portion of the partnership's income attributable to the short taxable year may be determined either by an interim closing of the partnership books or, if the partners agree, by prorating the partnership's tax results over the year according to time or any other reasonable method. Reg. § 1.706–1(c)(2)(ii).

If a partner disposes of only a portion of her partnership interest, the taxable year of the partnership does not close even with respect to that partner. § 706(c)(2)(B). At the end of the year, however, the partners' distributive shares of partnership items must be determined by taking into account their varying interests in the partnership. § 706(d)(1). For purposes of determining gain or loss, the selling partner's outside basis also must be adjusted as of the date of the disposition. Reg. § 1.705–1(a)(1).

2. Characterization of Gain or Loss
a. General Rule: § 741
Section 741 provides that the gain or loss recognized from the sale or exchange of a partnership interest is capital gain or loss, except as otherwise provided in § 751. If § 751 applies, it overrides the general rule in § 741. Consequently, § 751 is the starting point in characterizing a partner's gain or loss from the sale of a partnership interest.

b. Definition of § 751 Assets
Section 751(a) provides that the consideration received by a selling partner in exchange for all or part of his interest in "unrealized receivables" or inventory items, shall be considered as an amount realized from the sale or exchange of property producing ordinary income rather than capital gain. In applying § 751(a), the critical questions are: (1) does the partnership have unrealized receivables or inventory items? and (2) if so, what portion of the selling partner's gain or loss is attributable to those assets?

1) Unrealized Receivables
Unrealized receivables are rights (contractual or otherwise) to payment for goods delivered, or to be delivered (to the extent sale of the property would produce ordinary income), and services rendered or to be rendered to the extent they have not previously been included in income under the partnership's accounting method. § 751(c)(1), (2). Unrealized receivables also include the gain that would be characterized as ordinary income on a disposition of an asset for fair market value under the depreciation recapture provisions (e.g., § 1245) and other rules requiring recapture of deductions. § 751(c).

The classic unrealized receivable is a cash method partnership's accounts receivable for services performed. A similar account receivable in the hands of an accrual method partnership would not be an unrealized receivable, however, because it would have been previously included in income. The courts have construed the term "unrealized receivables" broadly. Thus, a partnership's rights in a contract or agreement to earn ordinary income in the future generally will be considered an unrealized receivable. See, e.g., *Ledoux v. Comm'r,* 77 T.C. 293 (1981), aff'd per curiam, 695 F.2d 1320 (11th Cir.1983), where the Tax Court held that a management agreement under which a partnership had the right to manage a dog track for 20 years was an unrealized receivable.

2) Inventory Items

"Inventory items" are defined as all property of the partnership (including § 1221(1) "dealer" property) which if sold by the partnership or the selling partner would not be considered a capital or § 1231 asset. § 751(d)(1), (2), (4).

The definition of "inventory items" is broad enough to include all of a partnership's unrealized receivables since they are property which if sold by the partnership would produce ordinary income. Reg. § 1.751–1(d)(2)(ii). Even though an asset may be both an unrealized receivable and an inventory item, it will be taxed only once under § 751(a).

Example (1): Assume the ABCDE cash method, calendar year general partnership has the following balance sheet:

Assets	A.B.	F.M.V.
Cash	$ 5,000	$ 5,000
Accounts Receivable for Services	0	20,000
Dealer Property	12,500	15,000
Capital Asset	2,500	35,000
Building (no recapture)	80,000	100,000
	$100,000	$175,000

The accounts receivable are unrealized receivables. § 751(c)(2). The dealer property is an inventory item. § 751(d)(1). The accounts receivable are also considered inventory items but they are only counted once. Thus, both the accounts receivable and the dealer property are § 751 assets.

Example (2): If the dealer property in Example (1) were a capital asset to the partnership but would have produced ordinary income if sold by the selling partner (because she is a dealer in such property), it still would be an inventory item. § 751(d)(4).

Example (3): If the gain in the building in Example (1) were all § 1250 recapture income, that portion of the building would be considered a separate unrealized receivable with a $20,000 fair market value and a zero adjusted basis. Reg. § 1.751–1(c)(4), (5). The recapture gain also would be an inventory item.

Example (4): If the ABCDE general partnership in Example (1) used the accrual method of accounting, the accounts receivable would have been previously included in income and would not be unrealized receivables. The inventory items would still include the dealer property and the accounts receivable (which would have a $20,000 basis as a result of previously being included in income).

c. Computation of § 751 Gain or Loss

Once the partnership's unrealized receivables and inventory items are identified, the selling partner must determine the portions of the gain or loss characterized as ordinary under § 751(a) and capital under § 741. This is accomplished by first determining the amount of income or loss from § 751 property that would have been allocated to the selling partner if the partnership had sold all of its property in a fully taxable transaction for cash in an amount equal to the fair market value of such property. Reg. § 1.751–1(a)(2). Special allocations and allocations required under § 704(c) (including remedial allocations) are taken into account in determining the selling partner's share of income or loss from § 751 property in the hypothetical sale. Id. The gain or loss attributable to § 751 property is ordinary income or loss. The difference between the selling partner's total gain or loss and the § 751 gain or loss is § 741 capital gain or loss. It is possible for the selling partner to have a gain under § 751(a) and a loss under § 741 or vice versa. The long-term or short-term character of the § 741 portion of the sale will be determined with reference to the selling partner's holding period in the partnership interest.

Example (1): Assume the ABCDE cash method, calendar year general partnership has the following balance sheet:

Assets	A.B.	F.M.V.
Cash	$ 5,000	$ 5,000
Accounts Receivable for Services	0	20,000
Dealer Property	10,000	15,000
Capital Asset	5,000	35,000
Building (no recapture)	80,000	100,000
	$100,000	$175,000

If A sells her one-fifth partnership interest in which she has a $20,000 adjusted basis for $35,000 cash on January 1, A's total gain would be $15,000 ($35,000 amount realized less $20,000 adjusted basis). The accounts receivable and the dealer property are § 751 assets. The accounts receivable are unrealized receivables as well as inventory items and the dealer property is an inventory item. In a hypothetical sale of all the § 751 assets for cash equal to the fair market value of those assets, A would be allocated $5,000 of income ($4,000 from the accounts receivable and $1,000 from the dealer property). Thus, A has $5,000 of ordinary income under § 751(a). The difference between A's total gain ($15,000) and A's § 751(a) gain ($5,000) would be § 741 capital gain, long-term or short-term depending on A's holding period for her partnership interest.

Example (2):   If in Example (1) A's amount realized consisted of $25,000 cash and $10,000 of liability relief instead of $35,000 of cash, under § 752(d) her total amount realized would still be $35,000 and her tax results on the sale of her partnership interest would be the same.

Example (3):   If in Example (1) A sold her partnership interest for $15,000 cash instead of $35,000 because the capital asset and building were only worth a total of $35,000, the § 751 portion of the transaction does not change. A still has a $5,000 § 751 gain (the share of income she would be allocated from the accounts receivable and dealer property). Under § 741, the difference between A's $5,000 total loss ($15,000 amount realized less $20,000 adjusted basis) and her $5,000 § 751(a) ordinary income is $10,000, which is characterized as capital loss. This variation illustrates that a selling partner can have an overall loss on a sale of her partnership interest but still recognize ordinary income under § 751.

Example (4):   If in Example (1) A sold her entire partnership interest mid-year when her share of ABCDE income to that date was $5,000, the ABCDE taxable year will close with respect to A and she will include the $5,000 in income which will increase the basis of her partnership interest to $25,000. If the buyer now pays A $40,000 cash for her interest because he acquires her right to the $5,000, the results under § 751 and § 741 are the same. If only a portion of A's partnership interest were sold mid-year, ABCDE's taxable year would not close but a basis adjustment would have to be made to the interest sold to reflect ABCDE's tax results prior to the sale.

Example (5): If in Example (1) A had contributed the accounts receivable to the partnership when their fair market value was $20,000 and adjusted basis was zero, she would be allocated $21,000 of income on a hypothetical sale of the § 751 assets ($20,000 from the accounts receivable under § 704(c) and $1,000 from the dealer property). Thus, A would have $21,000 of ordinary income under § 751(a). Under § 741, the difference between A's total gain ($15,000) and her § 751(a) gain ($21,000) is $6,000, which is characterized as capital loss.

d. Capital Gains Look–Through Rules

The regulations apply a "look-through rule" for determining the character of gain or loss on sales or exchanges of interests in a partnership, an S corporation, or a trust. Reg. § 1.1(h)–1. Thus, a partner who sells a partnership interest held for more than one year may recognize § 751 ordinary income, collectibles gain (taxed at up to a 28% rate), unrecaptured § 1250 gain (taxed at up to a 25% rate), and residual capital gain (taxed at up to a 20% rate). Id. See §§ 1(h)(6), (7), (11), and (12). Any gain from a partnership interest held for more than one year that is (1) attributable to unrealized appreciation in the value of the partnership's collectibles is treated as gain from the sale or exchange of a collectible, and (2) attributable to unrecaptured § 1250 gain in the partnership's assets is treated as unrecaptured § 1250 gain. The selling partner's share of collectibles gain and unrecaptured § 1250 gain is determined under a hypothetical-sale approach where you ask: how much of each type of gain would the selling partner be allocated if the partnership transferred all of those assets in a fully taxable transaction for cash equal to the fair market value of the assets immediately before the transfer of the partnership interest? Reg. §§ 1.1(h)–1(b)(2)(ii), (3)(ii). This determination takes into account special allocations and § 704(c) allocations (including remedial allocations). The selling partner's share of residual capital gain is equal to the amount of the § 741 long-term capital gain or loss minus the partner's shares of collectibles and unrecaptured § 1250 gains. Reg. § 1.1(h)–1(c).

e. Holding Period

A partner's holding period in a partnership interest may be part long-term and part short-term. This could result from contributions of property made to the partnership during the prior year or because a portion of the partnership interest was purchased during the prior year. Reg. § 1.1223–3(a). If a partner sells a partnership interest with a divided holding period, any capital gain or loss must be divided between long-term and short-term capital gain or loss in the same proportion as the long-term and short-term holding periods for the partnership interest. Reg. 1.1223–3(c)(1), (2)(ii). To apply the capital gains look-through rule, the regulations first identify the portions of the selling partner's § 741 capital gain or loss that are long-term or short-term gain or loss. Then a proportionate amount of any collectibles or unrecaptured § 1250 gain is deemed to be part of the long-term capital gain or loss.

If a partner sells her partnership interest, some special rules may apply to determine the holding period for the interest. If a partner makes cash contributions to and receives cash distributions from the partnership during the one-year period before the sale of her partnership interest, the partner may reduce the cash contributions made during the year by the cash distributions on a last-in-first-out basis, generally treating all cash distributions as if they were made immediately before the sale or exchange. Reg. § 1.1223–3(b)(2); see Reg. § 1.1223–3(f) Example (3). Contributions of § 751 assets (§ 751(c) unrealized receivables and § 751(d) inventory items) within one year of a sale or exchange of partnership interest generally are disregarded for holding period purposes if the partner recognizes ordinary income or loss on such § 751 assets in a fully taxable transaction (e.g., on a sale of the partnership interest or a sale by the partnership of the contributed asset). Reg. § 1.1223–3(b)(4). Thus, a contribution of § 751 assets generally will not both produce ordinary income to the contributing partner and result in a short-term holding period.

Example (1): Assume the ABC cash method, calendar year general partnership has the following balance sheet. All partnership assets have been held long-term.

	A.B.	F.M.V.
Cash	$9,000	$9,000
Accounts Receivable	0	15,000
Capital Asset	15,000	39,000
	$24,000	$63,000

Assume A sells her one-third partnership interest in which she has an $8,000 adjusted basis for $21,000 cash on January 1 and A's holding period in the interest is 50% long-term and 50% short-term. A's total gain would be $13,000 ($21,000 amount realized less $8,000 adjusted basis). The accounts receivable are unrealized receivables and § 751 assets. In a hypothetical sale of the accounts receivable, A would be allocated $5,000 of income (one-third of $15,000). Thus, A has $5,000 of ordinary income under § 751(a). The $8,000 difference between A's total gain ($13,000) and A's § 751(a) gain ($5,000) would be § 741 capital gain. The § 741 capital gain would be 50% long-term capital gain ($4,000) and 50% short-term capital gain ($4,000).

Example (2): Assume that in Example (1) the capital asset is two capital assets. One is a collectible with a fair market value of $9,000 and a basis of $3,000 and the other is land with a fair market value of $30,000 and a basis of $12,000. Assume A's holding period is all long-term. A would again have the same § 751(a) and § 741 gains except that all of the § 741 capital gain would be long-term capital gain. In a hypothetical sale of all the collectibles for cash equal to the fair market value of the collectibles, A would be allocated $2,000 of collectibles gain (one-third of the $6,000 of collectibles gain). Therefore, A will recognize $2,000 of collectibles gain and $6,000 of residual long-term capital gain (the difference between $8,000 of § 741 long-term capital gain and A's $2,000 share of collectibles capital gain).

Example (3): If in Example (2) A's holding period for the partnership interest were 50% long-term and 50% short-term, then the gain attributable to the collectibles ($2,000) that is allocable to the portion of the interest sold with a long-term holding period is $1,000 (50% per holding period allocations). Thus, A would recognize $1,000 of collectibles gain, $3,000 of residual long-term capital gain, and $4,000 of short-term capital gain, in addition to $5,000 of § 751(a) ordinary income. See Reg. § 1.1(h)–1(f) Example 5.

Example (4): If collectibles held by the partnership have a built-in loss (i.e. the basis exceeds the fair market value of the collectibles), the loss in the collectibles is ignored and not recognized at the time of the transfer of the partnership interest. See Reg. § 1.1(h)–1(f) Example 3.

3. Related Issues
a. Installment Sale of a Partnership Interest

An installment sale of a partnership interest raises many issues if the partnership has assets which are not eligible for installment sale reporting treatment. For example, § 453 precludes installment reporting on the sale of assets such as publicly traded stock and personal property inventory, and recapture income may not be deferred under § 453. § 453(b)(2)(B), (i), (k)(2)(A). If a partner sells an interest in a partnership under the installment method, must the gain attributable to these types of assets be recognized immediately? Congress and the Service have begun to provide guidance on this issue. Section 453(i)(2) denies installment reporting for § 1245 and § 1250 recapture income in partnership property. Thus, a partner selling an interest in a partnership which has gain subject to recapture under these provisions must recognize the gain in the year of sale. The Service has ruled that the installment method also is not available for income attributable to inventory items which would not be eligible for installment reporting if sold directly. Rev.Rul. 89–108, 1989–2 C.B. 100. The ruling concludes that the portion of any gain on the sale of a partnership interest that is attributable to "Section 751 property" may be reported under the installment method only to the extent the income could have been reported under § 453 if the asset had been sold directly. An unrealized receivable other than § 1245 or § 1250 recapture income must be separately analyzed to determine whether it was eligible for installment reporting if sold directly.

b. Exchange or Conversion of Partnership Interests

1) Exchanges of Partnership Interests

   An exchange of partnership interests does not qualify for nonrecognition as a like-kind exchange. § 1031(a)(2)(D). This rule applies regardless of whether the interests exchanged are general or limited partnership interests, or interests in the same partnership or different partnerships. Reg. § 1.1031(a)–1(a)(1).

2) Conversions of Partnership Interests

   A conversion of a general partnership into a limited partnership, or vice versa, is governed by §§ 721 and 731, relating to contributions to and distributions from a partnership, and is not to be treated as an exchange of partnership interests. See Rev.Rul. 84–52, 1984–1 C.B. 157.

3) Conversions into LLC or LLP Interests

   The conversion of a domestic partnership into an interest in a domestic limited liability company that is classified as a partnership for tax purposes, or into a limited liability partnership, also is governed by §§ 721 and 731. Rev. Rul. 95–37, 1995–1 C.B. 130; Rev. Rul. 95–55, 1995–2 C.B. 313.

C. Tax Consequences to the Buying Partner

1. Introduction

The buyer of a partnership interest takes the interest with a cost basis. For this purpose, "cost" includes the buying partner's share of partnership liabilities attributable to the interest. §§ 742; 752(d); 1012.

At the partnership level, § 743(a) provides that the transfer of a partnership interest generally has no impact on the basis of partnership property. This rule produces distortions in the timing and character of the buying partner's income or loss. To help remedy these distortions a partnership may elect under § 754 to adjust the basis of its assets pursuant to § 743(b), which is considered below.

Example: Partner A purchases a 25% interest in a cash method partnership for $50,000, the fair market value of the interest. One of the partnership's assets is a $40,000 account receivable in which the partnership has a zero basis. In the absence of a § 754 election, if the partnership collects the receivable in a later year, A's distributive share will be $10,000 of ordinary income despite the fact that A, in effect, paid $10,000 for his share of that asset. A will receive a $10,000 upward adjustment in the basis of his partnership interest which will result in a loss or less income when he sells his interest or the partnership is liquidated. But those events may not occur for many years and the loss or income offset will be capital under § 741 despite the fact that the account receivable produced ordinary income.

2. Operation of § 743(b)
a. Requirement of § 754 Election

The inside basis adjustments under § 743(b) are made only if the partnership has made an election under § 754. Once made, the election applies to all subsequent taxable years of the partnership and may be revoked only with the Service's consent. A § 754 election also triggers the inside basis adjustments required by § 734 in the case of distributions of property by the partnership. See XIX.B.2., at page 445, *infra*.

b. Adjustments to Inside Basis Under § 743(b)
1) The Overall § 743(b) Adjustment

If a partnership has a § 754 election in effect, § 743(b) requires that if there is a sale or exchange of a partnership interest the partnership shall: (1) increase its inside basis by an amount equal to the excess of the buying partner's outside basis over his proportionate share of inside basis, or (2) decrease its inside basis by the excess of the buying partner's share of inside basis over his outside basis. The allocation of the total inside basis adjustment required under § 743(b) is made in accordance with the rules in § 755 and is personal to the buying partner, who will have a special basis for purposes of computing that partner's depreciation, depletion, gain or loss, and basis on distributions. § 743(c); Reg. § 1.743–1(j)(1).

The basic purpose of a § 743(b) inside basis adjustment is to give the purchasing partner the equivalent of a cost basis in his share of the partnership's assets. In a situation where there are no special allocations or § 704(c) allocations, the total amount of the § 743(b) adjustment generally is equal to the new partner's outside basis (e.g., a cost basis in the case of a purchased partnership interest or a date-of-death basis in the case of an inherited interest) and that partner's proportionate share of the partnership's inside basis. To accommodate special allocations and the complexities of § 704(c), the regulations provide a detailed formula for determining the transferee partner's share of the partnership's inside basis. Under the formula, a transferee partner's share of inside basis is equal to the sum of (1) the transferee's interest as a partner in the partnerships "previously taxed capital," plus (2) the transferee's share of partnership liabilities. The transferee partner's interest in the partnership's previously taxed capital is generally determined by considering a hypothetical, fully taxable, disposition of all the partnership's assets for cash equal to their fair market value. The transferee's interest in the partnership's previously taxed capital is equal to the cash the partner would receive on a liquidation following the hypothetical sale, increased by the amount of tax loss and decreased by the amount of tax gain that would be allocated to the transferee partner in the hypothetical sale. Reg. § 1.743–1(d)(1) and (2).

Example (1):   The ABC cash method, general partnership has a § 754
                 election in effect and the following balance sheet:

	A.B.	F.M.V.
Accounts Receivable	$ 0	$ 30,000
Capital Asset	45,000	60,000
Depreciable Business Property (no recapture)	105,000	150,000
	$150,000	$240,000

If Nupartner purchases A's one-third interest in the
partnership for $80,000 cash, her outside basis will be
$80,000. Under § 743(b), Nupartner's § 743(b) total
upward inside basis adjustment will be $30,000, the
difference between her $80,000 outside basis and her
$50,000 share of the partnership's inside basis. Under the
regulations, Nupartner's share of the partnership's inside
basis would equal her interest in the partnership's
previously taxed capital. If there were a hypothetical cash
disposition of all the partnership's assets, Nupartner
would receive $80,000 of cash on the liquidation of the
partnership. That amount is reduced by the $30,000 of tax
gain ($10,000 in the accounts receivable, $5,000 in the
capital asset, and $15,000 in the depreciable business
property) that would be allocated to Nupartner in the
hypothetical sale and liquidation. Thus, Nupartner's
interest in the partnership's previously taxed capital and
her share of the partnership's inside basis is $50,000.
Note that under the formula in the regulations,
Nupartner's share of the partnership's inside basis is
simply her one-third proportionate share of the $150,000
total inside basis. That is because there are no special or
§ 704(c) allocations in the example.

Example (2):   Assume that in Example (1) A contributed the accounts
                 receivable when they had a fair market value of $30,000
                 and a basis of zero. If Nupartner buys A's interest for
                 $80,000 cash, her outside basis is again $80,000. Under
                 § 743(b), Nupartner's § 743(b) total upward inside basis
                 adjustment will now be $50,000, the difference between
                 her $80,000 outside basis and her $30,000 share of the
                 partnership's inside basis. Under the regulations,
                 Nupartner's share of the partnership's inside basis would
                 equal her interest in the partnership's previously taxed
                 capital. Again, in a hypothetical sale of assets followed by
                 a liquidation of the partnership, Nupartner would receive

$80,000 cash. That amount is reduced by the $50,000 of tax gain ($30,000 in the accounts receivable, $5,000 in the capital asset, and $15,000 in the depreciable business property) that would be allocated to Nupartner in the hypothetical sale and liquidation. Nupartner, as a transferee of A steps into A's shoes with respect to the § 704(c) gain in the accounts receivable. Reg. 1.704–3(a)(7). Thus, Nupartner's interest in the partnership's previously taxed capital and her share of the partnership's inside basis in $30,000.

2) Allocation of the Adjustment

Section 755 and its regulations set out the process for allocating the total § 743(b) adjustment to the partnership's assets. First, the partnership's assets are divided into two classes: (1) capital assets and § 1231(b) property, and (2) all other partnership property. Then the allocation is made to each of the two classes and within each class based on the allocations of income, gain, or loss (including remedial allocations under § 704(c)) that the transferee partner would receive if, immediately after the transfer of the interest, all of the partnership's property were sold for cash equal to the fair market value of such property. Reg. § 1.755–1(b). The regulations specifically allow an increase to be made to one class of property while a decrease is made to the other class. Reg. § 1.755–1(b)(1). Also, an increase can be made in the basis of one asset in a class while a decrease is made to another asset in the class. Id. Basis is first allocated to the class of all other (i.e., ordinary income) property. Keep in mind that the goal of the allocation is to produce the equivalent of a cost basis for the purchasing partner.

Example (1):   Assume the same facts as Example (1) on page 432. Nupartner's $30,000 § 743(b) total inside basis adjustment will be allocated under § 755. If all of the partnership's assets were sold in a fully taxable transaction for fair market value, Nupartner would be allocated $10,000 of gain from the class of all other property (the accounts receivable) and $20,000 of gain from the class of capital assets and § 1231(b) property (capital asset and depreciable business property). Thus, the $30,000 adjustment would be allocated $10,000 to the accounts receivable and $20,000 to the capital asset and depreciable business property. Nupartner would be allocated $5,000 of gain from the capital asset and $15,000 from the depreciable business property so the $20,000 adjustment to that class would be allocated $5,000 to the capital asset and $15,000 to the depreciable business property.

Example (2):   Assume the same facts as Example (2) on page 432. Nupartner's $50,000 total inside basis adjustment will again be allocated according to the allocations of income, gain, or loss Nupartner would receive in a fully taxable sale of the partnership's assets. Nupartner would be allocated $30,000 of gain from the class of all other property (accounts receivable) and $20,000 of gain from the class of capital assets and § 1231(b) property. Thus, the $50,000 adjustment would be allocated $30,000 to the accounts receivable, $5,000 to the capital asset, and $15,000 to the depreciable business property.

Example (3):   The DEF cash method, general partnership has a § 754 election in effect and the following assets:

Assets	A.B.	F.M.V.
Accounts Receivable	$ 0	$45,000
Capital Asset	60,000	30,000
Total	$60,000	$75,000

DEF also has $30,000 of partnership liabilities. If Nupartner purchases D's one-third interest in the partnership for $15,000 cash, his outside basis will be $25,000, taking into account his share of partnership liabilities under § 752(d). Under § 743(b) Nupartner's total upward inside basis adjustment will be $5,000 ($25,000 outside basis less $20,000 share of the partnership's inside basis). Nupartner's share of the partnership's inside basis would be equal to his $10,000 interest in the partnership's previously taxed capital ($15,000 cash Nupartner would receive on a sale and liquidation of the partnership, plus $10,000 share of tax loss in capital asset, minus $15,000 share of tax gain in the accounts receivable) plus his $10,000 share of partnership liabilities. The regulations permit Nupartner to make a $15,000 upward basis adjustment to the accounts receivable and a $10,000 downward basis adjustment to the capital asset so the net adjustment equals the $5,000 total § 743(b) adjustment. Reg. § 1.755–1(b)(i); see Reg. § 1.755–1(b)(2)(ii) Example 1. The regulations also permit simultaneous upward and downward basis adjustments within a class of property. Reg. § 1.755–1(b)(1)(i); see Reg. § 1.755–1(b)(3)(iii) Example 1.

c. Effect of § 743(b) Adjustment

A basis adjustment under § 743(b) is personal to the transferee partner. The partnership's basis in its assets is not changed by the adjustment. Reg. § 1.743–1(j)(1). A partnership first computes all partnership items and each partner is allocated those items under § 704, without regard to any § 743(b) adjustments. The partnership then adjusts the transferee's distributive share of partnership items to reflect the adjustments. § 743(b) adjustments do not affect the transferee partner's capital account. Reg. § 1.743–1(j)(2). If a § 743(b) adjustment is made to a depreciable or amortizable asset, the adjustment generally is treated as being attributable to a newly purchased asset.

D. Review Questions

1. A sells her one-third interest in ABC for $150,000. A has an adjusted basis of $100,000 in her partnership interest and has held the interest for five years. None of the partnership's assets were contributed by A. ABC is a cash method partnership and has the following assets:

	A.B.	F.M.V.
Cash	$ 65,000	$ 65,000
Accounts Receivable	0	30,000
Dealer Property	60,000	90,000
Capital Asset	25,000	85,000
Equipment (all § 1245 gain)	150,000	180,000
	$300,000	$450,000

(a) Which of ABC's assets are § 751 assets?

(b) What is A's § 751 income?

(c) What is A's § 741 income?

(d) What is the character of A's § 741 income?

2. B sells her one-third interest in the ABC partnership for a $50,000 installment note payable in two years. B has an outside basis of $20,000. ABC has the following assets

	A.B.	F.M.V.
Capital Asset	$30,000	$ 60,000
Accounts Receivable	0	30,000
Equipment (all § 1245 gain)	30,000	60,000
	$60,000	$150,000

Must B recognize any gain in the year of the sale?

3. Nupartner purchases a one-third interest in the ABC cash method partnership for $30,000. ABC has the following assets:

	A.B.	**F.M.V.**
Cash	$15,000	$15,000
Accounts Receivable	0	15,000
Capital Asset	30,000	60,000
	$45,000	$90,000

(a) What is Nupartner's outside basis in her partnership interest?

(b) When the partnership collects the accounts receivable how much income will be allocated to Nupartner? Assume the partnership does not have a § 754 election in effect.

(c) Assume the partnership has a § 754 election in effect. What is Nupartner's personal inside basis in each partnership asset?

XIX

NONLIQUIDATING
DISTRIBUTIONS

Analysis

A. Consequences to the Partner

Because partners are taxed directly on partnership income under an aggregate theory, Subchapter K has rules which generally permit partners to receive distributions of that income without being taxed again. Those rules, however, are subject to a number of provisions designed to prevent easy avoidance of tax.

1. Cash Distributions
a. In General

A partner generally does not recognize gain or loss on the receipt of a cash distribution from a partnership. § 731(a). If, however, the money distributed exceeds the partner's outside basis, the excess is recognized as gain from the sale or exchange of the partner's partnership interest. § 731(a)(1). A partner's outside basis is reduced (but not below zero) by the amount of any money distributed by the partnership. §§ 705(a)(2); 733.

These rules apply only to distributions by a partnership. So, for example, if a partnership loans money to a partner, there is no distribution but a later cancellation of the partner's repayment obligation is considered a distribution. Reg. § 1.731–1(c)(2). Advances or draws of money or property by a partner against his distributive share of income are considered distributions on the last day of the partnership's taxable year because they are contingent on the profitability of the partnership and must be repaid to the extent the partnership does not have sufficient profits. Advances and draws thus are similar to loans. Reg. § 1.731–1(a)(1)(ii). The distribution rules apply to both actual cash distributions and deemed cash distributions under § 752(b), which occur as a result of a decrease in a partner's share of partnership liabilities. A deemed distribution of money under § 752(b) is treated as an advance or draw and is taken into account at the end of the partnership taxable year. Rev. Rul. 94–4, 1994–1 C.B. 196.

Example (1): A's outside basis is $10,000. If the partnership distributes $8,000 cash to A in a pro rata distribution to all partners, he will not recognize any gain or loss and his outside basis will be reduced to $2,000. If, instead, the partnership distributed $13,000 cash to A, he would recognize $3,000 of gain from the sale or exchange of his partnership interest and his outside basis would be reduced to zero. The results would be the same if under § 752(b) the $13,000 distribution resulted from a $13,000 decrease in A's share of partnership liabilities.

Example (2): B's outside basis is $8,000. On April 1, B receives a $6,000 cash "draw" against her share of partnership profits for the year, and on October 1 she receives a second $6,000 draw. B's distributive share of partnership profits for the year is $15,000

and the other partners also receive pro rata draws in April
and October. Because the $6,000 distributions are advances
against B's distributive share of profits, they are treated as
distributions on the last day of the partnership's taxable year.
At that time B's $15,000 distributive share of partnership
income increases her outside basis to $23,000 and the deemed
year-end distribution reduces her outside basis to $11,000.
§ 705(a)(1)(A), (a)(2). B will not recognize gain as a result of
the deemed year-end distribution because it does not exceed
her outside basis. If the April and October distributions were
not draws because B had no obligation to repay the amount in
excess of her distributive share of profits, the October
distribution would result in $4,000 of gain ($8,000 original
outside basis less total of $12,000 of distributions). In
addition, B would have to include in income her $15,000
distributive share of partnership profits. The characterization
of the mid-year distributions as "draws" or "advances" may
affect the tax results to the partners, and thus it is important
to establish the partner's obligation to repay excess
distributions if the partners wish a distribution to be treated
as a draw or advance against partnership profits.

b. Distributions of Marketable Securities

For purposes of the partnership distribution rules, "marketable securities" are
considered money to the extent of their fair market value on the date of the
distribution. § 731(c)(1). In effect, because marketable securities can be easily
valued and are as liquid as cash, distributions of such securities are taxed as
distributions of money. The partner's basis in the distributed securities is their
§ 732 basis (see XIX.A.2.b., at page 441, *infra*), increased by the amount of
gain recognized. § 731(c)(4)(A). Marketable securities are defined as financial
instruments (e.g. stocks, bonds, options, and futures) and foreign currencies
that are actively traded and include interests in mutual funds and instruments
convertible into marketable securities. § 731(c)(2). Various exceptions apply to
these rules, including exceptions for (1) investment partnerships, and (2) a
distribution of a security to the partner who contributed the security to the
partnership. See § 731(c)(3). The distributee partner also reduces the amount
of a § 731(c) distribution by the amount of the decrease in that partner's
distributive share of the net gain in the partnership's marketable securities.
§ 731(c)(3)(B).

2. Property Distributions
a. Recognition of Gain or Loss

When a partnership distributes property to a partner in a nonliquidating
distribution, generally neither the partner nor the partnership recognizes gain
or loss. § 731(a), (b). The principal exception is a distribution which is treated
as a constructive sale or exchange under § 751(b). See XIX.D.1., at page 452,

infra. Additionally, if a partner contributes property to a partnership and the property is distributed to another partner within seven years, the contributing partner must recognize the precontribution gain or loss inherent in the property. § 704(c)(1)(B). See XIX.C.2., at page 449, *infra.* Finally, if a partner contributes property to a partnership and the partnership distributes other property to the partner within seven years of the contribution, the partner must recognize gain as required by § 737. See XIX.C.3., at page 451, *infra.*

b. Basis Consequences

1) General Rule: Transferred Basis

   A partner generally takes a transferred basis in property distributed by a partnership, and the distributee partner's outside basis is reduced by the basis of the distributed property. §§ 732(a)(1); 733(2).

2) Basis Limitation

   A partner's basis in distributed property cannot, however, exceed the partner's outside basis less any money received in the same transaction. § 732(a)(2). For purposes of determining the amount of money distributed as a result of debt relief, the Service has ruled that decreases in a partner's share of partnership liabilities are offset by increases in the partner's individual liabilities. Rev.Rul. 79–205, 1979–2 C.B. 255; Reg. § 1.752–1(f).

3) Allocation of Basis

   If the outside basis limitation is reached, the basis to be allocated (i.e., the partner's outside basis less cash received in the transaction) must be allocated among the various properties received by the distributee partner. First unrealized receivables and inventory items are tentatively assigned basis equal to the adjusted basis of the partnership in those assets. § 732(c)(1)(A)(i). If the partnership's basis in the unrealized receivables and inventory items is greater than the basis to be allocated, then the bases of those assets is reduced (1) by first reducing the basis of assets with built-in losses (i.e., assets with an assigned basis greater their values) in proportion to the amount of such built-in losses (and only to the extent of such losses), and (2) by then making additional reductions in basis in proportion to the remaining adjusted basis of the unrealized receivables and inventory items. §§ 732(c)(1)(A)(ii), (3). If the basis to be allocated is greater than the partnership's basis in distributed unrealized receivables and inventory items, then each other distributed asset is tentatively assigned a basis equal to the partnership's basis in those assets. § 732(c)(1)(B)(i). The partnership's bases in those assets has to be reduced so that the sum of their bases equals the remaining basis to be allocated. Again, the reduction is accomplished by first reducing the basis of assets with built-in losses (in proportion to such losses), and then in proportion to the remaining adjusted bases of the properties. §§ 732(c)(1)(B)(ii), (3). For the definition of "unrealized receivables" and "inventory items," see XVIII.B.2.b., at page 423, *supra*.

4) Holding Period
Because a partner generally takes a transferred basis in distributed property, the partner's holding period for such property includes, or "tacks," the partnership's holding period for the property. §§ 735(b); 1223.

Example (1): C's outside basis is $30,000 and C receives a partnership distribution of $10,000 cash and undeveloped land with a fair market value of $25,000 and a $15,000 adjusted basis. The partnership makes identical pro rata distributions to the other partners. Under § 731(a), C recognizes no gain and reduces his outside basis to $20,000 ($30,000 less $10,000 cash distribution) under § 733. Under the general rule in § 732(a)(1), the land takes a $15,000 transferred basis and C's outside basis is reduced to $5,000 under § 733.

Example (2): If C's outside basis in Example (1) were $20,000 and he received the same distribution, again he would not recognize gain and his outside basis would be reduced to $10,000 as a result of the distribution of the cash. Since C's remaining outside basis of $10,000 is less than the $15,000 transferred basis for the land, § 732(a)(2) limits C's basis in the land to $10,000. His outside basis is reduced to zero under § 733.

Example (3): D's basis in her partnership interest is $10,000. D receives a partnership distribution of:

	A.B.	F.M.V.
Cash	$2,000	$2,000
Accounts Receivable	$ 0	$3,000
Inventory	$3,000	$5,000
Capital Asset	$4,000	$9,000

The partnership makes identical pro rata distributions to the other partners. Under § 731(a), D recognizes no gain or loss and reduces her outside basis to $8,000 ($10,000 less $2,000 cash distribution) under § 733. Under the general rule in § 732(a)(1), the accounts receivable, inventory, and capital asset take a zero, $3,000, and $4,000 transferred basis, respectively, and D's outside basis is reduced to $1,000 under § 733.

Example (4):   Assume the same facts as Example (3) except D's outside basis is $3,000. D does not recognize gain or loss and her outside basis is reduced to $1,000 as a result of the distribution of the cash. Under § 732(a)(2) and (c), D's remaining outside basis of $1,000 must be allocated to the distributed assets. First, the accounts receivable and the inventory items are assigned a basis equal to the partnership's bases in those assets (zero and $3,000 respectively). Since neither asset has a built-in loss the required $2,000 reduction is made in proportion to the remaining bases in those assets (all to the inventory). Thus, the basis in the accounts receivable is zero, the basis in the inventory is $1,000, and the basis in the capital asset is zero. D's outside basis is reduced to zero.

Example (5):   E's basis in his partnership interest is $5,000. E receives a partnership distribution of:

	A.B.	F.M.V.
Cash	$ 2,000	$ 2,000
Inventory—Lot 1	$12,000	$10,000
Inventory—Lot 2	$ 5,000	$18,000

The partnership makes identical pro rata distributions to the other partners. Under § 731(a), E recognizes no gain or loss and reduces his outside basis to $3,000 ($5,000 less $2,000 cash distribution) under § 733. Under § 732(a)(2) and (c), E's remaining outside basis of $3,000 is allocated between the two lots of inventory. Both lots of inventory initially are assigned a basis equal to the partnership's basis in the lots ($12,000 to Lot 1 and $5,000 to Lot 2). To apply the § 732(a)(2) basis limitation, Lot 1's basis is first reduced by the amount of built-in loss in that asset ($2,000). The remaining bases in the two lots of inventory ($15,000 total) must then be reduced to a total of $3,000 (the basis to be allocated). The $12,000 reduction is accomplished by reducing the bases of the lots in proportion to their respective remaining bases. Thus, $8,000 of the reduction (two-thirds) is made in the basis of Lot 1 and $4,000 (one-third) is made in the basis of Lot 2. Thus, Lot 1 takes a $2,000 basis and Lot 2 takes a $1,000 basis. E's outside basis is reduced to zero.

c. Section 732(d) Election

Under § 732(d), a distributee partner who acquires her partnership interest in a transfer (by sale or exchange or upon the death of a partner) when there is no § 754 election in effect may elect, with respect to distributions within two years after the transfer, to treat the bases of the partnership's assets as if § 743(b) adjustments had taken place. As a result of a § 732(d) election, a distributee partner will take § 743(b) adjustments into account in determining the basis of distributed property under § 732(a) and (c). See XVIII.C.2., at page 431, *supra,* for the operation of § 743(b). The Service may require application of § 732(d) in the case of a distribution (within two years or later) if, at the time the partner acquired her partnership interest, the fair market value of the partnership property (other than money) exceeded 110% of its adjusted basis. The regulations limit this rule to situations where there would otherwise be a shift in basis from nondepreciable to depreciable property. Reg. § 1.732–1(d)(4).

Example: B purchases a one-fourth interest in a partnership for $60,000 at a time when the partnership has not made a § 754 election. The partnership's balance sheet is as follows:

	A.B.	F.M.V.
Accounts Receivable	$ 0	$ 40,000
Nondepreciable Capital Asset	80,000	200,000
Total	$80,000	$240,000

Within two years of B's purchase, the partnership distributes $10,000 of the accounts receivable to each of its four partners. If B does not make a § 732(d) election, he will take a zero basis in the $10,000 of accounts receivable under § 732(a)(1) and his outside basis will continue to be $60,000. If B makes a § 732(d) election, there would be a $10,000 upward adjustment under § 743(b) and § 755 to the basis of the receivables distributed to him. See XVIII.C.2.b., at page 431, *supra,* for the operation of § 743(b) and § 755. Under § 731(a)(1), the $10,000 basis in the receivables would carry over to B and his outside basis would be reduced to $50,000 under § 733.

3. Dispositions of Distributed Property
a. General Rules: § 735

Under § 735(a), any gain or loss recognized with respect to distributed "unrealized receivables" is characterized as ordinary, and any gain or loss recognized with respect to "inventory items" (whether or not substantially appreciated) within five years after the distribution is characterized as ordinary. See XVIII.B.2.b., at page 423, *supra,* for the definitions of "unrealized receivables" and "inventory items." For purposes of this rule, the long-term holding period requirement in § 1231(b) is disregarded, and thus property otherwise described in § 1231(b) is not an "inventory item" even if it has not been held long-term. §§ 735(c)(1); 751(d)(2)(B). If a partner disposes of either a distributed unrealized receivable or a distributed inventory item in a nonrecognition transaction, any substituted basis property (other than C corporation stock received in a § 351 exchange) resulting from the transaction retains the taint of the distributed property. The same rule applies to a series of nonrecognition transactions. § 735(c)(2).

Example (1): Partner C receives a parcel of real property from her partnership in a pro rata distribution. The parcel is an "inventory item" because the partnership held the parcel for sale to customers in the ordinary course of its business. § 751(d)(1). If C sells the parcel within five years, any gain or loss is characterized as ordinary. After five years, gain or loss on the parcel is characterized with reference to C's activities.

Example (2): Assume C holds the parcel in Example (1) for investment and it would be a capital asset in her hands. If C disposes of the parcel in a § 1031 exchange for property of like kind, the property C receives in the exchange will retain the § 735 ordinary income taint of the distributed parcel. If the new property is sold or exchanged within five years of the distribution of the original parcel, any gain or loss is characterized as ordinary.

b. Depreciation Recapture

If a partnership distributes depreciable property which has potential recapture income under § 1245 or § 1250 to a partner, the character of that income is preserved by the definition of "recomputed basis" in § 1245 and "depreciation adjustments" in § 1250(b)(3).

B. Consequences to the Partnership

1. Nonrecognition of Gain or Loss

Under § 731(b), generally, no gain or loss is recognized by a partnership when it distributes property (including money) to a partner. This nonrecognition rule extends to property with potential § 1245 or § 1250 depreciation recapture income. §§ 1245(b)(3); 1250(d)(3). The principal exception is distributions which are treated as sales or exchanges under § 751(b).

2. Impact on Inside Basis
a. General Rule: No Adjustment to Inside Basis

Under § 734(a), the inside basis of the partnership's assets is not adjusted as a result of a property distribution by the partnership unless it has a § 754 election in effect. In the absence of a § 754 election, liquidating and nonliquidating distributions may create an imbalance between the partnership's total inside basis and the total outside bases of the partners' partnership interests when: (1) a partner recognizes gain under § 731(a)(1) as a result of receiving a distribution of money in excess of his outside basis, or (2) the basis of distributed property is limited under § 732(a)(2) because the partner has insufficient outside basis. Liquidating distributions also may produce an imbalance between inside and outside basis in other situations. The resulting distortions may affect the timing and character of income and loss in a manner similar to the distortions resulting when a partner purchases an interest in a partnership which does not have a § 754 election in effect.

b. Section 734(b) Adjustment

Under § 734(b), if a partnership has a § 754 election in effect, it increases the inside basis of its assets by: (1) the amount of any § 731(a)(1) gain recognized by the distributee partner, and (2) if the § 732(a)(2) limitation applies, by the excess of the basis the distributed asset had to the partnership over the basis it has to the distributee partner.

c. Allocation of Basis Adjustment

An adjustment as a result of § 731(a)(1) gain recognition by the distributee partner must be allocated to capital assets and § 1231(b) property. Reg. § 1.755–1(c)(1)(ii). The basis increase as a result of a distribution of property is allocated under § 755 to the same class of property (capital assets and § 1231 property or all other property) which gave rise to the adjustment. Reg. § 1.755–1(c)(1)(i). If a basis increase is allocated within a class of property, the increase is first allocated to properties with unrealized appreciation in proportion to their appreciation. Any remaining increase is allocated in proportion to the fair market values of the properties. Reg. § 1.755–1(c)(2)(i). Decreases in the basis of partnership assets may result from a distribution that liquidates a partner's interest. See § 734(b)(2) and XX.A.2.b., at page 461, *infra*. If a basis decrease is allocated within a class of property, the decrease is allocated first to properties with unrealized depreciation in proportion to their respective amounts of unrealized depreciation before the reduction. Any remaining decrease must be allocated among the properties within the class in proportion to their adjusted bases (after adjustment for unrealized depreciation). Reg. § 1.755–1(c)(2)(ii). The basis of a property cannot be reduced below zero. Reg. § 1.755–1(c)(3). If a partnership does not have property of the character to be adjusted or if the basis of all property of like character has been reduce to zero, the adjustment carries over until the partnership acquires property of a like character to which an adjustment can be made. Reg. § 1.755–1(c)(4).

Example (1): The ABC partnership has the following balance sheet:

	Assets			Partners' Capital	
	A.B.	**F.M.V.**		**A.B.**	**F.M.V.**
Cash	$11,000	$11,000	A	$10,000	$11,000
Capital					
Asset	19,000	22,000	B	10,000	11,000
			C	10,000	11,000
Total	$30,000	$33,000		$30,000	$33,000

If A receives $11,000 in cash in liquidation of his entire interest in the partnership, he will recognize $1,000 of gain under § 731(a)(1). If the partnership does not have a § 754 election in effect, under § 734(a) there will be no adjustment to the inside basis of the capital asset and its balance sheet will be as follows:

	Assets			Partners' Capital	
	A.B.	F.M.V.		A.B.	F.M.V.
Capital Asset	$19,000	$22,000	B	$10,000	$11,000
			C	10,000	11,000
Total	$19,000	$22,000		$20,000	$22,000

Because no adjustment is made under § 734(a), the partnership's asset still has $3,000 of gain potential even though A recognized $1,000 of gain on the distribution. Thus, if the partnership sold the capital asset, B and C would each recognize $1,500 of gain which would increase their outside bases to $11,500. B and C would each have $500 of potential loss built into their partnership interests which would be recognized only if they dispose of their partnership interests or if the partnership liquidates.

If the partnership had a § 754 election in effect, it would increase its inside basis by $1,000 as a result of A recognizing gain under § 731(a)(1). § 734(b)(1)(A). That $1,000 adjustment must be allocated to partnership capital assets and § 1231(b) property with unrealized appreciation in proportion to the relative appreciation in each asset. Thus, the basis of the capital asset would increase to $20,000 and the partnership's balance sheet would be as follows:

	Assets			Partners' Capital	
	A.B.	F.M.V.		A.B.	F.M.V.
Capital Asset	$20,000	$22,000	B	$10,000	$11,000
			C	10,000	11,000
Total	$20,000	$22,000		$20,000	$22,000

Note that the § 734(b) adjustment brought the inside and outside bases into balance and eliminated the potential distortion which resulted from the no-adjustment rule in § 734(a). Now if the partnership sells the capital asset there will be $2,000 of gain and B and C will each recognize their $1,000 share.

Example (2):   The DEF Partnership has the following balance sheet:

	Assets			**Partners' Capital**	
	A.B.	**F.M.V.**		**A.B.**	**F.M.V.**
Cash	$ 4,000	$ 4,000	D	$10,000	$11,000
Capital Asset # 1	11,000	5,000	E	10,000	11,000
Capital Asset # 2	15,000	24,000	F	10,000	11,000
Total	$30,000	$33,000		$30,000	$33,000

If the partnership distributes Capital Asset #1 to D, she will take a $10,000 basis in the asset under § 732(a)(2). If there is no § 754 election in effect, the loss of $1,000 of basis will again create distortions among the partners. If a § 754 election has been made, the partnership will receive a $1,000 increase in its inside basis which must be allocated to Capital Asset #2 because it is in the same class of property which gave rise to the adjustment. Thus, the basis of Capital Asset #2 would become $16,000 and the partnership's balance sheet would be:

	Assets			**Partners' Capital**	
	A.B.	**F.M.V.**		**A.B.**	**F.M.V.**
Cash	$ 4,000	$ 4,000	D	$ 0	$ 6,000
Capital Asset # 2	16,000	24,000	E	$10,000	$11,000
			F	10,000	11,000
Total	$20,000	$28,000		$20,000	$28,000

Note that the inside and outside bases are now in balance as a result of the § 734(b) adjustment. One problem remains. Without a special allocation, the recognition of income on Capital Asset #2 will be distorted. Originally there was $6,000 of loss in Capital Asset #1, which would have been shared equally among the partners ($2,000 each). As a result of the distribution, D would recognize $5,000 of that loss if she sold the asset ($5,000 fair market value less $10,000 adjusted basis under § 732(a)(2)). To compensate E and F for not receiving their $4,000 share of loss, D should recognize the first $4,000 of gain in Capital Asset #2. And to compensate E and F for the loss of $1,000 of basis in Capital Asset #1, D should also recognize an additional $1,000 of gain in Capital Asset #2. The remaining $3,000 of gain in Capital Asset #2 should be shared equally ($1,000 each) among the partners. Thus, the $8,000 of gain in Capital Asset #2 should be allocated $6,000 to D, $1,000 to E, and $1,000 to F. Such an allocation would not have substantial economic effect. It is not tax motivated, however, and should be recognized. For an allocation which is similar in purpose and is respected, see Reg. § 1.704–1(b)(5) Example 14(i).

3. Adjustments to Capital Accounts

A partner's capital account is reduced by the fair market value of property received in a distribution from the partnership. Reg. § 1.704–1(b)(2)(iv)(b). In order to account for the variation between the distributed property's fair market value and its book value, the regulations require that the capital accounts first be adjusted to reflect the manner in which the unrealized gain or loss would be allocated if there were a taxable disposition of the property for its fair market value. Reg. § 1.704–1(b)(2)(iv)(e)(1).

C. Mixing Bowl Transactions

1. Introduction

Subchapter K includes two anti-abuse provisions to combat "mixing bowl transactions," an income-shifting strategy that generally involves a partner first transferring appreciated property to a partnership and the partnership later either distributing the contributed property to another partner or distributing other property to the contributing partner. The tax planning goal is to shift or defer the recognition of the contributing partner's precontribution gain by exploiting the nonrecognition rules for contributions to (e.g., § 721) and distributions by (e.g., § 731) a partnership.

2. Distributions of Contributed Property To Another Partner
a. The Attempted Strategy

As discussed earlier, a partner who contributes property with a built-in gain or loss to a partnership is generally allocated that gain or loss when the partnership subsequently disposes of the property. § 704(c)(1)(A). See XVII.C.3. at page 387, *supra*. When first enacted, § 704(c) did not apply to distributions of contributed property. As a result, a contributing partner could avoid an allocation of precontribution gain or loss if the partnership distributed the contributed property to another partner instead of selling it. Neither the partnership nor the contributing partner normally would recognize gain or loss on the distribution, and built-in gain often was shifted to the distributee partner. This type of income-shifting is contrary to the policy of § 704(c).

b. General Rule of § 704(c)(1)(B)

Section 704(c)(1)(B) provides that if property contributed by a partner is distributed to another partner within seven years of its contribution, the contributing partner must recognize gain or loss from the sale or exchange of the property in an amount equal to the gain or loss that would have been allocated to that partner under § 704(c)(1)(A) if the property had been sold by the partnership for its fair market value. § 704(c)(1)(B)(i). The character of the gain or loss is determined as if the partnership had sold the property. § 704(c)(1)(B)(ii). The contributing partner's outside basis is increased or decreased by the gain or loss recognized as a result of the distribution. § 704(c)(1)(B)(iii). To avoid double recognition of gain or loss, the partnership's inside basis in the distributed property is increased or decreased prior to the distribution to reflect the contributing partner's gain or loss. Id. A successor to the contributing partner (e.g., a purchaser of the partnership interest) is treated in the same manner as the contributing partner. § 704(c)(3).

Example (1): On the formation of the ABC equal partnership, A contributed Gainacre with a fair market value of $100,000 and a basis of $40,000. If the partnership distributes Gainacre to C two years later when it is worth $130,000, A recognizes $60,000 of gain (the built-in gain at the time of contribution). The character of A's gain is the same as it would have been if the partnership had sold the property. If A had sold his partnership interest to D during the two-year period, D would be treated in the same manner as A—i.e., D would recognize $60,000 gain.

Example (2): Same facts as Example (1), except that Gainacre is worth only $80,000 when the partnership distributes it to C. If the partnership makes § 704(c) allocations using the traditional method, the ceiling rule would limit A's gain on the distribution to $40,000 because that is the gain the partnership would have recognized if it had sold Gainacre for $80,000.

c. Exceptions

The general rule of § 704(c)(1)(B) is subject to two statutory exceptions: (1) it does not apply if the contributed property is distributed back to the contributing partner or her successor (§ 704(c)(1)(B)), and (2) relief is provided to a contributing partner who receives a distribution of § 1031 like-kind property within 180 days after the contributed property is distributed to another partner, or if earlier, the due date for the contributing partner's tax return (§ 704(c)(2)). For purposes of the second exception, the contributing partner is treated as if she received the same property that she originally contributed to the partnership up to the value of the like-kind property actually received. The policy is that gain should not be recognized under § 704(c)(1)(B) if the contributing partner would have qualified for nonrecognition if the transaction had taken place outside the partnership (e.g., with the other partner). The regulations also provide that § 704(c)(1)(B) does not apply if there is a constructive termination of the partnership under § 708(b)(1)(B). Reg. § 1.704–4(c)(3). See XX.B.2. at page 470, *infra.*

Example (3): Assume in Example (1), above, that the partnership again distributes Gainacre (value, $130,000) to C two years after A's contribution. If the partnership distributes like-kind property to A that is worth at least $130,000 within the prescribed time limits, A does not recognize gain on the distribution of the contributed property.

3. Distributions of Other Property To The Contributing Partner
a. The Attempted Strategy
A second potential abuse identified by Congress was a transaction where a partner contributes appreciated property to a partnership and later receives a distribution of other property, with the partnership retaining the contributed property. The concern in this scenario is that, if the normal contribution and distribution rules of Subchapter K applied, a contributing partner would be able to avoid recognition of gain on a swap of properties when a similar transaction outside the partnership would not have qualified for nonrecognition.

b. General Rule of § 737
Section 737 requires a contributing partner to recognize gain if she contributes appreciated property to a partnership and within seven years of the contribution receives property other than money as a distribution from the partnership. § 737(a). The amount of the gain recognized is the lesser of: (1) the fair market value of the distributed property (other than cash) less the partner's outside basis immediately before the distribution (reduced, but not below zero, by any cash received in the distribution), or (2) the net gain that the partner would have recognized under § 704(c)(1)(B) if all of the property contributed by the partner within seven years of the current distribution had been distributed to another partner at the time of the distribution to the contributing partner ("net precontribution gain"). § 737(a), (b). In effect, § 737 requires a contributing partner to recognize precontribution gain on contributed property to the extent that the value of other property distributed by the partnership to that partner exceeds the partner's outside basis. In so doing, it permits the partner to limit potential gain recognition by netting any precontribution losses against precontribution gains.

The distributee partner's outside basis is increased by the partner's § 737 recognized gain; this adjustment is treated as occurring immediately before the distribution. § 737(c)(1). The partnership increases its inside basis in the contributed property to reflect any § 737 recognized gain. § 737(c)(2).

Example: A and B form the equal AB partnership, with A contributing Gainacre (value $40,000, basis $24,000), and B contributing $10,000 cash and Land (value and basis $30,000). Three years later, when A's outside basis is still $24,000, the partnership distributes Land (value still $30,000) to A. A recognizes $6,000 gain, which is the lesser of: (1) $6,000, the $30,000 value of Land reduced by A's $24,000 outside basis, or (2) $16,000, A's net precontribution gain. After determining the § 737 gain but immediately before the distribution, A increases his outside basis by $6,000, to $30,000. A recognizes no further gain on the distribution but reduces his outside basis by $30,000 (the partnership's inside basis in Land) to zero. The partnership's basis in Gainacre is increased by $6,000, to $30,000.

c.   Exceptions

Section 737 is subject to two statutory exceptions: (1) if any portion of the distributed property consists of property contributed by the distributee partner, that property is not taken into account in determining § 737(a) gain or net precontribution gain under § 737(b), and (2) § 737 does not apply to the extent that § 751(b) applies. § 737(d). For a discussion of § 751(b), see XIX.D. at page 452, *infra*. The regulations also provide that § 737 does not apply to a constructive termination of the partnership under § 708(b)(1)(B). Reg. § 1.737–2(a). See XX.B.2. at page 470, *infra*.

D.   Distributions Which Shift the Partners' Interests in § 751 Assets: § 751(b)

1.   Purpose and Scope of § 751(b)

Section 751(b) is designed to prevent shifts of ordinary income and capital gain among the partners through property distributions. It provides that if a partner receives in a distribution (1) unrealized receivables or substantially appreciated inventory ("§ 751 property") in exchange for some or all of her interest in other partnership property (including money), or (2) other property (including money) of the partnership in exchange for some or all of her interest in the partnership's § 751 property, then the distribution is to be treated as a sale or exchange of that property between the partner and the partnership. Section 751(b) does not apply, however, to distributions of property which the distributee partner contributed to the partnership, payments governed by § 736(a), draws or advances against the partner's distributive share, and distributions which are gifts or payment for services or the use of capital. § 751(b)(2); Reg. § 1.751–1(b)(1)(ii).

2.   Section 751(b) Assets

Section 751(b) generally applies to both nonliquidating and liquidating distributions that shift the partners' interests in the same types of property which § 751(a) singles out for ordinary income or loss treatment when a partner sells some or all of a partnership interest (i.e., unrealized receivables and inventory items). See XVIII.B.2.b., at page 423, *supra*, for the definition of unrealized receivables and inventory items, and the operation of § 751(a). In the case of § 751(b), however, inventory items are treated as § 751 property only if they have "appreciated substantially in value." § 751(b)(1)(A)(ii). Inventory items are considered to have appreciated substantially in value if their fair market value exceeds 120% of their adjusted basis. § 751(b)(3)(A). Remember that the definition of inventory items is broad enough to include all of a partnership's unrealized receivables since they are property which if sold by the partnership would produce ordinary income. Reg. § 1.751–1(d)(2)(ii). The inclusion of unrealized receivables as inventory items is important for purposes of testing whether the inventory items are substantially appreciated. But if the inventory items (including the unrealized receivables) are not substantially appreciated, the unrealized receivables nevertheless retain their separate § 751 taint.

To prevent abuses, inventory acquired by a partnership with the principal purpose of avoiding the 120% test is disregarded for purposes of determining whether the inventory items are substantially appreciated in value. § 751(b)(3)(B).

3. **Operation of § 751(b)**
   The operation of § 751(b) breaks down into four steps:

   a. First, the distributee partner's interest in § 751 property and non–§ 751 property before and after the distribution must be compared to determine whether a § 751(b) exchange has occurred. If so, the amount and nature of the partnership property given up (the "exchanged" property) and the property received in the exchange (the "property received from the partnership") also must be identified. The partners are free to agree as to the composition of the exchanged property. Reg. § 1.751–1(g) Example (3)(c).

   b. Second, a constructive distribution is created in which the exchanged property is distributed by the partnership to the partner. The normal rules governing partnership distributions (§§ 731, 732 and 733) apply to this constructive distribution. This step places the partner in a position to complete the fictional exchange required by § 751(b).

   c. Third, after the constructive distribution, the partner is deemed to transfer the exchanged property for the property received from the partnership in a taxable transaction.

   d. Finally, the tax results of the remainder of the distribution (i.e., the distributed property which is not part of the § 751(b) exchange) must be determined under §§ 731, 732, and 733.

   Example: The ABC equal partnership has the following balance sheet:

Assets	A.B.	F.M.V.		Partners' Capital A.B.	F.M.V.
Cash	$12,000	$12,000	A	$ 9,000	$12,000
Inventory	9,000	12,000	B	9,000	12,000
			C	9,000	12,000
Capital Asset	6,000	12,000			
Total	$27,000	$36,000		$27,000	$36,000

Assume A receives a distribution of the $12,000 of inventory in liquidation of her partnership interest. Before the distribution, each partner had a one-third interest in each partnership asset and would have recognized $1,000 of ordinary income if the inventory were sold and $2,000 of capital gain if the capital asset were sold. If the distribution to A were respected, A would take the $12,000 of inventory with a $9,000 basis and have $3,000 of ordinary income potential. B and C, the remaining partners, each would have $3,000 of capital gain potential in the capital asset. Thus, in the absence of § 751(b), the distribution to A would shift $2,000 of capital gain to B and C, and A would have $2,000 of additional ordinary income preserved in the inventory.

The first step in applying § 751(b) is to identify the § 751 (b) exchange. Before the distribution, A had a one-third, or $4,000, interest in each of the cash, the inventory, and the capital asset. After the distribution, A has $12,000 of inventory (which is § 751(d) substantially appreciated inventory) and no interest in the cash and capital asset. As a result, a § 751(b) exchange has taken place in which A has exchanged her $4,000 interests in the cash and capital asset (non–§ 751 property) for an additional $8,000 of inventory (§ 751 property).

The second step is to set the stage for the § 751(b) exchange. The partnership constructively distributes the exchanged property ($4,000 of cash and $4,000 of the capital asset with a $2,000 basis) to A. Under § 731, A would recognize no gain or loss as a result of this constructive distribution and would receive a $2,000 transferred basis in the $4,000 capital asset under § 732. Following the constructive distribution to A, the partnership's balance sheet would be as follows:

	Assets			**Partners' Capital**	
	A.B.	**F.M.V.**		**A.B.**	**F.M.V.**
Cash	$ 8,000	$ 8,000	A	$ 3,000	$ 4,000
Inventory	9,000	12,000	B	9,000	12,000
			C	9,000	12,000
Capital					
Asset	4,000	8,000			
Total	$21,000	$28,000		$21,000	$28,000

The third step is for A to transfer the exchanged property ($4,000 of cash and $4,000 of capital asset with a $2,000 basis) to the partnership for the property received from the partnership—the $8,000 of inventory in excess of her one-third, or $4,000 share. The $8,000 of inventory has a $6,000 basis. This exchange is taxable and A will recognize $2,000 of gain on the capital asset ($4,000 amount realized less $2,000 basis) and the partnership will recognize $2,000 of ordinary income on the inventory which is taxed $1,000 to both B and C and increases their outside basis. Reg. § 1.751–1(b)(2)(ii), (b)(3)(ii). The partnership also receives $4,000 of cash and $4,000 of capital asset with a $4,000 cost basis as a result of the exchange. After the § 751(b) exchange the partnership's balance sheet is as follows:

	Assets			Partners' Capital	
	A.B.	F.M.V.		A.B.	F.M.V.
Cash	$12,000	$12,000	A	$ 3,000	$ 4,000
Inventory	3,000	4,000	B	10,000	12,000
			C	10,000	12,000
Capital Asset	8,000	12,000			
Total	$23,000	$28,000		$23,000	$28,000

Finally, to complete the transaction, the partnership distributes the remaining $4,000 of inventory (her original share of that property) to A. Under § 731, neither A nor the partnership recognizes gain as a result of the distribution and A takes the $4,000 of inventory with a $3,000 basis. Following the distribution the partnership's balance sheet is:

	Assets			Partners' Capital	
	A.B.	F.M.V.		A.B.	F.M.V.
Cash	$12,000	$12,000	B	$10,000	$12,000
Capital Asset	8,000	12,000	C	10,000	12,000
Total	$20,000	$24,000		$20,000	$24,000

When the dust settles, A will have recognized $2,000 of capital gain and will hold $12,000 of inventory with an $11,000 basis, consisting of the $8,000 cost basis from the § 751(b) exchange and a $3,000 transferred basis as a result of the non–§ 751(b) distribution. B and C will have recognized their $1,000 shares of ordinary income in the inventory and have $2,000 of potential capital gain lurking in the capital asset.

In more complicated situations, the principal difficulty in applying § 751(b) is identifying the exchanged property and the property received from the partnership. The property exchanged under § 751(b) can be identified by focusing on the distributee partner's share of either § 751 property or non–§ 751 property.

4. Criticisms of § 751(b)

Section 751(b) has been criticized on a number of grounds. As the examples in the text illustrate, the section is extremely complex. And despite its complexity, § 751(b) does not reach all shifts in income among partners. Non-pro rata distributions within a class of property (§ 751 or non–§ 751) are not reached by § 751(b). Because of these deficiencies, the American Law Institute and other commentators have called for the repeal of § 751(b).

E. Review Questions

1. A has a basis in his partnership interest of $20,000. What is A's outside basis after each of the following pro rata distributions? What gain or loss, if any, does A recognize as a result of the distributions?

   (a) The partnership distributes $15,000 cash to A.

   (b) The partnership distributes $25,000 cash to A.

   (c) The partnership distributes $15,000 cash, accounts receivable with $0 A.B. and $10,000 F.M.V., and inventory with $10,000 A.B. and $25,000 F.M.V. to A.

   (d) The partnership distributes $10,000 cash, accounts receivable with $0 A.B. and $15,000 F.M.V., inventory with $10,000 A.B. and $20,000 F.M.V., and a capital asset with a $10,000 A.B. and $20,000 F.M.V. to A.

2. If a partner receives a cash distribution and recognizes gain under § 731(a)(1), the partnership will not adjust its inside basis unless a § 754 election has been made. True or False?

3. The ABC Partnership has the following balance sheet:

	Assets			Partners' Capital		
	A.B.	**F.M.V.**			**A.B.**	**F.M.V.**
Cash	$15,000	$15,000	A		$12,000	$15,000
Inventory	12,000	15,000	B		12,000	15,000
Capital Asset	9,000	15,000	C		12,000	15,000
Total	$36,000	$45,000			$36,000	$45,000

Assume B receives a distribution of the $15,000 of inventory in exchange for his partnership interest.

   (a) *Step 1:* What is B's interest in § 751 and non–§ 751 property before and after the distribution?

   (b) *Step 2:* Determine the tax consequences of the constructive distribution by the partnership to B to set the stage for the § 751(b) exchange.

   (c) *Step 3:* Determine the tax consequences of the § 751(b) exchange.

   (d) *Step 4:* To complete the distribution, the partnership transfers the remaining inventory to B. Does B recognize any gain or loss on this distribution? What is B's total basis in the inventory?

XX

LIQUIDATING DISTRIBUTIONS

Analysis

A. Liquidation of a Partner's Interest

1. Introduction

A partner may terminate her interest in a partnership by selling the interest to a third party and recognize capital gain except to the extent provided in § 751. See XVIII.B., at page 422, *supra,* for the tax treatment of a sale of a partnership interest. Alternatively, the partner's interest may be liquidated. A "liquidation" is "the termination of a partner's entire interest in a partnership by means of a distribution, or series of distributions, to the partner by the partnership." § 761(d). A partner whose interest is being liquidated is often referred to as "the retiring partner."

Section 736 is the starting point for determining the tax consequences of payments in liquidation of a partner's interest in a partnership. It applies only to payments made to retiring partners or to a deceased partner's successor in interest. Reg. § 1.736–1(a)(1)(i). Section 736 classifies such payments into two broad categories, and the tax treatment of the payments is then determined under other provisions of Subchapter K. Under § 736(b), payments for a partner's interest in partnership property generally are treated as distributions by the partnership and taxed under the rules applicable to nonliquidating distributions. See generally Chapter XIX, *supra.* In the case of a general partnership interest in a partnership in which capital is not a material income-producing factor, payments for the partner's share of unrealized receivables and goodwill, except to the extent the partnership agreement provides for a specific payment with respect to goodwill, are excluded from § 736(b). § 736(b)(2), (3). Under § 736(a), payments not within § 736(b) (i.e., (1) payments for unrealized receivables and "unstated goodwill" for a general partnership interest in a services partnership, and (2) "premium" payments paid to the partner in excess of her share of partnership property) are considered to be: (1) a distributive share if the amount of the payment is dependent on partnership income or (2) a § 707(c) guaranteed payment if the amount is determined without reference to partnership income.

Under general tax principles, capital is not a material income-producing factor where substantially all of the income comes from compensation for services (e.g., fees and commissions). Thus, a partnership of doctors, lawyers, architects or accountants is not a business where capital is a material income-producing factor even though the business may require a large capital investment (e.g., in equipment or a physical plant) if that investment is incidental to the professional practice.

2. § 736(b) Payments

Under § 736(b), payments to a partner for his interest in partnership property generally are treated as partnership distributions. Excluded from this treatment, however, are payments for a general partnership interest in a services partnership attributable to § 751(c) unrealized receivables and unstated goodwill. § 736(b)(2)–(3). For purposes of § 736, recapture items are not unrealized receivables and thus payments made by a partnership to a retiring partner for recapture items are § 736(b) payments. § 751(c). If a partner's interest in partnership property is determined in an arm's length agreement, that value generally is accepted as correct. Reg. § 1.736–1(b)(1).

a. Tax Consequences of § 736(b) Payments to the Partner

1) Recognition of Gain

Section 736(b) payments generally are treated like nonliquidating distributions. Gain is recognized only if the retiring partner receives cash in excess of his outside basis. § 731(a)(1).

2) Recognition of Loss

Because the liquidation of a partner's interest is a closed transaction, § 731(a)(2) provides that a partner may recognize a loss on a liquidating distribution if only cash, § 751(c) unrealized receivables, and § 751(d)(2) inventory items are distributed. In that situation, loss is recognized to the extent that the partner's outside basis exceeds the sum of the money distributed and the partner's transferred basis in the unrealized receivables and inventory items. The loss is considered as arising from the sale or exchange of a partnership interest and is thus a capital loss. These rules are designed to permit nonrecognition for the partner to the extent possible and preserve the retiring partner's share of ordinary income or loss.

3) Basis of Distributed Property: In General

The partner's basis in any property distributed by the partnership is equal to his outside basis reduced by any cash distributed in the same transaction. § 732(b).

4) Allocation of Basis

If the outside basis limitation is reached, the basis to be allocated (i.e., the partner's outside basis less cash received in the transaction) must be allocated among the various properties received by the distributee partner. First, unrealized receivables and inventory items are tentatively assigned basis equal to the adjusted basis of the partnership in those assets. § 732(c)(1)(A)(i). If the sum of the partnership's bases in the distributed unrealized receivables and inventory items exceeds the basis to be allocated, then the partnership's bases in those properties must be reduced by the amount of such excess. § 732(c)(1)(A)(ii). The reduction is achieved (1) by first reducing the basis of assets with built-in losses (i.e., assets with an assigned basis greater than their value) in proportion to the amount of such built-in losses (and only to the extent of such losses), and (2) by then making additional reductions in basis in proportion to the remaining adjusted basis of the unrealized receivables and inventory items. § 732(c)(1)(A)(ii), (3). If the basis to be allocated is greater than the partnership's basis in the distributed unrealized receivables and inventory items, then each other distributed asset is tentatively assigned a basis in those assets equal to the partnership's basis in those assets. § 732(c)(1)(B)(i). Basis increases or decreases then must be allocated to the other distributed assets if the partner's remaining basis (after allocation to unrealized receivables and inventory items) is greater or less than the sum of the partnership's bases in those assets. § 732(c)(1)(B)(ii). If an overall increase is required, the increase is allocated (1) first among properties with unrealized appreciation in proportion to such appreciation (and only to the extent of the appreciation), and (2) then in proportion to the fair market values of the properties. § 732(c)(2). If an overall decrease is required, the decrease is allocated (1) first among properties with unrealized depreciation in proportion to such depreciation (and only to the extent of the depreciation), and (2) then in proportion to the remaining adjusted bases of the properties. § 732(c)(3). For the definition of "unrealized receivables" and "inventory items" see, XVIII.B.2.b., at page 423, supra.

5) Holding Period

The distributee partner may tack the partnership's holding period in distributed property under § 735(b). Section 735(a) preserves the ordinary income character indefinitely in distributed unrealized receivables and for five years in distributed inventory items.

Example (1):   A, a retiring partner, has an outside basis of $25,000. In a liquidating distribution to which § 751(b) does not apply, A receives $15,000 cash and inventory items of the partnership which have an inside basis of $5,000. A first reduces her outside basis to $10,000 as a result of the cash distribution; $5,000 of the remaining basis is allocated to the inventory items under § 732(b) and (c)(1)(A)(i). Finally, under § 731(a)(2), A recognizes $5,000 of capital loss (the excess of her $25,000 outside basis over the sum of the $15,000 cash and $5,000 transferred basis in the inventory).

Example (2):   Assume that A in Example (1) received $15,000 cash, inventory items with a $5,000 inside basis, and a capital asset with a $2,000 inside basis. A again reduces her outside basis to $10,000 as a result of the cash distribution; $5,000 of the remaining basis is allocated to the inventory items under § 732(b) and (c)(1)(A)(i) and the remaining $5,000 basis is all allocated to the capital asset under § 732(c)(1)(B) and (c)(2). No loss is recognized. Instead, since the partner received partnership property in addition to the cash and inventory items (the capital asset), the partner's unrecognized gain or loss is preserved in that property through the basis rules.

b. Tax Consequences of § 736(b) Payments to the Partnership

A partnership generally does not recognize gain or loss on a distribution of property and the distribution has no impact on the inside basis of the partnership's retained assets. §§ 731(b); 734(a). But if the partnership has a § 754 election in effect, it may adjust the inside basis of its retained assets to prevent certain distortions. Under § 734(b), the partnership increases the inside basis of its retained assets by the amount of any gain recognized by the distributee partner and decreases the basis in the event the distributee partner recognizes a loss. § 734(b)(1)(A), (2)(A). These adjustments must be allocated only to capital assets or § 1231(b) property. Reg. § 1.755–1(c)(1)(ii). In addition, if the basis rules for distributed property result in a difference between the partnership's inside basis for an asset and the asset's basis in the hands of the distributee partner, the partnership adjusts the inside basis of its retained properties. § 734(b)(1)(B), (2)(B). For example, if a partner takes a distributed asset with a reduced basis because the partner has insufficient outside basis, the partnership increases its inside basis in property in the same class by the amount of the reduction. § 734(b)(1)(B); Reg. § 1.755–1(c)(1)(i). And if the basis of a distributed capital asset or § 1231(b) property is increased above its inside basis under § 732(c)(2), the partnership must reduce its inside basis in property of that class by the amount of the increase. § 734(b)(2)(B); Reg. § 1.755–1(c)(1)(i). See generally XIX.B.2., at page 445, *supra,* for the operation of § 734 and allocation of § 734 adjustments under § 755.

c. Interaction of § 736 and § 751(b)

If a distribution shifts the distributee partner's interests in § 751 property and non–§ 751 property, the shift is identified and considered a sale or exchange of the property between the partner and the partnership. § 751(b). See XIX.D.1., at page 452, *supra,* for a discussion of the operation of § 751(b). Because § 736(b) payments are considered a distribution by the partnership, they may trigger § 751(b). But § 736(b) does not apply to the distributee partner's share of unrealized receivables and unstated goodwill, two types of property which normally must be analyzed in applying § 751(b), when those payments are for a general partner's interest in a services partnership. Section 751(b)(2)(B) addresses these jurisdictional questions by providing that § 751(b) does not apply to payments described in § 736(a). As a result, in the case of a general partnership interest in a services partnership, the distributee partner's pre-and post-distribution shares of unrealized receivables and unstated goodwill are ignored in applying § 751(b) to § 736(b) payments. Note, however, that unrealized receivables are still inventory items for purposes of determining whether the partnership's inventory items are substantially appreciated.

Example: The ABC partnership, which is a services partnership in which capital is not a material income-producing factor, has three equal general partners and the following balance sheet:

| | **Assets** | | | **Partners' Capital** | |
	A.B.	**F.M.V.**		**A.B.**	**F.M.V.**
Cash	$60,000	$ 60,000			
Accounts Receivable	0	15,000	A	$30,000	$ 60,000
Inventory	27,000	30,000	B	30,000	60,000
Capital Asset	3,000	45,000	C	30,000	60,000
Goodwill	0	30,000			
Total	$90,000	$180,000		$90,000	$180,000

Assume A's partnership interest is liquidated and A receives $60,000 cash from the partnership with no designation that $10,000 is paid for his share of partnership goodwill. A will be taxed on $15,000 of ordinary income (the amount of his share of unrealized receivables and unstated goodwill) under § 736(a). See XX.A.3., at page 463, *infra.* The inventory items of the partnership (unrealized receivables and the inventory) are substantially appreciated in value because their $45,000 fair market value exceeds 120% of the basis of those assets. While payments for the unrealized receivables are characterized under § 736(a) and the unrealized receivables are not considered in the § 751(b) analysis, those assets are inventory items for purposes of testing for substantial appreciation.

A's share of § 736(b) assets (cash, inventory and capital asset) prior to the distribution is $20,000 of cash, $10,000 of inventory, and $15,000 of capital asset. After the distribution, A has $45,000 of cash disregarding the payments under § 736(a). Thus, in the § 736(b) distribution A exchanged $10,000 of inventory and $15,000 of capital asset for $25,000 of cash. Only the inventory-for-cash exchange is governed by § 751(b) because the cash and capital asset are both non–§ 751 property. Under § 751(b), A is deemed to have received $10,000 of inventory with a transferred basis of $9,000 and sold the inventory to the partnership for $10,000 cash, recognizing $1,000 of ordinary income.

The last step is to determine the tax results of the distribution of the remaining $35,000 of cash. A's outside basis after the § 751(b) constructive distribution and exchange is $21,000 ($30,000 less $9,000 transferred basis in inventory constructively distributed to A). The $35,000 cash distribution will reduce A's outside basis to zero and A will recognize $14,000 of capital gain under § 731. If the partnership had a § 754 election in effect, it would receive a $14,000 upward inside basis adjustment under § 734(b)(1)(A), which would be allocated to the partnership's capital asset and goodwill (the capital assets and § 1231(b) property of the partnership).

3. **§ 736(a) Payments**

   a. **Definition of § 736(a) Payments**

   Section 736(a) payments are all liquidating payments for property not within § 736(b). This is a deceptively broad category. As a practical matter, § 736(a) only applies to payments for: (1) § 751(c) unrealized receivables (excluding recapture items) and goodwill, unless the partnership agreement expressly provides for payment with respect to goodwill, and only when the payments are for a general partnership interest in a partnership in which capital is not a material income-producing factor, and (2) "premium" amounts paid in addition to the partner's share of partnership property that are in the nature of mutual insurance. Reg. § 1.736–1(a)(2).

   Only "payments" (cash or otherwise) for the retiring partner's share of § 736(a) assets are governed by § 736(a). Thus, an in-kind distribution of unrealized receivables to a retiring general partner in a services partnership is governed by § 736(b), not § 736(a). In addition, to the extent of a partner's share of inside basis in unrealized receivables and goodwill (including special basis adjustments under § 732(d) or § 734(b)), those assets are excluded from § 736(a) and treated as § 736(b) property. Reg. § 1.736–1(b)(2), (3).

   b. **Tax Treatment of § 736(a) Payments**

   Section 736(a) payments are taxed to the distributee partner as either a distributive share or a guaranteed payment, depending upon whether the amount of the payment is dependent on partnership income. § 736(a)(1), (2). If the amount of the payment is determined with regard to partnership income, the payment is considered a distributive share that will have the effect of reducing the distributive shares of other partners (which is equivalent to a deduction). Reg. § 1.736–1(a)(3)(i), (4). If the payment is determined without regard to partnership income, it is a guaranteed payment that is deductible by the partnership. Reg. § 1.736–1(a)(3)(ii), (4).

   c. **Timing of § 736(a) Payments: In General**

   A § 736(a) payment characterized as a distributive share is included by the distributee partner in the taxable year within which the partnership's taxable year ends. If a § 736(a) payment is characterized as a guaranteed payment, it is included in income in the year in which the partnership is entitled to deduct the payment. Reg. § 1.736–1(a)(5).

   d. **Special Treatment for Partnership Goodwill**

   Section 736(b) generally permits the distributee partner to take advantage of the nonrecognition/capital gain regime generally applicable to partnership distributions under § 731. And since § 736(b) payments are considered a distribution of partnership property, the partnership (i.e., the remaining partners) receives no deduction. Section 736(a) payments, on the other hand, produce ordinary income to the distributee partner and a reduction in the income of the other partners via either reduced distributive shares or a partnership deduction. Section 736 permits a distributee general partner and a services partnership to select which of these tax results they desire for payments with respect to partnership goodwill. Absent a provision in the partnership agreement providing for payment with respect to goodwill, such payments are taxed under § 736(a). § 736(b)(2)(B). For this purpose, the partnership agreement includes any modifications (oral or written) made up to the time for filing the partnership's return in the year of liquidation. § 761(c); Reg. § 1.761–1(c). The courts generally require that the partnership agreement specifically state that a payment is for goodwill. See *Smith v. Comm'r*, 313 F.2d 16 (10th Cir.1962). If, however, there is a statement about a payment in the partnership agreement but the statement is ambiguous, a court will attempt to ascertain the intentions of the parties concerning whether the payment is for goodwill. See *Comm'r v. Jackson Inv. Co.*, 346 F.2d 187 (9th Cir.1965).

4. Allocation and Timing of § 736 Payments
a. Allocation

If liquidating distributions are made to a partner over more than one year, allocation and timing issues are raised. First, the payments made each year must be allocated between the § 736(b) portion and the § 736(a) portion. The distributee partner and the partnership may agree on the allocation provided that the total amount allocated to § 736(b) property does not exceed the value of that property at the date of retirement. Reg. § 1.736–1(b)(5)(iii). In the absence of an agreement, the regulations provide different allocation rules depending on the nature of the payments. If the payments are fixed in amount and paid over a fixed number of years, the § 736(b) portion each year is equal to the agreed fixed payment for the year, multiplied by a ratio of the total fixed payments under § 736(b), and divided by the total fixed payments under § 736(a) and (b). The remainder of the amount received in the year is treated as a § 736(a) payment. If the total agreed payment for the year is not made, the amount actually paid is first considered to be the § 736(b) payment. Reg. § 1.736–1(b)(5)(i).

If the payments are not fixed in amount, they are first treated as § 736(b) payments to the extent of the partner's interest in partnership property and, thereafter, as § 736(a) payments. Reg. § 1.736–1(b)(5)(ii).

b. Timing

Section 736(a) payments which are considered a distributive share are included in income in the taxable year in which the partnership's taxable year ends. Section 736(a) payments which are considered a guaranteed payment are included in the year in which the partnership is entitled to a deduction. Section

736(b) payments are taken into account in the year in which they are made by the partnership. Reg. § 1.736–1(a)(5). A partner is permitted to receive actual and constructive cash distributions under § 736(b) until her outside basis is recovered before recognizing gain under § 731. Reg. § 1.731–1(a)(1). A loss is recognized in the year of the final distribution, but only if the property distributed consists only of money, unrealized receivables and inventory items. Reg. § 1.731–1(a)(2). Alternatively, a partner receiving a fixed sum may elect to report a pro rata portion of the total gain or loss as each § 736(b) payment is made. Reg. § 1.736–1(b)(6).

Example (1):   The ABC general partnership, a services partnership in which capital is not a material income-producing factor, has the following balance sheet:

	Assets			Partners' Capital	
	A.B.	**F.M.V.**		**A.B.**	**F.M.V.**
Cash	$45,000	$ 45,000	A	$24,000	$ 40,000
Accounts Receivable	0	15,000	B	24,000	40,000
Capital Asset	12,000	24,000	C	24,000	40,000
Goodwill	15,000	36,000			
Total	$72,000	$120,000		$72,000	$120,000

Assume A receives $44,000 cash in liquidation of her partnership interest and the partnership agreement has no provision regarding goodwill. A's interest in the accounts receivable and appreciation in the goodwill is not within § 736(b). § 736(b)(2), (3); Reg. § 1.736–1(b)(2), (3). A's share of § 736(b) assets is $28,000 ($15,000 of cash, $8,000 of capital asset, and $5,000 of the basis in the goodwill). The remaining $16,000 that A receives ($44,000 less $28,000) is the § 736(a) payment which is attributable to A's $5,000 share of accounts receivable, $7,000 of appreciation in the goodwill, and $4,000 of premium payments. The $16,000 § 736(a) payment is paid without regard to partnership income and is a § 736(a)(2) guaranteed payment which will result in ordinary income to A and produce a deduction for B and C.

The $28,000 § 736(b) payment is not subject to § 751(b) because the partnership has no inventory items other than the accounts receivable which are disregarded under § 751(b)(2)(B) and § 736(a)(2). The $28,000 § 736(b) payment will result in $4,000 of capital gain to A under § 731(a)(1) ($28,000 distribution less $24,000 basis). If the partnership has made a § 754 election, it will receive a $4,000 upward inside basis adjustment which will be allocated to the capital asset and goodwill.

Example (2):   If the partnership in Example (1) paid the $44,000 to A at the rate of $11,000 per year for four years, then each year's payment will have to be allocated between § 736(a) and (b) payments. Since the payments are fixed in amount for a fixed period, $28,000/$44,000 or 7/11 of each payment is treated as a § 736(b) payment. The other 4/11 of each payment is treated as a § 736(a) payment. Thus, on A's receipt of each $11,000 payment, $7,000 is treated as a § 736(b) payment and $4,000 is ordinary income under § 736(a)(2), and B and C each receive a $2,000 deduction. The $7,000 each of § 736(b) payment can be treated as all outside basis recovery in each of the first three years and A will have $4,000 of capital gain in the fourth year. Alternatively, A can elect to prorate the total $4,000 capital gain over the four $11,000 payments, $1,000 per year.

Example (3):   Assume that in Example (1) A is to receive 40% of the partnership profits for four years in liquidation of her partnership interest and the profits share turns out to be $11,000 per year. Since the payments are not fixed, under the regulations they are considered to first be § 736(b) payments. Thus, the first $28,000 of payments (all of the first and second years payments and $6,000 of the third year payment) are treated as cash distributions and A will recognize $4,000 of capital gain in the third year after full recovery of her $24,000 inside basis. The remaining $5,000 of the third year payment and the full $11,000 of the fourth year payment will be a distributive share of partnership profits (characterized by the profits) which will reduce the distributive shares allocable to B and C.

Example (4):   Assume that in Example (1) A's basis in her partnership interest is $32,000 and the partnership distributes $11,000 per year for four years to A in liquidation of her partnership interest. On these facts the § 736(a) and (b) portions of each payment would still be 4/11 and 7/11, respectively. Thus, on receipt of each year's payment A would have $4,000 of ordinary income under § 736(a)(2) and the partnership (B and C) would receive a corresponding $4,000 deduction. Under § 736(b), A would have a $4,000 capital loss under § 731(a)(2) ($32,000 adjusted basis less $28,000 § 736(b) payments). A can elect to recognize the full $4,000 of loss in the final year of the payments or recognize the loss pro rata, $1,000 per year, as payments are made.

5. Liquidation vs. Sale
a. In General

A retiring partner can structure his departure from the partnership as either a liquidation of the interest under § 736 or as a sale of the interest to the continuing partners. The choice can have a significant effect on the tax consequences to the retiring and continuing partners. The critical difference is that § 736(a) liquidating distributions generally produce ordinary income to the retiring partner and reduce the income reportable by the continuing partners, while a sale of an interest to the continuing partners produces capital gain to the retiring partner, except as provided in § 751(a), and the continuing partners must capitalize the purchase price as part of their outside bases. The partners are free to structure the transaction in whatever manner they select. In a liquidation of a general partnership interest in a services partnership, the partners can decide whether to expressly provide for payment for goodwill and can determine the allocation and timing of § 736(a) payments. When the parties disagree over the sale versus liquidation issue, the courts will characterize the transaction according to its "substance" by reviewing the partnership agreement and other relevant documents to determine the intent of the parties. See generally, *Foxman v. Comm'r*, 352 F.2d 466 (3d Cir.1965) (transaction characterized as a sale); and *Cooney v. Comm'r*, 65 T.C. 101 (1975) (transaction characterized as a liquidation of the partner's interest).

b. Abandonment of a Partnership Interest

A variation on the liquidation vs. sale issue arises when a partner abandons a worthless partnership interest. In Rev.Rul. 93–80, 1993–2 C.B. 239, the Service ruled that a loss incurred on the abandonment or worthlessness of a partnership interest results in an ordinary loss. But if there is an actual or deemed distribution to the partner, or if the transaction is in substance a sale or exchange, the partner recognizes a capital loss except to the extent § 751(b) provides otherwise. See XIX.D.1., *supra,* at page 452, A deemed distribution for this purpose includes a decrease in the partner's share of partnership liabilities which under § 752(b) is considered a distribution of money to the partner.

B. Liquidation of the Entire Partnership

1. Voluntary Liquidation
a. In General

The tax consequences of a complete liquidation of a partnership are different from the tax consequences of liquidating a single partner's interest. The rules in § 731, § 732 and § 735 regarding partnership distributions determine the tax results of liquidating distributions to the partners. Section 736, however, does not apply to the liquidation of an entire partnership because that section contemplates payments by an ongoing partnership. But § 736 will apply to payments made to a retiring partner in a situation where termination of the partnership is contemplated at the end of the payments. Reg. § 1.736–1(a)(6).

Section 751(b), however, is applicable to distributions in complete liquidation of a partnership. See XIX.D.1., at page 452, *supra,* for the operation of § 751(b). If a partner receives disproportionate amounts of unrealized receivables, substantially appreciated inventory, or non–§ 751 property in a liquidation of a partnership, § 751(b) will treat that portion of the distribution as an exchange of such property between the partner and the partnership. In Revenue Ruling 77–412, 1977–2 C.B. 223, the Service ruled that in the case of a two-person partnership, § 751(b) is applied by treating the distribution as a sale or exchange between the distributee partner and the partnership even though after the distribution the partnership consisted of a single partner.

b. Incorporation of a Partnership

If partners decide to terminate their partnership and incorporate its business, the transaction may take any one of three forms: (1) the partnership may transfer its assets and liabilities to the newly formed corporation in exchange for stock and then transfer the stock to its partners, (2) the partnership may liquidate by distributing its assets and liabilities to its partners who then transfer the assets to the newly formed corporation in exchange for stock, or (3) the partners may transfer their partnership interests to the newly formed corporation in exchange for stock. Assuming the requirements of § 351 (see IV, *supra*) are met, the incorporation will be a nonrecognition transaction. In Revenue Ruling 84–111, 1984–2 C.B. 88, the Service ruled that it will follow the form of incorporation selected by the partners in applying the provisions of Subchapter K. This ruling permits partners to select the most favorable method of incorporating if there are differences between inside and outside basis or the holding period of partnership assets and the partners' partnership interests.

c. Partnership Mergers and Divisions

1) Merger or Consolidation

If two or more partnerships merge or consolidate, the resulting partnership is considered the continuation of any merged or consolidated partnership whose members own more than 50% in the capital and profits of the resulting partnership. § 708(b)(2)(A). If the resulting partnership can be considered a continuation of more than one of the merged or consolidated partnerships under that test, it is considered a continuation of solely the partnership that contributed assets with the greatest fair market value (net of liabilities) to the resulting partnership. Reg. § 1.708–1(c)(1). Any other merged or consolidated partnership is considered terminated. If the members of none of the merged or consolidated partnerships have an interest of more than 50% in capital and profits of the resulting partnership, then all of the merged or consolidated partnerships are terminated and a new partnership results. Id. A merger or combination of partnerships can take three forms: (1) the terminated partnership can contribute its assets and liabilities to the resulting partnership in exchange for a partnership interest and then distribute interests in the resulting partnership to its partners in liquidation (assets-over form), (2) the terminating partnership could distribute all of its assets to its partners in liquidation of the partners' interests and then the partners could immediately contribute the distributed assets to the resulting partnership in exchange for partnership interests (assets-up form), or (3) the partners in the terminating partnership can transfer their partnership interests to the resulting partnership in exchange for partnership interests and then the resulting partnership can liquidate the terminating partnership (interest-over form). The tax results of a merger of partnerships may vary depending on the form the transaction takes. For example, the mixing bowl rules (§§ 704(c)(1)(B) and 737) may potentially apply in an assets-up merger but not apply in an assets-over merger. Reg. §§ 1.704–4(c)(4), 1.737–2(b)(1). The adjusted basis of the assets in the resulting partnership also may vary depending on the form of the transaction.

Under the regulations, the form selected for a merger will be respected if the partners select the assets-over or assets-up form. Reg. § 1.708–1(c)(3). If no particular form is used or if the interest-over form is selected, the merger is treated as taking the assets-over form. Reg. § 1.708–1(c)(3)(i). Increases and decreases in partnership liabilities associated with a merger are netted by the partners in the terminating and resulting partnerships to determine the effect under § 752. Reg. § 1.752–1(f); see Reg. § 1.752–1(g) Example 2. If the resulting partnership transfers cash to the terminating partnership (in addition to partnership interests) in order to buy out a partner in the terminating partnership in an assets-over transaction, the sale of the partner's interest will be respected if the parties specify (1) that the resulting partnership is purchasing an interest from a particular partner, and (2) the consideration that is transferred for each interest sold. Reg. § 1.708–1(c)(4).

2) Divisions

If a partnership divides into two or more partnerships, the resulting partnerships are considered a continuation of the prior partnership if members of the resulting partnership had an interest of more than 50% in the capital and profits of the prior partnership. § 708(b)(2)(B). Any other resulting partnership is considered a new partnership. Reg. § 1.708–1(d)(1). Partnership divisions can be accomplished through an assets-over or assets-up form. The regulations respect whichever of those two forms is selected. If no form is selected or if the assets-up form is not selected, the division is treated as taking the assets-over form. Reg. § 1.708–1(d)(3).

In a partnership division taking the assets-up form, the mixing bowl rules (§§ 704(c)(1)(B) and 737) may be triggered. In an assets-over division, the partnership interest in the resulting partnership is treated as § 704(c) property to the extent that the interest is received in exchange for § 704(c) property. Reg. § 1.704–4(d)(1). Consequently, the distribution of interests may (1) trigger § 704(c)(1)(B) to the extent interests are received by partners who did not contribute § 704(c) property, or (2) trigger § 737 if a partner who contributed § 704(c) property receives an interest in the resulting partnership that is not attributable to § 704(c) property.

2. Termination Forced by Statute

a. § 708(b)(1)(B)

Under § 708(b)(1)(B), a partnership is considered to have terminated if within a 12–month period there is a sale or exchange of 50% or more of the total interests in partnership capital and profits. Because the interests sold or exchanged making up the 50% requirement must be different partnership interests, resales within 12 months of the same interest are not counted. Sales between partners are counted for the test but dispositions by gift, bequest, inheritance, and through liquidation of a partnership interest are not counted as "sales or exchanges." Reg. § 1.708–1(b)(2).

b. Effect of Termination

If a partnership is terminated under § 708(b)(1)(B), the partnership is deemed to contribute its assets and liabilities to a new partnership in exchange for a partnership interest. Reg. § 1.708–1(b)(4). The terminated partnership then liquidates by distributing partnership interests in the new partnership to the purchaser and the other partners. Id. The capital account of any transferee partner and the capital accounts of the other partners carry over to the new partnership and termination of the partnership is disregarded in the maintenance and computation of capital accounts. Reg. § 1.704–1(b)(2)(iv)(l). If the terminated partnership has a § 754 election in effect (including one made on its final return for the year in which the sale occurs), the election applies to the incoming partner and the bases of the partnership's assets are adjusted under §§ 743 and 755 before the deemed contribution. A partner with a basis adjustment in property held by the partnership that terminates continues to have the same basis adjustment with respect to property deemed contributed to the new partnership, even if the new partnership does not make a § 754 election. Because a § 708(b)(1)(B) termination does not result in a distribution of assets to the partners, the mixing bowl rules (§§ 704(c)(1)(B) and 737) do not apply to the termination. Reg. §§ 1.704–4(c)(3), 1.737–2(a). A new seven-year period also does not begin to run under the mixing bowl rules. Reg. §§ 1.704–4(a)(4)(ii), 1.737–2(a). But a later distribution of § 704(c) property by the new partnership is subject to the mixing bowl rules to the same extent that a distribution by the terminated partnership would have been subject to the mixing bowl rules. Reg. §§ 1.704–4(c)(3), 1.737–2(a). For holding period purposes, the Tax Court has held that a partner who acquired a partnership asset by way of a purchase which terminated the partnership could not tack the partnership's holding period in the asset. *McCauslen v. Comm'r,* 45 T.C. 588 (1966). The court reasoned that since the purchase terminated the partnership, the asset was acquired by purchase rather than through a distribution from the partnership.

Example (1): The equal AB partnership has the following balance sheet:

| | Assets | | | Partners' Capital | |
	A.B.	F.M.V.		A.B.	F.M.V.
Cash	$30,000	$30,000	A	$25,000	$40,000
Accounts Receivable	0	10,000	B	$25,000	$40,000
Capital Asset	20,000	40,000			
Total	$50,000	$80,000		$50,000	$80,000

None of the partnership's assets were contributed by A or B. On July 1 of the current year, A sells his interest to C for $40,000. Assume the partnership has never made a § 754 election. As a result of A's sale to C, the partnership will terminate under § 708(b)(1)(B). The partnership is then deemed to contribute all of its assets to a new BC partnership in exchange for an interest in the new partnership. Under § 722 the BC partnership will take the assets with the same basis as the AB partnership. Under § 723 the AB partnership will take the partnership interest with a basis of $50,000 (the basis of the contributed assets). The AB partnership will then liquidate and distribute one-half interests in the BC partnership to B and C. B will take the partnership interest with a $25,000 basis under § 732(b). C will take the partnership interest with a $40,000 basis under § 732(b). C will succeed to A's capital account and the termination will have no effect on the maintenance of capital accounts. The BC partnership will have the following balance sheet:

| | Assets | | | Partners' Capital | |
	A.B.	F.M.V.		A.B.	F.M.V.
Cash	$30,000	$30,000	B	$25,000	$40,000
Accounts Receivable	0	10,000	C	40,000	40,000
Capital Asset	35,000	40,000			
Total	$65,000	$80,000		$65,000	$80,000

Example (2): If the partnership in Example (1) had a § 754 election in effect, C would receive a $15,000 personal inside basis adjustment ($40,000 outside basis less $25,000 share of the partnership's previously taxed capital) on the purchase. That adjustment would be allocated $5,000 to the accounts receivable and $10,000 to the capital asset, which would provide C with a total personal inside basis of $5,000 in the accounts receivable and $20,000 in the capital asset. The terminated AB partnership would again contribute all its assets to the new BC partnership for an interest in the new partnership. Under § 722, the BC partnership will take the assets with the same basis (including the inside basis adjustments) as the terminated partnership. Under § 723, the AB partnership will take the partnership interest with a $65,000 basis (the basis of the contributed assets). The AB partnership will then liquidate and distribute one-half interests in the BC partnership to B and C. B will take the partnership interest with a $25,000 basis under § 732(b). C will take the partnership interest with a $40,000 basis under § 732(b). C will succeed to A's capital account and the termination will have no effect on the maintenance of capital accounts. The BC partnership will have the following balance sheet:

| | **Assets** | | | **Partners' Capital** | |
	A.B.	**F.M.V.**		**A.B.**	**F.M.V.**
Cash	$30,000	$30,000	B	$25,000	$40,000
Accounts Receivable	5,000	10,000	C	40,000	40,000
Capital Asset	30,000	40,000			
Total	$65,000	$80,000		$65,000	$80,000

C will continue to have a personal inside basis adjustment of $5,000 in the accounts receivable and $10,000 in the capital asset even if the BC partnership does not make a § 754 election.

C. Review Questions

1. Name the types of partnership property for which § 736(a) payments are made.

2. Section 736(a) payments are considered a distributive share if the amount is dependent on partnership income or a § 707(c) guaranteed payment if the amount is determined without reference to partnership income. True or False?

3. The ABC general partnership, which is a services partnership in which capital is not a material income-producing factor, has the following balance sheet:

| | **Assets** | | | **Partners' Capital** | |
	A.B.	**F.M.V.**		**A.B.**	**F.M.V.**
Cash	$60,000	$60,000	A	$30,000	$50,000
Accounts Receivable	0	30,000	B	30,000	50,000
Capital Asset	15,000	30,000	C	30,000	50,000
Goodwill	15,000	30,000			
Total	$90,000	$150,000		$90,000	$150,000

Assume A receives a $50,000 cash liquidating distribution for his partnership interest and the partnership agreement has no provision regarding payment for goodwill. Determine the tax consequences of the distribution to A.

*

XXI

DEATH OF A PARTNER

Analysis

A. Introduction

When a partner dies, his partnership interest may be disposed of in one of three ways: (1) the interest may pass to the partner's designated successor in interest who continues as a partner; (2) the interest may be sold at the partner's death pursuant to a preexisting buy-sell agreement; or (3) the interest may be liquidated pursuant to a preexisting agreement among the partners. Each of these possibilities has different tax consequences to the deceased partner and the partnership.

B. The Deceased Partner's Distributive Share In The Year Of Death

When a partner dies, his taxable year closes as of the date of death. § 443(a)(2). In general, the partnership's taxable year does not close when a partner dies. § 706(c)(1). The taxable year of the partnership, however, does close with respect to a partner whose interest in the partnership terminates, whether by reason of death, liquidation, or otherwise. § 706(c)(2). Thus, a deceased partner's final tax return includes a distributive share of partnership income or loss for the portion of the partnership's taxable year prior to death.

> *Example:* Partner B is a calendar year taxpayer and is a member of the ABC partnership, which has a taxable year ending on November 30. If B dies on September 15, 2003, his "decedent's final return" for January 1 to September 15, 2003, will include a distributive share from the partnership for its November 30, 2003 taxable year.

C. Estate Tax, Income in Respect of a Decedent, and Basis Consequences

1. Federal Estate Tax
The fair market value of the deceased partner's partnership interest, including any distributive share earned prior to death, is includible in the partner's gross estate for federal estate tax purposes. §§ 2031; 2033.

2. Income in Respect of a Decedent ("IRD")
a. In General
Property passing from a decedent generally takes a basis equal to its fair market value at the date of the decedent's death or the § 2032 alternate valuation date. § 1014(a). The "date of death" basis rule does not apply to property which constitutes a right to an item of "income in respect of a decedent" under § 691. § 1014(c). In general, income in respect of a decedent ("IRD") is a right to income which was earned by the decedent but not previously taxed. A classic example of IRD is salary earned by a cash method taxpayer who dies before the salary is paid. The decedent's taxable year ends

as of the date of death and since the salary is not paid it is not included in the decedent's final income tax return. §§ 443(a)(2); 451(a). Since the right to the salary payment is IRD, it is not eligible for the date of death basis rule. The decedent's successor in interest thus recognizes the salary as gross income when it is paid. Other common forms of IRD are accounts receivable earned by a cash method taxpayer and installment sale obligations under § 453. But tangible property, including appreciation in value (whether or not subject to recapture), is subject to the date of death basis rule and is not IRD.

b. Distributive Share in Year of Death

The distributive share for the partnership's taxable year ending after a deceased partner's death is not IRD because it must be included in the deceased partner's final tax return. See § 706(c)(2)(A).

c. Income in Respect of a Decedent in a Sale at Death or Continuing Interest

The courts have used an aggregate approach to determine whether partnership items constitute IRD. Thus, a decedent partner's share of accounts receivable of a cash method partnership is IRD. *Quick's Trust v. Comm'r*, 54 T.C. 1336 (1970), aff'd per curiam, 444 F.2d 90 (8th Cir.1971); *Woodhall v. Comm'r*, 454 F.2d 226 (9th Cir.1972).

d. Income in Respect of a Decedent in a Liquidation of a Partnership Interest

Under § 753, all § 736(a) payments (payments for a general partnership interest in a services partnership for unrealized receivables and unstated goodwill as well as premium payments made to any liquidated partner) made by a partnership to an estate or other successor in interest of a deceased partner also are IRD. If a partnership interest held by an estate or successor in interest is liquidated by the partnership, any § 736(a) payments are not eligible for a date of death basis. Payments for depreciation recapture are not within § 736(a) and are not IRD. An aggregate theory also could classify payments for § 736(b) property (e.g., unrealized receivables within § 736(b)) as IRD.

3. Outside and Inside Basis

The basis of a partnership interest acquired from a decedent is the fair market value of the interest at the date of her death or at the alternate valuation date, increased by the successor's share of partnership liabilities and reduced by the value of IRD items. Reg. § 1.742–1. The Service has ruled that since a successor's outside basis is reduced by IRD items, § 743 cannot be applied to give the successor the benefit of an inside basis adjustment in such items. Rev.Rul. 66–325, 1966–2 C.B. 249.

Example (1):   A is an equal general partner in the ABCD services partnership which on January 1 of the current year had the following balance sheet:

	Assets			Partners' Capital	
	A.B.	**F.M.V.**		**A.B.**	**F.M.V.**
Cash	$24,000	$24,000	A	$15,000	$24,000
Accounts Receivable	0	12,000	B	15,000	24,000
Depreciable Property (all § 1245 gain)	20,000	40,000	C	15,000	24,000
Capital Asset	16,000	20,000	D	15,000	24,000
Total	$60,000	$96,000		$60,000	$96,000

Both A and the partnership are cash method, calendar year taxpayers. On June 1 of the current year A dies. In addition to the balance sheet assets listed above, the partnership earned $8,000 of income in the current year prior to June 1 of which A's share is $2,000.

For federal estate tax purposes, A's gross estate will include $26,000 as the fair market value of the partnership interest ($24,000 plus $2,000 share of income). The partnership's taxable year will close with respect to A and her $2,000 share of the partnership's income for the current year will be included in her final tax return and will not be IRD. See § 706(c)(2)(A). Under case law, A's $3,000 share of the accounts receivable is IRD. A's estate or successor in interest will take a $23,000 basis in the partnership ($26,000 fair market value less $3,000 of income in respect of a decedent). If the partnership had a § 754 election in effect, A's successor would obtain a $8,000 inside basis adjustment ($23,000 less $15,000 share of the adjusted basis to the partnership of its property) which would be allocated to the $2,000 share of this year's income, depreciable property ($5,000) and capital asset ($1,000).

Example (2): If A's entire partnership interest in Example (1) were sold as of the date of her death pursuant to a preexisting buy-sell agreement, the partnership's taxable year would close with respect to A and she would include her $2,000 share of partnership income and that item would not be IRD. § 706(c)(2)(A). A's share of the partnership's accounts receivable is still IRD and the basis of A's partnership interest for purposes of the sale would be $23,000 ($26,000 less $3,000 of income in respect of a decedent). If the partnership had a § 754 election in effect, A's partnership interest would obtain a $8,000 inside basis adjustment which would be allocated to the $2,000 share of this year's income, depreciable property ($5,000) and capital asset ($1,000).

Example (3): If A's entire partnership interest in Example (1) were liquidated, the partnership's taxable year closes as to A. § 706(c)(2)(A). Thus,

A will include her $2,000 distributive share of the partnership's income and the distributive share will not be IRD. In addition, under § 753, the amount of § 736(a) payments will be IRD. This will include the $3,000 paid for A's share of partnership unrealized receivables ($3,000 of accounts receivable). The depreciation recapture is not an unrealized receivable for purposes of § 736. § 751(c). If the partnership had unstated goodwill or A's successor were paid a premium for the interest, those amounts also would be IRD. A's successor's outside basis will be $23,000 ($26,000 fair market value less $3,000 of income in respect of a decedent). If the partnership had a § 754 election in effect or a § 732(d) election were made, A's partnership interest would obtain a $8,000 inside basis adjustment which would be allocated to the $2,000 share of this year's income, depreciable property ($5,000) and capital asset ($1,000).

D.   Review Questions

1. When a partner dies, the partnership's taxable year closes with respect to the partner regardless of the date of death. True or False?

2. If the deceased partner's partnership interest is sold at death pursuant to a buy-sell agreement, the partnership's taxable year closes with respect to the partner and the deceased partner's final return will include his distributive share of partnership income or loss for the short taxable year. True or False?

3. Which of the following is "income in respect of a decedent":

   (a) The distributive share for the partnership's taxable year ending after a deceased partner's death?

   (b) The portion of a deceased partner's interest held by a successor in interest attributable to a cash method partnership's accounts receivable?

   (c) The portion of a deceased partner's interest held by a successor in interest attributable to depreciable equipment, including depreciation recapture?

   (d) § 736(b) payments attributable to depreciation recapture?

*

XXII

PARTNERSHIP ANTI–ABUSE RULES

Analysis

A. Introduction

The flexible rules for taxing partnership activities provide taxpayers with considerable tax saving opportunities. That flexibility may lead to abuse if the statutory rules are applied literally. To combat improper reduction of income taxes, the Treasury promulgated Reg. § 1.701–2, which gives it the power to recast transactions that attempt to use partnerships in an abusive manner that is inconsistent with the intent of Subchapter K or the Code and regulations. The partnership anti-abuse regulations contain two main provisions. The first allows the IRS to recast a transaction as appropriate to achieve tax results that are consistent with the intent of Subchapter K. Reg. § 1.701–2(a)–(c). The second rule permits the IRS to disregard the partnership entity and treat a partnership as an aggregate of its partners (in whole or in part) as appropriate to carry out the purposes of the Code or regulations. Reg. § 1.702–2(e).

In addition to these general regulations, the IRS has included anti-abuse rules in some regulations interpreting specific Code sections. For example, the regulations under both § 704(c)(1)(B) and § 737 contain anti-abuse rules that require the Code and regulations to be applied in a manner consistent with the purpose of the statute. Reg. §§ 1.704–4(f), 1.737–4. Under those anti-abuse rules the Commissioner is given the power to recast a transaction to achieve appropriate tax results. Id.

B. Abuse of Subchapter K Rules

1. In General
a. "Common Law" Requirements of Subchapter K

The partnership anti-abuse regulations acknowledge that Subchapter K is intended to permit taxpayers to conduct joint business or investment activities through a flexible economic arrangement without incurring an entity-level tax. Reg. § 1.701–2(a). Implicit in the intent of Subchapter K, however, are the following common law requirements:

1) The partnership must be bona fide and each partnership transaction must be entered into for a substantial business purpose;

2) The form of each partnership transaction must be respected under substance over form principles; and

3) The tax consequences under Subchapter K to each partner of partnership operations and transactions between the partner and the partnership must accurately reflect the partners' economic agreement and clearly reflect the partner's income. Reg. § 1.701–2(a)(1)–(3).

b. Administrative Convenience Exception

The regulations recognize one exception to the three common law principles. Certain provisions of Subchapter K and the regulations were adopted to promote administrative convenience and other policy objectives. Thus, if the business purpose and substance over form requirements are satisfied, the clear reflection of income requirement is deemed to be met if the ultimate tax results of a transaction, taking into account all relevant facts and circumstances, are contemplated by an applicable provision of Subchapter K. Reg. § 1.701–2(a)(3).

Example: Partner withdraws from Partnership and receives a § 732(b) basis in the distributed assets, but Partnership does not make a § 754 election in order to avoid a reduction in inside basis. If the transaction satisfies the business purpose and substance-over-form requirement, the clear reflection of income requirement is deemed satisfied even though distortions may result because no § 754 election is made. The § 754 election is provided for administrative convenience and the ultimate tax consequences that follow from the failure to make the election are clearly contemplated by § 754. Reg. § 1.701–2(d) Example (9). Thus, the transaction will be respected.

c. Impermissible Tax Reduction Purpose

The regulations also provide that if a partnership is formed or availed of in connection with a transaction a principal purpose of which is to reduce substantially the present value of the partners' aggregate federal tax liability in a manner inconsistent with the intent of Subchapter K, the IRS can recast the transaction to achieve appropriate tax results. Reg. § 1.701–2(b). The regulations employ an all facts and circumstances test to determine whether a partnership is formed or availed of for an impermissible purpose.

2. Facts and Circumstances Analysis
a. In General

All facts and circumstances, including a comparison of the purported business purpose for a transaction and the claimed tax benefits resulting from the transaction, are examined to determine whether a partnership is formed or availed of to reduce tax liability in a manner inconsistent with Subchapter K. The regulations provide a nonexclusive list of factors which may indicate, but do not establish, that a partnership was used in such a manner. The presence or absence of any of the listed factors also does not create a presumption that a partnership was or was not used in an impermissible manner.

b. Specific Factors

The factors listed in the regulations are:

1) The present value of the partners' aggregate federal tax liability is substantially less than had the partners owned the partnership's assets and conducted the activities directly;

2) The present value of the partners' aggregate federal tax liability is substantially less than it would be if the purported separate transactions are integrated and treated as steps in a single transaction;

3) One or more partners either have nominal partnership interests or are substantially protected from any risk of loss from partnership activity or have little or no participation in partnership profits except for a preferred return that is a payment for use of capital;

4) Substantially all of the partners (measured by number of partnership interests) are related directly or indirectly to one another;

5) Partnership allocations are inconsistent with the purpose of § 704(b);

6) The benefits and burdens of property nominally contributed to the partnership are substantially retained by the contributing partner or a related party; and

7) The benefits and burdens of partnership property are shifted to a distributee partner before or after the property is actually distributed to the partner or a related party. Reg. § 1.701–2(c).

c. **Examples**

The regulations illustrate the abuse of Subchapter K rules with 11 detailed examples. The examples generally suggest that the IRS will not challenge transactions designed to take advantage of the principal features of Subchapter K, such as avoidance of an entity-level tax or the ability to make special allocations with substantial economic effect under § 704(b). In contrast, transactions involving a partner with a nominal interest, a temporary partner, or a plan to duplicate losses, are viewed as not consistent with the intent of Subchapter K. Although helpful, the examples specifically state that they "do not delineate the boundaries of either permissible or impermissible types of transactions" and that the addition or deletion of any fact in an example may alter the outcome of the transaction. Reg. § 1.701–2(d). Thus, the regulations can be relied upon as guidance in specific transactions only with a great deal of caution. The examples below are illustrative of the IRS's facts and circumstances analysis.

Example (1): B, an individual, and A Corp., form a limited partnership with A Corp. having a 1% general partnership interest and B having a 99% limited partnership interest. The arrangement is properly classified as a partnership for federal tax purposes. A limited partnership was selected so that B could have limited liability without being subject to an entity-level tax. Reg. § 1.702–1(d) Example (1) concludes that the IRS will not recast this transaction.

Example (2): Corporations X and Y make equal contributions to form a bona fide partnership to make joint investments. The partnership purchases common stock of Z, an unrelated corporation which historically has paid a $6 per share dividend. The partnership allocates dividend income on the Z stock to X to the extent of an established rate for inter-bank loans on the record date applied to X's contributions and allocates the remainder of the dividend income to Y. The allocation has substantial economic effect. The purposes for the arrangement were to avoid an entity-level tax, provide X with a floating-rate return based on an established index, and permit X and Y to claim a dividends received deduction under § 243. The IRS will not recast this transaction. Reg. § 1.702–2(d) Example (5).

3. Commissioner's Power to Recast Transactions

Under the anti-abuse regulations, the Commissioner can recast a transaction to achieve tax results that are consistent with the intent of Subchapter K. The Commissioner can determine that:

a.   the purported partnership should be disregarded;

b.   one or more purported partners should not be treated as a partner;

c.   the partnership's or partner's method of accounting should be adjusted;

d.   the partnership's items of income, gain, loss, deduction, or credit should be reallocated; or

e.   the claimed tax treatment should otherwise be adjusted or modified.

Reg. § 1.701–2(b).

C.   Abuse of Partnership Entity

Under the second anti-abuse rule, the Commissioner can treat a partnership as an aggregate of its partners in whole or in part as appropriate to carry out the purpose of any Code or regulation provision. Reg. § 1.701–2(e)(1). This rule is designed to prevent the use of a partnership to avoid other Code provisions and does not depend on a showing of the taxpayer's intent. An exception is made when (1) a Code section or regulation prescribes the treatment of a partnership as an entity, and (2) that tax treatment and the ultimate tax results are clearly contemplated by that provision. Reg. § 1.701–2(e)(2).

Example: Corporation X is a partner in the XYZ partnership which has conducted substantial business activities for several years. As part of its business activities, XYZ purchases shares in Corporation R which announces an extraordinary dividend under § 1059 six months later. Under § 1059(a), if a corporation receives an extraordinary dividend and it has not held the stock for more than two years before the dividend announcement date, the basis in the stock held by the corporation is reduced by the nontaxed portion of the dividend. X takes the position that § 1059(a) does not apply because XYZ is a partnership and not a corporation. Under the partnership anti-abuse rule, the IRS will treat XYZ as an aggregate of its partners. Section 1059(a) does not prescribe the treatment of a partnership as an entity for purposes of that section and the treatment of XYZ as an entity could result in corporate partners receiving dividends through partnerships contrary to the intent of § 1059. See Reg. § 1.701–2(f) Example (2).

D.   Review Questions

1. If the partnership anti-abuse regulations are violated, what remedies are available to the IRS?

2. Will the following transaction likely be challenged by the IRS under the partnership anti-abuse regulations? A U.S. corporation and foreign corporation conduct a bona fide joint venture through a foreign partnership rather than a foreign corporation so the U.S. corporation can achieve better foreign tax credit results.

II. CLASSIFICATION

1. No. A joint undertaking merely to share expenses is not a separate entity for federal tax purposes and X and Y will not be partners. Reg. § 301.7701–1(a)(2).

2. If A and B form a limited liability company or limited partnership to conduct their business venture, the entity will be classified as a partnership. If A alone forms a limited liability company to operate the business, the entity will be treated as a disregarded entity for tax purposes—i.e., a sole proprietorship if A is an individual or as part of A if A is a corporation. In both cases an election could be made to classify the entity as a corporation.

III. THE C CORPORATION AS A TAXABLE ENTITY

1. **(a)** X Corp.'s taxable income is determined as follows:

Gross Income:	
Income from Operations	$230,000
Dividends	25,000
§ 1231 Gain (LTCG)	30,000
Total	$285,000

Deductions and Losses:
   Operating Expenses 85,000
   LTCL (to extent of LTCG) 30,000
   Bad Debt 10,000
   Sub Dividend (100% Deduction) 20,000
   IBM Dividend (70% Deduction) 3,500
   ACRS Depreciation 45,000
   Total $193,500
Taxable Income .... $ 91,500

(b) X Corp.'s regular tax liability is $19,360, determined as follows:

$$
\begin{array}{ll}
15\% \text{ of first } \$50{,}000 = & \$\ 7{,}500 \\
25\% \text{ of next } \$25{,}000 = & 6{,}250 \\
34\% \text{ of next } \$16{,}500 = & \underline{5{,}610} \\
\text{Total § 11 tax} & \$19{,}360
\end{array}
$$

(c) X Corp.'s alternative minimum taxable income is determined as follows:

Taxable Income	$ 91,500
Tax Preference Items:	
Private Act. Bond Int.	22,500
§ 56 Adjustments:	
AMT Depreciation Adj.	15,000
AMTI before ACE adjustment	$129,000
ACE Adjustment (see below)	13,875
Alternative Minimum Taxable Income	$142,875
ACE Adjustment:	
Adjusted Current Earnings:	
Pre–ACE AMTI	$129,000
Tax–Exempt Bond Interest	15,000
Dividends Received Deduction	
(IBM stock only)	3,500
	$147,500
Less: Pre–ACE AMTI	129,000
Excess of ACE over pre-ACE AMTI	$ 18,500
75% of Excess	13,875

(d) X Corp.'s alternative minimum tax liability is determined as follows:

Alternative Minimum Taxable Income	$142,875
Less: Exemption Amount	40,000
Difference	$102,875
Alternative Minimum Tax at 20%	$ 20,575

IV. FORMATION OF A CORPORATION

1. **(a)** Yes. A and B each exchanged property solely in exchange for Newco stock and, immediately after the exchange, A and B collectively own 100% of the total value of Newco's only class of stock.

   (b) A's § 358 basis in the Newco stock is: basis of property transferred ($15,000), less liabilities assumed by Newco ($8,000) = $7,000. A's holding period for the stock includes the period that A held the van. B takes a $7,000 cost basis and his holding period begins as of the date of the exchange. Newco takes a § 362 transferred basis of $15,000 in the van, and Newco's holding period includes the period that A held the van.

   (c) Yes. A donative transfer after the incorporation will not cause the transaction to violate the "immediately after the exchange" requirement.

   (d) A must recognize $1,000 gain on the transfer under § 357(c) because liabilities assumed by Newco ($8,000) exceed the aggregate adjusted basis of the property transferred by A ($7,000). The gain is ordinary income under the depreciation recapture rule in § 1245.

   (e) A could have avoided gain by contributing $1,000 cash or property with up to a $1,000 basis, or under *Lessinger* or *Peracchi*, by contributing a $1,000 promissory note to Newco.

2. **(a)** Yes. Although B, as a service provider, is not considered a transferor of property, A has transferred property and, as an owner of 90% of Newco's only class of stock, A has "control" of Newco immediately after the exchange.

   (b) A recognizes $5,000 gain under § 351(b). A's basis in the Newco stock is: basis of land transferred ($30,000), less money received ($5,000), plus gain recognized ($5,000) = $30,000. A's holding period for the stock includes his holding period for the land.

   (c) If § 83(a) applies, B recognizes income to the extent that the shares received for services are not subject to a substantial risk of forfeiture. Since half the shares are not subject to such a risk, B recognizes $2,500 income when he receives the Newco stock. When the restrictions lapse on the other shares, B recognizes ordinary income in the amount of the fair market value of the stock at that time. If B makes the § 83(b) election, he recognizes $5,000 ordinary income in year 1.

   (d) B may not recognize any loss on the forfeiture. If B had paid an amount for the stock, he could deduct the amount paid on a forfeiture even if he made a § 83(b) election. Reg. § 1.83–2(a).

3. **(a)** The cash received by A is boot. The $10,000 boot is allocated to the two assets transferred by A in proportion to their relative fair market values—i.e., 80%

($8,000) to Gainacre, and 20% ($2,000) to Lossacre. Thus, A recognizes $8,000 gain, which is the boot allocated to Gainacre, but A may not recognize any of his loss on Lossacre.

(b) A's basis in the Newco stock is: basis in Gainacre ($8,000) plus basis in Lossacre ($15,000), less boot received ($10,000), plus gain recognized ($8,000) = $21,000. Newco's basis in Gainacre is: A's basis in Gainacre ($8,000), plus gain recognized by A ($8,000) = $16,000. Newco takes a $15,000 transferred basis from A in Lossacre.

4. **(a)** A's realized gain is $45,000. A's recognized gain is $20,000 (the $5,000 cash and the $15,000 note) under § 351(b). Under Prop.Reg. § 1.453–1(f), A is treated as having exchanged $30,000 of Gainacre for $30,000 of Newco stock; A's entire $5,000 basis in Gainacre is allocated to this § 351(a) nonrecognition transaction. The remaining $20,000 of Gainacre (with a zero basis) is treated as having been exchanged for $5,000 cash and the $15,000 note in a § 453 installment sale. The "selling price," "total contract price" and "gross profit" are all $20,000, and the gross profit fraction is thus 100%. Payments in the year of sale are limited to the $5,000 cash. A thus recognizes $5,000 gain in the year of the incorporation and $3,000 gain per year over the next five years as principal payments are made on the note.

A's basis in the Newco stock is: basis in Gainacre ($5,000), less cash received ($5,000), less other boot received ($15,000), plus gain recognized ($20,000) = $5,000. § 358(a). The upward adjustment for the entire gain recognized is permitted even though some of the gain is deferred under § 453. Prop.Reg. § 1.453–1(f)(3)(ii).

(b) Newco's basis in Gainacre is: A's basis in Gainacre ($5,000), plus gain recognized by A in the year of incorporation ($5,000) = $10,000. Newco may increase its basis in Gainacre by $3,000 per year over the next five years as A recognizes gain on the installment method. See Prop.Reg. § 1.453–1(f)(3)(ii).

V. CAPITAL STRUCTURE

1. The five factors specified in § 385 that are taken into account in distinguishing debt from equity are:

   (1) The form of the obligation;

   (2) Subordination;

   (3) The debt/equity ratio;

   (4) Convertibility; and

   (5) Proportionality of the purported debt to the shareholders' equity interests in the corporation.

The courts have considered many other factors, including the intent of the parties to create a debtor/creditor relationship, and whether a third party lender would have made a loan on the same terms.

2. There are several approaches to determining a corporation's debt/equity ratio. Debt generally includes all long-term liabilities, including shareholder loans. In determining equity, the courts disagree as to whether to reflect assets at their adjusted tax basis or at fair market value, and whether to include certain intangibles, such as goodwill. If the assets here are reflected at current value, the debt/equity ratio is $400,000/$600,000, which is very favorable. If assets are reflected at adjusted basis, the debt/equity ratio is $400,000/$100,000, which is riskier but not excessive. Even if the shareholder loans are proportionate to stock holdings, the risk of reclassification is minimal when the debt/equity ratio is not excessive.

3. A's $50,000 loss on the stock is a long-term capital loss under the worthless security rules in § 165(g). The promissory note is not a "security," as defined in § 165(g)(2), and thus A's $100,000 loss on the note is characterized by the bad debt rules in § 166. Since it is likely that A's dominant motivation in making the loan was to protect her investment interest in the corporation rather than her stake as an employee, the loss is a non-business bad debt under the *Generes* case and is treated as a short-term capital loss under § 166(d), not an ordinary loss under § 166(a).

VI. NONLIQUIDATING DISTRIBUTIONS

1. False. Although taxable income is typically the starting point, various additions, subtractions and adjustments are made to determine earnings and profits.

2. Yes. Able must amortize the § 179 expense ratably over five years for purposes of determining E & P. § 312(k)(3)(B).

3. Earnings and profits is a tax accounting concept that is used to measure the extent to which a distribution is made from a corporation's economic income. E & P are relevant even when a corporation makes no current distributions because the corporation also must keep track of its "accumulated" earnings and profits in order to determine if future distributions are dividends.

4. The entire distribution is a dividend out of current E & P, which are determined as of the end of the taxable year without reduction for distributions made during the year.

5. Calder recognizes $10,000 gain on the distribution under § 311(b). Calder must increase current E & P by that $10,000 gain, and, following the distribution, it may reduce accumulated earnings and profits by the $50,000 fair market value of the property. § 312(a)(3), (b). This treatment is equivalent to the result if the corporation had first sold the appreciated property and then distributed the net

cash proceeds. The amount of the distribution is $50,000 (§ 301(b)), and A's basis in the distributed property is $50,000 (§ 301(d)).

6. Yes as to Calder but no as to A. Calder would not be permitted to recognize its $10,000 loss. § 311(a). It could have avoided this result by first selling the property and recognizing the loss, and then distributing the cash proceeds. Calder's accumulated E & P would be reduced by $60,000 under § 312(a)(3). The consequences to A are unchanged.

7. A corporation may be deemed to have made a constructive dividend in the following situations: payment of unreasonable compensation; low-interest loans; loans without expectation of repayment; purported "interest" payments on debt that is reclassified as equity; bargain sales or leases with shareholders; excessive payments to shareholders for the purchase or rental of property; payment of shareholders' personal expenses; and certain transactions between commonly controlled corporations.

VII. STOCK REDEMPTIONS AND PARTIAL LIQUIDATIONS

1. H constructively owns 300 shares: 100 shares from his Wife under § 318(a)(1); 100 shares from the Trust through his Children (who are sole beneficiaries of the Trust) under § 318(a)(2)(B) and § 318(a)(1); and 100 shares from the HYZ Partnership under § 318(a)(2)(A). Although 100 shares are attributed from the HYZ Partnership to Y and then reattributed to his daughter, W, these shares may not be reattributed to H because of the rule in § 318(a)(5)(A) prohibiting double family attribution. Double family attribution also may not be used to attribute Y's 300 shares to H.

H and W's children constructively own 500 shares: 200 shares from their father (H); 100 shares from their mother (W); 100 shares from the Trust for their benefit (§ 318(a)(2)(B)); and 100 shares from HYZ Partnership through their father (H). The shares actually owned and constructively owned from the Partnership by Y are not attributed to his grandchildren because § 318(a)(1) does not provide for grandparent to grandchild attribution.

Z constructively owns 100 shares from the HYZ Partnership under § 318(a)(2)(A).

Y constructively owns 300 shares: 100 shares from the HYZ Partnership; 100 shares from his daughter (W); and 100 shares from the Trust through his grandchildren.

2. Before the redemption, the Trust actually owns 100 shares and constructively owns an additional 400 shares (300 from H and W through the children, and 100 from the HYZ Partnership through H and the children), for a total of 500 out of the 1,000 outstanding shares of X Corp., or 50%. After the redemption, the Trust owns no shares actually but continues to own 400 shares constructively, for a total of 400 out of the 900 outstanding shares of X Corp., or 44.4%. This does not qualify as a

substantially disproportionate redemption under § 302(b)(2) because the Trust does not own less than 40% of X Corp.—i.e., less than 80% of its 50% percentage ownership of X Corp. immediately before the redemption.

The redemption may qualify as a complete termination under § 302(b)(3) if the Trust satisfies the waiver of family attribution by entity rules in § 302(c)(2)(C). To qualify, the Trust and all "related persons" (here, the children, to whom ownership of stock is attributable under family attribution and then is reattributable to the Trust) must satisfy the 10–year look back and forward rules in § 302(c), and the Trust and the children must agree to be jointly and severally liable for any tax deficiency that may result if a prohibited interest is acquired during the 10–year-look-forward period. If § 302(b)(3) applies, the redemption is treated as an exchange, and the Trust recognizes capital gain or loss equal to the difference between the amount distributed in the redemption and its adjusted basis in the stock.

If § 302(b)(3) does not apply, the redemption may qualify under § 302(b)(1) as "not essentially equivalent to a dividend" because the Trust's interest fell from 50% (enough to cause a deadlock) to below 50%. This might be a meaningful reduction under the Service's rulings, but it would be safer to qualify the redemption under the § 302(b)(3) rules discussed above.

If the redemption is not treated as an exchange, the entire amount distributed will be a dividend because X has ample E & P. Since the Trust will not own any more shares, its basis in the redeemed stock would be added back to the basis of stock held by related shareholders under § 318. See Reg. § 1.302–2(c).

3. The distribution likely will be treated as a partial liquidation. X has undergone a significant contraction of its operations by selling the Depression division and may even qualify for partial liquidation treatment under the "termination of business" safe harbor in § 302(e)(2). Although the Depression division was opened only three years ago, it could be considered as an expansion of a trade or business that had been actively conducted throughout the five-year period ending on the date of the distribution. The fact that none of the shareholders surrendered any shares will not change this result because the sales proceeds were distributed pro rata. If the transaction qualifies as a partial liquidation, it will be treated as an exchange, and the shareholders will be entitled to capital gains treatment and recovery of a proportionate share of their stock basis.

If shareholder A were a corporation, it could not qualify for partial liquidation treatment. § 302(b)(4). In that event, the distribution to A would be a dividend. Although A Corp. would be entitled to a § 243 dividends received deduction, the distribution would be an "extraordinary dividend" under § 1059(e)(1) and A Corp. would be required to reduce its basis in its X Corp. stock by the untaxed portion of the dividend.

4. Section 304 applies because A has "control" (i.e., 50% ownership) of both X Corp. (the "issuing corporation") and Y Corp. (the "acquiring corporation") and has sold

stock in X to Y in exchange for property. This is a "brother-sister" acquisition under § 304(a)(1). The $30,000 is treated as received by A as a distribution in redemption of Y Corp. stock. The redemption is tested by reference to A's stock ownership in X Corp. Before the constructive redemption, A owned 70% of X Corp. (700 out of 1,000 outstanding shares). After the redemption, A owns 55% of X Corp. (550 out of 1,000 shares–400 shares actually and 150 constructively through Y Corp.). The redemption thus will not qualify as an exchange but rather as a § 301 distribution. Y is deemed to have acquired the X stock from A in a § 351(a) transaction, and then Y is treated as having distributed $30,000 to A in redemption of its stock. The distribution is treated as a dividend to the extent of $25,000 (the combined E & P of both corporations). The remaining $5,000 is first treated as a reduction of A's $800 basis in his Y Corp. stock under § 301(c)(2) and the remaining $4,200 is a long-term capital gain under § 301(c)(3). (Note that A's $500 basis in his Y Corp. stock was increased by his $300 basis in the X stock that A transferred to Y.)

X and Y each reduce their E & P to zero. Y Corp. takes a $300 transferred basis in the 300 shares of X Corp. that it acquires from A.

VIII. STOCK DISTRIBUTIONS AND § 306 STOCK

1. These distributions are not taxable because they do not have the effect of increasing the shareholders' proportionate interests in the corporation. A tax-free "preferred on common" stock distribution, however, will be labelled as § 306 stock.

2. A receives 10 shares of nonconvertible preferred stock with a total value of $100. The distribution is not taxable to A under § 305(a). A must allocate her $1,000 basis in the common between the common and the new preferred based on the relative fair market values of the two classes of stock after the distribution—i.e., $1,900 (95%) and $100 (5%), respectively. § 307(a). A thus takes a $950 basis in the common stock and a $50 basis in the preferred, and she may tack her holding period in the common to the preferred. X Corp. does not recognize gain on the distribution, and its E & P are unaffected. §§ 311(a)(1); 312(d)(1)(B).

3. All shareholders, including A, who received preferred stock are treated as having received a § 301 distribution of $10 per share. The result is the same whether or not any shareholders elect to take cash in lieu of the preferred stock. This is an application of § 305(b)(1), which treats a stock distribution as taxable if, at any shareholder's election, it is payable either in stock of the distributing corporation or in cash or other property.

4. This falls within § 305(b)(3), which provides that a stock distribution (or series of distributions) is taxable if the effect is that some common shareholders receive preferred stock and others receive common stock. All shareholders, including A, will be treated as having received a § 301 distribution.

5. The preferred stock is § 306 stock because it was received as a tax-free stock distribution that was other than "common-on-common." A's amount realized on any

sale of this § 306 stock must be treated as ordinary income to the extent that the preferred stock distribution would have been a dividend at the time of the distribution if cash rather than stock had been distributed. § 306(a)(1). Since X has $100,000 of current E & P and distributed a total of $1,000 in preferred stock to its common shareholders, the entire distribution would have been a dividend to A if she had received $100 in cash instead of the preferred stock. On the sale, A thus must treat the first $100 of the $250 amount realized as ordinary income; the $150 balance is treated first as a reduction of her $50 basis (see Answer #2, above) in the preferred, and then as $100 long-term capital gain from a sale of the stock ($250 less $100 less $50).

6. A's entire $80 amount realized is treated as ordinary income under § 306(a)(1). A may add her $50 basis in the preferred back to her basis in the common stock.

7. Although the preferred is still § 306 stock, § 306(a) does not apply on the sale because A has completely terminated her entire stock interest in the corporation. § 306(b)(1)(A). A thus recognizes a $200 long-term capital gain on the sale ($250 amount realized less $50 basis in the preferred).

IX.   COMPLETE LIQUIDATIONS AND TAXABLE CORPORATE ACQUISITIONS

1. **(a)** X Corp. recognizes $400,000 gain on the distribution of Gainacre. § 336(a). X has distributed 80% ($400,000) of Lossacre, with a $640,000 basis, to A, and 20% ($100,000), with a $160,000 basis, to B. Under § 336(d)(1)(B), X may not recognize its $240,000 loss on the distribution of 80% of Lossacre because A, as a more than 50% shareholder, is a § 267 "related person," and Lossacre, having been acquired by X in a § 351 transaction within the five-year period preceding the distribution, is "disqualified property." X may recognize its $60,000 loss on the distribution of 20% of Lossacre to B, however, because B is not a related person and thus § 336(d)(1)(B) does not apply.

     Ignoring (for convenience) any adjustment resulting from the corporate-level tax imposed on X as a result of the distribution, A receives $800,000 in the liquidation and recognizes $500,000 long-term capital gain, and B receives $200,000 and recognizes $400,000 long-term capital loss. § 331(a). Each shareholder takes a fair market value basis for his or her respective interests in the distributed parcels. § 301(d).

    (b) X recognizes $400,000 gain on the distribution of Gainacre. § 336(a). As discussed in the answer to (a), above, X may not recognize its $240,000 loss on the 80% of Lossacre distributed to A. § 336(d)(1)(B). Under § 336(d)(2), X must reduce its $160,000 adjusted basis in the 20% of Lossacre distributed to B by $20,000, which represents 20% of the $100,000 precontribution built-in loss at the time X acquired Lossacre in a § 351 transaction. As a result, X's adjusted basis is decreased to $140,000, and it may only recognize $40,000 of its $60,000 realized loss on the distribution to B. This assumes that Lossacre was acquired as part of a plan the principal purpose of which was to recognize loss by X in connection with its subsequent liquidation. Property acquired within the two-year period preceding the adoption of a liquidation plan is presumed to have been acquired as part of a plan to recognize loss if there is no clear and substantial relationship between the contributed property and the conduct of the corporation's current or future business. § 336(d)(2)(B)(ii). If no such avoidance plan is present, B may recognize its entire $60,000 loss on the distribution to B.

The results to A and B are the same as in (a), above.

(c) X recognizes $400,000 gain on the distribution of Gainacre. § 336(a). If the § 351 transfer of Lossacre occurred six years prior to the liquidation, it is no longer "disqualified property." As a result, X may recognize its entire $300,000 loss on the distribution of Lossacre to A and B.

(d) This qualifies as a liquidation of a controlled subsidiary under §§ 332 and 337. X does not recognize gain or loss on the distribution of 80% of each parcel to A. X must recognize $80,000 gain on the distribution of 20% of Gainacre to B, who is a minority shareholder, but it may not recognize its $60,000 loss on the distribution of 20% of Lossacre to B. § 336(d)(3).

A Corp. does not recognize gain on the liquidation of X (§ 332) and takes a transferred basis in its 80% interest in Gainacre ($80,000) and Lossacre ($640,000), respectively. Ignoring the effect of any corporate-level tax imposed on X, B receives a $200,000 distribution and recognizes $400,000 long-term capital gain on the liquidation of X. B takes a fair market value basis in its 20% interest in the two parcels. § 334(a).

2. This qualifies as a liquidation of a controlled subsidiary under §§ 332 and 337. S distributes 90% of Gainacre ($90,000 value, $63,000 basis) to P Corp. and 10% of Gainacre ($10,000 value, $7,000 basis) to B. S does not recognize gain on the distribution to P (§ 337(a)) but recognizes $3,000 gain on the distribution to B (§ 336(a)).

P does not recognize gain on the liquidation. § 332(a). P's $50,000 basis in its S stock disappears, and P takes a $63,000 transferred basis in its 90% interest in Gainacre. § 334(b). B recognizes $8,000 gain on the liquidation (§ 331(a)) and takes a $10,000 fair market value basis in its 10% interest in Gainacre (§ 334(a)). P succeeds to 90% of S's earnings and profits. § 381(a).

3. (a) Three methods for structuring the acquisition are: (1) P acquires T's assets from T, and T liquidates, distributing the cash (less any corporate-level tax imposed on the liquidating sales) to its shareholders; (2) T liquidates, distributes its assets to its shareholders, and the shareholders sell the assets directly to P; or (3) P purchases 100% of T's stock from S and I. As an

alternative to method (1), T could stay in existence rather than liquidating after selling its assets to P. In connection with method (2), P must decide whether or not to make a § 338 election.

(b) On an asset sale followed by a liquidation, T recognizes $250,000 gain, resulting in a corporate tax liability of $85,000 (assuming, for convenience, a 34% flat corporate rate). T then distributes $415,000 ($500,000 sale proceeds less $85,000 corporate-level tax) to its shareholders: $332,000 (80%) to S and $83,000 (20%) to I. S recognizes $232,000 long-term capital gain, and I recognizes $33,000 long-term capital gain on the liquidation. § 331(a). Note that the problem assigns a fair market value to each of the assets, including goodwill, and thus it avoids any asset allocation issues under § 1060.

The results would be the same on a liquidation followed by an asset sale by the shareholders. T recognizes $250,000 gain on the distribution of its assets in complete liquidation. § 336(a). The amount realized by the shareholders is $415,000 (the $120,000 cash is reduced by the $85,000 corporate-level tax liability). The shareholders take a fair market value basis in the distributed assets and recognize no further gain when they sell the assets to P. P takes a fair market value (cost) basis in the assets.

On a stock sale, each shareholder recognizes long-term capital gain in an amount equal to the difference between the amount realized on the sale and the shareholder's adjusted basis in his stock. If P does not make a § 338 election, T does not recognize gain on its assets, and its asset bases and other tax attributes are preserved. If P makes a § 338 election, T recognizes gain on the deemed sale of its assets to "new T," and "new T's" aggregate basis in its assets (on these simple facts) equals the price paid by P for the T stock, increased by the income tax liabilities of old T triggered by the deemed asset sale. P would bear the economic burden of any corporate-level tax imposed on the deemed sale of T's assets. Since P bears the economic burden of this corporate-level tax, it logically would pay less than $500,000 for the T stock. New T's aggregate basis in its assets would be the consideration paid by P for the T stock plus T's tax liability on the deemed sale. The basis would be allocated among T's assets using the residual method prescribed by the regulations.

(c) In general, the most favorable acquisition method on these facts is a stock purchase without a § 338 election. This method results in a deferral of corporate-level tax.

(d) Yes. In this situation, P would purchase T's stock, and P and S would make a joint election under §§ 338 and 338(h)(10). S's gain on its sale of T stock to P is ignored, and T is treated as having sold its assets for their $500,000 fair market value to "new T," which takes a fair market value basis in the noncash assets. The gain is includible on S and T's consolidated return, where it can be offset by S's net operating losses.

X. ANTI–AVOIDANCE PROVISIONS

1. False. Under § 533(a), if a corporation permits its earnings and profits to accumulate beyond the reasonable needs of its business, that fact establishes a tax avoidance purpose unless the corporation proves it does not have such a purpose by a preponderance of the evidence. It is generally difficult for a corporation to rebut the presumption of a tax avoidance purpose once one arises. The regulations provide a nonexclusive list of factors which indicate whether earnings and profits have been accumulated beyond the reasonable needs of the business. Reg. § 1.537–2(b), (c).

2. Under § 542(a), a "personal holding company" is a corporation which meets both an income and a stock ownership requirement. To meet the income requirement, at least 60% of the corporation's adjusted ordinary gross income for the taxable year must be personal holding company income. § 542(a)(1). To meet the stock ownership requirement, more than 50% in value of a corporation's stock must be owned, directly or indirectly, at any time during the last half of the taxable year by five or fewer individuals. § 542(a)(2). Special attribution rules are applied to determine stock ownership. § 544.

3. Section 341(b)(1) defines a collapsible corporation as a corporation formed or availed of principally for the manufacture, construction or production of property, or for the purchase of "§ 341 assets," with a view to: (1) the sale or exchange of its stock by its shareholders or a distribution to its shareholders before the corporation realizes two-thirds of the taxable income to be derived from the property, and (2) the realization by the shareholders of gain attributable to such property.

4. Section 341(d) provides three exceptions under which the gain recognized by a shareholder on stock of a collapsible corporation is not converted to ordinary income. Under § 341(d)(1), the collapsibility rules do not apply to any shareholder who owns 5% or less of the stock of the corporation at any time after the manufacture, construction, etc. of property begins. Under § 341(d)(2), the collapsibility rules do not apply to a shareholder's gain unless 70% of such gain is attributable to collapsible property. Under § 341(d)(3), the collapsibility rules do not apply to gain recognized more than three years following the completion of the manufacture, construction, etc. of property.

    Section 341(e) generally provides that a corporation is not considered collapsible with respect to sale or exchange of stock by a shareholder if the net unrealized appreciation in the corporation's "subsection (e) assets" does not exceed 15% of its net worth.

    Section 341(f) provides that the collapsibility rules do not apply to a sale of stock (other than to the issuing corporation) if the corporation consents to recognize its gain on any disposition of a "subsection (f) asset." A "subsection (f) asset" is defined as any property which on the date of the stock sale is not a capital asset and is owned, or subject to an option to purchase, by the corporation.

XI. TAX–FREE REORGANIZATIONS

1. **(a)** No. The use of nonvoting preferred stock disqualifies the transaction as a Type B reorganization.

    (b) Yes. If, as is likely, the liquidation of T was part of the overall reorganization plan, the transaction is tested as a Type C reorganization. Rev.Rul. 67–274, 1967–2 C.B. 141. The acquisition qualifies as a Type C reorganization under the boot relaxation rule in § 368(a)(2)(B) because at least 80% of T's assets were acquired in exchange for P voting stock.

    (c) This acquisition fails as a § 368(a)(2)(E) reverse triangular merger because P did not acquire "control" (i.e., 80%) of T in a single transaction in exchange for P voting stock. Under the regulations, however, the acquisition qualifies as a Type B reorganization if, as here, S is a transitory subsidiary formed solely to facilitate the merger. See Reg. § 1.368–2(j)(6) Example (4). This question illustrates that creeping acquisitions ordinarily will not qualify as reverse triangular mergers, but creeping Type B acquisitions are possible if P's earlier cash acquisitions are "old and cold."

    (d) No, under the Service's regulations and ruling guidelines. Although the transaction meets the continuity of proprietary interest test (75% of the consideration is stock), it fails the continuity of business enterprise requirement because P does not continue to conduct T's historic business or use a significant portion of T's historic business assets in a business. Reg. § 1.368–1(d).

    (e) No. As a stock-for-assets acquisition, the transaction must meet the requirements for a Type C reorganization. It fails because P only acquired $150,000 out of T's $200,000 in assets (75%) for P voting stock, and thus the boot relaxation rule in § 368(a)(2)(B) has not been satisfied. For this purpose, the $25,000 of T liabilities taken over by P is treated as cash consideration.

2. **(a)** The transaction qualifies as a Type A reorganization. There is 100% continuity of interest even though T shareholders only receive nonvoting preferred stock. A and B do not recognize gain on the exchange of their T stock for P stock. § 354(a). A's and B's basis in the P stock received is the same as the basis of the T stock surrendered—$200,000 for A and $400,000 for B. It is unlikely that the P preferred stock received by A and B is § 306 stock because, under the *Clark* case, the receipt of cash rather than preferred stock would not have the effect of a dividend. Cf. § 356(a)(2). T does not recognize gain on the transfer of its assets to P or with respect to the assumption of its liabilities. §§ 361(a); 357(a). P takes a transferred basis in the T assets. § 362(b). P does not recognize any gain on the issuance of its stock in connection with the acquisition. § 1032(a). T's tax attributes (E & P, etc.) transfer to P. § 381(a).

    (b) This transaction is not a statutory merger but rather a stock-for-assets acquisition. As such, it must meet the requirements for a Type C reorganization. It fails to do so because P has not used any of it voting stock. Because this is a failed reorganization, it is treated as a taxable asset acquisition followed by a taxable complete liquidation of T. T recognizes $500,000 gain on the sale of its assets to P. Assuming a 34% corporate tax rate, T's tax liability is $170,000. Since T has no cash to pay these taxes, A and B will be liable as transferees. P takes a cost (i.e., fair market value) basis in the T assets it acquires. Although § 336(a) applies, T has no gain when it distributes the P stock to its shareholders in complete liquidation because T took a $1,000,000 fair market value basis in that stock on the taxable asset exchange. The amount realized by each shareholder on the complete liquidation of T is $500,000 less the $85,000 corporate tax liability for which each is responsible, or $415,000. A thus recognizes $215,000 long-term capital gain, and B recognizes $15,000 long-term capital gain under § 331(a).

(c) The transaction qualifies as a Type A reorganization despite the use of P bonds because there is 60% continuity of interest. Although the P long-term bonds are "securities," they are treated as boot because A and B are receiving but not surrendering any securities. §§ 354(a)(2); 356(d). Each shareholder's realized gain must be recognized to the extent of the boot received. Thus, A recognizes $200,000 gain, but B only recognizes his $100,000 realized gain. The recognized gain is treated as a dividend to the extent that the exchange "has the effect of a distribution of a dividend." § 356(a)(2). Under the *Clark* case, the exchange is tested for dividend equivalency by treating A and B as having received only P stock, a portion of which is then redeemed by P for an amount equal to the bonds actually received. Without knowing the exact number of shares of P stock that A and B received, we are unable to determine whether the hypothetical redemption meets the tests for exchange treatment in § 302(b)(1) or § 302(b)(2). Since P is a publicly traded company with many shares outstanding, it is likely that one of those tests would be met. As a result, A and B would recognize long-term capital gain which they could report on the § 453 installment method.

A's basis in the P stock received is $200,000 ($200,000 basis of T stock surrendered less $200,000 boot received plus $200,000 gain recognized). B's basis in the P stock received is $300,000 ($400,000 basis of T stock surrendered less $200,000 boot received plus $100,000 gain recognized).

T recognizes no gain, either on the transfer of its assets and liabilities to P (§ 361(a)), or on the distribution of the P stock and securities (both are "qualified property") to A and B. P does not recognize gain on the issuance of its stock or bonds, and it takes a transferred basis in the T assets.

(d) Since P acquires all of T's operating assets solely for P voting stock, the transaction should qualify as a Type C reorganization.

T does not recognize gain on the transfer of its operating assets for P voting stock. § 361(a). It also does not recognize gain on the transfer of $200,000 of the P voting stock to its creditors (a transfer of "qualified property" to creditors to satisfy T liabilities is treated as a distribution under § 361(b)(3)), or the distribution of the remaining voting stock to A and B. § 361(c). P recognizes no gain on the issuance of its voting stock (§ 1032(a)), and P takes a $600,000 transferred basis in the T assets. § 362(b).

The $200,000 of liquid assets distributed to A and B are treated as boot under §§ 354 and 356. Assuming the distribution is pro rata, A and B each recognize $100,000 gain. The remainder of A's realized gain is not recognized under § 354. The gain would be characterized under the principles of the *Clark* case. (See #2(c), above.) A's basis in the P voting stock received is $200,000 ($200,000 basis in T stock surrendered less $100,000 boot received plus $100,000 gain recognized). B's basis in the P voting stock received is $400,000 ($400,000 basis in T stock surrendered less $100,000 boot received plus $100,000 gain recognized).

(e) The first step is a taxable stock acquisition. A and B each recognize gain on the sale of their stock but, since no § 338 election was made, T has no gain and the bases of its assets are unchanged. The second step is a tax-free liquidation of T under §§ 332 and 337. P takes a transferred basis in T's assets. The step transaction doctrine is not applied here in deference to the policy of § 338. If it were applied, P would have been treated as having acquired T's assets for cash and would have taken a cost basis even though no § 338 election was made. Rev. Rul. 90–95, 1990–2 C.B. 67 would not permit application of the step transaction doctrine on these facts.

(f) Under Rev. Rul. 2001–46, the two steps will be integrated because the overall transaction qualifies as a Type A reorganization. A and B recognize their realized gain to the extent of the cash received. T does not recognize any gain and P takes a transferred basis in T's assets under § 362.

XII. CORPORATE DIVISIONS

1. False. The distributing corporation may distribute stock of a preexisting controlled subsidiary. § 355(a)(2)(C). In that case, the division would not be pursuant to a Type D reorganization plan.

2. Probably not because there is no business purpose for the distribution. The business purpose requirement is not met if the distributing corporation's goals could have been achieved through a nontaxable transaction that would not have required the distribution of stock of the controlled corporation and was neither impractical nor unduly expensive. On these facts, P could have met its objectives simply by transferring the assets of one business to a new corporation in a § 351 transaction. Reg. § 1.355–2(b)(3).

3. **(a)** No, because S's ownership of investment securities is not an actively conducted trade or business. Reg. § 1.355–3(b)(2)(iv).

(b) The answer depends on whether the hat business, which only has been conducted for two years, may be considered to be an expansion of the pants business that P has conducted for more than the requisite five-year period. If so, the active trade or business test is met. The regulations look to whether the new activity effects such a change in character that it constitutes a new or different business. Reg. § 1.355–3(b)(3)(ii). P will argue that it is merely expanding a diversified apparel business. The Service likely would contend that the hat business is different from the pants business and has not been actively conducted for five years.

(c) Although P acquired control of the radio station corporation within the five years preceding the distribution, it did so in a transaction in which gain or loss was not recognized to the seller. As a result, the active business test is satisfied because the radio station business has been conducted for 15 years. § 355(b)(2)(D). It does not matter that P has owned the radio station for less than five years.

4. Under § 355(a)(1)(B), the "mere fact" that stock or securities of either the distributing or controlled corporations are sold subsequent to a distribution shall not be construed to mean that the distribution was used as a device unless the sale was negotiated or agreed upon prior to the distribution. Under the regulations, any sale or exchange of S stock after a spin-off is evidence of a device. The strength of the evidence increases as more stock is sold and decreases as more time passes between the distribution and subsequent sale. Prearranged sales are substantial evidence of a device, while other sales are only evidence. Reg. § 1.355–2(d)(2). The corporate business purpose for a distribution is evidence of a nondevice, the strength of which depends on all the facts and circumstances. Reg. § 1.355–3(d)(3)(i). The fact that federal law requires the divestiture may be helpful in weighing the device and nondevice factors, but the Service still might contend that the shareholders were not required to sell the S stock after the spin-off.

5. A does not recognize gain on the spin-off. § 355(a). A allocates his old basis in the P stock between the P and S stock in proportion to their relative fair market values as of the date of the distribution. The combined value of the P and S stock after the distribution is $800,000, of which 75% ($600,000) is attributable to the P stock and 25% ($200,000) is attributable to the S stock. A thus takes a $75,000 basis in the P stock and a $25,000 basis in the S stock. A's holding period in the S stock includes the period that she held the P stock.

    P does not recognize gain on the distribution of the S stock to A. § 355(c). (Note that § 361(c) does not apply because the distribution was not preceded by a Type D reorganization, but § 355(c) provides essentially the same result.) S's basis in its assets remain unchanged after the distribution, but P's basis in its S stock disappears.

6. These are the facts of Rev.Rul. 93–62, 1993–2 C.B. 118. Under the ruling, the determination of whether a boot payment in a § 355 distribution is treated as a

dividend under § 356(a)(2) is made prior to the exchange by applying § 302 principles. A's interest in P immediately before the exchange is compared to the interest A would have retained if A had surrendered only the P shares equal in value to the boot. On these facts, A owned 40% of the outstanding P stock before the distribution. If A had surrendered only the 200 shares for which he received boot, A still would hold 200 of the 800 remaining shares, or 25% of the P stock outstanding after the exchange. This represents less than 50% of P's voting stock, and 62.5% of A's pre-exchange stock interest in P. Thus, the hypothetical redemption would be treated as an exchange because it qualifies as substantially disproportionate under § 302(b)(2). The transaction does not have the effect of the distribution of a dividend.

XIII. CARRYOVERS OF CORPORATE TAX ATTRIBUTES

1. Section 382 limits the use of a loss corporation's net operating loss carryforwards if there is a substantial change in ownership of the corporation. After an ownership change, if the new corporation does not continue the business enterprise of the old loss corporation for at least two years, the pre-acquisition NOLs are disallowed. § 382(c)(1). If the continuity of business requirement is met, the taxable income permitted to be offset by pre-acquisition NOL's is limited to the value of the loss corporation multiplied by the long-term tax-exempt rate. § 382(b)(1).

2. **(a)** This is an ownership change. It is an owner shift involving a 5% shareholder in which a 5% shareholder's (P's) percentage ownership of the loss corporation (T) increased by more 50 percentage points. § 382(g)(1), (2).

    (b) This is not an ownership change because P's percentage ownership of T does not increase by *more than* 50 percentage points.

    (c) This is an equity structure shift and the less than 5% shareholders in each corporation are treated as one 5% shareholder. § 382(g)(4)(A), (B). P is the loss corporation for purposes of testing whether an ownership change has taken place. § 382(k)(1). An ownership change has taken place since the percentage of stock of the loss corporation (P) owned by one or more 5% shareholders (the T shareholders) has increased by more than 50 percentage points.

XIV. AFFILIATED CORPORATIONS

1.

	W Co.	X Co.	Y Co.	Z Co.	Identical Ownership
A	35%		25%		25% (W, Y)
B		50%		35%	
C	47%	25%	60%	10%	47% (W, Y)
Total	82%	75%	85%	45%	

W Co. and Y Co. are a brother-sister controlled group because A and C own over 80% of the shares of each corporation and have aggregate identical ownership of more than 50% in the two corporations. See Reg. § 1.1563–1(a)(3) Example (1).

2. The Service will most likely scrutinize intercompany transactions under § 482 when there is evidence that the transactions were not made at arm's length and when the potential for abuse is present. The Service, under these circumstances, may make adjustments to the books of the entities and allocate the appropriate tax effects of the transactions among the participants.

XV.   S CORPORATIONS

1. Yes. Under pre–1997 law, C would be an ineligible corporation because it had an active 80% owned subsidiary. Under current law, however, C corporation subsidiaries are permitted.

2. No. C has 76 shareholders and therefore does not satisfy the 75–shareholder limit in § 1361(b)(1)(A). F and J are counted as one shareholder since they are husband and wife. A and B are unmarried joint tenants and therefore are considered to be two separate shareholders.

3. No. Although C now satisfies the 75–shareholder limit, a small business corporation may not have a partnership as a shareholder. § 1361(b)(1)(B).

4. A trust which has stock transferred to it pursuant to a will can be a shareholder in a small business corporation but only for a two-year period beginning on the day of transfer. § 1361(c)(2)(B)(iii).

5. According to the regulations, the second class of authorized but unissued stock will not cause C to be in violation of the one class of stock requirement of § 1361(b)(1)(D). Therefore, assuming C meets all of the other requirements, it would qualify as a small business corporation.

6. A majority of shares of stock must vote in favor of revocation. § 1362(d)(1)(B). Thus, A will need 41 additional votes to revoke the election.

7. Any effective date on or after the date of revocation may be selected. If a date is not selected, then the revocation is effective on the first day of the taxable year if made before the sixteenth day of the third month of such year or on the first day of the next taxable year if it is made after the fifteenth day of the third month of the year. § 1362(d)(1)(C), (D). Thus, if S's taxable year ends on December 31, 1998 and the revocation is approved on March 10, 1998, if no prospective effective date is selected the revocation will be effective on January 1, 1998. Alternatively, if the revocation is approved on June 10, 1998, the revocation will be effective on January 1, 1999.

8. The termination is effective on the date it acquired its 76th shareholder and terminated its S corporation status. § 1362(d)(2).

9. Yes. The corporation may argue that the termination was inadvertent under § 1362(f). If the Treasury agrees that the termination was inadvertent, the corporation takes steps to correct the terminating event within a reasonable period, and the corporation agrees to make any adjustments required by the Treasury, the corporation will be treated as continuing to be an S corporation.

10. Recent cases (e.g., *Estate of Leavitt* and *Harris*) have supported the Service's contention that such loan guarantees do not result in basis credit to the shareholder until the shareholder makes an economic outlay pursuant to the guarantee. There is some authority (*Selfe*) that a shareholder may receive basis credit for the loan guarantee under debt-equity analysis.

11. Even if a loss pass-through is allowed because it is less than the shareholder's adjusted basis in the corporation's stock and debt, the at-risk limitations in § 465 and the passive loss limitations in § 469 may limit the amount of loss that is currently deductible by the shareholder.

12. A will include her pro rata share of income and capital loss for the year and the basis of her S stock will be:

$$
\begin{array}{r}
\$4,000 \\
\underline{+8,000} \\
\$12,000
\end{array} \quad \text{§ 1367(a)(1)(B)}
$$

Since S has no earnings and profits, the $10,000 distribution will be considered recovery of stock basis, and A's stock basis will be reduced to $2,000. A may deduct $2,000 of the long-term capital loss, and the remaining $4,000 of loss may be carried forward under § 1366(d)(2).

13. The accumulated adjustments account (otherwise known as the "AAA") is relevant to characterizing distributions by an S corporation with E & P. The AAA is a running total of the undistributed earnings of the corporation which have been taxed to its shareholders since it became an S corporation. Distributions are treated as recovery of stock basis and gain from the sale or exchange of the stock to the extent of the corporation's AAA. § 1368(c).

14. The § 1374 tax on built-in gains generally is relevant to an S corporation which was once a C corporation. Section 1374 imposes a corporate level tax on the appreciation in a corporation's assets which arose while it was a C corporation, but which is recognized within 10 years of its S election. The tax is designed to reduce the incentive for C corporations to elect S status to avoid corporate-level tax on preelection gains. The tax does not apply to a corporation which has always been an S corporation except to the extent the corporation acquires assets from a C corporation with a transferred basis. § 1374(c)(1), (d)(8).

XVI. FORMATION OF A PARTNERSHIP

1. **(a)** No gain or loss is recognized by A or AB. § 721(a).

(b) A's outside basis is $70,000, the sum of the money and the adjusted basis of property contributed by A. § 722.

(c) AB's inside basis is $15,000 in the installment obligations, $20,000 in the equipment, and $30,000 in the land. § 723.

2. **(a)** G bears the economic risk of loss for the liability. As the general partner, G is obligated to make a contribution to GL to pay the liability in the event of a doomsday liquidation.

(b) G's outside basis is $80,000, consisting of the $20,000 contribution and the $60,000 share of partnership liabilities which is treated as a cash contribution. §§ 722, 752(a).

(c) L's outside basis is $20,000.

3. **(a)** D recognizes $100,000 of income in Year Five when the property is no longer subject to a substantial risk of forfeiture. § 83(a).

(b) ABC will recognize $90,000 of gain ($100,000 fair market value less $10,000 basis) on the transfer of the 25% capital interest to D.

(c) D recognizes $25,000 of income (the fair market value of 25% of the assets) in Year One. § 83(b).

(d) D is not entitled to a deduction when the partnership interest is forfeited. § 83(b).

(e) In part (a), D's outside basis is $100,000. In part (c), D's outside basis is $25,000.

4. The organization expenses under § 709 are (a), (d), and (e). The registration fees for issuing interests (b) and fees relating to the prospectus or offering materials ((c), (f) and (g)) are syndication expenses.

XVII. OPERATIONS OF A PARTNERSHIP

1. The ABC Partnership can adopt a November 30 or August 30 taxable year. Using the mechanical rules of § 706(b)(1)(B), ABC can adopt November 30 because partners owning more than 50% of ABC's profits and capital (A and B) use a November 30 taxable year. Using the business purpose standard of § 706(b)(1)(C), ABC can adopt an August 31 taxable year because ABC has earned more than 25% of its gross receipts in the last two months of the requested year in each of the prior three years.

2. ABC must separately state interest income, § 1231 loss, and the charitable contributions. The interest income must be separately stated so various deduction

limitations may be applied at the partner level. See, e.g., § 163(d). The § 1231 loss is separately stated so it can be combined with the partners' other § 1231 gains and losses. The partnership is not allowed a charitable deduction in determining its taxable income. § 703(b)(2)(C). But contributions pass through to the partners, who may combine their distributive share of partnership charitable contributions with their personal contributions and then apply the § 170 percentage limitations on charitable deductions. ABC's nonseparately computed income is $183,000, computed as follows:

$200,000	Gross Business Revenue
+25,000	§ 1245 Gain
−20,000	Salary Expense
− 8,000	Depreciation Expense
−14,000	Maintenance Expense
$183,000	

3. False. Elections affecting the determination of partnership taxable income generally are made by the partnership. § 703(b).

4. **(a)** A's portion of the partnership's taxable income for the year is $35,200 (80% of $20,000 LTCG plus 80% of $24,000 nonseparately computed income). A also has $12,800 (80% of $16,000) of tax-exempt interest.

(b) A's outside basis is computed as follows:

$20,000	Beginning Basis
+35,200	§ 705(a)(1)(A)
+12,800	§ 705(a)(1)(B)
$68,000	

5. AB's operations resulted in a $4,000 ordinary loss and a $12,000 capital loss. A's distributive share is $3,000 of ordinary loss (75% of $4,000) and $9,000 of capital loss (75% of $12,000). A's allowable deduction under § 704(d) is $10,000, which will be characterized as follows:

$$\frac{\$\ 3,000}{\$12,000} \times \$10,000 = \$2,500 \text{ ordinary loss}$$

$$\frac{\$\ 9,000}{\$12,000} \times \$10,000 = \$7,500 \text{ capital loss}$$

A's carryover loss will be characterized as follows:

$$\$3,000 - \$2,500 = \$\ \ 500 \text{ ordinary loss}$$
$$\$9,000 - \$7,500 = \$1,500 \text{ capital loss}$$

B's distributive share is $1,000 of ordinary loss (25% of $4,000) and $3,000 of capital loss (25% of $12,000). Because B's basis is sufficient to accommodate the entire loss, there is no carryover.

6. **(a)** A's outside basis is $50,000 ($10,000 cash contributed plus $40,000 adjusted basis of property contributed). § 722. B's outside basis is $120,000 ($50,000 cash contributed plus $70,000 adjusted basis of property contributed). § 722.

(b) A and B will both have a balance of $100,000 in their capital accounts. These balances reflect their interests in partnership assets and are in accordance with their agreement to be equal partners.

7. At the end of Year 3, A's capital account has a balance of $20,000 ($50,000 beginning balance less $30,000 of cost recovery deductions), while B's capital account has a balance of $50,000. The $70,000 ($20,000 proceeds from the sale of the asset plus $50,000 cash) must be distributed in accordance with positive capital account balances, $20,000 to A and $50,000 to B.

8. Yes. The regulations provide that partnership agreements with allocations that fail to have economic effect will be deemed to have economic effect if, when interpreted according to state law, a liquidation would produce the same economic results as if The Big Three were satisfied. Reg. § 1.704–1(b)(2)(ii)(i).

9. **(a)** No, the economic effect of the allocation is not substantial. At the time the allocation was considered, there was a strong likelihood that tax-exempt interest and dividends realized would not substantially differ. As a result, the net increases and decreases in A's and B's capital accounts would be the same with the allocation as without the allocation, while the total taxes of A and B would be reduced as a result of the allocation.

(b) The amount will be reallocated to A and B in proportion to the net increases in their capital accounts due to the allocations of these items:

Allocations Per the Partnership Agreement

To A: 90% of $10,000 = $9,000
         10% of $5,000 = $ 500
                          $9,500

To B: 10% of $10,000 = $1,000
         90% of $5,000 = $4,500
                          $5,500

Reallocations as Follows:

To A: $\dfrac{9,500}{15,000} \times \$10,000 = \$6,333$ tax exempt interest

$\dfrac{9,500}{15,000} \times \$\ 5,000 = \$3,167$ dividends

To B: $\dfrac{5,500}{15,000} \times \$10,000 = \$3,667$ tax exempt interest

$\dfrac{5,500}{15,000} \times \$\ 5,000 = \$1,883$ dividends

10. **(a)** If AB sells the parcel of land for $70,000, the tax gain is $50,000 ($70,000 amount realized less $20,000 adjusted basis), and the book gain is $20,000 ($70,000 amount realized less $50,000 book value). The $30,000 difference between the tax gain and the book gain is allocated to A under the traditional method. § 704(c)(1)(A). The remaining $20,000 gain is divided equally between A and B according to the partnership agreement.

(b) If AB sells the parcel of land for $40,000, the tax gain is limited by the ceiling rule to $20,000 ($40,000 amount realized less $20,000 adjusted basis), and the book loss is $10,000 ($40,000 amount realized less $50,000 book value). The $20,000 tax gain is allocated to A. The $10,000 of book loss is allocated equally between A and B. The book loss only results in a book adjustment to capital accounts. See Reg. § 1.704–1(b)(5) Example 14(iii). The distortions created by the ceiling rule could be corrected through a curative allocation or by use of the remedial method.

11. **(a)** The amount of depreciation in Year 1 for book purposes is $10,000 ($50,000 book value/5–year useful life). The amount of depreciation in Year one for tax purposes is $4,000 ($20,000 book value/5–year useful life).

(b) Book depreciation is allocated equally between A and B, $5,000 each. The $4,000 of tax depreciation is allocated entirely to B, the noncontributing partner, under the traditional method. Even though B is entitled to receive $5,000 of depreciation deductions (an amount equal to his share of book depreciation), the ceiling rule limits the allocation to $4,000 (the actual amount of tax depreciation).

(c) A's outside basis in his partnership interest will remain at $70,000, while B's outside basis will be reduced to $96,000 ($100,000 beginning balance less $4,000 tax depreciation allocation).

(d) A's and B's capital accounts will be $95,000 at the end of Year 1 ($100,000 beginning balance less $5,000 of book depreciation).

12. **(a)** The receivables are "unrealized receivables" in the hands of A and the $50,000 of income realized would be allocated to A and would be characterized as ordinary income. §§ 704(c)(1)(A); 724(a); 751(c).

(b) Same answer as in (a) above. Gain or loss on the disposition or collection of the receivables will always be treated as ordinary income.

13. **(a)** The $40,000 of tax gain ($100,000 amount realized less $60,000 adjusted basis) will be allocated entirely to A. § 704(c)(1)(A). The gain will be characterized as ordinary gain because the cars were "inventory items" in the hands of A. § 724(b).

(b) The $40,000 of tax gain again is allocated to A. § 704(c)(1)(A). The gain will be characterized as long-term capital gain because the disposition was made more than five years after A's contribution and, therefore, is characterized at the partnership level. § 724(b).

14. AB is considered to have assumed the $60,000 nonrecourse loan upon B's contribution of the property. Therefore, B's individual liabilities decrease by $60,000. The partners' shares of nonrecourse liabilities will be determined under Reg. § 1.752–3. First, there is no partnership minimum gain because partnership minimum gain is computed using book value rather than tax basis. Next, under the traditional method for § 704(c) allocations, B is allocated $40,000 of the liability (the § 704(c) gain realized if the property was disposed of for full satisfaction of the debt). Finally, the remaining liability ($20,000) is allocated between A and B in accordance with their shares in partnership profits. Presumably, that is 50% each, but see Example 2, at p. 406, *supra,* for possible alternative allocations. Assuming B is allocated $10,000 of the remaining liability, the net decrease in B's liabilities is $10,000 ($60,000 decrease in individual liabilities and a $50,000 increase in share of partnership liabilities).

B's outside basis is:

$20,000	basis of property contributed
–10,000	§ 752(b) distribution (net decrease in liabilities—see §§ 731(a)(1), 733)
$10,000	Outside Basis

A's outside basis is:

$100,000	basis of property contributed
+10,000	§ 752 contribution (net increase in liabilities—see § 722)
$110,000	Outside Basis

15. A, B and C will all be allocated $10,500 of income. They each held a one-third interest for one-half of the year and a one-quarter interest for one-half of the year.

The pro rata income interest is calculated as follows: $(1/3 \times 1/2 \times \$36,000) + (1/4 \times 1/2 \times \$36,000) = \$10,500$. D will be allocated \$4,500 of income. D held a one-quarter interest for one-half of the year. D's pro rata income interest for the year is calculated as follows: $1/4 \times 1/2 \times \$36,000 = \$4,500$.

16. The allocation of the first \$30,000 of partnership gross income to A most likely will be classified as a § 707(a)(1) transaction between the partnership and a nonpartner under § 707(a)(2)(A). There is a transfer of property (use of the office space) and an allocation which, in effect, should be treated as prepaid rent assuming a distribution accompanies the allocation. Short-lived gross income allocations are particularly suspect. If the allocation and distribution are characterized as prepaid rent, A will have gross income and the partnership will have to amortize the payment over the five-year period that it uses the office space.

XVIII. SALES AND EXCHANGES OF PARTNERSHIP INTERESTS

1. **(a)** The accounts receivable and the § 1245 recapture are unrealized receivables. The accounts receivable, § 1245 recapture and dealer property are inventory items. Thus, the accounts receivable, § 1245 recapture and dealer property are all § 751 assets.

    (b) A's § 751 ordinary income is \$30,000, which is equal to the amount of income that would be allocated to A if the partnership sold all of its § 751 assets in a fully taxable sale for cash in an amount equal to the fair market value of such property. In such a sale, A would be allocated \$10,000 of gain from the accounts receivable, \$10,000 of gain from the dealer property, and \$10,000 of the § 1245 recapture.

    (c) A's § 741 capital gain is \$20,000, the difference between A's \$50,000 total gain (\$150,000 amount realized less \$100,000 adjusted basis) and her \$30,000 § 751(a) ordinary income.

    (d) A's capital gain will be characterized as long-term because she has held the partnership interest for 5 years.

2. In the year of sale, B must recognize \$10,000 of gain attributable to the § 1245 recapture income. § 453(i). The \$10,000 of gain attributable to the accounts receivable must also be recognized under an aggregate theory. Cf. Rev.Rul. 89–108, 1989–2 C.B. 100.

3. **(a)** Nupartner's outside basis in his one-third partnership interest is \$30,000. § 1012.

    (b) \$5,000 of ordinary income is allocated to Nupartner even though Nupartner paid \$5,000 for his share of the receivables and has no economic gain.

    (c) Nupartner's total § 743(b) inside basis adjustment is \$15,000 (\$30,000 outside basis less her \$15,000 share of the partnership's inside basis). Nupartner's

$15,000 share of inside basis is equal to her interest in the partnership's previously taxed capital ($30,000 cash received on a hypothetical sale of assets followed by a liquidation of the partnership, minus Nupartner's $15,000 share of tax gain in the accounts receivable and capital asset). Under § 755, the $15,000 adjustment would be allocated between the accounts receivable and the capital asset according to the allocations of income, gain, or loss to Nupartner from a fully taxable sale of those assets for cash equal to the fair market value of those assets. Thus, $5,000 of the adjustment would be allocated to the accounts receivable and $10,000 would be allocated to the capital asset. These adjustments give Nupartner a personal inside basis of $5,000 in the accounts receivable and $20,000 in the capital asset.

XIX. NONLIQUIDATING DISTRIBUTIONS

1. **(a)** A's outside basis would be reduced to $5,000 and A recognizes no gain or loss. §§ 731(a)(1); 733.

   (b) A's outside basis would be reduced to zero and A would recognize $5,000 gain from the sale or exchange of his partnership interest. §§ 731(a)(1); 733.

   (c) A's outside basis is reduced to $5,000 and A recognizes no gain or loss. §§ 731(a)(1); 733. The remaining basis ($5,000) must be allocated to the accounts receivable and inventory. First, those assets are each tentatively assigned a basis equal to the partnership's adjusted basis in those assets (zero in accounts receivable and $10,000 in the inventory). Since neither asset has a built-in loss, the basis of the inventory must be reduced by $5,000—i.e., according to the remaining inside basis of the accounts receivable and inventory. Thus, A's basis in the accounts receivable is zero and A's basis in the inventory is $5,000.

   (d) A's outside basis is reduced to $10,000 and A recognizes no gain or loss. §§ 731(a)(1); 733. The remaining basis ($10,000) must be allocated to the accounts receivable, inventory, and capital asset. First, the accounts receivable and inventory are each tentatively assigned a basis equal to the partnership's adjusted basis in those assets (zero in accounts receivable and $10,000 in inventory). Since there was sufficient basis to be allocated to those assets, A's basis in the accounts receivable is zero and A's basis in the inventory is $10,000. Since there is no remaining basis to be allocated, A's basis in the capital asset is zero.

2. True. § 734(a).

3. (a) Before the distribution, B had a one-third interest in each partnership asset as follows:

	A.B.	F.M.V.
Cash	$5,000	$5,000
Inventory	$4,000	$5,000
Capital Asset	$3,000	$5,000

After the distribution, B has the following interest in each partnership asset:

	A.B.	F.M.V.
Cash	$ 0	$ 0
Inventory	$12,000	$15,000
Capital Asset	$ 0	$ 0

Thus, as a result of the distribution, B exchanged $5,000 of cash and $5,000 of capital asset for $10,000 of inventory.

(b) The partnership constructively distributes B's interests in cash and the capital asset that B has given up as a result of the exchange. Cash in the amount of $5,000 and a capital asset with a $3,000 A.B. and $5,000 F.M.V are constructively distributed to B.

Under 731(a), B would not recognize any gain or loss as a result of the deemed distribution. A would take a $3,000 transferred basis in the capital asset and A's outside basis would be reduced to $4,000 ($12,000 beginning basis less $5,000 cash and $3,000 basis in capital asset).

The partnership's balance sheet after the deemed distribution is as follows:

Assets	A.B.	F.M.V.		Partners' Capital	A.B.	F.M.V.
Cash	$10,000	$10,000	A		$12,000	$15,000
Inventory	$12,000	$15,000	B		$ 4,000	$ 5,000
Capital Asset	$ 6,000	$10,000	C		$12,000	$15,000
	$28,000	$35,000			$28,000	$35,000

(c) B transfers his interest in cash and the capital asset to the partnership in exchange for the $10,000 of excess inventory. The exchange is taxable and B will recognize a $2,000 capital gain on the capital asset ($5,000 amount realized less $3,000 adjusted basis). The partnership recognizes $2,000 of ordinary income on the inventory ($10,000 amount realized less $8,000 adjusted basis) which is taxed to A and C.

(d) B's remaining outside basis is $4,000. Under § 731, B does not recognize any gain on the transfer of the remaining $5,000 of inventory. B takes a $4,000 transferred basis in that portion of the inventory and has a $14,000 total basis in the inventory ($10,000 cost basis plus $4,000 transferred basis).

XX. LIQUIDATING DISTRIBUTIONS

1. The types of partnership property are: 1) unrealized receivables as defined in § 751(c) (excluding depreciation recapture), and goodwill, unless the partnership agreement expressly provides for payment of goodwill, when the payments are for a general partnership interest in a partnership where capital is not a material income-producing factor; and 2) "premium" amounts paid in addition to the partner's share of partnership property which are in the nature of mutual insurance.

2. True. See § 736(a).

3. A's share of § 736(b) assets is $35,000 ($20,000 cash, $10,000 capital assets and $5,000 basis in goodwill). A's § 736(a) payment is $15,000 which is attributable to A's $10,000 share of accounts receivable and $5,000 share of appreciation in goodwill. The $15,000 § 736(a) payment is paid without regard to partnership income and will be a guaranteed payment. § 736(a)(2). The guaranteed payment will result in ordinary income to A and a deduction for B and C.

   Section 751(b) does not apply because the partnership has no inventory items other than the accounts receivable. § 751(b)(2)(B). The § 736(b) payment will result in $5,000 of capital gain under §§ 731(a)(1) and 741 since the payment is $35,000 and A's outside basis is $30,000.

XXI. DEATH OF A PARTNER

1. True. The partnership's taxable year does close with respect to a partner whose interest terminates by reason of death. § 706(c)(2)(A).

2. True. The taxable year of a partnership closes with respect to a partner who sells or exchanges his entire interest in a partnership. § 706(c)(2)(A).

3. The only item which is income in respect of a decedent is (b).

XXII. PARTNERSHIP ANTI–ABUSE RULES

1. Under the partnership anti-abuse regulations, the Service can disregard the purported partnership; treat a purported partner as a nonpartner; adjust the partnership's accounting method; reallocate items of partnership income, gain, loss, deduction or credit; or otherwise adjust or modify the claimed tax treatment. Reg. § 1.701–2(b).

2. The transaction likely will not be challenged under the partnership anti-abuse regulations. This problem is based on Reg. § 1.701–2(d) Example (3). The example

concludes that the decision to organize the partnership to take advantage of the look-through rules for foreign tax credit purposes is consistent with the intent of Subchapter K to permit taxpayers to conduct joint business activity through a flexible economic arrangement without incurring an entity-level tax.

*

APPENDIX B

PRACTICE EXAMINATION

QUESTION ONE

A, B and C, all individuals, wish to organize a "C" corporation to manufacture and sell computer software.

A will transfer the following assets to the new company:

Assets	A.B.	F.M.V.
Building	$30,000	$150,000
Land	15,000	50,000

The building is subject to a $50,000 nonrecourse mortgage, incurred by A many years ago for valid business reasons. The corporation will take the building subject to this mortgage.

B will transfer the following assets to the new company:

Assets	A.B.	F.M.V.
Cash	$50,000	$ 50,000
Accounts Receivable	0	200,000

517

In addition, the new corporation will assume $100,000 of accounts payable from B's cash basis sole proprietorship.

C will transfer a patent with a basis and appraised value of $60,000 and will be the "brains" behind the new enterprise.

A, B and C have agreed that each will own a one-third interest in the corporation in exchange for A and B's respective contributions of property and, in C's case, in exchange for his patent and future services.

Question:

Discuss and compare the tax consequences (gain realized and recognized, basis, etc.) to A, B, C *and* the corporation if they organize the corporation with A receiving $100,000 of unrestricted common stock and $50,000 of seven-year corporate notes bearing market rate interest, and B and C each receiving $150,000 of unrestricted common stock.

ANSWER TO QUESTION ONE

Qualification of the Exchanges Under § 351: A, B and C each transfer property to the newly formed corporation. The issue regarding qualification under § 351 is whether C will be considered part of the control group because C receives stock for both property and future services. If C is not part of the control group, all the exchanges fail under § 351 because A and B only own 62.5% of the corporation's stock after the exchanges.

A person who receives stock in exchange for both property and services is considered a transferor of property and may count all of the stock received for the 80% control requirement unless the value of the property transferred is of relatively small value compared to the stock received for services and the primary purpose of the property transfer is to qualify the exchanges of other transferors for nonrecognition. Under the Service's ruling position, if the stock received by a transferor in exchange for property is at least 10% of the value of stock received for services, the transferor is treated as a member of the control group. Here, the stock received by C in exchange for property ($60,000) is equal to more than 10% of the value of stock received for services ($90,000). Thus, the transferors of property (A, B, and C) control 100% of the new corporation and their exchanges qualify under § 351.

Tax Consequences to A: A realizes $120,000 of gain on the building and $35,000 of gain on the land. Under § 357(c), A must first recognize the excess of the mortgage relief over the aggregate basis of the transferred assets. That $5,000 of gain ($50,000 mortgage less $45,000 of aggregate basis) is characterized by allocating it to the transferred assets in proportion to their fair market values. Thus, $3,750 of the gain is characterized as from the building and $1,250 is characterized as from the land.

The $50,000 seven-year notes are boot which also will require recognition of gain. Those notes are allocated to the building and land in proportion to their fair market values:

$37,500 to the building and $12,500 to the land. The gain attributable to the notes will be recognized under the installment sale rules as payments on the notes are made. Under the § 453 proposed regulations, the basis of the transferred property is first allocated to the exchange of property for stock. Since the basis of the building and land is less than the value of the stock, no basis will be attributable to the exchange of property for the notes so the gross profit fraction is 100%, and thus A recognizes gain as principal payments are made on the notes.

A's basis in the stock under § 358(a)(1) is:

$45,000	Basis in Transferred Property
–50,000	Money Received (Debt Relief)
–50,000	Other Property (Notes)
+55,000	Gain Recognized
$ 0	

A is entitled to an upward basis adjustment for gain recognized even though part of his gain is deferred under § 453. Prop.Reg. § 1.453–1(f)(3)(ii). A's basis in the corporate notes is their face value ($50,000) less the income that will be taxable when they are satisfied in full ($50,000). § 453B(b). Thus, the notes take a zero basis. A's holding period in the stock will tack the holding period of the building and land assuming they are capital or § 1231 assets to A. If either the building or land has been held short-term by A, each share of stock will take a split holding period allocated in proportion to the fair market values of the transferred assets (75% building, 25% land). The seven-year notes will take a fresh holding period.

Tax Consequences to B: B's exchange is tax free. The assignment of income doctrine generally does not apply to a transfer of accounts receivable by a cash method taxpayer in a § 351 exchange. Under § 357(c)(3), the accounts payable are not considered a liability assumed or taken subject to by the corporation, so § 357(c) does not apply to B's exchange.

B's basis in the stock under § 358(a)(1) is $50,000, the basis of the exchanged property. The accounts payable are not treated as liabilities for purposes of calculating the stock's basis. § 358(d)(2). B will take a fresh holding period in the stock because the accounts receivable are not capital or § 1231 assets.

Tax Consequences to C: Even though C is considered a member of the control group, he must recognize ordinary income under § 61 on the value of the stock received for services. Since C's enjoyment of the stock is not subject to restrictions, he will have $90,000 of ordinary income in the year of the exchange. This result accepts the valuation placed on the common stock by the shareholders even though the net assets of the corporation may not support that valuation. Presumably, C's contribution of services adds to the value of the corporation.

C's basis in the stock is $150,000, which is the basis in the patent plus the amount included in income. C's holding period in the stock will tack the holding period of the patent, assuming it is a capital or § 1231 asset. Forty percent ($60/150$) of each share of stock will have the same holding period as the patent and 60% of each share will take a fresh holding period.

Tax Consequences to the Corporation: The corporation will not recognize gain or loss on the issuance of its stock and the seven-year notes. Under § 362, the corporation's basis in the building is $33,750 ($30,000 plus $3,750 of § 357(c) gain) and its basis in the land is $16,250 ($15,000 plus $1,250 of § 357(c) gain). In addition, the corporation will receive basis increases for those assets as A actually recognizes gain on the seven-year notes. Prop.Reg. § 1.4531(f)(3)(ii). The corporation's basis in the accounts receivable is zero and its basis in the patent is $60,000. The corporation's holding period for each asset includes the transferor's holding period. The corporation will be allowed a deduction as it pays the accounts receivable. The corporation also may deduct $90,000 for C's services as they are performed, assuming the services are not capital in nature.

QUESTION TWO

Target Corporation ("T"), a manufacturer of children's apparel, is a closely held "C" corporation. T, an accrual method taxpayer with a fiscal year ending March 31, has 1,000 shares of common stock outstanding, owned as follows:

Shareholder	No. Shares	Adj. Basis	F.M.V.
A	500	$ 30,000	$ 500,000
B	200	10,000	200,000
C Trust	200	100,000	200,000
D	100	200,000	100,000
TOTAL	1,000	$340,000	$1,000,000

A and B, the founders of T, are in their mid–60's and have held their stock for over 20 years. The C Trust is a trust created for the benefit of A and B's two children and four grandchildren. The Trustee (a bank) has complete discretion to distribute or to accumulate income or principal of the trust to the beneficiaries. D is A's brother and has held his stock for two years.

T is a profitable company. It has $400,000 of accumulated earnings and profits and the following assets (all held long-term) and liabilities:

Asset	Adj. Basis	F. Mkt. Value
Inventory	$ 50,000	$ 300,000
Capital Asset	50,000	200,000
Equipment ($50,000 § 1245 recapture)	100,000	300,000
Land	100,000	200,000
Securities	500,000	300,000
TOTAL	$800,000	$1,300,000

Liabilities	Amount
Accounts payable	$100,000
Bank loan	200,000
TOTAL	$300,000

Assume it is November 15, 2003 and T and its shareholders are concerned about the future of their company. They have read newspaper articles about converting to S corporation status and are intrigued by the possibility of avoiding the double tax. A friend has recommended that they conduct their apparel business as a partnership. They also are considering several offers to sell the Company. A and B are reaching retirement age and are inclined to sell. The Trustee of the C Trust is ambivalent. D, a chronic malcontent, is expected to oppose anything suggested by the others.

The details of the acquisition offers are as follows:

Fabric, Inc. ("F") has offered to buy the stock of T for $1,000 per share cash. Assume D is absolutely unwilling to sell his shares in 2003.

Genes, Inc. ("G"), a publicly held $50 million company with 1,000,000 common shares outstanding, would consider acquiring all T's assets *except* for the securities portfolio in exchange for up to $600,000 of G stock, with the remainder of the consideration consisting of short-term G notes. G would prefer not to assume T's liabilities. G does not wish to incur the expense of securing approval of its shareholders for the acquisition; such approval would be required on a straight merger of T into G.

Questions:

   (a) Discuss the tax advantages, disadvantages, obstacles (if any) and timing considerations of the proposals for T to convert to "S" corporation status or to operate the business as a partnership.

   (b) Discuss the tax consequences to all relevant parties of the acquisition offer from F.

   (c) Discuss the tax consequences to all relevant parties of G's acquisition offer and suggest a method of structuring this transaction in a manner that is compatible with what you know about the tax and nontax objectives of the parties. (For this purpose, assume that shareholder D is unalterably opposed to receiving any G stock but the other shareholders would accept a combination of G stock and other consideration.)

ANSWER TO QUESTION TWO

   (a) *Making an S Election:* The principal advantage of T making an S election and operating as an S corporation is avoidance of the double tax on future income. This advantage is limited somewhat by § 1374 (see below).

   T could not presently make an S election unless the C Trust makes an election under § 1361(e) to be an Electing Small Business Trust. Otherwise, the trust is an impermissible shareholder. If such an election is made, the income attributable to the S corporation stock will be taxed to the trust at the highest applicable individual marginal rates, and each trust beneficiary will be counted as a shareholder for purposes of the 75–shareholder limit.

An alternative would be to eliminate the C Trust as a shareholder. This could be accomplished by redeeming its shares or, alternatively, the trust could distribute the T stock to its beneficiaries and a voting trust, or qualified Subchapter S or grantor trusts could be established to hold the T shares. Another potential problem in T electing S status is shareholder D. All of the shareholders must consent to an S election, and D may not be cooperative. One option would be to redeem his shares prior to filing the election. If a redemption of D or the C Trust is planned, it would be a good idea to sell an appropriate amount of the securities to raise the funds needed to repurchase the stock. A sale would produce a tax loss for T and reduce the amount of its passive investment income following the election which would reduce: (1) the chances of T's election terminating, and (2) T's exposure to the § 1375 tax. (See below). If T distributed the securities in redemption of T stock, no loss would be allowed. § 311(a)(2).

If T makes an S election, its taxable year under § 1378 will be a calendar year or a year for which it can establish a business purpose. T also would be able under § 444 to select a taxable year with up to three months of deferral if it makes the payments required by § 7519. An S election by the T shareholders could be made (1) during the year preceding its first taxable year as an S corporation, or (2) on or before the 15th day of the third month of its taxable year. § 1362(b)(1).

If T makes an S election, its potential problems include the fact that under § 1362(d)(2) its election could terminate if more than 25% of its gross receipts in three consecutive years are passive investment income. If T's gross receipts are more than 25% passive investment income in any year, it also will be subject to the § 1375 tax. Both § 1362(d)(3) and § 1375 are potentially applicable because T has Subchapter C E & P.

T also will be subject to the § 1374 tax on the appreciation in its assets at the time of conversion to S status, up to the $500,000 net unrealized built-in gain (see § 1374(d)(1)) at that time. Thus, if an S election is made, it is important for T to obtain an appraisal of its assets on the effective date of the election. The tax applies to sales during the 10–year period following conversion to S status. One strategy for reducing the impact of § 1374 would be to time loss sales of the securities with sales of other assets which produce gains. That would be helpful because losses inherent in T's assets at the time of the S election may offset gains inherent in its assets at that time. § 1374(d)(2)(A)(i).

Conversion to a Partnership: Conversion of T to a partnership (or limited liability company) would not be advisable from a tax standpoint because it would require a liquidation of T which would cause T to immediately recognize all of its gains and losses and the shareholders to recognize their stock gains and losses. Since the T assets and shareholders (except D) have substantial appreciation, a liquidation would produce a large current tax liability.

(b) *Tax Consequences of the Acquisition Offer from F:* If F purchases the stock of the T shareholders for $1,000 per share, A will recognize a $470,000 gain, B will recognize a $190,000 gain, and the C Trust will recognize a $100,000 gain. Most likely, F will not want to make a § 338 election because such an election would trigger recognition of all of T's gains and losses in its assets. Note that T's potential tax liability makes the $1,000 per share price unrealistically high.

(c) *Structure of the Acquisition by G:* The T shareholders would like to structure the acquisition as a reorganization so that all or part of their realized gains do not have to be recognized. A Type A merger is not feasible because G wants to avoid obtaining approval of the transaction from its shareholders.

The terms proposed by G also do not qualify as a Type C reorganization. G does propose to obtain substantially all of T's assets. Under its plan, G would acquire $1,000,000 of T's assets which is at least 90% of the fair market value of its net assets ($1,000,000 x .90 = $900,000) and at least 70% of the fair market value of its gross assets ($1,300,000 x .70 = $910,000). T would be left with the securities which it could use to pay the liabilities. The problem with the acquisition qualifying as a Type C reorganization is the mix of consideration proposed by G. If G uses $600,000 of its stock and $400,000 of short-term notes, the acquisition cannot qualify under the boot relaxation rule in § 368(a)(2)(B) as a Type C reorganization since only 60% of the total consideration is G stock.

Based on the objectives of the parties, the best alternative may be a forward triangular merger under § 368(a)(2)(D). G could form a new subsidiary, S, by transferring its stock and $400,000 of its short-term notes for S stock in a § 351 exchange. T would then merge into S with the T shareholders receiving the G stock and notes. G ordinarily does not have to secure the permission of its shareholders to accomplish this type of merger. The exchange would qualify under § 368(a)(2)(D) because:

(1) S acquires substantially all of T's assets (see Type C reorganization discussion, above);

(2) No S stock is used; and

(3) The exchange would have qualified as a Type A merger if T had merged into G because the T shareholders as a group receive 60% G stock.

The remainder of the answer assumes that T and G undertake a forward triangular merger.

Consequences to the T Shareholders: The T shareholders, other than D, will receive a mixture of G stock and the short-term notes. The notes will be considered boot. Since D receives only boot, he will recognize his $100,000 loss. The other T shareholders (A, B and C Trust) will recognize their stock gains to the extent they receive G notes. The character of their gains will be determined under § 356(a)(2) by assuming that they received only G stock and then received the G notes in redemption of an appropriate portion of their G stock. These hypothetical redemptions will be tested for exchange or dividend treatment under § 302. Exchange treatment would entitle the shareholders to defer their recognized gain under § 453. See § 453(f)(6). The shareholders' bases in the G stock will be determined under § 358(a)(1). The stock will take a tacked holding period. The boot will take a fair market value basis and a fresh holding period.

Consequences to T: T recognizes no gain or loss on the exchange of its property for the P stock and short-term notes since the notes, which are § 361(c)(2)(B) "qualified property," are distributed to its shareholders. § 361(b)(1). Assuming T uses the retained securities to pay off the liabilities, it will recognize its $200,000 loss on that disposition.

Consequences to S: S recognizes no gain or loss on the exchange of the G stock and notes for the T assets. S will take a transferred basis in the T assets under § 362(b) and tack T's holding period for capital and § 1231 assets.

QUESTION THREE

X, Y and Z are equal general partners in the XYZ Services Partnership. On December 31, 2003, the XYZ Partnership will have the following balance sheet:

	Basis	FMV
Cash	$150	$150
Accounts Receivable	0	60
Inventory	45	90
Land (held for investment and		
subject to a $60 mortgage)	60	120
TOTAL	$255	$420

Partner X has decided to leave the partnership at the end of 2003 and is considering the following alternative transactions to achieve that result. X has requested that you evaluate all of the tax consequences to the various parties of each transaction. X also would appreciate any advice you may have which would improve her personal tax results. On December 31, 2003, X will have a $85 basis in her partnership interest. The XYZ Partnership has made a § 754 election.

(a) X will sell her interest to Buyer for $120 cash.

(b) The partnership will transfer $140 cash to X in liquidation of her partnership interest and Y and Z will continue to operate the partnership.

ANSWER TO QUESTION THREE

(a) *Tax Consequences to X:* On the sale of her partnership interest, X will have $55 of gain:

$140   Amount Realized ($120 cash
       plus $20 of debt relief)
 –85   Adjusted Basis
$ 55   Gain Recognized

The character of the gain will be determined under §§ 751(a) and 741. The accounts receivable are § 751(c) unrealized receivables. The accounts receivable and inventory are § 751(d) inventory items. In a hypothetical sale of all of the partnership's property, X would be allocated $35 of income from the accounts receivable and inventory. Thus, $35 of X's gain is ordinary and the remaining $20 of gain is capital gain under § 741. X's capital gain is long-term or short-term depending on the holding period for her partnership interest. None of X's § 741 gain is attributable to partnership collectibles or unrecaptured § 1250 gain.

Tax Consequences to Buyer: Since the partnership has a § 754 election in effect, Buyer will obtain a § 743(b) upward inside basis adjustment equal to $55, which is the difference between Buyer's outside basis ($140) and his $85 share of the adjusted basis to the partnership of its property. Buyer's interest in the partnership's previously taxed capital is $65 ($120, the amount of cash Buyer would receive if the partnership liquidated after a hypothetical sale of its assets, minus $55 of the gain in the accounts receivable, inventory, and land from the hypothetical sale). Buyer's share of the adjusted basis to the partnership of its property is $85 ($65 share of previously taxed capital, plus $20 share of the partnership's liabilities).

The next step is to allocate the $55 adjustment under § 755. If the partnership sold all of its assets in a fully taxable transaction at fair market value immediately after the transfer of the partnership interest to Buyer, the total amount of ordinary income that would be allocated to Buyer is equal to $35 ($20 gain from the accounts receivable and $15 gain from inventory). Buyer would also be allocated $20 of gain from the partnership's capital assets (the land). The amount of the adjustment that is allocated to the ordinary income property thus is $35 and the amount of the adjustment allocated to the land is $20. The final step is to allocate the $35 adjustment to the ordinary income property between the accounts receivable and the inventory according to the amounts of gain that would be allocated to Buyer from those assets: $20 to the accounts receivable and $15 to the inventory. These basis adjustments are personal to Buyer.

(b) Characterization of Payments: The total distribution to X is $160 which includes relief of her $20 share of liabilities. The § 736(b) payment is $120 and is for X's share of the cash ($50), inventory ($30), and land ($40). The remaining $40 of the distribution is a § 736(a) payment. The § 736(a) payment is $20 for X's share of unrealized receivables and the $20 premium paid to X in excess of the value of the partnership's assets.

Consequences to X of the § 736(b) Payment: The § 736(b) payment is subject to § 751(b). Here X exchanges her $30 share of inventory for $30 of cash. That exchange is taxable under § 751(b). The § 751(d) inventory items include both the inventory and the accounts receivable and those assets are substantially appreciated since the fair market value ($150) exceeds 120% of their basis ($54). To set the stage for the exchange, X is deemed to receive $30 of inventory with a $15 basis from the partnership in a distribution and then exchange the inventory with the partnership for $30 of cash. That exchange produces $15 of ordinary income for X and gives the partnership a $30 basis in that portion of the inventory so its total basis in the inventory becomes $60. The remaining $90 of § 736(b) payment exceeds X's $70 outside basis ($85 outside basis less $15 attributed to the § 751(b) inventory distribution) by $20 which is capital gain under § 731(a).

Consequences to X of the § 736(a) Payment: The $40 § 736(a) payment will be considered a guaranteed payment to X which will produce a $40 deduction for Y and Z.

Consequences to the Partnership: Since X recognized $20 of gain under § 731(a)(1) on the § 736(b) payment, the partnership will be entitled to a $20 increase in inside basis under § 734(b)(1)(A). That increase will be allocated to the land since it is a capital asset.

Advice to X. X was paid $20 more than her share of the fair market value of the balance sheet assets. If the partnership agreement stated that the $20 was a payment with respect to partnership goodwill, X would have $40 of capital gain on the § 736(b) payment and $20 less of ordinary income.

APPENDIX C

CORRELATION CHART

Topic in Outline	Coven, Peroni and Pugh (2d ed. 2002)	Doernberg and Abrams (3rd ed. 2000)	Kwall 2d ed. (2000)	Lind, Schwarz, Lathrope and Rosenberg (Corporate Tax) (5th ed. 2002)	McDaniel, McMahon and Simmons (Business Orgs.) (3d ed. 1999)	McDaniel, McMahon and Simmons (Corporate Tax) (3d ed 1999)	Lind, Schwarz, Lathrope and Rosenberg (Bus. Enterp. Tax) (2d ed. 2002)	Lind, Schwarz, Lathrope and Rosenberg (Partnership Tax) (6th ed. 2002)	McDaniel, McMahon and Simmons (Partnership Tax) (3d ed. 1999)	Shakow (2d ed. 1997)	Westin, McNulty and Beck (2d ed. 1999)	Andrews and Feld (3rd ed. 1994)
I. Introduction to Taxation of Business Organizations	782-786	1-6, 651-660	1-16	1-9	1-6	1-6	1-16	2-4	1-6	1-4, 28-37	1-3	
II. Classification	786-813	899-906	188-198	37-42	6-31, 412-416	39-49	16-32	4-25	6-32	156-159	3-22, 633-643	442-449
III. The C Corporation as a Taxable Entity		87-98, 559-572	17-29, 34-36, 65-65, 88-93	12-37	375-411, 417-434	6-38, 49-73	376-383			175-179, 492-493	223-236	
IV. Formation of a Corporation	44-125	7-85	37-38, 377-419	51-111	441-496	74-129	40-455, 474-477			38-86	247-294	195-224, 245-276
V. Capital Structure	163-163	98-117	48-54	112-143	497-550	130-183	455-474			4-27, 133-156	295-310	404-421
VI. Nonliquidating Distributions	164-193	119-175	29-33, 38-48, 58-64, 201-223	144-186	551-601, 873-880	184-234, 507-514	478-519			103-122, 127-133, 259-267	311-330	336-378
VII. Stock Redemptions and Partial Liquidations	194-261	177-247	223-283	187-277	602-657, 859-873	235-290, 492-507	520-600			234-259, 280, 487-492	339-375	467-535, 605-690
VIII. Stock Distributions and §306 Stock	262-298	249-290	725-750	278-309	658-697	291-330	601-622			280-294	330-337	13-35, 573-575, 583-615
IX. Complete Liquidations and Taxable Corporate Acquisitions	340-374	291-330, 347-380	283-302, 469-506	310-404	698-727, 831-857	331-360, 464-491	623-684			295-313, 316-330	377-409	163-179
X. Anti-Avoidance Provisions	299-339	535-558	65-85, 303-304	645-682	1145-1172	779-806	383-387			315-316	539-549	379-394
XI. Tax-Free Reorganizations	375-559	381-449, 493-501	507-629, 750-757	405-506, 560-593	881-1039	515-673	685-768			352-453, 470-489, 500-504	451-519	37-136, 179-194, 276-336, 551-566, 575-583, 690-720
XII. Corporate Divisions	560-618	451-491	667-724	507-559	1040-1094	674-728	769-813			453-469	413-449	137-147, 617-663
XIII. Carryovers of Corporate Tax Attributes	619-659	503-525	631-663	493-506, 594-614	1095-1144	729-778	814-837			493-500, 505-516	521-537	727-774
XIV. Affiliated Corporations	661-678	525-534, 572-585	615-644	615-644	434-440, 797-829	431-463	389-391			219-228	549-560	
XV. S Corporations	679-781	589-647	95-148, 305-319, 421-425	683-744	728-796	361-430	840-899	395-456	375-444	159-175, 179-187, 313-315	561-632	432-442

Topic in Outline	Coven, Peroni and Pugh (2d ed. 2002)	Doernberg and Abrams (3rd ed. 2000)	Kwall 2d ed. (2000)	Lind, Schwarz, Lathrope and Rosenberg (Corporate Tax) (5th ed. 2002)	McDaniel, McMahon and Simmons (Business Orgs.) (3d ed. 1999)	McDaniel, McMahon and Simmons (Corporate Tax) (3d ed. 1999)	Lind, Schwarz, Lathrope and Rosenberg (Bus. Enterp. Tax) (2d ed. 2002)	Lind, Schwarz, Lathrope and Rosenberg (Partnership Tax) (4th ed. 2002)	McDaniel, McMahon and Simmons (Partnership Tax) (3d ed. 1999)	Shakow (2d ed. 1997)	Westin, McNulty and Beck (2d ed. 1999)	Andrews and Feld (3rd ed. 1994)
XVI. Formation of a Partnership	818-850	660-662, 725-745	427-447, 454-458		34-70		34-77	28-72	34-70	86-97	23-48	
XVII. Operations of a Partnership	851-1013	671-723, 715-745, 779-800, 853-871, 906-909	149-188, 447-454, 458-463		71-246		78-245	73-249	71-246	97-102, 123-126, 187-219	49-119	
XVIII. Sales and Exchanges of Partnership Interests	1014-1057	801-826, 843-848, 883-898	341-345, 356-357, 363-363		247-291		246-275	250-282	247-291, 345-351	335-337	121-137	
XIX. Nonliquidating Distributions	1058-1103	562-668, 747-778, 874-882	321-336, 363-368		292-317, 368-373		276-310	283-318	292-317, 332-345, 368-373	337-344	139-154	
XX. Liquidating Distributions	1104-1169	669, 827-843, 848-852, 915-916	336-340, 346-355, 368-373		317-362		311-358	319-371	317-333, 351-362	330-335, 344-350	155-178, 183-206	
XXI. Death of a Partner	1170-1180				362-367		359-374	372-387	362-367		207-222	
XXI. Anti-Abuse Provisions	813-817		464-465		32-33		31-32	388-393	32-33	751	178-181	

*

+------------------------------+
| |
| APPENDIX D |
| |
+------------------------------+
| |
| |
| GLOSSARY |
| |
| |
+------------------------------+

This glossary is intended to provide the reader with brief definitions of some of the terms frequently encountered in a corporate or partnership tax course. More comprehensive definitions of many of these terms are included in the body of the outline.

A

Accumulated Adjustments Account (AAA): An account of the corporation which is adjusted for the period since the corporation has been an S corporation (beginning in 1983) in the same manner as adjustments are made to a shareholder's basis. The AAA is employed to characterize distributions by S corporations with E & P and, in general, represents the earnings of an S corporation previously taxed to the shareholders.

Accumulated Earnings Tax: An additional penalty tax which must be paid by any C corporation formed or availed of for the purpose of avoiding the individual income tax by accumulating rather than distributing E & P.

Active Trade or Business: A specific group of activities in which a corporation performs active and substantial management and operational functions for the purpose of earning income or profit. The concept is employed in connection with the qualification requirements for corporate divisions and partial liquidations.

Affiliated Group: One or more chains of corporations in which a parent corporation owns at least 80% of one corporation and at least 80% of each corporation is owned by other corporations in the group. An affiliated group may elect to file a consolidated tax return.

Aggregate Concept: An approach to taxing business organizations under which the organization is viewed as a collection of its individual owners rather than a separate taxable entity.

Aggregate Deemed Sales Price: The price for which a target corporation is treated as selling its assets if the target makes a § 338 election in connection with a taxable sale of 80% or more of its stock.

Alternate Economic Effect Test: A widely used test in the regulations under which a partnership allocation will be respected even though the partners are not unconditionally obligated to restore capital account deficits. For allocations to be respected under this test, the partnership agreement must contain a "qualified income offset."

Alternative Minimum Tax (AMT): In the case of C corporations, an additional broader-based tax payable to the extent that the AMT exceeds the corporation's regular tax liability. The AMT is 20% of a corporation's alternative minimum taxable income less an exemption amount. It was enacted to ensure that all C corporations pay at least some federal income tax.

Alternative Minimum Taxable Income (AMTI): The base for the alternative minimum tax. In general, AMTI is a C corporation's taxable income, adjusted to reflect certain timing differences (e.g., depreciation) and increased by specified "tax preference" items.

Association: An unincorporated entity with sufficient corporate attributes to be classified and taxed as a corporation.

Attribution Rules: Statutory rules that consider an individual or entity as owning stock owned by certain related family members or entities for purposes of various provisions of the Code where stock ownership is significant.

B

Bailout: A term used in tax parlance to describe a shareholder's attempt to withdraw profits accumulated by a C corporation in a transaction (e.g., a redemption, liquidation or sale) where the shareholder hopes to treat the amounts received first as a recovery of stock basis and then as a long-term capital gain instead of a fully taxable dividend.

The Big Three: A shorthand description of the basic test to determine whether a partnership allocation has economic effect. This test requires the partnership agreement to provide for proper maintenance of capital accounts, liquidating distributions to be made in accordance with positive capital account balances, and an unconditional obligation by each partner to restore a deficit capital account balance.

Bond: A long-term corporate debt obligation that is secured by particular corporate property.

Boot: Tax jargon for "other property or money" received in a transaction that otherwise qualifies for nonrecognition of gain or loss. In such transactions, a taxpayer ordinarily must recognize gain to the extent of the boot received but may not recognize any loss.

Bootstrap Sale: An integrated transaction where part of a shareholder's stock is redeemed and the balance is sold to an unrelated buyer. The term also is used to refer to a leveraged transaction in which the assets of a target corporation are used to pay for its own acquisition.

Built–In Gain or Loss: The difference between the fair market value and the adjusted basis of an asset (or assets)—i.e., the unrealized appreciation or depreciation inherent in an asset at a given point in time. The concept is employed for purposes of the § 1374 tax on S corporations, the carryover of tax attributes following a corporate acquisition, and partnership allocations with respect to contributed property under § 704(c).

Business Purpose Doctrine: A judicial doctrine that may be applied to deny tax benefits when a transaction has no substance, purpose or utility apart from tax avoidance. The doctrine is most frequently applied as an independent requirement for tax-free corporate divisions.

C

C Corporation: A corporation fully subject to the provisions of Subchapter C (§§ 301–385) of the Internal Revenue Code that has not made an S election. See S Corporation.

Capital Account: An account on a partnership's balance sheet which represents a partner's share of partnership capital. The regulations include specific requirements for maintenance of capital accounts for partnership allocations to be respected.

Capital Structure: The mix of debt and equity that a corporation has used to finance its operations.

Ceiling Rule: A limitation on a partnership's ability to make allocations (e.g., of gain or loss or depreciation) with respect to contributed property under § 704(c).

Collapsible Corporation: A corporation formed or availed of principally for the manufacture, production or sale of property with a view toward a sale or exchange of stock by the shareholders before the corporation recognizes two-thirds of the taxable income from the property and realization by the shareholders of gain attributable to the property.

Consolidated Return: A corporate return that may be filed by an affiliated group of corporations in which the group pays tax on its consolidated taxable income.

Constructive Dividend: An economic benefit provided by a corporation to a shareholder that is not a formal dividend but which in substance is a distribution of corporate earnings.

Continuity of Business Enterprise: A judicial test for reorganizations that requires the acquiring corporation either to continue the target corporation's historic business or to use a significant portion of the target's historic business assets in a business. The requirement also limits the carryover of a target's net operating losses following a change of ownership.

Continuity of Interest: A judicial test for acquisitive reorganizations that requires the shareholders of a target corporation to retain a continuing proprietary interest (i.e., as shareholders) in the acquiring corporation. As applied to divisive reorganizations, the test requires the shareholders of the distributing corporation to retain a continuing proprietary interest in both the distributing and controlled corporations after the distribution.

Contribution to Capital: A transfer of cash or property to a corporation by a shareholder or nonshareholder when no stock or other consideration is received in exchange.

Control: Used generically, "control" may connote more than 50% of the voting power of a corporation. Several provisions in Subchapter C use the term in specialized contexts and with varying definitions. "Control" typically is defined as ownership of a specified percentage (80% and 50% are common thresholds) of the stock of a corporation. The percentage requirement may apply to voting power, nonvoting stock and/or the value of stock.

Controlled Group of Corporations: A group of corporations which satisfies specific common ownership requirements. The members of a controlled group are limited with respect to certain tax benefits, such as the lower graduated rates in § 11(b). Examples include a "parent-subsidiary" or "brother-sister" controlled group.

Convertible Preferred Stock: Preferred stock that is convertible into common stock at a specified price or ratio.

Creeping Acquisition: An acquisition of a target corporation in a series of steps. The tax consequences of an acquisition often depend on whether the separate steps are treated as an integrated transaction and the type of acquisitive reorganization that the taxpayer is seeking to qualify for tax-free status. Creeping acquisitions are sometimes referred to as multi-step acquisitions.

D

Debenture: A long-term corporate debt instrument that is unsecured. Debentures are nonetheless frequently referred to as "bonds" in some contexts—e.g., "junk bonds" are often really high-yield debentures.

Debt Security: A corporate instrument representing funds borrowed by the corporation from the holder of the debt obligation.

Debt–Equity Ratio: The ratio between a corporation's debt and equity capital. The debt-equity ratio is relevant to whether or not a corporation is thinly capitalized and whether instruments labelled as debt will be reclassified as equity.

Device Limitation: A limitation in § 355 that is intended to prevent the use of a tax-free corporate division to bail out corporate earnings at capital gains rates and avoid tax through a recovery of basis.

Distribution: Used broadly, a term that refers to any kind of payment (of cash, property, debt obligations) by a corporation to shareholders with respect to their stock, or a transfer of cash or property by a partnership to a partner.

Distributive Share: The portion of a partnership's income, gain, loss or deduction that passes through to a partner and is reported on the partner's tax return. A partner's distributive share generally is determined in the partnership agreement unless the allocation does not have substantial economic effect.

Dividend: A distribution by a corporation to a shareholder out of the current or accumulated E & P of the corporation.

Dividends Received Deduction: A deduction of 70%, 80% or 100% of dividends received by corporate shareholders. The purpose of the deduction is to prevent multiple corporate-level taxation of income.

Double Tax: The result of the entity approach employed by Subchapter C, under which profits of C corporations are first taxed to the corporation when earned and taxed again to the shareholders when earnings are distributed as dividends.

E

Earnings and Profits (E & P): A corporate tax accounting concept that is used to measure the extent to which a distribution is made from a corporation's economic income. E & P are determined by making adjustments to a corporation's taxable income. The effects of various transactions on E & P are determined under § 312.

Economic Effect Equivalence: A test in the regulations under which partnership allocations which do not have economic effect under The Big Three or the alternative economic effect test are deemed to have economic effect if a liquidation of the partnership would produce the same results to the partners as The Big Three.

Economic Risk of Loss: A standard used for allocating partnership liabilities. A partner bears the economic risk of loss for a partnership liability to the extent that the partner would bear the economic burden of discharging the liability if the partnership were unable to do so.

Electing Small Business Trust: A trust that may make an election in order to become a permissible shareholder of an S corporation. The current beneficiaries of such a trust must otherwise be eligible S corporation shareholders.

Entity Concept: An approach to taxing business organizations under which the organization is considered to be an entity that is separate and distinct from its owners.

Equity: A corporate ownership interest evidenced by shares of stock.

Extraordinary Dividend: A dividend which exceeds 5% of the shareholder's adjusted basis in preferred stock or 10% of the shareholder's basis in the case of other stock. In some circumstances, a corporate shareholder that receives an extraordinary dividend must reduce its stock basis by the portion of the dividend not taxed as a result of the dividends received deduction and recognize gain once basis has been reduced to zero.

F

Family Partnership Rules: Rules in § 704(e) that are designed to prevent the shifting of income among partners who may not be dealing at arm's length, such as family members.

Forward Triangular Merger: An acquisition in which a subsidiary merges into the target corporation with the target shareholders receiving stock of the subsidiary's parent corporation. A forward triangular merger may qualify as a reorganization if the requirements in § 368(a)(2)(D) are met.

G

General Utilities Doctrine: A doctrine, named after an early Supreme Court case, under which a corporation did not recognize gain or loss on distributions of property to its shareholders and on certain sales of property pursuant to a plan of complete liquidation. The doctrine was repealed in the Tax Reform Act of 1986.

Grossed–Up Basis: An amount calculated under a formula which is used to determine a target corporation's aggregate basis in its assets resulting from a deemed asset sale triggered by a § 338 election. Grossed-up basis generally is the basis of the corporation's recently purchased stock multiplied by a fraction which is designed to equate purchases of less than 100% of the target's stock with purchases of all the stock.

Guaranteed Payment: Fixed payments to a partner for services performed as a partner or as a return on contributed capital.

H

Hypothetical Sale Approach: An approach used for various purposes (e.g., determination of the character of gain or loss on the sale of a partnership interest) in the partnership tax regulations. The approach assumes that a partnership sold all of its assets at their fair market value for cash and assumption of liabilities.

I

Inside Basis: A term used to refer to a partnership's basis in its assets.

Interim Closing of the Books: An accounting method used to apportion partnership items when a partnership's taxable year closes or interests in the partnership change during the year. Under this method, the portions of partnership items attributable to different periods in the partnership's taxable year are determined under the partnership's accounting method rather than simply pro rated on a daily basis throughout the year.

Inventory Item: A category of § 751 asset that generally consists of property which, if sold by a partnership or a selling or distributee partner, would not be a capital or § 1231 asset.

L

Limited Liability Company: A legal form of business entity that provides limited liability for each of its owners, who are usually known as "members." Limited liability companies with more than one member are usually classified as partnerships for federal tax purposes.

Limited Partnership: A partnership that has a general partner and at least one limited partner—i.e., one partner who is not liable for partnership debts beyond the partner's contributed capital.

Liquidation: A transaction in which a corporation ceases to be a going concern and its activities are merely for the purpose of winding up its affairs, paying its debts and distributing any remaining balance to its shareholders. A corporate liquidation may be preceded by sales of corporate assets. When used in connection with a partnership, a "liquidation" may connote a winding up of the entire partnership or simply a liquidation of the interest of a particular partner.

Liquidation–Reincorporation: A transaction designed to obtain a stepped-up fair market value basis for a corporation's assets, generally at the cost of a capital gain to the corporation's shareholders. The strategy is much less useful after repeal of the *General Utilities* doctrine.

M

Minimum Gain: A term used in the regulations governing allocations with respect to nonrecourse liabilities of a partnership. Partnership "minimum gain" with respect to a nonrecourse liability is the amount of gain which would be realized by the partnership if it disposed of the partnership property subject to the liability in full satisfaction of the liability and for no other consideration.

Minimum Gain Chargeback: A provision that must be inserted in a partnership agreement in order for allocations of nonrecourse deductions to be respected. Under a minimum gain chargeback, if there is a net decrease in partnership minimum gain for a partnership taxable year, each partner must be allocated items of income and gain for the year in proportion to, and to the extent of, the greater of: (1) the partner's portion of the net decrease in minimum gain allocable to the disposition of partnership property subject to nonrecourse liabilities, or (2) the deficit in the partner's capital account at the end of the year before any allocation for the year.

Mixing Bowl Transaction: A strategy used in the partnership setting to shift or defer recognition of precontribution gain on property contributed to a partnership by utilizing the nonrecognition rules for contributions and distributions. Mixing bowl transactions are now largely foreclosed by §§ 704(c)(1)(B) and 737.

N

Nonqualified Preferred Stock: Preferred stock with certain debt-like characteristics (such as a mandatory redemption feature). Nonqualified preferred stock is treated as boot rather than "nonrecognition property" for various corporate-shareholder transactions such as formations and reorganizations.

Nonrecourse Deductions: A technical term of art used in the § 704(b) allocation regulations. A partnership's nonrecourse deductions for the year equal the excess of the net increase in partnership minimum gain for the year over the aggregate of distributions during the year of proceeds of a nonrecourse liability that are allocable to an increase in partnership minimum gain.

Nonrecourse Liabilities: Any partnership liability (or portion thereof) for which no partner bears the economic risk of loss.

O

Old and Cold: A term used when analyzing the tax consequences of a series of transactions under the step transaction doctrine. Earlier steps that are not related to a later transaction for tax purposes are referred to as "old and cold."

Organizational Expenditures: Fees and expenses of organizing a corporation or partnership that normally would have to be capitalized but which may be amortized over 60 months if a corporation makes a § 248 election or a partnership makes a § 709 election.

Outside Basis: A partner's basis in her partnership interest.

P

Partial Liquidation: A corporate distribution resulting from a genuine contraction of the corporation's business, including the termination of a trade or business that the corporation has actively conducted for the five-year period preceding the distribution.

Passive Activity: A term used to describe trade or business activities in which a taxpayer does not materially participate and most rental activities. In general, for taxpayers affected by the passive activity loss limitations, losses from passive activities are currently deductible only to the extent of income from such activities.

Personal Holding Company: In general, an investment company with a small number of shareholders that is subject to a penalty tax if it does not distribute its net investment income to its shareholders.

Personal Service Corporation: A term used in the Code to describe a corporation substantially all of the activities of which involve the performance of service—i.e., corporations that perform services in particular specified fields, such as law, accounting, architecture, etc., and which are substantially owned by the employees who perform such services.

Preferred Stock: Stock which, relative to other classes of corporate stock outstanding, enjoys certain limited rights and privileges (generally dividend and liquidation priorities) but does not participate in corporate growth.

Previously Taxed Capital: A concept used in the formula to determine an elective § 743(b) basis adjustment. A transferee's share of a partnership's "previously taxed capital" equals: (1) the amount of cash the partner would have received on liquidation of the partnership immediately following a hypothetical sale of the partnership's assets at fair market value, increased by (2) the amount of tax loss that would be allocated to the transferee from the hypothetical sale, and decreased by (3) the amount of tax gain that would have been allocated to the transferee from the hypothetical transaction.

Publicly Traded Partnership: A partnership whose interests are traded on an established securities market or are readily tradable on a secondary market. Publicly traded partnerships generally are classified as corporations for tax purposes.

Q

Qualified Income Offset: Boilerplate language that must be included in a partnership agreement in order for a partnership allocation to be respected under the alternate test for economic effect. A qualified income offset requires that if a partner has a deficit capital account balance as a result of certain unexpected events (e.g., a distribution), that partner will be allocated items of income or gain in an amount and manner sufficient to eliminate the deficit as quickly as possible.

Qualified Subchapter S Trust: A type of irrevocable trust that may elect to be a qualified shareholder of an S corporation.

R

Recapitalization: A readjustment of the capital structure of a single corporation which may qualify as a Type E reorganization for tax purposes.

Recourse Liability: A partnership liability to the extent that any partner bears the economic risk of loss for the liability.

Redemption: An acquisition of stock by the issuing corporation in exchange for property.

Remedial Method: A method authorized by the regulations for making allocations with respect to contributed property under § 704(c) that seeks to remedy book/tax disparities created by the ceiling rule.

Reorganization: A term used in the Code to describe a variety of corporate combinations and adjustments falling into three broad categories: (1) acquisitive reorganizations, (2) nonacquisitive, nondivisive reorganizations (e.g., a recapitalization), and (3) divisive reorganizations.

Reverse Triangular Merger: An acquisition in which the target corporation merges into a subsidiary of the acquiring corporation. A reverse triangular merger may qualify as a reorganization if the target shareholders receive voting stock of the subsidiary's parent and certain other requirements in § 368(a)(2)(E) are met.

Rights: Short-term options, often distributed by a corporation to its shareholders with respect to their stock, to purchase a stock for a fixed price.

S

S Corporation: A corporation that qualifies to make an election to be treated as a pass-through entity subject to the provisions of Subchapter S (§§ 1361–1379) of the Code and which consequently avoids the double tax imposed on earnings of C corporations.

Section 732(d) Adjustment: An adjustment under which a distributee partner who acquired her partnership interest by a transfer when there is no § 754 election in effect may elect, with respect to distributions, within two years after the transfer, to adjust the bases of the partnership's assets as if a § 743(b) adjustment had taken place.

Section 734(b) Adjustment: A required adjustment to the inside basis of partnership assets that is triggered by certain partnership distributions if a partnership has a § 754 election in effect.

Section 743(b) Adjustment: An adjustment made following a transfer (by sale or exchange, or death of a partner) of a partnership interest if a partnership has a § 754 election in effect. The adjustment increases or decreases the inside basis of the partnership's assets by the difference between the transferee's outside basis and the transferee's proportionate share of inside basis.

Section 704(c) Allocation: An allocation of tax items with respect to property contributed by a partner to a partnership that takes into account the variation between the inside basis of the property and its fair market value at the time of the contribution. The most common § 704(c) allocations relate to precontribution gain or loss and cost recovery deductions on property contributed to a partnership.

Section 751 Assets: A category of assets described in § 751 that consists of a partnership's unrealized receivables and substantially appreciated inventory. Section 751 assets are sometimes referred to as "hot assets."

Section 338 Election: An election that may be made by a purchasing corporation following a purchase of 80% or more of a target's stock within a 12–month acquisition period. The election triggers a deemed sale of all of the target's assets.

Section 754 Election: If made by a partnership, a § 754 election triggers basis adjustments under § 734(b) (in the case of distributions) and § 743(b) (in the case of transfers of a partnership interest).

Section 306 Stock: In general, preferred stock received as a nontaxable stock dividend or in a reorganization that has bailout potential. All or part of the gain on a sale or redemption of § 306 stock may be characterized as ordinary income rather than capital gain.

Section 1244 Stock: Stock (usually of a closely held corporation) that qualifies for ordinary loss treatment on sale or worthlessness if certain requirements in § 1244 are met.

Security: A term of art in the Code used to refer to corporate debt obligations that represent a degree of continuing participation in the corporation that falls short of an equity interest but is greater than an interest held by a short-term creditor. Long-term bonds (10 years or more) generally qualify as securities but short-term notes (5 years or less) do not.

Spin–Off: A pro rata distribution of the stock of a controlled subsidiary corporation by a parent distributing corporation to its shareholders.

Split–Off: A non pro rata distribution of the stock of a controlled subsidiary corporation by a parent distributing corporation to its shareholders in redemption of some or all of their parent stock.

Split–Up: A distribution of the stock of more than one controlled subsidiary, either pro rata or non pro rata, by a parent corporation which owns no other assets to all of its shareholders in complete liquidation of the parent.

Stock Dividend: A distribution of stock which generally is not taxable when it does not increase the shareholders' proportionate interest in the company (e.g., common on common) but otherwise is treated as a distribution to which § 301 applies.

Subchapter C: Sections 301–385 of the Code. Subchapter C adopts an entity concept by treating corporations as separate taxpaying entities. When Subchapter S does not provide a specific rule, Subchapter C also may apply to S corporations and their shareholders.

Subchapter K: Sections 701–761 of the Code. Subchapter K is a pass-through taxing model under which partnerships are not treated as separate taxpaying entities, and partnership income and deductions pass through to the partners.

Subchapter S: Sections 1371–1379 of the Code. Subchapter S governs the tax treatment of S corporations and their shareholders.

Subordination: A status related to a debt or claim where the other creditors have a higher priority than the holders of the debt or claim. Subordination is a factor that may be considered in determining whether to reclassify nominal debt as equity.

Substantial Economic Effect: A standard for testing partnership allocations of income, deductions, etc., that is imposed by the Code and amplified by extensive regulations.

Substantially Appreciated Inventory: "Inventory items" of a partnership are "substantially appreciated" if their fair market value exceeds 120% of the adjusted basis of such property. Inventory acquired with a principal purpose of avoiding the 120% standard is disregarded for purposes of determining whether inventory items are substantially appreciated in value.

Syndication Expenses: Expenses connected with issuing and marketing of interests in a partnership. Syndication expenses are not deductible and may not be amortized as organizational expenses under § 709.

T

Tax–Book Disparity: The disparity (sometimes called "book-tax disparity") between the inside basis of an asset contributed to a partnership and the book value used to establish and maintain the partners' capital accounts. A tax-book disparity is often relevant in connection with allocations of gain, loss and cost recovery deductions with respect to contributed property under § 704(c).

Thin Capitalization: A term used to describe the capital structure of a corporation with a very high ratio of debt to equity.

Tiered Partnership: A structure where one partnership owns an interest in one or more "subsidiary" partnerships.

Traditional Method: A method authorized by the regulations for making allocations with respect to contributed property under § 704(c). Ceiling rule distortions resulting from the traditional method may be corrected by using the traditional method with curative allocations or the remedial method.

U

Unrealized Receivables: A category of § 751 assets that includes any rights to payment for goods or services that have not yet been included in income under the partnership's accounting method.

W

Warrant: A contractual right (in the nature of a long-term option) to purchase a certain number of shares of stock at a set price. Warrants generally are not considered stock or securities of a corporation.

*

APPENDIX E

TABLE OF CASES, IRC SECTIONS, TREASURY REGULATIONS, REVENUE RULINGS AND PROCEDURES

Table of Cases

541

Table of Internal Revenue Code Sections

Table of Treasury Regulations

Table of Revenue Rulings

*